Youth Employment and Joblessness in Advanced Countries

NBER Comparative Labor Markets Series

A National Bureau of Economic Research Series

Edited by Richard B. Freeman

Also in the series

David Card and Richard B. Freeman, editors
*Small Differences That Matter: Labor Markets and Income
    Maintenance in Canada and the United States*

Lisa M. Lynch, editor
Training and the Private Sector: International Comparisons

Rebecca M. Blank, editor
*Social Protection versus Economic Flexibility:
    Is There a Trade-off?*

Richard B. Freeman and Lawrence F. Katz, editors
Differences and Changes in Wage Structures

Joel Rogers and Wolfgang Streeck, editors
*Works Councils: Consultation, Representation, and
    Cooperation in Industrial Relations*

Youth Employment and Joblessness in Advanced Countries

Edited by **David G. Blanchflower and Richard B. Freeman**

The University of Chicago Press

Chicago and London

DAVID G. BLANCHFLOWER is professor in and chairman of the
Department of Economics at Dartmouth College and a research
associate of the National Bureau of Economic Research. RICHARD B.
FREEMAN holds the Herbert Ascherman Chair in Economics at
Harvard University and is director of the NBER Labor Studies
Program and codirector of the Centre for Economic Performance of
the London School of Economics.

331.34
Y 833

The University of Chicago Press, Chicago 60637
The University of Chicago Press, Ltd., London
© 2000 by the National Bureau of Economic Research
All rights reserved. Published 2000
Printed in the United States of America
09 08 07 06 05 04 03 02 01 00   1 2 3 4 5
ISBN: 0-226-05658-9 (cloth)

Library of Congress Cataloging-in-Publication Data

Youth employment and joblessness in advanced countries / edited by
    David G. Blanchflower and Richard B. Freeman
        p.   cm. — (NBER Comparative labor markets series)
        "This volume is a record of conference proceedings"—Cip's pub.
    info.
    Includes bibliographical references and index.
    ISBN 0-226-05658-9 (cl. : alk. paper)
    1. Youth—Employment—OECD countries Congresses.
    2. Young men—Employment—OECD countries Congresses.
    3. Young women—Employment—OECD countries Congresses.
    4. Unemployment—OECD countries Congresses.
    I. Blanchflower, David.   II. Freeman, Richard B. (Richard
    Barry), 1943– .   III. National Bureau of Economic Research.
    IV. Series.
    HD6270.Y674   2000
    331.3'4—dc21   99-39694
                                                           CIP

Contents

Introduction   1
David G. Blanchflower and Richard B. Freeman

I. The Situation Facing Young Workers

1. **The Declining Economic Status of Young
   Workers in OECD Countries**   19
   David G. Blanchflower and Richard B. Freeman

2. **Cohort Crowding and Youth Labor Markets:
   A Cross-National Analysis**   57
   Sanders Korenman and David Neumark

3. **Gender and Youth Employment Outcomes:
   The United States and West Germany,
   1984–1991**   107
   Francine D. Blau and Lawrence M. Kahn

II. Youth Responses to the Market

4. **Adapting to Circumstances: The Evolution
   of Work, School, and Living Arrangements
   among North American Youth**   171
   David Card and Thomas Lemieux

5. **Disadvantaged Young Men and Crime**   215
   Richard B. Freeman

6. **Child Development and Success or Failure
   in the Youth Labor Market**   247
   Paul Gregg and Stephen Machin

7. **The Rising Well-Being of the Young**   289
   David G. Blanchflower and Andrew J. Oswald

III. THE EFFECT OF PROGRAMS

8. **The Sensitivity of Experimental Impact
   Estimates: Evidence from the National
   JTPA Study**   331
   James J. Heckman and Jeffrey A. Smith

9. **The Swedish Youth Labor Market in Boom
   and Depression**   357
   Per-Anders Edin, Anders Forslund, and
   Bertil Holmlund

10. **Young and Out in Germany: On Youths'
    Chances of Labor Market Entrance
    in Germany**   381
    Wolfgang Franz, Joachim Inkmann,
    Winfried Pohlmeier, and Volker Zimmermann

11. **Minimum Wages and Youth Employment
    in France and the United States**   427
    John M. Abowd, Francis Kramarz,
    Thomas Lemieux, and David N. Margolis

    Contributors   473
    Author Index   475
    Subject Index   479

Introduction

David G. Blanchflower and Richard B. Freeman

Youth is the best time to be rich, and the best time to be poor.
—Euripides, *Heracles*

If a biotech firm developed a Ponce de León Fountain of Youth potion that would turn persons at the prime working ages of 35–55 into 25-year-olds, more older persons would buy the product than buy Viagra. Young people are generally healthier and stronger and have longer expected life spans than older people. They do not have to worry about thinning hair, expanding waistlines, and the other variegated signs of senescence. Only one thing would clearly worsen as a result of the trade: their labor market prospects.

Outside of sports or other highly physical activities, young workers almost invariably have lower wages and higher rates of joblessness than older workers. The lower wages of young workers presumably reflect their being less productive than older workers and their sacrificing some earnings potential to invest in on-the-job training. The higher rate of joblessness of young workers is due in part to their being in a transitional state, moving from the world of school to the world of work and moving from their parental families to living on their own.

In the 1970s the labor market situation of youths worsened noticeably, apparently because of the huge increase in supply resulting from the entry of baby boomers into the job market (Freeman 1979; Welch 1979; Berger 1984). Most analysts expected that the deteriorated position of youths in the job market would improve as baby boomers aged and as the youth

David G. Blanchflower is professor in and chairman of the Department of Economics at Dartmouth College and a research associate of the National Bureau of Economic Research. Richard B. Freeman holds the Herbert Ascherman Chair in Economics at Harvard University and is director of the NBER Labor Studies Program and codirector of the Centre for Economic Performance of the London School of Economics.

The editors thank the Ford Foundation for financial support of this project.

cohort declined in size (see OECD 1978). Most expected that increased education or training would substantially alleviate the problems of all youths save for a small hard core. The youth job market problem was expected to be a temporary one, readily curable by policy.

But to the surprise of most analysts, the traditional gap between adult and youth wages and employment rose substantially in the 1980s and 1990s. In virtually all advanced countries the youth cohort is much smaller and better educated than in the past, but the youth job market problem remains, and in most cases it has gotten worse rather than better.

In the United States the wages of less educated young men were 20 to 30 percent lower in the 1990s than at the end of the 1970s. The boom of the late 1990s raised pay and employment relative to adults but did not come close to restoring the position of youths to what it was even during the peak of the baby boomers' entry into the job market. An extraordinary proportion of the least educated young men, particularly black young men, were incarcerated.

In much of western Europe, youth unemployment rose in the 1980s and remained high in the 1990s. Many young workers waited long periods of time before they found jobs and remained in their parental homes longer and longer. In some countries youth unemployment was at levels that two or three decades ago might have led to serious social disorders, Spain, France, and Italy being most prominent.

1. What went wrong with the rosy expectations that demographic changes and additional schooling would resolve the youth job market problem?

2. How have youths responded to the deteriorated job market facing them?

3. How have economic policies focused on youths, particularly policies to improve their skills, worked in the period?

4. Why does the youth labor market problem seem to have become a constant scar rather than a temporary blemish (to use David Ellwood's 1982 expression)?

This volume contains 11 studies that cast light on these questions. The volume follows a long NBER tradition in studying the youth job market. In 1982 Richard Freeman and David Wise led an NBER research project that produced *The Youth Labor Market Problem.* In 1986, the NBER examined the specific problems of black youths (Freeman and Holzer 1986). This volume contains 10 studies that cast light on these questions. In 1994 Lisa Lynch led an NBER research effort, *Training and the Private Sector,* that placed particular emphasis on the training of young workers.

The 1980s research, based primarily on the U.S. experience, found that severe employment problems were concentrated among a small proportion of youths with distinctive characteristics but that for a vast majority of youths, lack of employment is not a severe problem. Aggregate economic activity was the major determinant of the level of youth joblessness in the United States, a result this volume confirms across all countries and in ensuing decades.

The current volume provides a detailed analysis of the situation facing young workers in a variety of countries besides the United States—Germany, France, Sweden, the United Kingdom, and Canada—and extends the traditional focus on wages and employment to other important outcome measures, such as living arrangements, crime, and measures of self-reported happiness. The biggest social change affecting youth since the earlier research is that a much larger proportion of youths attend school, largely full time, in all OECD countries. Concurrently, full-time entry into the job market takes longer now than it did in earlier years. Combining initial education and work is relatively more frequent in countries that have a dual-system apprenticeship program (Austria, Denmark, and Germany) or a relatively high incidence of part-time employment (Australia, Canada, Denmark, the Netherlands, the United Kingdom, and the United States).

The volume is organized around the first three questions listed above. They are questions that careful data analysis can in principle answer. While many of the papers address more than one of these questions, we have grouped the papers according to the area where they make their primary contribution. This introduction summarizes the answers these and other recent economic studies give to the empirically answerable questions.

The fourth question—why the youth job market problem has failed to lessen over time—is arguably the most important one, but it cannot be readily answered with tables of data. After summarizing what we know about the first three questions, we offer some speculative comments on the last question.

What's Gone Wrong with the Youth Labor Market?

The facts for young men are simple. Along a variety of dimensions the economic position of male workers in the age brackets 16–24 and 25–29 has worsened relative to that of older workers in virtually all OECD countries.

In the United States the worsening has largely taken the form of a drop in the relative earnings of youths, particularly those with less than college education. But relative earnings of young workers have fallen in other advanced countries as well (Blanchflower and Freeman, chap. 1 in this volume). The surprise is that the deterioration in relative earnings of the 1980s and 1990s followed a sharp drop in relative earnings attributed to the baby boom increase in the supply of young persons on the job market, despite favorable demographic changes. As Blanchflower and Freeman and Korenman and Neumark document, the demographic shift was large.

The youth proportion of the workforce declined sizably in the United States and in virtually every other OECD country in the 1980s and 1990s. Declining youth cohort size should lead to lower unemployment rates for youth and higher relative earnings for youth, and this trend should be particularly marked in countries like Japan, Ireland, Italy, Spain, and Portugal, where the fall in the relative size of youth cohorts was exceptional.

But the economic position of youths worsened rather than improved. That the demographic changes failed to improve the position of youths much does not mean that shifts in supply have no effect on the youth job market—the elasticity of the youth unemployment rate with respect to relative youth cohort size is still positive (Korenman and Neumark, chap. 2 in this volume). Rather, it means that other factors such as aggregate rates of unemployment or technological changes or increased trade with less developed countries with huge numbers of young, less skilled workers may have made domestic supply considerations less important than they were in the past.

In the European Union the relative wages of youths fell in most countries, even though wage-setting institutions maintained relatively narrow distributions overall. Regardless of the wage experience, however, youth unemployment rates rose substantially, save for Germany. In France, increased minimum wages reduced the employment of young, less skilled workers, with an effect concentrated on a narrow band of young workers in the immediately affected parts of the wage distribution (Abowd et al., chap. 11 in this volume). The country that dealt most successfully with the youth problem is Germany. While some German youths have great trouble in the job market, and while the apprenticeship system has run into some problems, young, less educated Germans have done markedly better in both employment and wages than comparable Americans (Franz et al., chap. 10 in this volume).

The situation for young women is less troubling, as young women have continued to move into the job market in increasing numbers and as female pay has improved relative to male pay. Still, in the late 1990s young women earned less than seemingly comparable young men and experienced a similar twist in the age-earnings profile against them. The unemployment rate for young women workers has risen in most countries, and in the United States and United Kingdom at least, poverty has become increasingly concentrated among single-parent female-headed households.

The contrast between how less skilled American and German youths fare in the job market is particularly striking. Young, less educated American men and women are less likely to be employed than their German counterparts, have much lower earnings relative to more highly educated youth than do comparable German youths, and earn less than less educated German youth in purchasing power parity terms. Young, less educated American women are far more likely to be single parents than young, less educated German women. Over time, the longitudinal growth rates of earnings are considerably higher for less educated Germans than less educated Americans. The large public sector in Germany was partly responsible for the economic situation of less educated youths by employing a sizable number of low-skilled youth. At the other end of the spectrum, Americans in the highest educational group outearned Germans by considerable amounts (Blau and Kahn, chap. 3 in this volume).

One simple statistic captures the overall change in the labor market position of young workers from the 1970s to the 1990s. This is the ratio of the young persons' share of labor market earnings to their share of the population of persons aged 15 and over. The share of income going to young workers depends on both their relative earnings and relative employment (and any changes in their share of non-labor-market income). Column (1) of table 1 records the share in the U.S. 15-plus population of two youth groups, ages 15–24 and 25–34, among men; column (2) gives the share of income going to those groups; and column (3) gives the ratio of shares. For both groups the share of income going to the young has fallen substantially more than the share of the population, producing a marked fall in the relevant ratios. The pattern among women in columns (4), (5), and (6) is similar. Since the relative pay of youths has fallen in other OECD countries, as well as in the United States, and relative employment of youths has trended downward rapidly as well, the findings in table 1 should generalize to other countries. Young persons are getting a proportionately smaller share of income than they did 20 or so years ago.

What makes the deterioration of the job market for young workers

Table 1   **Declining Share of National Income Accruing to the Young in the United States by Sex, 1980–97**

	Men			Women		
Age Group	Share of Population (1)	Share of Income (2)	Ratio (3)	Share of Population (4)	Share of Income (5)	Ratio (6)
Ages 15–24						
1980	25.5	8.9	.35	23.0	13.1	.57
1990	20.2	5.3	.26	17.4	7.5	.43
1997	19.3	4.8	.25	16.5	6.4	.39
Ages 25–34						
1980	21.9	24.7	1.14	16.4	25.1	1.53
1990	23.0	22.1	.96	21.3	23.3	1.09
1997	18.9	17.9	.95	17.7	19.7	1.11

Sources: U.S. Bureau of the Census, "Historical Income Tables: People," from www.census.gov/hhes/income/histinc/p08.html; U.S. Bureau of the Census, "Resident Population of the United States: Estimates, by Age and Sex," from www.census.gov/population/estimates/nation/intfile2-1.txt; U.S. Bureau of the Census (1995, table 14).

puzzling is that most of the basic economic forces that affect youth employment prospects operated to raise their relative position. In addition to the demographically induced decline in the number of young workers, the industrial composition of employment shifted toward sectors that hire relatively many workers, retail trade and services such as hotels and restaurants. This change should have increased the employment if not the wages of young workers. And the technological factor that many analysts cite as underlying the long-run rise of inequality and higher premium to skills—computerization—should have benefited the young, who have grown up with computers, relative to older workers, who have not. Finally, the increased years of schooling and skill of younger workers relative to those of older workers should have raised their relative pay and employment. In short, things did not work out as expected in the youth job market, creating a major puzzle for analysts of this market.

How Did Youths Respond to the Deteriorated Job Market Facing Them?

Perhaps the most important and positive way in which young persons can respond to poor labor market conditions is by postponing entry into the job market and remaining in school. Without a family to support, youths can invest in human capital rather than struggle to make a living in a difficult market.

In virtually all OECD countries, enrollments in school rose from the 1980s through 1990. The deterioration in the youth job market seems to have contributed to particularly large increases in enrollments in higher education. Among Americans the proportion of young men enrolled in college and university fell in the 1970s then rose from the mid-1980s to the late 1990s. The increase in college going was steady for women, so that by the 1990s approximately 25 percent more women were graduating with bachelor's degrees than were men. Figure 1 shows the rise in U.S. enrollments in college from 1980 to 1997. Enrollments increased even more rapidly in other OECD countries, so that the United States has lost much of its edge in producing college and university graduates. Partly as a result of the response of Canadian youths to high joblessness, enrollment rates in Canada, which traditionally had been lower than in the United States, came to exceed those in the United States.

In addition to enrolling in school, young persons shifted among fields of study and occupations. In the United States more students rejected sciences and liberal arts in favor of business-related areas, and Ph.D. degrees in favor of professional degrees (Bok 1993). The flow of students toward higher paying fields should have increased the earnings of young workers relative to the earnings of older workers, but even so the earnings of young, educated workers at best stayed even with those of older, educated workers.

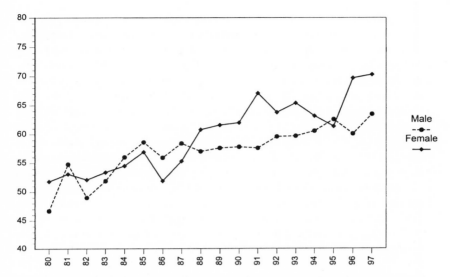

Fig. 1   College enrollment of recent high school graduates in the United States, 1980–97
Source: U.S. Bureau of the Census (1998, table 301).

A second important adjustment has been that young persons stay longer in their parents' homes or postpone setting up their own families. In Canada and the United States low youth wages increase the likelihood that young women remain living with their parents and attend school, while low employment rates raise the chances that women remain in their parents' homes but only marginally affect their rate of school attendance. Between 1971 and 1994, the proportion of 16–24-year-old American men who were heads or spouses in their own families fell from 22 to 11 percent, while in Canada the proportion dropped from 16 to 8 percent. Among women the trends were similar: a drop from 36 to 24 percent in the United States and a drop from 30 to 17 percent in Canada (Card and Lemieux, chap. 4 in this volume).

Taken together, increased schooling and residence in parental homes have elongated the period of youthful preparation for the job market and family formation. The "young" are older than they were several decades ago.

But this volume also documents another, more deleterious response of youths to the deterioration in their economic opportunities that is most marked in the United States. This response is increased involvement in crime. Large numbers of young American men committed sufficiently serious crimes in the 1980s and 1990s to make "prisoner" just about the fastest growing occupation. Young criminals come largely from disadvantaged backgrounds, including single-parent homes, have low AFQT scores, often suffer from child abuse, spend time in foster homes, have relatives who end up incarcerated, and have friends who are also involved in criminal activity. Similarly, in the United Kingdom, young men who have trouble with the police score low on academic tests, were disproportionately from single-parent homes, and were disproportionately placed in care. Many young persons involved in crime are employed before their arrest, suggesting that they have reservation wages for both legal and illegal work (Freeman, chap. 5 in this volume; Gregg and Machin, chap. 6 in this volume). While it is difficult to determine the supply elasticity of youths to crime, given the absence of good data on criminal earnings, the best evidence suggests that it is reasonably high, both to legitimate wages and unemployment (Gould, Weinberg, and Mustard 1998; Grogger 1995; Freeman, chap. 5 in this volume) and to criminal sanctions (Freeman 1999).

The reaction of youths to the deteriorated job market in terms of school enrollments, residence in parental homes, and criminal behavior indicates that the young have substantial supply responsiveness to economic incentives. The more responsive young people are to market conditions, the more likely is it that they undertake actions that bring about economic improvement for them and move the workforce into new areas. But this volume also shows that socially desirable supply responsiveness such as enrolling for additional education can be difficult for youths from disadvantaged backgrounds.

Gregg and Machin exploit a unique body of data for Great Britain to trace out the effects of early disadvantaged background on economic outcomes. The British survey has followed the social and economic progress of a cohort of persons born in a particular week in 1958. Young persons from disadvantaged backgrounds, as reflected by family income, living in a single-mother family, and, most striking, having been placed in a foster care home at some time, have lower employment and earnings even at age 33. An important transmission mechanism for the link between early childhood disadvantage and adult economic outcomes is educational attainment. In the United States a similar pattern is found in data on the family composition of youths going on to college. The huge rise of enrollments in college is concentrated among young persons from high-income families and has been minimal among those from families in the bottom quintile of the income distribution (Kane 1995).

The British data also show that children from disadvantaged backgrounds are more likely to get into trouble with the police at age 16, which in turn adds to the probability that they end up incarcerated (if male) or as a single parent (if female) as they mature. The math and reading scores of the children of parents in the 1958 cohort who are disadvantaged are also relatively low, suggesting that the pattern of disadvantage replicates itself across three generations.

Thus this volume finds truth both in the economists' model of young people responding in economically sensible ways to market conditions and in the sociologists' model of young people being greatly affected by their family backgrounds.

How Have Economic Policies to Help Youths Worked in the Period?

There are three major sorts of programs designed to help youths in the job market. On the supply side are programs that link schooling to work before youths encounter difficulties in the market and second-chance programs that try to increase the skills of youths having trouble in the job market. On the demand side are programs that raise youth wages, for instance through the minimum wage, or that direct some employment opportunities toward youths. The research in this volume examines German apprenticeships as the most highly developed school-to-work transition program, assesses Swedish active labor market programs, and assesses American JTPA training programs.

On the basis of aggregate outcomes, German apprenticeships seem to be a highly successful supply-side program. Less educated young workers have lower unemployment rates and higher relative earnings in Germany than in the United States. In the first five or so years of work, many fewer young Germans are jobless than young Americans. Apprenticeships offer a good return for most young persons. But the German apprenticeship system has its problems. The number of apprenticeship contracts has fallen, as more youths have chosen higher education. Youths who do not find jobs immediately after their apprenticeships face comparatively long periods of nonemployment, and those who fail in apprenticeship programs suffer long-term reductions in earnings. The apprenticeship system does not ameliorate the effects of family background: children of blue-collar and white-collar workers were more likely to be employed subsequently than children of nonemployed parents (Franz et al., chap. 10 in this volume).

By contrast, second-chance programs, including Sweden's much heralded active labor market programs, do not seem to be overly effective. For many years Sweden was viewed as having solved the problem of joblessness and economic inequality. During the 1970s and 1980s young workers fared reasonably despite sharply increasing youth relative wages. But the recession of the early 1990s proved that Sweden was not immune to substantial unemployment or to a major youth joblessness problem. In the 1990s youth unemployment has risen sharply, and the state has expanded youth participation in active labor market programs. This has reduced employment somewhat without solving the joblessness problem. Indeed, the increase in unemployment has been roughly proportional by age and education, implying that these programs have not altered the relative distribution of unemployment. The proportional growth of joblessness suggests that aggregate factors were more important in Sweden's jobless-ness than disaggregate shifts in demand for labor among different skill groups.

The evidence on U.S. second-chance programs is, if anything, even less positive for young men, though they seem to have benefited young women. Indeed, the argument over Job Training Partnership Act (JTPA) programs for disadvantaged young men focuses on whether they reduce the earnings of trainees rather than whether they have a benefit-cost ratio above one. U.S. studies of JTPA programs are particularly valuable because they are based on experimental evaluations of training programs. The 1995 evalua-tion of JTPA programs produced the startling result that youth training actually reduced the earnings of young male workers, inducing Congress to cut funding for the youth component of JTPA. But experimental evalu-ations involving humans are often imperfect. Some of the negative results appear due to details of the evaluation procedure: the specific way evalua-tors handled dropouts from the program, differences among sites, treat-ment of outliers, construction of earnings variables, and other technical decisions that could readily have gone differently. In addition, the fact that some youths in the "control sample" seek training outside of the program means that comparisons of the control and experimental groups give a downward bias to estimates of the effect of training per se (Heckman and Smith, chap. 8 in this volume).

France has a wide variety of youth programs and indeed leads the ad-vanced countries in the proportion of youths employed under some spe-cial program. France also has relatively high minimum wages, which can be expected to adversely affect youth employment: the real minimum hourly wage in France (the SMIC) has risen steadily since 1967, and ap-proximately 28 percent of French workers are in the range of the mini-mum—roughly 10 percent more than in the range of the U.S. minimum. In chapter 11 Abowd et al. find that young workers paid around the mini-mum wage in France were more likely to become unemployed or move out of the labor force than those paid over the minimum wage. But em-ployment effects in France are mitigated somewhat by participation in employment promotion programs that seem to shield workers from some of the effects of the increasing real SMIC. When this eligibility ends, the probability of subsequent nonemployment rises sharply.

In sum, the only policy that seems to have been effective in helping youths to make a successful transition into the job market is the highly structured German apprenticeship system. Whether this reflects the spe-cifics of the apprenticeship system or the fact that the policy affects youths before they enter the job market is uncertain. OECD (1997) data on liter-acy skills show that the bottom quintile of Germans have much higher reading, writing, and math skills than the bottom quintile of Americans, suggesting that the big U.S.-German difference is in premarket skills. But several other EU countries have more skilled bottom-quintile workers than the United States while still suffering from major youth job market problems.

Why Has the Youth Labor Market Problem Become a Constant Scar Rather Than a Temporary Blemish?

This volume examines some differences in how countries prepare youths for the job market and institutionalize the transition from school to work. In the United States, young workers shift jobs often as they search for a good match: spells of joblessness are short but frequent. In Italy and Spain, young workers wait extended periods of time to obtain permanent jobs: spells of joblessness are long, but youths eventually obtain fairly secure permanent jobs. In Germany and Austria, apprenticeship programs smooth the transition from school to work, which tends to shift forward the period where unemployment peaks. These institutions affect outcomes, but a consistent pattern of special "youth" differences remains, as does—save in Germany—a consistent worsening of the position of youths.

Why did the relative economic position of youths deteriorate despite their increased education and smaller cohort sizes? One reason is that aggregate unemployment was relatively high in OECD countries in the 1980s and 1990s. The demand for young workers is highly sensitive to aggregate economic conditions (Blanchflower and Freeman, chap. 1 in this volume; Clark and Summers 1982). As new entrants to the job market, young workers lack the specific training or seniority that buffers older workers from swings in market conditions. Their employment is highly dependent on the aggregate state of the labor market. High rates of unemployment in the European Union thus go a long way to explaining the prevailing rate of youth joblessness. The fall in joblessness in the United States in the late 1990s produced some rise in youth wages, as well as employment, after two decades or so of decline, but it did not come close to restoring the relative position of young workers (Freeman and Rodgers 1999).

The influx of women into the job market may also have affected the economic position of young workers. Many women workers are new entrants or reentrants into the job market who might fill jobs that younger workers would otherwise hold. But female pay has increased as the supply of women to the workforce has grown. Since we would expect the effects of an increase in the supply of women to be greater on women than on substitute young workers, this makes any *cherchez la femme* story difficult to sustain.

Increased trade with developing countries is another potential determinant of the deteriorated economic position of young workers. On a world scale the share of youths in the working age population is much larger than in advanced countries. Thus trade with less developed countries might be expected to reduce the relative position of young workers. But again, the sectors that compete most with less developed countries are those such as apparel that traditionally employ women workers, so one would expect trade to have devastated their wages or employment rather than that of young men.

All told, while the increased supply of competitive workers due to women or trade may have affected the position of young workers, these forces do not seem powerful enough to counteract the demographic and demand factors that favored young workers. To explain the observed deterioration in terms of labor supply, we must argue that workers in the baby boom generation are highly substitutable with younger workers so that the baby boom cohort reduced not only their own earnings but those of ensuing, smaller cohorts as well (Macunovich 1998). As the baby boom cohort gets older and older, however, and the economic position of young workers remains depressed, this becomes an increasingly tenuous claim.

Yet another supply-side possibility may resonate with those who need the Ponce de Léon potion: that young workers are simply not as good as older workers. Test scores for younger and older workers on the OECD international adult literacy survey reject this explanation save for the United States and Ireland. This survey, conducted in 1994, gave adults in several countries the same test of their literacy skills—prose, document, and literacy. The figures for all countries except the United States and Ireland show that younger workers are more skilled than older workers (OECD 1997). Because the survey does not include college students on campuses, however, it probably understates the skill level of younger Americans. Even if a decline in youth skills can help to explain the problems of young American workers, it cannot explain the fall in the relative position of youths across the OECD.

In sum, it is difficult to make a case that measurable market forces beyond high aggregate unemployment caused the worsened job market for young workers.

The Absence of Youth Protest

Given that the relative economic position of youths has declined, in some countries sharply, why have youths not protested collectively as their counterparts did in the late 1960s and early 1970s? With the sole exception of French youths, who protested a proposed youth subminimum wage in 1995 and demanded low pupil-teacher ratios and higher school quality in 1998, there has been virtually no collective youth response to worsened job prospects. High youth joblessness in Spain, Italy, and the United Kingdom has not generated Danny the Reds, mass student movements, or the conflict of the generations that marked the 1960s. In the United States the

American Association of Retired Persons raises the battle cry for the old, but there is no countervailing force on behalf of young workers.

One explanation this volume suggests is that, economics aside, youths are happier than in the past. Blanchflower and Oswald document that youths report greater happiness or life satisfaction than in the past. Perhaps sex, drugs, the end of the cold war, postponement of family responsibilities, and improved consumption have offset the fall in relative earnings and employment. But the increased happiness of youths is not evinced in one hard statistic: the relative number of suicides by young people, which have trended differently across countries. Suicide rates among young men rose between the 1970s and 1990s in English-speaking countries and Norway; fell in Japan, Sweden, Austria, and West Germany; and show little change elsewhere (Blanchflower and Freeman, chap. 1 in this volume). The increase in happiness occurs largely among the rising number of young persons who are unmarried, perhaps because they enjoy more personal freedom and greater social tolerance than similarly unmarried young persons in the past. But it leaves open the question of why youth suicide rates remain high.

Another explanation is that the worsened employment and earnings opportunities of young workers is a temporary state that simple aging will eliminate. Perhaps an extra year to find a permanent job or a drop in starting pay are transitional glitches with little or no consequences for lifetime income prospects. What matters is permanent income—the discounted present value of lifetime income—not transitory income. But if "temporary glitch" means that the lifetime income of young workers is unaffected by their entering the world of work in a depressed job market, this explanation is false. Cohorts who start off in worsened conditions historically do not recover from the initial adverse shock to their economic prospects. A cohort that enters the job market in a bad period will not "catch up" to the position it would have held had it entered in a good period. At best, the lifetime income profile of the cohort will follow a "normal" path, beginning at a lower starting point.

A third possibility is that while young workers may have suffered a permanent loss in real income compared to what they might have made absent the depressed market, the likelihood that they will have higher lifetime income than earlier generations has dissipated any discontent. In a world of rising per capita income, it would take an extraordinary shock for young cohorts to end up with lower income than older cohorts. Consider two groups of workers, parents and youngsters separated by 25 years. The income of both groups consists solely of labor market earnings. With a growth rate of real earnings of 1.5 percent per year due to technological change and human and physical capital accumulation, the younger generation will have a 45 percent higher discounted lifetime income than the older generation. Even a 20 percent permanent fall in the real earnings of the younger cohort relative to their parents will leave them with a 25 percent income advantage. Thus, if youths compare their lifetime income to that of older workers, the fact that they are better off (though less so than they might have been) may also dampen collective sentiments for protest.

Note also that the "rising tide" of growth argues against programs designed solely to redistribute income toward younger people. As long as the older generation provides the young with education and physical capital, the young have higher lifetime income than the old. Your local 20–25-year-old may have problems in the job market today, but he or she will still enjoy a higher standard of living than your local 45–50-year-old. In some situations, moreover, improvements in technology will make the lives of younger cohorts almost incommensurately better. Today medicine cannot cure the wealthiest person with AIDS, certain cancers, and so forth, but n years in the future medicine will presumably cure the poorest person with those diseases. From this perspective, the drop in the relative earnings of the young is an egalitarian redistribution. If you had to choose to reduce the earnings of older or younger workers or to have older or younger workers jobless, it is better to have the burden fall on the young. As Euripides said, "Youth is the best time to be rich, and the best time to be poor."

That each generation should (and will) do better than the previous generation is part and parcel of the modern economic world. To what extent has the depressed youth job market challenged this notion? Into the late 1990s surveys in the United States reported that a growing proportion of the population believed that their children would not enjoy the benefits of the rising tide. Sixty-seven percent of Americans said in 1997 that they thought the "economic situation" for their children would be worse than for their generation (Yankelovitch 1997). Given trends in the real earnings of median workers in the United States in the 1970s through 1990s, this was not an unrealistic expectation for many Americans, though Americans should have a more optimistic view as the economic boom of the late 1990s has continued.

But there is another possible comparison. Perhaps youths do not compare themselves much with the preceding generation. Older persons may remember that they had a relatively better employment situation when they were young, but the young do not look at historical age-earnings ratios and then take to the streets. Perhaps youths compare themselves largely with their peers. In this case, a fall in the ratio of youth income to that of older workers will not produce generational conflict. Everyone in a youth cohort may have a depressed income, but those at the top of the group might regard their situation as good rather than poor.

If the right comparison group consists of persons within a youth cohort, there are two telling statistics. For the United States at least, inequality in earnings has risen substantially among the young. And in the European Union, youth unemployment or inactivity has become highly concentrated in households where no other person is employed. In the majority of OECD countries for which trend data exist, moreover, the concentration of the unemployed in jobless homes has increased. From this perspective, the "real problem" in the youth job market is that society is sorting young people into two groups—the educated, skilled, and well paid and the less educated, unskilled, and unemployed or low paid.

One additional explanation for the lack of youth protest is that the weak labor market gives them little power to make demands on the rest of society. What can they do in politics or in the job market? The pre-baby boomers enjoyed a strong market that gives them a relatively good economic position. The baby boom generation, whose incomes fell relative to older workers, has the strength of numbers. The post-baby boomers have neither numbers nor a strong labor market. They cannot readily strike against more senior workers. With severe competition in the job market, who wants to risk his or her future by engaging in disruptive protests? And more skilled and educated young persons may have less in common with the less skilled and educated than they have with the older generation.

In sum, the experience of the 1980s and 1990s suggests that advanced countries can tolerate relatively high levels of youth joblessness and relatively high differentials between adult and youth earnings without risking social disorder. This does not mean that policies and programs designed to help youths fare better in the job market are not desirable—some policies may very well meet relevant benefit-cost tests—but that efforts to improve the youth job market are more likely to be successful as part of general reforms in the labor market than of more focused changes.

References

Berger, Mark. 1984. Cohort size and the earnings growth of young workers. *Industrial and Labor Relations Review* 37 (4): 582–91.

Bok, Derek. 1993. *The cost of talent: How executives and professionals are paid and how it affects america.* New York: Free Press.

Clark, Kim, and Lawrence Summers. 1982. The dynamics of youth unemployment. In *The youth labor market problem: Its nature, causes, and consequences,* ed. Richard B. Freeman and David A. Wise. Chicago: University of Chicago Press.

Ellwood, David T. 1982. Teenage unemployment: Permanent scars or temporary blemishes? In *The youth labor market problem: Its nature, causes, and consequences,* ed. Richard B. Freeman and David A. Wise. Chicago: University of Chicago Press.

Freeman, Richard B. 1979. The effect of demographic factors on the age-earnings profile in the U.S. *Journal of Human Resources* 14 (3): 289–318.

————. 1999. The economics of crime. In *Handbook of labor economics*, vol. 3, ed. Orley Ashenfelter and David Card. Amsterdam: Elsevier. Forthcoming.

Freeman, Richard B., and Harry J. Holzer, eds. 1986. *The black youth employment crisis.* Chicago: University of Chicago Press.

Freeman, Richard B., and William Rodgers. 1999. Area economic conditions and the labor market outcomes of young men in the 1990s expansion. NBER Working Paper no. 7073. Cambridge, Mass.: National Bureau of Economic Research, May.

Freeman, Richard B., and David A. Wise, eds. 1982. *The youth labor market problem: Its nature, causes, and consequences.* Chicago: University of Chicago Press.

Gould, Eric D., Bruce A. Weinberg, and David B. Mustard. 1998. Crime rates and local labor market opportunities in the United States, 1979–95. Paper presented at the annual meeting of the American Economics Association, Chicago.

Grogger, Jeffrey. 1995. The effect of arrests on the employment and earnings of young men. *Quarterly Journal of Economics* 110:51–72.

Kane, Thomas J. 1995. Rising public college tuition and college entry: How well do public subsidies promote access to college? NBER Working Paper no. 5164. Cambridge, Mass.: National Bureau of Economic Research, July.

Lynch, Lisa M., ed. 1994. *Training and the private sector: International comparisons.* Chicago: University of Chicago Press.

Macunovich, Diane J. 1998. The fortunes of one's birth: Relative cohort size and the wage structure of the U.S. Paper presented at the NBER Summer Institute Labor Workshop, Cambridge, Mass., July.

OECD (Organization for Economic Cooperation and Development). 1978. *Youth unemployment: A report on the high level conference.* Paris: Organization for Economic Cooperation and Development.

————. 1997. *Literary skills for the knowledge society, 1997.* Paris: Organization for Economic Cooperation and Development.

U.S. Bureau of the Census. 1995. *Statistical abstract of the United States, 1995.* Washington, D.C.: Government Printing Office.

————. 1998. *Statistical abstract of the United States, 1998.* Washington, D.C.: Bureau of the Census.

Welch, Finis. 1979. Effects of cohort size on earnings: The baby boom babies' financial bust. *Journal of Political Economy* 87, no. 5, pt. 2: S65–S97.

Yankelovitch Partners. 1997. CNN survey. 5–6 February.

I

The Situation Facing
Young Workers

The Declining Economic Status of Young Workers in OECD Countries

David G. Blanchflower and Richard B. Freeman

Throughout the OECD, young people had greater problems in the job market in the 1990s than in earlier decades. In some countries, this shows up in relatively high unemployment rates and low rates of employment to population. In other countries it takes the form largely of reduced wages for young workers. The worsened job market for the young occurred despite three trends favorable to them: a demographically induced decline in their relative supply; increased enrollments in school, which should have lowered the supply of youths to the job market; and an expansion of low-wage service industries that traditionally hire many youths. This chapter documents the dimensions of the deterioration in the youth job market and isolates the aggregate unemployment rate as the only variable that is consistently related to that deterioration. Finding that high aggregate unemployment excessively affected young workers in the 1990s is consistent with earlier NBER work (see Clark and Summers 1981). Our analysis also shows, however, that aggregate unemployment by itself falls far short of explaining the pattern of change. Conditional on aggregate unemployment, the male employment-population rate trended down while the female employment-population rate trended up, as did the employment-population rate for teenagers in school of both sexes.

David G. Blanchflower is professor in and chairman of the Department of Economics at Dartmouth College and a research associate of the National Bureau of Economic Research. Richard B. Freeman holds the Herbert Ascherman Chair in Economics at Harvard University and is director of the NBER Labor Studies Program and codirector of the Centre for Economic Performance of the London School of Economics.

The authors are deeply grateful to Norman Bowers for helping them with data and analysis. They also thank Peter Elias, Eric Hernaes, Max Tani, and John Wall. This project was partially funded by the Rockefeller Foundation.

1.1   The Transition into Work

Over a period of years any given cohort of young people moves from near full enrollment in school to negligible enrollment in school, and from negligible labor market activity to high levels of labor market activity. The length of the transition period depends on the pattern of elementary and secondary education and of higher education and vocational training in a country and on the economic attractiveness of work. In most advanced countries, the period covers 10 to 15 years: from roughly age 16 to ages 25–30. At age 16 the vast majority of the young are enrolled in school; by ages 25–30 school enrollment rates are 5 percent or less. At age 16 employment-population rates and labor force activity rates are low; by ages 25–30 they are high for both men and women. In this section we examine the pattern of this transition and the effects of aggregate unemployment on the transition.

Figure 1.1 shows the transition in terms of the percentage of youths in school in two or three age cohorts, separately by gender, as those cohorts age. The horizontal axis reports the years since age 16 for specified cohorts. The vertical axis gives the percentage of the youth cohort in school. The data for the European countries are derived from EUROSTAT-based surveys in which persons are asked if they are in school, regardless of their major activity. For most countries the figure covers the cohort aged 16 in 1983 and the cohort aged 16 in 1988. For the United States and Canada the data series is longer, covering the 1973 cohort for the United States and the 1976 cohort for Canada. The U.S. figures are limited to persons who report that their major activity is school and thus understate the numbers in school compared to most other countries.[1] The figure shows a universal decline in the percentage in school. In Europe and in Canada the curve for the 1988 cohort lies above the curve for the 1983 cohort, implying that years in school are increasing. Data for the individual countries show that this is due in large part to sharp upward shifts in schooling in Portugal, Spain, and France. In the United States, where postsecondary education increased earlier than elsewhere, the curves lie essentially on top of one another, implying a stable proportion enrolled in school as their major activity in the periods covered.

Figure 1.2 examines the transition from school to work in terms of the endpoint state of employment. This figure shows the percentage of youths

---

1. The extent of the understatement can be estimated for 16–24-year-olds, who, from the early 1980s to the early 1990s, were also asked directly if they were enrolled in school. The rates of enrollment so reported are approximately 10 percentage points higher than the proportion who report school as their major activity. In 1993, 21 percent of 16–24-year-olds who reported work as their major activity also said they were enrolled in school, largely in college, and over two-thirds were full-time students. Cross-country comparisons of school enrollment based on administrative data, as in OECD (1995), are also subject to problems, due to differences in the level of schooling, full-time versus part-time status, etc.

in a cohort who are employed whether they are in school or out of school. The pattern of cohort employment is a mirror image of the pattern for schooling shown in figure 1.1. The percentage working rises in a sigmoidal curve. For men the cohort employment curves approach 85 to 90 percent in most countries. But in Europe, where the aggregate unemployment rate is relatively high, the cohort employment curves are lower than in the United States, with lower aggregate unemployment rates. Similarly, cohorts who entered the job market in the late 1980s tend to have lower employment rates than cohorts who entered earlier. The fall in the cohort employment curves was greatest for France and Canada (see Blanchflower and Freeman 1992; OECD 1996). For women the curves also have a logistic shape, but the increases in the percentage working levels off at noticeably different levels among countries. In many countries the female employment rates approach 75 percent or so, but in some countries, such as Greece, Spain, and Italy, they level off at much lower rates.

How has the transition from school to work changed during the period under study? Table 1.1 provides a capsule picture of the activity status of young persons aged 18 and 22 in 1997 and 13 years earlier in 1984, by sex, as reported in labor force surveys. The table shows a general pattern of increased school enrollments, constant level of apprenticeships, increased proportion of the young neither in school nor in the labor force, decreased employment-to-population rates, and high rates of unemployment in most countries for youths of both genders. The rise in school enrollments is most marked outside the United States. Among 18-year-olds, in 1986 61 percent of U.S. men and 56 percent of U.S. women were in school, considerably above the OECD averages by gender (48.8 percent for men and 50.6 percent for women). By contrast in 1997, U.S. 18-year-old men are just slightly above the OECD average in the percentage enrolled in school and U.S. women are slightly below the OECD average. The proportion of young men who are idle—that is, neither in school nor in the labor force— has increased over the period 1984–97 and especially so in the United Kingdom and the United States, although the levels are considerably higher for the former: 11.4 versus 6.8 percent for 18-year-olds and 8.4 versus 5.6 percent for 22-year-olds. The proportion of young women who are idle decreased in the OECD as a whole but increased, as it did for men, in Germany, the United States, and the United Kingdom. With respect to employment, employment-population rates fell between 1984 and 1997 in virtually all the OECD countries in the table. The unweighted average shows that 35.4 percent of 18-year-old men were employed in 1997 compared to 43.8 percent employed in 1984, a drop of 8.4 percentage points, and that 29.9 percent of 18-year-old women were employed in 1997 compared to 36.6 percent in 1984, a drop of 6.7 percentage points. The comparable figures for 22-year-olds show drops in employment rates of 7.0 percentage points for men and 4.0 percentage points for women. Interestingly,

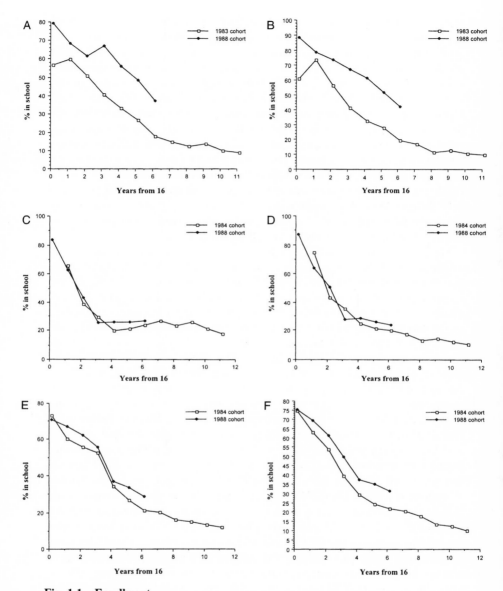

Fig. 1.1   Enrollment

Note: *A*, France, males; *B*, France, females. *C*, Germany, males; *D*, Germany, females. *E*, Italy, males; *F*, Italy, females. *G*, U.K., males; *H*, U.K., females. *I*, U.S., males; *J*, U.S., females.

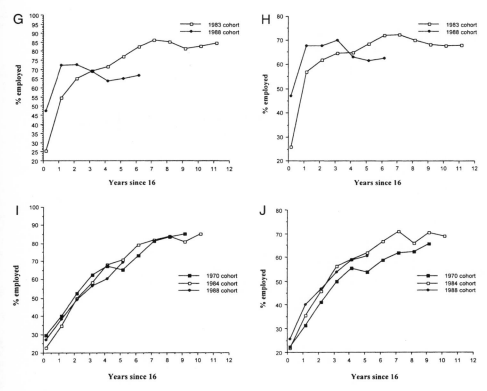

Fig. 1.2   (cont.)

result from tables 1.1 and 1.2 is that the transition period from school to work has grown longer.

One consequence of the longer transition period is an upward trend in the proportion of working youths at specific ages who are students.[2] This is shown in table 1.3 for young persons aged 18, 22, and 26. Among 18-year-olds the rise in the student proportion of youth employment is substantial in some countries. For instance, in Denmark, the in-school proportion of the employed rose from 23.9 percent in 1984 to 50.8 percent in 1994 among men and from 32.5 percent in 1984 to 63.5 percent in 1994 among women. The rise in the student share of the youth workforce is noticeable even in countries where students have not traditionally worked, such as France and Italy. Among all OECD countries in the sample the unweighted share of 18-year-old male employees who were students rose from 15.7 percent in 1984 to 25.1 percent in 1994. Similarly, the unweighted share of 18-year-old female employees who were students rose

2. This is not an algebraic necessity because nonstudents could have increased their employment while that of students fell. In fact, the opposite occurred. Increased employment of "in-school" youths helped raise the student share of the workforce.

Table 1.1   Labor Market Status, 1984–97

Gender and Country	Attending School (%) 1984	1997	In Some Apprenticeship (%) 1984	1997	Not in School and Not in Labor Force (%) 1984	1997	Employment-Population Ratio 1984	1997	Unemployment-Population Ratio 1984	1997
Men aged 18										
Australia[a]	26.4	41.6	18.1	11.9	2.1	3.8	66.0	53.7	17.2	16.3
Belgium	72.6	82.5	2.1	2.1	4.2	7.9	18.1	5.1	8.1	4.3
Canada[b]	58.8	72.5	n.a.	n.a.	6.1	5.6	43.8	43.2	15.3	12.3
Denmark[b]	41.5	51.7	30.6	29.1	1.7	2.3	66.3	70.3	8.0	9.3
France	54.8	80.7	8.1	8.3	3.2	2.6	27.2	15.0	15.3	5.2
Germany[b]	37.1	41.1	41.1	45.8	1.0	3.4	61.8	53.0	5.0	2.8
Greece[b]	56.8	69.1	0.6	0.5	5.5	6.0	33.4	18.1	7.1	8.3
Ireland[b]	41.8	63.5	6.1	2.4	1.3	3.4	43.5	27.1	18.3	8.6
Italy	56.4	68.7	0.4	0.0	2.9	6.4	30.8	18.9	12.2	8.1
Netherlands[c]	68.1	73.0	3.3	7.1	4.5	6.3	26.3	56.8	10.6	5.5
Portugal[d]	34.9	64.7	–	–	3.8	2.7	57.9	30.2	11.9	6.0
Spain[d]	49.3	69.7	–	–	1.6	5.0	25.8	18.0	23.8	13.9
United Kingdom	29.2	34.6	15.1	12.4	2.4	11.4	59.0	61.8	21.0	12.4
United States[d]	60.9	67.4	n.a.	n.a.	1.1	6.8	46.3	43.3	17.9	12.7
OECD average	48.8	63.6	11.3	11.5	3.0	4.7	43.8	35.4	13.0	9.1
Men aged 22										
Australia[a]	10.2	17.2	7.8	4.3	1.9	4.3	81.3	73.1	12.2	16.7
Belgium	36.9	38.0	1.7	0.9	2.4	6.0	51.8	46.7	14.7	11.9
Canada[b]	23.3	37.4	n.a.	n.a.	6.4	5.6	62.4	62.6	17.3	11.5
Denmark[b]	20.0	33.2	7.8	10.9	3.7	6.7	75.3	66.9	8.4	8.1
France	15.0	43.1	0.4	2.0	2.6	3.3	72.6	42.1	14.3	15.6

Germany[b]	23.8	26.1	5.1	9.0	1.4	4.2	68.3	66.4	8.3	8.4
Greece[b]	21.9	29.8	0.1	0.2	3.4	3.7	64.3	54.9	13.1	13.8
Ireland[b]	11.9	22.4	1.8	3.1	2.4	4.0	69.4	60.7	20.1	14.4
Italy	24.5	29.5	0.2	0.2	3.4	9.1	58.7	46.0	17.3	18.1
Netherlands[c]	39.6	48.5	2.4	3.9	2.8	4.9	58.2	72.7	16.0	3.6
Portugal[d]	19.6	36.4	–	–	4.9	2.9	70.9	62.4	11.9	9.6
Spain[d]	18.5	38.3	–	–	2.3	2.8	46.8	49.3	32.6	17.8
United Kingdom	14.6	18.2	1.3	3.5	2.3	8.4	76.0	72.8	15.1	11.5
United States[d]	25.5	29.6	n.a.	n.a.	0.9	5.6	76.1	78.2	12.4	5.0
OECD average	21.5	32.7	2.3	2.9	2.8	4.6	67.6	60.6	14.1	12.1
Women aged 18										
Australia[a]	28.6	51.4	6.5	7.5	6.9	5.5	59.3	50.9	14.6	17.5
Belgium	74.3	88.1	0.7	1.0	5.9	6.0	12.8	2.8	9.6	3.4
Canada[b]	59.5	73.6	n.a.	n.a.	7.9	5.6	43.6	44.8	11.8	10.3
Denmark[b]	50.2	78.3	21.3	6.1	3.3	1.7	57.3	54.4	7.1	12.1
France	61.0	86.5	2.3	3.8	4.4	2.7	16.3	6.3	20.5	5.7
Germany[b]	43.3	49.4	29.6	35.6	2.5	5.5	53.1	39.6	6.6	4.1
Greece[b]	49.5	69.8	0.2	0.1	22.4	8.8	18.3	10.1	14.4	14.6
Ireland[b]	50.6	77.0	1.4	1.0	2.2	3.8	37.1	16.4	18.6	7.9
Italy	54.3	75.3	0.4	0.2	11.9	9.0	20.5	10.3	16.6	7.2
Netherlands[c]	65.9	78.0	0.8	5.3	4.8	4.9	27.4	54.0	12.8	7.8
Portugal[d]	39.5	72.9	0.1	–	11.8	6.4	38.9	18.6	14.5	6.3
Spain[d]	48.9	76.5	–	–	15.2	4.3	15.6	10.1	20.3	15.2
United Kingdom	31.5	41.9	4.4	6.1	10.8	16.2	56.4	59.5	14.9	7.2
United States[d]	56.2	65.7	n.a.	n.a.	8.6	11.6	42.5	47.1	17.7	8.0
OECD average	50.6	70.6	5.8	6.5	8.1	5.8	36.6	29.9	13.5	9.4

(continued)

Table 1.1 (continued)

Gender and Country	Attending School (%)		In Some Apprenticeship (%)		Not in School and Not in Labor Force (%)		Employment-Population Ratio		Unemployment-Population Ratio	
	1984	1997	1984	1997	1984	1997	1984	1997	1984	1997
Women aged 22										
Australia[a]	10.8	20.3	3.4	4.0	20.5	13.5	67.2	67.9	7.7	11.8
Belgium	26.1	35.3	0.9	n.a.	9.2	11.7	50.1	43.9	19.1	12.2
Canada[b]	18.4	38.8	n.a.	n.a.	16.6	13.0	64.1	60.4	10.8	8.6
Denmark[b]	17.4	38.8	15.3	14.0	7.5	6.5	73.4	62.7	11.1	11.6
France	16.7	44.3	0.2	1.5	14.4	7.8	59.1	38.5	16.1	17.8
Germany[b]	19.7	23.7	3.4	9.2	12.7	15.2	63.3	59.5	7.2	7.4
Greece[b]	14.3	30.5	0.2	0.2	41.8	18.6	35.3	34.7	12.1	19.9
Ireland[b]	7.1	22.0	0.7	2.4	16.0	7.6	69.0	62.5	10.4	8.9
Italy	19.5	39.9	0.2	0.3	22.7	16.5	41.3	30.2	20.0	18.2
Netherlands[c]	24.0	48.2	1.1	1.2	14.0	8.6	64.3	72.6	9.3	4.8
Portugal[d]	24.2	45.4	–	–	21.3	5.0	45.5	51.3	14.3	6.7
Spain[d]	24.9	50.5	–	0.1	21.3	5.3	28.3	33.2	25.8	22.1
United Kingdom	30.3	38.2	9.8	9.4	6.6	13.7	57.8	60.7	17.9	9.9
United States[d]	58.6	66.6	n.a.	n.a.	4.7	9.2	44.4	45.2	17.8	10.2
OECD average	17.4	35.1	2.1	2.9	18.2	11.2	57.6	53.6	12.4	11.6

Source: OECD (1999).

Note: n.a. = data not available. OECD average is unweighted.

[a]Data refer to 1984 and 1994.

[b]Data refer to 1984 and 1996.

[c]Data refer to 1983 and 1997.

[d]Data refer to 1986 and 1997.

Table 1.2   Employment-Population Ratios, 1979–97

Country and Gender		1979 15–19	20–24	25–54	1989 15–19	20–24	25–54	1997 15–19	20–24	25–54
Australia	Men	52.5	82.6	91.7	51.9	82.1	89.0	42.2	71.3	84.6
	Women	43.8	63.6	48.8	48.8	71.4	62.3	43.7	66.2	64.1
Canada	Men	48.0	77.0	90.4	51.8	75.7	88.0	36.8	67.8	83.9
	Women	43.0	64.9	54.2	50.2	70.6	69.1	36.4	62.8	70.5
France	Men	22.8	73.8	93.3	12.9	59.0	89.8	7.5	40.5	85.6
	Women	13.5	59.0	59.5	7.0	45.5	64.0	2.7	30.4	67.3
Germany	Men	46.9	76.8	93.0	39.7	73.3	87.1	31.7	68.0	85.1
	Women	42.2	67.7	53.3	34.3	68.3	57.7	24.4	60.8	66.0
Ireland	Men	43.8	83.6	88.8	22.4	65.1	78.8	20.6	63.9	81.7
	Women	36.8	65.2	26.3	18.2	63.5	36.6	15.0	59.0	53.0
Italy	Men	24.3	58.9	91.5	17.4	53.6	86.4	14.8	41.1	79.1
	Women	17.2	41.9	36.2	11.6	40.3	42.3	9.4	29.7	44.2
Japan	Men	17.0	67.9	95.7	15.6	68.5	95.5	16.9	70.3	95.1
	Women	18.1	67.6	55.2	16.3	71.5	61.9	15.6	68.9	64.6
Norway	Men	39.4	59.5	92.1	38.6	72.4	89.7	40.4	72.3	89.7
	Women	35.8	58.4	64.9	39.7	63.6	76.2	36.5	62.5	80.4
Portugal	Men	58.8	82.9	92.1	48.2	76.2	92.0	23.0	58.8	87.7
	Women	38.4	54.1	49.6	33.6	59.3	63.6	15.2	47.3	71.1
Spain	Men	44.2	71.9	90.1	33.7	58.9	84.5	19.3	47.2	80.1
	Women	31.5	45.7	28.9	17.8	36.6	35.3	8.7	32.3	43.4
United Kingdom	Men	–	–	–	65.8	81.6	89.2	52.1	71.6	85.4
	Women	–	–	–	64.3	69.2	67.3	52.4	63.9	71.3
United States	Men	51.7	78.9	91.2	48.7	77.8	89.9	43.4	75.2	88.4
	Women	45.3	62.4	59.0	46.4	66.4	70.4	43.3	66.8	73.5
OECD	Men	41.6	74.6	91.6	36.4	70.3	89.3	29.1	63.8	86.8
	Women	34.5	60.9	53.3	31.7	59.9	59.6	24.1	53.2	63.9

Source: OECD (1999).

Note: OECD average is unweighted using a fuller set of countries.

Table 1.3   **Student Proportion of Youth Employment, 1984–94**

Gender and Country	Age 18		Age 22		Age 26	
	1984	1994	1984	1994	1984	1994
Men						
Australia	41.7	43.9	14.9	18.0	12.6	12.8
Belgium	7.1	11.5	4.9	3.8	6.9	3.0
Canada	46.1	68.1	14.0	22.8	7.0	12.2
Denmark	23.9	50.8	6.4	15.9	5.1	7.0
France	1.9	15.6	1.9	9.4	1.7	6.9
Germany	5.8	12.0	2.0	5.8	2.0	6.7
Greece	5.8	5.1	2.0	2.7	1.1	1.7
Ireland	5.9	10.8	3.5	3.7	1.9	1.9
Italy	2.1	2.6	2.4	3.0	2.2	1.7
Luxembourg	0.9	5.6	1.6	1.4	1.0	0.9
Netherlands[a]	23.7	55.1	13.7	25.6	12.5	7.4
Portugal[b]	10.2	16.6	7.9	10.2	2.1	8.7
Spain[b]	2.0	11.3	0.6	6.6	0.2	6.5
United Kingdom	14.6	21.9	6.6	7.9	3.9	5.1
United States[c]	43.8	46.3	9.2	12.0	2.1	2.1
OECD average	15.7	25.1	6.1	9.9	4.2	5.6
Women						
Australia	21.8	51.8	12.8	22.1	10.4	12.9
Belgium	3.2	6.7	2.5	2.7	5.6	2.8
Canada	47.1	72.1	14.6	27.9	10.2	6.0
Denmark	32.5	63.5	9.6	15.6	5.1	13.8
France	5.7	27.6	3.8	16.2	1.6	8.1
Germany	7.3	15.4	2.3	5.9	1.2	4.0
Greece	2.1	8.5	4.4	3.6	1.5	1.6
Ireland	6.9	23.3	2.3	3.7	3.1	1.7
Italy	2.5	2.3	2.1	3.5	2.5	3.4
Luxembourg	3.1	4.2	0	3.2	0.7	2.5
Netherlands[a]	18.8	65.7	10.3	16.5	9.3	5.1
Portugal[b]	4.0	15.8	8.0	16.4	6.2	9.0
Spain[b]	0.5	17.8	0.9	12.3	0.2	8.1
United Kingdom	18.1	33.0	3.2	7.8	2.6	5.8
United States[c]	42.9	45.6	7.3	13.2	1.8	1.5
OECD average	14.4	30.2	5.6	11.4	4.1	5.8

Source: OECD School Cohort Dataset.

Note: OECD average is unweighted.

[a]Data refer to 1993 and 1994.

[b]Data refer to 1986 and 1994.

[c]Data refer to 1983 and 1993.

from 14.4 percent in 1984 to 30.2 percent in 1994. Trends are similar for 22- and 26-year-olds, though for these age groups the student proportion of young workers remains generally small. Over all, working while in school is becoming a more important part of the school-to-work transition than the traditional model of school, then work.

Successful transition into the world of work varies considerably by educational attainment in every country. We illustrate this phenomenon across countries in tables 1.4 through 1.7. Table 1.4 presents unemployment rates for 1996 one year after leaving education by level of educational attainment. Unemployment rates are generally much higher for those with the least education. What does stand out from this table, though, is how low the unemployment rates for the least educated are in Germany (9.7 percent for men and 13 percent for women). This contrasts dramatically with most other countries, where more than one-third of such individuals were unemployed one year after completing their educations. Table 1.5 uses longitudinal data and reports labor market status in surveys taken one, three, and five years after completing initial education. It tells a story similar to that reported in table 1.4. Germany gets young people into jobs early and they stay employed. It takes much longer for young people in the United States, for example, to find work. Table 1.6 once again uses longitudinal data: young people report their labor market status in each of five years after they complete their educations. Youths in Germany are much less likely to report any unemployment experience than those in either Australia or the United States. Table 1.7 uses recall data to generate work histories over the five-year period after completion of initial education. Labor market status is reported in each month over the period; the table reports the proportion of the sample who have spent *any* time unemployed. Approximately 28 percent of youths in Germany experienced some unemployment, compared with 56 percent in the United States. There was no significant difference between men and women in the proportion who had experienced unemployment in either Germany or the United States.[3] What is noticeable is the much higher proportion of young people in Germany than in the United States who had never been unemployed (82 and 44 percent, respectively). Also, the experience of unemployment declines dramatically with level of educational attainment, with the rise in unemployment experience being much greater in the United States than in Germany. Unemployment duration in France for the least educated was especially long: over 58 percent of the least educated experienced at least 12 months of unemployment, compared with just under 10 percent in Germany and around 23 percent in the United States. What

---

3. In Germany 27.1 percent of men and 28.6 percent of women had experienced unemployment, compared with 56.4 percent of men and 58.0 percent of women in the United States.

Table 1.4   Unemployment Rates One Year after Leaving Initial Education, 1996

Country	Men			Women		
	Less Than Upper Secondary	Upper Secondary	University/ Tertiary	Less Than Upper Secondary	Upper Secondary	University/ Tertiary
Belgium	68.0	37.5	16.1	71.9	51.2	25.8
Denmark	41.6	11.8	3.2	24.6	10.7	29.1
Finland	31.0	48.8	22.6	58.4	58.3	28.2
France	38.7	30.8	27.4	38.3	37.6	31.3
Germany[a]	9.7	8.9	15.2	13.0	7.6	15.1
Greece	32.1	46.7	41.3	74.3	65.5	55.5
Ireland	33.7	17.5	15.8	12.9	16.4	9.9
Italy	43.0	53.2	63.4	64.5	72.6	61.8
Netherlands	30.6	16.9	23.7	42.5	24.2	30.6
Portugal	35.6	48.5	42.9	57.8	52.6	43.3
Spain	45.3	51.4	50.7	58.3	59.8	61.8
United Kingdom	25.6	22.6	25.9	19.3	19.6	12.7
United States[a]	25.6	12.0	11.5	61.6	15.0	9.3
OECD average	33.8	30.2	27.7	43.6	34.4	30.5

Source: OECD (1999).

Note: OECD unweighted average also includes Austria and Luxembourg.

[a]Data refer to 1995.

Table 1.5   **Employment Rates over First Three to Five Years after Leaving Initial Education**

Education and Country	Men			Women		
	First Year	Third Year	Fifth Year	First Year	Third Year	Fifth Year
Less than upper secondary						
Australia	65.1	65.9	75.9	55.4	45.5	39.2
France	77.5	81.3	78.1	68.3	73.0	69.0
Germany	87.5	91.9	88.5	73.7	79.2	72.6
Ireland	75.9	81.0	78.4	62.7	64.9	61.2
United States	49.5	64.8	79.8	31.6	31.9	39.3
Upper secondary						
Australia	74.9	74.9	82.5	78.2	75.4	74.2
France	n.a.	n.a.	n.a.	n.a.	n.a.	n.a.
Germany	88.2	96.3	95.0	83.6	89.9	86.0
Ireland	68.1	90.3	87.1	62.0	87.6	88.5
United States	71.6	77.7	85.9	61.1	68.0	71.1
University/tertiary						
Australia	78.2	84.0	87.0	79.0	77.6	77.6
France[a]	80.4	94.4	95.5	77.6	91.2	91.2
Germany	85.9	87.7	99.7	75.4	82.7	86.9
Ireland	73.7	83.6	n.a.	78.6	94.0	n.a.
United States	87.1	94.7	95.4	81.0	86.9	81.8

Source: OECD (1998).

Note: Employment rate is expressed as the percentage of the sample with a job. n.a. = data not available.

[a]Data refer to first, third, and fourth years after completion of education.

Table 1.6   **Employment during First Five Years after Leaving Initial Education**

Education and Country	Men		Women	
	Never Employed	Never Unemployed	Never Employed	Never Unemployed
Less than upper secondary				
Australia	8.3	39.8	37.3	65.7
Germany	1.5	71.8	7.9	72.9
United States	7.8	38.0	29.1	43.6
Upper secondary				
Australia	4.4	58.1	6.4	68.2
Germany	0	85.1	0.7	79.4
United States	2.9	58.3	8.4	62.0
University/tertiary				
Australia	5.2	68.8	2.0	62.9
Germany	0	79.5	5.2	81.6
United States	0.5	82.2	3.1	80.3

Source: OECD (1998). Data are as follows: Australia, Australian Youth Survey; Germany, German Socio-Economic Panel; and United States, National Longitudinal Survey of Youth (for details of data, see OECD 1998, annex 3B).

Table 1.7   Concentration of Youth Unemployment over Five-Year Period after Leaving Initial Education

Unemployment Duration	France		Germany				United States		
	Less Than Secondary	All	Less Than Secondary	Upper Secondary	University/ Tertiary	All	Less Than Secondary	Upper Secondary	University/ Tertiary
Percentage of Population Experiencing Unemployment									
None	17.9	82.2	61.8	74.9	77.6	43.8	15.9	30.4	53.0
1–3 Months	5.6	6.7	9.3	4.2	9.0	28.1	27.9	28.5	27.9
3–6 Months	5.9	9.5	9.1	9.8	9.4	10.8	16.3	12.3	9.4
6–9 Months	6.6	3.4	5.6	3.4	1.0	6.5	7.7	9.6	4.5
9–12 Months	5.6	3.1	4.5	3.5	0	3.5	9.0	5.8	1.6
12–24 Months	25.6	3.7	6.8	2.6	3.1	6.5	16.1	10.9	2.8
24–36 Months	16.8	0.8	1.4	0.8	0.0	1.5	5.1	2.2	0.8
36 Months or more	15.9	0.8	1.4	0.8	0.0	0.3	2.1	0.3	0.1
Percentage of All Weeks of Unemployment Accounted for by Each Duration									
1–3 Months	1.1	4.8	3.8	3.2	16.0	9.7	4.6	7.1	16.7
3–6 Months	2.7	17.3	9.7	19.1	37.1	13.4	8.7	10.8	20.0
6–9 Months	4.2	11.1	10.8	12.4	5.7	13.7	7.0	14.0	16.4
9–12 Months	4.4	14.2	13.4	17.5	0	10.9	10.8	11.7	9.5
12–24 Months	24.9	27.6	31.4	22.4	41.3	33.1	34.5	37.8	24.4
24–36 Months	25.2	10.2	11.9	10.9	0	15.2	22.4	15.8	10.6
36 Months or more	37.5	14.8	19.0	14.5	0	4.1	11.9	2.9	2.3

Source: OECD (1999).

is perhaps surprising is the similarity in the degree of concentration of unemployment in Germany and the United States. Among all Germans the 1.6 percent of the population who experienced at least two years of unemployment accounted for 25 percent of all weeks of unemployment over the five-year period examined. Analogously, in the United States the 1.8 percent of the population with at least two years of unemployment accounted for around 20 percent of total unemployment. This evidence is inconsistent with the view that the transition from school to work is dominated by short spells. Germany seems particularly successful in getting the vast majority of its young people into work. Just like the United States and France, Germany appears to have difficulties finding jobs for a small group of less educated individuals. Of particular concern is the fact that an increasing proportion of the unemployed in Germany reside in households where no other person is employed, and especially so for unemployed teenagers. Indeed, as table 1.8 shows, the proportion has more than doubled since 1985 with reunification. In 1996 a higher proportion of unemployed teenagers in Germany resided in households where nobody else was working than in any other country except Ireland (36.3 percent in Germany in 1996 compared with an OECD average of 22.2 percent).

Does the extension of the period of schooling and delay of working reflect the state of the macroeconomy or is it the result of other factors? To what extent is the schooling-employment status of youths sensitive to aggregate economic forces?

To answer these questions, we developed a data file that gives the number of young people who are working or in school by single year of age for the age group 16–35, separately by gender. Data are available for 15 countries: the United Kingdom, Belgium, Denmark, France, West Germany, Greece, Ireland, Italy, Luxembourg, the Netherlands, Portugal, Australia, and Spain for the period 1983–94; the United States for 1970–93; and Canada for 1976–94—making an overall total of 8,000 observations. The activities of youth fall into four disjoint states. The first state is the starting point for the transition: youths in school and not working (SN). The second state is being in school and employed (SE). The third state is being out of school and not working (ON). The fourth state is being out of school and employed (OE). SN and OE are the endpoints of the school-to-work transition process; while SE and ON are more transitional states.

We estimate the effect of aggregate demand on the distribution of youths among these four states by regressing the proportions of each age-gender group in the particular category on the rate of national unemployment in each year, a gender dummy, an age dummy, and a time trend.[4] We estimate a linear probability model for each country separately and then

---

4. For details of the data files and the means of the aggregate unemployment rates, see app. C in Blanchflower and Freeman (1996).

Table 1.8   Proportion of Unemployed Youths in Households Where No Other
                   Person Is Employed, 1985–96

| | Age 15–19 | | Age 20–24 | |
Country	1985	1996	1985	1996
Australia[a]	26.4	22.8	37.1	36.3
Austria	n.a.	18.4	n.a.	21.6
Belgium	20.2	33.9	28.3	38.8
Canada	21.7	24.1	39.7	40.9
Finland	n.a.	23.5	n.a.	64.6
France	19.2	25.8	27.9	29.8
Germany[b]	17.5	36.3	36.6	45.5
Greece	18.6	16.1	25.7	23.6
Ireland	27.9	40.5	35.0	43.5
Italy	12.4	21.5	21.1	27.2
Mexico	n.a.	8.5	n.a.	8.5
Netherlands[c]	22.3	17.8	48.6	44.5
Portugal	8.9	9.5	15.1	18.6
Spain	20.0	22.6	24.1	26.2
Switzerland	n.a.	4.8	n.a.	22.5
United Kingdom	26.6	32.4	44.1	48.7
United States[a]	20.6	18.8	39.6	40.1
European Union	19.4	24.9[d]	30.6	36.0[d]
OECD average	20.2	22.2[e]	32.5	34.2[e]

Note: n.a. = data not available.
[a]Data refer to 1986 and 1996.
[b]Data for Germany relate to West Germany in 1985 and the whole of Germany in 1996.
[c]Data refer to 1988 and 1996.
[d]The averages are respectively 25.6 and 34.6 for the 15–19 age group and 20–24 age group
when Austria and Finland are not included.
[e]The averages are respectively 24.3 and 36.7 for the 15–19 age group and 20–24 age group
when Austria, Finland, Mexico, and Switzerland are not included.

pool the regressions to cover all countries, with country dummies to allow
for different levels of outcomes. Table 1.9 summarizes the results in terms
of the coefficients on the rate of aggregate unemployment on the four categories and on two composite categories: the proportion in school and the
proportion employed. The effect of unemployment on schooling reveals
disparate results across countries. In some cases schooling is strongly positively related to unemployment (Germany, the Netherlands, Portugal, and
Denmark); in other cases it is negatively related to aggregate unemployment (Italy, Luxembourg, and Belgium); in yet other cases schooling and
aggregate unemployment have little relation (the United States, the United
Kingdom, Canada, Spain, Ireland, and Greece). Pooling all of the countries together, schooling is positively related to unemployment, but the
diverse country results gainsay any broad generalization.

Table 1.9   Estimated Effects of Aggregate Unemployment on the Proportion of Youths across Labor Market States

Country	SN (%)	SE (%)	In School (%)	ON (%)	OE (%)	Employed (%)
All	.4298 (7.58)	-.0136 (0.39)	.3890 (7.50)	.7336 (11.53)	-1.1538 (16.03)	-1.1267 (14.5)
Australia	.3954 (5.04)	-.2311 (3.26)	.0453 (0.77)	1.1694 (5.57)	-1.3337 (5.46)	-1.0520 (6.97)
Belgium	-.4004 (3.53)	.0852 (3.25)	-.3293 (2.80)	1.0309 (4.23)	-.7601 (2.95)	-.6059 (2.37)
Canada	.3513 (5.73)	-.2543 (3.61)	-.3442 (4.70)	.9958 (6.02)	-1.0928 (5.88)	-1.8338 (8.35)
Denmark	.3532 (2.66)	-.0788 (0.53)	.0970 (1.01)	1.0173 (7.98)	-1.3010 (7.06)	-1.3471 (7.48)
France	.2010 (0.76)	.2503 (5.98)	-.3205 (0.99)	.6898 (2.35)	-1.1682 (4.48)	-.8461 (2.29)
Germany	1.0375 (4.09)	.3212 (3.34)	.4588 (1.69)	.7121 (1.14)	-2.0347 (3.52)	-.9025 (3.48)
Greece	-.2010 (0.74)	.0166 (0.53)	1.3584 (4.51)	1.0537 (2.00)	-.8396 (1.39)	-1.7491 (3.03)
Ireland	-.3879 (1.29)	.0696 (0.91)	.2872 (1.38)	1.2333 (2.72)	-.8796 (2.39)	-1.3720 (8.98)
Italy	-.9559 (7.12)	-.0909 (5.82)	1.8998 (3.38)	.6545 (1.61)	.3922 (0.95)	-1.6295 (3.01)
Luxembourg	-.5497 (1.37)	.0338 (0.46)	-1.0467 (7.79)	1.3796 (1.97)	-1.7295 (1.97)	.3013 (0.86)
Netherlands	2.3066 (5.63)	-.4067 (1.37)	-.2016 (0.76)	-.6770 (1.16)	-1.2228 (2.09)	-.8348 (1.43)
Portugal	.7432 (4.07)	-.0989 (1.69)	-.9221 (2.68)	1.1955 (6.00)	-1.8397 (8.88)	-.3289 (0.41)
Spain	.0884 (1.53)	-.0836 (6.24)	-.0370 (0.72)	.9183 (5.34)	-.9215 (6.14)	-.6547 (3.58)
United Kingdom	.1733 (3.51)	-.5175 (7.25)	.1642 (1.46)	1.6606 (8.00)	-1.3164 (6.66)	-1.5841 (6.77)
United States	.1078 (2.37)	-.1413 (4.29)	.6442 (3.63)	.5499 (3.13)	-.5639 (3.13)	-1.9387 (9.13)

Source: OECD School Cohort Dataset.

Note: SN = in school and not working. SE = in school and employed. ON = out of school and not working. OE = out of school and employed. Controls include 19 age dummies, a time trend, a gender dummy, plus 14 country dummies in the overall equation. Numbers in parentheses are *t*-statistics.

By contrast, there is no ambiguity in the effect of aggregate economic conditions on the proportion of a cohort that is neither in school nor working or that is employed. The proportion neither in school nor working—sometimes called "idle"—falls with unemployment in nearly all countries. In the pooled OECD sample, an increase in aggregate unemployment raised the proportion idle by 0.73 percentage points. Contrarily, unemployment reduces the employment rate of youths by 1.13 percentage points.

Employment during school and employment when out of school generally play different roles in the lives of youths. In most cases, employment during school is a secondary activity (though for some, it may be the only way to fund their education), whereas for out-of-school youths, employment is potentially the dominant allocation of time. The coefficients on unemployment in the SE and OE columns show that the employment of youths in school is less sensitive to aggregate economic conditions than the employment of youths out of school.

The sensitivity of schooling and employment proportions to aggregate economic conditions varies considerably with age, declining as youths approach the end of the transition period. Table 1.10 documents this pattern using a pooled data set that includes all of the countries in the sample. The table records coefficients and standard errors on aggregate unemployment from regressions of the proportion of youths in school, employed, and unemployed by single age, with a dummy variable for gender, a time trend, and individual country dummies. The size of the coefficients on aggregate unemployment fall with age for all three outcome measures, but at very different rates. The percentage of persons enrolled in school is just as sensitive to unemployment for those in their mid-20s as for younger persons, and the employment rate is only modestly less sensitive for those in their mid- to late 20s than for teenagers. Only unemployment shows a steady drop in sensitivity to aggregate unemployment. One interpretation of the similarity between coefficients on the percentage in school and percentage employed variables through the mid- to late 20s is that responses are similar even as persons are aging 10 to 12 years because the transition period has become elongated.

Table 1.11 differentiates youth employment patterns by gender as well as by enrollment status. It records the results of linear probability estimates of the coefficients of aggregate unemployment and of the time trend on the employment of men and women separately, conditional on their schooling status. The coefficients on unemployment show that the employment of youths in school is less sensitive to aggregate economic conditions than the employment of youths out of school. This is true for all countries taken together for men (a coefficient on unemployment for the in-school group of -0.83 vs. -1.40 for the out-of-school group) and for women (a coefficient on unemployment for the in-school group of -0.90 vs. -1.03

Table 1.10   **Estimated Effects of Aggregate Unemployment on the Proportion of Youths across Labor Market States by Age and Gender**

Age	In School (%)	Employed (%)	Unemployed (%)
All	.3890 (7.50)	−1.1267 (14.45)	1.3492 (33.71)
16	.4429 (1.66)	−1.2778 (7.24)	2.2670 (9.61)
17	.5273 (1.87)	−1.3276 (7.42)	2.2113 (11.69)
18	.4552 (1.68)	−1.2436 (7.37)	1.8698 (9.48)
19	.3542 (1.31)	−1.2073 (7.18)	1.8333 (10.85)
20	.4201 (1.79)	−1.2706 (7.93)	1.8478 (13.09)
21	.4441 (2.28)	−1.2756 (7.65)	1.7088 (12.67)
22	.4976 (3.10)	−1.2777 (7.28)	1.5694 (11.97)
23	.4954 (3.70)	−1.2808 (7.55)	1.4347 (11.34)
24	.4507 (4.10)	−1.2607 (7.55)	1.3236 (11.19)
25	.3955 (3.96)	−1.1911 (7.22)	1.2284 (11.55)
26	.4663 (5.28)	−1.1567 (6.86)	1.1263 (11.56)
27	.4291 (5.45)	−1.1159 (6.40)	1.0727 (11.45)
28	.3906 (5.27)	−1.2054 (6.53)	1.0876 (12.12)
29	.3547 (4.62)	−.9872 (5.20)	.9925 (11.67)
30	.2928 (4.36)	−.9702 (4.81)	1.0219 (12.21)
31	.2968 (4.01)	−.9772 (4.68)	.9466 (11.78)
32	.2885 (4.13)	−.9060 (4.18)	.9438 (11.85)
33	.2551 (3.36)	−.8848 (3.97)	.9048 (11.65)
34	.2817 (3.54)	−.8446 (3.79)	.8679 (11.63)
35	.2605 (3.30)	−.8101 (3.52)	.8048 (11.17)
Women	.3793 (5.34)	−.9654 (10.73)	1.2491 (22.26)
Men	.3996 (5.46)	−1.2868 (16.19)	1.4554 (34.05)

Source: OECD School Cohort Dataset.

Note: Controls include 14 country dummies, a time trend, a gender dummy, plus 19 age dummies in the overall equation. Numbers in parentheses are *t*-statistics.

for the out-of-school group) and holds in 23 of 30 country-gender comparisons. Among out-of-school youths, moreover, the employment of men is more sensitive to aggregate conditions than is the employment of women. The major difference by gender in the calculations, however, is on the trend term. The coefficients on the trend show a rise in employment of women in virtually every country compared to trend decline in employment for men. Because unemployment rates have risen in most countries since the 1980s, this does not mean that the proportion of young out-of-school women has risen, but that it has risen relative to the rising rate of unemployment. The gap between the proportion of young women employed and the proportion of young men employed is declining over time.

The school-to-work transition can be a smooth process in which youths enter the job market and obtain relatively long term jobs or it can be more of a job-matching and shopping process in which youths enter and engage in a lengthy period of search before settling down. Germany and Japan

Table 1.11   Estimated Effects of Aggregate Unemployment on the Proportion of Youths Employed by Schooling Status and Gender

Country	Men				Women			
	In School		Out of School		In School		Out of School	
	Unemployment Rate (%)	Trend	Unemployment Rate (%)	Trend	Unemployment Rate (%)	Trend	Unemployment Rate (%)	Trend
All	−.8273 (5.39)	−.1095 (1.93)	−1.3975 (21.98)	−.3560 (15.30)	−.8992 (5.60)	.1620 (2.71)	−1.0295 (11.36)	.7345 (22.14)
Australia	−1.1048 (4.99)	−.8774 (9.16)	−1.8932 (15.76)	−.2084 (4.01)	−1.3754 (5.41)	.4250 (3.86)	−1.4457 (5.22)	.6286 (5.25)
Belgium	1.1388 (1.74)	−.1339 (0.37)	−1.4609 (5.84)	−1.0993 (7.96)	1.1944 (1.46)	−.0659 (0.15)	−1.3627 (4.01)	−.0452 (0.24)
Canada	−1.4660 (5.12)	−.1337 (1.59)	−2.0752 (20.84)	−.3294 (11.23)	−.2700 (1.03)	.2517 (3.27)	−1.0504 (5.13)	.7591 (12.59)
Denmark	−1.4041 (1.89)	−.2123 (0.65)	−1.4528 (7.16)	.1127 (1.28)	−1.0644 (1.39)	−.7137 (2.14)	−1.2616 (3.97)	.3316 (2.40)
France	.1327 (0.24)	.3163 (1.69)	−1.6863 (8.12)	−.0908 (1.30)	−.0797 (0.11)	−.3910 (1.60)	−1.1139 (5.35)	.3643 (5.19)
Germany	−.9212 (0.98)	2.1182 (7.72)	−.3503 (0.99)	−.0486 (0.47)	−.4543 (0.48)	1.6508 (5.94)	−.5836 (1.01)	.7693 (4.53)
Greece	1.4227 (1.04)	−1.1520 (4.45)	−.9029 (3.21)	−.2869 (5.34)	.0652 (0.05)	−.8721 (3.14)	−1.6912 (5.69)	.8090 (14.28)
Ireland	.2443 (0.36)	−1.3307 (4.53)	−1.6437 (5.81)	−.4309 (3.55)	−1.7319 (2.38)	−.7332 (2.36)	−1.2158 (3.04)	.7270 (4.25)
Italy	−2.4761 (3.86)	−.4522 (2.77)	−.4052 (1.90)	−.7384 (13.62)	−.9476 (1.47)	−.1203 (0.73)	−.1910 (0.81)	.1486 (2.47)
Luxembourg	−.5900 (0.31)	.2724 (0.78)	−2.1767 (4.03)	−.6542 (6.41)	−2.8387 (1.21)	−.6038 (1.31)	−2.1578 (2.97)	.0035 (0.03)
Netherlands	−4.3383 (6.01)	−3.4451 (5.79)	−.4907 (0.90)	.2297 (0.51)	−2.2364 (3.47)	−.5257 (0.99)	.6612 (1.29)	2.4205 (5.74)
Portugal	−1.0876 (2.17)	−.2931 (1.21)	−1.7686 (10.06)	−.3834 (4.51)	−1.7110 (2.92)	−.1604 (0.57)	−2.0144 (9.82)	1.1501 (11.60)
Spain	−1.2379 (5.50)	1.6958 (6.58)	−1.7209 (19.65)	.5046 (5.27)	−.6303 (3.11)	.3915 (1.66)	−1.0743 (14.36)	1.4230 (17.38)
United Kingdom	−1.6567 (4.38)	.5584 (3.27)	−2.3621 (14.72)	−.6422 (8.85)	−1.6592 (3.97)	1.0701 (5.66)	−1.6975 (9.33)	.5733 (6.96)
United States	−.7469 (2.43)	.1134 (1.90)	−1.6006 (21.36)	−.2784 (19.28)	−.2764 (1.09)	.3685 (7.46)	−.0500 (0.33)	.9290 (31.45)

Source: OECD School Cohort Dataset.

Note: Controls include 14 country dummies, a time trend, a gender dummy, plus 19 age dummies in the overall equation. Numbers in parentheses are *t*-statistics.

Table 1.12   **Numbers of Jobs Held by Young Persons between Ages 16 and 25**

Country	No. of Jobs Held Since Age 16 over Relevant Period	No. of Jobs per Year
United States: between age 16 in 1979 and age 25 in 1988		
Men	7.7	.86
Women	6.8	.76
Norway: from school leaving in 1988–89 to 1992 (age under 25 in 1989)		
Men	1.7	.57
Women	1.9	.63
United Kingdom: between age 16 in 1974 and age 23 in 1981		
Men	2.3	.26
Women	3.1	.34
Germany: between age 16 in 1974 and age 25 in 1984		
Men	2.6	.29
Women	2.0	.22
Japan: from school leaving to age 30 in 1985		
Men	1.6	.17
Women	1.5	.17

Sources: United States, National Longitudinal Survey of Youth; Norway, Norwegian Labor Market Survey, 1989–1992; United Kingdom, National Child Development Study; Germany, German Socio-Economic Panel; and Japan, Survey on Employment Conditions of Youth, 1985.

exemplify labor markets in which young persons enter the market and obtain relatively permanent jobs quickly. The United States and Canada are examples of labor markets in which youths enter the market and change jobs readily before settling down. Both mechanisms have benefits and costs. Youths who move from school to permanent work directly are likely to make greater firm- or sector-specific investments in human capital. Youths who go from school to many short-term jobs are likely to be more mobile across sectors and to pick up a more diverse set of employment experiences.

Table 1.12 shows that the differences between these modes of entry into employment produce huge differences in the number of jobs youths hold as they make the transition from school to work in various countries. It records the mean number of jobs youths held between ages 16 and 25 (or from school leaving to age 30 for Japan, and to age 25 for Norway), as given in longitudinal surveys (the United States and the United Kingdom) or in surveys that ask about jobs retrospectively (Germany, Japan, and Norway). The mean number of jobs held between ages 16 and 25 by American youths is an order of magnitude greater than that in the United Kingdom, Germany, or Japan and is considerably above that for Norwegian youths as well. This reflects the high degree of mobility in the U.S. job market that the OECD has found in other statistics as well. Many American youths work while attending school and during summer vacations, but this is not the reason for the sizable number of jobs. Young persons who have completed schooling also shift frequently among jobs during the school-to-work transition. National Longitudinal Survey of Youth (NLSY) data show that by age 26 almost no American youths had held just one job and 90 percent of women and men had changed jobs more than three times. By contrast, just 4 percent of Japanese men and 1 percent of Japanese women had changed jobs more than three times; 10 percent of German men under age 30 and 4 percent of German women under age 30; 10 percent of young Norwegian men and 13 percent of young Norwegian women; and only 30 percent of British men and 35 percent of British women (at age 23).[5]

In sum, the transition from school to work is sensitive to aggregate economic conditions, with the employment and unemployment of youths highly dependent on the rate of unemployment, particularly for younger youths and those out of school. The rising trend of employment for women has in part offset the adverse effects of aggregate unemployment on young women and shows that aggregate unemployment is not the "whole story" of what happened to youths in the job market. In addition, the institutions of the labor market produce very different job experiences during the transition period.

1.2   An Extreme Social Outcome: Suicide

The worsening of the youth job market in the 1980s and 1990s was accompanied by changes in several social outcomes for youths, including crime, living arrangements, reported happiness, and suicide. Some of these changes may be responses to changes in the job market and schooling of young people. Others may be simply correlates of those changes. Whichever they are, it is illuminating to go beyond the job market indicators of

5. The numbers for Japan relate to individuals from the time of leaving school to age 30, in 1985.

The German numbers are taken from the first sweep of the German Socio-Economic Panel of 1984. Respondents were asked how many jobs they had held over the preceding 10 years. The numbers reported here relate to individuals aged 16 or over.

The Norwegian numbers relate to individuals under age 25 who left education in 1989. The number of jobs is then counted over the period 1989–92.

The British numbers relate to the number of jobs held between 1974 and 1981 by respondents to the National Child Development Study, all of whom were born in March 1958.

For further details of all these data sources, see app. A3 in Blanchflower and Freeman (1996).

how youths have fared in the 1980s and 1990s to examine other social outcomes. Other chapters in this volume examine the criminal behavior of young men and the resultant outcome of incarceration (Freeman, chap. 5), the living arrangements of young men and women (Card and Lemieux, chap. 4), and reported life satisfaction and happiness (Blanchflower and Oswald, chap. 7). Here we focus on an extreme indicator of the well-being of youths, their death rate due to suicides.

Table 1.13 gives death rates per 100,000 by suicide and self-inflicted injury for young and older persons for 22 countries, for 1970, 1980, and 1992, separately by sex. Suicide is a reasonably well measured and powerful indicator of how people feel about themselves and their relation to society. The suicide rates are in all cases higher for men than for women. Across the countries, there is wide variation in both the adult and youth rates and considerable variation in the pattern of change.[6] In English-speaking countries—the United States, Canada, the United Kingdom, Australia, New Zealand, and Ireland—rates of suicide rose sharply, which could potentially reflect rising problems for youths in the job market in those countries, in particular the increase in inequality that marked the 1980s. But rates of suicide also rose among young men in Norway, where earnings inequality is small and the social safety net high. That youths in these countries report themselves as being happier or more satisfied with their lives (Blanchflower and Oswald, chap. 7 in this volume) further complicates any simple interpretation of these patterns and their link with the increasingly elongated transition from school to work.

1.3   Demography and Industrial Composition in the Youth Job Market

The supply of youths to the job market depends on the demographics of the youth population and the activity rates of youths with differing characteristics. The demand for youths in the job market depends in part on the composition of employment by sector and the ability of firms to substitute between youths and other inputs.

1.3.1   Demographic Factors

Because of fluctuations in fertility, the size of youth cohorts varies considerably over time. In the 1970s the baby boom generation reached the labor market, with significant consequences for youth unemployment and wages. The large influx of young workers depressed the opportunities for a typical entering worker. In the United States and other countries the result was a sharp twist in the age-earnings profile against the young. In

6. Suicide rates for young men declined between the 1970s and the 1990s in Japan, Austria, Sweden, and West Germany and fell for young women in three of these countries, Japan, Sweden, and West Germany. These are the countries where unemployment rates over the period 1970–90 were very low until the 1990s.

Table 1.13 **Death Rates by Suicide and Self-Inflicted Injuries, 1970–92 (deaths per 100,000 persons)**

Country	Men 15–19	Men 20–24	Men 25–54	Women 15–19	Women 20–24	Women 25–54
Australia						
1970	8.4	16.7	26.2	2.6	6.9	11.2
1980	9.9	25.6	22.9	2.4	6.7	8.4
1992	19.6	34.6	26.3	4.8	6.4	6.5
Austria						
1970	21.0	32.9	43.7	5.5	5.8	15.4
1980	18.5	40.4	45.6	7.3	6.0	15.1
1992	15.7	31.2	35.6	5.9	6.2	12.6
Canada						
1970	10.1	21.9	24.6	3.9	5.8	11.1
1980	19.4	30.4	28.5	3.8	7.0	9.8
1992	20.1	29.0	27.3	5.4	6.6	7.5
Denmark						
1970	3.7	17.8	39.4	1.1	9.9	20.8
1980	7.4	25.8	56.6	4.7	11.0	30.3
1992	5.5	19.2	35.0	2.3	4.4	16.1
France						
1970	6.7	12.1	25.7	4.3	4.4	8.8
1980	7.4	24.2	32.6	2.9	8.0	12.3
1992	6.7	20.7	37.5	2.5	5.9	12.3
Greece						
1970	0.6	2.7	5.5	1.4	1.7	3.6
1980	1.6	4.5	5.4	1.1	2.6	3.6
1992	1.4	4.0	5.9	1.3	2.1	3.6
Iceland						
1970	9.7	22.2	38.2	0	0	6.1
1980	8.7	9.0	24.3	0	9.6	12.7
1992	18.5	19.2	27.9	0	0	5.8
Ireland						
1970	0.7	6.6	3.6	0	1.0	0.9
1980	4.3	7.3	14.9	1.3	6.0	6.7
1991	14.9	29.2	24.8	1.3	2.9	4.4
Italy						
1970	2.6	4.5	7.9	2.3	2.3	3.7
1980	3.2	7.6	10.3	1.6	3.3	4.7
1990	3.3	8.3	10.5	1.6	2.4	3.8
Japan						
1970	8.7	18.8	19.4	6.9	16.2	12.8
1980	9.5	24.1	28.6	4.9	11.5	12.8
1992	5.3	15.3	25.9	3.2	6.3	10.1
Luxembourg						
1970	0	17.4	23.9	0	8.8	15.0
1980	7.0	13.8	24.1	0	0	14.7
1992	0	14.1	15.4	9.6	7.5	16.2

Table 1.13   (continued)

Country	Men 15–19	Men 20–24	Men 25–54	Women 15–19	Women 20–24	Women 25–54
Mexico						
1970	2.2	3.6	3.3	0.8	1.2	0.7
1980	3.2	4.3	4.0	1.3	1.4	0.8
1991	3.8	8.1	6.4	0.9	1.5	1.1
Netherlands						
1970	3.3	8.1	10.7	1.5	2.6	7.9
1980	3.7	13.1	15.6	0.8	6.6	9.5
1992	4.6	12.5	17.0	2.5	4.7	9.0
New Zealand						
1970	9.0	15.6	19.0	2.4	5.4	7.6
1980	12.4	27.8	17.5	9.2	6.9	10.2
1992	27.7	52.2	28.7	3.7	8.7	7.0
Norway						
1970	1.3	9.2	17.2	1.4	2.6	8.4
1980	14.3	26.5	21.8	1.3	5.3	9.7
1992	18.0	37.2	24.3	5.6	4.9	10.3
Portugal						
1970	5.1	6.4	15.3	3.2	4.2	3.4
1980	3.2	7.4	13.1	5.1	2.9	4.5
1992	3.5	8.1	12.6	2.2	2.1	4.8
Spain						
1970	1.3	2.7	6.8	1.0	0.8	2.2
1980	2.5	6.4	7.5	0.8	1.4	2.2
1991	4.7	9.4	10.4	1.4	3.0	3.0
Sweden						
1970	10.2	25.4	41.3	4.8	10.5	20.2
1980	5.8	28.2	37.6	4.3	7.4	14.8
1992	5.4	14.4	27.5	4.5	8.7	11.1
Switzerland						
1970	12.7	32.6	32.9	4.5	5.5	12.1
1980	22.9	48.0	40.9	6.9	18.4	17.6
1992	10.6	33.7	35.3	3.0	9.0	11.1
United Kingdom						
1970	3.0	8.5	11.5	1.4	3.4	7.5
1980	4.1	9.6	14.8	1.9	4.1	7.7
1992	6.4	16.9	17.8	1.6	2.9	4.5
United States						
1970	8.9	19.0	23.1	2.9	5.6	11.0
1980	13.8	26.6	23.6	3.0	5.5	8.2
1991	18.0	25.4	24.0	3.7	4.1	6.3
West Germany						
1970	15.7	24.6	34.0	5.5	8.5	17.3
1980	11.8	27.0	33.6	4.2	7.1	14.6
1990	9.6	18.6	23.8	2.4	5.9	8.6
1992[a]	8.6	16.0	26.3	2.4	4.0	8.5

Source: World Health Organisation Statistical Database.
[a]Data for 1992 refer to East and West Germany.

other countries the result was a twist in employment-population rates against the young. In the 1980s and 1990s the youth share of the population fell in most OECD countries, as the baby boomers aged and were replaced by smaller cohorts. The decline in the relative number of young persons is depicted in table 1.14, which shows the ratio of the population aged 15–24 to the population aged 25–54 in OECD countries in 1980, 1990, and 1994. The marked drop in the youth population relative to the 25–54-year-old population is substantial in all countries except Japan, where it *grew* from 30.8 percent in 1980 to 35.6 percent in 1994. Taking all the countries together, the ratio of 15–24-year-olds to the older group in 1980 averaged (unweighted) 44.2 percent, in 1990 it averaged 38.6 percent, and in 1994 it averaged 35.4 percent. The drops in the relative number of youths were particularly marked in Canada, the United States, and Germany. *All else the same, large declines in cohort size could be expected to raise the employment prospects and reduce the unemployment rates of*

Table 1.14   **Ratio of Population Aged 15–24 to Population Aged 25–54, 1980–94**

Country	1980	1990	1994
Australia	45.17	38.37	34.72
Austria	43.57	34.41	29.20
Belgium	41.03	32.96	29.97
Canada	50.25	32.89	29.67
Denmark	38.32	34.74	31.17
Finland	38.22	29.62	27.89
France	40.61	37.23	34.34
Germany	39.87	31.08	26.94
Greece	36.97	37.03	35.01
Iceland	54.32	41.58	38.18
Ireland	53.20	47.02	48.20
Italy	38.70	39.07	34.45
Japan	30.78	35.58	35.51
Luxembourg	37.25	29.59	28.18
Mexico	71.61	70.26	63.70
Netherlands	43.89	35.70	29.50
New Zealand	50.58	41.25	37.99
Norway	41.96	38.21	32.91
Portugal	48.09	43.07	39.83
Spain	43.19	43.39	40.12
Sweden	34.89	33.62	30.32
Switzerland	37.28	31.30	26.24
Turkey	64.13	59.06	53.41
United Kingdom	41.40	36.57	31.73
United States	49.56	34.77	31.59
OECD unweighted average	44.17	38.63	35.38
EEC 12 unweighted average	41.88	37.29	34.12

Source: United Nations Database.

youths relative to adults, and to raise their wages relative to adults. In many countries, indeed, youth labor market problems were expected to disappear as the youth cohort declined in size. But as we have seen in preceding sections, no such improvement in fact occurred.

1.3.2 Sectoral Employment

In most countries youths work in different economic sectors from adults. They are more likely to be found in retail trade industries and hotels and restaurants than in utilities, education, or public administration. Among men a disproportionate number of the young are employed in construction. Among women a disproportionate number of the young are employed in the health sector. Differences in the industrial distribution of employment for younger and older workers suggest a separation between the youth and adult labor markets. If the overall distribution of employment by industry is relatively stable or if youths are concentrated in declining sectors, they must switch industries to move into relatively permanent work.

One way to see which industries use youths disproportionately is to calculate the ratio of young workers to older workers in an industry (here the ratio of workers aged 16–24 to those aged 25–54) and to divide these coefficients by the economy-wide ratio of 16–24-year-old to 25–54-year-old employees. When the ratio exceeds one, an industry employs disproportionately more 15–24-year-old workers than it does older workers, making it a "youth-intensive" industry. When the ratio of the shares is below one, the industry employs relatively few younger workers. Table 1.15 records relative input coefficients for young workers in European OECD countries in the one-digit NACE industries where youths were highly concentrated in 1994. In every country, youths are disproportionately represented in hotels and restaurants and wholesale and retail trade and repair. These sectors are huge employers of youths. In Germany and France, for instance, the two sectors employed 39 percent of all young workers in 1994. When the youth workforce is disaggregated by sex, two other industries are highly youth intensive: construction, for men, and health, for women. The uniformity of these patterns across countries is striking and suggests that, differences in school-to-work transition patterns notwithstanding, what happens to the youth labor market depends critically on developments in a limited set of sectors in all countries.[7] If, for example,

---

7. The magnitude of the difference between the distributions of youths and adults across industries does, however, differ among countries. This is reflected in an index of structural dissimilarity between the two distributions: the sum of the absolute value of the difference between the percentage of 15–24-year-olds employed in an industry and the percentage of 25–54-year-olds employed in that industry. Blanchflower and Freeman (1996) show that Germany has the lowest index of industrial dissimilarity, especially for men. In part at least, this may reflect German reliance on apprenticeships in the school-to-work transition, which places youths in the sectors where they are likely to be permanently employed.

Table 1.15 Ratio of Age 15–24 Share of Employment to Age 25–54 Share of Employment in Youth-Intensive Industries, 1994

Country	All		Men		Women	
	Hotel and Restaurant	Wholesale and Retail Trade and Repair	Hotel and Restaurant	Construction	Hotel and Restaurant	Health
Belgium	2.03	1.41	2.66	1.62	1.48	1.19
Canada	3.92	1.96	4.43	0.77	3.46	1.99
Denmark	5.92	2.30	5.27	1.12	6.25	1.75
France	2.56	1.54	2.90	1.27	2.23	1.36
Germany	1.60	1.29	1.69	1.53	1.44	0.66
Greece	1.76	1.51	1.99	1.31	1.43	1.74
Ireland	2.01	1.66	2.39	0.87	1.52	1.16
Italy	1.63	1.06	1.89	1.36	1.29	1.29
Japan	1.60	1.27	2.73	0.90	1.00	0.78
Luxembourg	1.65	1.71	1.74	1.27	1.38	1.12
Netherlands	3.15	1.96	3.88	1.12	2.43	0.99
Portugal	1.44	1.22	1.46	1.81	1.43	0.88
Spain	1.64	1.45	2.01	1.26	1.17	1.39
United Kingdom	2.44	1.68	3.22	1.04	1.96	1.48
United States	2.44	1.68	–	0.75	–	1.14

Sources: OECD Industry Dataset and OECD, *Employment Outlook* (Paris, 1996).

the shares of employment in hotels and restaurants and wholesale and retail trade were falling, this would adversely affect the movement of youths into job markets and thus help us to explain why the youth job market worsened. But the opposite occurred: in nearly all of the countries employment in these sectors *grew* relative to total employment.

Table 1.16 shows this result for 20–24-year-olds for the period 1985–94 in selected OECD countries. It uses two-digit NACE industries to analyze the effect of changes in the composition of employment by industry on the employment of young workers. Column (1) records the age 20–24 share of total employment in 1985. Given the general decline in the age 20–24 share of the population, the age 20–24 share of employment should have fallen through 1994, and column (2) gives the 1994 demographically adjusted predicted share. It is obtained by multiplying the column (1) figures by the ratio of the age 20–24 share of the population in 1994 to the share in 1984. Column (3) shows the actual 1994 share of employment accounted for by 20–24-year-olds. Column (4) gives the difference between the actual share and the share that would have resulted simply from the drop in the youth share of the population: column (3) minus column (2). Column (5) gives the predicted effect of the change in industry mix. It is the sum of the changes in the share of total employment in each industry multiplied by the age 20–24 share of employment in that industry scaled for the change in the group's share of population.[8] In all of the countries save Belgium the change in industry share effect is positive, implying that the youth proportion of employment should have risen, not fallen, as a result of the changing mix of employment by sector.

1.4 The Youth Wage Discount

Youths invariably earn less than workers with more job market experience or age. To assess the "youth discount" we turn to data from the International Social Survey Programme (ISSP), which provides a single source, based on nominally similar definitions, for youth and adult earnings over time. Using the ISSP files for 1993, we regressed the log earnings of respondents on dummy variables for gender and age group across countries. For analysis of these wage data for earlier years, see Blanchflower (1999) and Blanchflower and Freeman (1992). The coefficients in this regression for workers aged 18–24 relative to those for workers aged 35–44 provide an estimate of the youth discount for a similarly defined group. The results, summarized in table 1.17, show a wide range of youth discounts among countries that roughly reflect the distribution of earnings

8. Specifically, let a_j be the age 20–24 share of employment in industry i in 1985, b_j be the share of industry j in total employment, and r be the ratio of the age 20–24 share of the population in 1994 to its share in 1995. The industry shift measure is then the sum over j of ra_j times the change in b_j, where the change is from 1985 to 1994.

Table 1.16   Youth Share of Employment and Change in Share Due to Demographic Change and Change in Employment by Industry, 1985–94

Country	Share of Total Employment, 1985 (1)	Expected Share of Employment, 1994, Given Change in Share of Population (2)	Actual Share of Employment, 1994 (3)	Actual Minus Expected Share (3) − (2) (4)	Change in Share of Employment Due to Changes in Industry Mix of Employment (5)
Belgium	11.7	10.2	8.8	−1.4	−0.1
Canada	14.5	10.3	9.8	−0.5	0.1
Denmark	11.4	10.2	9.5	−0.7	0.1
France	11.0	10.3	7.9	−2.4	0.2
Germany	12.4	9.4	8.9	−0.5	3.6
Greece	7.5	7.8	7.8	0.0	0.2
Ireland	16.9	16.6	14.0	−2.6	0.5
Japan[a]	12.2	12.9	13.3	+0.4	0.7
Luxembourg	14.5	12.0	10.4	−1.6	0.5
Netherlands	14.4	12.8	11.8	−1.0	0.2
Portugal[b]	9.9	10.2	9.7	−0.5	0.2
Spain[b]	10.2	9.8	9.9	+0.1	0.4
United Kingdom	13.0	11.0	10.4	−0.6	0.1
United States[c]	13.4	10.5	10.2	−0.3	0.2

Sources: Data for European countries supplied by EUROSTAT on the basis of each country's labor force survey. Data for Canada and the United States are based on each country's March labor force survey and were supplied by Statistics Canada. Data for Japan are from the 1992 Employment Status Survey from the Management and Coordination Agency, Statistics Bureau. See OECD, *Employment Outlook* (Paris, 1996), table 4.12.

Note: Age group is 20–24-year-olds.

[a]Data refer to ages 15–24. Years are 1982 and 1992.

[b]Data refer to 1986 and 1994.

[c]Data refer to 1983 and 1994.

Table 1.17   **Relative Earnings of 18–24-Year-Olds Compared with 35–44-Year-Olds, 1993**

Country	Coefficient	N
Canada	−1.2208	850
Great Britain	−.8111	868
Ireland	−.2282	365
Italy	−.4830	482
Japan	−.8500	685
Netherlands	−.2095	698
New Zealand	−1.0837	724
Norway	−.8106	772
Spain	−.5367	317
United States	−1.7148	895
West Germany	−.3820	822

Source: International Social Survey Programme, 1993.

Note: Coefficient on age dummy for 18–24-year-olds compared with the excluded category of 35–44-year-olds. All equations include five age dummies and a gender dummy. Sample consists of the employed (self-employed or employees).

and wage-setting institutions in the countries. The differentials are largest for countries with high levels of inequality and decentralized wage setting. The biggest adult-young wage differential is for the United States, followed by Canada and New Zealand. The United Kingdom and Japan also show sizable differentials, as does—surprisingly—Norway. Differentials are smaller in countries where wages are largely determined by collective bargaining: Germany, the Netherlands, Spain, and Italy, though Ireland also has a relatively small youth discount.

From the 1970s through the early 1980s the earnings of youths fell relative to the earnings of adults in several countries (OECD 1986). One important reason was the entry of the baby boom generation to the job market. Given this pattern, many analysts and governments expected youth labor market problems to lessen as the relative size of youth cohorts declined in the late 1980s and 1990s. As tables 1.1 and 1.2 showed, however, this demographic change did not produce favorable employment patterns. Did it show up in the relative wages of youths, particularly in countries like the United States or Canada, where wages are presumably highly responsive to shifts in supply or demand?

Figure 1.3 provides a clear answer to this question. It records the ratios of the earnings of workers aged 16–19 and 20–24, by sex, to the earnings of older workers in 11 OECD countries for which earnings by age are available. The precise age group for older workers in the comparisons differs depending on the country. For most countries, the older group consists of 35–44-year-olds or 40–49-year-olds, but the Swedish figures relate to 25–64-year-olds and the Japanese figures to 45–49-year-olds. There are other differences in the nature of the data across countries that make cross-

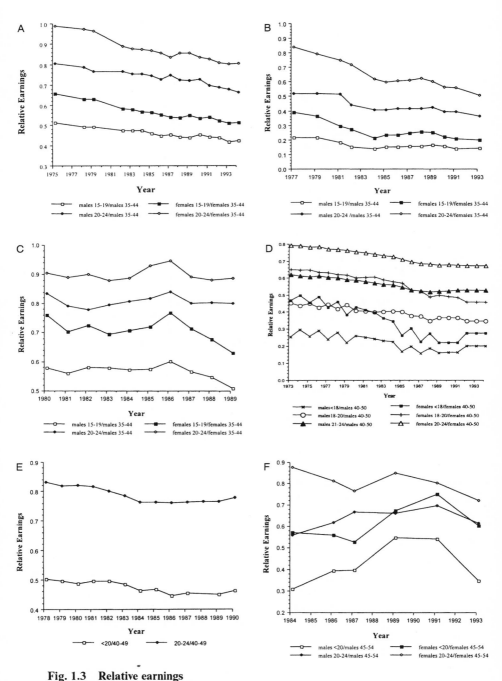

Fig. 1.3   Relative earnings

Note: A, Australia, 1975–94. *B*, Canada, 1977–93. *C*, Denmark, 1980–89. *D*, France, 1973–94. *E*, Germany, 1978–90 (both sexes together). *F*, Italy, 1984–93. *G*, Japan, 1973–92. *H*, Norway, 1980–91. *I*, Sweden, 1981–94. *J*, United Kingdom, 1970–95. *K*, United States, 1973–94.

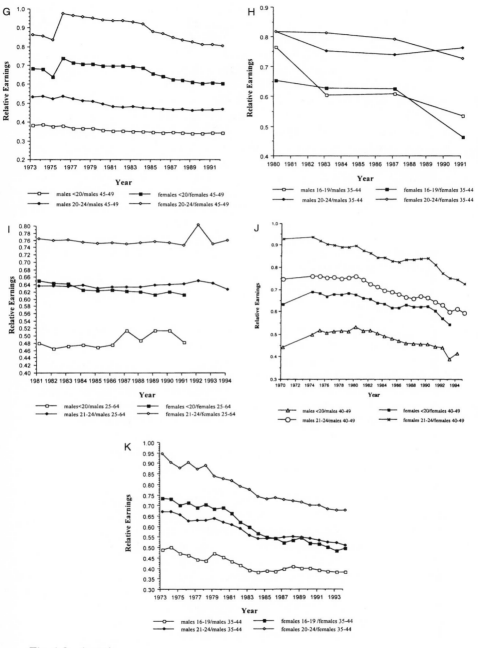

Fig. 1.3 (cont.)

country comparisons of the ratios imprecise (see Blanchflower and Freeman 1996, app. A2) but that do not affect changes over time. Figure 1.3 shows that in virtually all OECD countries workers aged 16–19 or 20–24 experienced declines in earnings relative to older workers through the 1990s. To be sure, there are some country differences in the magnitude and timing of the fall in relative youth earnings. The United States and Canada had steep drops from the mid-1970s; the United Kingdom's decline was larger from the mid-1980s to the mid-1990s than in the earlier period; Italian youth wages did not begin to fall sharply until the 1990s; and Swedish relative wages were roughly constant through 1991. But Sweden aside, despite the sharp fall in the relative size of youth cohorts, and despite differences in wage-setting institutions, the relative pay of youths dropped throughout the OECD. This implies that the presumably beneficial effect of the declining size of youth cohorts on youth wages was overwhelmed by other market forces. Wage-setting institutions may affect the magnitude of the youth-adult pay differential and possibly the magnitude of the response of that differential to market conditions, but they do not rule out qualitatively similar adjustments across countries.

1.5   Conclusion

Many analysts expected the problems faced by young workers in the job market to disappear as the baby boom generation aged and was replaced with a smaller generation of young persons. This did not occur. Despite declines in the relative number of youths and shifts among industries toward youth-intensive sectors, the employment and earnings position of youths deteriorated in almost all OECD countries. Differences in school-to-work transition affect the outcomes along some dimensions— for instance, in numbers of jobs that youths hold during the transition— but are generally dominated by whatever forces have caused an overall deterioration in the economic position of low-paid and less skilled workers.

Many analysts would expect the relative employment of youths to vary inversely over time with their relative wages. Perhaps greater youth discounts and greater declines in youth wages generated more jobs for them in some countries, but the declines that did occur, including the large drops in youth wages in the United States, did not suffice to stabilize, much less raise, youth employment-population rates. One interpretation is that the wage and employment numbers lie along labor supply curves, due to massively declining labor demand for young workers. Another interpretation is that the concordance of joblessness and falling pay reflects disequilibrium in the labor market, also the result of declining demand for young workers. Whichever, we have identified one basic pattern in the worsened job market for young workers: the disproportionately large response of youth employment or unemployment to changes in overall unemployment. The sensitivity of youth employment and unemployment to the overall rate of unemployment dominated sizable demographic and structural changes favorable to youth in determining how youths fare in the job market. Unless overall rates of unemployment are reduced, there is little prospect for improvements in youth outcomes, even if youth shares of the population continue to fall or remain relatively small or if the composition of employment shifts modestly toward service sectors that hire relatively many youths.

References

Blanchflower, D. G. 1999. Youth labor markets in twenty-three countries: A comparison using micro data. In *International perspectives on the school-to-work transition,* ed. D. Stern and D. Wagner. Cresskill, N.J.: Hampton.

Blanchflower, D. G., and R. B. Freeman. 1992. Going different ways: Unionism in the U.S. and other OECD countries. *Industrial Relations* 31 (1): 56–79. Reprinted in *Labor market institutions and the future role of unions,* ed. M. Bognanno and M. Kleiner. Oxford: Blackwell, 1992.

———. 1996. Growing into work. Centre for Economic Performance Discussion Paper no. 296. London: London School of Economics.

Clark, K. B., and L. H. Summers. 1981. The dynamics of youth employment. In *The youth labor market problem: Its nature, causes, and consequences,* ed. R. B. Freeman and D. A. Wise. Chicago: University of Chicago.

OECD (Organization for Economic Cooperation and Development). 1986. *Employment outlook.* Paris: Organization for Economic Cooperation and Development.

———. 1995. *Education at a glance.* Paris: Organization for Economic Cooperation and Development.

———. 1996. Growing into work. In *Employment outlook.* Paris: Organization for Economic Cooperation and Development.

———. 1998. Getting started, settling in: The transition from education to the labour market. In *Employment outlook.* Paris: Organization for Economic Cooperation and Development.

———. 1999. Preparing youth for the 21st century: The policy lessons from the past two decades. Background paper for conference organized by the OECD and the U.S. Departments of Labor and Education, Washington, D.C., 23–24 February.

Cohort Crowding and Youth Labor Markets
A Cross-National Analysis

Sanders Korenman and David Neumark

2.1 Introduction

Among the advanced economies, the European countries face a youth employment crisis. Over the period 1970–94 the average unemployment rate for youths aged 15–24 in the 11 European countries studied in this paper rose by over 16 percentage points (from 4.2 to 20.6 percent), while the average unemployment rate for adults aged 25–54 rose from 1.6 to 9.7 percent.[1] In contrast, in the United States in this period the youth unemployment rate rose from 11.0 to 12.5 percent, and the adult rate from 3.4 to 5 percent. Over the same period, the average youth employment rate in these European countries fell from 59 to 41 percent, while adult employment rates were generally flat or increasing. The deterioration of the youth labor market has been particularly severe in Finland, France, Ireland, Italy, Spain, and Sweden. The poor performance of the labor market for youths is in part due to aggregate cyclical fluctuations, with the most recent sharp increases in youth unemployment and decreases in youth em-

Sanders Korenman is professor in the School of Public Affairs at Baruch College, CUNY, and a research associate of the National Bureau of Economic Research. David Neumark is professor of economics at Michigan State University and a research associate of the National Bureau of Economic Research.

The authors are grateful to David Blanchflower for assistance with the data; to Daniel Hansen for outstanding research assistance; and to David Blanchflower, Richard Freeman, Ted Joyce, Thomas Lemieux, and Klaus Zimmerman for helpful comments. Neumark's research was partially supported by National Institute on Aging grant K01-AG00589.

1. The 11 European countries are Finland, France, Germany, Ireland, Italy, the Netherlands, Norway, Portugal, Spain, Sweden, and the United Kingdom. These averages are estimated using the first and last observations available on each country in the sample period, which are not always in 1970 and 1994, as explained below. We also use data on the United States, Canada, Australia, and Japan.

ployment in some countries (especially Finland and Sweden) likely to at least partly reverse course. However, the longer term trends suggest that the youth employment crisis goes beyond cyclical changes and may be symptomatic of more lasting changes, such as those that have affected the wage structure, favoring the more highly educated over those with fewer "skills," including favoring older workers over younger, less experienced workers. This concern raises the obvious question of what steps, if any, might be taken to ease the youth employment crisis.

Rather than focusing on policies to address youth employment problems, the purpose of this paper is to assess the evidence on the contribution of changes in the population age structure to the changing fortunes of youths in the labor market over the 1970s, 1980s, and early 1990s, and to use this evidence to project the likely effects of future cohort sizes on youth labor markets. This is intended to serve as a backdrop for broader labor market policy questions, by providing evidence on the extent to which youth labor market problems may be ameliorated by demographic change. A casual reading of the evidence provides little cause for optimism that demographic developments—in particular, projected declines in the size of young cohorts—will improve youth labor markets. Many countries experienced baby busts in the 1960s that produced relatively small entering cohorts in the 1980s and 1990s. For example, the ratio of the youth population to the adult population fell from 0.43 to 0.29 in the United States and from 0.51 to 0.28 in Finland from 1970 to 1994, while falling from 0.48 to 0.30 in the Netherlands from 1971 to 1994. These changes in the population age structure should have improved the labor market position of youths relative to older adults, as long as younger and older workers are not perfect substitutes in production. However, this period brought continuing deterioration of the youth labor market in many countries, rather than improvement. Why did youths do so poorly during a period when they became more scarce? One possible explanation is that the effects of changes in demand for young workers in this period due to downturns in the business cycle, technological changes, and changing patterns of international trade swamped the beneficial effects of supply-side changes. To some extent, this appears to be the case, because our results ultimately suggest that the independent effect of declines in relative youth cohort size is to improve the youth labor market.

We first review the recent literature on the effects of cohort size on labor market outcomes of youths. We then provide a descriptive overview of changes in population structure and youth labor markets. Following that, we turn to estimates of a series of regression models that attempt to isolate the effects of exogenous changes in potential youth labor supply on youth employment and unemployment rates, using a panel data set for 15 countries over more than 20 years.

Although there is a large literature in this area, we offer a number of innovations, as well as new information. First, we use a cross-national time-series sample that extends into the 1990s. This sample allows us to take advantage of variation across countries in the timing and magnitude of changes in youth cohort sizes to estimate cohort size effects, to better isolate the effects of cohort size from general trends that may have affected all young people during this period (e.g., rising relative demand for skilled labor).

Second, we address problems of potential bias from endogenous determination of relative youth cohort size in a country. In particular, we correct for the influence of endogenous migration decisions of youths and adults by using lagged births as an instrument for our measure of relative cohort size (the ratio of the youth population to the adult population).

Third, we estimate models that allow cohort size effects to vary according to the state of the macroeconomy, examining whether economies with tighter aggregate labor markets are able to absorb large cohorts more readily than those with slack aggregate labor markets.

Fourth, we carry out a variety of specification tests and sensitivity analyses, focusing on the specification of the error term, possible correlations between omitted variables and relative cohort size, and the appropriate dynamics.

Fifth, we relate the institutional features of labor markets to responses to population change. In particular, we focus on the effects of centralization in wage setting and the influence of policies (such as unemployment benefits) that may affect wage adjustments or the allocation of labor. We find some evidence, although it is statistically weak, to suggest that labor market institutions that decrease flexibility lead to greater response of youth unemployment and employment rates to fluctuations in youth cohort size.

The results are somewhat sensitive to alterations in estimation and specification, so the choice of estimation strategy affects the conclusions. Our preferred estimates indicate that large youth cohorts lead to large increases in the relative unemployment rate of youths, with elasticities as high as 0.5 or 0.6. On the other hand, we find little effect of relative cohort size on relative employment rates of youths.

Finally, we carry out a series of projections. Due to recent drops in fertility, several European countries (especially Ireland, Italy, Portugal, and Spain), as well as Japan, will experience marked reductions in the size of youth cohorts over the next 16 years. Projected declines of youth shares should improve youth labor markets in these countries, although the effects are not large compared with longer term changes in youth unemployment rates. Moreover, for countries that have experienced slack demand (reflected in rising adult unemployment rates), the improvements in youth labor markets from declining youth cohort sizes are small relative to the improvements that could be gained from increases in economic activity that reduce adult unemployment rates to earlier levels. Other countries cannot expect demographic changes to improve youth labor markets since youth population shares are projected to decline moderately (the United States, Finland, France, the Netherlands, and Australia) or to increase (Germany, Norway, Sweden, the United Kingdom, and Canada). Thus population change will probably do relatively little to reduce youth employment problems in the advanced economies.

2.2 Previous Literature on Cohort Size and Youth Labor Markets

In this section we review the literature on the effects of cohort size, with an emphasis on recent research. Although the empirical research in this paper examines effects on youth employment and unemployment only, our review also covers studies that estimate effects of relative cohort size on wages, in part because the employment and unemployment effects that we study may depend in part on wage changes induced by demographic changes.

Bloom, Freeman, and Korenman (1987) summarize 18 studies of the effects of cohort size on labor markets for youths. All the studies they review present evidence of some adverse effects of own cohort size on the relative wages or employment of youth. They conclude that "despite differences across studies, two clear areas of agreement emerge. First, in the U.S., Canada, and Israel, the entry of relatively large cohorts into the labor market did result in a decline in the earnings of those cohorts relative to the earnings of older, smaller cohorts. Second, the labor market entry of large cohorts tended to result in increased relative unemployment in most countries."

Most studies have relied on time-series variation in cohort size to estimate cohort size effects. Very few studies have taken advantage of cross-national variation in the size and timing of demographic fluctuations. Many studies note that there is potential confounding of cohort (size) and various period effects, especially those related to the business cycle (Fair and Dominguez 1991; Börsch-Supan 1993). The confounding of period and cohort effects is a particular concern in samples that cover short periods, and in those in which variation in cohort size is limited or where cohort size is trending smoothly.

The potential value of examining cross-national variation in demographic cycles is obvious. For example, in the United States the period 1973–84 was one of economic stagnation ending with a severe recession. Youths who reached age 20 between 1973 and 1984 were born between 1953 and 1964, a period containing the peak and trailing end of the U.S. baby boom. It is difficult with time-series evidence alone to determine the relative importance of two explanations of the labor market problems experienced by these baby boom cohorts in their youth: large cohort size and poor aggregate economic conditions at the time of labor market entry

(Fair and Dominguez 1991). However, fertility fluctuations were of different magnitudes and occurred at different times in different countries. As a result, fluctuations in labor supply due to the entry of young cohorts into the labor market also took place at different times. If cohort crowding is responsible for the adverse outcomes for large cohorts, then large cohorts should have poor outcomes in all economic environments. The cross-national approach should therefore provide a better test of the cohort crowding hypothesis.

Bloom et al. (1987) also conduct original analyses of a pooled cross-country cross-year sample. This is the only study we are aware of that takes advantage of cross-national variation in cohort sizes to estimate their effects.[2] (In the present paper, we are able to use data for a longer sample period, which exploits variation in cohort size in the 1980s and early 1990s produced by the baby bust in several countries in our data set.) Bloom et al. find that the expected relative wage (defined as the product of earnings and the employment rate) is lower for large cohorts. They also find evidence of a trade-off between relative employment and earnings: large youth cohorts experienced depressed earnings (e.g., in the United States) or increased relative unemployment rates (e.g., in Europe). Large youth cohorts appear to have been absorbed in all major industries, not simply through the expansion of youth-intensive industries, such as the service sector.

Bloom et al. also examine whether, in the United States, labor market disadvantages experienced in youth by large cohorts are permanent, by tracking the progress of large cohorts using the 1969–84 Current Population Surveys. They present evidence that the baby boom cohorts were able to "catch up," partly in relative wages, and completely in relative unemployment rates, within about a decade of labor market entry. Nonetheless, even though large cohorts may eventually obtain the economic status of smaller cohorts, large cohorts have lower lifetime wealth due to earnings lost during the catch-up period.

Several recent studies of cohort size effects have taken up the following questions (some of which were also discussed in earlier literature):

1. Do the same patterns of cohort size effects found mostly in studies of the United States appear in data for other countries?

2. Do the effects of cohort size on wages or employment persist?

3. How do demographic fluctuations (the size of own and surrounding cohorts) affect the shape of age-earnings or experience-earnings profiles? How do they affect investment in human capital?

4. Are cohort size effects larger for the more educated members of cohorts?

---

2. OECD (1980) presents separate models for 10 countries.

The findings from many of these recent studies are summarized in table 2.1.[3] Although researchers examine different aspects of cohort size effects on young workers using different samples and estimation techniques, it is possible to offer a tentative synthesis with respect to these questions. There seems to be evidence of an adverse effect of cohort size on youth unemployment, employment, and wages across a number of countries. There is also some consensus about the persistence of such effects; estimates run from partial to nearly full catch-up. Several authors predict that cohort size effects may differ depending on a cohort's "position" in the demographic cycle, although the evidence for this proposition is more mixed. Cohort size effects do appear to be stronger for more educated workers. In addition to these findings, there is also speculation based mainly on indirect evidence that the adverse effects of large cohort size are smaller for cohorts that happen to enter the labor market during favorable demand conditions. Finally, some authors have expressed concerns about endogeneity of relative cohort size due to various behavioral responses to cohort crowding such as migrating or delaying age of school leaving (when a relative labor force size variable is used), although this issue has not been adequately addressed. In the empirical work that follows, we consider evidence on many of these issues.

2.3 Empirical Analysis

2.3.1 Data

Most of the data we examine are from the United States, Canada, Australia, Japan, and the 11 European countries for which the OECD publishes time-series data on the variables used in this study for most or all of the period 1970–94.[4] The majority of the data on population, unemployment, and employment rates are from *Labor Force Statistics, Part III* and *Employment Outlook, July 1995: Statistical Annex,* both published by the OECD.[5] Population data for the United Kingdom prior to 1984 are from the *Demographic Yearbook* published by the United Nations. Employment and unemployment data for the United Kingdom prior to 1984 are from the aforementioned OECD sources and include only England and Wales (after 1984, the entire United Kingdom is included in the data).

Youth ages are defined as 15–24, with the following exceptions: 14–24

3. A more detailed discussion of these studies is provided in the appendix.
4. The exceptions are the former West Germany, 1970–93; Ireland, 1971, 1975, 1977, 1979, 1981, and 1983–93; Italy, 1970–93; the Netherlands, 1971–94; Norway, 1978–94; Portugal, 1974–93; Spain, 1972–94; and the United Kingdom, 1973, 1975–77, and 1980–94. We also have much more limited data on youth enrollment rates, discussed below.
5. The unemployment rates appear to be standardized unemployment rates. Leigh (1995, table 2.4) provides some comparisons of alternative unemployment rate measures across some of the countries in our sample.

Table 2.1   **Summary of Literature Review**

Study	Country	Outcomes	Prediction for Larger Cohorts	Evidence
Flaim (1979)	United States	Unemployment	Higher	Confirmed
Flaim (1990)	United States	Unemployment	Higher	Confirmed by fall in youth rate in 1980s
Levine and Mitchell (1988)	United States	Wages	Lower	Not confirmed
	United States	Wage growth	Lower	Confirmed
Nardone (1987)	United States	Unemployment	Higher	Not confirmed; small entering cohorts were hurt by early 1980s recession
Fair and Dominguez (1991)	United States	Wages	Lower	Not studied
	United States	Labor supply	Lower if substitution effect dominates income effect	Confirmed for women, not men; income effect may dominate for men
Stapleton and Young (1988)	United States	Returns to education	Lower	Not confirmed by later aggregate data
Berger (1989)	United States	College completion	Lower	Confirmed by later aggregate data
	United States	Age-wage profile	Flatter	Confirmed in his data
			Steeper if surrounded by large cohorts; low earnings but steeper profiles if born before or after peak	Not confirmed in later data; but demand factors may dominate supply in 1980s/1990s

(continued)

Table 2.1 (continued)

Study	Country	Outcomes	Prediction for Larger Cohorts	Evidence
Flinn (1993)	United States	Wages	Direct effect: lower return to human capital Indirect effect: increased human capital investment due to lower opportunity cost Following large cohorts is good due to low opportunity cost and high returns; leading a large cohort is bad due to high cost and low returns due to entry of large cohort soon to follow	Simulations confirm negative but modest direct effects of size of own cohort; small indirect effects
Zimmermann (1991)	Germany, preunification	Age-specific unemployment	Higher in short run Older workers hurt by large entry cohorts	Confirmed Possibly in long run
Wright (1991)	Great Britain	Wages	More depressed for more educated members of large cohorts	Education differential is confirmed but overall effect of large cohort on wages is temporary
Hartog et al. (1993)	Netherlands	Wages	Lower wages and steeper experience profiles	Not confirmed
Schmidt (1993)	Germany	Unemployment	Higher	Confirmed for a few age-sex groups, but adverse effects appear to fade with age
Nickell (1993)	Great Britain	Relative wage overall and in union sector	Lower relative wages if market conditions affect wages	Confirmed in both samples
Klevmarken (1993)	Sweden	Wages	Lower wages and wage growth	Not confirmed

in Italy and 16–24 in the United States, Norway, Spain, Sweden, and the United Kingdom. Adult ages are defined as 25–54, except for Italy, for which the range is 25–59.[6] Relative cohort size is measured as (Population 15–24)/(Population 25–54).

GNP figures are from *World Tables*, published by the World Bank. The GNP growth rate is defined as $100 \cdot (\text{GNP}_t - \text{GNP}_{t-1}) / \text{GNP}_{t-1}$. All of the figures are real values. The data series for the GNP growth rate are generally shorter than those for population and employment. These data are from 1975 through 1993 for most of the countries in the sample.[7]

Data for lagged births for the European countries are from *International Historical Statistics: Europe, 1750–1988* (Mitchell 1992). The same data for the United States are from *Vital Statistics of the United States, 1991*, published by the U.S. Department of Health and Human Services. Data for Japan and Australia come from *International Historical Statistics: Africa, Asia and Oceania* (Mitchell 1995).[8]

Population projections are taken from *World Population Prospects, 1994–95 Edition*, published by the World Bank. The projections are made in five-year intervals, beginning in 1995; we interpolate linearly to obtain estimates for each year. We have used the "medium-variant projections" from 2000 through 2010.

2.3.2   Time-Series Evidence by Country

Figure 2.1 displays data on relative youth cohort size for the 15 countries in our data set from approximately 1970 through 1994. The information displayed to the left of the 1994 vertical line is the actual data, while that to the right of the 1994 vertical line is projections, discussed in greater detail below. Looking first at the population share or relative cohort size variable, we see that the United States, Canada, Germany, Ireland, Portugal, and the United Kingdom experienced baby booms followed by busts, reflected in relative youth cohort sizes about 20 years later. Other countries—Finland, France, the Netherlands, Australia, and to some extent Sweden and Norway—have experienced fairly steady declines in the rela-

---

6. We use a relatively young cutoff to avoid the influence of changes in retirement policy or behavior that might have substantial effects on 55–64-year-olds. However, the results were not sensitive to using a wider age range.

7. The remaining countries have data as follows: Ireland, 1985–93; Norway, 1980–93; Portugal, 1976–93; and the United Kingdom, 1977 and 1982–93.

8. The estimation of lagged births is best illustrated by an example. We are interested in knowing how many 16–24-year-olds in 1970 were born in the United States. Births 16–24 year earlier (in the period 1946–54) will not include respondents who were born in 1945 but have not yet reached their birthdays (and so are still age 24). Similarly, this method would include some of the people born in 1954 who have not turned age 16 by the survey date. In the absence of information about the date of birth and survey date, we use the expected value of these dates (1 July) and so include one-half of 1945 births and exclude one-half of 1954 births. The age ranges for lagged births are chosen to match the age ranges in the population and employment data (which, as noted above, vary slightly across countries).

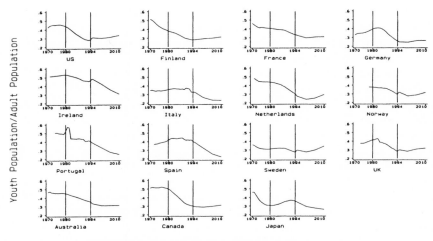

Fig. 2.1   Youth population shares with data through 1994 and projections through 2010

tive sizes of youth cohorts. Finally, in Italy and Spain there is no discernible trend, while Japan exhibits a sharp decline followed by a modest increase in the late 1980s and early 1990s. Based on the declines in relative youth cohort sizes over the latter part of the sample period (for all countries except Italy, Spain, and Japan), if smaller cohorts increase labor market prospects for young workers, then we should have seen higher youth employment rates and lower youth unemployment rates in recent years. Moreover, youth cohorts are projected to shrink in relative size for many of the countries—especially Ireland, Italy, Portugal, Spain, and Japan. Thus the cohort crowding hypothesis would suggest future improvements in youth labor markets in these countries.

However, data on youth unemployment and employment rates, depicted in figures 2.2 and 2.3 (displayed along with data on relative cohort sizes), raise doubts about the cohort crowding hypothesis. Figure 2.2, for example, shows youth unemployment rates (indicated by circles; population shares are indicated by solid lines). In some countries with declining or steady relative youth cohort sizes, youth unemployment rates rose steadily throughout the sample period (France and Ireland) or jumped toward the end of the period (Finland, Sweden, and to a lesser extent Australia and Canada). Similar phenomena are reflected in the youth employment rates displayed in figure 2.3. More generally, what we expect to see in these figures, if the cohort crowding hypothesis holds, is that (all else the same) youth unemployment rates and relative cohort sizes move in the same direction, whereas youth employment rates and relative cohort sizes move in opposite directions. With respect to unemployment, this prediction appears to be contradicted for Finland, France, Germany, Ireland, Norway,

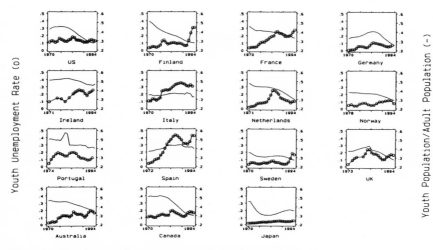

Fig. 2.2   Youth unemployment rates and population shares

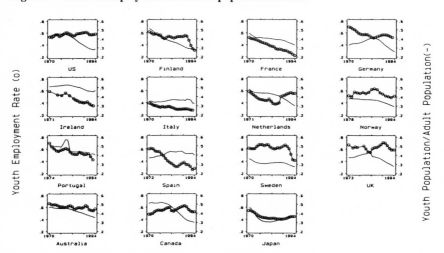

Fig. 2.3   Youth employment rates and population shares

Australia, and Canada, and for the early part of the sample period for the Netherlands. With respect to employment, this prediction appears to be contradicted for nearly all countries with the exceptions of Germany, Spain, and the United Kingdom, as well as the Netherlands in the late part of the sample period.

Of course, relative youth cohort size is not the only variable affecting youth unemployment and employment rates. Aggregate demand effects are likely to be important. In the regression estimates discussed below, we

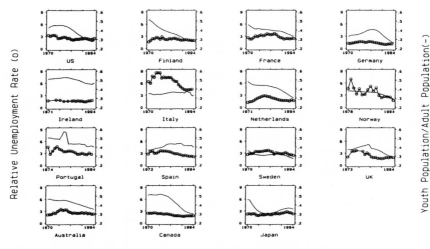

Fig. 2.4   Relative youth unemployment rates and population shares

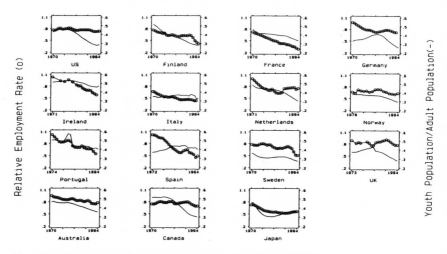

Fig. 2.5   Relative youth employment rates and population shares

include aggregate demand controls. In figures 2.4 and 2.5, we foreshadow the results by showing ratios of the youth unemployment or employment rate to the corresponding adult rate. These ratios will reduce the influence of aggregate changes that are also reflected in the adult rates, although they will not eliminate all aggregate influences, because youth unemployment and employment rates are more cyclically sensitive (Clark and Summers 1982). The relative unemployment rates graphed in figure 2.4 exhibit smaller movements; notably, the sharp increases in the unemployment rates in the past few years in Finland and Sweden, and the increase over a longer period in Spain, are not reflected in the unemployment rate ratios, suggesting that aggregate developments are an important contributor to changes in youth unemployment. Figure 2.4 appears to provide a little more support for the cohort crowding hypothesis, because relative youth unemployment rates and cohort sizes move in the same direction for more countries and longer sample subperiods. In contrast, the relative employment rates in figure 2.5 display time-series behavior similar to the absolute rates in figure 2.3, generally reflecting worsening youth labor markets coupled with declining youth cohort sizes.

2.3.3   Intervening Role of Schooling

It is possible, however, that the employment declines in figure 2.5 reflect trends in schooling or other labor market alternatives and therefore do not necessarily represent a social problem. Of course, it is difficult to untangle increased enrollment for exogenous reasons from increased enrollment that is spurred by slack labor markets for youths (for reasons other than demographic developments, which should have improved youth labor markets in many countries). Although this paper does not provide a detailed analysis of the relationships between youth enrollment, employment, and unemployment and demographic change, a cursory look at the evidence is nonetheless instructive.

Figure 2.6 plots relative youth cohort sizes and enrollment rates, based on school enrollment data for a subset of the countries for which the OECD has made such data available.[9] For the countries included in figure 2.6, those in which relatively strong declines in youth cohort size were not accompanied by increases in either the relative or absolute youth employment rate include France, Ireland, Portugal, and to a lesser extent Australia (see figs. 2.3 and 2.5). Figure 2.6 shows, however, that all four of these countries had rather steep increases in enrollment rates in the period for which data are available. At the same time, among countries in which youth employment rates and cohort sizes do appear to have a negative association, including Germany, Spain, the United Kingdom, the Netherlands, and to a lesser extent the United States and Canada, most had small increases in enrollment rates (the United States, Germany, the Netherlands, and the United Kingdom). Thus failure to account for sources of change in enrollment rates that in turn affect employment rates may help

9. These data were constructed by the OECD and supplied to us by David Blanchflower and Richard Freeman. For eight countries, actual enrollment rates for 16–24-year-olds are available. For these countries and three additional ones, enrollment rates by single-year ages and by sex are available, although we do not have the population weights at this level of disaggregation. We therefore report the average over all 16–24-year-olds of these disaggregated rates, which is equivalent to a fixed-weight enrollment rate. For the eight countries for which the true rates are available, the series are almost identical.

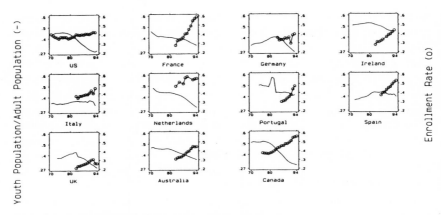

Fig. 2.6   Youth enrollment rates and population shares

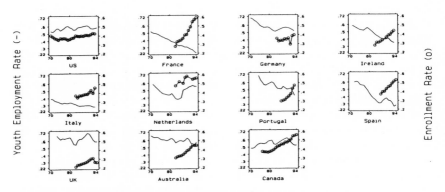

Fig. 2.7   Youth enrollment rates and employment rates

to explain the apparent lack of evidence for a negative relationship between youth employment rates and relative cohort sizes.

As additional evidence, figure 2.7 plots youth enrollment rates and employment rates. It is the case that some countries with steep declines in youth employment also experienced sharp increases in youth enrollment. However, it is not true that youth enrollment rates simply reflect the reverse of youth employment rates. While youth enrollment and employment rates generally moved in opposite directions, there are contrary occurrences, as in the United Kingdom and the Netherlands. Below, we look briefly at the implications of changes in enrollment rates within the regression framework in which we analyze the cohort crowding hypothesis more thoroughly.

Of course, nothing in this analysis says that the changes in youth enrollment rates were exogenous and therefore "explain" the failure of youth employment rates to conform to the cohort crowding hypothesis. The data are equally consistent with youth employment rates falling in some countries despite declining youth cohort sizes, and with enrollment rates rising in response to poor labor market prospects. Attempting to untangle the causality is a task for future research.

2.3.4   Grouping Countries by History of Cohort Size Changes

In the next set of figures (2.8–2.11), we aggregate countries according to their decade-by-decade changes in age structure. The countries are grouped into three categories for the 1970s and then for the 1980s and beginning of the 1990s: those in which a baby boom cohort reached youth ages, those in which a baby bust cohort reached these ages, and those with little trend in relative youth cohort size.[10] Figures 2.8 through 2.11 display, respectively, youth unemployment rates, relative (youth/adult) youth unemployment rates, youth employment rates, and relative youth employment rates for the six groups of countries. According to the cohort crowding hypothesis, youth labor market outcomes should deteriorate more (improve less) in periods when youth cohorts are increasing in size as compared to periods when they are decreasing in size or there is little variation in youth cohort size.

Consistent with the hypothesis, countries where a baby boom cohort entered the labor market in the 1970s experienced larger increases in youth unemployment than those where there was a baby bust cohort or little trend in cohort size (first row of graphs in fig. 2.8). Similarly, in the 1980s and 1990s countries in which a baby bust cohort entered the labor market experienced smaller increases in youth unemployment than countries with little trend, although the one country (Japan) in which a baby boom cohort entered did not experience a sharper rise in youth unemployment (second row of fig. 2.8, looking to the right of the vertical lines). Figure 2.9 shows the relative unemployment rates for the same set of countries. Here, too, the evidence is generally consistent with the cohort crowding hypothesis, at least as regards the comparison between boom and bust countries. For example, in the 1970s relative youth unemployment rates rose considerably more for those countries in which a boom cohort entered the labor market, compared with those in which a bust cohort entered.

Figures 2.10 and 2.11 turn to youth employment rates. Here, there is

10. These are defined, respectively, as whether relative cohort size grew by .04 or more, fell by .04 or more, or changed by an intermediate amount. In the 1970s, the countries in the "boom" category include Germany, Spain, and the United Kingdom. Those in the "bust" category include Finland, France, the Netherlands, Sweden, and Japan. All others are grouped in the category exhibiting little trend. For the 1980s and early 1990s, the boom countries include Japan only, while the bust countries include the United States, Finland, France, Germany, Ireland, the Netherlands, Norway, Portugal, the United Kingdom, Australia, and Canada.

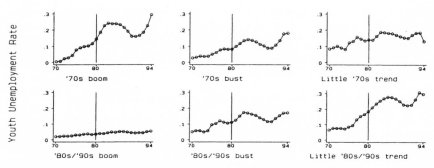

Fig. 2.8   Youth unemployment rates by cohort size history

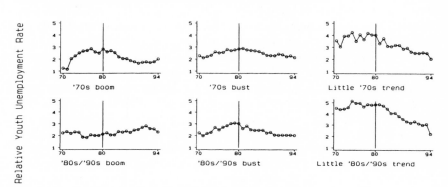

Fig. 2.9   Relative youth unemployment rates by cohort size history

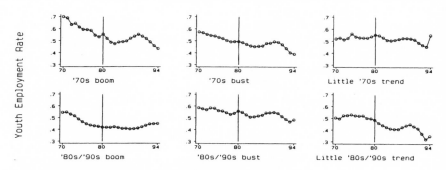

Fig. 2.10   Youth employment rates by cohort size history

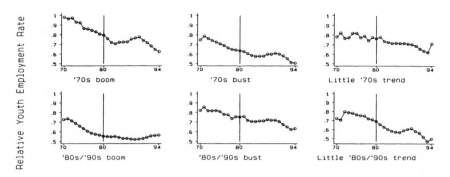

Fig. 2.11   Relative youth employment rates by cohort size history

much less evidence consistent with cohort crowding. In the 1970s employment rates (or relative employment rates) declined for boom and bust countries, although more so for the former. In the 1980s and early 1990s, however, youth employment rates (relative or absolute) rose for the boom countries and fell for the other countries, inconsistent with the cohort crowding hypothesis.

2.3.5   Interpretation

The data displayed in figures 2.2 through 2.11 lead to some tentative conclusions. First, youth unemployment rates appear to respond to changes in the relative sizes of youth cohorts in ways predicted by the cohort crowding hypothesis. On the other hand, youth employment rates appear at least sometimes to move in the opposite direction, falling as relative cohort sizes decline, or are unrelated to relative cohort sizes.

If wages are completely flexible, and the substitution effect dominates, then the employment rate should fall in response to the entry of a large cohort. Total employment of youths should increase, but at the lower equilibrium wage the employment *rate* should be lower as more youths choose not to work.[11] On the other hand, unemployment of youths should not necessarily increase, at least insofar as the unemployment rate reflects involuntary unemployment. The results for both unemployment and employment appear to be inconsistent with this characterization of labor markets for youths and the effects of cohort size. In contrast, if wages are rigid, or, alternatively, there is a fixed stock of jobs for youths, then in response to the entry of a large youth cohort, the employment rate of youths should fall (more sharply than if wages are flexible) and the unem-

11. Given that we are studying employment and not hours, it is natural to assume that the substitution effect dominates. In a static model, the wage exerts only a substitution effect on the labor force participation decision.

ployment rate should rise.[12] The evidence in figures 2.2 through 2.11 appears to be consistent with the rigid wage characterization with respect to unemployment rates, but not employment rates.

In fact, we expect that the reality is somewhere between these two extremes, which is why we expect large youth cohorts to increase youth unemployment rates and to decrease youth employment rates. Below, we look more closely at country differences in the response of youth unemployment and employment to demographic shifts and attempt to link these responses to institutional characteristics of labor markets related to the flexibility of wages. First, though, we turn to a more systematic analysis of the panel data set.

2.3.6   Analyzing the Panel Data

We begin by presenting estimates of specifications that are relatively standard in the literature, in particular

$$(1) \qquad YE_{it} = RCS_{it}\beta + AE_{it}\gamma + D_{it}\delta + \varepsilon_{it},$$

where i indexes country, t indexes year, and all variables are in logarithms. YE is the log of either the youth unemployment rate or the youth employment rate, defined as the rate for 15–24-year-olds (for most countries). RCS is the log relative cohort size. We include different cyclical controls, including the log adult unemployment rate, the log adult employment rate, or other measures; these are denoted AE.[13] D is a vector of dummy variables capturing the timing of changes in the definitions of various series in the data set, some described in the data section and others of a more technical nature indicated in the original data sources.

We interpret equation (1) as a reduced-form employment rate or unemployment rate equation, with the adult unemployment and employment variables capturing demand influences and the relative cohort size variable capturing supply influences. Assuming that workers of different ages are imperfectly substitutable, and controlling for demand shifts, larger co-

12. One could argue that the implications for unemployment are more ambiguous because the unemployment rate depends on the decisions of individuals to remain in the labor force. Singell and Lillydahl (1989) provide a summary of this issue and other problems with respect to the measurement and interpretation of youth unemployment rates.

13. Note that once we include the adult rate corresponding to the youth rate on the left-hand side (e.g., the adult unemployment rate on the right-hand side of the equation for the youth unemployment rate), the specification is essentially identical to one in which the dependent variable is the log of the youth rate relative to the adult rate. In particular, the estimate of β is unaffected by the form of the dependent variable used. This follows because the variables are entered in logs. To see this, note that eq. (1), when AE is the log adult unemployment rate and RE is the log of the youth unemployment rate relative to the adult unemployment rate, can be written as

$$RE_{it} = RCS_{it}\beta + AE_{it}(\gamma - 1) + D_{it}\delta + \varepsilon_{it}.$$

horts face lower wages. When the dependent variable is the youth employ-ment rate, the cohort crowding hypothesis predicts that β is negative. In contrast, when the dependent variable is instead the relative unemploy-ment rate, the cohort crowding hypothesis predicts that β is positive.

2.3.7 Basic Regression Results

In table 2.2 we present estimates of the effects of relative youth cohort size on youth unemployment and employment rates, focusing on the ap-propriate specification of the error term in equation (1). We control for adult unemployment and employment rates. Panel A reports OLS esti-mates in which we treat the error term ε as orthogonal to the regressors and independently (and identically) distributed both within and across

Table 2.2   **Estimates of Effect of Youth Population Share on Youth Unemployment and Employment Rates**

| | Independent Variables | | | |
Dependent Variable	Youth/Adult Population	Adult Unemployment Rate	Adult Employment Rate	ρ
A. Pooled data				
Youth unemployment rate	.035	.853**	−.230	n.a.
	(.126)	(.025)	(.181)	
Youth employment rate	.481**	−.070**	.903**	n.a.
	(.058)	(.012)	(.083)	
B. Fixed country effects				
Youth unemployment rate	.363**	.923**	−.002	n.a.
	(.094)	(.018)	(.277)	
Youth employment rate	.133**	−.171**	.691**	n.a.
	(.045)	(.009)	(.133)	
C. Fixed year and country effects				
Youth unemployment rate	.292**	.800**	−1.057**	n.a.
	(.095)	(.034)	(.374)	
Youth employment rate	−.112**	−.080**	1.468**	n.a.
	(.050)	(.018)	(.197)	
D. Fixed year and country effects with AR correction				
Youth unemployment rate	.181	.689**	−1.148**	.652
	(.149)	(.040)	(.473)	
Youth employment rate	.117*	−.047**	1.441**	.855
	(.070)	(.013)	(.177)	

Note: $N = 342$ in panels A through C. $N = 320$ in panel D. All variables are expressed in log form. The data are from 1970 through 1994, although most of the countries do not have data for all of the years. The regressions include dummy variables that account for changes in the data series for some countries. Numbers in parentheses are standard errors.

*Significant at the 10 percent level.

**Significant at the 5 percent level.

countries. Larger relative youth cohort size is associated with a higher relative youth unemployment rate, as predicted by the cohort crowding hypothesis, although the estimated coefficient is small (.035) and not statistically significant. Larger relative youth cohort size is also associated with a *higher* relative youth employment rate (with the effect statistically significant), inconsistent with the cohort crowding hypothesis.

In panel B we consider the inclusion of common country components in the error, reporting estimates from specifications with country-specific fixed effects. It seems plausible that there are country-specific factors (although they are not necessarily time invariant) that influence relative youth unemployment and employment rates.[14] In comparison to the OLS estimates in panel A, the fixed-effect estimates indicate a much larger and significant positive effect of cohort size on the youth unemployment rate, and a much smaller positive effect on the youth employment rate.[15]

We next add fixed year effects, in panel C, maintaining the fixed country effect specifications. Figure 2.3, discussed above, shows a downward trend in the youth employment rate in many countries that will be captured by the year dummy variables. The inclusion of fixed year effects has little impact on the estimated equation for the youth unemployment rate, as the estimated effect of relative cohort size is still positive and significant, with an elasticity of 0.29. However, the estimated effect of relative cohort size on the youth employment rate becomes negative (and significant), as predicted by the cohort crowding hypothesis, with an elasticity of -0.11.[16]

Thus a plausible specification that appears to be consistent with the data (conditional on the specification of the observable variables) produces evidence consistent with the cohort crowding hypothesis. Large relative youth cohorts are associated with lower youth employment rates and higher youth unemployment rates. Given the results in panels A, B, and C, in the remainder of the paper we estimate specifications with fixed country and fixed year effects.

Finally, we estimate specifications accounting for serially correlated errors, as well as fixed country and year effects. Such serial correlation renders the estimates in panel C inefficient and likely biases the estimated

---

14. E.g., the apprenticeship system in Germany is thought to be responsible for the relatively low ratio of youth to adult unemployment in that country (Sorrentino 1993), and unemployment rates may systematically differ in some countries (such as Sweden) because of active labor market policies or other policy or measurement differences.

15. We also computed estimates with random country effects. The resulting estimates were very similar to the fixed-effect estimates. Large changes in the coefficients in going from OLS to random effects indicate that the random-effect specification is inappropriate because the random-effect estimator is a weighted average of the within and the between estimator. Thus, although Hausman tests do not reject random effects in favor of fixed effects, we proceed with fixed country effects.

16. In contrast, estimates with random year effects were little different from those in panel B. Hausman tests reject the random-effects specification in favor of fixed effects (in one case the p-value was .00; in the other the matrix difference of the variance-covariance matrices was not positive definite).

standard errors downward. Panel D of table 2.2 reports estimates incorporating an AR(1) process into the error term of equation (1).[17] The estimated effect of relative cohort size on the youth unemployment rate falls to .18, which, coupled with a sizable increase in the standard error, is not significant. In the equation for the youth employment rate, the sign of the estimated coefficient reverts to being positive, inconsistent with the cohort crowding hypothesis. The high estimated degree of autocorrelation in the data (with the estimates of the first-order serial correlation parameter ranging from .65 to .86) suggests that the AR(1) error specification is preferred; we therefore maintain it in the analyses that follow.[18]

2.3.8   Endogeneity of the Relative Cohort Size Variable

In the next set of analyses we explore the importance of potential endogeneity of the relative cohort size variable. In particular, the youth population (and to a lesser extent the adult population) may be endogenous if immigration flows respond to labor market conditions. In panel A of table 2.3 we address the endogeneity of the youth population by instrumenting for relative cohort size with the ratio of lagged births (i.e., births from the years in which the current youth cohort was born) to the adult population.[19] If we expect the currently resident youth population to be relatively larger when youth labor markets are doing well, then the relative cohort size variable will be positively correlated with the youth employment rate, biasing the estimate of β upward in the regressions for the employment rate. Similarly, the estimate of β would be biased downward in the regressions for the youth unemployment rate.

In the first row of panel A, we see that in fact the estimated effect of relative cohort size on the unemployment rate becomes more positive, consistent with endogeneity bias, and is now statistically significant. Also consistent with endogeneity bias, in the second row the estimated coefficient of relative cohort size in the specification for the youth employment rate falls, although it remains positive (and becomes insignificant).

In panel B of table 2.3, we instrument using the lagged births variable only. On theoretical grounds, lagged births (only) is a better instrument

17. We lose some observations (in addition to the first) because of breaks in the data series. The estimates for the smaller samples—not accounting for serial correlation—were very similar to those for the full sample. E.g., for the specification corresponding to the first row of panel C, the estimate (standard error) of β was .329 (.094); for the specification corresponding to the second row, it was $-$ .127 (.050).

18. The qualitative results were similar when we introduced dynamics by including relative cohort size lagged one year (along with the contemporaneous value), instead of allowing for serial correlation, although the estimates of the individual coefficients were much less precise. In these specifications, however, significant serial correlation in the error remained.

19. Other researchers have raised the endogeneity issue and, e.g., used population shares rather than labor force shares to measure cohort sizes. However, population shares are still affected by endogenous migration. We are not aware of other attempts to remedy this problem by using lagged births as an instrument for a relative labor force or relative cohort size variable.

Table 2.3 **Fixed Year and Country Effects Estimates Correcting for Serial Correlation and Instrumenting for Youth Population Share**

Dependent Variable	Independent Variables			Hausman Test (p-value)	ρ
	Youth/Adult Population	Adult Unemployment Rate	Adult Employment Rate		
A. Using lagged births/adult population as an instrument					
Youth unemployment rate	.344**	.693**	−1.036**	.20	.651
	(.168)	(.040)	(.479)		
Youth employment rate	.059	−.048**	1.411**	.67	.855
	(.087)	(.014)	(.181)		
B. Using lagged births as an instrument					
Youth unemployment rate	.503**	.695**	−.946*	.13	.651
	(.202)	(.040)	(.486)		
Youth employment rate	−.066	−.052**	1.323**	.11	.866
	(.105)	(.014)	(.187)		

Note: $N = 318$. All variables are expressed in log form. The Hausman tests are for the reported variables only (no dummies are included in the test). The data are from 1970 through 1994, although most of the countries do not have data for all of the years. The regressions include dummy variables that account for changes in the data series for some countries. Two observations are lost relative to panel D of table 2.2 because of missing lagged births data for Japan. Numbers in parentheses are standard errors.

*Significant at the 10 percent level.

**Significant at the 5 percent level.

for relative cohort size because it should not be affected by endogenous migration decisions of adults (or youths). The results are qualitatively consistent with those in panel A, although the effects of instrumenting are more profound. The estimated effect of relative cohort size on youth unemployment becomes stronger, while the estimated effect on youth employment becomes negative, although it is insignificant.[20]

Although the Hausman tests tend not to lead to rejection of the exogeneity of relative cohort size, the results of instrumenting are qualitatively different, with little increase in the standard errors. Thus we maintain the IV estimation in the following analyses. In our view, the lagged births instrument is theoretically superior to the ratio of lagged births to the adult population (reflected also, perhaps, in the lower p-values, between .10 and .15, from the Hausman test). Thus we retain this instrument in the following tables.

Overall, consideration of the endogeneity of relative cohort size leads to stronger evidence of cohort crowding effects on youth unemployment. In addition, it eliminates the anomalous positive effect of relative cohort size on the youth employment rate.

2.3.9   Alternative Aggregate Demand Controls

In table 2.4 we explore the sensitivity of our results to using a measure of the business cycle that is more exogenous with respect to labor market developments. After all, given some substitutability between younger and older workers, adult employment and unemployment rates may be affected by the youth population share. In addition, other factors may affect youth employment or unemployment, which in turn may affect adult employment or unemployment, although the endogeneity bias could probably go in either direction.[21] We therefore instead use the lagged growth rate of GNP (which was more strongly related to youth employment and unemployment rates than was the contemporaneous growth rate, consistent with unemployment and employment being lagging indicators). The results are reported in panel A.

The estimated effects of lagged GNP growth are consistent with expectations, as it has a negative effect on the youth unemployment rate and a positive effect on the youth employment rate. In the equation for the youth unemployment rate, the estimated effect of relative cohort size more than doubles, to 1.12, and remains statistically significant, while the estimated

20. In all cases discussed in this section, the F-statistic for the instrument in the first-stage regression was huge, suggesting that small sample biases are unlikely to be a problem (Bound, Jaeger, and Baker 1995).

21. E.g., a higher minimum wage that reduces the employment rate for young workers may increase the employment rate for older workers toward whom employers substitute, leading to downward endogeneity bias in the estimated coefficient of the adult employment rate. Conversely, a negative demand shock for firms employing young workers could increase youth unemployment and via multiplier effects also increase adult unemployment.

Table 2.4 Fixed Year and Country Effects Estimates Correcting for Serial Correlation and Instrumenting for Youth Population Share with Lagged Births, Including Lagged GNP Growth Rate as a Cyclical Indicator

	Independent Variables				
Dependent Variable	Youth/Adult Population	Lagged GNP Growth Rate	Adult Unemployment Rate	Adult Employment Rate	Hausman Test (p-value)
A. Only including the lagged GNP growth rate					
Youth unemployment rate	1.119**	−.018**			.08
	(.429)	(.004)			
Youth employment rate	−.036	.003**			.97
	(.154)	(.001)			
B. Adding the other cyclical indicators					
Youth unemployment rate	.603**	−.005**	.667**	−1.075**	.06
	(.219)	(.003)	(.045)	(.505)	
Youth employment rate	−.030	.001	−.064**	1.285**	.48
	(.114)	(.001)	(.016)	(.199)	

Note: $N = 293$. All variables are expressed in log form. The Hausman tests are for the reported variables only (no dummies are included in the test). The data are from 1970 through 1994, although most of the countries do not have data for all of the years. The regressions include dummy variables that account for changes in the data series for some countries. Observations are lost relative to panel B of table 2.3 because of missing data on the lagged GNP growth rate. The mean of the lagged GNP growth rate is 2.715 with a standard deviation of 2.603. The results for panel B of this table without the lagged GNP growth rate, but using the smaller sample size, are qualitatively the same as the results in table 2.3. Numbers in parentheses are standard errors.

**Significant at the 5 percent level.

effect of relative cohort size on the youth employment rate remains negative, but small and insignificant. In panel B, we include adult employment and unemployment rates, as well as lagged GNP growth. The estimated effect of relative cohort size falls to .6 for youth unemployment and remains small, negative, and insignificant for youth employment. It is not entirely clear which estimates in table 2.4 are better. Our sense is that while the adult employment and unemployment measures are prone to endogeneity bias, this bias is likely to be minor, and the bias from omitting variables that affect labor markets but are not captured by lagged GNP growth may be more severe.

2.3.10 Results Disaggregated by Sex

In table 2.5 we reestimate the preferred specification from the preceding analysis separately for men and women. Specifically, in equation (1) our youth unemployment and employment rate variables are now the rates for either young men or young women. We continue to define the relative cohort size variable for men and women together because (barring war) the fraction of the youth cohort that is one sex or the other is presumably stable over time and because we do not think that young men and women in the countries included in our sample compete in entirely distinct labor markets. The specification of the aggregate demand controls is perhaps more problematic here. When we use the adult employment and unemployment rates, we use the rates for men and women together, so as not to confound different effects of cohort crowding on youth labor markets for men and women with trends or changes in employment and unemployment rates of women. Nonetheless, the adult rates could still have rather different relations with the youth rates for men and women because of changing trends, rather than because the cycle has different effects. As a consequence, we also estimate specifications using the lagged GNP control to capture cyclical effects.

The results indicate that the cohort size effect on young men's unemployment is less severe than the effect on young women's unemployment. In the specifications using adult employment and unemployment rates as controls, we actually find that only young women's unemployment rises in response to a larger youth cohort. In the specifications with the lagged GNP control, there are sizable effects for both young men and young women, although the effect is still considerably larger for women. For neither sex do we find much effect on the youth employment rate.

These results suggest that young women bear a disproportionate burden of unemployment when youth cohorts are large.[22] One interpretation of

---

22. We obtain the same qualitative result whether or not we instrument for relative cohort size, and whether or not we correct for serial correlation.

Table 2.5 Fixed Year and Country Effects Estimates Correcting for Serial Correlation and Instrumenting for Youth Population Share with Lagged Births, by Sex

| | Independent Variables | | | | |
Dependent Variable	Youth/Adult Population	Adult Unemployment Rate	Adult Employment Rate	Lagged GNP Growth Rate	Hausman Test (p-value)
A. Men					
Youth unemployment rate	.123	.827**	−.466		.35
	(.228)	(.049)	(.582)		
Youth employment rate	−.008	−.074**	1.058**		.37
	(.119)	(.017)	(.228)		
Youth unemployment rate	.836*			−.023**	.12
	(.474)			(.005)	
Youth employment rate	.046			.005**	.82
	(.166)			(.001)	
B. Women					
Youth unemployment rate	.899**	.568**	−1.220**		.09
	(.221)	(.045)	(.537)		
Youth employment rate	−.142	−.023*	1.743**		.01
	(.104)	(.013)	(.182)		
Youth unemployment rate	1.435**			−.013**	.04
	(.408)			(.004)	
Youth employment rate	−.142			.002*	.09
	(.159)			(.001)	

Note: $N = 318$ in the first two rows of panels A and B. $N = 293$ in the second two rows. Observations are lost because of incomplete data on lagged GNP growth rate. All variables are expressed in log form. The Hausman tests are for the reported variables only (no dummies are included in the test). The data are from 1970 through 1994, although most of the countries do not have data for all of the years. The regressions include dummy variables that account for changes in the data series for some countries. Numbers in parentheses are standard errors.

*Significant at the 10 percent level.

**Significant at the 5 percent level.

this result is that employers tend to hire young men first and turn to young women when supply conditions are tight. Another possibility is that labor markets and marriage markets interact. When cohort size rises, because women tend to marry slightly older men, marriage rates for women may fall, leading to higher labor force participation rates for women that could, in principle at least, raise their unemployment rate but not their employment rate. For men, in contrast, this channel of influence of cohort size would not operate because of the weaker connection between marriage and labor force participation. While we regard the differences by sex as interesting, in the ensuing analysis we continue to look at all young workers together since from a policy perspective the overall effects of population changes on youth labor markets may be of most interest. But sex differences in cohort crowding effects merit further research.

2.3.11   Variations in Specifying the Effects of Cohort Crowding

As discussed earlier, it is possible that the effects of relative cohort size on employment and unemployment of youths vary over the business cycle, with large youth cohorts having a more depressing effect on youth labor markets when overall labor markets are slack. To address this issue, we estimate augmented specifications of the form

$$(2) \qquad YE_{it} = RCS_{it}\beta + AE_{it}\gamma + RCS_{it} \cdot AE_{it}\gamma' + D_{it}\delta + \varepsilon_{it},$$

where the adult unemployment rate is interacted with relative cohort size. The hypothesis is that γ' is negative in the employment rate regression, so that the youth employment rate falls by more in response to a large cohort in a slack labor market, and similarly that γ' is positive in the unemployment rate regression.

The results for equation (2) are reported in table 2.6.[23] Although the estimated coefficients of the population share/adult unemployment rate interactions are statistically significant (at the 5 or 10 percent level) for both the unemployment and employment rate regressions, the signs are not as expected. For example, the estimates suggest that the effect of a large youth cohort in raising youth unemployment is lower when adult unemployment is high. (Note that this does not imply that youth unemployment is lower, because a higher adult unemployment rate is also associated with higher youth unemployment.) One possible interpretation of this finding is that periods of high unemployment generally are characterized by high rates of job destruction (Davis, Haltiwanger, and Schuh

23. We instrument by forming the fitted value of the relative cohort size variable, and using this variable and its interaction with the adult unemployment rate as instruments for relative cohort size and its interaction with the adult unemployment rate. This is the method of "internal instruments" (Bowden and Turkington 1984).

Table 2.6   **Fixed Year and Country Effects Estimates Correcting for Serial Correlation and Instrumenting for Youth Population Share with Lagged Births, Including Interactions of Adult Unemployment Rate**

		Independent Variables			
Dependent Variable	Youth/Adult Population	Interaction with Youth Population Share	Adult Unemployment Rate	Adult Employment Rate	Hausman Test (p-value)
Youth unemployment rate	.626**	−.399**	.304*	−.843*	.11
	(.204)	(.158)	(.160)	(.484)	
Youth employment rate	−.082	.095*	.041	1.314**	.05
	(.104)	(.053)	(.054)	(.187)	

Note: N = 318. All variables are expressed in log form. The Hausman tests are for the reported variables only (no dummies are included in the test). The data are from 1970 through 1994, although most of the countries do not have data for all of the years. The regressions include dummy variables that account for changes in the data series for some countries. The youth population share is interacted with (adult unemployment rate − mean adult unemployment rate). Numbers in parentheses are standard errors.

*Significant at the 10 percent level.

**Significant at the 5 percent level.

1996), which lead to relatively more openings for young workers to be hired than would otherwise be the case.[24]

2.3.12 Incorporating Enrollment Rates

Earlier, we discussed the potential confounding influence of changes in school enrollment rates, noting that there was evidence that youth enrollment rates rose the most in countries with sharp declines in youth employment rates, and raising the possibility that exogenous changes in factors influencing enrollment rates help to explain the failure of the results for youth employment rates to conform to the cohort crowding hypothesis.

Table 2.7 touches briefly on this evidence in the regression context, reporting estimates of our preferred specifications for the countries and years for which enrollment data are available and then adding the enrollment rate as a control.[25] The evidence in table 2.7 has two important limitations. First, the sample is much smaller because we lose countries as well as years. This may underlie the differences in the estimated coefficients of the relative cohort size variable in the first two rows of this table, compared with the comparable specifications for the full sample in table 2.3; for this subsample, the estimated effects of relative cohort size are insignificant in the regressions for youth unemployment and employment rates, but the evidence is more consistent with an effect primarily on youth employment. Second, because enrollment may be endogenous and we expect negative endogeneity bias in the coefficient of enrollment, we may overstate the influence of enrollment on employment. Nonetheless, the third and fourth rows of table 2.7 indicate that the results are little affected by adding the youth enrollment rate as a control. As expected, its estimated coefficient is negative (and significant at the 10 percent level) in the youth employment equation. But the estimated coefficient of the relative cohort size variable is largely unaffected in both equations. Thus the intervening influence of changes in youth enrollment rates does not appear to explain the failure of youth employment rates to behave as predicted by the cohort crowding hypothesis.

2.3.13 Interpreting the Estimates

On the basis of the results presented in this section, it appears that the most reliable estimates of the average effects of relative cohort size on youth unemployment and employment rates are similar to those found in panel B of table 2.3. While the estimated employment rate elasticity is near

---

24. This may seem like a contradictory argument since there is most likely more hiring of young workers in periods of low unemployment. But we are conditioning on the adult unemployment rate and are therefore referring to a cohort size/unemployment interaction net of the relationship between adult unemployment and youth unemployment.

25. Again, for the eight countries for which unweighted enrollment rates are available, the results were insensitive to using the unweighted rates or the fixed-weight rates.

Table 2.7 Fixed Year and Country Effects Estimates Correcting for Serial Correlation and Instrumenting for Youth Population Share, Including Enrollment Rate

Dependent Variable	Independent Variables				Hausman Test (p-value)	ρ
	Youth/ Adult Population	Adult Unemployment Rate	Adult Employment Rate	Youth Enrollment Rate		
Youth unemployment rate	.073	.700**	−.192		.49	.573
	(.421)	(.095)	(.691)			
Youth employment rate	−.383	−.098*	.556		.75	.683
	(.284)	(.051)	(.377)			
Youth unemployment rate	.123	.696**	−.197	−.029	.59	.548
	(.422)	(.097)	(.704)	(.126)		
Youth employment rate	−.343	−.075	.604	−.130*	.99	.603
	(.250)	(.053)	(.386)	(.070)		

Note: $N = 120$. All variables are expressed in log form. The Hausman tests are for the reported variables only (no dummies are included in the test). The data are from 1970 through 1994, although most of the countries do not have data for all of the years. Figures 2.6 and 2.7 show the data series of enrollment rates available for each country. The regressions include dummy variables that account for changes in the data series for some countries. Numbers in parentheses are standard errors.

*Significant at the 10 percent level.

**Significant at the 5 percent level.

zero and insignificant, the unemployment rate elasticity is about 0.5. Given the declines in relative youth cohort sizes that are projected to occur in the near future in many of the countries in our sample, an interesting question is how much these demographic changes will contribute to lowering youth unemployment rates. We also noted that adult unemployment rates were considerably higher in recent years than in earlier years for many of the countries in our sample. Since the estimated elasticity of the youth unemployment rate with respect to the adult unemployment rate is high (0.7 in panel B of table 2.3), it is instructive to compare the consequences of declining youth cohorts for youth unemployment with the consequences of improved aggregate labor market conditions. We focus on the youth unemployment rate because relative cohort size appears to affect this rate and because, as indicated earlier, the youth employment rate may be affected by enrollment decisions.

We present such information in two ways. First, in figure 2.12 we attempt to provide a sense of the relative strength of adult labor market developments and youth cohort size on youth unemployment rates. In figure 2.12A, we show estimated year effects on youth unemployment rates, first with no cyclical or demographic controls, then including a cyclical control, and finally including the relative cohort size variables.[26] All specifications include year and country dummy variables and dummy variables for changes in the data series. We define the year effects relative to the overall mean, rather than any specific year, as in Suits (1984). For the youth unemployment rate, with no controls the year effects reflect increases in youth unemployment rates in the early to mid-1980s, and again in the early 1990s. When the adult unemployment rate is included as a control, the pattern changes somewhat. In particular, the year effects display more persistently high youth unemployment rates during the 1980s, presumably revealing more of the effects of large youth cohorts. In the early 1990s, the positive year effects are eliminated because adult and youth unemployment rates rose sharply together in many countries. Finally, when the relative cohort size variable is included, most year effects diminish further, suggesting that large youth cohorts raised youth unemployment rates in these years. However, most of the year effects remain, indicating that cohort size effects account for only part of the movements in youth unemployment rates that are common across countries.

Figure 2.12B shows the estimated country effects from the same specification. Relative youth cohort size explains relatively little of the persistent cross-country differences in youth unemployment rates. In contrast,

---

26. To focus more sharply on demographic changes vs. cyclical effects, this analysis is based on a specification that includes only the adult unemployment rate as a control. The results for this specification were very similar to those including the adult employment rate as a control as well.

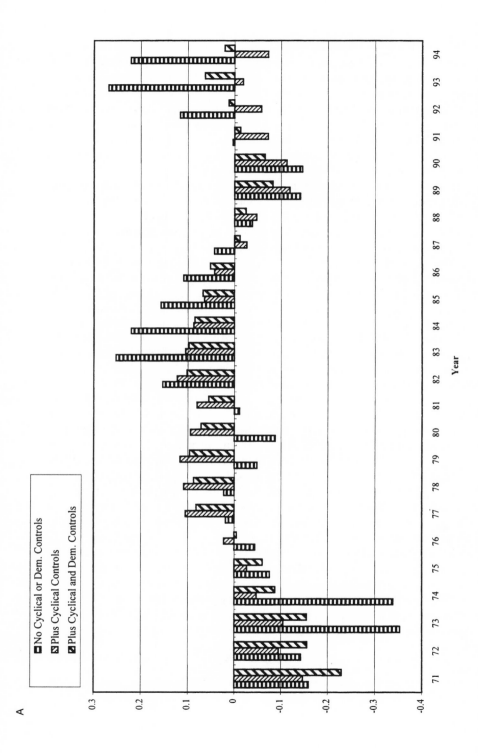

A

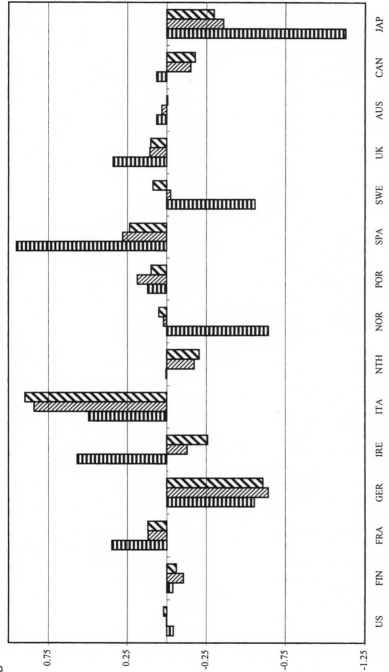

Fig. 2.12   Year and country effects on youth unemployment rates

Note: A, Year dummies from table 2.3, panel B, unemployment regression. *B,* Country dummies from table 2.3, panel B, unemployment regression.

for many countries the estimated country effect shrinks considerably once the cyclical control is included.

These results suggest that while declining youth cohorts may hold the promise of improved youth labor markets in the future, any such benefits are likely to pale in comparison with the benefits that might accrue from improved labor markets for all workers. Of course, this conclusion could be affected by the fact that in figure 2.12 we first include the adult unemployment rate and then look at the incremental effect of adding relative youth cohort size; however, if we include the relative youth cohort size variable first, the conclusion is unchanged. To make this point in a simpler fashion, we next report projections of future youth unemployment rates, based on projected youth cohort sizes and alternative scenarios regarding future adult unemployment rates.

Projecting relative cohort size is easy because youth cohorts that will enter the labor market in the next 16 years have already been born, although immigration and other influences can intervene. The future course of the adult unemployment rate is more uncertain. We therefore present three simple scenarios: (1) Adult unemployment rates in each country remain at their mean for the 1990–94 period (the most pessimistic scenario for almost all countries). (2) Adult unemployment rates revert to their means computed over the entire sample period. (3) Adult unemployment rates return to their means for the 1975–80 period (the most optimistic scenario for almost all countries). We regard the first and third scenarios as providing plausible bounds on the future course of adult unemployment rates.[27]

Figure 2.13 displays the projections for each country. In each figure, the plain solid line is the projection of relative youth cohort size (we show the projections for the years 2000, 2005, and 2010).[28] The other three lines are the projected youth unemployment rates for each of the three adult unemployment rate scenarios. The figure indicates much bigger changes in youth unemployment rates associated with changes in adult unemployment rates over the range seen in the past two decades than with the projected changes in youth shares over the next 10 to 15 years. Spain and Italy provide relatively extreme illustrations of this point. In Spain, the range of variation in future youth unemployment rates given alternative scenarios regarding the adult unemployment rate is much greater than that associated with the sharp projected decline in the youth share. In Italy, the persistence of recent high adult unemployment rates would completely offset the beneficial effects of sharply declining youth cohorts.

27. The other issue that arises is the treatment of time trends in youth unemployment rates. The models estimated to this point include year dummy variables. In the absence of information on future trends, we simply project based on the year effect for the last year in the sample; however, as fig. 2.12A shows, this year effect is very close to the sample mean.

28. These were also displayed in fig. 2.1, although the scale is different in that figure.

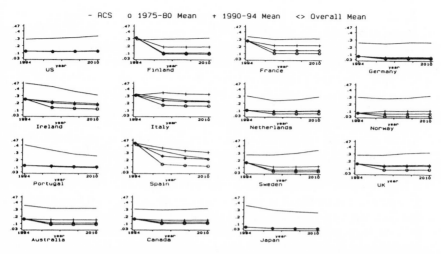

Fig. 2.13   Youth unemployment rate projections using various averages to predict the adult unemployment rate

The greater importance of differences in the level of aggregate economic activity is partly due to the higher estimated elasticity of the youth unemployment rate with respect to the adult unemployment rate than with respect to relative cohort size (in panel B of table 2.3). It is also partly due to the fact that the range of variation in adult unemployment rates is much larger than that of projected youth shares; that is, even though youth shares are projected to decline in many countries, the declines are too small to produce sharp reductions in youth unemployment rates. Portugal provides a good example: relative youth cohort size is projected to decline relatively dramatically, but the adult unemployment rate scenarios are very similar. The relatively sharp decline in youth cohort size from about .4 to .28 produces a decline in the youth unemployment rate of about 2 percentage points to about 10 percent. Although this change is not negligible, it is small relative to the declines in youth unemployment rates that (in other countries) are associated with declines in adult unemployment rates. Thus the qualitative conclusion is that improving aggregate labor markets has much more influence on the health of youth labor markets than do even large reductions in relative youth cohort sizes.

2.4   The Role of Institutions in the Response of Labor Markets to Demographic Change

Having explored the consequences of demographic change for youth labor markets, we now turn to the interaction between demographic change and labor market institutions and policy. Specifically, we consider whether the responses of youth employment and unemployment rates to changes in relative cohort size depend on institutional features of labor markets that affect the flexibility of those markets. For example, in a market with relatively inflexible wages, the response of youth unemployment and employment rates to changes in relative youth cohort size should be greater. This hypothesis is of particular interest given recent attempts to increase labor market flexibility, especially in the European countries (see, e.g., Blank and Freeman 1994).

While centralized wage setting and other institutions and policies that make wages less flexible may make absorption of large youth cohorts more difficult, associated institutions may improve the quality of entry-level labor, so as to offset adverse impacts on firms during baby busts. In particular, countries with more centralized wage setting tend also to have institutions that support worker training (Lynch 1994). Employers in countries where institutions that support worker training are weak or lacking may have difficulty finding qualified young workers, particularly during a baby bust. Training may therefore help employers to offset any "numbers loss." Perhaps it is not a coincidence that there appears to be growing interest in training institutions in the United States at precisely the time when young workers have become more scarce (e.g., Lynch 1994; U.S. Office of Technology Assessment 1990).

We begin with rather broad brush strokes, examining differences in the response to population changes between the European countries and the other countries in our data set. Freeman (1994) details differences between labor markets in Europe and the United States; European labor markets are less flexible, in general, being characterized by stronger unions, higher income support for the unemployed, more generous safety nets, and higher mandated nonwage labor costs.[29] We therefore first estimate a specification similar to equation (2), but allowing for differential effects of population change in Europe, as in

$$(3) \quad YE_{it} = RCS_{it}\beta + RCS_{it} \cdot EUR_i\beta' + AE_{it}\gamma + AE_{it} \cdot EUR_i\gamma'$$
$$+ D_{it}\delta + \varepsilon_{it},$$

where EUR is a dummy variable for the European countries and we allow for different responses of youth unemployment and employment rates to the adult rates in the two sets of countries. If the European countries are characterized as having less flexible labor markets, we might expect both

29. On the other hand, Allen and Freeman (1995) caution against exaggerating the differences in flexibility. They report some evidence that European labor markets are less flexible, manifested in less frequent movements between employment and unemployment. But they do not find evidence of less sectoral reallocation of labor in European labor markets. They also suggest that European labor markets became more flexible relative to the United States in the 1980s, compared with earlier decades.

a stronger response of youth unemployment rates to large youth cohorts and a stronger response of employment rates (because wages are less flexible downward).

Results are reported in panel A of table 2.8. For youth unemployment and employment rates, the results indicate little difference between European and non-European countries. For example, the association between large youth cohorts and higher youth unemployment rates is positive and marginally significant for the non-European countries (with a coefficient estimate of .419), and the interaction for the European countries is positive (.169), but not significantly so.

We next attempt to identify some of the institutional characteristics of labor markets that might underlie the differences between European and non-European countries. It seems appropriate to classify countries with respect to two characteristics that may affect labor market adjustments to population change. The first is the centralization of wage setting, which is thought to be inversely related to the flexibility of wages (e.g., Bruno and Sachs 1985). Of course, centralization or lack thereof may have more to do with the flexibility of aggregate wage levels than with the flexibility of wages for workers in particular age groups or skill categories. The second institutional characteristic is labor market policies that may inhibit wage adjustments and the reallocation of labor, such as the support given to unemployed or nonemployed workers. For example, Burtless (1987) argues that higher unemployment rates in Germany (and other European countries) are attributable to more generous unemployment compensation that allows workers to be more selective about the jobs they take.

The industrial relations literature provides classifications of countries according to the degree of centralization, three of which we use here (Crouch 1985; Blyth 1979; Calmfors and Driffill 1988).[30] The first of these classifies countries as corporatist or noncorporatist (with the former implying centralization), and the latter two as having high, medium, or low centralization. The countries in our data set that are classified as highly centralized according to all three of these classifications are Norway and Sweden, while Germany and Finland are classified as highly centralized according to two of the three classifications. In all three classifications, the United Kingdom, the United States, Japan, Canada, and Italy are classified as having a low degree of centralization.[31]

Our empirical strategy is to compare the responsiveness of youth

---

30. These are discussed in more detail in Blanchflower and Freeman (1992).

31. The complete classifications are listed in table 2.8. Ireland, Portugal, and Spain are not included in these classifications, so they are omitted from the estimation.

Blanchflower and Oswald (1994, chap. 7) review literature that tends to classify the United States, the United Kingdom, and Italy as economies with low centralization and Germany and Norway as economies with high centralization. Freeman (1994), Card, Kramarz, and Lemieux (1996), and Leigh (1995), among others, also discuss the flexibility of wages but do not provide as complete a classification of countries.

Table 2.8 Fixed Year and Country Effects Estimates Correcting for Serial Correlation and Instrumenting for Youth Population Share with Lagged Births, Including Interactions with Various Groupings of Countries

			Independent Variables				
Dependent Variable	Youth/Adult Population	Interaction with Youth Population Share	Interaction with Adult Unemployment Rate	Interaction with Adult Employment Rate	Adult Unemployment Rate	Adult Employment Rate	Hausman Test (p-value)
A. European countries							
Youth unemployment rate	.419	.169	.002	-1.224	.697**	.055	.15
	(.256)	(.331)	(.075)	(.956)	(.080)	(.946)	
Youth employment rate	-.058	-.035	-.062*	-.792*	.002	2.000**	.20
	(.118)	(.157)	(.034)	(.468)	(.034)	(.431)	
B. Countries classified as highly centralized							
Youth unemployment rate	.221	.719**	.220**	-.816	.402**	-2.599**	.99
	(.194)	(.321)	(.069)	(.954)	(.076)	(.952)	
Youth employment rate	.096	-.161	-.034	.164	.018	2.390**	.38
	(.066)	(.111)	(.023)	(.337)	(.023)	(.296)	
C. Countries with indefinite support							
Youth unemployment rate	.350*	.274	.273**	1.637**	.591**	-1.639**	.83
	(.194)	(.284)	(.058)	(.779)	(.047)	(.666)	
Youth employment rate	-.019	-.206	-.024	-1.093**	-.022	2.429**	.40
	(.096)	(.130)	(.024)	(.334)	(.017)	(.254)	

Note: $N = 318$ in panel A, $N = 196$ in panel B, and $N = 299$ in panel C. Panel A includes all of the countries. In Panel B, the highly centralized countries are Finland, Germany, Norway, and Sweden. Countries with a low degree of centralization are the United States, Italy, the United Kingdom, Canada, and Japan. All other countries are excluded from the regressions in panel B. In panel C, the countries that provide indefinite support are Finland, Germany, Ireland, the Netherlands, the United Kingdom, and Australia. Portugal is excluded from the regressions in panel C. All variables are expressed in log form. The Hausman tests are for the reported variables only (no dummies are included in the test). The data are from 1970 through 1994, although most of the countries do not have data for all of the years. The regressions include dummy variables that account for changes in the data series for some countries. Numbers in parentheses are standard errors.

*Significant at the 10 percent level.

**Significant at the 5 percent level.

unemployment and employment rates to population changes in these two subsets of countries. However, there are a few reasons to be cautious about the relation between centralization and the response of labor markets to demographic change. First, other institutional features of labor markets may offset the effects of wage rigidity. For example, Leigh (1995) suggests that the Trade Union Confederation in Sweden sought centralized wage bargaining with wage equalization across industries and regions but also encouraged active labor market policies to increase the employability of workers at prevailing wages.[32] Second, labor market flexibility may change over time. For example, labor markets in the United Kingdom increased in flexibility with some of the reforms introduced after 1979 (Cappelli 1993), and Blank and Freeman (1994) describe numerous changes implemented in European countries to attempt to increase labor market flexibility in the 1980s. Third, a priori classifications of countries based on centralization of labor markets may not always be reflected in actual wage adjustments across skill groups and the like (Card et al. 1996).[33]

We estimate an augmented version of equation (3) of the form

$$(4) \quad YE_{it} = RCS_{it}\beta + RCS_{it} \cdot H_i\beta' + RCS_{it} \cdot M_i\beta'' + AE_{it}\gamma$$
$$+ AE_{it} \cdot H_i\gamma' + AE_{it} \cdot M_i\gamma'' + D_{it}\delta + \varepsilon_{it},$$

where H is a dummy variable set equal to one for those countries classified as having a high degree of centralization and M is a dummy variable set equal to one for those countries classified as neither high nor low, so that the reference group is those classified as having a low level of centralization.[34] The hypothesis is that β' is positive in the youth unemployment rate regression and negative in the youth employment rate regression.

Panel B of table 2.8 presents the results. The evidence is consistent with centralization leading to considerably stronger positive effects of large youth cohorts on youth unemployment. The estimated difference in the effect of relative cohort size on youth unemployment, between the countries classified as highly centralized and those classified with low centralization, is large (the estimated coefficient of the interaction is .719) and is statistically significant. Looking at the youth employment rate, the estimated coefficient of this interaction is not significant, although it is negative as predicted. Thus the evidence that centralization of wage setting leads to larger responses of youth labor markets to population change is relatively strong when the outcome is the youth unemployment rate.

32. However, Forslund and Krueger (1994) argue that Sweden's active labor market policies have contributed to higher unemployment.
33. However, Card et al. compare the United States and Canada with France, the latter of which is not generally characterized as highly centralized according to the classifications described above.
34. We do not need to add the dummy variables H and M to the regressions because they are subsumed in the country dummy variables.

There are a multitude of ways to attempt to classify economies in terms of other features that affect labor market flexibility. We focus in particular on the support provided to the able-bodied nonemployed, which should be related to the degree to which fluctuations in cohort size elicit market-clearing wage movements. In particular, we follow Layard et al. (1991) in classifying countries according to whether they provide essentially indefinite support to these individuals (through a combination of unemployment insurance, supplemental benefits, and means-tested programs). The list of countries in our data set that do so includes Germany, Ireland, the Netherlands, the United Kingdom, Australia, and Finland.[35] Because this list of countries is quite different from the list of countries with highly centralized wage setting, we obtain independent information. We estimate a specification of the form

$$(5) \quad YE_{it} = RCS_{it}\beta + RCS_{it} \cdot I_i\beta' + AE_{it}\gamma + AE_{it} \cdot I_i\gamma' + D_{it}\delta + \varepsilon_{it},$$

where I is a dummy variable set equal to one for those countries with indefinite support. The hypothesis is that β' is positive in the youth unemployment rate regression and negative in the youth employment rate regression.

The results, reported in panel C of table 2.8, are somewhat supportive of this hypothesis, as the signs of the estimates of β' are consistent with expectations, but only the estimated coefficient in the youth employment rate regression ($-.206$) is marginally significant.

To summarize, there is little evidence that European labor markets in general have sharper responses of youth employment and unemployment to fluctuations in the size of youth cohorts.[36] The results suggest that centralized wage-setting institutions, and possibly greater support given to the unemployed, may inhibit absorption of large entering cohorts. However, the evidence is rather weak statistically and is based on relations estimated at the aggregate level that clearly need to be explored at other levels as well.

Ironically, because flexible wages tend to dampen the response of youth unemployment rates to fluctuations in the size of youth cohorts, increasing wage flexibility should not be viewed as a tool to help exploit the projected declines in youth population shares in order to reduce youth unemployment rates over the next 10 to 15 years; increased flexibility may directly reduce unemployment of youths and adults, but it weakens the relation between cohort size and youth unemployment.[37]

---

35. For details, see table 6 and appendix A1 in Layard, Nickell, and Jackman (1991).

36. The results reported in this section are very similar if we do not instrument for the relative cohort size variables.

37. Our evidence does not speak to the direct effects of flexibility on youth unemployment rates because the various measures of flexibility are country specific and fixed over time and hence are indistinguishable from the country dummy variables. Some measure of flexibility

2.5 Conclusions

In this paper we report evidence from a cross-national study of the effects of cohort crowding on youth unemployment and employment, using data on most of the OECD countries from 1970 to 1994. The use of data from many countries, with a relatively long panel, offers advantages over the existing literature for reducing the influence of period and other cohort effects and for avoiding faulty inferences from strongly trended data. In addition, we consider a number of issues not addressed in earlier studies, including the potential endogeneity of relative cohort size measures, augmentation of the model to allow for variation in the effects of cohort size over the business cycle, and the influence of labor market institutions on the response of youth labor markets to demographic change. Our preferred estimates indicate that the response of the youth employment rate to relative youth cohort size is close to zero. But they indicate an elasticity of the youth unemployment rate with respect to relative youth cohort size on the order of 0.5.

We use our estimates to project the likely course of relative youth unemployment rates, since the model estimates suggest that projected declining youth population shares in at least some of the countries in our sample should lead to lower unemployment rates for youths. All in all, the lessons from the projection exercises are fairly clear: falling youth population shares should improve youth labor market outcomes over the next 10 to 15 years in some countries—particularly those with relatively high youth unemployment rates in which large declines in youth population shares are projected (Ireland, Italy, Spain, and Portugal). But even for these countries, and even with an optimistic scenario regarding future adult unemployment rates, the projections never indicate a return to the lower youth unemployment rates seen in the 1970s. Youth unemployment rates are much more responsive to general labor market improvements than to declines in cohort size. In particular, in many countries a return to the tighter labor markets that produced the low adult unemployment rates of the 1970s and 1980s would do far more to improve youth labor markets. Thus, while changes in population age structure may yield some improvements in youth labor markets in some countries, more substantial reductions in youth unemployment will have to be generated from other sources.

One source of improved youth labor markets over the long term may be institutional changes, especially in European labor markets, that will increase flexibility, allowing cohort fluctuations to have greater wage effects and hence smaller employment and unemployment effects. The evi-

---

that changed over time would be required for this purpose, but the analysis of such changes is beyond the scope of this paper. For evidence on the relation between labor market flexibility and unemployment, see Layard et al. (1991).

dence, while not strong, suggests that greater centralization of wage setting in some European labor markets, and generous support for the unemployed, may increase the response of youth unemployment and employment rates to cohort size fluctuations. However, while increased flexibility may have advantageous direct effects on youth unemployment or the labor market more generally, it does not offer any particular advantage in exploiting future declines in youth population shares. Again, improvements in aggregate labor market performance offer the principal means of reducing youth unemployment rates. Whether these aggregate improvements can be more effectively encouraged through supply-side (institutional) changes or aggregate demand policies remains an open question.

Appendix
Literature Review

This appendix reviews the findings of recent studies, which are summarized in table 2.1 of the paper (along with some studies not discussed below). In general, recent studies continue to confirm earlier studies in finding effects of cohort size on relative earnings and employment or unemployment. However, this is not always the case. Few studies examine both employment and earnings. A few have analyzed longitudinal data sources in an attempt to distinguish period from cohort effects and to examine effects on age-earnings profiles, but they have yielded limited insight due to the short length of panels.

Looking first at evidence for the United States, Flaim (1979) studies the effects of demographic changes on the U.S. unemployment rate. Simple decomposition exercises suggest that 1 percentage point of a 2.7 percentage point increase in the unemployment rate in the United States between 1957 and 1977 is due to changing demographic (age and sex) composition of the labor force. Allowing interactions suggests that the "pure" effects of changing demographic composition are lower, the remainder being accounted for by positive interactions between changes in size and changes in group-specific unemployment rates (e.g., cohort crowding). Flaim also finds a positive correlation between the percentage of teens in the population and the gap between the unemployment rates of teens and adults. He predicted that the overall unemployment rate would fall about 0.4 percentage point between 1977 and 1990 (from about 7.0 percent). In a follow-up study published in 1990, Flaim shows indeed that the unemployment rate fell by about 0.5 percentage point between 1979 and 1989 and argues that the decrease is accounted for by declining youth cohort sizes. However, there appears to be no attempt to control for the state of the macroeconomy or for wage changes. One must wonder why, if supply shifts (smaller youth cohorts) explain declining unemployment rates, youth wage rates fell relative to the wages of older workers in this period.

Nardone (1987) shows that the early 1980s recession hurt youths even though they were a small fraction of the labor force. This finding seems to conflict with the results of Flaim, but it also underscores the difficulty of distinguishing period, age, and cohort effects. The present difficulty arises from a well-known age-period interaction: that is, labor market outcomes for younger workers appear to be more responsive to economic recessions than are outcomes for older workers (e.g., Clark and Summers 1981). This finding suggests that researchers should control for the business cycle even when studying *relative* unemployment rates (or employment rates) between youths and adults.

Fair and Dominguez (1991) predict that entry of large cohorts should depress wages of young workers, lowering labor supply if the substitution effect dominates the income effect in labor supply decisions. Estimates of a simple empirical model indicate that the income effect dominates for men but not for women.[38] They admit, however, that both cohort size and age effects could be contaminated by business cycle effects.

Other researchers have examined additional implications of changing population age structure. Stapleton and Young (1988) note that U.S. baby boomers affected the rate of return to education as well as the average level of educational attainment. If substitutability between younger and older workers declines as education increases, the present value of lifetime earnings is depressed more for highly educated workers from large cohorts, reducing incentives to invest. This implies that the returns to education and college completion rates would fall for baby boomers, while educational attainment should increase for post–baby boomers. They study a sample from 1973 to 1980 and note a decrease from 30 to 23 percent in the fraction of 22-year-old males who completed college, although completion among females increased steadily. They project that college completion rates would rise in the mid-1980s and continue to climb, as in fact occurred.

Berger (1989) studies a sample of white males drawn from the March Current Population Survey from 1968 to 1984, arguing for the importance of accounting for position in the demographic cycle, in addition to cohort size, in estimating the effect of demographic change on youth labor markets. Members of large cohorts can expect flatter wage profiles, those surrounded by large cohorts can expect steeper profiles, and those in cohorts born just before or after demographic peaks should expect lower initial earnings but steeper profiles. Berger argues that larger cohorts will invest

---

38. The implied magnitudes of the substitution and income effects are consistent with the labor supply literature (e.g., Killingsworth 1983).

less in human capital because they anticipate low returns; young and old workers are poor substitutes *if* they are highly educated, so the returns to education will be relatively low for members of large cohorts. His model assumes static demand for educated labor. In the 1980s and 1990s increases in the demand for educated workers may have swamped the effects of any changes in supply, although in some countries the entry of smaller cohorts may have contributed to the increase in the returns to education.

Building on the work of Stapleton and Young, Berger, and his own earlier work, Flinn (1993) develops a model of cohort size and human capital investment. In particular, he examines the effects of changes in the number of "investors" on the returns to investment, assuming different cohorts are perfect substitutes, in two models: one in which investors have perfect foresight and the other in which expectations are static. The focus is on investment in on-the-job training. There are time-dependent demand shifts such as trade or productivity shocks. The cohort size sequence is known and the returns to investment are given. Entrants maximize present value of lifetime income. All cohort size effects are reflected in the sequence of rental rates for human capital, which are determined by cohort size and investment decisions. Cohort size perturbations have direct and indirect effects. Direct effects are those holding investment constant; indirect effects allow human capital to adjust. The model is calibrated with U.S. data on white male age distributions from 1880 to 2010 at 10-year intervals and average white male wages in U.S. manufacturing from 1925 to 1985. Youths are aged 15–24.

Results from the simulation suggest that the elasticity of own wage with respect to cohort size is negative but small. The reason is that increases in cohort size reduce the opportunity cost of investment, which serves to offset the lower returns. Flinn also predicts that being a member of a cohort that "follows" a large cohort has a large positive effect on one's wages because opportunity costs of investment decline with no decreased return; similarly, he predicts a large adverse effect of being on the leading edge of a demographic cycle because many highly trained workers will follow in the near future, driving down the returns to investment. The elasticity of wealth with respect to cohort size is negative (about −0.25 for own cohort size). Also, Flinn finds little difference between direct and indirect effects. Simulations suggest that wealth was depressed 20 to 30 percent for baby boomers (compared to a scenario of constant population sizes).

A number of researchers have also considered evidence on these questions using data from European countries. Zimmermann (1991) examines the effects of aging and cohort size on age-specific unemployment rates in preunification Germany. He uses aggregate time-series data from 1967 to 1988 on younger workers (aged 15–34) and older workers (aged 35–54). Preunification Germany makes an interesting country study because there are large within-country variations between men and women in relative cohort size due to high male mortality during World War II. The effects of cohort size are larger in the short run than the long run, confirming the hypothesis of (at least partial) catch-up. In particular, he finds a significant positive effect of cohort size on unemployment that appears to decline with age, controlling for the business cycle. Large cohorts of younger workers do not affect the unemployment rates of older cohorts in the short run, suggesting a short-run adverse effect of cohort size on relative unemployment of youth. However, his estimates suggest that older workers, especially males, may be hurt in the long run by the entry of a large cohort.

Wright (1991) studies cohort size and earnings in Great Britain. The sample is composed of male heads of household from the General Household Survey for 1973–82. Wright hypothesizes a greater impact of cohort crowding for more educated workers. Therefore, he conducts separate analyses for three educational groups and 31 age groups, over 10 years, although he does not create education-specific cohort size controls because educational attainment is thought to be endogenous. Wright finds that the effects of cohort size are indeed bigger for more educated individuals. He finds some evidence of lower earnings in larger cohorts, but these earnings differences do not persist as the cohort ages. However, the period 1973–82 may not have been a good choice for the study of cohort size effects on the relative earnings of youth because of a modest and approximately linear increase in the size of the young-old population ratio (where the young are aged 15–29 and the old 30–64; Wright 1991, fig. 2).

Hartog, Oosterbeck, and Teulings (1993) study effects of cohort size in a sample of Dutch males in 1979, 1985, and 1988, stratified by educational group. They find significant positive effects of cohort size on earnings and negative cohort size/experience interactions, which are significant for workers with lower levels of educational attainment. These signs are the reverse of those found in other studies. Their table 8.9 presents a specification check. First, in a simple cross section, they do find a significant negative cohort size "main effect." Second, with experience and age controls, the effect is small, negative, and not significant. Third, when they drop school and age controls, significant negative effects return. Finally, when they control for age alone, there is no significant effect. Hartog et al. note that the sensitivity of the cohort size estimates may be due to collinearity between age and cohort size in a single cross section. In his discussion of this paper, Wright (1993) comments that the reverse effects may not be a mystery because the authors neglect to measure cohorts' positions in the demographic cycle.

Schmidt (1993) examines population aging and unemployment in Germany. He does not consider relative wages because "wage adjustment is hampered by a strong monopoly union" (216). In recent years in Germany, there has been a reversal of relative unemployment rates, with those for older workers actually exceeding those for younger workers. He finds adverse effects of large cohort size for a few age-sex groups. In particular, effects of cohort size on unemployment are positive and significant for ages 15–19, 20–24, and 55–59 (males and females) but not for other ages. This result is consistent with a cohort size effect on unemployment that does not persist into prime working ages. Consistent with Flinn, Schmidt notes that two issues—the persistence of cohort size effects and the effects on investment in human capital—are linked. He finds that the relative wage structure is fairly constant but notes that births are not the only demographic factor to affect the relative size of the labor force at different ages.

Nickell (1993) examines effects of relative cohort size on the relative wages of young men in Britain from 1961 to 1989. He carries out two sets of analyses: one for the general labor market, the other for the unionized sector. Both analyses suggest substantial adverse effects of cohort size on the relative wages of youth, controlling for the proportion of youth enrolled in school and cyclical demand factors.

Klevmarken (1993) focuses more on the effects of population aging on earnings mobility. Age-earnings profiles should be sensitive to supply and demand shifts (see his figs. 7.1 and 7.2). For example, secular increases in productivity will lead cross-sectional estimates of age-earnings profiles to be biased downward. Entry of large youth cohorts will tend to steepen cross-sectional age-earnings profiles. Klevmarken reviews studies of the effects of cohort size on age-earnings profiles (Freeman 1979; Welch 1979; Berger 1985, 1989; Stapleton and Young 1988; Martin and Ogawa 1988; Wright 1991; Jonsson and Klevmarken 1978; Tasiran and Gustaffson 1991; Murphy, Plant, and Welch 1988). The point of greatest contention appears to be the extent of catch-up in earnings for members of large cohorts. Klevmarken in particular questions Berger's (1989) results, which suggest that catch-up does not take place. Murphy et al. (1988) find an "initial" (short-run) elasticity of 10 percent with respect to cohort size that falls to 3 percent on a lifetime basis. Tasiran and Gustaffson (1991) find that wages of Swedish shop assistants are depressed by large cohort size but profiles are steeper.

Klevmarken conducts an analysis of a Swedish panel data set for the period 1984–88 at two-year intervals. His relative cohort size measure is the weighted average of own and surrounding age groups. He notes that immigration flows are large and poorly measured. He finds that all cohort size variables are insignificant and concludes that "another result, supported both by this and previous studies, is that earnings profiles are more sensitive to changes in demand than to supply side changes" (Klevmarken 1993, 167). However, we note that the models contain many interaction terms that make interpretation difficult.[39]

---

39. Börsch-Supan (1993) provides comments on the Klevmarken paper and remarks that the panel studied is far too short to distinguish age and cohort effects.

References

Allen, Steven G., and Richard B. Freeman. 1995. Quantitative flexibility in the U.S. labor market. Raleigh: North Carolina State University. Mimeograph.

Berger, Mark C. 1985. The effect of cohort size on earnings growth: A reexamination of the evidence. *Journal of Political Economy* 93:561–73.

———. 1989. Demographic cycles, cohort size, and earnings. *Demography* 26: 311–21.

Blanchflower, David G., and Richard B. Freeman. 1992. Unionism in the United States and other advanced OECD countries. *Industrial Relations* 31 (1): 56–79.

Blanchflower, David G., and Andrew J. Oswald. 1994. *The wage curve.* Cambridge, Mass.: MIT Press.

Blank, Rebecca M., and Richard B. Freeman. 1994. Evaluating the connection between social protection and economic flexibility. In *Social protection versus economic flexibility,* ed. Rebecca M. Blank. Chicago: University of Chicago Press.

Bloom, David E., Richard B. Freeman, and Sanders Korenman. 1987. The labour market consequences of generational crowding. *European Journal of Population* 3:131–76.

Blyth, C. 1979. Level of national bargaining. In *Collective government and national policies.* Paris: Organization for Economic Cooperation and Development.

Börsch-Supan, Axel. 1993. Comment on Klevmarken. In *Labour markets in an ageing Europe,* ed. Paul Johnson and Klaus F. Zimmermann. Cambridge: Cambridge University Press.

Bound, John, David A. Jaeger, and Regina M. Baker. 1995. Problems with instrumental variables estimation when the correlation between the instruments and the endogenous explanatory variables is weak. *Journal of the American Statistical Association* 90:443–50.

Bowden, Roger J., and Darrell A. Turkington. 1984. *Instrumental variables.* Cambridge: Cambridge University Press.

Bruno, Michael, and Jeffrey Sachs. 1985. *The economics of worldwide stagflation.* Cambridge, Mass.: Harvard University Press.

Burtless, Gary. 1987. Jobless pay and high European unemployment. In *Barriers to European growth: A transatlantic view,* ed. Robert Z. Lawrence and Charles L. Schultze, 105–74. Washington, D.C.: Brookings Institution.

Calmfors, L., and J. Driffill. 1988. Centralisation of wage bargaining and macroeconomic performance. *Economic Policy* 6:13–61.

Cappelli, Peter. 1996. Youth apprenticeship programs in Britain: Lessons for the United States. *Industrial Relations* 35 (1): 1–31.

Card, David, Francis Kramarz, and Thomas Lemieux. 1996. Changes in the relative structure of wages and employment: A comparison of the United States, Canada, and France. NBER Working Paper no. 5487. Cambridge, Mass.: National Bureau of Economic Research.

Clark, Kim B., and Lawrence H. Summers. 1981. Demographic differences in cyclical employment variation. *Journal of Human Resources* 16 (1): 61–79.

———. 1982. The dynamics of youth unemployment. In *The youth labor market problem: Its nature, causes, and consequences,* ed. Richard Freeman and David Wise, 199–235. Chicago: University of Chicago Press.

Crouch, Colin. 1985. Conditions for trade union restraint. In *The politics of inflation and economic stagflation,* ed. Leon N. Lindberg and Charles S. Maier, 105–39. Washington, D.C.: Brookings Institution.

Davis, Steven J., John C. Haltiwanger, and Scott Schuh. 1996. *Job creation and destruction.* Cambridge, Mass.: MIT Press.

Fair, Ray C., and Kathryn M. Dominguez. 1991. Effects of changing U.S. age distribution on macroeconomic equations. *American Economic Review* 81 (5): 1276–94.

Flaim, Paul O. 1979. The effect of demographic change on the nation's unemployment rate. *Monthly Labor Review* 102:13–23.

———. 1990. Population changes, the baby boom, and the unemployment rate. *Monthly Labor Review* 113:3–10.

Flinn, Christopher J. 1993. The implications of cohort size for human capital investment. In *Labour markets in an ageing Europe,* ed. Paul Johnson and Klaus F. Zimmermann. Cambridge: Cambridge University Press.

Forslund, Anders, and Alan B. Krueger. 1997. An evaluation of Swedish active labor market policy: New and received wisdom. In *The welfare state in transition: Reforming the Swedish model,* ed. Richard B. Freeman, Robert Topel, and Brigitta Swedenborg. Chicago: University of Chicago Press.

Freeman, Richard B. 1979. The effect of demographic factors on age earnings profiles. *Journal of Human Resources* 14:289–318.

———. 1994. How labor fares in advanced economies. In *Working under different rules,* ed. Richard B. Freeman, 1–28. New York: Russell Sage Foundation.

Hartog, Joop, Hessel Oosterbeek, and Coen Teulings. 1993. Age, wages, and education in the Netherlands. In *Labour markets in an ageing Europe,* ed. Paul Johnson and Klaus F. Zimmermann. Cambridge: Cambridge University Press.

Jonsson, A., and N. A. Klevmarken. 1978. On the relationship between cross-sectional and cohort earnings profiles. *Annales de l'INSEE,* 331–53.

Killingsworth, Mark R. 1983. *Labor supply.* Cambridge: Cambridge University Press.

Klevmarken, N. Anders. 1993. On ageing and earnings. In *Labour markets in an ageing Europe,* ed. Paul Johnson and Klaus F. Zimmermann. Cambridge: Cambridge University Press.

Layard, Richard, Stephen Nickell, and Richard Jackman. 1991. *Unemployment: Macroeconomic performance and the labour market.* Oxford: Oxford University Press.

Leigh, Duane. 1995. *Assisting workers displaced by structural change.* Kalamazoo, Mich.: W. E. Upjohn Institute for Employment Research.

Levine, Phillip B., and Olivia S. Mitchell. 1988. The baby boom's legacy: Relative wages in the twenty-first century. *American Economic Review* 78 (2): 66–69.

Lynch, Lisa, ed. 1994. *Training and the private sector: International comparisons.* Chicago: University of Chicago Press.

Martin, Linda G., and Naohiro Ogawa. 1988. The effect of cohort size on relative wages in Japan. In *Economics of changing age distributions in developing countries,* ed. Ronald D. Lee, W. Brian Arthur, and Gerry Rodgers. Oxford: Oxford University Press.

Mitchell, B. R. 1992. *International historical statistics: Europe, 1750–1988.* 3d ed. Basingstoke, England: Macmillan; New York: Stockton Press.

———. 1995. *International historical statistics: Africa, Asia and Oceania, 1750–1988.* 2d rev. ed. New York: Stockton Press.

Murphy, Kevin, Mark Plant, and Finis Welch. 1988. Cohort size and earnings in the United States. In *Economics of changing age distributions in developing countries,* ed. Ronald D. Lee, W. Brian Arthur, and Gerry Rodgers. Oxford: Oxford University Press.

Nardone, Thomas. 1987. Decline in youth population does not lead to lower jobless rates. *Monthly Labor Review* 110:37–41.

Nickell, Stephen. 1993. Cohort size effects on the wages of young men in Britain: 1961–1989. *British Journal of Industrial Relations* 31 (3): 459–69.

OECD (Organization for Economic Cooperation and Development). 1980. *Youth unemployment: The causes and consequences.* Paris: Organization for Economic Cooperation and Development.

Schmidt, Christoph M. 1993. Ageing and unemployment. In *Labour markets in an ageing Europe,* ed. Paul Johnson and Klaus F. Zimmermann. Cambridge: Cambridge University Press.

Singell, Larry D., and Jane H. Lillydahl. 1989. Some alternative definitions of youth unemployment: A means for improved understanding and policy formation. *American Journal of Economics and Sociology* 48 (4): 457–71.

Sorrentino, Constance. 1993. International comparisons of unemployment indicators. *Monthly Labor Review* 116 (March): 3–24.

Stapleton, David C., and Douglas J. Young. 1988. Educational attainment and cohort size. *Journal of Labor Economics* 6 (3): 330–61.

Suits, Daniel B. 1984. Dummy variables: Mechanics v. interpretation. *Review of Economics and Statistics* 66:177–80.

Tasiran, A., and B. Gustaffson. 1994. Wages in Sweden since World War II: Gender and age specific salaries in wholesale and retail trade. *Scandanavian Economic History Review* 42 (1): 77–100.

U.S. Office of Technology Assessment. 1990. *Worker training: Competing in the new international economy.* Washington, D.C.: Government Printing Office, September.

Welch, Finis. 1979. Effects of cohort size on earnings: The baby boom babies' financial bust. *Journal of Political Economy* 87:S65–S97.

Wright, Robert E. 1991. Cohort size and earnings in Great Britain. *Journal of Population Economics* 4:295–305.

———. 1993. Comment on Hartog, Oosterbeek and Teulings. In *Labour markets in an ageing Europe,* ed. Paul Johnson and Klaus F. Zimmermann. Cambridge: Cambridge University Press.

Zimmermann, Klaus F. 1991. Ageing and the labor market: Age structure, cohort size and unemployment. *Journal of Population Economics* 4:177–200.

Gender and Youth Employment Outcomes
The United States and West Germany, 1984–1991

Francine D. Blau and Lawrence M. Kahn

3.1 Introduction

During the past 15 years, the labor market prospects facing less educated young workers in the United States have seriously deteriorated as part of a dramatic trend toward widening wage inequality. For example, Katz and Murphy (1992) find that real wages *fell* by 15.8 percent for young men with less than a high school education from 1979 to 1987, and a recent study by Burtless (1994) similarly documents the deteriorating wage prospects of young women with limited education. Perhaps as a result of their falling real wages, young, less educated men and women have also experienced decreasing labor market attachment relative to their more highly educated counterparts.[1]

In contrast to the poor and declining prospects of many, especially less

Francine D. Blau is the Frances Perkins Professor of Industrial and Labor Relations at the School of Industrial and Labor Relations, Cornell University, and a research associate of the National Bureau of Economic Research. Lawrence M. Kahn is professor of labor economics and collective bargaining at the School of Industrial and Labor Relations, Cornell University.

This work was partially supported by a grant from the Rockefeller Foundation to the National Bureau of Economic Research. Earlier versions of this paper were presented at the NBER–Universität Konstanz conference and the preconference held at Konstanz, Germany; as well as at the American Economic Association/Industrial Relations Research Association meetings in New Orleans, January 1997; the Sloan Conference on the Growth in Labor Market Inequality in Madison, Wisconsin, February 1997; and workshops at Cornell University, the University of Toronto, and the University of Rochester. The authors are indebted to Brian Levine, Deborah Anderson, and Wen-Jui Han for excellent research assistance and to Katherine Abraham, Danny Blanchflower, Richard Freeman, Robert Hutchens, Stephen Nickell, Jörn-Steffen Pischke, Jane Waldfogel, and conference and workshop participants for helpful comments and suggestions.

1. For other discussions of these trends, see Bound and Johnson (1992), Juhn, Murphy, and Pierce (1993), Juhn (1992), Blau (1998), and Blau and Kahn (1997).

educated U.S. youths, young workers in Germany appear to be well pre-
pared for the labor market and to have better labor market outcomes.
German youths typically have lower relative unemployment rates than
youths in the United States. For example, in 1989, at a time when the
overall unemployment rate in Germany was 8.0 percent, it was 8.1 percent
among 15–20-year-olds and 7.4 percent among 20–30-year-olds. In contrast, in the United States, where the overall rate was 5.3 percent in that
year, it was 15 percent for 16–19-year-olds, 8.6 percent for 20–24-year-
olds, and 5.7 percent for 25–29-year-olds (Abraham and Houseman 1995,
400; ILO 1993, 653; USBLS 1990, 162). Further, the low-skilled in Germany were spared the declining relative and absolute real wages that
afflicted those in the United States and several other OECD countries in
the 1980s: wage inequality in Germany was stable to declining, and real
wages of the low-skilled in particular rose. The relative earnings of young
workers were also stable to rising over the 1980s (OECD 1993a; Abraham
and Houseman 1995). Thus young workers and the low-skilled in general
had better labor market outcomes over the 1980s in Germany than in the
United States. This difference in labor market performance suggests that
the United States may have much to learn from Germany's relative success.

In this paper, we examine differences between the United States and
West Germany in employment outcomes of young workers over the
1984–91 period. In light of the employment problems of less educated
youth in the United States, we place special emphasis on how those at
relatively low educational levels fared in the labor market. We especially
focus on less educated young women. Given recent U.S. welfare reform
legislation, this group will be increasingly dependent on their own employment and earnings prospects. We use nationally representative databases
for each country, which allow us to measure young workers' employment
outcomes and also permit comparisons across age groups: principally the
German Socioeconomic Panel for Germany and the Current Population
Survey for the United States.

German society is structured in several ways to ensure relatively good
outcomes for those at the bottom. For example, the vast majority of
youths participate in Germany's vocational training system, although
women do not participate to the same extent as men. In the United States,
no corresponding training system on a large scale imparts skills to workers
at the lower end of the educational distribution. However, not everyone
in Germany completes an apprenticeship. In this paper, we emphasize a
comparison of German youths who are left out of that system with a
group in the United States who are also left out—high school dropouts.

Even for the group of Germans who drop out of the apprentice training
system, institutions exist to improve labor market outcomes. First, the
German educational system appears to provide better basic skills than the
American system at the bottom of the distribution of academic achieve-

ment. Second, German wage-setting institutions disproportionately raise the wages of the low-skilled. The U.S. labor market is largely nonunion, while wages in Germany are set in industry-wide contracts that are extended by law to (or in almost all cases imitated by) the nonunion sector. In addition, the U.S. minimum wage is low by international standards and has generally been declining in real terms since the late 1970s (Minimum pay 1992). Thus we expect German wage-setting institutions to disproportionately raise the pay of young, less educated workers. However, there may be negative employment effects of this system, and we will attempt to determine whether this is the case. If such effects exist, they should be strongest for unskilled youths in general and young women in particular, since they are the ones most likely to be affected by wage floors. Third, Germany has a larger public sector than the United States, and government employment can be a mechanism for reducing potential adverse employment effects of administered wages (see Edin and Topel 1997; Björklund and Freeman 1997; Kahn 1998). We will investigate this possibility as well.

For women, while wage floors are expected to have demand-side effects on relative employment, public policy toward the support of children and maternity and parental leave may have supply-side effects.[2] For example, maternity and parental leave policies in Germany are considerably more generous than those in the United States, and became even more so over the late 1980s. While relatively short leaves are likely to increase women's labor force attachment, extended leaves may arguably do the opposite. And German schools do not provide lunch for students, forcing families to provide lunch at home; this feature of German society is also likely to reduce women's labor force attachment because mothers are usually the ones responsible for arranging lunch for children. In earlier work we indeed found higher labor force participation rates for U.S. than for German women (Blau and Kahn 1995). On the other hand, the U.S. welfare system places a particularly strong penalty on work for low-income, single mothers, implying possible negative employment effects for low-skilled women. Below we will attempt to shed light on the impact of the U.S. welfare system on young, hard-to-employ women.

We find that less educated youths do indeed fare considerably better in Germany, experiencing both higher employment rates and higher relative earnings than is the case in the United States. Both these differences are particularly pronounced for women. While welfare may play a role, our findings suggest that it accounts for very little of the U.S.-German difference in employment rates. It is also the case that the German women's

---

2. Of course, high wage floors can attract potential workers into the labor force in search of good jobs. In contrast, low and freely falling real wages for the less skilled may have led many U.S. workers to leave the labor force. See Mincer (1976) and Juhn (1992).

employment advantage exists despite Germany's more generous maternity and parental leave policies, which our results suggest do negatively affect German women's employment rates, especially their full-time employment rates, all else equal. This suggests that low and declining real wages are likely an important explanation for the lower labor force attachment of both young men and women in the United States. The relatively high employment rates of less educated German youths combined with their relatively high wages raise the question of how they are successfully absorbed into the labor market. Our findings suggest that the public sector in Germany in effect functioned as an employer of last resort during this period, absorbing some otherwise unemployable low-skilled youths.

3.2 Overview of West German and U.S. Labor Market Conditions and Institutions in the 1980s

3.2.1 Training and Wage-Setting Institutions

In designing policies to help young workers in the United States, analysts have looked increasingly to several aspects of the German educational system and its labor market institutions for guidance, including its basic formal secondary schooling system, its apprentice training programs, and its wage-setting mechanisms. First, its basic educational system has been found to produce a superior level of learning, particularly for those at the bottom of the ability distribution (Nickell and Bell 1996). For example, on international mathematics tests for 13-year-old students, young Germans outscored young Americans at both the top and the bottom of the distribution. Thus, in particular for those at the bottom of the distribution of math ability, Germany produces a more highly trained potential labor force.

Second, Germany's apprentice training system, which many believe greatly facilitates the school-to-work transition there, is often held up as an example for the United States to emulate (Buechtemann, Schupp, and Soloff 1993). Following secondary education in Germany, students typically locate themselves on one of two tracks: (1) higher education—universities and four-year technical colleges; or (2) one- to four-year full-time vocational schools and the "dual system" consisting of apprentice training and part-time attendance at vocational schools coordinated with firm-based training.[3] This arrangement is a partnership among government, training schools, and firms in which the transition from postsecondary education (vocational schools) to employment is enhanced. These programs have been credited with reducing youth unemployment, and as we

---

3. This description of Germany's training institutions is based on Buechtemann et al. (1993), Soskice (1994), and Steedman (1993).

have seen, relative unemployment rates for German youths are indeed lower than those for U.S. youths (see also Buechtemann et al. 1993).

Finally, Germany's system of centrally determined industry wage bargains with contract extensions to nonunion workers has been shown to raise the pay of low-skilled workers disproportionately (Blau and Kahn 1996a). It is possible that German wage-setting institutions allowed its wage distribution to resist the effects of changing supply and demand conditions in the 1980s and to remain stable, in contrast to the widening U.S. distribution.[4]

These latter two aspects of the German labor market—its elaborate system of apprentice training and its union-negotiated industry-wide wage minima—resemble the kinds of policies advocated by Robert Reich, former U.S. secretary of labor, who in 1995 called for an expansion of investment in education and skills, a rise in the federal minimum wage, and changes in U.S. labor law to make it easier for unions to achieve recognition (Bureau of National Affairs 1995a, 1995b).

While participation in some form of postsecondary education or training is near universal in Germany, about 21 percent of German youths had not attained a training certificate or postsecondary education degree 12 years after leaving secondary school (Buechtemann et al. 1993, 8). It is these youths whom we categorize as "hard to employ" and who are the focus of this paper. A potential drawback to the German labor market setup, particularly for hard-to-employ youths, concerns the possible disemployment effects of administered wages. While in the United States, minimum wages have generally been found to have small or no employment effects,[5] several studies have found evidence consistent with the existence of disemployment effects of high wage floors in Europe, although this finding is not unanimous.[6]

While we expect wage floors to reduce the relative employment of the low-skilled, an alternative response is for the government to act as employer of last resort, as argued by Björklund and Freeman (1997) for the case of Sweden. They show that the share of all unskilled workers who were employed by the government rose during a period of severe wage

---

4. However, Abraham and Houseman (1995) find that while growth in the supply of highly educated workers decelerated in the 1980s in the United States, in Germany this growth rate appeared stable. Thus it is possible that some of the stability in the German wage distribution in the 1980s reflects more stable growth in the supply of highly trained workers there.

5. Card and Krueger (1995) find that minimum wages did not have negative employment effects for teenagers, while Neumark and Wascher (1992) find relatively small negative effects. Larger negative effects have been obtained by Deere, Murphy, and Welch (1995).

6. These include Edin and Topel (1997), Katz, Loveman, and Blanchflower (1995), Abowd et al. (chap. 11 in this volume), Blau and Kahn (1996a), and Kahn (1998). However, Card, Kramarz, and Lemieux (1995) find no evidence that inflexible relative wages in France over the 1982–89 period led to larger employment losses among low-wage workers there than in the United States. And Machin and Manning (1994) find that minimum wages in the United Kingdom did not have disemployment effects in the 1980s.

compression induced by Sweden's solidarity wage policy. Others have also found evidence of such government employment responses, including Edin and Topel (1997) for Sweden and Kahn (1998) for Norway. In light of possible public employment responses, we also examine this outcome below. Data in Nickell (1997) show that relative spending on active labor market policies during the 1989–94 period was about eight times as high in Germany as in the United States (this was defined as spending per unemployed person as a percentage of GDP per member of the labor force). To the extent that such policies are disproportionately directed at youths and provide public sector jobs, they may help to account for the relative success of German youths. We also note that such employment responses by the government need not solely reflect explicit policies. Rather, the pattern of government employment may be such that, for whatever reason, it has the effect of absorbing otherwise unemployable youths.

3.2.2   Gender and Labor Market Success:
Germany versus the United States

The gender wage gap among employed workers was lower in West Germany than in the United States in 1979, when American women's wages were 60 percent of men's compared to 71 percent in West Germany. But by 1991, the gender ratio was virtually the same, about 74 percent in both countries, and by 1994, the ratio was actually somewhat higher in the United States (76.4 percent) than in West Germany (74.2 percent).[7] American women have considerably higher labor force participation rates than German women, especially among married women, and are more likely to work full time. They are also less occupationally segregated and outearn a larger percentage of men than their German counterparts, implying that U.S. women have higher relative qualifications or enjoy more favorable treatment by employers than German women (Blau and Kahn 1995).

It is possible that Germany's more generous maternity and parental leave policies play a role in producing these differences in women's labor market attachment. Provisions for parental leave in West Germany, according to the 1979 amendments to the Maternity Protection Act, call for 14 weeks of fully paid maternity leave, of which two months are mandatory, and protection of job security during pregnancy and through the end of the fourth month after childbirth. Beginning in January 1986, a 12-month parental leave with a paid allowance was additionally mandated (ILO 1988; Demleitner 1992). In 1990, the German parental leave provision was expanded to 18 months, and in 1992, which is outside our sample period, it was increased even further to three years. Moreover, German

---

7. See Blau and Kahn (1995), ILO (1993, 1995), and USBLS (1992, 1995). Figures for 1991 and 1994 are for average hourly earnings of nonagricultural employees in West Germany and for median weekly earnings of full-time wage and salary workers in the United States.

parental leave is paid as long as the parent taking the leave works no more than 19 hours per week, a provision encouraging part-time work. This is almost always the mother, as roughly 99 percent of people taking parental leave as of 1992 were women (Demleitner 1992).[8] In contrast, there was no mandated parental leave policy in the United States prior to the passage of the Family and Medical Leave Act in 1993, which requires up to 12 weeks of unpaid parental leave for women or men. However, prior to the passage of the act it was (and continues to be) required that pregnancy be treated the same as any other medical disability by the firm. Thus leave for the physical aspects of childbearing must be covered under a firm's medical disability plan, if it has one. And in the late 1980s, roughly 40 percent of employees of large and medium-size establishments worked at firms that voluntarily granted some kind of parental leave beyond this, 92 percent of them unpaid (Hyland 1990). While there was some provision for parental leave in the United States prior to the 1993 legislation, it is clear that parental leave policies were considerably more generous in Germany.

The impact of parental leave on women's labor force attachment is unclear a priori. On the one hand, by guaranteeing women's right to return to their jobs after pregnancy, parental leave may strengthen their labor force attachment. On the other hand, such policies, particularly if they are generously paid and of long duration, could increase the incidence or duration of workforce withdrawals associated with pregnancy. It is possible that by 1991 Germany's relatively generous parental leave policies— 18 months of partially paid parental leave after 14 weeks of fully paid maternity leave—encouraged labor force withdrawals among mothers of young children relative to the United States. In addition, the 19-hour provision unambiguously encouraged part-time work among employed women. Moreover, throughout our period, it was legal in Germany for employers to deny job offers to pregnant women (Demleitner 1992, 246). Finally, as noted earlier schoolchildren are sent home for lunch in Germany, making the family (usually the mother) responsible for arranging this meal (OECD 1988, 142). Each of these special features of the German labor market may be expected to discourage labor force attachment by women and, most particularly, full-time employment.

In addition to parental and maternity leave policies that likely reduce the incidence of employment or full-time employment among women, Germany maintains a system of child allowances. This is a universal system with increasing benefits paid to families with larger numbers of children. While the child allowance is less generous for high-income families,

---

8. In fact, fathers had to get special permission to take family leave. Since firms bear some of the direct costs of the paid leave, it has been argued that they have an incentive to discriminate against women in hiring (Demleitner 1992). The 19-hour provision was part of the original legislation that went into effect in January 1986 (ILO 1988, 103–4).

it is available whether or not one works (U.S. Social Security Administration 1995). In contrast, in the United States, there were direct cash benefits paid only to low-income families with children, through the Aid to Families with Dependent Children (AFDC) program, as it was called until 1996. This program paid benefits almost exclusively to female-headed, low-income families and greatly penalized work among recipients by reducing benefits virtually dollar for dollar with increased earnings. Welfare has been found to have only moderate effects on labor supply in the United States (Moffitt 1992), but to the extent that it does have a negative effect, we would predict that it would disproportionately affect low-skilled, unmarried women with children in the United States.[9]

3.3 Data

Our data sources for examining gender differences in young workers' labor market outcomes are principally the German Socio-Economic Panel (GSOEP) and the March Current Population Survey (CPS).[10] The CPS has the advantages of large sample size and, like the GSOEP, coverage of all individuals. However, unlike the GSOEP, the CPS does not have information on actual labor market experience, a factor that has been found to be important in explaining the gender pay gap (Mincer and Polachek 1974; O'Neill and Polachek 1993; Blau and Kahn 1997). Because of this omission, we also perform some examination of actual experience using the Michigan Panel Study of Income Dynamics (PSID).[11] However, the PSID contains labor market information only on household heads and spouses, thus excluding those who are living in the homes of their parents or of other relatives. This is of particular concern in a study of youths. Moreover, as discussed below, actual experience is not available for new

9. In addition, the U.S. income tax system in effect rewards larger families through the personal exemption, which allows the family to exclude from taxable income a given amount of money ($2,550 as of 1996) per person in the family. This system is similar to the German universal system (at least among U.S. taxpayers), but the AFDC program for the United States with its work disincentives for low-income individuals was significantly different from the German system. AFDC was replaced in 1996 with a reformed welfare system that has strict limits on the duration of benefits. We expect the new system to encourage labor force participation and note that in the period we examine in this paper, 1984–91, the AFDC system was in place. Working in the opposite direction during our period was the expansion of the earned income tax credit starting in 1987, which worked to increase the participation rate of single mothers, all else equal (Eissa and Liebman 1996).

10. See Burkhauser (1991) for a detailed description of the GSOEP and Katz and Murphy (1992) for a discussion of the CPS.

11. The PSID is a nationally representative survey and is structured very similarly to the GSOEP; see Blau and Kahn (1997) for a description. In addition to the nationally representative portion of the sample, the PSID collected data on an oversample of those living in high-poverty areas. We used these data as well in order to have larger samples of hard-to-employ youths and applied the PSID's sampling weights in our analyses of these data to correct for the oversampling.

members of the GSOEP after 1984. Thus we focus on analyses comparing the CPS and the GSOEP.

We use the 1984 wave of the GSOEP because it has the largest sample size, is not affected by attrition, and is the only one for which we can compute actual labor market experience for all respondents. It is a nationally representative sample of the population living in West Germany, including West Berlin, in that year. In our main analyses, we use data only on Germans from the GSOEP, since education and training information is less detailed for immigrants.[12] However, we also present some findings for immigrants that suggest focusing on Germans gives an accurate picture of the labor market for less skilled youths in this country. We define "young" as aged 18–29, a relatively inclusive definition. We do this in part for reasons of sample size and in part because, in Germany, schooling and formal training usually continue into the middle to late twenties (Buechtemann et al. 1993). By extending our age cutoff to 29, we thus increase the chances of observing the school-to-work transition.

In view of the important changes in the labor market in the United States and other countries in the 1980s, and because we wish to observe what happens to young workers as they mature, we also examine the 1991 GSOEP and CPS. In examining what happens to young individuals as they age, we rely primarily on "synthetic cohorts." That is, we compare a random sample of 18–29-year-olds in 1984 to a random sample of 25–36-year-olds in 1991 to make inferences about what happened to people as they aged over the 1984–91 period. While it is possible to construct panels of individuals in the GSOEP (and of course the PSID), and we do so in a supplementary analysis, one loses about 45 percent of the GSOEP panel through attrition and the sample sizes become too small for meaningful analysis. Similarly, while it is possible to construct a 1991 sample with information on actual experience by following the original 1984 sample members, the small sample size problem precludes this.

A final data issue relates to employment. We use two measures of employment: the probability of being employed and the probability of being employed full time (both relative to the population). The measure of employment refers to current (survey week) employment status. Full-time employment corresponds to usual weekly hours for the currently employed of 35 or more in the preceding year (United States) or on the current job (Germany). We examine both variables because the latter gives additional information regarding the extent of labor force attachment.

Some data issues arise in defining "employment" in the presence of pa-

---

12. In particular, the GSOEP does not include detailed information on basic schooling obtained outside Germany for immigrants. The survey asks whether the respondent earned a "degree," but it does not specify what kind of degree. There is better information on whether immigrants completed postsecondary training outside (or inside) Germany and whether they earned German basic school degrees, information we use below.

rental leaves. Neither the CPS nor the 1984 GSOEP separately identify such individuals. In the CPS, individuals on parental leave are considered employed ("with a job but not at work"; Klerman and Leibowitz 1997). The same likely applies to the 1984 GSOEP. Only the 1991 German data give the option of separately identifying individuals on "maternity leave." One question this raises is what is meant by "maternity leave." Since we found that a relatively high proportion of young women fell into this category, we assumed that this meant both maternity and parental leave.[13] A second question relates to how this category should be treated. Since our interest is in actual work, we chose to exclude individuals on maternity leave from the employed category. This raises some compatibility issues with the CPS, as well as the 1984 GSOEP. However, it may be recalled that only 14 weeks of maternity leave were mandated in Germany in 1984 and there were no mandates in place in the United States at this time. Thus the inclusion of women who were on leave as employed is likely to have had relatively little effect compared to the situation in Germany in 1991, when an additional 18 months of parental leave had become available. In terms of possible effects on our results, had we included women out on maternity leave in 1991 as employed, the German employment advantage that we find for less educated German women would have been still larger. On the other hand, the larger negative effect on employment of children that we estimate for German women in 1991 compared to 1984 would have been reduced.

3.4 U.S.-German Differences in Labor Market Preparedness and Outcomes of Youths

3.4.1 Education

Our major focus is on gender differences in the labor market for hard-to-employ youths in West Germany and the United States. Since, in each country, the less educated are the hardest to employ, comparing the two countries requires a standardized definition of education. For the United States, a measure of years of formal schooling completed is readily available in the CPS and PSID data sets. However, since classroom, vocationally related training is far more important in Germany than in the United States, it would be desirable to take into account both academic and vocational schooling in creating a comparable years of schooling measure for Germany. Krueger and Pischke (1995) have created a mapping from the GSOEP's educational and training measures into a years of school variable, and we use their scheme here.

---

13. The following proportions of young women (aged 18–29) were in this category: .037 (low-education group), .089 (middle-education group), and .087 (high-education group). See the next section for definitions of the educational categories.

Based on German and U.S. measures of years of schooling, we create three educational groups for each country that encompass roughly the same proportions of the nonenrolled population and thus account for differences between the two countries in average years of schooling completed: Edlow, Edmid, and Edhigh, respectively, referring to groups with low, middle, and high education. For the United States, the groups are Edlow, less than 12 years; Edmid, 12–15 years; and Edhigh, 16 or more years. For Germany, the groups are Edlow, 9–10 years; Edmid, 11–12 years; and Edhigh, over 12 years.[14]

We chose educational groups according to categories instead of, say, quartiles of the distribution of educational attainment, for several reasons. First, we believe that for both countries, the Edlow category corresponds to an identifiable group made up of the hard to employ. In West Germany, individuals in that category had completed at most only basic secondary education and had no formal degree from a high school (gymnasium), university, college, or any vocational school. This group is outside the system of formal certification. In the United States, those in the Edlow category have less than a high school education, which surely places them at great risk of severe difficulties in the labor market. Second, because the distribution of years of schooling is lumpy, it is not possible to construct categories that correspond exactly to particular percentiles of the population, such as the middle two quartiles. For example, among American men aged 18–29 who were not in school, 48 percent had exactly 12 years of schooling in 1984 (CPS tabulation). Third, looking ahead to table 3.2, we see that among those not currently in school, the percentages of the 18–29-year-old population in the three educational categories as we have defined them are quite similar for the United States and Germany. Thus, for our target group, the educational categories we have created in fact correspond roughly to a breakdown by distribution percentiles.

Tables 3.1 and 3.2 provide evidence on educational participation and attainment by age-gender group. Several findings emerge that provide a picture of the relative labor market preparedness of men and women in each country. In table 3.1, we focus on current school attendance. The German data allow people with jobs to also report that they are in school, while the CPS asks respondents to state their "major activity." Thus, in the CPS, only those who say their major activity is school are reported as being in school. In contrast, in the U.S. Census of Population, people are asked if they are currently enrolled in school, whether or not employment is their major activity. Since it is possible for one to be employed and in

---

14. For Germany, we include those with an *Abitur* degree only (i.e., with no postsecondary schooling) in the middle-education group even though Krueger and Pischke (1995) code an *Abitur* as requiring 13 years of schooling. Our decision was based on our impression that these people, who made up only about 1 percent of the sample, were more similar in their employment experience to the middle- than to the high-education group. Because the group is so small, this coding did not affect our results.

Table 3.1   Educational Participation and Attainment

| | Ages 18–29 | | | Ages 25–36 | | |
Country	Proportion in School	Years of School Completed	Sample Size	Proportion in School	Years of School Completed	Sample Size
Germany (GSOEP)						
1984 Men	.418	11.60	1,069	.157	12.59	973
Women	.304	11.56	1,028	.063	11.95	958
1991 Men	.425	11.67	953	.183	12.71	883
Women	.320	11.52	894	.065	12.25	857
United States (CPS)						
1984 Men	.175	12.46	16,271	.029	13.16	15,801
Women	.154	12.49	17,062	.023	12.91	16,792
1991 Men	.175	12.45	13,241	.025	12.95	15,153
Women	.171	12.61	14,381	.031	12.99	16,297
United States (PUMS)[a]						
1990 Men	.287	—	—	.101	—	—
Women	.290	—	—	.111	—	—

[a]PUMS is the Census of Population Public Use Microdata Sample 1/100 sample.

school at the same time, we also report in table 3.1 U.S. figures for school enrollment using the 1990 Census of Population (PUMS) information.

Using either the CPS or the PUMS definition, among both 18–29- and 25–36-year-olds, German men are more likely than American men to be in school.[15] The differences are substantial. For example, in the younger group, the most likely to be in school, over two-fifths of German men were in school in each year, compared to 29 percent of American men in 1990 (PUMS). For women in the census data—that is, using a definition of being in school comparable to that in Germany—18–29-year-olds are slightly less likely than Germans to be in school (29 percent in the United States for 1990 and 32 percent in Germany in 1991). However, among 25–36-year-olds, American women are more likely than Germans to be in school (11.1 vs. 6.5 percent).

Among young men and women, aged 18–29, gender differences in years of schooling completed are small in both countries in each year. However, using either the CPS or the PUMS as the American comparison group, women are about equally likely as men to be currently in school in the United States but substantially less likely than men to be currently in school in Germany. The German gender gap in current school attendance implies that educational attainment differentials will increase as a cohort ages and finishes its schooling. This effect can be seen in table 3.1 by noting that among 25–36-year-olds in Germany in 1991, the gender gap in years of schooling was 0.46, while among 18–29-year-olds in 1984 (i.e., the same cohort seven years earlier), it was only 0.04 years. In contrast, in the United States, there was a negligible gender difference in years of school completed for men and women aged 18–29 in 1984, and this remained true as the cohort aged.

Table 3.2 explores educational attainment in more detail, focusing on those currently not in school. This population is the focus of our subsequent analyses. We again note that in both Germany and the United States, gender differences in years of school among 18–29-year-olds are small. However, in Germany, they widen with age, and in the full population (aged 18–65), women are considerably more likely than men to be in the low-education group and considerably less likely to be in the high-education group. Gender differences in educational attainment are small in all age groups in the United States, with the major difference in the full population being women's lesser likelihood of being in the high-education group and their greater likelihood of being in the middle group.

There is some evidence of an increase in women's relative educational attainment among recent cohorts in both countries. As may be seen in table 3.2, the gender gap in years of school completed for 25–36-year-olds

---

15. The longer period of German than American schooling has been noted by Buechtemann et al. (1993).

Table 3.2   Educational Attainment for Individuals Currently Not in School

Country	Years of School Completed	Proportion in Category			Sample Size
		Edlow	Edmid	Edhigh	
A. Ages 18–29					
Germany (GSOEP)					
1984 Men	11.69	.122	.743	.135	622
Women	11.69	.209	.637	.154	716
1991 Men	11.77	.185	.622	.193	482
Women	11.71	.187	.667	.146	561
United States (CPS)					
1984 Men	12.39	.191	.668	.140	13,421
Women	12.43	.177	.688	.136	14,441
1991 Men	12.37	.198	.654	.148	10,926
Women	12.55	.180	.657	.163	11,924
B. Ages 25–36					
Germany (GSOEP)					
1984 Men	12.37	.090	.638	.272	820
Women	11.78	.203	.626	.171	898
1991 Men	12.59	.108	.574	.318	721
Women	12.12	.160	.625	.215	801
United States (CPS)					
1984 Men	13.12	.139	.599	.262	15,343
Women	12.89	.143	.637	.220	16,400
1991 Men	12.91	.149	.619	.232	14,772
Women	12.97	.141	.624	.234	15,796
C. Ages 18–65					
Germany (GSOEP)					
1984 Men	12.15	.112	.632	.256	2,971
Women	11.10	.344	.540	.115	3,267
1991 Men	12.36	.117	.599	.285	2,246
Women	11.50	.274	.578	.148	2,425
United States (CPS)					
1984 Men	12.52	.222	.561	.216	44,531
Women	12.24	.216	.630	.154	48,427
1991 Men	12.75	.188	.578	.234	43,645
Women	12.60	.180	.626	.193	47,177

and 18–65-year-olds in Germany was slightly smaller in 1991 than in 1984. And the gender gap in the incidence of Edlow among 18–65-year-olds fell from about 23 percentage points in 1984 to 16 percentage points in 1991.[16]

16. In table 3.2, the incidence of Edlow in Germany among 18–29-year-old men not in school actually rose between 1984 and 1991, from .122 to .185, while that for women fell from .209 to .187. These changes may reflect an improvement in the job market for young men over the 1980s. As noted above, male youth unemployment in Germany declined both absolutely and relatively over the 1980s (Abraham and Houseman 1995, 400).

However, among 18–29-year-olds in Germany, the gender gap in current school attendance was about the same in 1991 as in 1984, and the gender gap in school attendance among 25–36-year-olds in Germany was actually a bit larger in 1991 than in 1984 (table 3.1). These differences in school enrollment suggest that there will continue to be a gender gap in completed schooling among mature adults in Germany in the future. In the United States, the gender gap in schooling completed was never large and appears to be even smaller for newer cohorts (actually favoring women among 18–29-year-olds). Particularly notable is the rise in women's relative incidence of college graduation.[17] An implication of these findings is that the target group of this study, less educated youths, is one in which German, but not American, women are overrepresented.

3.4.2   Employment

Our goal in this paper is to compare how well less educated youths fare in the German and American labor markets and to attempt to provide some explanations for differences across the two countries. To do this we examine the employment and earnings of workers by age, education, and gender, beginning with the incidence of employment. The most striking pattern evident in the raw comparisons shown in table 3.3 and figure 3.1 is the relatively low employment rate of young, less educated Americans, particularly women, in comparison to their German counterparts.[18] In 1984, the employment rate of 18–29-year-old women in the Edlow group was only 35 percent in the United States, and their full-time employment rate (i.e., percentage of the out-of-school population with full-time jobs) only 21 percent, in comparison to rates of 55 and 43 percent, respectively, in Germany. This difference continued to hold in 1991 when the employment and full-time rates for this group were 38 percent and 23 percent in the United States compared to 57 and 42 percent in Germany. Young, less educated American men were also less likely to be employed or employed full time than Germans, particularly in 1991 but also in 1984. Similar, although smaller differences prevail for men in the middle-education group.

The differences between the United States and Germany for young, less educated women are particularly noteworthy, since among the other educational groups, young Americans tend to be at least as employable and often more so than Germans. And among the less educated population as a whole (Edlow for 18–65-year-olds), Americans fared much better than among youths. For example, in table 3.3, we see that among the full low-education group (aged 18–65), American women are about as likely as German women to be employed and actually more likely to be employed

17. In addition, relative female enrollment in marketable degree programs in law, business, and medicine increased in the United States in the 1970s and 1980s (Blau and Kahn 1997).
18. This pattern was also found in the PSID.

Table 3.3   Employment Measures by Selected Age and Educational Group

Country	Edlow		Edmid		Edhigh	
	Employed	Full Time	Employed	Full Time	Employed	Full Time
A. Ages 18–29						
Germany (GSOEP)						
1984 Men	.750	.684	.900	.803	.905	.762
Women	.553	.427	.664	.575	.782	.618
1991 Men	.899	.798	.947	.840	1.000	.911
Women	.571	.417	.735	.591	.841	.756
United States (CPS)						
1984 Men	.687	.545	.855	.686	.936	.806
Women	.353	.210	.678	.472	.867	.704
1991 Men	.696	.564	.861	.742	.950	.856
Women	.375	.232	.720	.520	.888	.745
United States/Germany						
1984 Men	.916	.797	.950	.854	1.034	1.058
Women	.638	.492	1.021	.821	1.109	1.139
1991 Men	.774	.707	.909	.883	.950	.940
Women	.657	.556	.980	.880	1.056	.985
B. Ages 25–36						
Germany (GSOEP)						
1984 Men	.824	.689	.948	.883	.960	.771
Women	.412	.209	.589	.342	.675	.448
1991 Men	.910	.855	.966	.927	.974	.928
Women	.602	.291	.657	.378	.663	.482

United States (CPS)							
1984	Men	.743	.652	.890	.803	.961	.888
	Women	.388	.262	.655	.478	.802	.645
1991	Men	.743	.674	.886	.841	.958	.914
	Women	.419	.290	.710	.543	.838	.693
United States/Germany							
1984	Men	.902	.946	.939	.909	1.001	1.152
	Women	.942	1.254	1.112	1.398	1.188	1.440
1991	Men	.816	.788	.917	.907	.984	.985
	Women	.696	.997	1.081	1.437	1.264	1.438

C. Ages 18-65

Germany (GSOEP)							
1984	Men	.777	.687	.863	.782	.918	.742
	Women	.366	.179	.531	.300	.645	.387
1991	Men	.767	.710	.860	.816	.933	.876
	Women	.451	.229	.613	.349	.667	.442
United States (CPS)							
1984	Men	.675	.586	.846	.747	.934	.870
	Women	.382	.253	.630	.446	.773	.604
1991	Men	.659	.580	.844	.781	.923	.877
	Women	.402	.276	.678	.505	.813	.655
United States/Germany							
1984	Men	.869	.853	.980	.955	1.017	1.173
	Women	1.044	1.413	1.186	1.487	1.198	1.561
1991	Men	.859	.817	.981	.957	.989	1.001
	Women	.891	1.205	1.106	1.447	1.219	1.482

Note: Includes only those out of school.

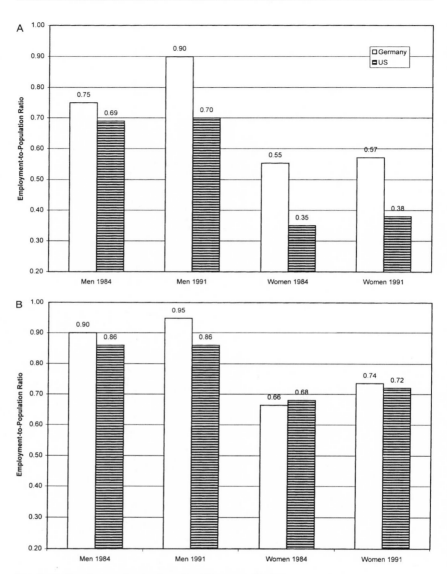

Fig. 3.1   Employment rates by education, ages 18–29
Note: A, Low education; B, middle education; C, high education.

full time, in a major contrast to the 18–29-year-olds. And while less educated German men aged 18–65 had higher employment rates than Americans, the German-U.S. differences were generally smaller than for youths. Thus, in an absolute and a relative sense, the low employment rates of less educated young people in the United States compared to Germany are particularly notable.

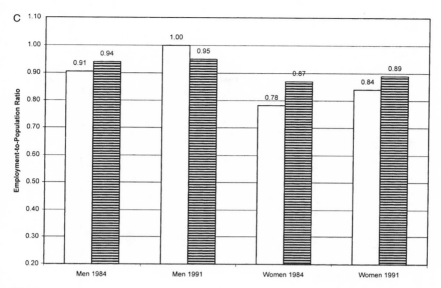

Fig. 3.1   (cont.)

Table 3.4 provides some evidence on the progress of the 18–29-year-old cohort over the 1984-91 period.[19] Focusing on the less educated, the table shows that employment-population ratios rose for men and women in both countries with age, with the largest increases for German men. Significantly, however, by the time its members reached their late twenties and early thirties (ages 25–36), the 1984 German youth cohort of less educated men and women remained considerably more likely to be employed than those in the United States. The same conclusions for full-time jobs hold for men. However, in all educational groups, including the least educated, German women's full-time attachment fell dramatically as they aged. By 1991, less educated German women were no more likely than Americans to have full-time jobs. In the other educational groups, American women either caught up to and surpassed German women or added to their 1984 lead in employment incidence and especially in their full-time employment rates. In contrast, American men in the middle- and high-education groups fell behind Germans in employment (but not as far as the Edlow group did) and had a mixed set of outcomes for full-time employment.

Overall, the synthetic cohort analysis shows that at least during the 1984–91 period, the employment disadvantage faced by less educated young men and women in America compared to Germany was not reversed with age. The one exception was that due to a strong general

19. Note that in this synthetic cohort analysis, the members of, say, the low-education group in 1984 are compared with those who remained in that educational category in 1991.

Table 3.4   Employment Measures by Educational Group for Synthetic Cohort Aged 18–29 in 1984

Country	Edlow		Edmid		Edhigh	
	Employed	Full Time	Employed	Full Time	Employed	Full Time
Germany (GSOEP)						
1984 Men	.750	.684	.900	.803	.905	.762
Women	.553	.427	.664	.575	.782	.618
1991 Men	.910	.855	.966	.927	.974	.928
Women	.602	.291	.657	.378	.663	.482
United States (CPS)						
1984 Men	.687	.545	.855	.686	.936	.806
Women	.353	.210	.678	.472	.867	.704
1991 Men	.743	.674	.886	.841	.958	.914
Women	.419	.290	.710	.543	.838	.693
United States/Germany						
1984 Men	.916	.797	.950	.854	1.034	1.058
Women	.638	.492	1.021	.821	1.109	1.139
1991 Men	.816	.788	.917	.907	.984	.985
Women	.696	.997	1.081	1.437	1.264	1.438

pattern of declining full-time employment rates with age among German women in all educational categories, the less educated American women's full-time rate equaled that of German women by 1991. This equality, however, stands in marked contrast to the considerably higher rates of full-time employment for American compared to German women in the middle- and high-education categories and thus still indicates considerable relative disadvantage for less educated American women.

The stronger association of education (particularly Edlow) with employment or full-time employment for American youths than for German youths shown in tables 3.3 and 3.4 holds up in probit analyses when we control for age, age squared, marital status, presence of children, and, for the United States, a race indicator. The point estimates and asymptotic standard errors are presented in appendix tables 3A.1 and 3A.2. Table 3A.3 calculates the estimated effects of education based on these results, both as partial derivatives of the employment probability with respect to education and as semielasticities (the derivative divided by the mean). Both absolutely and relative to the mean, we find that educational differences play a stronger role in leading to differences in employment opportunities or willingness to work in the United States than is the case in Germany.

So far we have analyzed labor market attachment solely by examining whether or not one is currently employed or employed full time. Table 3.5 takes a closer look at the workforce attachment of young workers by considering patterns of actual experience for panels of workers for whom experience during the 1984–91 period was observable. Recall that in the GSOEP, experience is collected only as of 1984. For the original panel members who remain, experience after 1984 can be computed. However, we cannot observe experience for those who join the GSOEP after 1984. For comparability, we construct a similar panel of individuals from the PSID. Table 3.5 shows experience and full-time experience as of 1984 and 1991. It should also be noted that since experience is measured from age 15 in the GSOEP and from age 18 in the PSID, the raw levels of experience are not directly comparable across countries. We can, however, compare relative levels of experience for educational groups.

The results are quite consistent with what would be expected based on the employment rates. For both men and women, Americans with low levels of schooling have lower relative experience levels (compared to those with middle or high levels of education) than those in Germany. The differences in amounts of experience across educational levels are particularly dramatic for young American women: less educated American women had only 40 percent of the total or full-time experience of middle educated women in 1984, while less educated German women had 11 to 18 percent more experience than middle educated women. These U.S.-German differences continue to be observed as the 18–29-year-old cohort

Table 3.5   Years of Experience and Full-Time Experience by Educational Group for Individuals Aged 18–29 in 1984

Work Experience		Edlow as of 1984		Edmid as of 1984		Edhigh as of 1984	
		Germany	United States	Germany	United States	Germany	United States
Total experience							
1984	Men	5.70	6.07	4.76	6.81	4.08	7.29
	Women	5.19	1.68	4.39	4.24	2.93	6.06
1991	Men	11.98	12.55	11.35	13.73	10.96	14.23
	Women	9.43	6.01	9.33	9.93	7.92	12.06
Full-time experience							
1984	Men	5.44	5.58	4.74	6.00	3.82	3.99
	Women	4.45	1.38	3.99	3.52	2.62	3.49
1991	Men	11.54	11.14	11.27	12.37	10.56	10.62
	Women	6.96	3.33	7.53	7.21	6.05	7.55

Sources: Panels for 1984–91 from the German Socio-Economic Panel and Michigan Panel Study of Income Dynamics.

Note: Includes only those out of school as of 1984.

aged into 1991, although the cross-country differences decline somewhat. Among men, the low-education group in the United States has about 90 percent of the total or full-time experience of the middle educated in each year, while in Germany the less educated men's advantage ranges from 2 to 20 percent depending on the year and measure. Overall, the data on experience levels reinforce our conclusion that less educated young men and women in America have relatively low labor market attachment compared to their German counterparts.

3.4.3 Earnings

In this section we consider the earnings of youths. Earnings are of course important in themselves as an indicator of economic well-being. In addition, an analysis of earnings may provide some evidence regarding the reasons for the lower labor market attachment of less educated American youths detailed above. For example, if these workers have particularly poor labor market opportunities (i.e., low wages), then movements along a supply curve would be a possible explanation for their low attachment to the labor force.

To analyze wages, we focus on people who are not currently self-employed and who did not have any self-employment income during the previous year. In both the GSOEP and the CPS, it is possible to compute average monthly wage and salary income over the previous year, including wages and salaries, as well as bonuses. Thus earnings for the 1984 and 1991 samples refer to 1983 and 1990. Unfortunately, it is not possible in the GSOEP to calculate hourly earnings since we lack information on weeks worked. However, both data sets contain information on hours worked per week. We use this information to simulate hours-corrected earnings as follows. Suppose that for each country and year we can express log monthly earnings of person i:

$$(1) \qquad \ln Y_i = a_1 PART_i + a_2 HRPART_i + a_3 HRFULL_i + B'X_i + u_i,$$

where Y is monthly labor income in 1983 U.S. dollars for both countries,[20] *PART* is a dummy variable for part-time workers (defined as working less than 35 hours per week), *HRPART* and *HRFULL* are interactions of work hours with part-time and full-time employment, X is a vector of explanatory variables, and u is a disturbance term. The following variables are included in X: age and its square, marital status (Mar), presence of children (Childyes), educational dummies (Edlow and Edmid), and, for the United States, a race dummy variable for whites (White). For the reasons discussed above, we are forced to use age rather than actual experience in equation (1). We include controls for marital status and especially children

---

20. This is obtained using the OECD's (1996) index of purchasing power parity (German marks per U.S. dollar) for 1983 and 1990 and the U.S. consumer price index as deflator.

to pick up some of the effects of workforce interruptions for women associated with these events (e.g., Waldfogel 1998). Equation (1) is estimated separately for men and women in each age group.

We then simulate full-time earnings for each individual as follows:

$$(2) \qquad \ln YFULL_i = \ln Y_i - a_1 PART_i - a_2 HRPART_i$$
$$- a_3 (HRFULL_i - 40).$$

Equation (2) estimates what a worker's monthly earnings would have been had he or she worked 40 hours per week.[21]

Table 3.6 presents log real hours-corrected monthly earnings in 1983 U.S. dollars for both countries, by age-gender-education group for 1984 and 1991; figure 3.2 highlights the results for young workers. We see the same pattern among men and women: German youths with low education levels outearned Americans. In 1984, the German advantage was 11 to 15 percent and grew to 27 to 35 percent by 1991 (compare the first and second columns of table 3.6).[22] In American purchasing power, real wages of less educated German youths rose 9 to 12 percent between 1984 and 1991, while they fell by 7 to 8 percent for American youths over this period. Although American youths with middle levels of education also lost ground to inflation and relative to Germans, they remained closer to the German level of purchasing power in 1991 than American less educated workers. Finally, among highly educated youths, Americans started with a small advantage over Germans (1 to 5 percent) in 1984 that widened to 20 to 22 percent by 1991. The changes in relative wages by educational group for the labor force as a whole (ages 18–65) were similar to those for 18–29-year-olds but less dramatic. The changes in the relative purchasing power of high- and low-education groups illustrate the considerably greater widening of the American wage distribution in the 1980s compared to Germany (Abraham and Houseman 1995).

Table 3.7 shows the progress in real wages within the cohort of 18–29-year-olds as it aged during the 1984–91 period. Real hours-corrected earnings rose for all gender-education groups in this cohort within Germany and the United States; however, by 1991 less educated Germans outearned Americans by 15 to 22 percent. American men's real wages rose substantially less quickly than German men's among the low-education group, while American less educated young women maintained their position at roughly 15 percent lower purchasing-power-corrected wages than Germans. In contrast, young, highly educated Americans experienced very

---

21. In earlier work on international differences on the gender gap in pay, we used a similar procedure since we lacked data on hourly earnings there as well; see Blau and Kahn (1995, 1996b).

22. The percentage differences cited in the text are approximations based on the differences in the logs.

Table 3.6 Log Real Hours-Corrected Earnings

Gender	Edlow 1984	Edlow 1991	Edmid 1984	Edmid 1991	Edhigh 1984	Edhigh 1991	All 1984	All 1991
A. Ages 18–29								
Men								
Germany (GSOEP)	6.834	6.926	7.002	7.067	7.305	7.148	7.019	7.059
United States (CPS)	6.724	6.652	7.020	6.940	7.316	7.347	7.020	6.963
U.S.-German difference	−0.110	−0.274	0.018	−0.127	0.011	0.199	0.001	−0.096
Women								
Germany (GSOEP)	6.653	6.777	6.745	6.867	7.029	6.989	6.776	6.875
United States (CPS)	6.504	6.423	6.768	6.752	7.075	7.213	6.801	6.820
U.S.-German difference	−0.149	−0.354	0.023	−0.115	0.046	0.224	0.025	−0.055
B. Ages 25–36								
Men								
Germany (GSOEP)	6.915	7.093	7.186	7.175	7.450	7.364	7.226	7.224
United States (CPS)	6.979	6.869	7.306	7.230	7.545	7.571	7.333	7.268
U.S.-German difference	0.064	−0.224	0.120	0.055	0.095	0.207	0.107	0.044
Women								
Germany (GSOEP)	6.805	6.709	6.955	6.978	7.195	7.223	6.978	6.993
United States (CPS)	6.663	6.560	6.967	6.943	7.272	7.391	7.027	7.039
U.S.-German difference	−0.142	−0.149	0.012	−0.035	0.077	0.168	0.049	0.046
C. Ages 18–65								
Men								
Germany (GSOEP)	7.022	7.057	7.198	7.235	7.577	7.566	7.269	7.313
United States (CPS)	7.047	6.938	7.301	7.266	7.668	7.709	7.339	7.326
U.S.-German difference	0.025	−0.119	0.103	0.031	0.091	0.143	0.070	0.013
Women								
Germany (GSOEP)	6.751	6.810	6.921	6.968	7.261	7.303	6.925	6.992
United States (CPS)	6.662	6.612	6.917	6.951	7.276	7.410	6.954	7.024
U.S.-German difference	−0.089	−0.198	−0.004	−0.017	0.015	0.107	0.029	0.032

Note: Earnings are in 1983 U.S. purchasing-power-equivalent dollars.

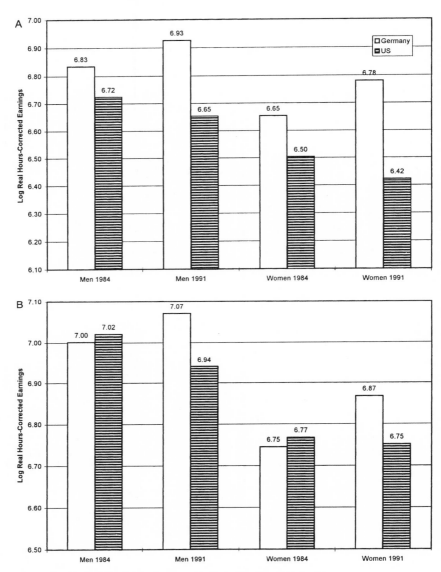

Fig. 3.2   Log real hours-corrected earnings by education, ages 18–29
Note: A, Low education; *B*, middle education; *C*, high education.

large gains relative to the Germans. As was the case for employment, less educated American workers did not close the gap with Germans as they aged but rather continued to do substantially worse than their German counterparts.

The general findings suggested by the tabulations in tables 3.6 and 3.7

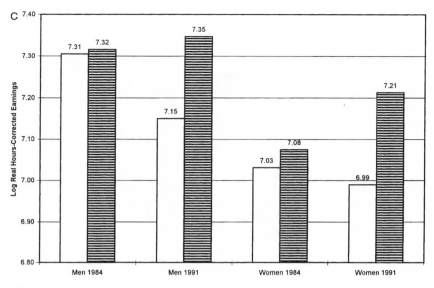

Fig. 3.2 **(cont.)**

are confirmed by the education effects obtained in regression analyses controlling for age, age squared, marital status, presence of children, and, for the United States, race, in addition to the hours variables. These results, which are shown in table 3.8, indicate the greater importance of education in determining American than German wages and the increased importance of education in the United States relative to Germany over the 1984–91 period. The rising returns to education in the United States occur both across cohorts over time and within the youth cohort as it ages from 18–29 in 1984 to 25–36 in 1991.

The gender gap in pay is explored in table 3.9, which shows male-female differences in the log of hours-corrected earnings by age-education group. Among the youth cohort overall, the gender pay gap was slightly smaller (by .024 to .041 log points) in the United States than in Germany in both years and fell by similar amounts in both countries. However, for the low-education group, the American gender pay gap was larger than the German gap, by .039 to .080 log points, reflecting the especially poor labor market position of less educated, young American women.[23] As expected based on published data and previous studies, for the labor force as a whole (ages 18–65, all), the gender pay gap was larger in the United States than in Germany in 1984 (by .041 log points), but by 1991, the German gap was a bit greater (by .019 log points). Interestingly, *within* each

23. However, within the cohort that was 18–29 years old in 1984, the U.S.-German gender gap difference fell between 1984 and 1991 (from .039 to −.075) for the less educated but rose for the other educational groups.

Table 3.7   Log Real Hours-Corrected Earnings for Synthetic Cohort Aged 18–29 in 1984

Gender	Edlow		Edmid		Edhigh		All	
	1984	1991	1984	1991	1984	1991	1984	1991
Men								
Germany (GSOEP)	6.834	7.093	7.002	7.175	7.305	7.364	7.019	7.224
United States (CPS)	6.724	6.869	7.020	7.230	7.316	7.571	7.020	7.268
U.S.-German difference	−0.110	−0.224	0.018	0.055	0.011	0.207	0.001	0.044
Women								
Germany (GSOEP)	6.653	6.709	6.745	6.978	7.029	7.223	6.776	6.993
United States (CPS)	6.504	6.560	6.768	6.943	7.075	7.391	6.801	7.039
U.S.-German difference	−0.149	−0.149	0.023	−0.035	0.046	0.168	0.025	0.046

Note: Earnings are in 1983 U.S. purchasing-power-equivalent dollars.

Table 3.8   **Ceteris Paribus Effects of Education on Log Earnings**

	1984		1991	
Country	Edlow	Edmid	Edlow	Edmid
	A. Ages 18–29			
Germany (GSOEP)				
Men	−.324	−.185	−.110	−.016
	(.070)	(.053)	(.077)	(.059)
Women	−.246	−.188	−.098	−.050
	(.083)	(.065)	(.076)	(.056)
United States (CPS)				
Men	−.423	−.158	−.565	−.303
	(.023)	(.018)	(.022)	(.017)
Women	−.424	−.193	−.634	−.345
	(.026)	(.017)	(.026)	(.017)
	B. Ages 25–36			
Germany (GSOEP)				
Men	−.506	−.253	−.237	−.180
	(.057)	(.034)	(.060)	(.037)
Women	−.377	−.225	−.463	−.199
	(.083)	(.063)	(.089)	(.066)
United States (CPS)				
Men	−.558	−.227	−.698	−.334
	(.019)	(.013)	(.017)	(.012)
Women	−.584	−.285	−.803	−.429
	(.024)	(.014)	(.022)	(.013)

Note: Other explanatory variables include age, age squared, marital status (Mar), presence of children (Childyes), *PART, HRPART, HRFULL,* and, for the United States, a race dummy (White).

educational group, the American pay gap for all workers (ages 18–65) was larger than the German pay gap in 1991, possibly reflecting a more egalitarian German wage structure. The fact that not controlling for education, the overall gender pay gap was smaller in the United States than in Germany reflects the superior relative educational qualifications of American women.

3.4.4   Patterns for Immigrants in Germany

As we noted earlier, the basic analyses for Germany in this paper are performed for German natives only, due to the lower quality of schooling information on immigrants. However, the GSOEP does provide some evidence on immigrants' education, as well as on their family status and labor market outcomes. In this section, we explore the schooling, employment, and earnings of young immigrants in Germany, with a special focus on those without German technical school, high school, or postsecondary

Table 3.9   Gender Gap in Log Real Hours-Corrected Earnings

Country	Edlow		Edmid		Edhigh		All	
	1984	1991	1984	1991	1984	1991	1984	1991
				A. Ages 18–29				
Germany (GSOEP)	.181	.149	.257	.200	.276	.159	.243	.184
United States (CPS)	.220	.229	.252	.188	.241	.134	.219	.143
U.S.-German difference	.039	.080	−.005	−.012	−.035	−.025	−.024	−.041
				B. Ages 25–36				
Germany (GSOEP)	.110	.384	.231	.197	.255	.141	.248	.231
United States (CPS)	.316	.309	.339	.287	.273	.180	.306	.229
U.S.-German difference	.206	−.075	.108	.090	.018	.039	.058	−.002
				C. Ages 18–65				
Germany (GSOEP)	.271	.247	.277	.267	.316	.263	.344	.321
United States (CPS)	.385	.326	.384	.315	.392	.299	.385	.302
U.S.-German difference	.114	.079	.107	.048	.076	.036	.041	−.019

degrees. We conclude that even if one were to include immigrants in what we have termed the low-skilled group, young people without formal credentials living in Germany would still have employment and wage outcomes far superior to those of low-skilled young Americans.

Appendix table 3A.4 contains schooling, employment, and wage information for young immigrants in Germany for 1984 and 1991. Panels A and B show that in comparison to natives, immigrants are less likely to be in school and less likely to have postsecondary training or German technical or high school degrees (cf. tables 3.1 and 3.2 above). Thus, overall, immigrants tend to be a relatively low skilled group. Panel B examines employment and hours-corrected earnings for all young immigrants who are not in school. Overall, men are about as likely to be employed as German natives in the low-education group, while women are somewhat less likely to be employed than German natives; however, immigrant women are much more likely than low-skilled Americans to be employed. And German immigrants' wages are about the same as those of German natives with low levels of education.

If we treat all immigrants, regardless of their training, as competing with low-skilled native workers, then according to the GSOEP's weights, immigrants would make up only about 16 percent of the low-skilled population among individuals in Germany for 1984.[24] Under this assumption, we still conclude that young people with low skill levels (immigrants and natives aggregated) in Germany have much better employment and wage outcomes than Americans. However, panel B of table 3A.4 indicates that a considerable portion of the immigrant population had German schooling that would place them in the middle- or high-education group by our definition. A sharper comparison between immigrants and natives may be drawn by examining lower skilled immigrants, as we now do.

To focus on immigrants without German formal skills, we present labor market information on young immigrants without German technical, high school, or postsecondary degrees in panel C of table 3A.4. In panel D, we additionally exclude immigrants who have received vocational or university degrees from other countries. Our conclusions are the same in either case. We find the levels of male employment and wages to be quite similar to those for German low-skilled workers. However, while low-skilled immigrant women's wages are about the same as their native German counterparts, their employment rates are considerably lower than those of

24. The GSOEP immigrant files are an oversample of that population. While the GSOEP version we used had sampling weights for 1984, it did not include sampling weights for 1991, so we cannot produce a similar figure for that year. But according to the OECD (1993b), foreign individuals made up 7.4 percent of the population in West Germany in 1984 and 8.2 percent in 1990 (falling to 7.3 percent for eastern and western Germany combined for 1991). Thus our conclusions about the small relative size of the immigrant population in the youth labor market are likely to hold for 1991 as well.

natives. Young, low-skilled immigrant women in Germany are only a little more likely to be employed than low-skilled American young women in 1984, and equally likely to be employed in 1991; full-time employment rates are somewhat higher for low-skilled immigrant women in Germany than for low-skilled Americans. Nonetheless, since for 1984 immigrants without German formal skills were only 11 to 13 percent of all young Germans without formal skills, our basic finding that young, low-skilled individuals in Germany have much more labor market attachment than those in the United States would not be affected were we to include immigrants.

The finding that the hours-corrected earnings of low-skilled immigrants of both sexes are virtually identical to those of German natives is quite consistent with the high administered wages in Germany. The fact that employment rates of less educated male immigrants are similar to those of natives suggests that they too do not pay a price in terms of employment for these relatively high wages. While the lower employment rates of less educated immigrant women could indicate an employment cost of high wages for them, we strongly suspect much of the immigrant-native employment difference for women in Germany reflects cultural factors operating on the supply side. A substantial proportion of young immigrant women come from countries with relatively low female labor force participation rates, including 45 percent from Turkey and an additional 38 percent from Italy, Greece, and Spain.[25]

3.5 Explanations for the Low Labor Market Attachment of Less Educated American Youths

As we have seen, real wages are lower for less educated youth in America than in Germany, both absolutely and relative to their more highly educated counterparts. Our wage findings are consistent with the operation of high wage floors in Germany from which less educated employed youths disproportionately benefit. The low labor market attachment of Americans may reflect movements along a supply curve in response to these lower wages, and below, we use existing estimates of American labor supply elasticities to simulate the effect of raising American wages to German levels. However, to the extent that the higher relative wages of less educated German youths reflect high administered industry minimum wages, we would expect to observe demand-induced employment reductions in Germany. Yet we find that employment rates of less

25. All of these countries had a lower female-male labor force participation rate ratio than West Germany during the 1985–88 period (Blau and Ferber 1992, 300–304). While 12 percent of young immigrant women came from Yugoslavia, which had a female-male labor force participation rate ratio slightly higher than that in West Germany for the 1985–88 period, this group is far outweighed by those from countries for which the ratio favors Germany.

educated youths are higher in Germany. This pattern is particularly striking among young women, where Americans lag behind Germans substantially in both wages and employment. At least two features of German and American government policy may help to explain Germany's relatively high youth employment rates, which occur despite its system of relatively high, administered wages.

First, Germany has a larger public sector, which can potentially absorb those who would otherwise be out of work. Second, the U.S. welfare system, for which less educated women are most likely to qualify, strongly penalizes market work. We attempt to shed light on these possible explanations for German-U.S. differences in employment outcomes below. In addition, it is of interest that the lower employment rates of less educated U.S. women occur in the face of a countervailing factor that would work to reduce labor market attachment among German women: Germany's system of maternity and parental leave, which is considerably more generous than that in the United States and was expanded between 1984 and 1991. This could mean either that German family leave does not have the expected negative effect or that other factors are sufficiently strong to outweigh its impact among less educated women. We also investigate this question below.

3.5.1 Government Employment

As several authors have argued, public employment can be an outlet for the labor supply induced by high wages. The descriptive results in table 3.10, showing the fraction of workers in each gender-age-education group who are government workers in each country, are consistent with this ar-

Table 3.10 **Fraction of Employment in Government: Levels**

Year		Edlow		Edmid		Edhigh	
		Germany	United States	Germany	United States	Germany	United States
A. Ages 18–29							
1984	Men	.158	.049	.161	.077	.208	.167
	Women	.218	.043	.229	.107	.442	.276
1991	Men	.189	.027	.188	.114	.241	.163
	Women	.267	.036	.256	.096	.304	.208
B. Ages 30–65							
1984	Men	.164	.101	.245	.142	.359	.258
	Women	.236	.104	.235	.184	.561	.453
1991	Men	.158	.073	.242	.145	.318	.233
	Women	.274	.093	.260	.170	.503	.384

Note: Includes only those out of school.

gument. Public employment is more extensive in Germany. While in both countries it is disproportionately taken by the highly educated, the less educated appear to have greater representation in the public sector in Germany than in the United States.

Table 3.11 subjects these impressions to greater scrutiny by comparing differences between the two countries in the incidence of public employment by age-education group. For government employment to explain the higher employment rates of less educated German youths, we expect to find that low education is less of a barrier to public employment in Germany than in the United States. Further, we might expect this effect to be particularly strong for young workers, who are potentially the most affected by wage floors, and to be strongest for young women, who are the lowest wage group. These expectations are at least partly borne out by the data.

Most significantly, the results in table 3.11 strongly suggest that low education is less of a barrier to public employment among less educated youths in Germany than in the United States: for each comparison (Edlow vs. Edmid and Edlow vs. Edhigh) and each year, the German-U.S. difference is positive, indicating that the treatment of less educated youths is more favorable in Germany than in the United States. However, this favorable effect does not tend to be larger for young women than for young men. Among males, our additional expectation that low education is more of a barrier to public employment among older than among young workers within Germany is confirmed as well: the Edlow-Edmid and Edlow-Edhigh differences by age group in panel C are larger for Germany than for the United States in all cases. This finding is consistent with a larger private sector disemployment effect of high wage floors on young male workers that provide a stronger impetus for government employment. Our additional expectations are not, however, consistently borne out among women. Less educated, younger workers face lower barriers than older workers to obtaining government employment only in the Edlow-Edhigh comparisons. In addition, in only one case—the 1991 Edlow-Edhigh comparison—is the relative advantage of younger women larger in Germany than in the United States. It may be that older, less educated German women are also minimum wage constrained so that they may seek government employment. In any case, the data in table 3.11 support the notion that in Germany the government potentially plays an important role in providing jobs for less educated, young workers even if in the case of women this effect is not necessarily greater than for older, less educated women.[26] We may note that we are not necessarily arguing that this reflects

26. These findings are largely confirmed when we estimate the probability of government employment as a function of educational group, age, age squared, marital status, presence of children, and, for the United States, a race indicator. The results are shown in appendix table 3A.5.

Table 3.11   Fraction of Employment in Government: Differences

| | Edlow vs. Edmid | | | | | | Edlow vs. Edhigh | | | | | |
| | Germany | | United States | | Germany-U.S. | | Germany | | United States | | Germany-U.S. | |
Year	Absolute	Divided by Mean	Absolute	Divided by Mean	Absolute	Divided by mean	Absolute	Divided by Mean	Absolute	Divided by Mean	Absolute	Divided by Mean
						A. Ages 18–29						
1984 Men	−.003	−.018	−.028	−.322	.025	.304	−.050	−.299	−.118	−1.311	.068	1.012
Women	−.011	−.041	−.064	−.489	.053	.447	−.224	−.839	−.233	−1.779	.009	.940
1991 Men	.001	.005	−.087	−.806	.088	.811	−.052	−.260	−.136	−1.259	.084	.999
Women	.011	.041	−.060	−.526	.071	.568	−.037	−.139	−.172	−1.509	.135	1.370
						B. Ages 30–65						
1984 Men	−.081	−.340	−.041	−.246	−.040	−.095	−.195	−.819	−.157	−.940	−.038	.121
Women	.001	.003	−.080	−.611	.081	.614	−.325	−1.042	−.349	−2.664	.024	1.622
1991 Men	−.084	−.422	−.072	−.667	−.012	.245	−.160	−.804	−.160	−1.481	.000	.677
Women	.014	.050	−.077	−.675	.091	.725	−.229	−.812	−.291	−2.553	.062	1.741
					C. Difference by Age: (Ages 18–29) − (Ages 30–65)							
1984 Men	.078	.322	.013	−.076	.065	.399	.145	.520	.039	−.371	.106	.891
Women	−.012	−.044	.016	.122	−.028	−.167	.101	.203	.116	.885	−.015	−.683
1991 Men	.085	.427	−.015	−.139	.100	.566	.108	.544	.024	.222	.084	.322
Women	−.003	−.008	.017	.149	−.020	−.157	.192	.673	.119	1.044	.073	−.371

Note: Includes only those out of school. "Mean" refers to the mean fraction employed by government for the relevant age-gender group.

an explicit government policy to function as an employer of last resort. It may simply be that, given the large size of the government sector and the composition of employment in it, these groups are more readily absorbed than in the United States.

To assess the potential size of the effect of government employment in causing young, less educated Germans' greater labor market attachment, we present table 3.12 showing the fraction of the population of less educated youths having government jobs. Among both young men and women, a much larger share of this population has government jobs in Germany than in the United States. Further, the percentage point gap between the two countries in this share (9 to 15 points for men and 11 to 14 points for women) is large compared to the German-U.S. differences in employment-population ratios shown in table 3.3. These latter differences are about 20 percentage points for women and range from 6 to 20 points for men. Of course, each government job may not add a total of one net new job for the population, but the large differences between the two countries shown in the table imply that government employment has a potentially important effect in increasing the employment rates of young, less educated Germans compared to their counterparts in the United States.

As noted above, we found that young German men with low education especially improved their relative economic status over the late 1980s. Their employment increased both absolutely and relative to young, low-skilled Americans, while their real earnings increased relative to less educated youths in the United States and more highly educated German youths. Our results suggest that public sector employment played a role in this improvement. Table 3.12 shows a sharp increase in the fraction of the population of young, less educated German men with government jobs (from 12 percent in 1984 to 17 percent in 1991). It is true that the Edlow-Edmid and Edlow-Edhigh comparisons for young German men in table 3.11 indicate that there was no *relative* increase in the government employment incidence of the less educated between 1984 and 1991. That is, less educated German young men appear to have benefited from a general increase in the incidence of government employment for young males in all educational groups. However, for the Edlow-Edmid comparison, the

Table 3.12   Fraction of the Population with Government Jobs for Ages 18–29 with Low Educational Levels

Year		Germany	United States
1984	Men	.119	.034
	Women	.121	.015
1991	Men	.170	.019
	Women	.152	.014

Note: Includes only those out of school.

German-U.S. difference did increase in absolute value. This suggests that low education had an increasingly important effect in the United States relative to Germany in keeping young men out of government jobs over the 1984–91 period. Thus, in this relative sense, we can say that the government played a role in raising young, less educated men's employment in Germany compared to that in the United States.

The sharply higher real wages, labor market attachment, and incidence of government employment among young, less skilled Germans than among Americans are consistent with the following scenario. German unions negotiate high wage floors, having a relatively large positive effect on wages of the low skilled. The government in effect functions as an employer of last resort and provides jobs for the additional workers looking for employment as a result of the higher wages, although this may or may not reflect an explicit government policy. The additional workers finding government jobs include those disemployed by the wage floors and those brought into the labor market by the prospect of high wages. An important question in interpreting our U.S.-German comparisons is the degree to which this scenario can account for the employment attachment differences of less educated youths in the two countries. In particular, given American labor supply elasticities, could German-level real wages, coupled with government jobs for those not able to find private sector work, entice enough Americans into the labor force to bring the employment-population ratio to the German level?

In order to answer this question, we need estimates of the wage elasticity of labor force participation for young, low-skilled workers in the United States. The labor supply literature typically estimates the supply elasticity for total work hours (Killingsworth 1983); however, we have found some studies of the participation elasticity that would allow us to simulate the effects of raising Americans' real wages. For women, Schultz (1980) finds for white married women in 1967 an elasticity of 1.5 for ages 14–24 and 1.0 for ages 25–34. A second study by Kimmel (1996) obtains a participation elasticity of 1.5 for single mothers aged 18–55 in 1987. While these samples are not identical to our low-skilled group, 1.5 seems a reasonable estimate for the female elasticity for simulation purposes. For men, Juhn (1992) estimates the derivative of the employment probability with respect to wages as a step function that depends on one's position in the wage distribution. For white men in the bottom 20 percent in 1970, a group comparable in relative size to our low-skilled group, she finds a derivative of .288. While Juhn (1992) does not report an elasticity for this group, we can approximate one by using as a base the employment-population ratio for white high school dropouts. When we do this, we obtain an employment-population ratio elasticity of 0.3 for low-skilled men.

For young, low-skilled women, table 3.6 shows that American real wages were lower than those for Germany by .15 log points in 1984 and

.36 in 1991. Applying the 1.5 elasticity to wage increases of this magnitude implies increases in the labor force participation rate of .079 in 1984 and .201 in 1991. These movements along the women's supply curve constitute about 40 percent of the German-U.S. employment rate gap in 1984 and 103 percent in 1991. However, these studies relate to labor force participation rather than employment. While the GSOEP did not collect unemployment information in 1991, it is available for 1984, allowing us to calculate labor force participation rates for the earlier year. We find that the labor force participation gap between the United States and Germany is slightly smaller than the gap for the employment-population ratios so, at least for that year, the proportion explained would be roughly the same were we to focus on participation.

For low-skilled young men, the U.S.-German real wage differences were .11 log points in 1984 and .27 in 1991. According to Juhn's (1992) estimates, these wage increases would raise the American employment-population ratio by .023 in 1984 and .057 in 1991, or about 37 percent of the German-U.S. employment gap in 1984 and 28 percent in 1991.[27]

These simulations of the effects of equalizing German and U.S. real wages among young workers with low educational levels imply that the high-wage, public employment demand response scenario could account for all of the German-U.S. difference in employment rates for low-skilled young women in 1991. But for young women in 1984 and young men in both years, something more is needed to explain higher employment rates among German low-skilled youths.

One possible explanation for the remaining differences for young males and for young females in 1984 is that German youths have lower unemployment rates than young Americans, and it is likely that labor force participation depends on unemployment as well as wages. As just noted, the GSOEP allows us to compare U.S. and German unemployment rates for 1984, and we find that less educated young men and women both have higher unemployment rates in the United States. For women, the unemployment rate was 11.8 percent in the United States and 10.0 percent in Germany, while for men it was 19.8 percent in the United States and 18.4 percent in Germany. What are the labor supply implications of these unemployment rate gaps between the United States and Germany? If the American unemployment rate were lowered to the German level for these workers and if the labor supply elasticity of the employment-population ratio with respect to the unemployment rate were .76 for men and 1.91 for women, then labor supply responses to unemployment rate and wage differences could together account for all of the employment-population

---

27. Since Juhn's (1992) estimates are for employment (rather than for labor force participation), applying elasticities based on her results to our employment-population ratios is appropriate.

ratio gap between young, less skilled Germans and Americans in 1984.[28] And the higher incidence of public employment in Germany would allow the greater labor supply there to result in actual employment.

3.5.2   Welfare

While we have seen that higher government employment provides a plausible explanation for a substantial portion of the U.S.-German differences in the employment rates of the low skilled, it is also possible that the U.S. welfare system plays a role. As we see in table 3.13, single motherhood in the United States is highly negatively correlated with education. In 1984, for example, 33 percent of young U.S. women with low levels of education were single mothers, compared to 20 percent in the middle-education group and only 6 percent in the high-education group.[29] The United States also has a much higher incidence of single motherhood among women with low educational levels than is the case for Germany. In 1984, the German rate of single motherhood was about 10 percentage points lower than the U.S. rate in the low- and middle-education groups and about the same in the high-education group. Moreover, between 1984 and 1991, the incidence of single motherhood in the United States increased by a bit more (4 percentage points) in the Edlow group than in the Edmid group (3 points) while actually declining slightly for women in the Edhigh group. In Germany, if anything, single motherhood appears to have diminished. The difference between the United States and Germany in female headship may itself be due in part to AFDC in the United States, although research generally does not indicate a strong welfare effect on fertility or marital status within the United States (Ellwood and Bane 1985; Moffitt 1992).

In addition to possibly affecting family formation decisions (we attempt to assess the employment consequences of family structure below), the welfare system could also of course reduce labor market attachment among recipients. Tables 3.14 and 3.15 shed light on this issue by examining the employment rates of young women in each country by family composition and education. If the welfare system is important in reducing employment, we expect this impact to be primarily confined to those who

---

28. These implied elasticities were computed as follows. Taking the case of men for illustrative purposes, we note that wage differences between Germans and Americans account for 2.3 percentage points of the 6.3 percentage point differential in the employment-population ratio. Thus unemployment rate differences would have to account for the remaining 4.0, which would imply a 5.8 percent increase on the U.S. base employment-population ratio of 68.7 percent. The American unemployment rate in 1984 for young, low-skilled men was 7.6 percent higher than that for Germans (i.e., .198/.184). Thus the required American elasticity of the employment-population ratio with respect to the unemployment rate is 5.8/7.6, or 0.76. An analogous computation leads to a required elasticity for women of 1.91.

29. The heavy concentration of single motherhood among less educated women in the United States is particularly emphasized by Blau (1998).

Table 3.13 Family Composition of Women Aged 18–29

Country	Marital Status		Children Present			No Children Present		
	Married	Not Married	Total	Married	Not Married	Total	Married	Not Married
United States (CPS)								
1984 Edlow	.510	.490	.761	.436	.325	.239	.073	.166
Edmid	.509	.491	.550	.349	.200	.450	.160	.290
Edhigh	.500	.500	.272	.215	.057	.728	.285	.443
1991 Edlow	.430	.570	.736	.365	.371	.264	.066	.199
Edmid	.451	.549	.537	.312	.225	.463	.139	.324
Edhigh	.457	.543	.223	.183	.040	.777	.274	.503
Germany (GSOEP)								
1984 Edlow	.500	.500	.613	.393	.220	.387	.107	.280
Edmid	.559	.441	.465	.362	.103	.535	.197	.338
Edhigh	.464	.536	.310	.255	.055	.691	.209	.482
1991 Edlow	.408	.592	.562	.359	.203	.437	.049	.388
Edmid	.450	.550	.401	.306	.095	.599	.144	.455
Edhigh	.451	.548	.183	.159	.024	.817	.293	.524

Table 3.14   Employment by Family Composition and Education for Women Aged 18–29: Levels

| | 1984 | | | | 1991 | | | |
| | Not Married | | Married | | Not Married | | Married | |
Country	Without Children	With Children	Without Children	With Children	Without Children	With Children	Without Children	With Children
United States (CPS)								
Employment-population ratio								
Edlow	.526	.308	.455	.303	.526	.316	.468	.335
Edmid	.842	.645	.791	.508	.846	.660	.842	.578
Edhigh	.957	.856	.898	.642	.949	.885	.923	.670
Full-time employment-population ratio								
Edlow	.303	.157	.342	.192	.325	.175	.333	.220
Edmid	.606	.398	.642	.326	.619	.433	.710	.396
Edhigh	.796	.649	.756	.457	.793	.679	.831	.499
Germany (GSOEP)								
Employment-population ratio								
Edlow	.643	.667	.875	.339	.850	.476	n.a.	.243
Edmid	.883	.787	.856	.321	.970	.657	.943	.301
Edhigh	.887	n.a.	1.000	.429	.953	n.a.	.958	.231
Full-time employment-population ratio								
Edlow	.619	.545	.750	.136	.800	.286	n.a.	.027
Edmid	.844	.745	.833	.133	.929	.371	.811	.053
Edhigh	.774	n.a.	.826	.143	.860	n.a.	.875	.154

Note: n.a. = cell size equal to 10 or fewer observations.

Table 3.15   Employment by Family Composition and Education for Women Aged 18–29: Differences

| | 1984 | | | | 1991 | | | |
| | Not Married: With Children vs. Without Children | | With Children: Not Married vs. Married | | Not Married: With Children vs. Without Children | | With Children: Not Married vs. Married | |
Country	Absolute Difference	Divided by Mean	Absolute Difference	Divided by Mean	Absolute Difference	Divided by Mean	Absolute Difference	Divided by Mean
United States (CPS)								
Employment-population ratio								
Edlow	−.218	−.618	.005	.014	−.210	−.560	−.019	−.051
Edmid	−.197	−.291	.137	.202	−.186	−.258	.082	.114
Edhigh	−.101	−.116	.214	.247	−.064	−.072	.215	.242
Edlow-Edmid	−.021	−.327	−.132	−.188	−.024	−.302	−.101	−.165
Edlow-Edhigh	−.117	−.501	−.209	−.233	−.146	−.488	−.234	−.293
Full-time employment-population ratio								
Edlow	−.146	−.695	−.035	−.167	−.150	−.647	−.045	−.194
Edmid	−.208	−.441	.072	.153	−.186	−.358	.037	.071
Edhigh	−.147	−.209	.192	.273	−.114	−.153	.180	.242
Edlow-Edmid	.062	−.255	−.107	−.319	.036	−.289	−.082	−.265
Edlow-Edhigh	.001	−.486	−.227	−.439	−.036	−.494	−.225	−.436
Germany (GSOEP)								
Employment-population ratio								
Edlow	.024	.043	.328	.593	−.374	−.655	.233	.559
Edmid	−.096	−.145	.466	.702	−.313	−.548	.356	.854
Edhigh	n.a.	n.a.	n.a.	n.a.	n.a.	n.a.	n.a.	n.a.
Edlow-Edmid	.120	.188	−.138	−.109	−.061	−.107	−.123	−.295
Full-time employment-population ratio								
Edlow	−.074	−.173	.409	.958	−.514	−1.233	.259	.621
Edmid	−.099	−.237	.612	1.468	−.558	−1.338	.318	.763
Edhigh	n.a.	n.a.	n.a.	n.a.	n.a.	n.a.	n.a.	n.a.
Edlow-Edmid	.025	.064	−.203	−.510	.044	.106	−.059	−.141

Note: n.a. = cell size equal to 10 or fewer observations. "Mean" refers to the mean outcome for the relevant education group.

are eligible for benefits. By and large, this group is limited to unmarried women with children, although in a very small number of cases, married couples with children can also qualify. Moreover, among this group of single mothers, the less educated are far more likely to qualify for welfare benefits and to find welfare an attractive option. These considerations suggest several possible comparisons that can yield evidence on the importance of welfare.

First, among unmarried women, one can compare the employment rates of those with and without children. In the United States, the former can conceivably qualify for welfare benefits, while the latter cannot. Further, employment differences between these two groups can be contrasted for the less educated and those with middle or high educational levels, since less educated, single mothers are the most likely welfare recipients. And both these comparisons can be contrasted for Germany and the United States, since only the U.S. welfare system has strong work disincentives built in. Second, among women with children, one can compare the employment rates of married and unmarried women. In Germany, neither group has an AFDC-like program available, while in the United States, again, single mothers can qualify. In either comparison, if less educated, single mothers in the United States stand out with especially low relative employment levels, then this would provide some evidence that welfare may have a role to play in explaining the lower employment rates of at least some American women.

The levels of the relevant variables are shown in table 3.14. We focus on table 3.15, which provides the type of comparisons discussed above. We focus on the employment-population ratio rather than work hours, since AFDC taxed away virtually all earnings except for a small exemption (Ehrenberg and Smith 1997). First, looking at unmarried American women, we see that for each educational group, those with children are less likely to be employed than those without children. Further, the largest differences either in absolute value or (especially) relative to the mean of the educational group are for less educated American women. This is the case in both 1984 and 1991. In contrast, in Germany among less educated unmarried women in 1984, those with children actually are more likely to be employed than those without children, while the reverse is true among those with middle levels of education. In 1991, mothers are less likely to work among both less and middle educated women in Germany, but relative to the mean, the contrasts between the Edlow and the Edmid groups are bigger in the United States than in Germany. This comparison between the German and the U.S. experience implies that welfare may play a role in lowering American women's employment. This does not mean, however, that welfare necessarily explains a substantial portion of the U.S.-German difference. We attempt to shed light on the potential size of the effects of welfare below.

Second, among those with children, the unmarried in the United States are as likely or more likely than married women to be employed. Although it is the case that as education rises, unmarried women's relative employment levels compared to those who are married also rise, we find a similar result for Germany (when data are available). Thus this contrast between educational groups is not strong evidence of a welfare effect. Finally, we note that among less educated women with children, the unmarried are much more likely to work than married women (by 23.3 to 32.8 percentage points) in Germany, while in the United States the married are about as likely to work as the unmarried. However, the German employment advantage for unmarried women with children is even larger among the middle-education group, so this comparison again does not provide evidence of a welfare effect.

While tables 3.13, 3.14, and 3.15 provide some suggestive (although mixed) evidence that the U.S. welfare system plays a role in explaining U.S.-German differences in labor market attachment among the less educated, how large an effect can it have? This issue is addressed in table 3.16, which examines the impact of family structure. It shows what the employment and full-time employment rates among less educated young American women would be if they had the same population shares for marital-status–presence-of-children groups as German women (i.e., married with children, married without children, unmarried with children, and unmarried without children). The table shows that the U.S.-German difference in labor market attachment would be almost as large in each year under this simulation as it actually is. Specifically, 81 to 86 percent of the German advantage in employment rates would remain. (Similar results are obtained for full-time employment.) Thus family structure is

Table 3.16   **Actual and Hypothetical Employment Rates for Women Aged 18–29 with Low Educational Levels**

Year	Employment		Full-Time Employment	
	Actual	German Shares	Actual	German Shares
1984				
Germany	.553	.553	.427	.427
United States	.353	.382	.210	.231
U.S.-German difference	.200	.171	.217	.196
1991				
Germany	.563	.563	.417	.417
United States	.375	.411	.232	.257
U.S.-German difference	.188	.152	.185	.160

Note: Employs German shares for marital-status–presence-of-children groups.

not an important factor in producing the German employment advantage, at least not in an accounting sense. Thus, even if the welfare system were responsible for the entire U.S.-German difference in family structure, its effects would be small.

The results in table 3.16 imply that the source of the U.S.-German differences is located within marital-status-children groups. This could still mean that welfare is important, but not necessarily. As may be seen in table 3.14, where data are available, German employment rates are higher than American rates even among two groups not eligible for welfare, married and unmarried women without children, and in 1984, this was also the case for married women with children. If we restrict the U.S.-German comparison entirely to the three groups who are largely not eligible for U.S. welfare (i.e., married women with and without children and unmarried women without children) and use the German shares for these groups (to focus on the within-group differences in employment rates), the average employment rate for Germany was .522 in 1984; in the United States, this simulated rate was only .375. Thus, for welfare-ineligible groups, using a fixed-weight average for both countries, Germans were 14.7 percentage points more likely to be employed than Americans in 1984. This difference is almost as large as the 17.1 percentage point gap in the family-composition-corrected employment rates for the entire population of young women with low educational levels shown in table 3.16. This means that in 1984 the bulk of the employment rate gap between the United States and Germany for less educated young women occurred within groups who were not eligible for AFDC in the United States. While unfortunately the data do not permit a similar computation for 1991, the results for 1984 strongly suggest that welfare is not an important cause of the German women's greater attachment to the labor market.

3.5.3 Parental Leave

While low real wage offers, less access to public employment, and, to a considerably lesser extent, welfare may all potentially reduce young, less educated American women's labor market attachment relative to German women's, a countervailing factor is Germany's maternity and parental leave policies. Throughout our period of observation (1984–91) Germany has had more generous maternity leave policies than is the case in the United States. Moreover, in 1986 additional parental leave was mandated in Germany, reaching 18 months by 1990, and provisions were adopted to require paid parental leave for those working under 19 hours per week. As a test of the effect of this law, we compare the impact of children on young married mothers' labor market attachment in the United States and Germany for 1984 (before the new law) and 1991.

The results of this comparison are shown in table 3.17, which contrasts

Table 3.17   **Employment by Family Composition and Education for Women Aged 18–29: Differences**

| | Married: With Children vs. Without Children | | | |
| | 1984 | | 1991 | |
Country	Absolute Difference	Divided by Mean	Absolute Difference	Divided by Mean
United States (CPS)				
Employment-population ratio				
Edlow	−.152	−.431	−.133	−.355
Edmid	−.283	−.417	−.264	−.367
Edhigh	−.256	−.295	−.253	−.285
Full-time employment-population ratio				
Edlow	−.150	−.714	−.113	−.487
Edmid	−.316	−.669	−.314	−.604
Edhigh	−.299	−.425	−.332	−.446
Germany (GSOEP)				
Employment-population ratio				
Edlow	−.536	−.969	n.a.	n.a.
Edmid	−.539	−.812	−.642	−.873
Edhigh	−.571	−.730	−.727	−.864
Full-time employment-population ratio				
Edlow	−.614	−1.438	n.a.	n.a.
Edmid	−.700	−1.217	−.758	−1.283
Edhigh	−.683	−1.105	−.721	−.954

Note: n.a. = cell size equal to 10 or fewer observations.

employment and full-time employment by educational group for young married women with and without children. In all cases, married women with children have lower employment rates than married women without children. Further, for each year and educational group, this difference is considerably larger for Germany than for the United States, particularly for full-time employment. This pattern holds for both absolute differences and for differences relative to the mean for the relevant educational group.

The larger difference in employment rates between married women with children and those without children for Germany than for the United States likely reflects a variety of factors in addition to Germany's more generous maternity and parental leave policies, including cultural differences between the two countries, the need to supply lunches at home for schoolchildren in Germany, and the legality of employment discrimination against pregnant women. However, the parental leave system became steadily more generous between 1984 and 1991, whereas the need to provide lunches for schoolchildren and the legal situation of pregnant women did not change. We do not know what happened to attitudes toward mothers working; however, since female participation rates in general increased over this period, it is unlikely that these became *less* favorable. Thus, if the effect of children became more negative between 1984 and 1991, an adverse effect of the policy changes on German women's employment will be suggested.

The results in table 3.17 indicate that the "effect" of children (i.e., the difference in employment rates between mothers and nonmothers) tended to rise for Germany, although this pattern is most consistent for employment rather than for full-time employment. In contrast these effects stayed the same or declined slightly in the United States.[30] These results are largely confirmed in appendix table 3A.6, which uses the probit analyses of tables 3A.1 and 3A.2 to examine partial derivatives and semielasticities of employment and full-time employment with respect to marriage and children. Moreover, in these analyses, which control for other factors (i.e., age, age squared, marital status, Edlow, Edmid, and race for the United States), the rise in the absolute value of the effect of children (both the derivative and the semielasticity) in Germany is larger for full-time employment than for overall employment. The larger impact on full-time work in Germany may well be due to the 19-hour provision enacted into the 1986 law, which strongly discourages full-time work. The results in tables 3.17 and 3A.6 thus provide some evidence in support of an impact of the German parental leave law.

These findings serve to highlight the strength of the factors raising the employment rates of young, less educated German women relative to similar women in the United States. Their higher wages and greater access to government employment were strong enough to outweigh the more generous German policies for maternity and parental leave, which our results suggest did negatively affect German women's employment behavior in the 1980s, as well as other factors including the possibility of legal discrimination against pregnant women and the lack of school lunch programs in Germany.

3.6 Conclusions

This paper has examined gender differences in labor market outcomes for hard-to-employ youths in the United States and West Germany during the 1984–91 period. We find that young, less educated American men and especially women are far less likely to be employed than their German counterparts. Moreover, less educated young women and men in the United States have lower earnings relative to more highly educated youths

---

30. The declining relative effect of children on women's labor force participation in the United States has been noted in other studies (see, e.g., Leibowitz and Klerman 1995).

in their own country and also fare much worse than less educated German youths in absolute terms, correcting for purchasing power. At the same time, for those in the highest educational group, Americans outearned Germans by considerable margins.

The evidence that young, less educated women in the United States are more weakly attached to the labor market than those in Germany is especially surprising in light of Germany's lower labor force participation rates for other groups of women and its considerably more generous family and maternity leave policies. We present evidence suggesting that all else equal these policies do negatively affect the labor force attachment of German women, particularly their full-time employment rates. While welfare may play a role, our findings suggest that it accounts for very little of the U.S.-German difference in employment rates. Employment rates of less educated women are also substantially lower in the United States than in Germany for categories of women who would not be eligible for welfare—in particular, for married and unmarried women without children. And most of the difference in labor market attachment between less educated young German and American women is accounted for by groups who are not eligible for welfare in the United States. This suggests that poor labor market opportunities are more important than our welfare system in explaining young American women's lower labor force attachment.

The relatively high employment rates of less educated German youths combined with their relatively high wages, raise the question of how they are successfully absorbed into the labor market. One possibility is that less educated German youths are more productive than their American counterparts. We lack the data to examine this issue directly; however, other evidence suggests that less educated German youths may well have higher skills (Nickell and Bell 1996) and thus that productivity differences could play a role in explaining this pattern. However, given the considerable evidence discussed above that institutions affect wage inequality, we believe that productivity differences are unlikely to account fully for the extremely large differences that we have documented between Germany and the United States in the wages and employment of hard-to-employ youths.

An alternative explanation that we were able to explore is that the public sector in Germany in effect functions as an employer of last resort, absorbing some otherwise unemployable low-skilled youths. Consistent with this idea, we find that while government employment is selective of the highly educated in both the United States and Germany, low education has a much larger negative effect on government employment of young workers in the United States. Moreover, among German males, the effect of low education on government employment is more negative for older than for younger workers, supporting the idea that public employment in Germany is particularly an outlet for younger, less skilled workers. This makes sense in that they are more likely to be minimum wage constrained. While this pattern did not hold consistently among women, it may well be that older, less educated German women are also minimum wage constrained. A simple accounting suggests that the effects of the public sector on youth employment in Germany could be large indeed. Public sector jobs may well allow the German labor market to absorb the additional workers attracted by high wages for the low skilled, relative to the U.S. labor market. This does not require that Germany explicitly pursue a policy of utilizing the government as employer of last resort. The large size of the government sector in Germany combined with the composition of employment in government jobs could well have this effect even in the absence of a conscious policy.

Appendix

Table 3A.1   Probit Results for the Determinants of Employment and Full-Time Employment, Ages 18–29

| | Germany | | | | United States | | | |
| | Men | | Women | | Men | | Women | |
Explanatory Variables	Coefficient	S.E.	Coefficient	S.E.	Coefficient	S.E.	Coefficient	S.E.
A. Employment 1984								
White					.428	.037	.331	.033
Age	−.577	.397	.318	.275	.107	.065	.080	.055
Agesq	.012	.008	−.005	.006	−.002	.001	−.001	.001
Mar	.489	.189	−.647	.131	.550	.036	−.354	.026
Childyes	−.236	.150	−1.049	.118	−.163	.031	−.680	.025
Edlow	−.443	.262	−.321	.189	−.925	.055	−1.192	.048
Edmid	.126	.220	−.100	.166	−.381	.050	−.461	.041
Constant	7.692	4.736	−2.955	3.292	−.455	.766	.052	.656
N	622		716		13,421		14,441	
Log likelihood	−210.947		−371.638		−5,480.21		−8,013.24	
B. Full-time employment 1984								
White					.397	.035	.180	.033
Age	.277	.325	.485	.276	.424	.058	.528	.055
Agesq	−.005	.007	−.010	.006	−.007	.001	−.010	.001
Mar	.434	.157	−.744	.125	.483	.029	−.197	.024
Childyes	−.256	.129	−1.215	.115	−.124	.027	−.679	.024
Edlow	.006	.227	−.122	.185	−.476	.044	−.881	.044

	Coef.	S.E.	Coef.	S.E.	Coef.	S.E.	Coef.	S.E.
Edmid	.334	.177	.195	.158	−.173	.038	−.302	.035
Constant	−3.455	3.888	−4.857	3.292	−5.623	.687	−6.439	.657
N	622		716		13,421		14,441	
Log likelihood	−309.091		−363.485		−7,671.28		−8,735.83	
C. Employment 1991								
White					.359	.041	.270	.034
Age	−.048	.067	.604	.429	.139	.072	.087	.062
Agesq	.001	.001	−.011	.009	−.002	.002	−.001	.001
Mar	.038	.027	−.675	.169	.432	.041	−.214	.028
Childyes	−.022	.027	−1.732	.166	−.046	.036	−.662	.028
Edlow	−.074	.035	−.327	.275	−1.055	.063	−1.235	.051
Edmid	−.038	.028	.042	.236	−.498	.058	−.421	.044
Constant	1.485	.820	−5.936	5.238	−.717	.857	.018	.741
N	473		554		10,926		11,924	
Log likelihood	—		−201.802		−4,376.31		−7,430.67	
D. Full-time employment 1991								
White					.302	.039	.120	.034
Age	−.213	.472	.182	.435	.530	.066	.656	.061
Agesq	.007	.010	−.004	.009	−.009	.001	−.012	.001
Mar	.043	.213	−.723	.158	.543	.036	−.090	.027
Childyes	.117	.203	−1.955	.154	−.082	.033	−.650	.027
Edlow	−.127	.264	−.556	.262	−.653	.051	−.928	.046
Edmid	−.060	.224	−.135	.209	−.210	.044	−.278	.037
Constant	1.942	5.673	−.328	5.304	−6.709	.786	−7.940	.737
N	473		554		10,926		11,924	
Log likelihood	−187.373		−195.551		−5,702.66		−8,264.56	

Note: S.E. = asymptotic standard error. The employment regression for German men in 1991 is OLS, due to convergence problems.

Table 3A.2   Probit Results for the Determinants of Employment and Full-Time Employment, Ages 25–36

| | Germany | | | | United States | | | |
| | Men | | Women | | Men | | Women | |
Explanatory Variables	Coefficient	S.E.	Coefficient	S.E.	Coefficient	S.E.	Coefficient	S.E.
A. Employment 1984								
White					.355	.039	.028	.031
Age	.456	.425	.121	.276	-.107	.083	-.020	.061
Agesq	-.007	.007	-.002	.005	.002	.001	.001	.001
Mar	.601	.197	-.364	.125	.546	.040	-.275	.026
Childyes	-.285	.196	-1.303	.131	-.037	.040	-.704	.028
Edlow	-.725	.242	-.320	.154	-1.111	.049	-.974	.037
Edmid	-.053	.187	.077	.131	-.543	.042	-.324	.029
Constant	-5.897	6.431	-.775	4.190	2.646	1.246	1.460	.921
N	820		898		15,343		16,400	
Log likelihood	-169,496		-512.271		-4,823.43		-9,526.76	
B. Full-time employment 1984								
White					.358	.035	-.137	.030
Age	.181	.320	-.030	.300	.073	.070	.061	.059
Agesq	-.003	.005	-.00005	.005	-.001	.001	-.001	.001
Mar	.406	.145	-.569	.119	.476	.033	-.322	.024
Childyes	-.225	.142	-1.484	.119	-.010	.033	-.781	.025
Edlow	-.233	.184	-.136	.171	-.804	.040	-.819	.037
Edmid	.455	.121	.154	.137	-.357	.031	-.276	.026
Constant	-2.003	4.885	1.839	4.543	.738	3.167	.033	.895
N	820		898		15,343		16,400	
Log likelihood	-349.708		-399.363		-7,069.55		-10,073.8	

C. Employment 1991

White								
Age	.719	.499	.224	.301	.280	.039	.147	.031
Agesq	−.012	.008	−.003	.005	−.062	.082	−.180	.065
Mar	.393	.248	−.434	.138	.001	.001	.003	.001
Childyes	−.071	.255	−1.497	.142	.459	.038	−.099	.026
Edlow	−.516	.276	.183	.169	.029	.039	−.640	.028
Edmid	−.079	.218	.285	.134	−1.082	.049	−1.035	.038
Constant	−9.176	7.537	−2.451	4.547	−.531	.043	−.303	.030
					2.287	1.245	3.765	.992
N	696		789		14,472		15,796	
Log likelihood	−108.36		−410.331		−4,919.14		−8,720.72	

D. Full-time employment 1991

White								
Age	.466	.399	−.125	.341	.280	.036	.006	.030
Agesq	−.007	.007	.002	.006	.023	.075	−.077	.062
Mar	.076	.186	−.587	.135	−.0004	.001	.001	.001
Childyes	.043	.193	−2.066	.133	.509	.035	−.192	.024
Edlow	−.346	.223	−.098	.197	.062	.035	−.707	.025
Edmid	.020	.161	.109	.147	−.924	.043	−.888	.037
Constant	−5.897	6.041	2.776	5.159	−.376	.035	−.248	.026
					.459	1.128	2.033	.939
N	696		789		1,472		15,796	
Log likelihood	−191.227		−296.014		−6,116.72		−9,824.16	

Note: S.E. = asymptotic standard error.

Table 3A.3   Partial Derivatives and Semielasticities of Employment Probabilities with Respect to Education

Country	Partial Derivative				Semielasticity			
	1984		1991		1984		1991	
	Edlow	Edmid	Edlow	Edmid	Edlow	Edmid	Edlow	Edmid
				A. Ages 18–29				
Germany								
Men	−.087	.025	−.074	−.038	.099	.028	.078	.040
	(.051)	(.043)	(.035)	(.028)	(.058)	(.049)	(.037)	(.030)
Women	−.118	−.037	−.110	.014	−.179	−.056	−.153	.020
	(.069)	(.061)	(.093)	(.079)	(.105)	(.092)	(.129)	(.110)
United States								
Men	−.231	−.095	−.256	−.121	−.277	−.114	−.304	−.144
	(.014)	(.012)	(.015)	(.014)	(.017)	(.014)	(.018)	(.017)
Women	−.443	−.171	−.439	−.150	−.686	−.265	−.641	−.219
	(.018)	(.015)	(.018)	(.016)	(.028)	(.023)	(.026)	(.023)
U.S.-Germany difference								
Men	−.144	−.120	−.182	−.083	−.376	−.142	−.382	−.184
	(.053)	(.045)	(.038)	(.031)	(.060)	(.051)	(.041)	(.034)
Women	−.325	−.134	−.329	−.164	−.507	−.209	−.488	−.239
	(.071)	(.063)	(.095)	(.081)	(.109)	(.095)	(.132)	(.112)

B. Ages 25-36

Germany								
Men	−.086	−.006	−.042	−.006	−.092	−.007	−.043	−.007
	(.029)	(.022)	(.022)	(.018)	(.031)	(.024)	(.023)	(.018)
Women	−.126	.030	.068	.106	−.221	.053	.105	.163
	(.061)	(.052)	(.063)	(.050)	(.107)	(.091)	(.097)	(.077)
United States								
Men	−.212	−.103	−.215	−.106	−.239	−.116	−.244	−.120
	(.009)	(.008)	(.010)	(.009)	(.010)	(.009)	(.011)	(.010)
Women	−.361	−.120	−.360	−.106	−.556	−.185	−.515	−.152
	(.014)	(.011)	(.013)	(.010)	(.022)	(.017)	(.019)	(.014)
U.S.-Germany difference								
Men	−.126	−.097	−.173	−.100	−.147	−.109	−.201	−.113
	(.030)	(.023)	(.024)	(.020)	(.032)	(.026)	(.026)	(.021)
Women	−.235	−.150	−.428	−.212	−.335	−.238	−.620	−.315
	(.063)	(.053)	(.064)	(.051)	(.109)	(.092)	(.098)	(.078)

Note: Based on coefficients from tables 3A.1 and 3A.2. Derivatives are evaluated at the sample mean of the dependent variable. The semielasticity is defined as the derivative divided by the sample mean. Other explanatory variables include age, age squared, marital status (Mar), presence of children (Childyes), and for the United States a race dummy (White). Numbers in parentheses are asymptotic standard errors.

Table 3A.4   **Average School Attendance, Educational Attainment, Employment, and Log Wages for Immigrants in Germany Aged 18–29**

	1984		1991	
Sample	Men	Women	Men	Women
A. All immigrants				
In school	.275	.144	.286	.257
German technical or high school degrees	.041	.039	.066	.085
German postsecondary degrees	.300	.209	.347	.232
Vocational/university degrees outside				
Germany	.137	.094	.063	.037
N (including the nonemployed)	437	436	378	354
B. Individuals not in school				
German technical or high school degrees	.025	.027	.048	.038
German postsecondary degrees	.325	.204	.407	.289
Vocational/university degrees outside				
Germany	.167	.105	.081	.049
Employed	.823	.456	.889	.487
Full-time employed	.779	.373	.863	.384
Log hours-corrected earnings among				
employed	6.889	6.617	6.991	6.731
N (including the nonemployed)	317	373	270	263
C. Individuals not in school and without				
German technical, high school, or				
postsecondary degrees				
Vocational/university degrees outside				
Germany	.222	.119	.132	.072
Employed	.830	.400	.848	.376
Full-time employed	.778	.314	.835	.276
Log hours-corrected earnings among				
employed	6.882	6.607	6.952	6.770
N (including the nonemployed)	213	293	158	181
D. Individuals not in school, without				
German technical, high school, or				
postsecondary degrees, and without				
vocational/university degrees outside				
Germany				
Employed	.824	.403	.854	.381
Full-time employed	.782	.318	.839	.280
Log hours-corrected earnings among				
employed	6.879	6.602	6.934	6.770
N (including the nonemployed)	165	258	137	168

Note: Native earnings equations were used to simulate hours-corrected earnings for immigrants.

Table 3A.5 **Partial Derivatives and Semielasticities of Government Employment Probabilities with Respect to Edlow and Edmid**

Gender		Ages 18–29		Ages 30–65	
		Edlow	Edmid	Edlow	Edmid
		A. Derivatives			
Men					
1984	United States	−.095	−.063	−.171	−.108
		(.010)	(.007)	(.008)	(.005)
	Germany	.001	−.008	−.208	−.110
		(.068)	(.048)	(.039)	(.022)
1991	United States	−.176	−.043	−.181	−.079
		(.015)	(.009)	(.008)	(.005)
	Germany	−.025	−.032	−.179	−.070
		(.067)	(.050)	(.052)	(.025)
Women					
1984	United States	−.230	−.130	−.376	−.247
		(.018)	(.009)	(.011)	(.007)
	Germany	−.165	−.172	−.283	−.291
		(.072)	(.053)	(.043)	(.039)
1991	United States	−.200	−.103	−.320	−.198
		(.018)	(.009)	(.011)	(.006)
	Germany	−.009	−.026	−.237	−.241
		(.083)	(.062)	(.047)	(.040)
		B. Semielasticities			
Men					
1984	United States	−1.090	−.723	−1.025	−.649
		(.118)	(.078)	(.045)	(.031)
	Germany	.003	−.049	−.766	−.405
		(.409)	(.289)	(.144)	(.079)
1991	United States	−1.631	−.400	−1.130	−.493
		(.137)	(.079)	(.052)	(.030)
	Germany	−.130	−.162	−.675	−.266
		(.340)	(.257)	(.197)	(.093)
Women					
1984	United States	−1.758	−.989	−1.488	−.921
		(.138)	(.067)	(.053)	(.029)
	Germany	−.619	−.644	−1.008	−1.034
		(.268)	(.199)	(.155)	(.138)
1991	United States	−1.753	−.902	−.320	−.198
		(.161)	(.076)	(.011)	(.006)
	Germany	−.032	−.096	−.760	−.773
		(.311)	(.232)	(.151)	(.128)

Note: Based on a probit model controlling for age, age squared, marital status (Mar), presence of children (Childyes), Edlow, Edmid, and for the United States, a race dummy (White), estimated among those with jobs. Derivatives are evaluated at the sample mean of the dependent variable. The semielasticity is defined as the derivative divided by the sample mean. Numbers in parentheses are asymptotic standard errors.

Table 3A.6   Partial Derivatives and Semielasticities of Employment Probabilities with Respect to Marriage and Presence of Children for Women

Age Group	Employment Probability				Full-Time Employment Probability			
	1984		1991		1984		1991	
	Marriage	Presence of Children	Marriage	Presence of Children	Marriage	Presence of Children	Marriage	Presence of Children
A. Derivatives								
Ages 18–29								
Germany	−.237	−.385	−.227	−.583	−.294	−.481	−.282	−.763
	(.048)	(.043)	(.076)	(.056)	(.049)	(.046)	(.062)	(.060)
United States	−.132	−.253	−.076	−.235	−.078	−.269	−.036	−.259
	(.010)	(.009)	(.010)	(.010)	(.010)	(.010)	(.011)	(.011)
Ages 25–36								
Germany	−.143	−.512	−.162	−.558	−.270	−.442	−.279	−.754
	(.049)	(.052)	(.051)	(.053)	(.045)	(.042)	(.061)	(.059)
United States	−.102	−.261	−.034	−.223	−.128	−.311	−.076	−.280
	(.009)	(.010)	(.009)	(.009)	(.010)	(.010)	(.009)	(.010)
B. Semielasticities								
Ages 18–29								
Germany	−.360	−.584	−.316	−.810	−.535	−.874	−.484	−1.309
	(.073)	(.066)	(.111)	(.078)	(.090)	(.083)	(.106)	(.103)
United States	−.204	−.391	−.111	−.343	−.171	−.589	−.071	−.513
	(.015)	(.014)	(.015)	(.015)	(.021)	(.021)	(.021)	(.021)
Ages 25–36								
Germany	−.252	−.902	−.251	−.866	−.812	−1.326	−.701	−1.895
	(.087)	(.091)	(.080)	(.082)	(.136)	(.126)	(.153)	(.149)
United States	−.157	−.402	−.049	−.319	−.265	−.643	−.141	−.518
	(.014)	(.016)	(.012)	(.013)	(.020)	(.021)	(.017)	(.018)

Note: Based on coefficients from tables 3A.1 and 3A.2. Derivatives are evaluated at sample means of the dependent variable. The semielasticity is defined as the derivative divided by the sample mean. Other explanatory variables include age, age squared, Edlow, Edmid, and for the United States a race dummy (White).

References

Abraham, Katherine, and Susan Houseman. 1995. Earnings inequality in Germany. In *Differences and changes in wage structures,* ed. Richard B. Freeman and Lawrence F. Katz, 371–403. Chicago: University of Chicago Press.

Björklund, Anders, and Richard B. Freeman. 1997. Generating equality and eliminating poverty, the Swedish way. In *The welfare state in transition: Reforming the Swedish model,* ed. Richard B. Freeman, Robert Topel, and Birgitta Swedenborg, 33–78. Chicago: University of Chicago Press.

Blau, Francine D. 1998. Trends in the well-being of American women, 1970–1995. *Journal of Economic Literature* 36 (March): 112–65.

Blau, Francine D., and Marianne A. Ferber. 1992. *The economics of women, men, and work,* 2d ed. Englewood Cliffs, N.J.: Prentice-Hall.

Blau, Francine D., and Lawrence M. Kahn. 1995. The gender earnings gap: Some international evidence. In *Differences and changes in wage structures,* ed. Richard B. Freeman and Lawrence F. Katz, 105–43. Chicago: University of Chicago Press.

———. 1996a. International differences in male wage inequality: Institutions versus market forces. *Journal of Political Economy* 104 (August): 791–837.

———. 1996b. Wage structure and gender earnings differentials: An international comparison. *Economica* 63 (May suppl.): S29–S62.

———. 1997. Swimming upstream: Trends in the gender wage differential in the 1980s. *Journal of Labor Economics* 15 (January, pt. 1): 1–42.

Bound, John, and Richard B. Freeman. 1992. What went wrong? The erosion of relative earnings and employment among young black men in the 1980's. *Quarterly Journal of Economics* 107 (February): 201–32.

Bound, John, and George Johnson. 1992. Changes in the structure of wages in the 1980's: An evaluation of alternative explanations. *American Economic Review* 82 (June): 371–92.

Buechtemann, Christoph, Juergen Schupp, and Dana Soloff. 1993. Roads to work: School-to-work transition patterns in Germany and the United States. *Industrial Relations Journal* 24:97–111.

Bureau of National Affairs. 1995a. *Daily Labor Report,* no. 100 (24 May).

———. 1995b. *Daily Labor Report,* no. 107 (7 June).

Burkhauser, Richard V. 1991. An introduction to the German Socio-Economic Panel for English-speaking researchers. Syracuse, N.Y.: Syracuse University, September.

Burtless, Gary. 1994. The employment prospects of welfare recipients. Washington, D.C.: Brookings Institution, August. Working paper.

Card, David, Francis Kramarz, and Thomas Lemieux. 1995. Changes in the relative structure of wages and employment: A comparison of the United States, Canada, and France. Princeton, N.J.: Princeton University, December. Working paper.

Card, David, and Alan B. Krueger. 1995. *Myth and measurement: The new economics of the minimum wage.* Princeton, N.J.: Princeton University Press.

Deere, Donald, Kevin M. Murphy, and Finis Welch. 1995. Employment and the 1990–1991 minimum-wage hike. *American Economic Review* 85 (May): 232–37.

Demleitner, Nora V. 1992. Maternity leave policies of the United States and Germany: A comparative study. *New York Law School Journal of International and Comparative Law* 13 (1): 229–55.

Edin, Per-Anders, and Robert Topel. 1997. Wage policy and restructuring: The Swedish labor market since 1960. In *The welfare state in transition: Reforming the Swedish model,* ed. Richard B. Freeman, Robert Topel, and Birgitta Swedenborg, 155–201. Chicago: University of Chicago Press.

Ehrenberg, Ronald, and Robert Smith. 1997. *Modern labor economics,* 6th ed. New York: HarperCollins.

Eissa, Nada, and Jeffrey B. Liebman. 1996. Labor supply response to the earned income tax credit. *Quarterly Journal of Economics* 112 (May): 605–37.

Ellwood, David, and Mary Jo Bane. 1985. The impact of AFDC on family structure and living arrangements. In *Research in labor economics,* ed. Ronald Ehrenberg, 137–207. Greenwich, Conn.: JAI.

Hyland, Stephanie L. 1990. Helping employees with family care. *Monthly Labor Review* 113 (September): 22–26.

ILO (International Labour Office). 1988. *Conditions of Work Digest,* no. 2 (February).

———. Various issues. *Yearbook of labour statistics.* Geneva: International Labour Office.

Juhn, Chinhui. 1992. Decline of male labor market participation: The role of declining market opportunities. *Quarterly Journal of Economics* 107 (February): 79–121.

Juhn, Chinhui, Kevin Murphy, and Brooks Pierce. 1993. Wage inequality and the rise in returns to skill. *Journal of Political Economy* 101 (June): 410–42.

Kahn, Lawrence M. 1998. Against the wind: Bargaining recentralisation and wage inequality in Norway, 1987–91. *Economic Journal* 108 (May): 603–45.

Katz, Lawrence F., Gary W. Loveman, and David Blanchflower. 1995. A comparison of changes in the structure of wages in four OECD countries. In *Differences and changes in wage structures,* ed. Richard Freeman and Lawrence Katz, 25–65. Chicago: University of Chicago Press.

Katz, Lawrence F., and Kevin M. Murphy. 1992. Changes in relative wages, 1963–1987: Supply and demand factors. *Quarterly Journal of Economics* 107 (February): 35–78.

Killingsworth, Mark. 1983. *Labor supply.* Cambridge: Cambridge University Press.

Kimmel, Jean. 1996. Reducing the welfare dependence of single-mother families. Upjohn Institute Staff Working Paper no. 96–43. Kalamazoo, Mich.: W. E. Upjohn Institute for Employment Research, March.

Klerman, Jacob Alex, and Arleen Leibowitz. 1997. Labor supply effects of state maternity leave legislation. In *Gender and family issues at the workplace,* ed. Francine D. Blau and Ronald G. Ehrenberg, 65–85. New York: Russell Sage Foundation.

Krueger, Alan B., and Jörn-Steffen Pischke. 1995. A comparative analysis of East and West German labor markets: Before and after unification. In *Differences and changes in wage structures,* ed. Richard Freeman and Lawrence Katz, 405–45. Chicago: University of Chicago Press.

Leibowitz, Arleen, and Jacob Alex Klerman. 1995. Explaining changes in married mothers' employment over time. *Demography* 32 (August): 365–78.

Machin, Stephen, and Alan Manning. 1994. The effects of minimum wages on wage dispersion and employment: Evidence from the U.K. wage councils. *Industrial and Labor Relations Review* 47 (January): 319–29.

Mincer, Jacob. 1976. Unemployment effects of minimum wage laws. *Journal of Political Economy* 84 (August): S87–S104.

Mincer, Jacob, and Solomon Polachek. 1974. Family investments in human capital: Earnings of women. *Journal of Political Economy* 82 (March/April): S76–S108.

Minimum pay in 18 countries. 1992. *European Industrial Relations Review,* no. 225 (October): 14–21.

Moffitt, Robert. 1992. Incentive effects of the U.S. welfare system: A review. *Journal of Economic Literature* 30 (March): 1–61.

Neumark, David, and William Wascher. 1992. Employment effects of minimum and subminimum wages: Panel data on state minimum wage laws. *Industrial and Labor Relations Review* 46 (October): 55–81.

Nickell, Stephen. 1997. Unemployment and labor market rigidities: Europe versus North America. *Journal of Economic Perspectives* 11 (summer): 55–74.

Nickell, Stephen, and Brian Bell. 1996. Changes in the distribution of wages and unemployment in OECD countries. *American Economic Review* 86 (May): 302–7.

OECD (Organization for Economic Cooperation and Development). 1988. *Employment outlook: September 1988.* Paris: Organization for Economic Cooperation and Development.

———. 1993a. *Employment outlook: July 1993.* Paris: Organization for Economic Cooperation and Development.

———. 1993b. *Trends in international migration: Annual report, 1993.* Paris: Organization for Economic Cooperation and Development.

———. 1996. *National accounts: Main aggregates, volume 1, 1960–1994.* Paris: Organization for Economic Cooperation and Development.

O'Neill, June, and Solomon Polachek. 1993. Why the gender gap in wages narrowed in the 1980s. *Journal of Labor Economics* 11 (January): 205–28.

Schultz, T. Paul. 1980. Estimating labor supply functions for married women. In *Female labor supply,* ed. James P. Smith, 25–89. Princeton, N.J.: Princeton University Press.

Soskice, David. 1994. Reconciling markets and institutions: The German apprenticeship system. In *Training and the private sector,* ed. L. Lynch, 25–60. Chicago: University of Chicago Press.

Steedman, Hilary. 1993. The economics of youth training in Germany. *Economic Journal* 103 (September): 1279–91.

USBLS (U.S. Department of Labor. Bureau of Labor Statistics). Various issues. *Employment and earnings.* Washington, D.C.: Bureau of Labor Statistics.

U.S. Social Security Administration. 1995. *Social security programs throughout the world, 1995.* Washington, D.C.: Government Printing Office.

Waldfogel, Jane. 1998. The family gap for young women in the U.S. and the U.K.: Can maternity leave make a difference? *Journal of Labor Economics* 16 (July): 505–45.

II

Youth Responses to the Market

4

Adapting to Circumstances
The Evolution of Work, School, and Living Arrangements among North American Youth

David Card and Thomas Lemieux

The past three decades have witnessed a series of challenges to the economic well-being of youths in Canada and the United States. During the 1960s and early 1970s the baby boom led to a substantial increase in the fraction of young people in the population. This massive supply shock is generally thought to have exerted downward pressure on the relative earnings of younger workers. In the late 1970s, just as the demographic bulge began to subside, the demand side turned against less skilled workers, resulting in falling real wages for youths and other groups at the bottom of the labor market (see Levy and Murnane 1992). Meanwhile, secular trends in family structure, including the rise in the fraction of children born out of wedlock and increasing divorce rates, have also worked to the relative disadvantage of youths.[1]

In this paper we take advantage of the rich microdata sets available for the United States and Canada to study the responses of young workers to

David Card is professor of economics at the University of California, Berkeley, and a research associate of the National Bureau of Economic Research. Thomas Lemieux is associate professor of economics at the University of British Columbia, a research director of the Centre Interuniversitaire de Recherche en Analyse des Organisations, and a research associate of the National Bureau of Economic Research.

The authors are grateful to Francine Blau, David Blanchflower, Richard Freeman, and François Vaillancourt for comments and suggestions. Card's research was funded in part by the National Institute of Child Health and Human Development and by a National Science Foundation grant to the Center for Advanced Study in the Behavioral Sciences. Lemieux's research was funded in part by the Social Science and Humanities Research Council of Canada, the Fonds pour la Formation de Chercheurs et l'Aide à la Recherch (of the province of Quebec), and the Hoover Institution.

1. Eggenbeen and Lichter (1991) conclude that changes in family structure between 1960 and 1988 account for a substantial fraction of the rise in child poverty rates in the United States over the period.

the external labor market forces that have affected the two countries over the past 25 years. Our key hypothesis is that young workers adjust to changes in labor market opportunities through a variety of mechanisms, including changes in living arrangements, changes in school enrollment, and changes in work effort. A comparative perspective offers at least two distinct benefits for evaluating this hypothesis. First, since the nature and timing of cyclical and secular shocks in the United States and Canada are slightly different, we gain valuable leverage for measuring the responses to these shocks. Second, a comparative perspective makes it immediately clear which modes of behavior are driven by country-specific policies or factors and which are attributable to broader forces.

Section 4.1 of the paper provides a descriptive overview of youth behavior in the two countries. Looking at such diverse outcomes as the fraction of youths who live with their parents and the fraction who work while attending school, we find similar behavior in the United States and Canada, with a general tendency toward *convergence* in outcomes over the period 1970–90. In particular, school enrollment rates, which were traditionally lower in Canada than in the United States, are now slightly *higher* in Canada. Very recently, U.S.-Canadian differences have been accentuated by the prolonged and severe recession in Canada. Some differences in family structure—associated with the higher fraction of female-headed families in the United States—stand out. Other differences arise because the distribution of family income has been more stable in Canada while widening sharply in the United States.[2]

In section 4.2 we develop and estimate a series of models for a variety of youth outcomes. Traditionally, economists have focused on youth employment or unemployment. Consistent with much of the existing literature, we interpret variation in youth employment as arising mainly from the demand side. On the supply side, we shift attention to three other behavioral outcomes that provide important mechanisms for adapting to external shocks: the decision to continue living with one's parents, the decision to attend school, and the decision to receive welfare benefits. Building on a standard choice framework, we emphasize two key "exogenous" variables: the wage rate available to young workers in the local labor market and a measure of cyclical conditions in the local labor market. We take as our unit of observation the set of individuals of a given gender and age in a specific regional market. This group-level analysis helps to solve a number of econometric issues (associated with the measurement of wages for nonworkers) while retaining substantial variation in the exogenous variables across observations. We use a pooled data set based on six prov-

---

2. This observation has been made by many other researchers, e.g., Blackburn and Bloom (1993).

inces/regions in Canada and nine census divisions in the United States over the period 1971–94 to estimate our models.

The results of our analysis suggest that youths in the United States and Canada exhibit a multidimensional response to changing labor market conditions. As in most of the literature, we find that the traditional focus of economists' interest—youth employment—is highly responsive to local cyclical conditions but relatively insensitive to changes in wages. But other aspects of youth behavior are also affected by local labor market conditions. In particular, "home leaving" behavior and enrollment decisions are relatively sensitive to cyclical conditions and to the relative level of youth wages.

4.1   An Overview of Youth Labor Markets and Outcomes

4.1.1   Aggregate Labor Market Data

We begin with an aggregate overview of youth labor markets in Canada and the United States. Columns (1), (2), and (3) of table 4.1 present data on the fraction of young workers in the population, the civilian labor force, and civilian employment.[3] In both the United States and Canada the youth share of population peaked around 1980 and has fallen steadily since then. Similar patterns hold for the labor force and for employment. A longer term perspective on the effect of the baby boom on employment shares is provided in figure 4.1, which plots the relative sizes of different age groups over the period since 1950. After a decade of stability in the 1950s, the fraction of jobs held by youths rose by over 200 percent in both countries from 1960 to 1980. The fractions of jobs held by the 25–34 and 35–44 age groups follow parallel paths with 10 and 20 year lags, respectively.[4]

Despite the relative supply shock created by the baby boom, the economies of Canada and the United States were able to create jobs for young workers at roughly comparable paces. Thus the ratio of the youth employment-population rate to the overall employment-population rate was constant (or even rising) in both countries over the 1970s and 1980s. Another aspect of the supply side that underlies the data in table 4.1 is the rising

---

3. The addition of members of the armed forces to the population and labor force has a modest effect on the trends in the data in table 4.1. E.g., there were roughly 500,000 fewer members of the armed forces in the United States in 1980 or 1990 than in 1970. Assuming that 80 percent of the difference were aged 16–24, the addition of armed forces members would raise the employment-population rate in 1970 (relative to later years) by 0.6 percentage points.

4. The sharp decline in the employment share of the 15–24 age group in the 1990s in Canada is due to the recession, which led to an unprecedented drop in the youth employment-population rate.

Table 4.1   Basic Data on Relative Labor Force Status of Youths

Year	Youth Share Pop. (1)	LF (2)	Emp. (3)	Unemp. (4)	Labor Force Participation Rate Youth (5)	All (6)	Youth/All (7)	Employment-Population Rate Youth (8)	All (9)	Youth/All (10)	Unemployment Rate Youth (11)	All (12)	Youth/All (13)
United States, ages 16–24													
1970	.22	.22	.20	.48	59.8	60.4	.99	53.2	57.4	.93	11.0	4.9	2.23
1975	.23	.24	.22	.45	64.6	61.2	1.06	54.2	56.1	.97	16.1	8.5	1.90
1980	.23	.23	.21	.45	68.1	63.8	1.07	58.7	59.2	.99	13.8	7.1	1.94
1985	.19	.21	.19	.39	68.3	64.8	1.05	59.0	60.1	.98	13.6	7.2	1.89
1990	.17	.17	.16	.35	67.3	66.4	1.01	59.8	62.7	.95	11.2	5.5	2.02
1995	.16	.16	.15	.35	66.3	66.6	.99	58.3	62.9	.93	12.1	5.6	2.16
Canada, ages 15–24													
1970	.26	.25	.24	.45	56.0	57.8	.97	50.3	54.5	.92	10.0	5.7	1.77
1975	.26	.27	.26	.47	62.9	61.1	1.03	55.3	56.9	.97	12.0	6.9	1.74
1980	.26	.27	.25	.47	67.8	64.6	1.05	59.0	59.7	.99	13.1	7.5	1.74
1985	.22	.23	.22	.36	68.1	65.8	1.03	57.0	58.9	.97	16.3	10.5	1.55
1990	.19	.19	.18	.30	69.2	67.3	1.03	60.4	61.9	.98	12.7	8.1	1.56
1995	.17	.16	.15	.27	62.2	64.8	.96	52.5	58.7	.90	15.6	9.5	1.63

Sources: Based on authors' tabulations of published data derived from the U.S. Current Population Survey and the Canadian Labour Force Survey.

Note: Population (Pop.), labor force (LF), and employment (Emp.) are for civilians and exclude members of the armed forces.

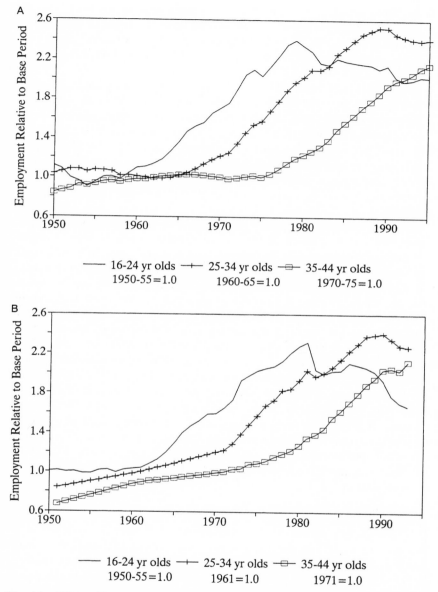

Fig. 4.1 Effect of baby boom on employment by age: relative size of age cohorts, *A*, United States; *B*, Canada

labor force attachment of women. This phenomenon accounts for the roughly 6 percentage point rise in overall labor force participation and employment from the 1970s to 1990. A similar trend occurred for young women, leading to proportional shifts in the youth employment and participation rates.

Columns (11), (12), and (13) of table 4.1 present data on unemployment rates. In the United States young workers historically have accounted for a disproportionate share of unemployment: the unemployment rate of 16–24-year-olds ranges from 1.9 to 2.2 times the overall unemployment rate. In Canada unemployment is more evenly distributed by age: the unemployment rate of 15–24-year-olds ranges from 1.6 to 1.8 times the overall rate. Interestingly, there is little evidence of a systematic *relative* trend in labor market opportunities for youths over the past 25 years in either country.

Both the U.S. and Canadian economies have strong regional components that lead to differential labor market outcomes for youths in different parts of the country.[5] The disparities in regional economic conditions are illustrated in figure 4.2, which shows overall employment-population rates and youth employment rates by province (for Canada) and by region (for the United States). All provinces and regions experienced a peak in employment in the late 1970s, followed by downturn in the early 1980s. The timing and strength of the subsequent recovery varies somewhat by region, with the sharpest gains in the East Coast, Midwest, and Pacific regions of the United States and in Ontario, Quebec, and British Columbia in Canada. The subsequent recession in the early 1990s was particularly pronounced in the New England and Pacific regions of the United States and in the eastern and central provinces (especially Ontario) of Canada. A prominent feature of figure 4.2 is the excess cyclical volatility of youth employment-population rates: national or regional fluctuations in overall employment are typically magnified by a factor of 1.5 to 2.0 in youth employment. We return to a more detailed analysis of this phenomenon in section 4.2.

4.1.2   The Relative Income Position of Youths

While the employment and unemployment data in table 4.1 show little evidence of a shift in the relative economic status of North American youths, a somewhat different conclusion emerges from an analysis of family income. Table 4.2 presents data on the family income distributions and the relative position of youths in Canada and the United States in 1970, 1980, 1990, and 1993. We divide individuals (aged 16 or over) into four

---

5. See Altonji and Ham (1990) for an interesting model of the regional components of the two economies.

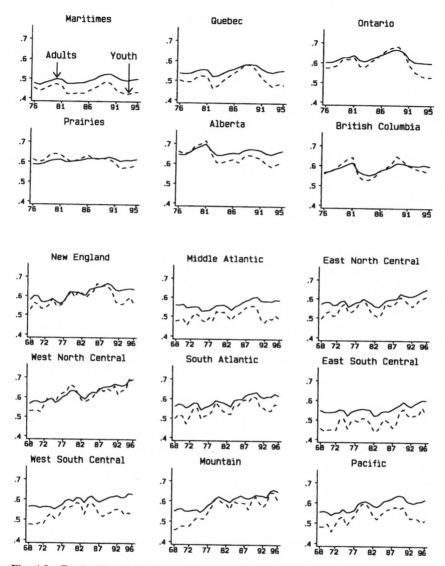

Fig. 4.2   Regional variation in employment

Table 4.2   **Inequality in Adjusted Family Income and Position of Youths in Family Income Distribution**

Quartile	United States				Canada			
	1970	1980	1990	1993	1970	1980	1990	1993
Share of Adjusted Family Income by Quartile among Individuals of All Ages (%)								
Bottom quartile	7.3	7.5	6.5	6.2	6.9	7.7	7.9	9.2
2d Quartile	17.2	17.3	16.1	15.7	17.1	17.3	17.6	18.4
3d Quartile	26.2	27.1	26.3	26.3	26.4	26.6	27.0	27.8
Top quartile	48.8	48.2	51.1	51.9	49.6	48.4	47.5	44.6
Fraction of Youth by Quartile of Adjusted Family Income Distribution (%)								
Bottom quartile	26.5	28.5	32.6	33.9	24.1	25.5	28.5	26.4
2d Quartile	26.5	25.9	24.9	25.6	25.7	25.7	24.0	24.1
3d Quartile	25.9	25.7	23.4	22.1	26.7	26.1	24.8	25.8
Top quartile	21.1	19.8	19.1	18.4	23.5	22.7	22.7	23.7

Sources: U.S. data based on the March Current Population Survey. Canadian data based on the census (1970, 1980, and 1990) and the Survey of Consumer Finances (1993). Families are "economic" families in the CPS and the SCF but "census" families in the Canadian census. See text for details.

Note: Adjusted family income is family income divided by the poverty level (low-income cutoff in Canada) for a family of this size.

quartiles on the basis of their adjusted family income.[6] The upper panel of table 4.2 shows the fractions of total adjusted family income received by individuals in each quartile. The table indicates that the distribution of family income has grown more unequal in the United States while remaining stable in Canada.[7]

The lower panel of table 4.2 shows the position of individuals aged 16–24 in the quartiles of the adjusted family income distribution in the United States and Canada. In both countries, the fraction of youths living in families in the lowest quartile of the income distribution has risen since 1970. The rise is particularly dramatic in the United States: whereas 26.5 percent of youths lived in bottom quartile families in 1970, the fraction had risen to 33.9 percent by 1993 (a 28 percent increase in concentration in the bottom quartile).

6. The data for the United States are based on the March 1971, 1981, 1991, and 1994 Current Population Survey. The data for Canada are based on the 1971, 1981, and 1991 census, and on the 1994 Survey of Consumer Finances (SCF). In constructing the table we use family income adjusted for family composition (i.e., family income divided by the poverty threshold income level for the appropriate family size and composition). Families are "economic" families in the CPS and the SCF (consisting of all related people who live in the same household) but "census" families in the Canadian census (i.e., related subfamilies are assigned their own family income, rather than the total income of all related individuals in their household).

7. As we note below, the Canadian distributional data are not strictly comparable between 1990 and 1993. However, consistent data from the SCF over the 1980s and 1990s show a very stable distribution of family income in Canada (see Beach and Slotsve 1996) over the past decade. The 1993 Canadian data are directly comparable to the 1993 U.S. data.

By contrast, in Canada the fraction of youths living in the lowest quartile only increased by 2.3 percentage points, from 24.1 percent in 1970 to 26.4 percent in 1993. Note, however, that the distribution of family income in 1993 is not strictly comparable to other years because of data differences. Whereas family income in the 1993 SCF represents total income of the *economic* family, in the census (1970, 1980, and 1990) it represents total income of the *census* family. Using census family as opposed to economic family income tends to understate the position of youths in the family income distribution.[8] To estimate the magnitude of this bias, we used the 1990 SCF to compute the fraction of youths in the lowest quartile of the distribution. In the 1990 SCF, only 25.7 percent of youths are in the lowest quartile, compared to 28.5 percent in the census. The fraction of youths in the lowest quartile is thus overstated by 2.8 percentage points in the census. Note, however, that even if we add this correction factor (2.8 percentage points) to the measured increase in the fraction of youths in the lowest quartile in Canada (2.3 percentage points), we still find a smaller increase in Canada (5.1 percentage points) than in the United States (7.4 percentage points).

In terms of relative purchasing power, the economic status of U.S. youths fell even further than suggested by their position in the relative income distribution. This is because, as shown in the upper panel of table 4.2, the fraction of total adjusted income earned by families in the bottom quartile fell by roughly 1 percentage point (a 14 percent decline) between 1970 and 1993. In Canada, on the other hand, the share of adjusted income earned by families in the bottom quartile actually rose from 1970 to 1990.

What can explain the relative deterioration of family incomes of youths over the past two decades—especially in the United States? One potential explanation is changing living arrangements: if youths who live with their parents have higher family incomes than those who live alone or head their own families, then a shift in the fraction who live with their parents would be expected to shift the relative family income status of youths. Table 4.3 describes the evolution of living arrangements among youths by year and gender for the United States and Canada, while table 4.4 illustrates the link between the living arrangements of youths and their family income quartile. In both tables, living arrangements are based on the composition of the economic family in which a young person lives. For example, a young woman who lives in the same household as her parents will be classified as "living with parents" even if she heads her own family (either as a single mother or as a married person). Appendix A explains

---

8. Since the economic family (all related people who live in the same household) is a broader concept than the census family, economic family income is more likely to include the income of the parents—which tends to improve the relative position of youths—than census family income. See appendix A for more detail.

Table 4.3   Living Arrangements of Youths (percent)

	United States				Canada			
	1971	1981	1991	1994	1971	1981	1991	1994
Men								
Living with parents	71.9	70.7	74.0	74.2	70.3	68.6	73.8	77.3
Husband/wife family	58.3	52.6	52.3	52.3	–	57.5	60.8	65.1
Single-headed family	13.6	18.1	21.7	22.0	–	11.1	12.9	12.1
Head or spouse of own family	21.7	15.9	11.2	10.6	15.5	15.3	9.9	7.8
Married	21.2	14.7	9.6	8.8	15.3	15.2	9.8	8.0
Single parent	.5	1.2	1.6	1.9	.2	.1	.1	.1
Living alone	6.4	13.4	14.8	15.1	14.5	16.1	16.3	14.9
Women								
Living with parents	57.8	58.7	62.5	62.3	55.0	55.3	62.4	66.3
Husband/wife family	47.2	43.9	44.2	43.0	–	46.7	51.7	56.7
Single-headed family	10.6	14.9	18.3	19.3	–	8.6	10.8	9.4
Head or spouse of own family	35.8	29.6	24.3	23.6	31.5	30.4	22.9	19.7
Married	33.2	25.1	17.9	16.0	30.4	28.4	20.0	16.8
Single parent	2.7	4.5	6.5	7.7	1.1	1.9	2.9	3.1
Living alone	6.4	11.6	13.1	14.1	13.5	14.3	14.7	14.1

Sources: U.S. data based on the March Current Population Survey. Canadian data based on the census (1971, 1981, and 1991) and the Survey of Consumer Finances (1994). See text for details.

in detail how the living arrangement status was determined in the U.S. CPS and in the Canadian census and SCF.

As shown in table 4.3, the overall fraction of youths who live with their parents has risen in the United States and especially in Canada. Table 4.4 documents that in both countries, youths who live with their parents are spread fairly evenly across the income distribution, whereas those who live alone or head their own families are disproportionately poor. Furthermore, the relative income position of youths who have left home has declined substantially between 1970 and 1993. Among youths who have left home, the fraction in the lowest quartile increased from 30 percent in 1970 to 50 percent in 1993 in both Canada and the United States. Among youths who live with their parents, the fraction in the lowest quartile is stable both in the United States (around 25 percent) and in Canada (15 to 20 percent).

Taken together, these tables support two important conclusions. First, the deterioration in the relative family income status of youths is mostly due to a sharp fall in the relative incomes of youths who have left home. This fall is attributable in part to a rise in the fraction of youths not living with their parents who live alone or head a single-headed family (vs. living with a spouse; see table 4.3) and in part to a relative decline in the income of younger individuals (see table 4.5 and the discussion below for more detail). Second, in the United States and especially in Canada, the rise in

Table 4.4   Effect of Living Arrangements on Fraction of Youths by Quartile of Adjusted Family Income

Quartile	1970			1993			
	Living Alone	Living with Parents	All	Living Alone	Living with Parents	All	1993 with 1970 Family Arrangements
Fraction of Youth by Quartile: United States							
Bottom quartile	31.2	24.0	26.5	50.1	26.4	33.9	34.8
2d Quartile	30.5	24.3	26.5	30.5	23.4	25.6	25.9
3d Quartile	24.6	26.7	25.9	14.6	25.5	22.1	21.7
Top quartile	13.7	25.1	21.1	4.8	24.7	18.4	17.7
Percentage of youth	35.4	64.6	100.0	31.7	68.3	100.0	100.0
Fraction of Youth by Quartile: Canada							
Bottom quartile	31.5	19.6	24.1	49.9	16.5	26.4	29.8
2d Quartile	25.9	25.6	25.7	24.6	23.9	24.1	24.1
3d Quartile	24.4	28.1	26.7	15.1	30.4	25.8	24.8
Top quartile	18.3	26.6	23.5	10.4	29.3	23.7	21.8
Percentage of youth	37.7	62.3	100.0	29.7	70.3	100.0	100.0

Sources: U.S. data based on the March Current Population Survey. Canadian data based on the census (1970) and the Survey of Consumer Finances (1993). The last column (1993 with 1970 family arrangements) indicates the distribution of youths that would have prevailed in 1993 if the fraction of youths living with their parents had remained as in 1970.

Note: The category "living alone" includes all youths who do not live with their parents. See text for details.

the fraction of 16–24-year-olds who remain with their parents has fore-stalled a potential deterioration in the relative income of youths. Indeed, the simple simulation reported in the last column of table 4.4 suggests that had the fraction of youths living with their parents remained at the 1971 level, the percentage of youths in the bottom quartile of the family income distribution would have risen by an additional 0.9 percentage points in the United States (34.8 − 33.9) and by an additional 3.4 percentage points in Canada (29.8 − 26.4). In other words, the larger "move back home" in Canada has reduced the percentage of youths in the bottom quartile by 2.5 percentage points.

Interestingly, we noted earlier that the percentage of youths in the bottom quartile of the family income distribution rose 2.3 percentage points more in the United States than in Canada between 1971 and 1994, taking account of differences in the definition of family income in the SCF (1993) and the Canadian census (1970, 1980, and 1990). Thus, if the move back home had not been more pronounced in Canada than in the United States, the fraction of youths in the lowest quartile would have risen by about as much in the two countries.

These results suggest that in the United States and especially in Canada, the family has played an important role in dampening the effect of the decline in the economic status of youths. The relative expansion of this family safety net for Canadian youths is potentially surprising, given the much wider public safety net in Canada (see, e.g., Blank and Hanratty 1993). There is certainly no indication that broader public safety net programs in Canada have "crowded out" the role of families in coping with adverse economic conditions.

4.1.3 Living Arrangements by Gender and Age

A striking feature of the data in table 4.3 is the difference in living arrangements between young men and young women. In both Canada and the United States, young women are less likely to live with their parents and more likely to head their own families than young men. In part this reflects the difference in average age at marriage between men and women. In addition, the much higher fraction of women who head their own single-parent families contributes to the male-female gap in living arrangements.[9]

A richer portrait of the changing living arrangements of youths in the two countries is provided in figures 4.3 and 4.4. Figure 4.3 shows the fraction of youths remaining with their parents, by age, for men and women in the two countries in 1971 and 1994. Almost all 16-year-olds live with

9. Note that for the United States we include women who have their own children but live with either or both of their parents as "living with parents" in table 4.3. If these women were considered as heading their own families, the fraction of single-head women would rise by about 3 percentage points in 1994.

their parents. By age 19, 10 to 20 percent of men have left home, while 30 to 35 percent of women have left. Between 1971 and 1994 the most noticeable shift is the rise in the fraction of Canadian women still at home. This change was associated with a very substantial increase in school enrollment of Canadian women (see below).

Close examination of figure 4.3 suggests a larger average increase in the fraction of youths living with parents between 1971 and 1994 than what is reported in table 4.3. A weighted average of the changes for individual age groups (with fixed 1971 weights) shows that the fraction of young men living with their parents increased by 4.9 and 9.0 percentage points in the United States and Canada, respectively (compared to 2.3 and 7.0 in table 4.3). The corresponding numbers for young women are 6.8 and 12.7 percentage points, respectively (compared to 4.5 and 11.3 percent in table 4.3). The source of discrepancy between fixed-weight averages and the averages for all youths is the changing youth age distribution. Since the youth population was younger—and thus more likely to be living with parents—in 1971 than in 1994, the fraction of all 16–24-year-olds living with their parents did not increase as much as it rose for any single-year age group (e.g., 24-year-olds). Note, however, that since the changes in the age compositon are very similar in the United States and Canada, these composition biases do not affect the relative trends in family arrangements in the two countries.

Figure 4.4 provides more detail on the changing living arrangements of youths by age and gender. Perhaps the most striking feature of this figure is the relatively high incidence of single motherhood among U.S. women in 1994. About 11 percent of American women aged 20–24 are currently supporting a family without a male head. Even restricting attention to white women, 8 to 9 percent of U.S. women aged 20–24 were single mothers in 1994, compared to 4 to 5 percent in Canada.[10]

The lower rate of single female headship in Canada also contributes to the higher relative income status of youths in Canada. In both countries, families headed by single mothers are very likely to be poor (Hanratty and Blank 1992). Among single mothers heading their own households in the United States in 1994, for example, 89 percent were in the lowest quartile of the adjusted family income distribution. The U.S.-Canadian gaps in both the fraction of young women heading single-parent families (about 5

---

10. We have not attempted to decompose the higher incidence of single motherhood in the United States into differences in out-of-wedlock births and differences in marital stability. Overall, the divorce rate is about twice as high in the United States as in Canada. According to vital statistics data (e.g., *Statistical Abstract of the U.S.* 1996, table 1358), the percentage of children born to unmarried mothers was about 18 percent in the United States in 1980 vs. 13 percent in Canada. By 1991 the rate was 30 percent in the United States and 29 percent in Canada. However, vital statistics data on the marital status of mothers are not strictly comparable across countries because of differences in common-law marriage rates and other factors.

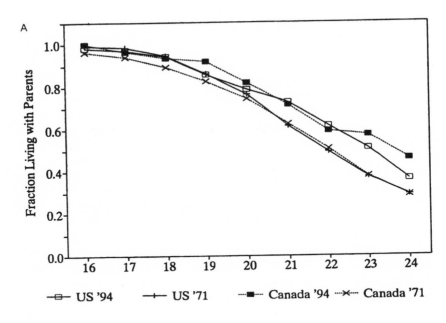

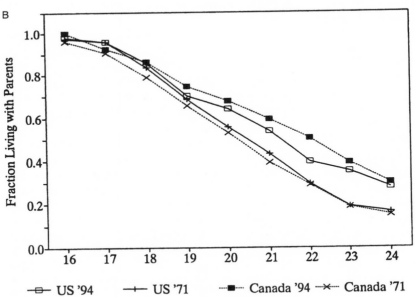

Fig. 4.3   Fraction of youths aged 16–24 living with parents by age: *A*, men; *B*, women

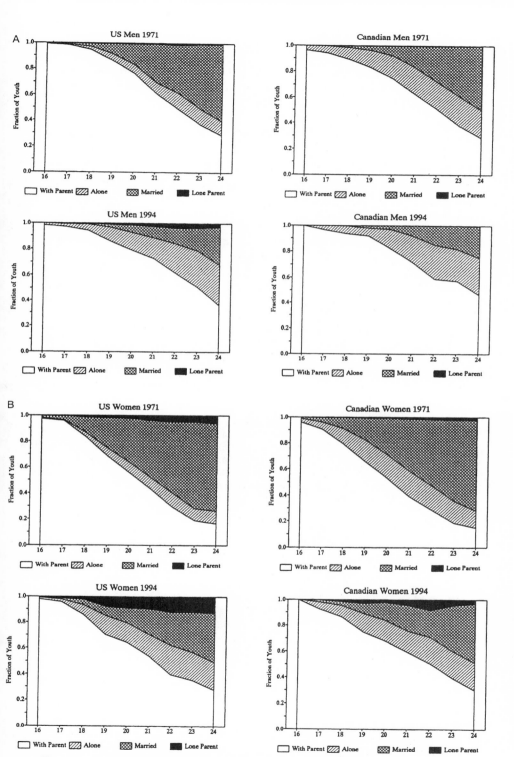

Fig. 4.4   Living arrangements of youths by age: *A*, men; *B*, women

percent in 1994) and the fraction of youths living in single-headed families (about 10 percent in 1994) thus accounts for some of the higher relative income status of youths in Canada.

4.1.4   Relative Earnings of Youths

A second explanation for the declining relative income status of youths is a decline in the relative earnings of young workers. This is in fact the primary explanation for the sharp decline in the relative income position of youths who live on their own. Table 4.5 shows the changing distribution of young men and women across the quartiles of the overall earnings distribution. In both Canada and the United States, a higher fraction of youths were concentrated in the bottom quartile of the earnings distribution in 1990 than in 1970. The increase is more pronounced for women than for men, and greater in Canada than in the United States. The greater effect for young women reflects the widening of age differentials among

Table 4.5   Inequality in Annual Earnings and Position of Youths in Earnings Distribution

	United States				Canada			
Quartile	1970	1980	1990	1993	1970	1980	1990	1993
Men								
Earnings Share by Quartile among Men Aged 16 and Over with Positive Earnings (%)								
Bottom quartile	4.7	4.6	4.8	4.2	5.8	5.5	4.7	4.0
2d Quartile	17.4	17.3	15.4	15.6	14.1	17.9	12.8	15.8
3d Quartile	28.0	29.3	28.0	26.3	32.4	28.8	32.8	28.9
Top quartile	48.7	49.8	51.8	53.8	47.7	48.4	49.7	51.3
Fraction of Young Men with Positive Earnings by Quartile of the Male Earnings Distribution (%)								
Bottom quartile	65.2	60.7	66.6	67.2	59.9	59.9	69.4	68.6
2d Quartile	23.0	27.8	24.3	25.1	29.3	26.8	23.5	23.5
3d Quartile	9.8	9.6	7.9	6.3	8.0	11.6	6.4	5.8
Top quartile	2.0	2.0	1.2	1.4	2.8	1.7	.7	2.1
Women								
Earnings Share by Quartile among Women Aged 16 and Over with Positive Earnings (%)								
Bottom quartile	2.7	3.5	3.8	3.5	4.0	3.7	4.1	3.8
2d Quartile	12.8	14.2	14.2	14.7	15.0	15.1	15.0	14.2
3d Quartile	29.1	28.7	27.6	26.7	29.0	29.0	28.6	28.7
Top quartile	55.5	53.5	54.4	55.1	52.0	52.2	52.3	53.3
Fraction of Young Women with Positive Earnings by Quartile of the Female Earnings Distribution (%)								
Bottom quartile	40.3	43.5	53.1	54.8	36.0	39.5	54.5	56.3
2d Quartile	28.3	27.4	27.4	28.3	25.8	28.6	27.5	26.7
3d Quartile	20.1	21.3	14.9	13.7	28.5	26.2	15.7	12.4
Top quartile	11.4	7.8	4.5	3.2	9.7	5.7	2.3	4.6

Sources: U.S. data based on the March Current Population Survey. Canadian data based on the census (1970, 1980, and 1990) and on the Survey of Consumer Finances (1993).

Note: Earnings are defined as all wages and salaries received during the year.

female workers in both countries over the 1980s. Whereas historically the wage gaps between younger and older women were much smaller than the corresponding gaps for men, over the past two decades age differentials among women have risen sharply.[11] The greater fall in the relative earnings of young workers in Canada than in the United States has been noted in other recent studies (e.g., DiNardo and Lemieux 1997). Compared to the United States, age differentials among male workers rose faster in Canada over the 1980s.

Table 4.5 also shows the fractions of overall earnings accruing to each earnings quartile in the United States and Canada over the past 25 years. Among male workers, earnings inequality increased in both countries, while among female workers the trend was ambiguous. Taken together with the trend toward an increasing fraction of young workers in the bottom earnings quartile, however, the growth in overall earnings inequality presents at least part of the explanation for the falling relative income of youths.

Although we have treated changes in family structure and changes in the relative earnings position of youths as separate phenomena, it is possible that family structure exerts some causal effect on earnings, or vice versa. For example, Korenman and Neumark (1991) have attempted to estimate the causal effect of marital status on male wages. While we place *no* causal interpretation on the correlation between wages and family structure, for completeness we estimated a series of linear regression models to measure the wage differentials associated with three living situations: living with one's parents, living alone, and heading one's own family. The results are summarized in appendix table 4B.1 and are fairly similar across countries. As one might expect, young men who live alone or head their own families earn higher average hourly or weekly earnings than those who live with their parents, with a generally larger differential (10 to 35 percent) for those who head their own families and a smaller effect (5 to 20 percent) for those who live alone.[12] Among young women the wage differentials associated with different living arrangements are smaller and tend to be close to zero in more recent years.

4.1.5 Work and School

While economists' attention is traditionally directed toward the labor force activities of youths, school attendance is at least as important an outcome for many youths. Figure 4.5 presents some simple aggregate statistics on overall employment and full-time enrollment rates among youths

---

11. It could be argued that the rising return to labor market experience among women reflects a tendency for women to take less time off work for child rearing and to choose careers with greater returns to experience.

12. These are estimated from linear regression models that control for age, education, race, and location, estimated by gender and country using data for log average weekly or hourly earnings in 1970, 1980, 1990, and 1993.

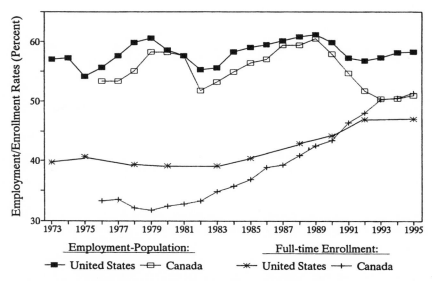

Fig. 4.5   Employment-population rate and full-time enrollment rate of youths

in the United States and Canada.[13] (Full-time enrollment rates exclude individuals who attend college part time; total enrollment rates are about 4 to 5 percentage points higher.)[14] In the early 1970s, full-time enrollment rates were 5 to 10 percentage points higher in the United States than in Canada. Throughout the 1980s, however, relative enrollment rates in Canada rose, so that by 1990 the fraction of 16–24-year-olds enrolled full time in Canada actually surpassed the U.S. rate. This crossover marks a historic turning point: throughout the twentieth century the United States has had a much better educated labor force than Canada (see, e.g., Freeman and Needels 1993). The data in figure 4.5 suggest that the rankings will be reversed within the next 25 years.

Table 4.6 gives a more detailed breakdown of work and school activity rates by gender and age group over our sample period. We distinguish four types of activities: school only, work and school, work only, and "inactivity" (neither work nor school).[15] Our data on school enrollment and

13. The Canadian data underlying this figure are for individuals aged 15–24 while the U.S. data are for individuals aged 16–24. We have adjusted the Canadian enrollment figures to a U.S. basis assuming that 100 percent of 15-year-olds are enrolled. We have not adjusted the Canadian employment rates; observe that any reasonable adjustment would *raise* the Canadian employment rates (by 4 to 5 percentage points).

14. The Canadian data in fig. 4.5 are from published tabulations from the October Labour Force Survey. The U.S. data are our own calculations using the October CPS files.

15. We classify as "inactive" individuals who do not actively participate in the labor market by working or investing in human capital (going to school). Many individuals classified as inactive are of course actively involved in home production activities such as child rearing. They are only inactive from a labor market point of view.

Table 4.6   **Activity Rates of Youths**

	United States				Canada			
Age Group and Year	School Only (1)	School and Work (2)	Work Only (3)	Inactivity (4)	School Only (5)	School and Work (6)	Work Only (7)	Inactivity (8)
				Men				
Ages 16–17								
1971	61.7	30.4	4.5	3.5	61.9	23.0	6.6	8.6
1981	58.0	31.6	5.5	4.8	55.3	22.2	10.7	11.8
1991	63.4	29.2	3.4	4.1	57.3	30.8	5.8	6.1
1991 (SCF)					53.6	38.8	3.2	4.5
1994	68.1	25.4	2.3	4.3	64.3	31.0	1.9	2.7
Ages 20–21								
1971	26.8	18.6	44.3	10.4	15.5	24.2	47.3	13.0
1981	18.4	15.7	51.8	14.1	10.4	24.0	54.0	11.5
1991	20.1	20.3	48.2	11.5	16.6	34.2	35.7	13.5
1991 (SCF)					26.1	14.3	38.6	21.0
1994	23.1	19.4	41.7	15.7	30.0	16.9	35.5	17.6
Ages 23–24								
1971	8.3	14.7	70.2	6.8	7.2	16.2	65.7	10.9
1981	5.9	10.0	70.4	13.6	5.7	18.7	66.2	9.5
1991	7.1	11.2	71.0	10.7	9.4	21.1	54.6	14.9
1991 (SCF)					13.2	10.1	56.0	20.7
1994	8.3	13.0	63.9	14.7	12.8	11.6	55.8	19.9

(continued)

Table 4.6   (continued)

| | United States | | | | Canada | | | |
Age Group and Year	School Only (1)	School and Work (2)	Work Only (3)	Inactivity (4)	School Only (5)	School and Work (6)	Work Only (7)	Inactivity (8)
Women								
Ages 16–17								
1971	64.8	24.6	3.2	7.4	67.8	15.2	6.5	10.5
1981	58.9	30.4	3.9	6.8	58.7	20.4	7.3	13.5
1991	63.5	28.9	2.7	4.9	59.6	29.9	4.6	6.0
1991 (SCF)					56.0	35.8	2.9	5.3
1994	65.1	28.0	1.7	5.2	61.6	34.0	1.5	2.9
Ages 20–21								
1971	15.3	11.7	41.5	31.5	13.0	14.5	44.5	28.0
1981	16.0	14.7	46.3	23.1	10.2	20.6	49.4	19.7
1991	17.3	21.8	38.6	22.4	18.4	36.4	30.9	14.3
1991 (SCF)					24.9	18.3	38.5	18.4
1994	21.5	25.2	31.2	22.1	30.2	22.6	30.6	16.5
Ages 23–24								
1971	3.4	5.8	47.4	43.5	4.4	8.3	46.3	40.9
1981	5.5	8.7	56.1	29.6	5.2	13.8	55.2	25.7
1991	5.9	11.3	58.3	24.6	9.0	20.8	50.2	20.1
1991 (SCF)					9.7	12.6	58.4	19.2
1994	7.6	13.2	55.6	23.6	14.9	10.2	53.0	21.9

Sources: U.S. data from the October Current Population Survey (1971, 1981, and 1991) and the March CPS (1994). Canadian data from the census (1971, 1981, and 1991) and the Survey of Consumer Finances (1994). Data from the 1991 SCF are also reported. In the SCF and the CPS, enrollment and work activities refer to the survey week (April in the SCF). In the Canadian census, enrollment refers to school attendance at any time over the nine-month period from September of the previous year to the "census week" (in June of the corresponding year), while work activity refers to the census week.

employment for the United States are taken from the October CPS and pertain to enrollment and employment as of the survey week. Our data on enrollment and employment for Canada are taken from two different sources. The rows labeled "SCF" present data from the Survey of Consumer Finances, a supplement to the Labour Force Survey much like the March CPS. Enrollment and work activities refer to the SCF survey week, in April of the corresponding year. The other rows present data from the Canadian censuses of 1971, 1981, and 1991. Enrollment in these data sources refers to school attendance at any time over the nine-month period from September of the previous year to the "census week" (in June of the corresponding year), while work activity refers to the census week. Complementing the data in table 4.6, figure 4.6 shows decompositions of work and school activities by age for U.S. and Canadian men and women in 1971 and 1994.

Among the notable features of table 4.6 and figure 4.6 is the rapid rise in school enrollment rates of women over the past two decades. For example, in 1981 the enrollment rate of 20–21-year-old women was about 30 percent in both the United States and Canada. By 1994 this rate was 46 percent in the United States and 52 percent in Canada. Coupled with this rise in school attendance (and an increase in employment rates) was a drop in inactivity rates. In 1971 over 40 percent of 23–24-year-old women in the United States and Canada were inactive (many of these were of course homemakers). By 1994 this rate had halved in both countries.

A more subtle feature of the data in table 4.6 is the relative propensity of enrolled youths in Canada to work compared to those in the United States. For example, among 16–17-year-old enrollees in 1994, 27 percent of U.S. men worked versus 33 percent of Canadian men. At higher ages, however, the relation was reversed. Among 23–24-year-old enrollees, for example, 61 percent of U.S. men worked versus 48 percent of Canadian men. A similar pattern holds among women: in Canada, younger students are more likely to work than their U.S. counterparts, while older students are less likely to work. It is interesting to speculate whether this pattern is driven by the higher average cost of U.S. colleges.

Schooling and work activities of youths are intimately connected to their choice of living arrangements. Many youths who want to attend school full time, for example, must live with their parents, while those who want to live alone are forced to work to support themselves. In appendix table 4B.2 we present cross-tabulations of work and school activity rates with living arrangements for men and women in 1971 and 1994. For simplicity we limited the analysis to older youths (20–24-year-olds) whose work, school, and living arrangements exhibit more variability than those of teenagers. The cross-tabulations show many of the expected patterns. For example, in both the United States and Canada, young men who live with their parents are *more* likely to be inactive, whereas young women

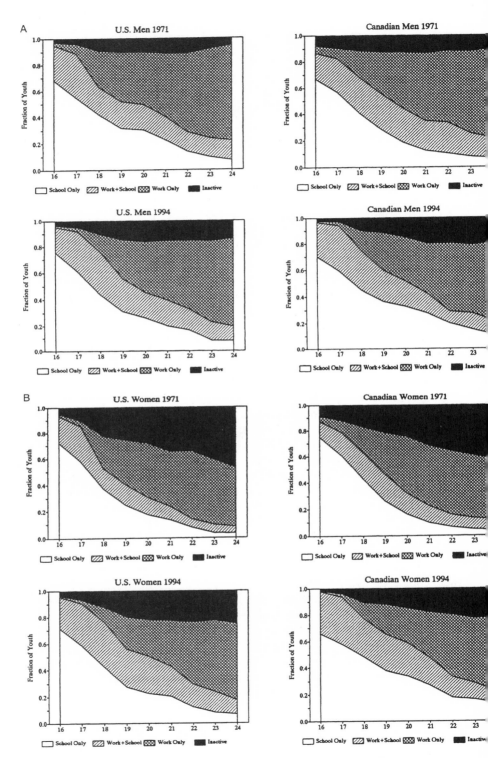

Fig. 4.6 School and work activities of youths by age: *A*, men; *B*, women

Table 4.7   **Proportion of Youths Receiving Welfare Payments**

	All Youths				Youths Not Living with Their Parents			
	United States		Canada		United States		Canada	
Year	Men	Women	Men	Women	Men	Women	Men	Women
1970	1.0	2.8	–	–	2.1	4.4	–	–
1980	1.2	5.7	–	–	1.8	8.8	–	–
1990	0.9	6.8	3.6	5.3	1.3	12.9	8.4	11.2
1993	1.0	7.9	6.3	7.4	0.9	14.1	15.4	17.8

Sources: U.S. data from the March Current Population Survey. Canadian data from the Survey of Consumer Finances.

who live with their parents are *less* likely to be inactive (presumably reflecting the importance of full-time homemakers in the group of women who head their own families). Interestingly, differences in school and work activity rates between young men and women who live with their parents and those who do not tended to narrow over the 1971–94 period in both countries.

4.1.6   Welfare Recipiency

A final important determinant of the overall income status of youths is participation in government transfer programs. Table 4.7 gives the fractions of all youths who reported receiving "welfare" payments in the two countries, and the fractions of youths *not* living with their parents who reported welfare recipiency.[16] The data reveal several interesting similarities and differences between the United States and Canada. First, in both countries overall recipiency rates have risen over the past 25 years. Second, despite the much higher rate of single headship among U.S. women (see fig. 4.4), welfare recipiency rates are similar for women in the two countries. This presumably reflects more generous Canadian benefits, as well as the availability of social assistance payments in Canada to dual-headed families and individuals living alone (see Blank and Hanratty 1993; Hanratty and Blank 1992). Third, welfare recipiency rates are much lower for young men than for young women in the United States, but only marginally lower for men than for women in Canada. We believe that this reflects the much greater availability of cash welfare benefits to men in Canada than in the United States. The major welfare benefit available to men in

16. In our U.S. data files, welfare receipt is defined as receipt of AFDC or public assistance. In our Canadian SCF files for 1990 and 1993, welfare receipt is defined as receipt of social assistance. We do not report numbers for earlier years in Canada because of data limitations in the Canadian census (welfare receipts cannot be distinguished from other transfers like workers' compensation in the 1981 census, and there is no information at all on transfers in the 1971 census).

the United States (food stamps) is not accurately recorded in the CPS and is not included in our tabulations.

4.2 Analytic Modeling of Youth Behavior

4.2.1 Theoretical Framework

Much of economists' attention to youths has focused on the determination of employment.[17] A conventional framework for modeling youth employment is a supply-demand model, in which wages and employment are jointly determined by demand-side factors (e.g., the state of the business cycle) and supply-side factors (e.g., the relative size of the youth population). As we have emphasized throughout this paper, however, youth behavior is characterized by far more than simply holding a job. In principle, the same exogenous factors that affect employment and wages also affect other aspects of youth behavior. Thus a natural approach to modeling the evolution of youth living arrangements, school enrollment, and program participation would be to estimate "reduced form" models, comparable to standard reduced-form models for employment and wages, which show the dependence of living arrangements, enrollment, and so forth, on such exogenous shift factors as the state of the business cycle and the relative size of the youth population.

On the other hand, most research on youth employment in both the United States and Canada has (at least implicitly) assumed that minimum wages or other institutional features lead to above-equilibrium wages in the youth labor market. In this case, the wage is exogenous to supply-side factors and employment is determined "on the demand curve" (see, e.g., Brown, Gilroy, and Kohen 1982). According to this view of the youth labor market, the youth wage rate and demand-side shift factors (such as the state of the business cycle) also determine other behavioral responses of youths, such as the decision to live with one's parents or the decision to attend school.

While a full investigation of the question of which (if either) of these two models of the youth labor market is correct is beyond the scope of this paper, we attempted a very simple test based on the effect of supply-shift factors on the youth wage. Specifically, we investigated the effect of changes in the relative youth population share on the level of youth wages in different regional labor markets in the United States and Canada.[18]

---

17. See, e.g., Freeman and Wise (1982). A voluminous literature focuses on the effect of minimum wages on youth employment. See Card and Krueger (1995).

18. We used data for nine regions in the United States and six provinces/regions in Canada for 1971, 1981, 1991, and 1994. In our models we regressed average youth wages on the fraction of the local population aged 16–24, the employment-population rate of adults, region dummies, and year-country dummies.

Contrary to the prediction of an unconstrained supply-demand model, but consistent with a model in which wages are held at above-equilibrium rates by minimum wage regulations or other institutional factors, we found no evidence that a larger youth population share is associated with a lower youth wage. (Indeed, our point estimates typically showed higher youth wages in regions or time periods with larger youth population shares.) Based on this evidence, we decided to adopt a modeling framework in which the youth wage and the state of demand (i.e., the business cycle) are taken as exogenous, with youth employment determined on the demand side (i.e., by employers' demand functions) and youth living arrangements, school enrollment, and program participation determined on the supply side (i.e., by individuals).

4.2.2   Regional Labor Markets

As noted in figure 4.2, labor markets in Canada and the United States exhibit significant regional differences. This regional variation provides a valuable tool for understanding the determinants of youth employment and other behaviors like leaving home or deciding to enroll in school.[19] For example, even in the presence of unspecified aggregate-level taste shifts, it is possible to identify the effect of changing business cycle conditions on the probability that a young person lives with his or her parents by correlating differences in living arrangements across regions with differences in local labor demand indicators. By pooling cross-sectional data for several years and including unrestricted region effects, it is also possible to account for any permanent differences in a particular outcome across different regions.

In this paper we combine region-specific data for the nine census divisions in the United States with data for the six major provinces/regions in Canada (the Maritimes, Quebec, Ontario, the Prairie provinces, Alberta, and British Columbia).[20] Our U.S. data are drawn from the 1971, 1981, 1991, and 1994 March CPS.[21] Comparable Canadian data are drawn from the 1971, 1981, and 1991 censuses and the 1994 SCF.

Table 4.8 provides a brief overview of the regional differences within the United States and Canada in three key youth outcomes: the fraction who live with their parents, the fraction employed, and the fraction enrolled in school. In both 1971 and 1994 the data for the two countries show sizable

19. Regional variation has been used in some studies of the effect of minimum wages; see Card and Krueger (1995).

20. The use of regional data (as compared to state data, e.g.) greatly increases the number of observations for youths in each age group.

21. We augment the March 1971 and 1981 data with enrollment data from the October 1970 and 1980 CPS. Beginning in the mid-1980s the March CPS contains enrollment information for youths—thus our 1991 and 1994 enrollment data are taken from the March CPS. A comparison of enrollment rates in the March 1991 and the October 1990 CPS reveals a high degree of consistency across regions and age groups in the two surveys.

Table 4.8   Fraction of Youths Living with Parents, Working, and Enrolled in School, by Region

Region	1971			1994		
	Living with Parents (1)	Working (2)	Enrolled (3)	Living with Parents (4)	Working (5)	Enrolled (6)
United States						
New England	69.5	53.2	51.0	75.2	56.9	55.2
Middle Atlantic	72.5	45.5	49.3	78.5	48.3	56.1
East North Central	64.5	50.9	46.2	68.0	59.5	52.6
West North Central	63.3	52.4	52.4	59.6	63.8	55.7
South Atlantic	64.4	47.1	43.4	68.2	53.1	49.2
East South Central	64.8	45.0	43.6	67.8	52.0	51.4
West South Central	62.4	48.4	46.9	68.4	51.5	52.3
Mountain	53.5	47.6	46.6	59.4	64.3	50.2
Pacific	58.7	45.7	50.4	64.8	51.0	52.9
National average	64.6	48.2	47.9	68.2	54.5	52.6
Canada						
Maritimes	66.4	46.0	45.9	78.1	40.0	53.8
Quebec	69.9	45.4	45.2	75.1	47.5	60.0
Ontario	60.1	57.5	49.7	75.1	51.1	60.3
Prairies	58.8	58.1	48.1	64.8	56.8	50.9
Alberta	53.3	59.2	48.3	59.9	59.6	48.7
British Columbia	55.6	55.4	45.6	62.2	58.3	47.9
National average	62.5	52.8	47.4	71.9	51.4	56.3

Sources: U.S. data based on the Current Population Survey. Canadian data based on the census (1971) and the Survey of Consumer Finances (1994). In the SCF and the CPS, enrollment and work activities refer to the survey week (April in the SCF). In the Canadian census, enrollment refers to school attendance at any time over the nine-month period from September of the previous year to the "census week" (in June of the corresponding year), while work activity refers to the census week.

differences across regions. For example, in 1971 the fraction of youths living with their parents ranged from 53.5 percent (Mountain region) to 72.5 percent (Middle Atlantic region) in the United States, and from 53.3 percent (Alberta) to 69.9 percent (Quebec) in Canada.[22] The range of interregional differences in the fraction living with their parents was comparable in 1994. Similarly, in 1971 the fraction of youths enrolled in school ranged from 43.4 percent (South Atlantic region) to 52.4 percent (West North Central region) in the United States, and from 45.2 percent (Quebec) to 49.7 percent (Ontario).[23] Interregional differences in school enrollment were even wider in 1994: for example, Canadian enrollment rates ranged from 47.9 percent (British Columbia) to 60.3 percent (Ontario).

A second fact revealed by the data in table 4.8 is that although interregional differences tend to persist, they are far from permanent. In the United States, for example, the New England and Middle Atlantic regions had among the highest enrollment rates and fractions of youths living with their parents in both 1971 and 1994. However, youths in the Mountain region moved from having among the lowest employment rates in 1971 to the highest in 1994. Another remarkable change is the school enrollment rate of youths in Quebec, which moved from the lowest in Canada in 1971 to the second highest in 1994.

4.2.3 Estimation Results

Our goal is to estimate the effects of changes in youth wages and local labor demand conditions on four youth outcomes: the probability of employment, the probability of living with one's parents, the probability of being enrolled in school, and the probability of receiving welfare payments. To analyze these outcomes we first compute the proportion P_{ijt} of youths of a given age ($i = 16, 17, \ldots, 24$) and a given region (j) and time period (t) who are employed, living with their parents, enrolled, or receiving welfare.[24] We then estimate "grouped linear probability models" of the form

$$(1) \quad P_{ijt} = \sum A_i \gamma_i + \sum R_j \alpha_j + \sum Y_t \delta_t + \beta_1 W_{jt} + \beta_2 D_{jt} + \varepsilon_{ijt},$$

where A_i is a set of age dummies, R_j is a set of region dummies, Y_t is a set of year dummies, W_{jt} is an index of youth wages in region j and year t,

22. One possible explanation for the high employment-population ratios and the low fraction living with parents in high-growth regions like Alberta is the internal migration of young workers. It would be interesting to analyze the role of migration as another form of adjustment to changing economic circumstances.

23. Note that the 1971 enrollment data for Canada are defined as enrollment at any time over the nine months prior to the census, as compared to a "point in time" enrollment rate in the United States and for the 1994 Canadian data.

24. Note that employment status, living arrangements, and enrollment are all measured as of the survey dates of the CPS, census, or SCF, whereas welfare recipiency is measured for the previous year.

and D_{jt} is a measure of local labor demand in region j and year t. Note that for each region-year observation we have nine age-specific observations on the fraction who exhibit the behavior in question. Since the key covariates—the wage index and the labor demand index—are the same for all age groups, and since the error terms for different age groups in the same region-year may have a shared component of variance, conventional standard errors reported for OLS estimates of equation (1) are likely to be biased (Moulton 1986). We therefore report corrected standard errors, which allow for an unrestricted covariance structure between observations for different age groups in the same region-year.

As an index for local labor market conditions we use the employment-population rate of 25–45-year-old adults of the same gender (estimated from the same sources as the dependent variables.[25] The derivation of an appropriate wage index is more difficult. For the later U.S. data (1981, 1991, and 1994), it is possible to use reported annual earnings, reported weeks of work, and reported hours per week over the previous calendar year to construct a measure of average hourly earnings of employed youth. However, neither the 1971 CPS nor the Canadian census files contain direct measures of hours per week in the previous year, and both the 1971 CPS and the 1971 and 1981 Canadian census files include only a categorical measure of weeks worked in the previous year. Thus a direct measure of the hourly wage cannot be computed from these data sets. For each year and each gender, we therefore computed a regional wage index for youth by running a regression of log annual earnings on a standard set of demographic variables, a set of controls for weeks worked last year and hours worked in the survey week, and a set of region dummies.[26] Our regional wage index is simply the coefficient on the corresponding region dummy from this regression.

In appendix figure 4B.1, we plot the values of the wage index in each region for young men and young women. In this figure, the wage index is expressed in terms of deviations from the annual mean for each gender in each country. One noticeable pattern is how the real price of oil (which increased sharply in the 1970s and then declined in the 1980s) drives rela-

---

25. After some experimentation, we found that the employment-population rate of 25–45-year-old women was a better proxy for local labor market conditions of young women than the employment-population rate of 25–45-year-old men.

26. The control variables are a set of age dummies, years of education, and years of education interacted with age. The weeks and hours variables for Canada are a set of five dummies for categories of "weeks worked last year" fully interacted with a dummy for part-time vs. full-time status last year and a set of eight dummies for categories of "hours worked last week." These hours variables are used because they are the broadest set that can be constructed on a comparable basis across years. A similar approach is used with the U.S. data. Note that the wage regressions are estimated using observations on youth (aged 16–24 in the survey month) who reported positive earnings and positive weeks of work in the previous calendar year. (Individuals who worked last year but not during the survey week are used in the estimation.)

tive youth wages in the oil-rich regions of Canada (Alberta) and the United States (West South Central). One can also see how the "Massachusetts miracle" pushed up youth wages in New England in the 1980s after these wages had declined sharply in the 1970s.

A final issue concerns the functional form of equation (1). As written, this equation implies that changes in the key covariates—the wage index and the local demand index—exert the same effects on the probabilities of a given outcome for all nine individual age groups. Since younger individuals have very high enrollment rates and very high rates of living with their parents (close to 100 percent for 16-year-olds) this specification is clearly inappropriate. One possibility would be to use the log odds of different outcomes as the dependent variables. As an alternative, we actually estimated an interacted version of equation (1), including both the levels of the wage and local demand indexes and their interactions with the age of the specific subgroup. This specification allows the effects of higher adult employment rates, for example, to exert a systematically larger effect on the enrollment rates of older individuals than on the rates of younger people.

Estimation results for this interacted version of equation (1) are reported in table 4.9. For simplicity, we report the effects of the two key covariates on 20-year-olds. The first part of the table shows results for men, and the second part shows results for women. For both genders, we report three sets of estimates: estimates for U.S. data alone, estimates for Canadian data alone, and estimates from a pooled U.S.-Canadian sample. In the latter case, we include country-specific year dummies, as well as region dummies for each of the 15 regions in the combined two-country sample. The estimates are derived from a weighted OLS procedure, using as a weight for each region-year-age observation the estimated population of individuals of that age in the region in that year.[27]

The results in the first part of table 4.9 indicate that, as expected, a rise in the employment-population rate of prime-age males has a strong positive effect on the employment rate of young men in the same region. The estimated coefficient in both the United States and Canada is larger than one, indicating that the employment rate of young men is more cyclical than the employment rate of prime-age males. Improving local demand conditions also tend to lower both the probability of living with parents and the probability of attending school among young men in the two countries. The cyclical effect on "living with parents" is larger in Canada while the cyclical effect on "attending school" is larger in the United States. The estimated effects of improving cyclical conditions on the probability of welfare receipt vary by country, although in the pooled model

---

27. In the pooled models, we multiply the weighted number of individuals in Canada by 10 to give a similar weights to the two countries in the regressions.

Table 4.9   **OLS Estimates of Impact of Wages and Cyclical Factors on Youth Outcomes**

	Dependent Variable: Proportion of Youths			
Variable	Living with Parents (1)	Working (2)	Attending School (3)	Receiving Welfare (4)
	Men			
United States				
Average log wage of men	−.127	.002	−.087	−.010
aged 16–24	(.057)	(.084)	(.042)	(.011)
Employment-population rate	−.378	1.326	−.722	−.064
of men aged 25–45	(.190)	(.252)	(.171)	(.032)
Canada				
Average log wage of men	−.190	.008	−.102	−.289
aged 16–24	(.071)	(.055)	(.044)	(.084)
Employment-population rate	−.472	1.173	−.105	.614
of men aged 25–45	(.238)	(.290)	(.229)	(.227)
United States and Canada				
Average log wage of men	−.163	.004	−.090	−.030
aged 16–24	(.049)	(.048)	(.032)	(.015)
Employment-population rate	−.434	1.232	−.368	−.032
of men aged 25–45	(.157)	(.204)	(.175)	(.053)
	Women			
United States				
Average log wage of women	−.110	−.041	−.088	−.039
aged 16–24	(.060)	(.095)	(.036)	(.031)
Employment-population rate	−.159	.687	.193	−.208
of women aged 25–45	(.134)	(.189)	(.089)	(.072)
Canada				
Average log wage of women	−.291	.095	−.131	.045
aged 16–24	(.054)	(.087)	(.087)	(.125)
Employment-population rate	−1.479	.861	.197	−.472
of women aged 25–45	(.262)	(.318)	(.344)	(.285)
United States and Canada				
Average log wage of women	−.102	.045	−.114	−.033
aged 16–24	(.048)	(.056)	(.059)	(.031)
Employment-population rate	−.688	.732	.198	−.234
of women aged 25–45	(.193)	(.166)	(.151)	(.071)

Note: Sample consists of age-region-year cells: all models also include unrestricted age, region, and year effects, as well as interactions between age and the wage and adult employment-population rate variables. The reported wage and employment-population rate effects are for youths aged 20.

There are six provinces/regions in Canada and nine regions in the United States (see table 4.8). Years are 1970, 1980, 1990, and 1993. The models are thus estimated using 234 age-region-year cells for the United States and 216 cells for Canada, except for the Canadian welfare models, in which only the years 1990 and 1993 are available.

Pooled U.S.-Canadian models include country-year effects.

Standard errors (in parentheses) are adjusted for arbitrary forms of heteroscedasticity and for residual correlation among age groups within each year-region cell.

(as in the United States) better local demand leads to a modest fall in welfare recipiency among young men. The positive and significant effect of local demand on welfare recipiency of Canadian men is an anomaly. It should be noted, however, that because of data limitations, comparable welfare recipiency rates are only available for the last two years of our sample period for Canada. Thus the welfare recipiency model for Canada is fit with only 12 observations on the underlying regional data.

The estimated effects of the wage index in the first part of table 4.9 are quite interesting. In the employment models in column (2), wages exert essentially no effect. It should be noted that these estimated wage coefficients may be upward biased by unobserved region-specific factors that lead to higher employment demand for youths and at the same time exert upward pressure on youth wages. We attempted to instrument the youth wage using the fraction of youths in the regional population (a "supply shift" variable) but as noted earlier this variable has an insignificant (and "wrong signed") effect on wage levels in the first-stage equation. In future work it would be interesting to evaluate the performance of other potential instruments, such as a minimum wage measure.

In contrast to the negligible effect of the wage index on employment, the estimates in table 4.9 suggest that higher wages exert a more systematic effect on the living arrangements and enrollment behavior of young men. In particular, rising wages are associated with a lower probability of living with one's parents and a lower probability of enrollment. Both effects are marginally significant in the country-specific models and in the pooled model.

Overall, the results in table 4.9 suggest that external labor market conditions exert a fairly strong effect on a wide range of behaviors among young men. In regions with stronger local demand conditions and higher wages, young men are more likely to work, more likely to strike out on their own and move away from their parents' homes, and less likely to go to school. In regions with depressed local demand conditions and lower wages, young men adapt by continuing to live with their parents and by attending school. The latter mechanism leads to an interesting paradox: a depressed labor market may lead to greater human capital accumulation and (presumably) to enhanced long-run growth.

In comparison to the results for men, the results for women in the second part of table 4.9 are more variable across countries. The employment models in column (2) show that young women's employment is less responsive to changes in the prime-age adult employment rate (the employment rate of adult women in this case) than the employment of young men. There is no indication that higher wages lower young women's employment. Better cyclical conditions (as measured by the employment rate of prime-age women) exert a strong negative effect on the probability of living with parents among Canadian women but only show a weak negative effect among U.S. women. Perhaps surprisingly, the estimated cyclical effects on enrollment are positive (but only significant in the United States) for the two countries.

As in the case of men, the estimates suggest that higher wages exert a systematic effect on the living arrangements and enrollment behavior of young women. In particular, rising wages are associated with a lower probability of living with one's parents and a lower probability of enrollment. Both effects are statistically significant in the country-specific models and in the pooled model.

The cyclical effects on welfare recipiency in the United States are relatively strong but for Canada are again "wrong signed," perhaps as a consequence of the limited amount of data used in the Canadian welfare model. On the other hand, the wage has a negative and significant impact on welfare recipiency in Canada, as expected.

Overall, the estimation results are fairly similar for young men and young women. Looking at the pooled models for outcomes other than welfare recipiency, the only systematic difference between men and women is that the employment-population rate of prime-age adults has a negative and significant effect on the probability of attending school for young men, but a positive and insignificant effect for young women. All the other estimated effects conform to our expectations, except perhaps for the effect of the wage on employment, which should be negative when wages move employment along a fixed demand curve.

4.2.4 Are U.S.-Canadian Differences in Youth Outcomes Driven by Regional Labor Markets?

The results presented in table 4.9 suggest that the state of the regional labor market has an important influence on youth decisions to live with parents, work, or enroll in school. We now turn to the question of whether changing regional labor market performance can account for differential U.S.-Canadian trends in these outcomes over the past 25 years.

Table 4.10 shows the changes in the U.S.-Canadian gaps in each "outcome" from 1971 to 1991 and from 1991 to 1994, along with the changes in each outcome predicted by our model as a consequence of changing regional labor market conditions and the "residual" component.[28] To measure the total changes and predicted changes in each outcome we fit pooled models for the six Canadian provinces/regions and nine U.S. regions using a full set of country-specific year effects. In the first specification we excluded the regional labor market variables (the wage index and the adult employment rate), while in the second specification these

---

28. Note that our regional wage indexes have the same mean in every year. By construction, then, the average changes in the wage index variable over time are zero for both countries, and this variable cannot "explain" any relative trends between the two countries.

Table 4.10   Effect of Labor Market Conditions on U.S.-Canadian Differences in Fraction of Youths Living with Parents, Working, and Enrolled in School

A. 1971–91

	Men			Women		
Change	Living with Parents	Working	Enrolled	Living with Parents	Working	Enrolled
Total change[a]	1.1	–.3	9.1	2.0	2.1	10.0
Changes explained by labor market conditions[b]	–1.4	.9	–.9	–3.6	3.7	–1.5
Unexplained change	2.5	–1.2	10.0	5.6	–1.6	8.5

B. 1991–94

	Men			Women		
Change	Living with Parents	Working[c]	Enrolled[d]	Living with Parents	Working[c]	Enrolled[d]
Total change[a]	2.7	–3.9	1.0	3.5	–2.9	.4
Changes explained by labor market conditions[b]	3.8	–5.6	2.7	2.7	–2.4	–.4
Unexplained change	–1.1	1.7	–1.7	.8	.5	.8

[a]Calculated from the estimated coefficients (translated into percentage points) on the full set of interactions between country and year effects when the labor market variables (adult employment-population rate and wage index) are not included in the pooled U.S.-Canadian model (see table 4.9).

[b]Indicates how the estimated coefficient changes when the labor market variables are included in the regression models.

[c]The change in the fraction of youth working has been adjusted to account for changes in the definition of employment in the Canadian data (work in the reference week in June in the 1991 census vs. work in the reference week in April in the 1994 SCF). The adjustment factor of 5.4 percentage points was obtained by comparing the fractions of youths working in the 1991 census and in the 1991 SCF.

[d]The change in the fraction of youth enrolled in school has been adjusted to account for changes in the definition of school enrollment in the Canadian data (enrolled at any time in the nine months before June in the 1991 census vs. enrolled in the reference week in April in the 1994 SCF). The adjustment factor of 7.1 percentage points was obtained by comparing the fractions of youths in school in the 1991 census and in the 1991 SCF.

variables were included. The total changes are measured by the differences in the differences of the U.S. and Canadian year effects between the base year and the end year (e.g., 1971 and 1991) in the model that excludes the labor market variables. The unexplained changes are measured by the differences in the differences between the base year and the end year in the model that includes the labor market variables. Finally, the explained changes are measured by the differences between the total and unexplained changes.

The first part of table 4.10 indicates that for both men and women, the proportion of youths living with their parents and the proportion of youths working evolved similarly in the two countries between 1971 and 1991. By contrast, the proportion of youths attending school increased much faster (10 percentage points more) in Canada than in the United States. In the case of men, the slightly better labor market conditions in Canada account for a small increase in the probability of working and a small decrease in the probability of living with parents. Note that these effects are substantially larger for women. This is due to the fact—not shown in the tables—that the employment rate of adult women increased substantially more in Canada than in the United States during this period.

Note also that labor market conditions do not account for any of the relative growth in the fraction of young Canadians enrolled in school. If anything, slightly better labor market conditions should have reduced this proportion in Canada relative to the United States. Overall, none of the relative changes in aggregate youth outcomes between the United States and Canada between 1971 and 1991 are explained by our labor market variables.

By contrast, the second part of the table shows that the poor performance of the Canadian labor market between 1991 and 1994 fully explains the "move back home" of young Canadians. For both men and women, the proportion of youths living with their parents increased by about 3 percentage points more in Canada than in the United States, which corresponds to the change predicted by the relative deterioration of the Canadian labor market. Similarly, the sharp drop in the relative employment rate of young Canadians is explained by the poor labor market conditions in Canada.[29] If anything, in fact, the employment rate of young men in Canada should have dropped slightly more than it actually did. The proportion of young Canadian men attending school also increased less than predicted between 1991 and 1994. Changing labor market conditions

---

29. In Canada, there is a spurious negative trend in the proportion of youths working or attending school because of changes in the definitions of these variables between 1991 (census) and 1994 (SCF). The numbers reported in the second part of table 4.10 have been adjusted using an adjustment factor computed by comparing the employment rate and enrollment rate in the 1991 SCF and those in the 1991 census. The adjustment factor is 5.4 percentage points for employment and 7.1 percentage points for school enrollment.

should have pushed up the enrollment rate by 2.7 percentage points more in Canada than in the United States, while the actual rate only increased by 1 percentage point. In the case of women, there was no substantial change (actual or predicted) in enrollment rates in Canada relative to the United States.

Overall, our findings suggest that young Canadians have adjusted to the poor conditions in the Canadian labor market during the 1990s by staying with their parents longer (and working less). By contrast, labor market conditions explain little of the sharp increase in enrollment rates in Canada relative to the United States between 1971 and 1991. The explanation for this increase has to be found elsewhere. One conjecture is that Canadian youths were simply catching up to American youths through the 1970s and 1980s. Lower tuition costs in Canada may also explain some of the change.

4.3   Conclusions

In this paper we take advantage of the rich microdata sets available for the United States and Canada to study the responses of young people to the external labor market forces that have affected the two countries over the past 25 years. Our key hypothesis is that young people adjust to changes in labor market opportunities through a variety of mechanisms, including changes in living arrangements, changes in school enrollment, and changes in work effort.

In the case of young men, the results support this hypothesis. In regions with stronger local demand conditions and higher wages, young men are more likely to work, more likely to strike out on their own and move away from their parents' homes, and less likely to go to school. In regions with depressed local demand conditions and lower wages, young men adapt by continuing to live with their parents and by attending school. The results for young women are similar except that local demand conditions (the employment-population rate of adult women) have no significant effect on school enrollment.

In fact, poor labor market conditions in Canada explain why the fraction of youths living with their parents has increased in Canada relative to the United States recently. Paradoxically, this move back home also explains why the relative position of Canadian youths in the distribution of family income did not deteriorate as fast as in the United States. Other factors like the relatively high rate of single-headed households in the United States also have a negative impact on the relative income position of U.S. youths. However, unlike the move back home in Canada, which is a recent phenomenon, the high incidence of single-headed households in the United States relative to Canada has persisted throughout the period considered here (1970–94). Short-run factors like the state of the labor market cannot account for the permanent difference in the fraction of youths who live in single-headed households in Canada and the United States.

The descriptive analysis presented in this paper raises a number of other interesting issues for future research. For example, enrollment rates were traditionally higher in the United States than in Canada but the situation has been reversed in the early 1990s. It would be interesting to know whether differences in college and university tuition levels and student loan programs can explain this reversal of historic trends. It would also be interesting to explore what analytical models of family behavior are consistent with our empirical observation that the family acts as a "safety net" for young people during difficult economic times.

Appendix A
Determination of Living Arrangements

U.S. Data

We used the household and family relationship variables in the Current Population Survey (CPS) to distinguish between three living arrangements: living with one's parents, living outside one's parent's home as a head (or wife) of one's own family, and living outside one's parent's home as a lone individual (with or without roommates). Individuals who head their own families but live with their parents (or parents-in-law) are considered to be living with their parents. In addition, individuals who live with some other relative (e.g., a grandmother or aunt) with or without their own families are classified as living with their "parents."

Individuals who head their own families but live with their parents (or parents-in-law) are classified as living in related subfamilies in the March CPS. For these individuals (and their children) we used the family information for the associated primary family to determine whether the parental family has dual heads, a single female head, or a single male head. For all other individuals we used the family information for their own family to determine whether the family has dual heads, a single female head, or a single male head.

Specific details for the various CPS years follow.

March 1971

We use "family relationship summary" (columns 43–44 of the person record) to determine living arrangements. This variable combines primary and related subfamilies. Individuals coded as children, grandchildren, or other relatives of the head (codes 3–9) are classified as living with their parents. Individuals coded as not in a family (codes 10–11) are classified as living alone. Individuals coded as heads or wives (codes 1–2) are classified as heading their own families.

March 1981

We use "relationship to householder" (column 103 of the person record) plus "subfamily relationship" (column 106 of the person record) to determine living arrangements. Individuals whose relationship to the householder is child or other relative (column 103 = 4–5) plus individuals who are unrelated subfamily members (column 103 = 6) and whose subfamily relationship is child or other relative (column 106 = 3–4) are classified as living with their parents. Individuals who are nonfamily householders or unrelated individuals (column 103 = 2, 7) are classified as living alone. Individuals whose relationship to the householder is householder or spouse (column 103 = 1, 3) plus individuals who are unrelated subfamily members (column 103 = 6) and whose subfamily relationship is reference person or spouse (column 106 = 1, 3) are classified as heading their own families.

March 1991 and March 1994

We use "family type" (column 31 of the person record) plus "family relationship" (column 32 of the person record) to determine living arrangements. Individuals whose family type is primary family or unrelated subfamily (column 31 = 1, 4) and whose family relationship is child or other relative (column 32 = 3–4) plus individuals whose family type is related subfamily (column 31 = 3) are classified as living with their parents. Individuals whose family type is nonfamily householder or secondary individual (column 31 = 2, 5) are classified as living alone. Individuals whose family type is primary family or unrelated subfamily (column 31 = 1, 4) and whose family relationship is reference person or spouse (column 32 = 1–2) are classified as heading their own families.

Canadian Data

1971, 1981, and 1991 Census

In the Canadian census (1971, 1981, and 1991), we use the variables "census family status" and "relationship with the head of household" to determine the same type of family arrangements as in the U.S. data. We classify as "living with parents" all individuals whose census family status is "child." By definition, these individuals live with their parents, have never been married, and have no children. We also classify as "living with parents" some individuals whose relationship with the head of household is "child" or "child-in-law" but who are not themselves children in a census family. Most of these individuals are either "heads" (husband or single parent) or "wives" of their own census families who happen to live with their parents or in-laws. We also classify as "living with parents" those individuals whose relationship with the head of household is "child" or "child-in-law" but whose census family status is "non-census family member living with relatives." Examples of these cases would be a divorced daughter living with her parents or a widower living with his in-laws.

Among individuals who were not classified as "living with parents," we classify as "living outside one's parent's home as a head (or wife) of one's own family" those who are heads (or wives) of census families. All other individuals do not live in a census family and are classified as "living outside one's parent's home as a lone individual (with or without roommates)." In the 1981 and the 1991 census, "census family status" can also be used to find out whether a child in a census family lives in a single- or dual-headed family. Since no such information is available for other individuals classified as "living with parents," we assume that all these individuals live in dual-headed households. This assumption is innocuous since only about 2 percent of individuals classified as "living with parents" are not children in census families. The "census family status" variable can also be directly used to classify individuals who are the heads of their own families as "head of a dual-parent family" or "head of a single-parent family."

In the 1971 census, however, the "census family status" variable provides no information on whether a family is single or dual headed. This explains why the subcategories that refer to living with parents in a single- or dual-headed family are left blank in table 4.3 in 1971. On the other hand, we use the martial status variable to classify as "single parent" an individual who is the head of a census family and is not married.

1994 Survey of Consumer Finances

In the 1994 SCF, we used three variables—census family status, economic family status, and family type—to determine the living arrangements of individuals. We classify all individuals whose economic family status is "child or child-in-law" as "living with parents." We also classify as "living with parents" individuals who are neither head, spouse, nor child or child-in-law in an economic family (the residual category "other" in the SCF) and are also in the "other" category for census family status.[30] A son living with his mother and his grandfather (head of the economic family) would fall into this particular category.

---

30. There are four possible categories for the census status variable: "head," "spouse," "not in a census family or lone parent," and "other." Logically, all individuals in the "other" category should be children in a census family, but few of them (0.21 percent of the sample) are also classified as head of an economic family. We classified this latter group of individuals as "living alone."

Individuals not classified as "living with parents" are classified as heads or spouses of their own families when the census family status is "head" or "spouse." Individuals in the census family category "not in census family or lone parent" are classified as heads of their own (single-headed) families when the "family type" variable indicates that they live in a single-parent household. All other individuals are classified as "living alone." Finally, the "family type" variable is also used to determine whether individuals who live with their parents live in single- or dual-headed families.

Appendix B

Table 4B.1   **Estimated Regression Coefficients of Living Arrangement Status on Log Wages of Youths**

	Young Men		Young Women	
	All	Ages 20+	All	Ages 20+
United States				
1. 1970 Weekly earnings, controlling for hours in survey week				
Living alone	.06	.07	.15	.16
	(.04)	(.04)	(.03)	(.03)
Living as head of own family	.34	.34	.10	.11
	(.02)	(.02)	(.02)	(.02)
2. 1980 Weekly earnings, controlling for hours in survey week				
Living alone	.16	.16	.12	.11
	(.02)	(.02)	(.02)	(.02)
Living as head of own family	.27	.27	.12	.12
	(.02)	(.02)	(.02)	(.02)
3. 1980 Hourly earnings				
Living alone	.11	.13	.04	.06
	(.01)	(.02)	(.01)	(.02)
Living as head of own family	.22	.23	.06	.08
	(.01)	(.02)	(.01)	(.01)
4. 1990 Hourly earnings				
Living alone	.06	.07	.05	.07
	(.02)	(.02)	(.01)	(.02)
Living as head of own family	.11	.12	.02	.03
	(.02)	(.02)	(.02)	(.02)
5. 1993 Hourly earnings				
Living alone	.13	.14	.01	.02
	(.02)	(.02)	(.02)	(.02)
Living as head of own family	.16	.17	.00	.01
	(.02)	(.02)	(.02)	(.02)

(continued)

Table 4B.1 (continued)

	Young Men		Young Women	
	All	Ages 20+	All	Ages 20+
Canada				
1. 1980 Weekly earnings (census), controlling for hours in survey week				
Living alone	.10	.09	.08	.07
	(.01)	(.01)	(.01)	(.01)
Living as head of own family	.19	.19	.10	.10
	(.01)	(.01)	(.01)	(.01)
2. 1990 Weekly earnings (census), controlling for hours in survey week				
Living alone	.10	.08	.07	.05
	(.01)	(.01)	(.01)	(.01)
Living as head of own family	.20	.19	.10	.08
	(.01)	(.02)	(.01)	(.01)
3. 1990 Weekly earnings (SCF), controlling for hours in survey week				
Living alone	.22	.22	.10	.10
	(.03)	(.03)	(.03)	(.03)
Living as head of own family	.23	.24	.00	−.01
	(.04)	(.04)	(.03)	(.03)
4. 1993 Weekly earnings (SCF), controlling for hours in survey week				
Living alone	.16	.15	.03	.05
	(.04)	(.04)	(.04)	(.04)
Living as head of own family	.29	.31	.01	−.02
	(.05)	(.04)	(.04)	(.04)

Note: Table entries are estimated coefficients of living arrangement status (living alone, living as head of one's own family) in a linear regression model for log average weekly earnings or log average hourly earnings over the previous calendar year. The omitted status is living with one's parents. Other covariates are age dummies, education, a nonwhite dummy, and region dummies for the United States and age dummies, education, and province dummies for Canada. The models in rows 1 and 2 also include the log of reported hours in the survey week (set to zero for nonworkers) and an indicator for individuals who did not work in the survey week. Samples include individuals aged 16–24—in the March Current Population Survey for the United States and in the census (1980 and 1990) and the Survey of Consumer Finances (1990 and 1993) for Canada—who reported positive earnings and weeks of work in the previous year.

Table 4B.2   **Activity Rates and Living Arrangements of Youths Aged 20–24**

	United States			Canada		
Activity	All Youth (1)	Living with Parents (2)	Living Alone (3)	All Youth (4)	Living with Parents (5)	Living Alone (6)

			1971			
Men						
Inactivity	9.0	12.6	5.7	11.9	15.0	8.6
School only	16.4	26.1	7.7	11.2	17.0	5.2
Work and school	16.1	17.1	15.2	20.9	24.1	17.5
Work only	58.5	44.1	71.4	56.1	43.9	68.7
Fraction of all youth	100.0	47.3	52.7	100.0	51.0	49.0
Women						
Inactivity	36.8	19.0	44.7	34.9	19.6	41.7
School only	9.0	20.9	3.7	8.1	17.4	4.0
Work and school	8.3	13.8	5.9	10.9	17.3	8.2
Work only	45.9	46.3	45.7	46.0	45.7	46.2
Fraction of all youth	100.0	30.8	69.2	100.0	30.6	69.4

			1994			
Men						
Inactivity	15.2	16.8	12.9	19.1	17.3	22.2
School only	15.4	20.9	7.3	21.0	26.4	11.9
Work and school	16.0	17.7	13.5	13.4	16.7	7.8
Work only	53.4	44.5	66.2	46.5	39.6	58.2
Fraction of all youth	100.0	59.0	41.0	100.0	63.2	36.8
Women						
Inactivity	23.0	16.3	28.2	19.1	11.4	26.5
School only	13.8	21.0	8.3	21.7	29.1	14.5
Work and school	18.6	26.0	12.8	16.4	23.9	9.2
Work only	44.6	36.7	50.7	42.9	35.6	49.8
Fraction of all youth	100.0	43.6	56.4	100.0	49.0	51.0

Sources: U.S. data based on the Current Population Survey. Canadian data based on the census (1971) and the Survey of Consumer Finances (1994). In the SCF and the CPS, enrollment and work activities refer to the survey week (April in the SCF). In the Canadian census, enrollment refers to school attendance at any time over the nine-month period from September of the previous year to the "census week" (in June of the corresponding year), while work activity refers to the census week.

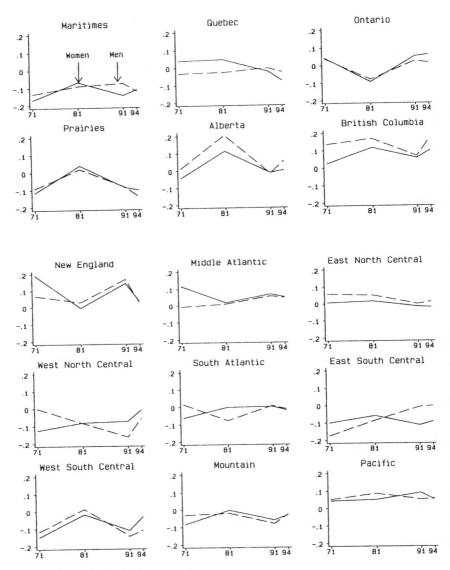

Fig. 4B.1   Regional variation in youth wages

References

Altonji, Joseph G., and John C. Ham. 1990. Variation in employment growth in Canada: The role of external, national, regional, and industrial factors. *Journal of Labor Economics* 8 (January): S198–S236.

Beach, Charles M., and George A. Slotsve. 1996. Are we becoming two societies? Income polarization and the myth of the declining middle class in Canada. Toronto: C. D. Howe Institute.

Blackburn, McKinley L., and David E. Bloom. 1993. The distribution of family income: Measuring and explaining changes in the 1980s for Canada and the United States. In *Small differences that matter: Labor markets and income maintenance in Canada and the United States,* ed. D. Card and R. B. Freeman, 233–66. Chicago: University of Chicago Press.

Blank, Rebecca M., and Maria J. Hanratty. 1993. Responding to need: A comparison of social safety nets in Canada and the United States. In *Small differences that matter: Labor markets and income maintenance in Canada and the United States,* ed. D. Card and R. B. Freeman, 191–232. Chicago: University of Chicago Press.

Brown, Charles, Curtis Gilroy, and Andrew Kohen. 1982. The effect of the minimum wage on employment and unemployment. *Journal of Economic Literature* 20 (June): 487–528.

Card, David, and Alan B. Krueger. 1995. *Myth and measurement: The new economics of the minimum wage.* Princeton, N.J.: Princeton University Press.

DiNardo, John, and Thomas Lemieux. 1997. Diverging male wage inequality in the United States and Canada, 1981–1988: Do institutions explain the difference? *Industrial and Labor Relations Review* 50 (July): 629–51.

Eggenbeen, David J., and Daniel T. Lichter. 1991. Race, family structure, and changing poverty among American children. *American Sociological Review* 56 (December): 801–17.

Freeman, Richard B., and Karen Needels. 1993. Skill differentials in Canada in an era of rising labor market inequality. In *Small differences that matter: Labor markets and income maintenance in Canada and the United States,* ed. D. Card and R. B. Freeman, 45–67. Chicago: University of Chicago Press.

Freeman, Richard B., and David A. Wise. 1982. *The youth labor market problem: Its nature, causes, and consequences.* Chicago: University of Chicago Press.

Hanratty, Maria J., and Rebecca M. Blank. 1992. Down and out in North America: Recent trends in poverty rates in the U.S. and Canada. *Quarterly Journal of Economics* 107 (February): 233–54.

Korenman, Sanders, and David Neumark. 1991. Does marriage really make men more productive? *Journal of Human Resources* 26 (spring): 282–307.

Levy, Frank, and Richard J. Murnane. 1992. U.S. earnings levels and earnings inequality: A review of recent trends and proposed explanations. *Journal of Economic Literature* 30:1333–81.

Moulton, Brent. 1986. Random group effects and the precision of regression estimates. *Journal of Econometrics* 32:385–97.

U.S. Department of Commerce. Bureau of the Census. 1996. *Statistical abstract of the United States.* Washington, D.C.: U.S. Government Printing Office.

5

Disadvantaged Young
Men and Crime

Richard B. Freeman

An extraordinary number of young disadvantaged American men commit crimes serious enough to put them under the supervision of the criminal justice system. These young persons have a "work"experience unlike that of persons engaged in legitimate activities. They make money doing illegal acts, commit violent crimes, are caught and arrested, are convicted and incarcerated or given a probationary sentence. Those who are incarcerated are paroled, work, commit other crimes, get arrested again, and so on. Some of these young men are "career criminals" who spend most of their work time at crime. But many more work at legal jobs when such jobs are available and also take criminal opportunities when they arise. Many youths combine legal and illegal work at the same time or over time. In poor communities in the United States crime in the 1980s and 1990s was not an aberrant or peripheral activity but rather a normal component of economic and social life for many young persons.

The massive involvement of young men in crime affects the national well-being. It harms the victims of crime.[1] It induces the government and private individuals to allocate substantial resources to crime prevention activities. The extent to which crime cuts into the public fisc was forcefully brought home to Americans in 1995, when the state of California announced that for the first time it spent more on prisons than on higher

Richard B. Freeman holds the Herbert Ascherman Chair in Economics at Harvard University and is director of the NBER Labor Studies Program and codirector of the Centre for Economic Performance of the London School of Economics.
1. Estimates of the costs of crime vary widely. The most recent U.S. study, which includes evaluation of the nonpecuniary costs of crime, suggests a total social cost of $450 billion (*New York Times,* April 1996).

education.[2] Crime also adversely affects the families of the criminals, the majority of whom have children under the age of 18 (U.S. Department of Justice 1994a, 10),[3] and the impoverished communities from which they usually come.[4]

Who are the young men involved in crime? What kinds of criminal and legal activities occupy their time? Is the incarceration of young criminals a sufficient strategy for reducing the crime rate?

5.1   The Magnitude of the Problem

That large numbers of Americans are involved in crime to the extent that they end up under the supervision of the criminal justice system has been widely publicized, particularly by the Sentencing Project, which every few years releases a report on the numbers incarcerated based on Justice Department statistics. Even so, each time I look at the data, my jaw drops. My jaw dropped when I looked at 1989 figures, which showed some 1.2 million persons in jail or prison and 4.3 million under the supervision of the criminal justice system. It dropped more with the 1997 figures (table 5.1) that show 1.9 million in jail or prison. Because the vast majority of prisoners are men, the 1.9 million figure translates into over one man incarcerated for every 36 men employed. Since, in addition, for every person incarcerated nearly 1.8 times as many are convicted and on probation and 0.4 times as many on parole, the 1997 figures translate into 5.9 million persons "under the supervision of the criminal justice system." This in turn means one man under supervision for every 14 men employed.[5] But even this statistic does not capture the full involvement of American men with the criminal justice system. Many young persons charged with a law violation are treated as juveniles. In 1995 courts with juvenile jurisdiction processed an estimated 1.7 million juvenile delinquency cases involving persons under age 18.[6] The number of offenses charged to juveniles has

2. Spending on prisons rose from 2 percent of the state budget in 1980 to 9.9 percent in 1995 whereas spending on higher education shrank from 12.6 percent in 1980 to 9.5 percent. The number of inmates increased from 23,500 to 126,100 over the period and 17 new prisons were built. This was *before* the state's "three strikes and you're out" law. See *New York Times,* 12 April, 1995, p. A21.

3. Some of these men were living with their children; others were not. In 1991, 31 percent of male inmates had been living with a child. See U.S. Department of Justice (1994a, 15).

4. Blacks are disproportionately the victims of crime. Among blacks, men aged 12–24, who constitute just 1.3 percent of the U.S. population, experience a 17.2 percent rate of single-victim homicide. See U.S. Department of Justice (1994b).

5. Ninety-three percent of those in jail or prison are men, 89 percent of those paroled are men, and 79 percent of those probated are men, so that approximately 87 percent of all those under supervision are men. This gives an estimate of 4.9 million men under supervision compared to male employment of 67 million aged 19 or over in 1997. This gives a ratio of 7.3 percent, or 1 in 14.

6. U.S. Department of Justice (1997a) lists the states with different juvenile justice procedures. Sickmund et al. (1998) give the 1995 figures on delinquency cases.

Table 5.1   Numbers of Adults Incarcerated and under Supervision of Criminal
                   Justice System

Year	Incarcerated in Prison or Jail	Probation	Parole	Under Supervision
1980	502,000	1,118,000	220,000	1,840,000
1990	1,146,000	2,670,000	531,000	4,347,000
1994	1,483,000	2,962,000	690,000	5,135,000
1997	1,855,000	3,285,000[a]	728,000[a]	5,868,000

Sources: U.S. Department of Justice, Bureau of Justice Statistics, "Correction Statistics,"
from www.ojp.usdoj.gov.bjsi.correct/.

[a] The 1997 figures for probation and parole are my estimates obtained by taking the 1996
figures of the Bureau of Justice Statistics (3,180,363 probated, 740,709 paroled) and updating
them by the 3.3 percent increase in these numbers over the 1990s. See U.S. Department of
Justice, Bureau of Justice Statistics, "Nation's Probation and Parole Population Reached
Almost 3.9 Million Last Year," news release, 14 August 1997.

also trended upward, rising by 45 percent from 1986 to 1995, with a 99
percent increase in the juvenile violent crime index. Finally, the Bureau of
Justice Statistics estimates that 9.0 percent of U.S. men and 28.5 percent
of black men will be confined to a state or federal prison during their
lifetimes (U.S. Department of Justice 1997b). Because these figures ignore
persons who go to jail but not prison, they understate the chance that an
American man will be incarcerated during his life.[7]

The vast majority of the crime-involved population are young men. Figure 5.1 shows that the likelihood of arrest rises sharply in the midteens,
remains relatively high through the early twenties, then declines steadily
with age. The age of prisoners is somewhat higher than that of arrestees
because it often takes several arrests before a court will convict a young
person and send him or her to prison. In 1991, 2.9 percent of 25–34-year-
old American men were incarcerated, and approximately 10 percent were
under the supervision of the criminal justice system.[8] Given the growth of
the prison population, this figure is likely to have exceeded 4 percent by
1997. A disproportionate number of those incarcerated are black. In 1991
about 7 percent of black men over age 18 were incarcerated, and 12 percent of black men aged 25–34 were incarcerated. In 1996 the Sentencing

7. Many persons who go to jail later end up in prison, so one cannot simply use the
chances of going to jail for the first time by age to estimate lifetime chances of any incarceration. According to the U.S. Department of Justice (1997b, table 3), 31.4 percent of persons
who were admitted to state or federal prison had had a prior sentence to local jail, including
juvenile facilities. In 1996, 59.5 percent of jail inmates had been previously incarcerated (U.S.
Department of Justice 1998, table 7).

8. Figures on the demographic characteristics of state prisoners are provided by the Bureau
of Justice Statistics in the *Survey of State Prison Inmates,* which is conducted every five years.
Figures on the demographic characteristics of jail inmates are provided by the Bureau of
Justice Statistics in the *Profile of Jail Inmates.* At this writing, the 1996 *Survey of State Prison
Inmates* is not available, so I have used the 1991 data.

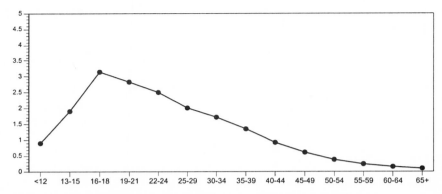

Fig. 5.1   Arrest rates of men and women by age relative to national arrest rate, 1995
Source: Tabulated from Maguire and Pastore (1997, table 4.4).

Project estimated that almost one in three young black males in the age group 20–29 was under some type of correctional control. Approximately two-thirds of men in prison were dropouts from high school in 1991. Among 25–34-year-olds approximately 12 percent of male dropouts were incarcerated in 1991. Combine race, age, and education and you discover that in 1991, 34 percent of high-school-dropout black men aged 25–34 were incarcerated. Since many of those noninstitutionalized are on probation or parole, moreover, a majority of young black male high school dropouts are likely to be under the supervision of the criminal justice system.

With a more than threefold increase in the number of criminals in jail or prison between the 1960s and 1990s, one would expect the rate of crime in the United States to be low and falling. One reason is the incapacitation of proven criminals: if we lock up the most crime-prone individuals, they cannot commit crimes (save in prison, against other criminals). Another reason is deterrence. If we increase the probability that a criminal will be apprehended or incarcerated, fewer people will commit crimes. In fact, the rate of crime reported by police departments in the Uniform Crime Report (U.S. Department of Justice) stabilized in the 1980s and then fell in the 1990s while the rate of crime in the National Crime Victimization Survey fell significantly in the 1980s and 1990s. But neither of these changes come close to the virtual elimination of crime that a threefold increase in incarcerations should have produced through incapacitation. The explanation for the discrepancy is that the rate of involvement in crime by the nonincarcerated population rose (Freeman 1996). Many youths who had not previously committed crimes elected to do so. The new supply was large enough to maintain a high rate of crime despite the massive "incarceration experiment." The number of juveniles involved in crime rose substantially in the period, moreover, leading some analysts to fear a future wave of violent crime (Fox 1996).

Why has crime become more attractive to young men than in the past? One likely cause is falling real wages for legitimate work and continued high joblessness for the less skilled (Freeman 1996; Grogger 1997). Another is the expansion of the demand for drugs and arrest of persons for drug-related offenses (U.S. Department of Justice Statistics 1995). Another part of the story is that the incapacitation of a criminal creates an "opening" or opportunity in the crime market for someone else to take over his activity. Arrest one member of the criminal gang, and the gang finds a replacement. Lock up Joe the 15th Street drug dealer, and Harry decides to sell drugs on that block. Some criminologists also hypothesize that as more and more young men are involved in crime, the disincentive of incarceration becomes less potent: I may care less about going to prison if many of my peers also go. Similarly, if my friends are in a gang, I may join and commit crimes that I would otherwise not.

Whatever the cause, the fact is clear: the number of young men engaged in crime is large and growing, even in the face of a huge incarcerated population. Who are these young men who choose to be involved in crime? What crimes do they commit?

5.2   Who They Are and What They Do: NLSY

In this section I use the National Longitudinal Survey of Youth (NLSY) to examine the characteristics of the youths who commit crimes, the crimes they commit, and the relation between engaging in crime and legitimate employment. The NLSY asked a crime module in 1980, which provides some information on criminal behavior. In ensuing years, the survey interviewed some youths in prison or jail, providing additional information on involvement with the criminal justice system. The NLSY contains fairly detailed information on the personal characteristics of youths and the extent of youth crime that allows us to differentiate among youths who commit the most serious crimes, those more marginally involved in criminal activity, and those who eschew crime completely. (See Center for Human Resource Research 1979–88.)

Table 5.2 contrasts selected background characteristics of young men who engage in varying levels of crime with those of young men who do not engage in crime. The table uses two pieces of information to categorize criminal involvement: (1) self-reported criminal activity on the 1980 crime module and (2) whether the young men were interviewed in jail or prison in any year through 1989. Measures of crime based on self-reported criminal activity are contaminated by reporting bias. If people do not admit to criminal activity, self-reported crime would understate criminal participation. If, on the other hand, young men think it "cool" to claim to commit

Table 5.2   Background Correlates of Male Youths by Criminal Involvement

	Youths in Mutually Exclusive Groups w/ Given Characteristics[a]					Ratio of Proportions		
Characteristic	No Crime (1)	Stopped (2)	Charged (3)	Probation (4)	Jail (5)	Jail/ No Crime (6)	Jail/ Probation (7)	Probation/ No Crime (8)
Characteristics of family at age 14								
Black	.27	.26	.21	.22	.42	1.56	1.91	.81
Not father/mother family	.32	.32	.43	.39	.54	1.69	1.38	1.22
Family on welfare	.19	.17	.15	.24	.41	2.16	1.71	1.26
Mother less than high school	.42	.4	.42	.5	.59	1.4	1.18	1.19
Father less than high school	.44	.41	.36	.48	.63	1.43	1.31	1.09
Alcoholic relatives	.43	.47	.5	.57	.57	1.33	1.0	1.33
Mother white collar	.43	.46	.43	.46	.25	.54	.54	1.07
Mother laborer, service	.34	.32	.37	.37	.47	1.38	1.27	1.09
Father white collar	.32	.36	.37	.24	.13	.41	.54	.75
Father laborer, service	.18	.15	.17	.19	.25	1.39	1.32	1.06
Runaway from home								
One or two times	.013	.025	.029	.035	.051	3.9	1.46	2.7
More than two times	.006	.007	.021	.035	.061	10.2	1.74	5.8
School experience								
Expelled from school	.06	.07	.1	.16	.24	4	1.5	2.7
Truant from school, over four times	.034	.074	.115	.128	.11	3.3	.87	3.76
Drug and alcohol use								
High drug use	.05	.05	.07	.15	.13	2.6	.87	3.0
Uses needles for drugs	.01	.01	.02	.03	.07	7	2.33	3.0
Drinks a lot	.1	.18	.19	.21	.15	1.5	.71	2.1

Source: Tabulated from the National Longitudinal Survey of Youth. Maximum sample sizes for the various groups are no crime, 4,029; jail, 454; stopped, 855; charged, 243; and probation, 313.

[a]Each statistic gives the proportion of youth in each column who have the characteristic of each row.

crimes, self-reported numbers would overstate criminal participation. Criminologists have explored these biases by asking people whether they were arrested and then comparing their responses to police records. The evidence shows that young white males report criminal activity roughly accurately, but that young black males underreport criminal participation (Hindelang, Hirschi, and Weis 1981), possibly because criminal involvement among blacks extends beyond hard-core youths who may take pride in being "bad guys." The NLSY evidence that a youth was interviewed in jail or reported having been in prison or jail is thus probably a more valid indicator of criminal activity than the youth's self-report of crimes committed. Still, both types of information have value, and I use both in this study.

Table 5.2 summarizes the information about youth involvement in crime according to the seriousness of the offense and involvement with the criminal justice system. The numbers give the percentage of youths involved in different aspects of crime who had the given characteristic. For instance, column (1) gives the percentage of youths who report that they did not commit crimes: the .27 number for "black" tells us that 27 percent of the youths who did not commit crimes were black (and thus that 73 percent of the youths who did not commit crimes were nonblack). Similarly, the other numbers show that 26 percent of those who were stopped were black, that 21 percent of those who were charged with a crime were black, and so on. Column (5) shows the characteristics of youths who went to jail or prison. Columns (2), (3), and (4) show the characteristics of youths who engaged in crime but did not end up incarcerated in succeeding years. These categories are defined as discrete nonoverlapping groups, with youths classified in the group of their most serious involvement with the criminal justice system. Thus youths who were stopped by police but did not end up charged or probated or sent to jail are in the "stopped" group, those charged with crime but not probated or sent to jail are in the "charged" group, and so on. Columns (6), (7), and (8) give the ratios of figures in earlier columns and thus indicate how much different characteristics varied with differing levels of criminal activity. For instance, column (6) measures the relative difference in the probability that a youth would end up in jail as opposed to having no criminal involvement due to the given characteristic.[9]

The table highlights four aspects of the characteristics of young men who end up incarcerated or otherwise involved in crime. First, there are strong family background correlates to being incarcerated. Youths who go to jail or prison are disproportionately black, disproportionately from

9. The proportion of youths in the noncriminal set with characteristic x is N_x/N, and the proportion of youths in the jailed set with characteristic x is J_x/J; so the ratio is $(J_x/J)(N/N_x)$. This is just $(J_x/N_x)/(J/N)$, the relative increase in the chance that someone will be in the jailed set due to characteristic x.

families that did not have both parents present at age 14, and disproportionately from families that were on welfare. More of these youths than other youths have relatives who are alcoholic. More have parents employed in lower paying blue-collar jobs, and fewer have parents in white-collar jobs. Most striking, a disproportionate number of young men who end up in jail have run away many times from home. While the NLSY contains no information that would let us determine whether these youths were running away from bad home environments or running away to escape parental supervision that might have limited their criminal activity, evidence from surveys of prison inmates, which I examine later (table 5.7), shows that a large number of prisoners were physically or sexually abused as children, suggesting that many at least are running away from dysfunctional family situations rather than to escape normal adult supervision.

Second, the skills of youths who end up incarcerated are lower than those of youths not involved in crime. The youths who end up incarcerated are more likely to be expelled from school and to be truant many times when enrolled in school. Consistent with this, figure 5.2 shows that the youths who are incarcerated have lower scores on the Armed Forces' Qualification Test (AFQT), and they have fewer years of educational attainment in 1980 and eight years later.

Third, the youths who are engaged in crime are only moderately more likely to use drugs than other youths but are much more likely to use a needle for drugs. It is serious drug abuse, not modest "recreational use," that is associated with crime. There is only a modest difference in alcohol use between youths who end up incarcerated and those who commit no crimes.

Fourth, while the background characteristics of youths are monotonically related to their involvement in crime, the relation seems to be highly nonlinear. Youths who are only moderately involved in crime—having been stopped by police, charged with crime, and even probated—have background characteristics that are more similar to the noncriminal group than they are to those who end up incarcerated. This nonlinear break is demonstrated in columns (7) and (8) of the table, which give the ratios of the percentage with given characteristics among those receiving probationary sentences to the percentage with those characteristics among those who committed no crimes and similar ratios for the characteristics of the probated and those of the incarcerated. Despite the fact that both incarcerated and probated youths have been convicted of crimes, those given probationary sentences are closer in background characteristics to those who committed no crimes than they are to the incarcerated group.

The cross-tabulations in table 5.2, while valuable in showing the characteristics of youths who commit crimes, do not show the independent influence of any of the background factors on the criminal activity of youths. To isolate the independent effect of the various factors and determine

YEARS OF SCHOOLING, 1980

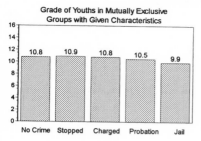

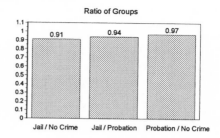

YEARS OF SCHOOLING, 1988

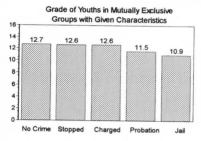

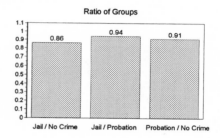

AFQT SCORES

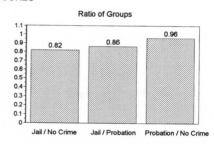

Fig. 5.2   Skill of youth
Source: Tabulated from the National Longitudinal Survey of Youth.

which factors have the most substantial effect on crime, I examine next the relation between the factors taken together and the dichotomous variable, whether the youth was ever incarcerated from 1980 to 1988, using a logistic equation. The results of these calculations are summarized in table 5.3. Column (1) gives the estimated coefficients and standard errors for selected personal and skill measures. All of these variables affect the probability of ending up incarcerated, but what stands out is the substantial impact of AFQT on incarceration, conditional on age, race, and years of

Table 5.3   **Logistic Curve Estimates of the Probability of Going to Jail**

Variable	(1)	(2)	(3)
Basic personal			
Age	.15 (.03)	.20 (.04)	.10 (.04)
Black	.33 (.12)	.32 (.16)	.31 (.16)
Grade in 1980	−.11 (.04)	−.18 (.05)	−.13 (.05)
AFQT	−.018 (.002)	−.020 (.003)	−.021 (.003)
Characteristics of family at age 14			
Not father/mother family		.37 (.17)	.29 (.16)
Family on welfare		.35 (.17)	.32 (.17)
Mother less than high school		−.35 (.17)	−.26 (.17)
Father less than high school		.33 (.17)	.28 (.17)
Alcoholic relatives		.47 (.4)	.35 (.15)
Runaway from home		.87 (.18)	.67 (.19)
Behavior of youth			
Expelled from school			1.04 (.19)
Truant from school, over four times			.06 (.06)
High drug use			1.15 (.25)
Uses needles for drugs			1.19 (.38)
Drinks a lot			0
N	4,970	3,692	3,686
Pseudo *R*²	0.11	0.15	0.19
Percentage incarcerated, predicted:			
Yes	24	27	31
No	7	5	5

Source: Tabulated from the National Longitudinal Survey of Youth.
Note: Numbers in parentheses are standard errors.

schooling. Column (2) gives the results of calculations in which I have added the family background characteristics of youths. Absence of a two-parent family and being on welfare increase the chances that someone is incarcerated, as in the cross-tabulation. But other major indicators of family background do not show clear or consistent effects. The education of fathers is positively related to incarceration while the education of mothers is negatively related to incarceration. Measures of the occupational status of parents had such negligible effects on the chance of going to prison that I dropped the variables from the table. By contrast, the measure of whether the youth ran away from home remains a strong powerful predictor of incarceration.

The weak effect of parental education and parental occupation on going to jail or prison compared with the stronger effect of family composition, welfare, and the runaway variable suggests that criminal behavior among disadvantaged youths is due more to dysfunctional family activity than to poverty itself. If your family life was unpleasant enough that you ran away from home several times, you have problems of the kind that produce criminal behavior. If your parents are poorly educated and in low-wage occupations, you are not so disadvantaged.

Finally, column (3) of the table records the coefficients and standard errors for logistic equation estimates that include measures of youth behavior in school and use of drugs or alcohol. Being expelled from school is a strong predictor of future incarceration, as is using a needle to take drugs.

The importance of running away from home and expulsion from school in determining criminal behavior suggests that social isolation—what Europeans call "social exclusion"—may also play a part in inducing youths into serious criminal behavior. Those isolated from normal family influences and school are more prone to crime than otherwise similar youths. At the minimum these factors are important advance or early warning indicators that a youth is likely to get into serious criminal justice system trouble.

How well do the background factors predict which youths are incarcerated? Since the dependent variable is a 0/1 variable while the logistic predictions give probabilities, one cannot simply apply the usual summary statistics to determine the overall success of the equations. One meaningful way to judge the predictive power of the equations is to rank the youths by the predicted probability that they are incarcerated, determine a cutoff probability so that the number of persons with a probability above the cutoff equals the actual number incarcerated in the sample, and then compare how many youths with above-cutoff and below-cutoff probabilities were incarcerated. If the equations do a good job of predicting involvement in crime, the proportion incarcerated in the above-cutoff group should greatly exceed the proportion incarcerated in the below-cutoff group. The bottom lines of table 5.3 show that the individuals in the group that the model predicts would end up incarcerated were in fact from 3.4 times (col. [1]) to 6.3 times (col. [3]) more likely to end up in jail or prison than persons predicted not to be incarcerated. From one perspective, a sixfold odds ratio for predicting an infrequent event is rather good. Still, the best model (col. [3]) predicted an erroneous incarceration outcome for over twice as many persons (69 percent) as it predicted a correct outcome for (31 percent). Thus, while there are strong background identifiers of the form of criminal behavior that leads to incarceration, these factors still lead to considerable misclassification. Many highly disadvantaged youths do not engage in crime or do so sufficiently infrequently or lightly to avoid incarceration.

5.2.1   Working at Crime

What crimes do young men commit? Which crimes result in prison or jail sentences? Do young men who engage in crime do so exclusively, or do they also work?

There are various ways to estimate the crimes that young men commit: through self-reports of crime by young people, through data on the charges made when the police arrest young person, through victimization reports, and through the crimes prisoners report that they committed before they were locked up. None of these measures is an ideal random sample of the crimes youths commit, but each still provides reasonably valid information of the type of criminal activities in which youths engage.[10]

The NLSY gives respondents the following instructions:

> On this form are descriptions of types of activities that some young people can get into trouble for. I want you to read each item and put a check mark after the category that best describes the number of times in the last year you have done the activities described.

The form lists 17 particular crimes, ranging from shoplifting to attacking someone with the idea of seriously hurting or killing that person. In table 5.4 I record the incidence of 15 of these crimes (I have excluded smoking marijuana or using drugs), ordered from the least to the most violent. The survey allows youths to report that they committed crimes 50 or more times, and some do so report. For ease of presentation the table aggregates the distribution between youths who commit a crime once or twice and those who commit a crime three or more times.

The column on the incidence of crime shows that a substantial minority of youths admit to committing a large array of crimes at least one or two times and that many admit to committing them three or more times. The proportion of youths involved in crime, including violent and serious crime, is quite high in this population. Overall, 82 percent of young men in the NLSY report having committed some crime; 77 percent admit that they committed a crime beyond either smoking marijuana or taking drugs. Thirty-seven percent report having committed at least one crime three times or more, and nearly the same percentage reported having committed at least three different crimes. Figure 5.3 records the distribution of the number of crimes exclusive of smoking marijuana or taking drugs committed by youths: the number is the sum of the number of times youths said they had committed each individual crime, with the top-coded category of 50 or more given the value 50. Even with this extremely conservative assumption, the distribution of crimes committed by youths is highly skewed, with a mean number of crimes of 20 for youths who commit crimes but a median number of about 5.5 crimes. Approximately 18 percent of crimes are committed by the 1 percent of the sample at the far right-hand tail of the distribution, and 59 percent of crimes are committed by youths in the top decile of the distribution. In this sample 8 percent of

---

10. The self-reported data suffer from youths' underreporting crimes. Victimization surveys suffer because victims will not know the ages of the criminals who victimized them. Arrest data miss crimes that the police do not clear with an arrest—roughly 80 percent of crimes (Maguire and Pastore 1997, table 4.20).

Table 5.4   Crimes Committed in Past Year by Young Men and Involvement with Criminal Justice System

Crime	Incidence (%)	Outcome (%)				
		None	Stopped	Charged	Probation	Jail
Property crime						
Times intentionally damaged property						
None	73	69	14	4	5	6
1–2	18	50	20	6	9	12
3 or more	10	41	22	5	9	17
Shoplift						
None	70	69	14	4	4	6
1–2	19	52	20	6	8	11
3 or more	10	39	21	5	11	17
Petty theft						
None	75	69	14	4	4	6
1–2	17	52	20	6	8	11
3 or more	8	39	21	5	11	17
Grand theft						
None	91	66	16	4	5	6
1–2	6	36	13	8	15	22
3 or more	3	15	16	4	16	43
Times sold marijuana/hashish						
None	86	67	15	4	5	7
1–2	6	40	23	7	12	15
3 or more	8	32	21	10	14	18

(continued)

Table 5.4 (continued)

Crime	Incidence (%)	Outcome (%)				
		None	Stopped	Charged	Probation	Jail
Times sold hard drugs						
None	97	64	16	5	6	7
1–2	2	31	20	4	16	24
3 or more	2	22	19	8	13	31
Times conned someone						
None	74	66	15	4	5	7
1–2	16	56	20	6	7	10
3 or more	10	48	20	5	9	15
Times auto theft						
None	89	66	15	4	5	7
1–2	8	43	19	5	10	9
3 or more	3	31	27	10	18	16
Times broken into building						
None	89	67	16	4	5	6
1–2	8	35	20	7	12	20
3 or more	3	20	20	7	14	32
Times sold/held stolen goods						
None	82	68	15	4	5	6
1–2	12	45	19	7	11	14
3 or more	6	29	20	6	14	26

Times aided in gambling operation						
None	92	64	16	4	6	7
1–2	2	39	24	5	9	22
3 or more	2	32	20	9	9	25
Violent crime						
Times fought in school/work						
None	60	69	14	4	4	6
1–2	25	58	18	6	7	9
3 or more	15	43	21	5	10	17
Used force to obtain things						
None	92	65	16	4	5	7
1–2	6	43	18	5	12	20
3 or more	2	30	21	10	9	25
Threatened to hit or hit someone						
None	54	71	14	4	4	6
1–2	27	57	18	6	7	9
3 or more	19	48	21	5	9	13
Times attacked someone or seriously hurt/kill						
None	86	67	15	4	5	6
1–2	10	42	19	8	9	16
3 or more	4	31	28	5	11	22

Source: Calculated from the National Longitudinal Survey of Youth.

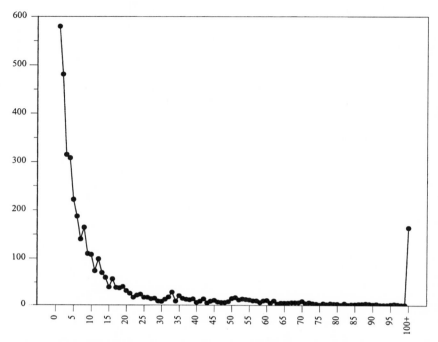

Fig. 5.3   Distribution of crimes among out-of-school young men who commit at least one crime
Source: Tabulated from the National Longitudinal Survey of Youth.
Note: Number of crimes (*x-axis*) vs. number of youths committing that number of crimes (*y-axis*).

young men engage in crime to such an extent that they end up incarcerated at some point over the ensuing period.

The crimes that youths commit range from the violent crime of attacking someone with the intent of causing injury (14 percent of the youths) to selling marijuana/hashish (also 14 percent), to various forms of theft (25 percent petty theft, 29 percent shoplifting, 9 percent grand theft, and 11 percent automobile theft), to dealing with stolen goods, damaging property, and so on. Because these patterns are similar to those shown in arrest figures for teenagers and young adults in FBI arrest records, they are probably reasonably accurate.[11]

The numbers under the heading "outcome" in table 5.4 show what happened to people who committed various levels of crime. They are row

11. The arrest statistics show that most arrests are for property crimes but that the proportion of arrests for violent crimes rises from the early teens until age 24 and then declines (Maguire and Pastore 1997, table 4.7).

percentages or conditional frequencies. For example, the 69 in the first row says that 69 percent of individuals who never intentionally damaged property had no involvement with the criminal justice system. By contrast, only 41 percent of those who said they had damaged property three or more times had no involvement with the criminal justice system; 17 percent of them spent time in jail or prison. Overall, the youths who were most intensively involved in crime were more likely to end up in jail than others, although some of those who report no involvement in particular crimes also end up incarcerated. One of the reasons for this is that some persons who did not commit a particular crime committed other serious offenses. Another reason is that some youths who did not commit a crime as of 1980 committed crimes after 1980. A third reason is that some youths presumably understated their criminal activity. Still, the table shows that the more involved youths were with crime in 1980, the more likely they were to have been incarcerated at some time. In one sense, the linkage between crimes reported in 1980 and ensuing incarceration provides a check on the reliability of 1980 reports of criminal involvement and suggests that the reports are reasonably valid, at least as indicators of differential criminal involvement.

To what extent does the chance of incarceration rise with the extent of criminal activities? I examine this question by estimating the relation between incarceration and a summary measure of criminal involvement: the number of crimes a youth committed.

The set of logistic regressions in table 5.5 shows that conditional on the other major determinants of incarceration, the number of crimes youths report significantly raises the chances that they are incarcerated at some point in the 1980s. In column (1) I enter the number of crimes as a linear variable, with a separate dummy for youths who commit no crimes. In column (2), I enter the number of crimes as a set of discrete dummy variables, with youths who commit crimes placed in the quartile of the distribution of crimes in which they fit. Here there is some evidence that the relation between the number of crimes and the chance of incarceration is nonlinear. The biggest impact of the number of crimes on the chance of incarceration comes between the top quartile and the third quartile. There are other ways to organize these data to explore the nonlinear relation between the extent of criminal involvement and ensuing imprisonment or other involvement with the criminal justice system,[12] but the basic result is clear: youths deeply involved in crime end up incarcerated whereas those less involved are more likely to avoid this outcome.

---

12. One way of looking for nonlinearity that does not work is to enter the squared number of crimes. Some youths commit so many crimes that the huge squared term produced obscures the basic nonlinear relation.

Table 5.5   **Logistic Curve Estimates of Effect of Numbers of Crimes and Illegal Share of Income on Ever Being Incarcerated**

Variable	(1)	(2)	(3)	(4)
Number of crimes	.010		.009	
	(.001)		(.001)	
No crimes				
Bottom quartile		.69		
		(.22)		
2d Quartile		.77		
		(.23)		
3d Quartile		1.25		
		(.22)		
Top quartile		1.98		
		(.22)		
Age	.22	.26	.22	.21
	(.04)	(.04)	(.04)	(.04)
Black	.29	.21	.22	.15
	(.14)	(.4)	(.15)	(.15)
AFQT score	−.017	−.019	−.018	−.015
	(.002)	(.002)	(.002)	(.002)
Weeks worked (1979)	−.020	−.021	−.020	−.020
	(.004)	(.004)	(.004)	(.004)
Years of schooling	−.199	−.204	−.186	−.206
(1980)	(.040)	(.040)	(.043)	(.043)
Share of illegal income			.81	1.86
			(.35)	(.30)
Summary statistics				
N	3,738	3,738	3,493	3,493
ln likelihood	−901	−889	−812	−839
Pseudo R^2	.170	.181	.171	.143

Source: Tabulated from the National Longitudinal Survey of Youth.

Note: Measure of number of crimes gives 50 for the top group, which reports 50 or more crimes. Numbers in parentheses are standard errors.

5.2.2   Crime and Work

Does engaging in criminal activity mean that a young person does not do any normal work, or do many young criminals combine crime and work? At one point, many social scientists and policy analysts viewed legal and illegal economic activities as mutually exclusive. The dividing line between making money from crime and making money from legal work was supposedly a sharp one. Many considered unemployment to be a major contributing factor to crime, and evidence that ex-offenders had lower employment rates than other workers suggested that many had made a permanent break with the legitimate job market. But there is no logical reason for an either/or relationship between crime and work. Several ethnographic studies suggest a blurring of distinctions between legal and

Table 5.6   **Percentage Employed in Survey Week in 1980 by Criminal Behavior of Out-of-School Nonmilitary Youth**

	Responses to Criminal Questions		Sample Sizes	
Criminal Activity	Yes	No	Yes	No
Admitted committing property crime	70.3	73.3	2,369	1,847
Reported positive illegal income	66.0	73.2	951	3,265
Charged with crime	58.6	71.5	744	3,279
Jail in following year	30.4	65.6	46	4,223

Source: Tabulated from the National Longitudinal Survey of Youth, with youths in school coded as missing. In these tabulations I have also excluded those in the military. Inclusion of youths in the military reduces the employment difference between those who reported crimes and those who did not (strengthening the argument in the text) but does not noticeably affect the difference in employment rates for those in jail the following year.

illegal work among disadvantaged youths (Sullivan 1989; Williams 1989; Padilla 1992; Adler 1985; Taylor 1990).

To see how much, if any, overlap exists between legal and illegal work in the NLSY, I have examined the work activity of persons who did and did not commit property crimes, which one would expect to be most negatively related to work. Table 5.6 records the employment status of young men according to four measures of criminal activity: admitted committing a property crime, earning illegal income, being charged with a crime, and ending up incarcerated in the following year. The sample is limited to out-of-school youths not involved in military service. There are differences in employment between those involved in crime and those not involved in crime, but they are relatively modest between those who committed and those who did not commit crime (3 percentage points) and between those with positive incomes from crime and those without such income (7 percentage points). The difference is larger but still not massive between those charged with crime and those not charged (13 percentage points). None of these differences support a crime-employment dichotomy. The only grouping that yields something close to that is between youths who end up incarcerated a year later and the rest of the sample—a 35 percentage point difference in employment.

Treating the decision to engage in crime as a dichotomous choice between legal and illegal work thus misses an important aspect of criminal activity. Because most offenders work outside of criminal organizations, and because the U.S. job market is characterized by considerable mobility and flexibility, it is easy to combine work with crime at a point in time or to move between the two activities over time. And many youths do this. One fruitful way to think about this type of behavior is to expand the concept of a reservation wage for work to allow for a reservation wage for legal work and a separate reservation wage for illegal work. Consider a youth who faces an opportunity to commit a crime—say, to help some drug dealer sell or deliver his wares. The youth must decide whether to engage in that activity. At some rate of pay, he will accept this opportunity—his reservation wage for crime. He may the very next day hear about a short-term low-paying legal job and decide to take it, as long as the wage exceeds his reservation wage for normal work.

In some sense, the youth "forages" in his neighborhood for income opportunities, legal or illegal, much as animals forage for food, making decisions in a short period of time whether to "prey" on a particular food source or to turn that prey down to search for better prey, whether to exploit opportunities in a given patch or to search for new opportunities, and so forth (Stephens and Krebs 1986).

The foraging model directs attention to the factors that determine differing reservation wages for legal and illegal money-making activities, which presumably depend on the risk associated with the activities and the moral sentiment, be it guilt or pride, that accompanies those activities, and to the factors that determine the legal and illegal opportunities that a youth encounters. Freeman (1992) shows that young men in inner city poverty areas encounter many illegal and legal opportunities in a relevant (and short) time period: McDonald's may be hiring this week, Jones Construction may need a laborer, robbers may need someone to fence stolen goods, an elderly woman may wander along the wrong street, a car with an expensive stereo system may be parked in an alley, and so forth. In a world where short-run legal and illegal earnings opportunities arrive more or less randomly, it is natural for individuals to move between them, commit crimes while working, or take a legitimate job when available without giving up less time-intensive criminal pursuits. If this hypothesis is correct, and the behavior of crime-prone youths is similar to that of foraging animals rather than to that of adults with permanent careers, the supply of youths to crime will be quite elastic with respect to the number of criminal opportunities (and thus possibly to police presence in crime-intensive areas) or to the relative rewards from crime as opposed to legal work.

How might we examine the elasticity of youth to crime? In its 1980 crime module the NLSY asked youths the proportion of their income that came from illegal sources. I use responses to this question to assess the possible responsiveness of youths to economic incentives to commit crime. Let w be the legal wage, H the hours spent on legal work, i the wage from illegal work, and C the hours spent at crime, so that the share of income from illegal sources ($ILLSHARE$) is $Ci/(Ci+wH)$. The share of income from illegal sources has five nonzero values: very little (to which I assign the value .05), about a quarter (.25), about half (.50), about three-quarters (.75), and almost all (.95). Using this numeric scale the variable has a mean value of .17 for out-of-school youths who said that they made illegal income. Conditional on C and H, the share of income from illegal sources will vary with the relative rewards to crime i/w. A 10 percent increase in the relative rewards from crime will raise the proportion of income from illegal sources by about 8 percent. NLSY data on weeks worked in 1979 provide a measure of H while data on the number of crimes committed in the past year provide a measure of C.[13] Then the following equation provides some notion of the responsiveness of youth criminal behavior to economic incentives:

(1)   Prob(*Incarceration*) $=$ $a + b$ *ILLSHARE* $+ c$ *Weeks Worked*

$+ d$ *NUMCRIMES*.

Columns (3) and (4) of table 5.5 present logistic estimates of equation (1) for young out-of-school men in the NLSY. In column (3), where I enter both the number of crimes committed and the percentage of income that is illegal, the estimated logit coefficient of .81 on the illegal share of income variable suggests that an increase in the share of illegal income of, say, 0.10 percentage points would raise the proportion of youths ending up incarcerated by somewhat less than 1 percentage point, which is fairly substantial given that it takes many crimes to get a youth incarcerated. In column (4), I drop the number of crimes from the regression on the argument that decisions to engage in crime depend not only on the relative money rewards of crime but also on the number of criminal opportunities that face young people, which is reflected in the number of crimes committed. Because the number of crimes and the share of income from illegal sources are closely linked, the result is a large increase in the estimated effect of illegal earnings on future incarceration—a coefficient of 1.8. Given the crudity of the data and model, I would not put much weight on any of the specific estimated response parameters in the table. What the NLSY data show is that the proportion of income from crime is positively related to future incarceration in a way that is consistent with significant responsiveness of young men to the relative economic rewards from crime.

5.3   Who They Are and What They Do: Prison and Jail Inmate Surveys

Surveys of inmates in prisons and jails provide an alternative source of information on the characteristics of young criminals. These surveys have several advantages over the NLSY: They cover persons who have unquestionably committed serious crimes and provide detailed data on the criminal activity of these persons. They ask questions about family background that standard labor surveys do not ask and gather information about work

---

13. Since different crimes take different amounts of time, and since for some crimes the amount of time taken is very fuzzy, this is only a crude control.

Table 5.7   Percentage of Prison and Jail Inmates, by Characteristic

	Male Prisoners, 1991		Jail Inmates, 1996
Characteristic	Ages 18–24	Ages 25–34	
Personal			
Black	51	49	41
Noncitizen	5	5	8
Less than high school graduate	80	66	51[a]
High school graduate	16	23	35
More than high school graduate	4	10	14
Married	8	18	16
Have children	44	62	
Parental family			
When growing up lived mostly with both parents	30	42	40
Lived in foster home	11	9	14
Parents abused drugs	8	4	8
Parents abused alcohol	25	27	30
Physically/sexually abused	13	17	13[b]
Parent served time	12	7	17
Brother/sister served time	30	35	36
Any family member served time	37	38	46

Source: Tabulated from U.S. Department of Justice (1993, 1998).
[a]For comparability I report those who finished high school, excluding persons who earned GEDs or high school equivalencies.
[b]For comparability this is for males only.

activity prior to the arrest that led to incarceration. The 1991 prison inmate survey asked, in addition, a battery of questions about the activities of friends of the prisoners. The disadvantage of inmate surveys is that they do not contain information on the comparison group of nonincarcerated young persons.

Table 5.7 summarizes the personal and family characteristics of young men aged 18–24 and 25–34 from the 1991 prison inmate survey and the characteristics of all inmates in jail from the 1996 survey of jail inmates.[14] Some of the results mirror those found in the NLSY. The panel on personal characteristics shows that prisoners are disproportionately black and disproportionately high school dropouts. Jail inmates are somewhat

14. At this writing the Bureau of Justice Statistics has not yet reported results from the 1996 *Survey of State Prison Inmates* or made the data files publicly available. It has reported some results from the 1996 *Profile of Jail Inmates,* though the data files are not yet available for analysis. Thus I have patched together my analysis of the 1991 *Survey of State Prison Inmates* with the Bureau of Justice Statistics report on the 1996 *Profile of Jail Inmates.*

less likely to be black or to be high school dropouts, but these groups are still overrepresented in jail. In addition, while relatively few prisoners are married, a substantial number have children: 44 percent of the 18–24-year-old prisoners and 62 percent of the 25–34-year-old prisoners. The panel on parental background characteristics shows that relatively few prisoners grew up in a two-parent family. In 1991 just 30 percent of the 18–24-year-old prisoners and 42 percent of the 25–34-year-old prisoners report that when they were growing up, they lived mostly with both parents, while just 40 percent of jail inmates report that they lived mostly with both parents. These statistics compare to approximately 72 percent of all youngsters living with both parents.[15] Roughly one in ten of those in prison and one in seven of those in jail lived in a foster home or institution at one time. Eight percent of the 18–24-year-old prisoners and 8 percent of jail inmates report that their parents abused drugs, but just 4 percent of 25–34-year-old prisoners report drug abuse by their parents. These differences potentially reflect the rising use of drugs over time. Over a quarter of all the groups in table 5.7 report that their parents abused alcohol.

What is particularly striking, however, is that 13 to 17 percent of male prisoners report that they had been physically or sexually abused, mostly before age 18, and presumably by relatives. Child maltreatment is a significant social problem, but as best as I can tell, the rate of victimization of children in the country as a whole falls far short of these figures. In 1995 the rate of victimization of young persons under age 18 was approximately 1.5 percent, with an estimated 80 percent of the perpetrators being the parents of the victims (U.S. Department of Health and Human Services 1998, 1). While it is possible that 1.5 percent in a given year could cumulate to a double-digit figure close to that for the prisoners, the likelihood is much higher that many child abusers are repeat abusers, so that 1.5 percent in a given year cumulates to something far short of 13 to 17 percent. This is consistent with the stress that many criminologists place on the role of childhood experiences, particularly child abuse (Widom 1991), as a determinant of youth criminal behavior.

Finally the table shows that criminal behavior has a strong family component. Twelve percent of 18–24-year-old prisoners, 7 percent of 25–34-year-old prisoners, and 17 percent of jail inmates report that a parent had served time. Roughly a third reported that a brother or sister had served time. Taken together, nearly half of the jail inmates said that some family member had been incarcerated at one point. This remarkable statistic highlights the extent to which criminal behavior runs in families, for rea-

---

15. Men aged 18–24 in 1990 were in the parental home from roughly 1970 to 1990; those aged 25–34 were in the parental home from roughly 1965 to 1980. In 1970, 64 percent of black families had two parents; in 1980, 48 percent; and in 1990, 39 percent. The proportion for the total population varied from 87 percent in 1970 to 69 percent in 1990.

Table 5.8   Income and Work of Prison Inmates Prior to Incarceration (percent)

	Ages 18–24	Ages 25–34
Held job month before arrest	60	72
Work full time	79	87
Work part time	21	13
No job month before arrest	40	28
Looking for work	52	57
Not looking for work	48	43
Most important reason not looking		
Illegal activity	31	23
Drugs/alcohol	10	19
Total income year before arrest ($)		
0–4,999	45	31
5,000–7,499	13	11
7,500–9,999	8	9
10,000–14,999	13	19
15,000–24,000	10	18
25,000–49,000	5	8
50,000	6	5
Mean[a]	11,150	13,525
Admitted getting income from illegal		
sources	30	21
Amount of income from illegal		
sources		
Most of it	73	58
Some of it	16	21
Very little of it	11	21
Have children	44	62
Have children month before arrest		
and supported child	26	38
Family supported by welfare		
Before arrest	43	46
After arrest (now)	53	53

Source: Tabulated from U.S. Department of Justice (1993). The survey gives several figures on receipt of income from illegal sources. The figure in the table is based on variable 896: how much income from illegal sources.

[a]Calculated by using the median value in each category, except for the top category, which was assigned $50,000.

sons of genetic predisposition, or upbringing, or most likely some mixture thereof.

Table 5.8 summarizes these data for male prisoners aged 18–24 and 25–34 in 1991. The data on employment in the month before arrest provide further support for the claim that the boundary between legal and illegal work is quite porous. Some 60 percent of 18–24-year-old prisoners and 72 percent of 25–34-year-old prisoners reported that they held a job in the month prior to their arrest, with the vast majority holding a full-time job. A similar pattern is found in data on jail inmates for 1996: 64 percent of inmates report holding a job prior to arrest, largely (77 percent) full-time jobs (U.S. Department of Justice 1998, 3). Both of these figures fall short of the employment rates for similarly aged men—an employment rate of 74 percent for nonincarcerated men who are not enrolled aged 16–24[16] in the late 1980s and an employment rate of 88 percent for men aged 25–34—but they still decisively reject the old dichotomous view of legal and illegal work. In addition, over one-half of the prison inmates and jail inmates who did not have a job in the month before they were arrested were looking for work. Among the prison inmates who said that they were neither working nor looking for work, 31 percent of the 18–24-year-olds and 23 percent of the 25–34-year-olds said that they were not looking for work because they were involved in illegal activity. This group constitutes about 5 percent of the prisoner population and gives a crude estimate of the proportion for whom the old dichotomy holds.

The income figures in the table show that inmates report relatively low income for the year prior to their arrest. Most 18–24-year-old prisoners had yearly incomes below $7,500 and most 25–34-year-old prisoners had incomes below $10,000. Jail inmates also reported low prearrest personal incomes, with 46 percent earning less than $600 per month. While low, these incomes are not "off the map" of the U.S. income distribution. In 1989, for example, just 17 percent of U.S. men aged 25–34 reported money income less then $10,000. Overall, the income of prisoners puts them in the lower third of the income distribution of similarly aged men in the United States.

Only a minority of prisoners said that they made income from illegal sources. As this is inconsistent with the fact that most have been arrested for property crimes, I am dubious of these figures. For what it is worth, the majority of those who admitted that they got income from illegal activities said it was the bulk of their income.

5.3.1   Social Interactions?

Social interaction models posit that individual behavior depends not only on the incentives facing the individual but also on the behavior of the individual's peers or neighbors. These models predict that with the same expected return from crime, a young person may be more likely to commit crimes if his peers commit crimes than if they do not commit crimes. His decision, in turn, affects their behavior. When the reservation wage for crime by individuals is influenced by the behavior of others in this manner, one gets a "behavioral multiplier" that can blow up elasticities of individual responses.

Ethnographic evidence on the role of youth gangs in crime suggests that social interaction models have some empirical validity. Gangs are an important social institution in the United States. The 1995 National Youth Gang Survey reported that over 665,000 young Americans were in gangs

---

16. Tabulated from U.S. Bureau of the Census (1990, table 633).

(Moore 1996). Much illegal work is organized within ethnic gangs that combine economic and cultural interests, often in very narrow geographic areas. In Boston, for instance, virtually all youth gangs are found in an area of 1.7 square miles, about 4 percent of the city's area (Kennedy, Piehl, and Braga 1996). The Rochester Youth Study found that gang members commit a disproportionate share of serious crimes and that youths commit twice as many crimes when they are gang members than when they are not (Thornberry and Christenson 1984). Taylor (1990) and Padilla (1992) stress the importance of money in inducing young blacks and Latinos into gangs and crime. Drug-selling groups function as economic units with management structures oriented toward the maintenance of profitability and efficiency.

Table 5.9 summarizes information from the 1991 prison inmate survey on youth gangs and the social groups with whom young criminals are involved. The upper panel of the table shows the proportions of inmates aged 18–24 and 25–34 who said that their friends were involved in various criminal activities. Two-thirds of the 18–24-year-old prisoners and over half of 25–34-year-old prisoners said that they had friends who did some illegal act. Roughly half of their friends used drugs, and sizable numbers engaged in a wide variety of criminal acts. The fact that criminals report having friends engaged in crime does not show that social interactions are a potentially important contributor to criminal behavior. But it is consis-

Table 5.9   Percentage of Prisoners Whose Friends Engage in Illegal Activities and Percentage of Prisoners Who Are Gang Members

	Ages 18–24	Ages 25–34
Has friends who		
Do some illegal act	66	55
Use drugs	49	47
Damage property	27	20
Fight	40	26
Shoplift	22	22
Steal motor vehicle	27	20
Fence stolen goods	29	25
Break into homes	27	23
Sell drugs	19	32
Mug or rob	18	13
Characteristics of gangs inmates joined		
Formal membership	12	8
Leader	15	10
Common clothing	18	9
Group name	17	9
Members from area	40	30
Have turf	25	15

Source: Tabulated from U.S. Department of Justice (1993).

tent with such an interpretation. Finally, the lower panel of table 5.9 focuses more narrowly on gang membership and activity. It shows a larger proportion of younger inmates than of older inmates were members of gangs and gives some of the characteristics of the gangs themselves.

5.4 The Payoff to Reducing Youth Involvement in Crime

The United States responded to the crime wave of the late 1960s to mid-1980s by massively increasing the number of persons incarcerated. Since incarceration is expensive, a natural question is whether such an expensive policy for controlling crime pays off. The answer to the question hinges on the marginal cost of crime to society, the marginal reduction in crime due to incarceration, and the cost of incarceration.

Estimates of the average cost of crime, much less of the marginal cost, are difficult to make. The National Crime Victimization Survey estimates direct monetary losses due to crimes by asking victims to estimate losses from theft or damage, medical expenses, and pay loss due to injury. The 1992 estimates were that the average burglary cost $834, the average auto theft $3,990, the average robbery $555, and so on (Klaus 1994). The average crime nominally cost victims 3.4 days of working time. The total economic loss to victims of crime, including medical costs and lost work time, was estimated to be $532 per crime, or $17.6 billion for all reported crimes in 1992.

But these figures do not cover the nonpecuniary costs of crime in the form of the misery created for victims. Some criminologists have estimated a more inclusive cost of crime, based on jury evaluation of nonpecuniary costs (Cohen 1988). These estimates are rough. Jury cases may involve greater misery than other victimizations. Some estimates include the lost legitimate earnings of incarcerated criminals, which may affect the well-being of spouses or children; others exclude earnings, on the argument that the criminal consumes most of those earnings (Levitt 1995). None include the suffering of the families of criminals or the cost to taxpayers of providing subsidies for families where the male earner is incarcerated. Miller, Cohen, and Rossman (1994) stress the medical cost of injuries to victims, including psychological problems. All of these estimates exceed reported monetary losses by massive amounts. For example, the estimated average pain and suffering and cost of risk of death created by a robbery is approximately 11 times the direct monetary loss (Cohen 1988, table 3). Estimates of the cost of pain, suffering, and economic loss for the average crime are on the order of $2,300 (DiIulio and Piehl 1991) to $3,000 (Levitt 1995).[17]

---

17. Levitt (1995) reports $45,000 as the estimated cost per criminal and estimates that criminals commit 15 crimes per year, for the $3,000 estimate that I use.

Estimating the marginal reduction in crime associated with increased incarceration is more problematic. Most analyses are based on the incapacitative effect of incarceration. The analyst multiplies estimates of the average cost per crime by an estimate of the number of crimes committed per criminal to obtain costs per criminal. In incapacitation models, the value of locking up someone is the number of crimes he or she would have committed, so the social benefit of putting the criminal in prison or jail is simply the cost of crimes committed per criminal. Using an estimated 180 crimes per criminal, Zedlewski (1987) found that the benefits of imprisonment exceeded the costs of imprisonment by 17 to 1. But 180 crimes per criminal is at the upper end of estimates of crimes committed by prisoners and almost certainly exceeds the number of crimes committed by marginal offenders.[18] At more moderate estimates of crimes per criminal, the benefit-cost ratio falls greatly. For instance, if each criminal committed 15 crimes per year, Zedlewski's (1987) benefit-cost ratio would fall to 1.4:1. Using estimates of the distribution of crimes per criminal, DiIulio and Piehl (1991) have shown that the benefit-cost ratio of incarceration exceeds one at the median number of crimes per criminal but falls below one for those in the lower quartile or so of the distribution of crimes. They conclude that the costs of crime are high enough to justify incarceration of offenders at current U.S. levels, though perhaps not at much greater levels. Since incarcerating an additional person costs society $20,000,[19] the marginal prisoner must cost society a similar amount of money. Given costs per crime of $2,000 to $3,000, incapacitating someone who commits 10 or so crimes a year passes their benefit-cost test.

Estimates of the marginal effect of incarceration on crime based on an incapacitation model should, however, be viewed cautiously. The incapacitation model ignores both labor supply responses to criminal opportunities (the replacement of one criminal with another, which will lower the marginal reduction in crime due to incarceration) and the deterrent effect of incarceration on crime (which will raise the marginal reduction in crime due to incarceration) and thus can be misleading.[20] Still, the studies of the social value of incarceration provide a useful benchmark for assessing

18. There are definitional problems with the number of crimes that prisoners and others report. If you sell drugs ten times, should this be counted as ten crimes or as one?

19. In 1993, $25 billion were spent on corrections. With 1.14 million persons in prison or jail in that year, the average cost is $22,000 per person. Annual current operating expenditures for prisoners are on the order of $15,000 (DiIulio and Piehl 1991). Estimates of the amortized value of prisons are on the order of $4,000 to $5,000 (Cavanaugh and Kleiman 1990, table 2). The annual operating costs and amortized construction costs thus also come out around $20,000.

20. That the biases are in opposite directions is mildly reassuring. Both Marvell and Moody (1994) and Levitt (1995) have examined the effect of increased incarceration on crime using aggregate data that should embody the replacement and deterrent effects. Levitt exploits the fact that overcrowding of prisons forced some states to let some prisoners out early, while Marvell and Moody exploit the fact that increases in crime do not show up quickly in increased prison populations. Both find that incarceration reduces crimes noticeably.

other crime prevention programs. Assume that the analyses are roughly right, so that on average the social benefit of incarceration exceeds the social cost, while the marginal benefit roughly equals the marginal cost. Given that incarceration is extremely costly, the implication is that any modestly effective crime prevention program focused on crime-prone disadvantaged youths should have a high social payoff. Society benefits from any crime prevention program in two ways: through the value of the reduction in crime and through the savings in the cost of incarcerating the criminal later. If we could make contracts with potential criminals to forgo crime or devise policies to train them or to subsidize their employment so that they would forgo crime, we would be willing to spend the $20,000 or so that they cost society and the $20,000 or so that it costs us to incarcerate them—or $40,000 per potential criminal. In fact, the favorable benefit-cost assessments of some social programs—such as the Job Corps or the Ypsilanti Perry Preschool Program—hinge critically on large estimated savings in criminal justice expenses due to reduced crime by participants.

To be sure, society cannot offer large sums to any takers who promise they will not commit crimes, but since so much crime is committed by disadvantaged young men, highly targeted programs could pass benefit-cost tests even if a substantial portion of the funds went to disadvantaged youths who would not have committed crimes in any case. For instance, if 50 percent of inner city black male high school dropouts are likely to commit crimes and end up incarcerated, a program that spent $4,000 per youth and reduced the proportion who committed crime to 40 percent would just pay off. The reduction in crime would save $2,000 per youth and the reduction in incarceration would save $2,000 per youth.[21] While I know of no "magic bullet" job or crime prevention program, meta-analyses show that the average juvenile delinquency program has some modest deterrent effect (Lipsey 1992), which given the likely modest cost could readily justify expanding the resources of such programs. In short, the high costs of crime and incarceration imply a potentially large payoff to finding programs that effectively deter some at-risk young men from crime, be they employment subsidies, job training programs, increased policing, or whatnot. If incarceration pays off, so too does any modestly effective crime prevention program.

References

Adler, Patricia. 1985. *Wheeling and dealing: An ethnography of an upper-level dealing and smuggling community.* New York: Columbia University Press.

---

21. Since the reduction in incarceration is due solely to the reduction in crime, the deterrent effect of incarceration remains the same in this situation.

Cavanaugh, David P., and Mark A. R. Kleiman. 1990. A cost benefit analysis of prison cell construction and alternative sanctions. Cambridge, Mass.: BOTEC Analysis Corp., June.

Center for Human Resource Research. 1979–88. *National longitudinal surveys of youth.* Columbus: Ohio State University, Center for Human Resource Research.

Cohen, Mark A. 1988. Pain, suffering, and jury awards: A study of the cost of crime to victims. *Law and Society Review* 22 (3): 537–55.

DiIulio, John, and Anne Piehl. 1991. Does prison pay? *Brookings Review* 9 (4): 29–35.

Fox, James Alan. 1996. *Trends in juvenile violence.* Washington, D.C.: Department of Justice, March.

Freeman, Richard B. 1992. Crime and the employment of disadvantaged youth. In *Urban labor markets and job opportunity,* ed. George Peterson and Wayne Vroman. Washington, D.C.: Urban Institute.

———. 1996. Why do so many young American men commit crime and what can we do about it? *Journal of Economic Perspectives* 10 (1): 25–42.

Grogger, Jeffrey. 1997. Market wages and youth crime. NBER Working Paper no. 5983. Cambridge, Mass.: National Bureau of Economic Research, March.

Hindelang, M. J., T. Hirschi, and J. Weis. 1981. *Measuring delinquency.* Beverley Hills, Calif.: Sage.

Kennedy, David M., Anne M. Piehl, and Anthony A. Braga. 1996. Youth violence in Boston: Gun markets, serious youth offenders, and use reduction strategy. *Law and Contemporary Problems* 59, no. 1 (winter): 147–96.

Klaus, Patsy. 1994. The costs of crime to victims. Crime Data Brief. Washington, D.C.: Department of Justice, February.

Levitt, Steven. 1995. The effect of prison population size on crime rates: Evidence from prison overcrowding litigation. Cambridge, Mass.: Harvard University, February.

Lipsey, Mark W. 1992. Juvenile delinquency treatment: A meta-analytic inquiry into the variability of effects. In *Meta-analysis for explanation,* ed. T. D. Cook et al. Beverly Hills, Calif.: Sage.

Maguire, Kathleen, and Ann L. Pastore, eds. 1997. *Sourcebook of criminal justice statistics, 1996.* Washington, D.C.: Government Printing Office.

Marvell, Thomas, and Carlisle Moody. 1994. Prison population growth and crime reduction. *Journal of Quantitative Criminology* 10 (2): 109–40.

Miller, Ted R., Mark A. Cohen, and Shelli B. Rossman. 1994. Victim costs of violent crime and resulting injuries. *Health Affairs* 12:186–97.

Moore, J. P. 1996. The 1995 youth gang survey. Report to the OJJDP. Tallahassee, Tenn.: National Youth Gang Center.

Padilla, F. 1992. *The gang as an American enterprise.* New Brunswick, N.J.: Rutgers University Press.

Sickmund, Melissa, Anne Stahl, Terence Finnegan, Howard Snyder, Rowen Poole, and Jeffrey Butts. 1998. *Juvenile court statistics.* Washington, D.C.: Office of Juvenile Justice and Delinquency Prevention.

Stephens, David W., and John R. Krebs. 1986. *Foraging theory.* Princeton, N.J.: Princeton University Press.

Sullivan, Mercer. 1989. *Getting paid: Youth crime and work in the inner city.* Ithaca, N.Y.: Cornell University Press.

Taylor, C. 1990. Gang imperialism. In *Gangs in America,* ed. C. Ronald Huff, 103–15. Newbury Park, Calif.: Sage.

Thornberry, Terence, and R. L. Christenson. 1984. Unemployment and criminal involvement: An investigation of reciprocal causal structures. *American Sociological Review* 56:609–27.

U.S. Bureau of the Census. 1990. *Statistical abstract of the United States.* Washington, D.C.: Government Printing Office.

U.S. Department of Health and Human Services. Administration for Children and Families. 1998. *The scope and problem of child maltreatment: Highlights of findings,* accessible through the ACF website: http://www.acf.dhhs.gov/programs/cb/ncanprob.htm (July).

U.S. Department of Justice. Office of Justice Programs. Bureau of Justice Statistics. 1993. *Survey of state prison inmates, 1991.* Washington, D.C.: Bureau of Justice Statistics.

————. 1994a. *Profile of inmates in the U.S. and in England and Wales, 1991.* Washington, D.C.: U.S. Government Printing Office, October.

————. 1994b. *Young black male victims,* by Lisa D. Bastian and Bruce M. Taylor. Washington, D.C.: Department of Justice, December.

————. 1995. *Drugs and crime facts, 1994.* Rockville, Md.: Department of Justice, June.

————. 1997a. *Juveniles prosecuted in state criminal courts,* by Carol J. DeFrances and Kevin J. Strom. Washington, D.C.: Department of Justice, March.

————. 1997b. *Lifetime Likelihood of going to state or federal prison,* by Thomas P. Bonczar and Alan J. Beck. Washington, D.C.: Department of Justice, March.

————. 1998. *Profile of jail inmates, 1996.* NCJ 164620. Washington, D.C.: Bureau of Justice Statistics, April.

————. Various years. *Uniform crime reports of the United States.* Washington, D.C.: U.S. Government Printing Office.

Widom, Cathy Spatz. 1991. *Child abuse, neglect, and violent criminal behavior in a Midwest metropolitan area of the United States, 1967–1988.* Ann Arbor, Mich.: Inter-University Consortium for Political and Social Research.

Williams, Terry. 1989. *The cocaine kids: The inside story of a teenage drug ring.* Reading, Mass.: Addison Wesley.

Zedlewski, Edwin. 1987. Making confinement decisions. Washington, D.C.: Department of Justice.

Child Development and Success or Failure in the Youth Labor Market

Paul Gregg and Stephen Machin

6.1 Introduction

Economic success or failure in the early years of adulthood is the outcome of a number of potentially complex interactions involving an individual's development as a child, family background, school experience, and the state of the labor market. In this chapter we consider the determinants of relative success in the initial years of working life, focusing specifically on the associations that disadvantages in the childhood years have with later economic outcomes. We use a large unique cohort database of British individuals to examine a range of issues to do with child development and subsequent outcomes (mostly economic, though broader social outcomes are also to be considered in places).

The basic idea of the paper is, first, to try to pin down the factors associated with childhood disadvantage. We try to do so by using data on detailed characteristics of the families in which children grow up and on child-specific factors such as school attendance, staying on at school, and

Paul Gregg is a programme director at the Centre for Economic Performance at the London School of Economics. He is also a member of the Council of Economic Advisers and Her Majesty's Treasury. Stephen Machin is professor of economics at University College London and director of the Industrial Relations Programme at the Centre for Economic Performance, London School of Economics.

The authors thank the Joseph Rowntree Foundation for financial support. They are grateful to John Abowd, David Blanchflower, Richard Freeman, John Hills, Peter Robinson, Jonathan Thomas, participants in the Konstanz and Winston-Salem conferences and in seminars at the Centre for Economic Performance (LSE), the Centre for Labour Market Studies (Aarhus), the University of Newcastle, and the Norwegian School of Economics and Business Administration (Bergen) for comments and suggestions. They also thank Susan Harkness for help with the National Child Development Study data and Tanvi Desai and David Wilkinson for producing the Labour Force Survey tabulations reported in the paper.

contact with the police. We use these variables to characterize individuals' childhood experiences into classifications that suggest whether or not they may be at some kind of disadvantage at age 16.[1] We choose to focus on two groups of measures, the first based on family circumstances in the years of childhood, the second based on child-specific individual behavioral attributes.

We then go on to relate measures of economic success at later ages (e.g., going on to higher education, higher wages, or being in work) and failure (spells of unemployment or poor educational attainment) as a function of these childhood factors. Our empirical analysis is based on the National Child Development Study (NCDS), a survey of all individuals born in a week of March 1958 that currently contains detailed information (from parents, schools, nurses, and the cohort members themselves) at ages zero, 7, 11, 16, 23, and 33. Because the data source follows a cohort of people through time it allows us to adopt a sequential modeling approach in which we build up progressively more detailed econometric models as we sample individuals at older ages. This enables us to fix initial conditions (by effectively standardizing the characteristics of individuals at an early age) and then to identify the transmission mechanisms that underpin the determinants of economic success or failure in adulthood.

The remainder of the paper is structured as follows. Section 6.2 sets the scene by briefly describing trends in the youth labor market in Britain, using annual cross sections from the Labour Force Survey from the mid-1970s onward. Section 6.3 uses NCDS data to estimate individual-level models of the determinants of age 16 economic and social outcomes. We then define various measures of juvenile delinquency or disadvantaged backgrounds that we use as independent variables in the models of relative success or failure at ages 23 and 33. These models are presented in sections 6.4 (age 23) and 6.5 (age 33). As already noted, we are interested in the transmission mechanisms that may underpin any link with success or failure, and therefore, because we view educational attainment as a key potential transmission mechanism, we report models that do and do not condition on highest educational qualification (by age 23). We do this because we are interested in whether delinquency and disadvantage variables have an impact over and above education or whether it is simply that delinquents and the disadvantaged do worse because of their massively lower educational attainment. We also try to identify whether disadvantaged individuals who invest in education at later ages have any scope to catch up with their counterparts who obtained educational qualifications at earlier ages. In the last part of section 6.5 we also introduce an intergenerational

---

1. Other work focuses specifically on child disadvantage in terms of children living in poor families or those dependent on welfare: an excellent up-to-date survey of (mostly American) work is given in Currie (1995). For a recent study of trends in child poverty and the evolution of the income distributions of families with and without children in Britain, see Gregg, Harkness, and Machin (1999).

aspect to our analysis by considering the relation between the early age cognitive skills of children of NCDS cohort members and the childhood disadvantage status of the cohort member. Finally, section 6.6 concludes.

6.2   Trends in the British Youth Labor Market

In this section we provide a background description of trends in labor force and student status among young British individuals from the Labour Force Survey (LFS).[2] Up to (and including) 1991 the LFS was an annual survey carried out each spring that covered individuals in a sample of about 60,000 responding households.[3] From 1992 it became a quarterly survey, with a longitudinal component. We define two age cohorts of youths to examine the state of the youth labor market between 1975 and 1995. The two age cohorts are defined (by date of birth) to cover school year cohorts aged 16/17 (one year after the compulsory school leaving age) and aged 18/19 (one year after individuals would have taken A levels).[4] So the first year of data matches with our NCDS cohort of individuals, who if they left at the compulsory school leaving age, would have left school in the summer of 1974.

Table 6.1 reports labor force and schooling status for the full populations of the two age cohorts between 1975 and 1995.[5] Labor force status is broken down into three categories, employed, unemployed, and inactive (where employed includes individuals participating in government training schemes), and given the increased likelihood of students' combining student and work status in recent years, student status is defined as whether an individual carried on full time in the educational system after O and A levels broken down by working and not working (after 1984, when information on this first became available).

The numbers in table 6.1 make it very clear that the youth labor market has changed dramatically since the 1970s. There is a very clear rise in staying on rates, coupled with a massive decline in employment as an individual's sole labor market state. And while unemployment displays a cyclical pattern there is a persistent rise in inactivity rates. For example, in 1975, 61 percent of male 16/17-year-olds were employed while 34 percent

---

2. See Blanchflower and Freeman (1996) for an international comparison of the evolution of youth labor markets across the OECD.

3. From 1983 to 1991 the survey was conducted annually. Before that (starting in 1975) it was carried out once every two years.

4. The "standard" pattern of schooling in Britain is that individuals take ordinary level ("O" level) exams in their last year of compulsory schooling when aged 15/16 and then advanced level ("A" level) exams two years after that, when aged 17/18.

5. As is well known, the relative sizes of these cohorts, in terms of their shares in the working age population, shifted over this time period. In 1975, 2.5 percent of the working age population was in the age 16/17 cohort. This share rose and peaked at 2.9 percent in 1981 and then fell continuously to 1.9 percent by 1995. For the age 18/19 cohort the percentage was 2.3 in 1975, which rose and peaked at 2.7 percent in 1985 and then fell to 2.0 percent by 1995.

Table 6.1   Labor Force Status and Staying on in Education for British Youths, 1975–95

First Year after O Levels: 16/17-Year-Olds

| | Males (%) | | | | | Females (%) | | | | |
| | | | | Student | | | | | Student | |
Year	Employed	Unemployed	Inactive	Not Working	Working	Employed	Unemployed	Inactive	Not Working	Working
1975	60.5	4.8	0.4	34.2	n.a.	52.7	5.4	3.3	38.5	n.a.
1977	55.8	6.4	0.7	37.1	n.a.	46.0	6.5	2.7	44.9	n.a.
1979	58.0	5.5	1.0	35.6	n.a.	50.7	5.0	2.9	41.4	n.a.
1981	50.5	15.4	1.9	32.2	n.a.	47.1	13.5	4.4	35.0	n.a.
1983	48.2	13.2	2.6	36.0	n.a.	40.6	8.2	3.6	47.6	n.a.
1984	47.6	10.8	2.5	39.1	n.a.	40.4	8.7	3.4	47.6	n.a.
1985	48.9	8.6	2.9	30.4	9.4	40.1	7.0	5.2	30.4	17.3
1986	47.8	8.6	2.7	29.8	11.2	38.3	7.9	6.8	29.4	17.6
1987	46.1	9.2	3.0	29.4	12.2	40.5	6.3	5.0	30.2	18.0
1988	48.6	7.8	2.9	26.5	14.2	40.6	6.1	4.8	27.5	21.0
1989	51.2	5.1	3.1	26.5	14.2	37.8	5.3	4.5	30.6	21.8
1990	45.5	6.5	2.5	28.4	17.1	34.5	3.5	4.3	32.0	25.7
1991	40.3	7.4	2.6	31.6	18.2	29.8	5.8	3.4	34.5	26.5
1992	30.5	7.4	3.7	37.0	21.4	24.0	4.9	5.1	39.2	26.9
1993	30.1	5.5	4.2	44.2	16.0	19.1	5.2	4.0	45.8	26.0
1994	24.7	6.1	3.0	43.3	22.9	21.3	4.3	4.3	43.6	26.5
1995	26.0	6.3	2.6	43.2	22.0	21.0	3.6	4.4	39.8	31.2

First Year after A Levels: 18/19-Year-Olds

Year										
1975	76.8	7.0	0.7	15.4	n.a.	69.1	6.1	11.3	13.6	n.a.
1977	78.0	7.1	1.5	13.4	n.a.	70.6	6.7	10.2	12.5	n.a.
1979	79.7	5.3	1.3	13.7	n.a.	72.7	5.9	10.9	10.5	n.a.
1981	69.2	16.9	2.6	11.3	n.a.	65.2	12.2	11.4	11.4	n.a.
1983	61.7	20.6	3.8	13.9	n.a.	60.8	14.9	11.0	13.3	n.a.
1984	61.2	22.3	4.2	12.3	n.a.	55.2	17.0	15.3	12.6	n.a.
1985	63.9	17.3	5.7	10.7	2.4	60.0	14.2	13.7	9.2	2.9
1986	63.1	18.0	6.2	10.5	2.1	59.8	13.2	14.3	9.4	3.2
1987	63.6	17.5	5.5	10.3	3.1	64.5	11.4	10.0	9.4	4.6
1988	66.6	14.4	5.4	10.1	3.5	63.0	9.4	13.5	9.9	4.3
1989	68.9	11.0	5.5	10.6	4.1	64.5	8.6	12.8	9.6	4.5
1990	67.3	9.9	5.8	12.0	5.0	61.2	8.1	13.0	10.9	6.7
1991	57.8	15.1	5.0	15.1	7.0	59.7	8.8	13.2	11.3	7.0
1992	51.0	13.5	6.5	21.6	7.4	49.2	8.7	13.0	20.2	9.0
1993	45.6	15.7	5.8	24.9	8.0	42.3	9.1	12.8	26.1	9.6
1994	43.9	12.9	5.8	27.0	10.3	39.7	7.2	12.8	27.3	12.9
1995	42.8	10.7	5.2	28.9	12.5	41.9	6.6	12.2	26.0	13.3

Source: Labour Force Survey.
Note: n.a. = data not available.

stayed on in education. By 1995, only 26 percent were in employment and 65 percent stayed on. For women aged 16/17 the pattern is even more marked: in 1975, 53 percent were employed and 39 percent stayed on; by 1995, only 21 percent were in work and a massive 71 percent stayed on. Around half of the rise in staying on after 1985 was from people combining study and (normally part time) employment.[6]

The same kind of pattern is observed for the older, age 18/19 cohort. Employment rates fell sharply between 1975 and 1995: by 34 percentage points (from 77 to 43 percent) for males and by 27 percentage points (from 69 to 42 percent) for females. Looking at those who stayed on in higher education after A-level age illustrates the magnitude of the expansion of the educational system: for men 15 percent stayed on in 1975, while by 1995 this more than doubled to 41 percent; for women the staying on rate also more than doubled, going from 14 percent in 1975 to 39 percent by 1995. At the same time, simultaneously combining work and study seems even more relevant for this older cohort in the 1990s.

The data described in table 6.1 clearly demonstrate that large changes in the educational system and in the youth labor market occurred between the 1970s and 1990s. The higher educational system greatly expanded, as is made evident by the sharp rise in staying on rates for both age cohorts.[7] At the same time the employment rates of teenagers fell very sharply, with about a quarter (fifth) of male (female) 16/17-year-olds and about 40 percent of male and female 18/19-year-olds being employed in 1995. Also, despite the expansion of the educational system, male unemployment rates (while displaying a cyclical evolution) were higher by 1995 than in the 1970s and male inactivity among youths rose very sharply. On the whole, it seems that women did better than men, but that the youth labor market displayed a growing polarization between the 1970s and 1990s, with far more individuals going on to higher education, but this trend was mirrored by a rise in nonemployment (especially for men). These trends, and the gender differences they suggest, are important to bear in mind in the analysis that follows.

6.3 Models of Economic and Social Outcomes at Age 16

6.3.1 Data Description

The National Child Development Study is an ongoing survey of all persons born between 3 and 9 March 1958. To date, follow-up surveys of the participants have occurred in 1965 (NCDS1), 1969 (NCDS2), 1974

6. See Robinson (1994) for more details on changes in the educational system in the United Kingdom.

7. The bulk of the increase took place after 1989, following the introduction of a new examination system (the General Certificate of Secondary Education—GCSE) that was first relevant to students sitting for examinations in the summer of 1989.

(NCDS3), 1981 (NCDS4), and 1991 (NCDS5). NCDS1 to NCDS3 include interviews with the parents of the children involved on a wide range of topics concerning the background, environment, health, and education of the child. These are backed up by questionnaires given to the child's school and the child. NCDS4 and NCDS5 are based on detailed interviews with the subjects themselves (by then aged 23 and 33, respectively). For our purposes, the data are an extremely rich source that allows us to model youth labor market outcomes as a function of children's development through environmental, parental, and individual-specific factors.

6.3.2   Modeling Approach

We begin by modeling age 16 outcomes so as to try to isolate factors that are associated with being in a less advantaged position at that age.[8] We will then, in the subsections that follow, use these classifications to see the extent to which being in a disadvantaged position at age 16 is associated with various economic and social outcomes at later ages (ages 23 and 33). These models build up in a sequential manner, and we implement our estimation procedure as essentially a block recursive system that builds up by age (i.e., identification comes from the aging of the cohort).

The general form of the initial econometric model we intend to estimate treats an outcome measure for youths as a function of various individual, parental, and environmental factors. We consider three age 16 outcomes:

school attendance in the autumn term of the last year of school (age 15/ 16), which comes from school records and is defined as the proportion of possible half-days attended by the cohort member = (number of possible half-day attendances − number of half-day absences)/number of possible half-day attendances,
contact with the police, which comes from the question "Has the child ever been in contact with the police or probation office?" and
staying on at school after the compulsory school leaving age.[9]

The NCDS is an extremely useful data source for analyzing the determinants of these outcomes because it contains very rich information on individuals as they grow up. We are able to specify a fairly rich set of independent variables that go back to the earlier years of an individual's life.

We choose to model the three outcomes as a function of the characteristics of individuals and their families at various points in time. As was noted above NCDS interviews took place at ages zero, 7, 11, and 16, so we prefer to split the cohort members' childhood development into an early stage and a late stage. Given the survey construction we take the

---

8. The compulsory school leaving age in Britain is 15/16 years depending on date of birth—given that respondents were all born in March 1958 it would be age 16 for the cohort we study.

9. See also Micklewright (1989) for an analysis of staying on at age 16 using the NCDS3 data.

former to be age 7 and before and the latter to be between ages 7 and 16 (these can be loosely thought of as preschool and during-school timings).

In terms of our modeling strategy we then estimate our first-stage econometric models for cohort member i of the form.[10]

$$Y_i^{\text{age 16}} = \Gamma_1 X_i^{\text{pre 16}} + \varepsilon_1,$$

where Y^{age16} is the appropriate age 16 outcome under consideration and X^{pre16} is a set of childhood factors as follows: (1) age 7 individual-specific characteristics—ethnicity, age 7 cognitive skills (measured by math and reading test scores), indicators of illness and behavioral problems,[11] and whether the child was classified as an educational special needs child; (2) parental educational status; (3) the pre-7 and age 7–16 outcomes of interest. In our empirical models these outcomes are the following: whether the child was living in a lone-mother family, whether the father figure was unemployed at the survey date, whether the family was in financial difficulties in the year prior to the survey date,[12] whether the child has ever been in care.

We prefer to think of the inclusion of the variables in items 1 and 2 as fixing what we might call the "initial conditions" (i.e., standardizing the characteristics of individuals at an early age) so that we can then follow a sequential modeling approach as individuals grow older. Put alternatively, we are interested in the relation between our age 16 outcomes and the variables in item 3 above in models that hold constant these initial conditions.

6.3.3   Descriptive Statistics

Table 6.2 reports some simple descriptive statistics on the age 16 outcomes. They are reported separately for male and female cohort members, as are all the empirical models that we present. Mean school attendance for males was .88 and for females was .87 in autumn 1973, and there are clear differences for both sexes in terms of childhood characteristics: school attendance is lower for children of lower age 7 ability, for children who have ever been in care, and for those from families with less educated

10. Notice that the subscript "1" attached to the parameter vector and the error term is there simply to denote that this is the first stage in our sequential modeling approach.

11. The illness variables correspond to the age 15/16 school year and are included in the school attendance and staying on models to ensure that we are not classifying children as low school attendance individuals or poor school performers if they are ill. The behavioral problem variable are defined from the following eight "syndrome" scores given in NCDS: unforthcomingness, withdrawal, depression, anxiety, hostility toward adults, anxiety for acceptance by children, restlessness, and "inconsequential" behavior. They are entered into the empirical models as 0/1 dummies indicating positive scores on one, two or three, and four or more of the eight measures (with no positive scores being the reference group).

12. To be precise the age 11 and 16 questions on family financial difficulties related to the previous year, but at age 7 the question referred to the child's early years.

Table 6.2   Age 16 Outcomes and Child and Family Characteristics

Characteristic	School Attendance	Sample Size	Contact with Police/Probation	Sample Size	Stay on at School	Sample Size
			Males			
All individuals	.883	6,381	.108	5,995	.289	6,267
White	.895	4,759	.100	4,708	.303	4,449
Nonwhite	.891	203	.130	200	.355	141
Bottom quintile of age 7 reading test	.829	1,288	.171	1,209	.080	1,248
Top quintile of age 7 reading test	.926	944	.081	896	.567	928
Bottom quintile of age 7 math test	.855	1,027	.139	944	.117	987
Top quintile of age 7 math test	.916	1,223	.082	1,129	.476	1,236
Ever in care	.841	277	.388	304	.123	244
Never in care	.886	5,960	.093	5,688	.295	5,884
Father left school aged 15 or less	.876	3,739	.121	4,455	.207	3,522
Father left school after age 15	.937	1,047	.052	1,233	.600	987
Mother left school aged 15 or less	.876	3,860	.121	4,615	.207	3,615
Mother left school after age 15	.934	1,054	.056	1,238	.597	994
Ever in lone-mother family	.847	731	.181	747	.202	636
Never in lone-mother family	.888	5,514	.097	5,248	.298	5,497
Father ever unemployed	.812	492	.203	528	.152	447
Father never unemployed	.890	5,753	.096	5,467	.299	5,686
Family ever in financial difficulties	.817	1,111	.204	1,151	.126	982
Family never in financial difficulties	.898	5,080	.084	4,826	.320	5,101

(continued)

Table 6.2 (continued)

Characteristic	School Attendance	Sample Size	Contact with Police/Probation	Sample Size	Stay on at School	Sample Size
			Females			
All individuals	.866	6,135	.038	5,696	.289	6,270
White	.880	4,622	.037	4,702	.299	4,436
Nonwhite	.879	174	.027	152	.364	121
Bottom quintile of age 7 reading test	.792	818	.062	747	.081	790
Top quintile of age 7 reading test	.910	1,300	.029	1,229	.496	1,386
Bottom quintile of age 7 math test	.824	1,134	.059	1,041	.122	1,103
Top quintile of age 7 math test	.899	970	.032	913	.480	1,056
Ever in care	.813	228	.664	231	.175	223
Never in care	.869	5,968	.032	5,459	.292	5,910
Father left school aged 15 or less	.862	3,626	.043	4,224	.207	3,522
Father left school after age 15	.927	1,003	.013	1,180	.565	982
Mother left school aged 15 or less	.859	3,721	.042	4,340	.215	3,584
Mother left school after age 15	.928	1,054	.022	1,239	.563	1,024
Ever in lone-mother family	.815	725	.064	747	.186	683
Never in lone-mother family	.895	5,282	.034	4,949	.300	5,461
Father ever unemployed	.787	499	.063	506	.141	466
Father never unemployed	.874	5,508	.035	5,790	.300	5,678
Family ever in financial difficulties	.780	1,109	.074	1,100	.128	1,057
Family never in financial difficulties	.887	4,867	.029	4,583	.321	5,050

Source: National Child Development Study, waves 1, 2, and 3 (at ages 7, 11, and 16).

Note: Ever/never refers to any of age 7, 11, or 16.

parents, from lone-mother families, or from families where fathers were unemployed at the survey date. It is also considerably lower for individuals whose families reported being in financial difficulties during the childhood years. The same pattern holds for females.

In terms of whether cohort members had ever been in contact with the police or probation services, the mean is (not surprisingly) higher for males than females, and the qualitative pattern of differences across characteristics is broadly the inverse of the school attendance breakdown.

Finally, the third outcome of interest, whether the cohort member stayed on at school, is the same on average for males and females, and for both sexes, the breakdown by characteristics is displays a similar qualitative pattern to the school attendance variables and the converse pattern to the police/probation contact variable. Staying on at school is higher for higher ability children, for children who have never been in care, for children from more educated parents, and where the family has not had financial difficulties or not suffered from father's unemployment or lone-mother status.

6.3.4   Econometric Estimates

A number of the patterns in the raw data remain statistically significant in the econometric models reported in table 6.3, which reports Tobit models of school attendance (as there is upper censoring at complete school attendance equal to one) and probit models of police/probation contact and staying on at school. For males "good" outcomes, higher school attendance or staying on at school, are more likely with higher reading ability (staying on is also more likely for children with higher math ability). Better school performance (i.e., better attendance or staying on) at this stage is also more likely for those whose parents stayed on at school after age 15. It is also more likely for children who live in families without financial difficulties (in early or late childhood) or who have never been in a lone-mother family or had an unemployed father. These last three variables are strongly related to one another, and in the models we report the financial difficulty variable seems to dominate: leaving it out of the specification, however, produced much stronger effects of living in a lone-mother family or having an unemployed father (and this was true in all the models of table 6.3). We take this strong interrelation into account when we move on to characterizing children into disadvantaged states below.

Turning to the "bad" outcome variable, whether the child had been in contact with the police or probation services, it is reassuring that the effects of the independent variables largely go in the opposite direction. Better reading ability (for males) and math ability (for females) are associated with less police contact. Whether the child was in care during the childhood years has a very strong positive association with police contact as does whether the family was in financial difficulties during the child's years of growing up.

Table 6.3   **Estimates of the Determinants of Age 16 Outcomes**

Characteristic	School Attendance (Tobit)	Contact with Police/Probation (probit)	Stay on at School (probit)
	Males		
Constant	.995 (.010)	−1.981 (.113)	.022 (.097)
Individual characteristics			
Nonwhite	−.003 (.012)	.029 (.127)	.129 (.126)
2d Lowest quintile of math test scores (age 7)	−.000 (.007)	.102 (.078)	−.036 (.077)
Middle quintile of math test scores (age 7)	−.015 (.008)	.160 (.082)	.129 (.075)
2d Highest quintile of math test scores (age 7)	−.010 (.008)	.165 (.085)	.186 (.076)
Highest quintile of math test scores (age 7)	−.008 (.008)	.249 (.091)	.315 (.076)
2d Lowest quintile of reading test scores (age 7)	.025 (.007)	−.073 (.071)	.174 (.074)
Middle quintile of reading test scores (age 7)	.047 (.007)	−.156 (.079)	.448 (.074)
2d Highest quintile of reading test scores (age 7)	.069 (.008)	−.206 (.086)	.748 (.075)
Highest quintile of reading test scores (age 7)	.068 (.008)	−.384 (.097)	1.035 (.078)
Behavioral response 1	−.015 (.006)	.043 (.074)	−.105 (.054)
Behavioral response 2/3	−.022 (.006)	.234 (.066)	−.207 (.053)
Behavioral response 4	−.025 (.007)	.435 (.072)	−.324 (.068)
Ever educational special needs	.015 (.011)	−.077 (.110)	−.269 (.129)
Ever sick in last school year, minor ailments	−.095 (.005)		−.351 (.052)
Ever sick in last school year, more serious ailments	−.124 (.008)		−.303 (.082)
Family structure and parental characteristics			
Ever in care	−.004 (.011)	.814 (.084)	−.276 (.122)
Father left school aged 15 or less	−.036 (.007)	.257 (.074)	−.612 (.055)
Mother left school aged 15 or less	−.023 (.007)	.191 (.072)	−.633 (.055)
Lone-mother family at child age 7	−.011 (.012)	.050 (.122)	−.097 (.127)
Lone-mother family at child age 11 or 16	−.016 (.008)	.120 (.074)	.010 (.078)
Father unemployed at child age 7	−.043 (.015)	.035 (.140)	−.210 (.196)
Father unemployed at child age 11 or 16	−.026 (.009)	.057 (.083)	−.078 (.096)
Family in financial difficulties at child age 7	−.039 (.010)	.279 (.089)	−.474 (.122)
Family in financial difficulties at child age 11 or 16	−.042 (.007)	.254 (.062)	−.232 (.071)
Proportion censored (Tobit)/mean proportion (probit)	.161	.108	.289
Log likelihood	1,264.17	−1,845.58	−2,974.84
Sample size	6,381	5,995	6,267

Table 6.3 (continued)

Characteristic	School Attendance (Tobit)	Contact with Police/Probation (probit)	Stay on at School (probit)
	Females		
Constant	.978 (.011)	−2.532 (.166)	−.140 (.101)
Individual characteristics			
Nonwhite	.020 (.014)	−.338 (.242)	.288 (.130)
2d Lowest quintile of math test scores (age 7)	.013 (.007)	−.178 (.108)	.137 (.071)
Middle quintile of math test scores (age 7)	−.003 (.008)	−.109 (.109)	.311 (.070)
2d Highest quintile of math test scores (age 7)	−.003 (.008)	−.263 (.124)	.312 (.071)
Highest quintile of math test scores (age 7)	.004 (.009)	−.057 (.124)	.530 (.073)
2d Lowest quintile of reading test scores (age 7)	.026 (.008)	.027 (.119)	.100 (.088)
Middle quintile of reading test scores (age 7)	.043 (.009)	.085 (.126)	.318 (.086)
2d Highest quintile of reading test scores (age 7)	.057 (.009)	.112 (.128)	.544 (.085)
Highest quintile of reading test scores (age 7)	.070 (.009)	.188 (.134)	.826 (.086)
Behavioral response 1	−.009 (.006)	.335 (.091)	−.124 (.049)
Behavioral response 2/3	−.023 (.007)	.371 (.097)	−.140 (.059)
Behavioral response 4	−.017 (.008)	.460 (.115)	−.357 (.085)
Ever educational special needs	−.024 (.015)	.324 (.160)	.196 (.156)
Ever sick in last school year, minor ailments	−.098 (.005)		−.363 (.047)
Ever sick in last school year, more serious ailments	−.132 (.008)		−.435 (.074)
Family structure and parent characteristics			
Ever in care	−.012 (.012)	.702 (.113)	−.071 (.112)
Father left school aged 15 or less	−.023 (.007)	.375 (.117)	−.503 (.054)
Mother left school aged 15 or less	−.037 (.007)	.070 (.100)	−.583 (.053)
Lone-mother family at child age 7	−.002 (.013)	.032 (.163)	−.148 (.125)
Lone-mother family at child age 11 or 16	−.023 (.008)	.047 (.107)	−.136 (.078)
Father unemployed at child age 7	−.052 (.016)	.085 (.209)	.100 (.162)
Father unemployed at child age 11 or 16	−.016 (.009)	−.054 (.117)	−.194 (.096)
Family in financial difficulties at child age 7	−.053 (.010)	.159 (.121)	−.343 (.108)
Family in financial difficulties at child age 11 or 16	−.059 (.007)	.258 (.087)	−.238 (.068)
Proportion censored (Tobit)/mean proportion (probit)	.121	.038	.289
Log likelihood	1,361.30	−829.88	−3,103.87
Sample size	6,135	5,696	6,270

Note: Behavioral response variables are based on eight sets of teacher-reported answers to questions about interactions between the cohort member and adults and other children (see n. 11 in the text). Scores 1, 2/3, and 4 denote a score for one set, two or three, and four or more of the eight scores indicating behavioral difficulties. Numbers in parentheses are standard errors.

In table 6.4 we illustrate the relative magnitude of these effects by computing school attendance, police contact, and staying on on probabilities for a base group individual and then examining deviations from the base. These are of interest because they give some indication of the relative magnitude of the estimated effects. They also let us combine the effects of more than one variable in our examination of the deviations from the base set of characteristics (as in the last two rows of the table). The largest positive effect on school attendance comes from higher age 7 reading ability and on staying on rates from better reading and math ability at age 7 for both males and females: for example, the second to last row of the table combines the two effects, showing that being in the highest quintile of both raises staying on rates by a huge .406 over the base for males and .444 for females. On the down side the most negative effects on school attendance are from growing up in a family facing financial hardship, and the same is true for staying on rates, along with a strong negative effect from low parental education. The last row of the table highlights this pattern, showing that school attendance is .099 and .136 points lower than the base and the staying on rate is .482 and .409 points lower than the base for males and females who grew up in families with low parental education that faced financial difficulties during the childhood years. Finally, contact with the police or probation services is much higher for children who have ever been in care, at .098 higher than the .024 base for males and .028 higher than the .006 base for females. Children growing up in families with low parental education that had financial difficulties during the childhood years are also much more likely to have contact with the police (with positive deviations of .134 and .042 for males and females, respectively).

6.3.5   Characterizing Delinquency and Disadvantage

For the remainder of the paper we require some measures of delinquency and disadvantage that we can use as independent variables in our models of success or failure at later ages. To ensure that the analysis is manageable and to facilitate a clear interpretation of the reported effects we choose two sets of variables as measures. The first set consists of variables based on individual behavioral attributes that we stylize as juvenile delinquency, and the second consists of measures based on family circumstances that we stylize as describing disadvantaged social background in the years of childhood.

We model juvenile delinquency in terms of school attendance and contact with the police. First, we define a variable for low school attendance that equals one if school attendance is less than or equal to .75 (unless the child was ill, in which case we do not code the child as low attendance). Second, we consider the dummy variable indicating whether the individual has been in contact with the police. We use these two variables to characterize individuals who have delinquent tendencies at age 16.

Table 6.4   Variations in Age 16 Predicted Outcomes

Characteristic	Males			Females		
	School Attendance	Contact with Police/Probation	Stay on at School	School Attendance	Contact with Police/Probation	Stay on at School
Base individual[a]	.853	.024	.509	.841	.006	.444
Deviations from base						
Nonwhite	−.001	+.001	+.050	+.010	−.004	+.114
Top quintile of math test scores	−.003	+.018	+.123	+.002	−.002	+.208
Top quintile of reading test scores	+.018	−.015	+.346	+.025	+.004	+.310
Ever in care	−.001	+.098	−.109	−.006	+.028	−.027
Father left school aged 15 or less	−.019	+.018	−.232	−.013	+.010	−.184
Mother left school aged 15 or less	−.012	+.013	−.239	−.022	+.001	−.209
Lone-mother family at child age 7	−.005	+.003	−.039	−.001	+.000	−.057
Lone-mother family at child age 11 or 16	−.010	+.007	+.003	−.013	+.001	−.053
Father unemployed at child age 7	−.024	+.002	−.086	−.033	+.001	+.040
Father unemployed at child age 11 or 16	−.013	+.003	−.032	−.009	−.001	−.075
Family in financial difficulties at child age 7	−.021	+.020	−.186	−.033	+.003	−.129
Family in financial difficulties at child age 11 or 16	−.023	+.018	−.092	−.038	+.006	−.091
Top quintile of math and reading test scores	+.017	−.007	+.406	+.026	+.002	+.444
Father and mother left school aged 15 or less, family in financial difficulties at child age 7, 11, or 16	−.099	+.134	−.482	−.136	+.042	−.409

Note: Derived from Tobit and probit models in table 6.3.

[a]The base individual is white, lowest quintiles of test scores, never in care, father and mother left school after age 15, never in lone-mother family, father never unemployed, never in family with financial difficulties, not sick in last school year, and behavioral response score of zero.

We model childhood disadvantage on the basis of the ways in which the family-based measures enter the age 16 equations discussed above. Four particular variables are considered: whether the cohort member was ever placed in care during his or her childhood, whether the family was ever in financial difficulties, whether the cohort member ever lived in a lone-mother family, and whether the cohort member's father was unemployed at any of the age 7, 11, and 16 interview dates.

Because of the clear overlap among the last three variables in terms of their correlations with age 16 outcomes we enter the financial difficulty variable directly but then define two dummies for the lone-mother and father unemployed variables conditional on not having financial difficulties. That is, the actual variables entered into the econometric model are (1) ever lived in a lone-mother family but without facing financial difficulties and (2) ever had an unemployed father without facing financial difficulties. This is because, as noted above, when they coincide the financial difficulty variable and the lone-mother family and father unemployed variables tend to capture similar effects in the reported regressions. We define the variables in this particular way because the financial difficulty variable seems to dominate in the table 6.3 models.

Of course, there are clear issues associated with characterizing children and their families in this rather coarse way, but because we intend to examine a large number of outcomes at different ages, we require some parsimony in our approach. We have, however, estimated fuller specifications, and it is reassuring that for the most part, our classifications seem to parameterize the concepts of age 16 delinquency and disadvantage relatively well.

6.4   Models of Economic and Social Outcomes at Age 23

In this section we treat a variety of age 23 outcomes as functions of our measures of juvenile delinquency and social disadvantage.[13] We begin by considering educational attainment and then go on to look at economic and social outcomes in models that do and do not condition on education. We choose to do the following as it is of interest whether or not any significant correlations are affected by netting out educational achievement.

6.4.1   Age 23 Educational Attainment

Table 6.5 breaks down age 23 educational attainment by the juvenile delinquency and social disadvantage variables. Educational attainment is measured by a ninefold ordered ranking of educational qualifications ranging from no educational qualifications to a degree or higher (see the

---

13. See also some early work using the NCDS up to age 23 by Elias and Blanchflower (1987) and the more recent study by Kiernan (1995). Blanchflower and Elias (1993) also examine some of the economic outcomes that we consider here in their work on NCDS twins.

Table 6.5   Age 23 Educational Qualifications and Age 16 Delinquency and Social Disadvantage

Characteristic	Sample Size	No Qualification	Lower Academic	Lower Vocational	Intermediate Vocational	Intermediate Academic	Advanced Vocational	Advanced Academic	Higher Vocational	Higher Academic
Males										
All	6,267	.257	.014	.018	.022	.280	.163	.057	.081	.109
School attendance < .75 (and not ill)	264	.606	.034	.023	.038	.208	.049	.008	.023	.011
Contact with police/probation	463	.477	.026	.024	.052	.242	.123	.015	.030	.011
Ever in care	244	.520	.008	.033	.025	.238	.094	.016	.033	.033
Family ever in financial difficulties	982	.458	.014	.024	.030	.275	.097	.024	.043	.035
Ever in lone-mother family (but no financial difficulties)	331	.254	.024	.024	.024	.317	.151	.066	.054	.085
Father ever unemployed (but no financial difficulties)	183	.279	.022	.044	.016	.311	.164	.055	.060	.049
Females										
All	6,270	.298	.023	.012	.007	.368	.060	.051	.088	.093
School attendance < .75 (and not ill)	261	.663	.023	.011	.023	.211	.011	.008	.038	.012
Contact with police/probation	162	.525	.025	.012	.000	.296	.049	.012	.049	.031
Ever in care	223	.547	.013	.013	.000	.251	.067	.022	.054	.031
Family ever in financial difficulties	1,057	.535	.017	.016	.005	.304	.023	.023	.052	.026
Ever in lone-mother family (but no financial difficulties)	348	.305	.026	.009	.000	.376	.055	.043	.089	.098
Father ever unemployed (but no financial difficulties)	174	.356	.017	.017	.006	.368	.046	.023	.069	.098

Note: The educational attainment variable is defined as: 0 = no qualifications; 1 = lower academic (certificates of secondary education, no O levels); 2 = lower vocational/other; 3 = intermediate vocational (craft qualifications, apprenticeships); 4 = intermediate academic (O levels only); 5 = advanced vocational (national or general certificate or diploma/ordinary national certificate); 6 = advanced academic (A levels only); 7 = higher vocational (higher national certificate/higher national diploma, teaching, nursing); 8 = higher academic (degree or higher degree).

note to the table for the precise definitions). The table makes it very clear that in the raw data, our groups of interest do much worse in terms of educational attainment. For example, in the full sample 26 percent of males have no educational qualifications, while the same is true of 61 percent of males with low school attendance and 48 percent of males who had been in contact with the police or probation services in their adolescent years. Young men with no educational qualifications are also overrepresented in the disadvantaged family groups, with the percentages for men being 52 percent of those who have ever been in care and 46 percent of those from poor families. Things are better in the lone-mother and father unemployed cases in the absence of family financial difficulties, where the percentages are 25 and 27 percent, respectively. For females the contrast is equally stark with delinquent and disadvantaged females having much higher probabilities of having no educational qualifications.

The picture is equally bleak for higher levels of educational attainment. At the upper end of the educational spectrum about 11 and 9 percent of men and women, respectively, have a degree or higher qualification. Hardly any of the low school attendance individuals possess a degree, and with the exception of the lone-mother (no financial difficulties) group, the percentages with a degree are much lower for the delinquency and disadvantage groups.

We can now move to stage two in our modeling procedure. If we define the delinquency measures as $DELINQ_i$ and the family disadvantage measures as $DISADV_i$ this involves estimating educational attainment equations of the form:

$$ED_i^{\text{age }23} = \alpha_2 + \beta_2 DELINQ_i + \psi_2 DISADV_i + \Gamma_2 X_i^{\text{pre }16} + \varepsilon_2,$$

where $ED^{\text{age}23}$ is the age 23 educational attainment variable (and the subscript "2" denotes that we are now at stage two in our sequential modeling procedure).

Table 6.6 reports ordered probit estimates of educational attainment equations. It reports six specifications, three each for males and females, which differ in which of the $DELINQ$, $DISADV$, and $X^{\text{pre}16}$ variables are included. We basically build the specifications up, first looking at the correlation between $ED^{\text{age }23}$ and the $DISADV$ variables (i.e., setting $\beta = \Gamma_2 = 0$), then entering the $X^{\text{pre}16}$ variables, and finally including the $DELINQ$ variables.

It is clear from table 6.6 that the main thrust of the results holds for both groups as the estimated specifications are qualitatively very similar for males and females and there is a strong linkage between worse educational achievement and delinquency or disadvantage among this cohort of British young adults. Even after conditioning on the pre-16 variables.[14]

14. Of the pre-16 variables it is very clear that (in results nor reported here, but available on request) doing better on tests administered to NCDS children at age 7 leads to higher

there remains a strongly negative association between age 23 educational attainment and age 16 juvenile delinquency or social disadvantage for males and females.

The bottom of the table converts the ordered probit coefficient estimates on the key dummy variables of interest into marginal effects. These are defined as

$$\Pr[ED = j \mid D = 1] - \Pr[ED = j \mid D = 0]$$
$$= \Phi(X\theta + \tau_j + \Theta) - \Phi(X\theta + \tau_j)$$

for the ordered educational variable ED, which is modeled as a function of a set of control variables X with associated coefficients θ, a threshold parameter τ_j and a dummy independent variable D with an estimated coefficient Θ ($\Phi(\cdot)$ is the standard normal distribution function, and we evaluate it at the sample means of the X variables). This can be interpreted as the ceteris paribus impact of D on the probability of being in a given educational qualification category.

The reported marginal effects are sizable. Males with low school attendance or who had been in contact with the police or probation services are 11 and 8 percentage points less likely to be in the higher academic category and 17 and 10 percentage points more likely to have no educational qualifications as compared to the other NCDS cohort members (for females comparable marginal effects are 8 and 4 percentage points for degrees or higher and 23 and 9 percentage points for no qualifications).

Growing up in a socially disadvantaged background characterized by ever being placed in care renders males 6 percentage points less likely to have a degree and 6 percentage points more likely to have no educational qualifications (from the fullest specification). For females comparable figures are −3 and 6 percentage points. Finally, being in a family facing financial difficulties during the childhood years has a strong effect, even when all other delinquency and disadvantage variables and the $X^{pre\ 16}$ variables are included. The marginal effects here correspond to a 7 (5) percentage point lower probability of being in the top educational group and a 7 (10) percentage point increased chance of being in the bottom group for males (females).

Despite the coarseness of our measures of disadvantage these results are striking. Educational attainment by age 23 is very strongly hampered by child development factors, and children growing up in relatively disadvantaged situations have strikingly worse levels of educational attainment.

---

educational attainment, because being in a higher quintile of the age 7 math or reading score distribution strongly raises the probability of having a higher educational qualification by age 23. There is also a strong relation between educational attainment and whether one's parents left school at the compulsory school leaving age. Estimated coefficients on dummy variables for whether an individual's father or mother left school at age 15 or less are significantly negative in all cases.

Table 6.6   Models of Educational Attainment at Age 23

Variable	Males			Females		
	(1)	(2)	(3)	(4)	(5)	(6)
Low school attendance			-.699 (.054)			-.733 (.054)
Contact with police/probation			-.448 (.057)			-.322 (.096)
Ever in care	-.590 (.075)	-.360 (.078)	-.286 (.079)	-.454 (.079)	-.283 (.083)	-.234 (.084)
Family ever in financial difficulties	-.672 (.039)	-.450 (.041)	-.348 (.041)	-.731 (.039)	-.452 (.041)	-.358 (.042)
Ever in lone-mother family (but no financial difficulties)	-.204 (.060)	-.178 (.061)	-.139 (.062)	-.134 (.060)	-.133 (.061)	-.100 (.062)
Father ever unemployed (but no financial difficulties)	-.307 (.080)	-.253 (.081)	-.235 (.082)	-.255 (.084)	-.183 (.087)	-.123 (.087)
Age 7 controls and parental characteristics	No	Yes	Yes	No	Yes	Yes
Log likelihood	-11,219.10	-10,319.16	-10,165.62	-10,204.05	-9,219.37	-9,073.99
Sample size	6,267	6,267	6,267	6,270	6,270	6,270

Pr[ED = 8|Low school attendance = 1] − Pr[ED = 8|Low school attendance = 0]			−.111			−.078
Pr[ED = 0|Low school attendance = 1] − Pr[ED = 0| Low school attendance = 0]			.172			.225
Pr[ED = 8|Police/probation = 1] − Pr[ED = 8|Police/probation = 0]			−.080			−.041
Pr[ED = 0|Police/probation = 1] − Pr[ED = 0|Police/probation = 0]			.095			.087
Pr[ED = 8|Care = 1] − Pr[ED = 8|Care = 0]	−.090	−.059	−.055	−.066	−.030	−.032
Pr[ED = 0|Care = 1] − Pr[ED = 0|Care = 0]	.199	.091	.060	.159	.090	.063
Pr[ED = 8|Financial difficulties = 1] − Pr[ED = 8|Financial difficulties = 0]	−.109	−.075	−.067	−.104	−.048	−.048
Pr[ED = 0|Financial difficulties = 1] − Pr[ED = 0|Financial difficulties = 0]	.226	.116	.074	.276	.155	.103

Note: These are ordered probit coefficient estimates where the dependent variable is the ordered educational attainment variable defined in table 6.5. All models include X^{prel6} as defined in the text. Numbers in parentheses are standard errors.

As such, education must play a potentially important role as an intermediating factor, or transmission mechanism, that may underpin any association with economic success or failure. We now consider this explicitly in models of age 23 economic and social outcomes.

6.4.2   Age 23 Economic and Social Outcomes

For male NCDS cohort members we consider four economic and social outcomes at age 23:

In hourly wages if in employment in 1981,
unemployment time since age 16, defined by a count of the number of months spent unemployed,
probability of being in employment in 1981, and
whether an individual has ever had a spell of prison or borstal (since age 16).

For female NCDS cohort members we consider four outcomes, the first three being the wage, unemployment time, and employment outcomes listed for males and the fourth outcome being:

whether a female cohort member was a lone mother by age 23.

These variables enable us to consider a relatively wide range of outcomes (from higher wages through prison attendance for males and through lone motherhood for females) in our search for factors that shape relative success or failure in the early years of adulthood.

Table 6.7 reports descriptive statistics for the economic and social outcomes for all NCDS cohort members and broken down by the delinquency and disadvantage variables. In these raw data descriptions hourly wages and the probability of being employed are lower than average in almost all cases. On the other hand, time spent unemployed since age 16 and the probability of having had a prison or borstal spell (for males) or being a lone mother (for females) are higher in almost all cases. There is some variation across the different groups, with low school attendance being strongly associated with lower wages and employment and higher unemployment. Also, ever being placed in care during the childhood years and being in contact with the police or probation services between ages 10 and 16 are associated with much higher incidence of prison or borstal spells for men.

Again following our modeling strategy of building up progressively more detailed models as the individuals age, the age 23 models we estimate are of the following form:

$$ Y_i^{\text{age 23}} = \alpha_3 + \beta_3 DELINQ_i + \psi_3 DISADV_i + \Gamma_3 X_i^{\text{pre 16}} + \Omega_3 ED_i^{\text{age 23}} + \varepsilon_3, $$

where Y^{age23} denotes the relevant age 23 economic or social outcome variable.

Table 6.7   Age 23 Outcomes and Age 16 Juvenile Delinquency and Social Disadvantage

Characteristic	Hourly Pay	Unemployment Time	Pr[Employment]	Pr[Prison] for Males; Pr[Lone Mother] for Females
		Males		
All	2.710	4.707	.861	.011
Low school attendance	2.496	10.788	.723	.042
Police/probation	2.610	9.309	.767	.050
Ever in care	2.562	10.734	.721	.074
Ever in financial difficulties	2.595	8.746	.773	.025
Ever in lone-mother family (no financial difficulties)	2.707	5.849	.855	.009
Father ever unemployed (no financial difficulties)	2.647	6.497	.780	.016
		Females		
All	2.380	3.614	.661	.080
Low school attendance	2.051	7.388	.467	.199
Police/probation	2.022	6.086	.438	.191
Ever in care	2.215	6.009	.511	.170
Ever in financial difficulties	2.243	5.757	.485	.163
Ever in lone-mother family (no financial difficulties)	2.416	3.448	.678	.075
Father ever unemployed (no financial difficulties)	2.161	5.011	.618	.080

Table 6.8 reports models of the determinants of age 23 outcomes. For each outcome four specifications are reported, the first three being the same as the education models in table 6.6, plus a further specification that enters age 23 educational attainment. In some sense this is a key distinction because we are interested in models that set either set $\Omega_3 = 0$ or estimate Ω_3 along with the other parameters of the model. The reason for doing this is that we are interested in the role that educational attainment may play as a transmission mechanism, and some information on this can be gleaned from considering models that do and do not condition on educational attainment.

The first part of table 6.8 reports least squares estimates of wage equations, Tobit estimates of the determinants of unemployment time (as there is censoring at zero), and probit models of employment and prison or borstal status for male cohort members. The overall picture that emerges is one that shows a marked relation between delinquency and disadvantage and economic and social outcomes. What is also clear is that educational attainment acts as an important transmission mechanism because an important part of the association is usually wiped out by including the education variable (if coefficients in cols. [3] and [4] and witness the fall in the absolute value of the estimated effects). Nevertheless, some important associations with the delinquency and disadvantage results remain intact (and significant in most cases). The main exception to this is the wage results, but we would argue that looking at wages at age 23 is probably too early in the life cycle to identify any important effects—this is borne out when we consider the age 33 results below. For females, all four outcomes are significantly worse for most of the delinquency and disadvantage variables (except for the lone-mother and father unemployed variables, whose effects are more mixed) and remain so (albeit smaller) once one controls for education.

Looking in a little more detail, the quantitatively most important effects in the models that control for educational attainment are the following: poor school attendance is associated with about five months more of unemployment between ages 16 and 23 for both men and women; individuals growing up in a family facing financial difficulties have about five months (males) and three months (females) more of unemployment and joblessness rates about 6 percent higher for both sexes; being in contact with the police or probation services results in much lower employment probabilities (5 percent for men, 13 percent for women) and significantly higher probabilities of a prison or borstal spell for men (the marginal effect is .016) and lone motherhood for women (the marginal effect is .045).

It is also interesting that table 6.8 shows that conditioning on education reduces the estimated coefficients by somewhere up to 50 percent (the "typical" reduction is probably about a third). As these estimated models include the early age "ability"-related measures (what we earlier called the

Table 6.8   Models of Attainment by Age 23

A. Males

Variable	(1)	(2)	(3)	(4)
	Ln Hourly Wage: Least Squares			
Low school attendance			-.011 (.023)	.028 (.023)
Police/probation			-.010 (.025)	.011 (.024)
Ever in care	-.049 (.034)	-.009 (.034)	-.009 (.034)	.006 (.034)
Family ever in financial difficulties	-.035 (.018)	-.015 (.018)	-.013 (.018)	.005 (.018)
Ever in lone-mother family (but no financial difficulties)	.010 (.027)	.011 (.027)	.009 (.028)	.015 (.027)
Father ever unemployed (but no financial difficulties)	-.035 (.038)	-.029 (.038)	-.029 (.038)	-.017 (.038)
Age 7 controls and parental education	No	Yes	Yes	Yes
Controls for age 23 educational qualifications	No	No	No	Yes
R^2	.002	.036	.037	.056
Sample size	4,720	4,720	4,720	4,720
	Unemployment Time: Tobit			
Low school attendance			7.049 (.817)	5.012 (.813)
Police/probation			5.499 (.903)	4.371 (.891)
Ever in care	8.319 (1.217)	5.364 (1.201)	4.289 (1.199)	3.511 (1.176)
Family ever in financial difficulties	8.774 (.669)	7.133 (.668)	5.842 (.670)	4.835 (.660)
Ever in lone-mother family (but no financial difficulties)	4.330 (1.093)	3.877 (1.065)	3.350 (1.063)	3.030 (1.043)
Father ever unemployed (but no financial difficulties)	4.280 (1.455)	4.098 (1.416)	3.726 (1.397)	3.295 (1.367)
Age 7 controls and parental education	No	Yes	Yes	Yes
Controls for age 23 educational qualifications	No	No	No	Yes
Log likelihood	-14,285.69	-14,171.01	-14,105.10	-13,998.81
Proportion censored at zero	.541	.541	.541	.541
Sample size	6,263	6,263	6,263	6,263

(continued)

Table 6.8   (continued)

A. Males

Variable	(1)	(2)	(3)	(4)
	Pr[Employed]: Probit			
Low school attendance	-.436 (.089) [-.115]	-.265 (.093) [-.064]	-.314 (.066) [-.075]	-.244 (.068) [-.055]
Police/probation			-.261 (.073) [-.061]	-.220 (.074) [-.049]
Ever in care	-.417 (.051) [-.104]	-.335 (.054) [-.080]	-.197 (.095) [-.045]	-.168 (.096) [-.037]
Family ever in financial difficulties	-.105 (.089) [-.023]	-.079 (.091) [-.017]	-.277 (.055) [-.128]	-.241 (.056) [-.053]
Ever in lone-mother family (but no financial difficulties)			-.035 (.092) [-.007]	-.028 (.094) [-.006]
Father ever unemployed (but no financial difficulties)	-.415 (.107) [-.109]	-.419 (.108) [-.108]	-.398 (.109) [-.101]	-.408 (.110) [-.101]
Age 7 controls and parental education	No	Yes	Yes	Yes
Controls for age 23 educational qualifications	No	No	No	Yes
Log likelihood	-2,461.11	-2,394.26	-2,371.89	-2,322.38
Sample size	6,251	6,251	6,251	6,251
	Pr[Prison/Borstal since Age 16]: Probit			
Low school attendance			.385 (.140) [.008]	.284 (.143) [.004]
Police/probation			.692 (.140) [.022]	.651 (.142) [.016]

	(1)	(2)	(3)	(4)
Ever in care	.844 (.135)	.714 (.143)	.592 (.153)	.556 (.156)
	[.050]	[.028]	[.017]	[.013]
Family ever in financial difficulties	.373 (.110)	.304 (.116)	.231 (.124)	.165 (.127)
	[.012]	[.007]	[.004]	[.002]
Ever in lone-mother family (but no financial difficulties)	.070 (.223)	.039 (.232)	−.042 (.254)	−.029 (.259)
	[.002]	[.001]	[−.001]	[−.000]
Father ever unemployed (but no financial difficulties)	.280 (.247)	.289 (.260)	.304 (.268)	.272 (.275)
	[.009]	[.007]	[.006]	[.004]
Age 7 controls and parental education	No	Yes	Yes	Yes
Controls for age 23 educational qualifications	No	No	No	Yes
Log likelihood	−353.21	−334.24	−317.22	−306.07
Sample size	6,267	6,267	6,267	6,267

B. Females

Variable	(1)	(2)	(3)	(4)
	Ln Hourly Wage: Least Squares			
Low school attendance			−.125 (.027)	−.073 (.026)
Police/probation			−.105 (.053)	−.084 (.052)
Ever in care	−.060 (.045)	−.013 (.044)	−.002 (.044)	−.028 (.021)
Family ever in financial difficulties	−.113 (.021)	−.063 (.021)	−.049 (.021)	.011 (.042)
Ever in lone-mother family (but no financial difficulties)	.036 (.031)	.033 (.030)	.032 (.030)	.038 (.029)
Father ever unemployed (but no financial difficulties)	−.100 (.044)	−.077 (.042)	−.071 (.042)	−.052 (.041)
Age 7 controls and parental education	No	Yes	Yes	Yes
Controls for age 23 educational qualifications	No	No	No	Yes
R²	.011	.085	.096	.151
Sample size	3,777	3,777	3,777	3,777

(*continued*)

Table 6.8 (continued)

B. Females

Variable	(1)	(2)	(3)	(4)
	Unemployment Time: Tobit			
Low school attendance	3.341 (1.168)		5.049 (.727)	4.550 (.738)
Police/probation	5.333 (.587)		2.713 (1.328)	2.720 (1.324)
Ever in care		2.146 (1.162)	1.892 (1.158)	1.751 (1.155)
Family ever in financial difficulties		4.131 (.600)	3.454 (.604)	3.171 (.607)
Ever in lone-mother family (but no financial difficulties)	1.055 (.979)	1.102 (.967)	1.175 (.974)	.998 (.972)
Father ever unemployed (but no financial difficulties)	4.598 (1.308)	4.088 (1.291)	3.695 (1.280)	3.511 (1.277)
Age 7 controls and parental education	No	Yes	Yes	Yes
Controls for age 23 educational qualifications	No	No	No	Yes
Log likelihood	−12,823.45	−12,768.56	−12,737.43	−12,722.38
Proportion censored at zero	.586	.586	.586	.586
Sample size	6,267	6,267	6,267	6,267
	Pr[Employed]: Probit			
Low school attendance	−.288 (.087) [−.110]		−.345 (.057) [−.131]	−.167 (.058) [−.061]
Police/probation			−.406 (.105) [−.156]	−.333 (.107) [−.126]
Ever in care		−.184 (.090) [−.069]	−.146 (.091) [−.054]	−.104 (.092) [−.038]
Family ever in financial difficulties	−.548 (.044) [−.210]	−.403 (.046) [−.153]	−.340 (.047) [−.128]	−.253 (.048) [−.094]
Ever in lone-mother family (but no financial difficulties)	−.053 (.072) [−.020]	−.065 (.074) [−.024]	−.042 (.076) [−.015]	−.007 (.078) [−.002]

Father ever unemployed (but no financial difficulties)	−.225 (.099) [−.085]	−.166 (.101) [−.062]	−.130 (.102) [−.048]	−.087 (.104) [−.032]
Age 7 controls and parental education	No	Yes	Yes	Yes
Controls for age 23 educational qualifications	No	No	No	Yes
Log likelihood	−3,915.25	−3,768.87	−3,725.31	−3,553.67
Sample size	6,256	6,256	6,256	6,256

Pr[Lone Mother by Age 23]: Probit

Low school attendance			.347 (.071) [.053]	.220 (.072) [.025]
Police/probation			.389 (.125) [.063]	.342 (.126) [.045]
Ever in care	.364 (.105) [.065]	.285 (.108) [.044]	.237 (.110) [.035]	.204 (.112) [.024]
Family ever in financial difficulties	.553 (.055) [.100]	.420 (.059) [.066]	.360 (.060) [.054]	.290 (.061) [.034]
Ever in lone-mother family (but no financial difficulties)	.117 (.104) [.018]	.126 (.108) [.017]	.099 (.110) [.013]	.073 (.114) [.008]
Father ever unemployed (but no financial difficulties)	.150 (.142) [.023]	.106 (.148) [.015]	.082 (.148) [.013]	.042 (.151) [.004]
Age 7 controls and parental education	No	Yes	Yes	Yes
Controls for age 23 educational qualifications	No	No	No	Yes
Log likelihood	−1,688.32	−1,617.80	−1,595.51	−1,518.13
Sample size	6,270	6,270	6,270	6,270

Source: National Child Development Study, wave 4.

Note: Numbers in parentheses are standard errors. Numbers in brackets are marginal effects.

"initial conditions" variables) this reflects education's role as an important transmission mechanism that underpins the relation between disadvantage and inferior economic and social outcomes.

While we have only summarized some of the key results here, all in all we feel they are strong evidence that childhood factors linked to delinquency or social disadvantage have important linkages with age 23 economic and social outcomes. Even after netting out a variety of pre-labor-market factors and educational attainment the less advantaged individuals in the NCDS cohort are much less likely to be employed and are much more likely to have experienced longer unemployment spells and experienced detrimental social experiences. In this sense we view our measures of social disadvantage as important, albeit noisy, characterizations of the "at-risk" population of the worse performers in the early years of adulthood. In the next section we examine whether the economic effects of such disadvantages persist to age 33.

6.5   Models of Economic and Social Outcomes at Age 33

6.5.1   Age 33 Economic and Social Outcomes

The most up-to-date wave of the NCDS that we can currently access is the age 33 survey that was carried out in 1991. In this section of the paper we consider wage and employment outcomes at age 33 and relate them to our measures of delinquency and disadvantage in the same kind of approach as above where we build up progressively more detailed models that net out factors from earlier ages. The second issue on which we focus is the difficult question of whether there is potential for a "late developer" effect. We operationalize this by asking whether there exist wage returns from late educational upgrading and, perhaps more important, whether they differ for our measures of social disadvantage. A third issue we consider is the possibility of a cross-generational effect as we look at the potential for intergenerational spillovers onto the early age cognitive skills of cohort members' children.

Table 6.9 reports a set of descriptive statistics for the pay and employment of NCDS cohort members at age 33 in 1991. The structure of the table is the same as for the earlier 1981 data. Hourly wages and employment rates are clearly lower for the first four measures (low school attendance, police/probation, ever in care, and ever in financial difficulties) though there is less difference for the family structure (in the absence of financial difficulties) variables.

Continuing with the same kind of modeling approach that we have adopted thus far in the paper, our fourth-stage multivariate models take the form:

Table 6.9   **Age 23 Outcomes and Age 16 Juvenile Delinquency and Social Disadvantage**

Characteristic	Hourly Pay	Pr[Employment]
Males		
All	7.628	.905
Low school attendance	5.796	.805
Police/probation	6.429	.816
Ever in care	6.355	.752
Ever in financial difficulties	6.276	.834
Ever in lone-mother family (no financial difficulties)	7.729	.905
Father ever unemployed (no financial difficulties)	7.191	.907
Females		
All	5.240	.760
Low school attendance	3.947	.615
Police/probation	4.489	.627
Ever in care	4.781	.620
Ever in financial difficulties	4.223	.649
Ever in lone-mother family (no financial difficulties)	5.939	.702
Father ever unemployed (no financial difficulties)	4.751	.691

$$Y_i^{\text{age 33}} = \alpha_4 + \beta_4 DELINQ_i + \psi_3 DISADV_i + \Gamma_4 X_i^{\text{pre 16}} + \Omega_4 ED_i^{\text{age 23}} + \varepsilon_4,$$

where Y^{age33} denotes the relevant age 33 outcomes (wages and employment).

Table 6.10 reports least squares estimates of wage equations and probit models of employment for males and females in 1991. The structure of the table is the same as for the age 23 models reported in table 6.8. The estimated models make it clear that the effects of childhood disadvantage do not die out by age 33. This is especially the case for men where there are negative wage effects, after controlling for education, from low school attendance or growing up in a family facing financial difficulties or in a lone-mother family. Male employment rates are significantly lower for low school attendance and ever being in care. For females, significant associations are less common, but there do seem to be significant negative wage effects for the financial difficulty variable. There is much less of an effect on female employment rates at age 33. The male-female comparisons are interesting because it is clear that between ages 23 and 33, the position of disadvantaged females did not worsen and some of the earlier effects were ameliorated. These gender-based differences after age 23, with

Table 6.10   Age 33 Wage and Employment Models

A. Males

Variable	(1)	(2)	(3)	(4)
	Ln Hourly Wage: Least Squares			
Low school attendance	-.114 (.044)	-.037 (.042)	-.123 (.031)	-.042 (.030)
Police/probation	-.204 (.024)	-.107 (.023)	-.045 (.033)	-.005 (.032)
Ever in care	-.077 (.039)	-.070 (.037)	-.032 (.042)	.009 (.040)
Family ever in financial difficulties	-.080 (.046)	-.029 (.044)	-.088 (.023)	-.049 (.023)
Ever in lone-mother family (but no financial difficulties)			-.067 (.037)	-.058 (.035)
Father ever unemployed (but no financial difficulties)			-.026 (.044)	.002 (.041)
Age 7 controls and parental education	No	Yes	Yes	Yes
Controls for age 23 educational qualifications	No	No	No	Yes
R^2	.026	.137	.144	.229
Sample size	3,367	3,367	3,367	3,367
	Pr[Employment]: Probit			
Low school attendance	-.593 (.112) [-.130]	-.409 (.118) [-.075]	-.350 (.090) [-.060]	-.234 (.091) [-.035]
Police/probation	-.369 (.069) [-.067]	-.241 (.073) [-.039]	-.218 (.098) [-.035]	-.152 (.100) [-.022]
Ever in care			-.367 (.121) [-.028]	-.324 (.122) [-.052]
Family ever in financial difficulties			-.184 (.075) [-.028]	-.128 (.076) [-.018]

	(1)	(2)	(3)	(4)
Ever in lone-mother family (but no financial difficulties)	−.087 (.121) [−.013]	−.071 (.124) [−.010]	−.059 (.126) [−.009]	−.028 (.129) [−.004]
Father ever unemployed (but no financial difficulties)	−.161 (.152) [−.027]	−.131 (.156) [−.020]	−.117 (.157) [−.018]	−.075 (.159) [−.010]
Age 7 controls and parental education	No	Yes	Yes	Yes
Controls for age 23 educational qualifications	No	No	No	Yes
Log likelihood	−1,338.75	−1,272.94	−1,261.19	−1,221.94
Sample size	4,655	4,655	4,655	4,655

B. Females

Variable	(1)	(2)	(3)	(4)
		Ln Hourly Wage: Least Squares		
Low school attendance	−.041 (.057)	−.001 (.055)	−.125 (.033)	−.023 (.031)
Police/probation			−.027 (.061)	.019 (.056)
Ever in care			.014 (.055)	.040 (.050)
Family ever in financial difficulties	−.230 (.026)	−.132 (.026)	−.107 (.026)	−.068 (.024)
Ever in lone-mother family (but no financial difficulties)	.048 (.042)	.048 (.040)	.071 (.041)	.079 (.037)
Father ever unemployed (but no financial difficulties)	−.090 (.056)	−.069 (.053)	−.056 (.053)	−.045 (.049)
Age 7 controls and parental education	No	Yes	Yes	Yes
Controls for age 23 educational qualifications	No	No	No	Yes
R^2	.024	.126	.137	.268
Sample size	3,540	3,540	3,540	3,540

(continued)

Table 6.10 (continued)

B. Females

Variable	(1)	(2)	(3)	(4)
	Pr[Employment]: Probit			
Low school attendance	−.043 (.104)	.039 (.106)	−.142 (.064)	−.053 (.067)
	[−.015]	[.014]	[−.051]	[−.019]
Police/probation			.009 (.121)	.032 (.122)
			[.003]	[.011]
Ever in care	−.071 (.051)	−.011 (.053)	.045 (.107)	.069 (.108)
	[−.025]	[−.004]	[.015]	[.024]
Family ever in financial difficulties	.080 (.083)	.066 (.083)	.000 (.054)	.037 (.054)
	[.028]	[.023]	[.000]	[.013]
Ever in lone-mother family (but no financial difficulties)	.057 (.113)	.085 (.114)	.046 (.085)	.062 (.086)
	[.020]	[.029]	[.016]	[.021]
Father ever unemployed (but no financial difficulties)			.093 (.114)	.107 (.115)
			[.032]	[.036]
Age 7 controls and parental education	No	Yes	Yes	Yes
Controls for age 23 educational qualifications	No	No	No	Yes
Log likelihood	−3,067.09	−3,034.55	−3,031.27	−2,995.44
Sample size	4,972	4,972	4,972	4,972

Source: National Child Development Study, wave 5.

Note: Numbers in parentheses are standard errors. Numbers in brackets are marginal effects.

disadvantaged men doing worse than womenn in terms of economic success, seem to be in line with recent labor market trends for younger cohorts of men and women in Britain (as discussed in section 6.2 above).

6.5.2   Late Developers and the Potential to Catch Up

We now go on to see if there exists any potential for catch-up or late development for individuals who look relatively unsuccessful in the early years of adult life (i.e., as characterized by our relative disadvantage measures). We consider one possible route through which this might happen, namely, educational upgrading. We defined a variable *Upgrade* equal to one if individuals improved their educational qualifications between 1981 and 1991 and entered this into equations modeling wage growth between ages 23 and 33.[15] Basic regressions show clear evidence of wage gains associated with educational upgrading for both men and women, with slightly larger gains for women:

Males: $\ln Wage^{age\ 33} - \ln Wage^{age\ 23} = .122\ Upgrade,$
$$(.025)$$

Females: $\ln Wage^{age\ 33} - \ln Wage^{age\ 23} = .171\ Upgrade.$
$$(.133)$$

These are least squares estimates; standard errors in parentheses.

This pattern of results remains robust to the inclusion of the 1981 wage and a variable *Outtime* measuring the number of months spent out of the labor force between ages 23 and 33 (which, especially in the case of women in this age group, is an important variable to control for in wage change equations):

Males: $\ln Wage^{age\ 33} - \ln Wage^{age\ 23} = .120\ Upgrade$
$$(.025)$$

$- .628\ \ln Wage^{age\ 23} - .677\ Outtime,$
$\ \ \ (.027) \qquad\qquad\ \ \ (.071)$

Females: $\ln Wage^{age\ 33} - \ln Wage^{age\ 23} = .139\ Upgrade$
$$(.027)$$

$- .487\ \ln Wage^{age\ 23} - .874\ Outtime.$
$\ \ \ (.024) \qquad\qquad\ \ \ (.050)$

Next we consider whether the potential returns to upgrading one's education differ for individuals whom we characterize as childhood delinquents or from disadvantaged backgrounds. To do this we estimate wage

---

15. Upgrading one's educational qualifications is significantly more likely for individuals with higher age 7 math and reading scores and for those with parents with lower educational attainment. It is not significantly related to the measures of delinquency and disadvantage.

growth models including interactions between *Upgrade* and the delinquency and disadvantage measures considered above. This produced the following estimates:

Males:
$$\ln Wage^{\text{age }33} - \ln Wage^{\text{age }23} = \underset{(.026)}{.145} \; Upgrade$$

$$- \underset{(.086)}{.134} \; Upgrade * Low \; school \; attendance$$

$$- \underset{(.112)}{.040} \; Upgrade * Ever \; in \; care$$

$$- \underset{(.097)}{.038} \; Upgrade * Contact \; with \; police/probation$$

$$- \underset{(.064)}{.102} \; Upgrade * Ever \; in \; financial \; difficulties$$

$$- \underset{(.097)}{.102} \; Upgrade * Ever \; in \; lone\text{-}mother \; family \; (no \; fin. \; diff.)$$

$$+ \underset{(.150)}{.050} \; Upgrade * Father \; ever \; unemployed \; (no \; fin. \; diff.)$$

$$- \underset{(.023)}{.629} \ln Wage^{\text{age }23} - \underset{(.069)}{.677} \; Outtime,$$

Females:
$$\ln Wage^{\text{age }33} - \ln Wage^{\text{age }23} = \underset{(.035)}{.152} \; Upgrade$$

$$+ \underset{(.122)}{.002} \; Upgrade * Low \; school \; attendance$$

$$+ \underset{(.236)}{.030} \; Upgrade * Ever \; in \; care$$

$$- \underset{(.268)}{.145} \; Upgrade * Contact \; with \; police/probation$$

$$- \underset{(.093)}{.103} \; Upgrade * Ever \; in \; financial \; difficulties$$

$$+ \underset{(.111)}{.068} \; Upgrade * Ever \; in \; lone\text{-}mother \; family \; (no \; fin. \; diff.)$$

$$- \underset{(.150)}{.171} \; Upgrade * Father \; ever \; unemployed \; (no \; fin. \; diff.)$$

$$- \underset{(.025)}{.488} \; \ln Wage^{\text{age }23} - \underset{(.051)}{.873} \; Outtime.$$

Because these are wage change equations, the delinquency and disadvantage variables cannot be entered in levels (as they would be differenced out), but their interactions with *Upgrade* can be considered. The results that emerge show that if anything, men with low school attendance in their last year or who were in low-income families benefit less from educational upgrading. For women, the picture is less depressing because all interaction terms are insignificant, suggesting no difference in the potential to achieve wage gains from increasing levels of education at a later age. This gender difference is clearly in line with the background trends we presented in section 6.2, with women doing better than men in the 1980s and early 1990s.

6.5.3 Children of NCDS Cohort Members in 1991

Because the NCDS cohort members are old enough to have their own children, the survey coordinators have now incorporated information on cohort members' children in the survey. The NCDS contains data on test score outcomes from a battery of tests administered to the cohort members' children. These data permit us to introduce an intergenerational aspect to our study and to ask the very important question of whether social disadvantage faced by NCDS cohort members in their childhood years has any clear relationship with their own children's cognitive abilities.

Table 6.11 reports information on two tests administered to cohort members' children aged 6–9. The tests are the well-known Peabody Individual Achievement Tests (for math and reading recognition) and are standardized for age differences (see Social Statistics Research Unit, n.d., for more details). Children have been classified into percentiles of the test score distribution, and we report the mean percentile broken down by parents' social disadvantage in the table. A clear and strong pattern emerges. For math and reading tests children of a parent who faced social disadvantages in his or her own childhood have lower percentile rankings.

Table 6.12 reports regressions that include social disadvantage measures and also consider the intergenerational correlations of test scores.[16] Two specifications are reported for the math and reading tests, and these differ in whether they include the parental test score quintile dummy variables. The results show a strong negative relation between the cognitive skills of cohort members' children and whether (one of) their parents faced social disadvantages while growing up. In almost all cases the effects are large

---

16. Notice that the tests are not identical for cohort members and their children. As noted above the children's tests are Peabody Individual Achievement Tests and the tests administered to NCDS cohort members at age 7 were the Southgate Group reading test and a problem arithmetic test. For more work on intergenerational mobility in terms of the earnings and education of NCDS cohort members and their parents, see Dearden, Machin, and Reed (1997).

Table 6.11   Math and Reading Test Score Percentiles for Children of NCDS Cohort Members

Characteristic	Math: Peabody Individual Achievement Test Score (percentile)	Sample Size	Reading: Peabody Individual Achievement Test Score (percentile)	Sample Size
All	51.89	1,007	51.28	1,008
Parent had low school attendance	48.31	104	44.48	105
Parent was in contact with police/probation	41.45	56	37.16	56
Parent was ever in care	37.49	37	34.84	37
Parent grew up in family ever in financial difficulties	45.17	182	43.96	183
Parent ever in lone-mother family (no financial difficulties)	55.88	65	52.69	65
Parent's father ever unemployed (no financial difficulties)	54.19	31	47.58	31

Note: The age range of children is 6 years, 0 months to 9 years, 0 months inclusive (at the time of taking the tests).

and show that test scores are somewhere between 5 and 10 percentile points lower for each of the parental disadvantage measures. The results also show an important intergenerational correlation of test scores (especially for reading), and while boys do better on the math test, girls seem to outperform boys on the reading test.

These results demonstrate a further effect of social disadvantage when growing up, namely, the existence of an intergenerational spillover. The children of parents who grew up in socially disadvantaged situations are more likely to have lower scores on tests administered to them at an early age. Because early age math and reading ability are important determinants of economic and social success or failure as an adult this suggests that the effects of childhood disadvantage persist over generations (see also Machin 1997).

6.6   Concluding Remarks

The basic message of this study is clear. Economic and social disadvantages faced during childhood display a persistent association with the subsequent economic success of British individuals. We use unique longitudinal data from a cohort of all individuals born in a week of March 1958 to examine models of relative success or failure in the early years of adulthood. Our results suggest that individual and family characteristics, especially those associated with adverse economic and social child

Table 6.12   Math and Reading Test Score Percentiles for Children of NCDS Cohort Members: Intergenerational Correlations

Variable	Math: Children's Peabody Individual Achievement Test Score (percentile)		Reading: Children's Peabody Individual Achievement Test Score (percentile)	
	(1)	(2)	(3)	(4)
Parent had low school attendance	−2.680 (3.099)	−2.008 (3.106)	−5.792 (3.044)	−3.305 (3.000)
Parent was in contact with police/probation	−7.289 (4.107)	−7.253 (4.093)	−10.950 (4.048)	−9.623 (3.953)
Parent was ever in care	−10.018 (5.072)	−9.558 (5.054)	−13.163 (4.999)	−11.654 (4.890)
Parent grew up in family ever in financial difficulties	−6.762 (2.463)	−6.070 (2.469)	−7.742 (2.425)	−5.287 (2.388)
Parent ever in lone-mother family (no financial difficulties)	2.394 (3.844)	1.700 (3.838)	−.321 (3.789)	−.645 (3.701)
Parent's father ever unemployed (no financial difficulties)	1.477 (5.276)	2.948 (5.276)	−5.153 (5.200)	−1.452 (5.093)
Child = boy	2.975 (1.843)	2.920 (1.839)	−3.874 (1.815)	−4.193 (1.769)
Parents test scores (age 7)				
2d Lowest quintile of math and reading test scores		2.563 (2.800)		5.340 (2.711)
Middle quintile of math and reading test scores		3.171 (2.692)		11.655 (2.630)
2d Highest quintile of math and reading test scores		2.258 (2.777)		13.072 (2.828)
Highest quintile of math and reading test scores		10.142 (2.952)		19.604 (2.828)
R^2	.034	.046	.050	.102
Sample size	983	983	984	984

Note: Age range of children is 6 years, 0 months to 9 years, 0 months (at time of taking the tests). Numbers in parentheses are standard errors.

development, display an important association with subsequent success or failure in the labor market. In particular, children whom we characterize as juvenile delinquents or from socially disadvantaged backgrounds fare badly in terms of employment and unemployment, and their social disadvantages persist and still have a strong effect even at age 33.[17] An important transmission mechanism that underpins these links is educational attainment, which is vastly inferior for those we classify in the delinquent and disadvantaged groups. However, over and above this, factors such as poor school attendance and growing up in a family in financial distress matter (and in our work matter more than lone motherhood, which seems to be dominated by such family poverty measures). Furthermore, the children of parents who grew up in socially disadvantaged situations during their own childhoods have lower early age cognitive abilities, suggesting a potentially important cross-generational link that may well spill over to the subsequent economic fortunes of children of disadvantaged individuals.

17. For related work on an earlier cohort of British individuals born in 1946, see Kuh and Wadsworth (1991). They report that the earnings of men aged 36 were substantially affected by early life factors after controlling for education, social class, and early age abilities. In their study very few men from disadvantaged backgrounds achieved success in terms of reaching the upper third of the earnings distribution, and the impact of early life factors seemed to persist into the midlife years.

Appendix

Table 6A.1   Labor Force Status for People Aged 16/17 in 1975

Year	Males (%)					Females (%)				
				Student					Student	
	Employed	Unemployed	Inactive	Not Working	Working	Employed	Unemployed	Inactive	Not Working	Working
1975	60.5	4.8	0.4	34.2	n.a.	52.7	5.4	3.4	38.6	n.a.
1977	78.0	7.1	1.5	13.4	n.a.	70.6	6.7	10.2	12.5	n.a.
1979	82.0	6.6	1.5	9.9	n.a.	66.0	5.4	20.6	8.0	n.a.
1981	79.0	14.3	1.7	5.0	n.a.	61.1	7.6	28.8	2.6	n.a.
1983	78.9	14.6	4.0	2.6	n.a.	53.4	7.6	37.0	2.0	n.a.
1984	80.3	15.0	2.9	1.8	n.a.	54.3	9.1	35.3	1.3	n.a.
1985	78.0	13.0	6.6	0.5	0.0	53.9	8.8	37.0	0.2	0.1
1986	83.2	11.3	5.4	0.1	0.0	53.1	7.8	39.0	0.1	0.0
1987	84.6	11.1	4.0	0.3	0.0	54.8	9.3	35.7	0.3	0.0
1988	85.7	8.7	5.3	0.3	0.0	58.7	6.2	35.2	0.0	0.0
1989	88.7	6.6	4.5	0.2	0.1	59.2	5.7	35.2	0.0	0.0
1990	88.4	5.9	5.5	0.2	0.0	60.6	5.4	33.9	0.1	0.0
1991	87.1	7.9	4.8	0.2	0.1	65.4	4.4	30.1	0.1	0.0
1992	85.9	9.7	4.3	0.1	0.0	64.7	4.4	30.9	0.1	0.0
1993	86.0	8.3	5.6	0.1	0.0	65.2	4.4	30.3	0.1	0.0
1994	86.0	7.9	5.8	0.2	0.1	65.1	3.9	31.0	0.0	0.0
1995	85.4	7.2	7.3	0.1	0.0	70.4	3.4	26.2	0.0	0.0

Source: Labour Force Survey.
Note: n.a. = data not available.

References

Blanchflower, David, and Peter Elias. 1993. Ability, schooling and earnings: Are twins different? Hanover, N.H.: Dartmouth College. Mimeograph.

Blanchflower, David, and Richard Freeman. 1996. Growing into work. In *OECD employment outlook*. Paris: Organization for Economic Cooperation and Development.

Currie, Janet. 1995. Welfare and the well-being of children. Chur, Switzerland: Harwood.

Dearden, Lorraine, Stephen Machin, and Howard Reed. 1997. Intergenerational mobility in Britain. *Economic Journal* 107:47–64.

Elias, Peter, and David Blanchflower. 1987. The occupations, earnings and work histories of young adults: Who gets the good jobs? Department of Employment Research Paper no. 68. Coventry: University of Warwick Institute of Employment Research.

Gregg, Paul, Susan Harkness, and Stephen Machin. 1999. Child development and family income. York: Joseph Rowntree Foundation.

Kiernan, Kathleen. 1995. Transition to parenthood: Young mothers, young fathers—associated factors and later life experiences. Welfare State Programme Discussion Paper no. WSP/113. London: London School of Economics.

Kuh, Diana, and Michael Wadsworth. 1991. Childhood influences on adult male earnings in a longitudinal study. *British Journal of Sociology* 42:537–55.

Machin, Stephen. 1997. Intergenerational transmissions of economic status. In *Jobs, wages and poverty: Patterns of persistence and mobility*, ed. Paul Gregg. London: London School of Economics, Centre for Economic Performance.

Micklewright, John. 1989. Choice at sixteen. *Economica* 56:25–40.

Robinson, Peter. 1994. The comparative performance of the British education and training system. Centre for Economic Performance Working Paper no. 644. London: London School of Economics.

Social Statistics Research Unit. N.d. NCDS5: Child assessments. London: City University.

The Rising Well-Being of the Young

David G. Blanchflower and Andrew J. Oswald

7.1 Introduction

Many commentators believe that life in the industrialized nations is getting tougher for the young. They point to the increase in youth unemployment, the rise in young male suicides, the widening of the income distribution, the spreading use of drugs, and the high rate of divorce and of young single parenthood. But is so pessimistic a view justified? The evidence in this paper paints a different picture. The paper documents a rising level of happiness among young people in Western countries. It then discusses possible explanations for that secular trend.

This paper uses the numbers that people report when, in surveys, they are asked questions about how happy they feel and how satisfied they are with various aspects of their lives. There are obvious limitations to such statistics. Nevertheless, there are reasons to look at data on reported well-being.

1. A large psychology literature takes seriously the answers people give to "happiness" questions in surveys. Readable introductions include Argyle (1987) and Myers (1993). It would be extreme to argue that economists know more about human psychology than do psychologists.

2. People's reported well-being levels are correlated with observable events that appear consistent with genuine happiness. For example, those

David G. Blanchflower is professor in and chairman of the Department of Economics at Dartmouth College and a research associate of the National Bureau of Economic Research. Andrew J. Oswald is professor of economics at Warwick University, England.

For helpful ideas, the authors thank Andrew Clark, Nick Crafts, Jim Davis, Rafael Di Tella, Richard Freeman, Robert MacCulloch, and Claire Oswald. This research was funded by both the Rockefeller Foundation and the Leverhulme Trust.

who report high happiness scores tend to smile and laugh more, and to be rated by other people as happier individuals (Diener 1984; Pavot et al. 1991; Watson and Clark 1991; Myers 1993).

3. Reported well-being levels are correlated with scores obtained on standard psychiatric and mental stress tests.

4. The structure of well-being equations is similar in different countries over different periods. This is consistent with the idea that something systematic is being picked up in such data.

5. If the object is to study well-being, what people say about how they feel seems unlikely to contain zero information.

Statistical sources have for years collected individuals' answers to questions about well-being. These responses have been studied intensively by psychologists, studied a little by sociologists, and largely ignored by economists. Some economists will defend this neglect by emphasizing the unreliability of such data, but most are probably unaware that statistics of this sort are available and have not thought of how empirical measures for the theoretical construct called "utility" might be used in their discipline.[1]

Easterlin (1974) was one of the first economists to study data over time on the reported level of happiness. His paper's main concern is to argue that individual happiness appears to be similar across poor countries and rich countries. This finding, the author suggests, means that we should think of people as getting utility from a comparison of themselves with others close to them. Happiness, in other words, is relative.

On whether there is a trend in well-being over time, Easterlin's paper concludes: "In the one time series studied, that for the United States since 1946, higher income was not systematically accompanied by greater happiness" (1974, 118). This result, that GDP growth may have little or no effect on well-being, has become well known. Unfortunately, it is not obvious that Easterlin's data actually support it. For example, his longest *consistent* set of happiness levels for the percentages of Americans saying they were "very happy" and "not very happy" (the highest and lowest of three bands into which they could place themselves) are shown in table 7.1. Other data given by Easterlin—splicing together surveys with breaks and changes in definition—produce a different answer. But the data in table 7.1 form the longest consistent series and might be thought to command the most weight. A discussion of Easterlin's work is contained in Blanchflower, Oswald, and Warr (1993) and Veenhoven (1991). The former finds a statistically significant time trend in the year dummies of two decades of pooled U.S. cross sections.

This paper is divided into sections. Section 7.2 examines data from the

---

1. For a brief discussion of the quantitative literature that exists on well-being, see appendix B.

Table 7.1   Early U.S. Well-Being Data

Year	Very Happy (%)	Not Very Happy (%)	N
1946	39	10	3,151
1947	42	10	1,434
1948	43	11	1,596
1952	47	9	3,003
1956	53	5	1,979
1957	53	3	1,627

Source: Easterlin (1974, table 8) using U.S. AIPO poll data.

United States. It shows that reported well-being levels among the young rise from the early 1970s to the early 1990s. Section 7.3 studies European data, also from the early 1970s to the present. Life satisfaction data for a dozen countries reveal the same pattern as in the United States: the young report growing levels of well-being over time. Section 7.4 of the paper begins to explore why this might be. It considers various potential explanations: (1) the cessation of the cold war and thus increased chance of peace in young people's lifetimes, (2) declining discrimination against women and black people, (3) changing educational levels and the nature of work, (4) changing marital and personal relationships, and (5) the growth of consumer goods designed primarily for the young. The fourth of these is the one on which the paper eventually focuses. It shows that the increasing happiness of young unmarried individuals explains the bulk of the upward movement in the full sample of young people. Section 7.5 concludes.

7.2   Happiness in the United States from the 1970s

We begin with an examination of information from the General Social Surveys (GSS) of the United States for 1972–93, which have for decades been interviewing people about their levels of happiness. These surveys are of randomly selected individuals. Many issues—not just well-being—are covered in the surveys. GSS data have been collected annually in all but three of the years from 1972 to the early 1990s (no data are available for 1979, 1981, or 1991). The size of the sample averages approximately 1,500 individuals per year. Different people are interviewed each year: the GSS is not a panel.[2]

Are young Americans getting happier or less happy over time? Answers are available to the question:

2. Further details of the GSS are presented in appendix A.

> Taken all together, how would you say things are these days—would you say that you are very happy, pretty happy, or not too happy? (1994 GSS Cumulative Codebook, Question 157)

If young people use language in approximately the same way as they did 20 years ago (if not, our paper's analysis is potentially severely flawed), it should be possible to learn something about their changing sense of well-being.

The interpretation of people's well-being answers is difficult. It raises philosophical questions that cannot be resolved in this paper. Our approach is pragmatic. The analysis below assumes that individuals accurately know their own happiness or utility. What they cannot do is convey it to an interviewer in a way that is free of error. The errors can be viewed as arising from the fact that individuals do not know the common scale that the interviewer ideally wishes them to use. Thus respondents presumably implicitly use different scales (as they might if they were being asked to say whether they were very tall, fairly tall, or not too tall, rather than to state their height in inches). On this assumption, there is useful information in these data if it is possible to aggregate across individuals' answers.

The four parts of table 7.2 break happiness answers into responses for the whole sample, those over age 30, those under age 30, and those under age 30 and married. The first thing that is noticeable is that "pretty happy" is the typical answer and that "not too happy," which is the lowest score people can assign themselves, is given by slightly more than a tenth of the population. It is clear that in the whole sample reported well-being has changed little over two decades. This is in the spirit of Easterlin (1974). However, slightly fewer people in the 1990s say they are not too happy. There is also a small trend drop in the numbers saying "very happy." For the under-thirties, however, there have been more noticeable changes. Over the period, a declining number of young people say that they are not too happy (from approximately 14 percent in the 1970s to 10 percent in the 1990s), and slightly more state that they are pretty happy than did so in the 1970s. In working with well-being data, a change from 14 to 10 percent is a large movement. There is, nevertheless, little sign of a time trend in the answer "very happy." The proportion of young respondents giving this answer was around 30 percent both early in the 1970s and in the early 1990s.

Although the effect is not marked, for both the under-thirties and over-thirties, unhappiness is dropping secularly in the United States. The data are becoming more skewed—away from low happiness scores—over time. Table 7.2 reveals that the category "pretty happy" is expanding while "not too happy" is shrinking. Nevertheless, the effect is not dramatic, the range of years is comparatively short, and the "very happy" category also shrinks slightly. Interestingly, as the last columns of table 7.2 show, growth

Table 7.2 Happiness over Time: United States, 1972–96 (percent)

Year	All Ages			Age 30 and Over			Under Age 30			Under Age 30 and Not Married		
	Not Too Happy	Pretty Happy	Very Happy	Not Too Happy	Pretty Happy	Very Happy	Not Too Happy	Pretty Happy	Very Happy	Not Too Happy	Pretty Happy	Very Happy
1972	17	53	30	17	52	31	16	57	27	21	64	15
1973	13	51	36	13	49	39	14	58	28	18	64	18
1974	13	49	38	13	47	41	15	56	29	21	63	16
1975	13	54	33	13	53	35	14	58	28	19	63	18
1976	13	53	34	12	53	35	14	53	33	24	53	24
1977	12	53	35	12	51	37	13	59	28	14	63	23
1978	10	56	34	9	56	35	11	57	33	15	61	23
1980	13	53	34	13	52	35	14	56	29	17	58	25
1982	15	55	31	14	54	33	16	59	25	21	59	19
1983	13	56	31	12	56	32	14	57	29	14	59	27
1984	13	52	35	13	50	37	12	59	29	15	62	23
1985	11	60	29	12	59	29	9	62	29	12	62	26
1986	11	56	32	11	55	33	12	60	29	16	57	27
1987	13	57	29	13	57	30	14	60	27	17	62	22
1988	9	57	34	10	55	35	7	61	32	10	65	24
1989	10	58	33	10	57	33	10	60	30	11	59	31
1990	9	58	33	10	57	33	7	58	35	7	68	25
1991	11	58	31	12	56	32	7	65	27	10	66	24
1993	11	57	32	12	56	32	9	63	29	6	69	26
1994	12	59	29	12	58	30	12	63	25	15	67	18
1996	12	58	30	12	56	31	11	62	27	12	66	22

Source: General Social Surveys.

Note: Answers are to the question: "Taken all together, how would you say things are these days—would you say that you are very happy, pretty happy, or not too happy?"

in happiness seems to have occurred most among the young unmarried. We return to this subject later in the paper.

These are raw data. They may be being molded predominantly by a population that is changing its composition. To control for that, a more formal statistical method is required. Table 7.3 is a form of regression equation in which the happiness answers of survey respondents are explained by the list of variables shown in the table. Because happiness is measured by the ordering of "very happy" down to "pretty happy" and "not too happy," it is not possible to employ a simple method such as ordinary least squares (OLS). The equation is instead an ordered logit. The dependent variable can be viewed as the probability of reporting a high happiness score. In principle, the coefficients in ordered logit equations cannot routinely be read in the way possible in an OLS regression (because the estimated coefficients have to be weighted by changes in densities). However, our calculations suggest that in practice this is not a severe problem.

The columns of table 7.3 provide separate happiness equations for two groups: those under age 30 and those age 30 or over. Pooling from 1972 to 1993, the total sample size is approximately 28,000 Americans. Of these, approximately one-quarter are under age 30.

A number of personal characteristics are controlled for in table 7.3. Reported happiness is higher among women, whites, married individuals, and those in school or full-time work. There is a strong U-shaped age effect, which is captured by the quadratic in table 7.3. A literature on this kind of age-curve effect now exists, including Warr (1992) and Clark, Oswald, and Warr (1996). On average, happiness is lowest around approximately the end of one's twenties. Unemployment and marital breakdown are large sources of—or more precisely correlates with—unhappiness. Years of schooling is strongly positively correlated with reported well-being: the educated are happier. In columns (2) and (4) it is clear, as might be expected, that well-being is greater where (family) income is higher.[3]

For this paper, the main conclusion is found in the pattern in the time trend variable of table 7.3. Holding other factors constant, the young show a noticeable upward movement in reported well-being through the years. The trend term is effectively fitted through separate year dummies, as shown in figure 7.1. Figure 7.1 suggests that the trend terms for young people and old people are not being driven by one or two especially influential years.

If it is possible to trust these kinds of data, therefore, young Americans became steadily happier over the decades from the early 1970s. By contrast, older people in the United States apparently have not been getting

---

3. Where family income was missing its value was imputed and a dummy variable was included to identify where this was done. It was never significantly different from zero.

Table 7.3   Happiness Ordered Logits by Age: United States, 1970s–1990s

Variable	Under Age 30 (1)	Under Age 30 (2)	Age 30 and Over (3)	Age 30 and Over (4)
Time trend	.0166 (.0041)	.0091 (.0044)	−.0002 (.0022)	−.0116 (.0025)
Male	−.2871 (.0541)	−.3012 (.0543)	−.1984 (.0323)	−.2030 (.0324)
Black	−.7814 (.0725)	−.7379 (.0730)	−.4610 (.0424)	−.4125 (.0426)
Other nonwhite	−.2018 (.1539)	−.1641 (.1543)	−.0016 (.1002)	.0332 (.1003)
Part time	−.1615 (.0725)	−.1166 (.0766)	−.0514 (.0510)	.0175 (.0515)
Job but absent	−.1672 (.1791)	−.1659 (.1790)	−.2358 (.0911)	−.2238 (.0911)
Unemployed	−.6889 (.1134)	−.6624 (.1137)	−.7881 (.0943)	−.6692 (.0949)
Retired			−.0076 (.0498)	.0791 (.0505)
In school	.0947 (.0901)	.1727 (.0914)	−.2146 (.1516)	−.0902 (.1523)
Keeping house	−.0778 (.0774)	−.0183 (.0782)	−.1145 (.0417)	−.0261 (.0425)
Other	−.0093 (.2729)	.0559 (2.735)	−.6644 (.1122)	−.5145 (.1128)
Age	−.2751 (.1329)	−.2099 (.1338)	−.0089 (.0061)	−.0129 (.0061)
Age^2	.0054 (.0027)	.0040 (.0028)	.0001 (.0000)	.0002 (.00001)
Years schooling	.1157 (.0122)	.1084 (.0123)	.0446 (.0044)	.0288 (.0046)
Married	.5894 (.0602)	.5468 (.0608)	.8122 (.0528)	.6910 (.0538)
Widowed	−.1307 (.4406)	−.0768 (.4403)	−.2452 (.0664)	−.2540 (.0664)
Divorced	−.3918 (.1262)	−.3692 (.1263)	−.1390 (.0643)	−.1297 (.0644)
Separated	−.8090 (.1515)	−.7868 (.1519)	−.2655 (.0884)	−.2491 (.0885)
Log family income		.1508 (.0288)		.2243 (.0198)
Cut1	−4.0566 (1.5733)	−2.0173 (1.6320)	−1.2484 (.1902)	.5152 (.2479)
Cut2	−.9852 (1.5744)	1.0657 (1.6318)	1.5749 (.1901)	3.3525 (.2491)
N	6,819	6,819	21,472	21,472
Pseudo R^2	.0485	.0510	.0412	.0444
χ^2	615.75	647.74	1,691.8	1,823.62
Log likelihood	−6,042.5	−6,026.5	−19,672.8	−19,606.9

Source: General Social Surveys.

Note: Equations also include eight census area dummies and, where log family income is included, cases where mean family income was imputed. Numbers in parentheses are standard errors.

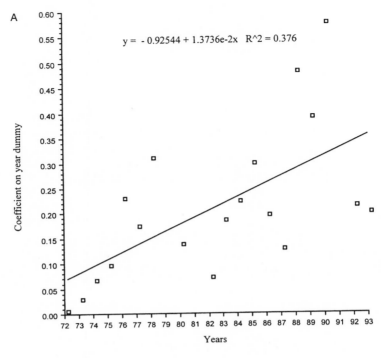

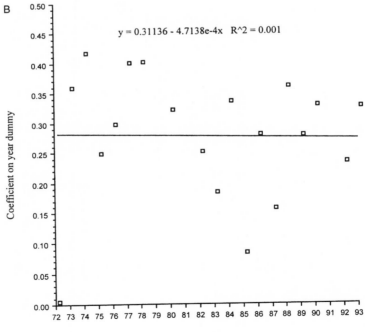

Fig. 7.1 Year dummies by age: United States, 1972–93
Note: *A*, Under age 30; *B*, age 30 and over.

happier through time. For those over age 30, the time trends in columns (3) and (4) of table 7.3 are small and negative.

Perhaps unexpectedly, the inclusion of family income in the equation (as in cols. [2] and [4]) has only small effects on most of the other coefficients. This suggests that the well-being derived from these characteristics is not complementary with income. In other words, the effect of income may be additively separable. The coefficient on the time trend is reduced by the inclusion of family income. It would be surprising if this did not happen. Prices have risen over the period, so a family income of $40,000 means less in real terms in the later years of the sample.

7.3 Life Satisfaction in Europe from the 1970s

There is similar information for most of the nations of Europe. Hence it is possible to test whether young Europeans also report rising levels of well-being.

Although economists seem rarely to have used the Eurobarometer survey series, these surveys ask:

> On the whole, are you very satisfied, fairly satisfied, not very satisfied, or not at all satisfied with the life you lead?

Answers are available for random samples, from 1973 to 1992, of approximately 1,000 people per year per country. The nations are Belgium, Denmark, West Germany, Greece, Spain, France, Ireland, Italy, Luxembourg, the Netherlands, Northern Ireland, Portugal, and Great Britain. Surveys have been held twice a year in each country. Because of their late entry into the European Community, there is no full run of data for Spain, Portugal, and Greece. A valuable source of information about the Eurobarometer surveys is the study by Inglehart (1990), who uses them to examine changing cultural values.[4]

Figure 7.2 plots the proportions of Eurobarometer respondents saying that they are "very satisfied" and "not at all satisfied" with their lives.[5] Various age groups are represented. As in the case of the United States, it is the young who stand out. From figure 7.2A, there was in the mid-1970s comparatively little difference among age groups in the percentage of people saying they were very satisfied with their lives. Approximately 20 percent of individuals gave this answer. Through time, the data fan out. Those in the youngest group, the under-twenties, end the data period with approximately 28 percent saying "very satisfied." The over-thirties show much less increase: by 1992 approximately 23 percent said they were very satisfied. This widening in the inequality of life satisfaction is especially

---

4. Further details of the Eurobarometer surveys are presented in appendix A.
5. The full sets of responses to this question by country are reported in appendix C.

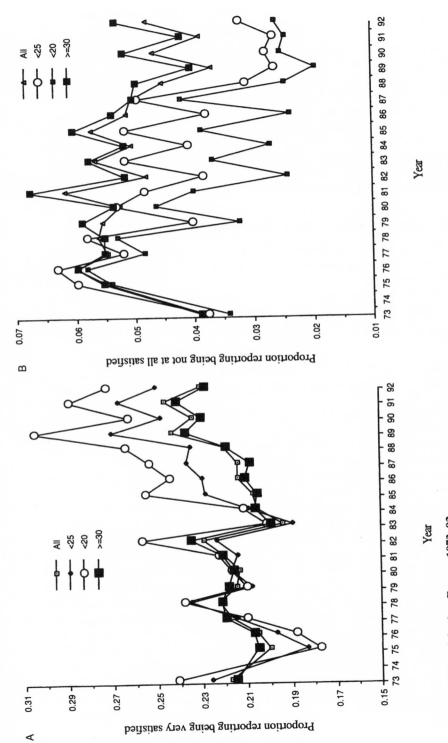

Fig. 7.2 Life satisfaction: Europe, 1973–92

Source: Eurobarometer series.

Note: Proportions reporting being (*A*) "very satisfied" and (*B*) "not at all satisfied" with their lives.

strong from the middle of the 1980s, but the underlying trend exists throughout the two decades. As can be seen, the upward trend is strongest for the under-twenties but still visible for the under-thirties.

A similar picture emerges from the dissatisfaction data. Figure 7.2*B* plots the percentage of individuals giving the answer "not at all satisfied." A sharp drop over the period is visible for young Europeans. By the start of the 1990s, less than 3 percent give this answer. The downward trend is again greater the younger the subsample. For those over age 30, the trend is flat across these two decades. Thus the low-satisfaction responses tell the same story as the high-satisfaction ones. Across these years, well-being apparently increases disproportionately among young individuals.

Table 7.4 is an ordered logit for life satisfaction in the European nations. The sample size is approximately 370,000. It includes both those who work and those who are retired or look after the home. The equations pool the individual Eurobarometer surveys from 1973 to 1992. To control for personal characteristics, the regressors include variables for male, self-employed, manual worker, white collar, holding an executive job, retired, housewife, student or military, unemployed, age and age squared of the respondent, a set of age left school (ALS) dummies, a further variable for studying, a set of marital status dummies, and country dummies, where France is the omitted category. Table 7.4 reveals that in a cross section the degree of satisfaction with life is greater among women, those who work for themselves, those in nonmanual jobs, and the highly educated. Being unemployed is associated with a heavily depressed level of life satisfaction. The same is true of those who are divorced or separated.

Table 7.4 reports four life satisfaction equations. Column (1) is for the full sample. There is a small positive time trend. In other words, through the two decades from the early 1970s, Europeans of given ages became more satisfied with their lives. Columns (2), (3), and (4) disaggregate by age group. They break the data into subsamples for the under-twenties, the under-thirties, and the over-thirties. The structures of the satisfaction equations for these groups are similar, in the sense that variables enter with approximately the same signs and sizes. What is noticeable is the difference in the time trend across these equations. The coefficient in the under-twenties column is approximately .02 while that in the over-thirties column is .003.[6] As in the simple time-series plots, therefore, the young are experiencing faster growth in life satisfaction than the old, even holding constant other factors.

One feature of table 7.4 is the apparently large differences in reported well-being across nations. The coefficients on country dummies vary from

---

6. Because *levels* of happiness differ greatly across groups the logit mapping is a reasonable transformation to a comparable scale. This allows us to draw comparisons of the relative orders of magnitude of the logit coefficients across equations. Thanks are due to Richard Freeman for this suggestion.

Table 7.4   Life Satisfaction Ordered Logits by Age: Europe, 1970s–1990s

Variable	Overall (1)	Under Age 20 (2)	Under Age 30 (3)	Age 30 and Over (4)
Time trend	.0066 (.0006)	.0196 (.0023)	.0169 (.0012)	.0034 (.0008)
Male	-.1270 (.0076)	-.0544 (.0224)	-.1171 (.0131)	-.1293 (.0095)
Self-employed 2	.3105 (.0278)	.1434 (.2359)	.1578 (.0673)	.3424 (.0307)
Self-employed 3	.1455 (.0233)	.2768 (.1748)	.0671 (.0605)	.1567 (.0253)
Manual	-.0462 (.0201)	-.0615 (.1336)	-.2132 (.0515)	-.0276 (.0221)
White collar	.1259 (.0207)	-.0324 (.1388)	-.0536 (.0523)	.1756 (.0229)
Executive	.3271 (.0241)	-.1310 (.1909)	.1752 (.0608)	.3503 (.0264)
Retired	.0563 (.0215)	-.1785 (.1857)	-.2942 (.0930)	.1064 (.0227)
Housewife	.0486 (.0206)	-.1971 (.1471)	-.1595 (.0544)	.0814 (.0225)
Student/military	.1397 (.0305)	-.0335 (.1351)	-.1394 (.0567)	-.0869 (.0782)
Unemployed	-.9665 (.0242)	-1.1715 (.1373)	-1.1982 (.0545)	-.9420 (.0295)
Age	-.0454 (.0012)	-1.0698 (.2310)	-.1965 (.0175)	-.0319 (.0021)
Age^2	.0005 (.0000)	.0285 (.0068)	.0033 (.0004)	.0005 (.0000)
ALS 15	.0700 (.0121)	-.0291 (.0638)	-.0108 (.0299)	.0644 (.0135)
ALS 16	.1479 (.0119)	.1306 (.0578)	.0630 (.0271)	.1597 (.0139)
ALS 17	.2340 (.0136)	.1480 (.0643)	.1538 (.0290)	.2456 (.0161)
ALS 18	.2832 (.0128)	.2067 (.0668)	.1746 (.0280)	.3084 (.0150)
ALS 19	.2724 (.0176)	.1883 (.0958)	.1814 (.0337)	.2970 (.0217)
ALS 20	.3293 (.0197)	.4434 (.2187)	.2331 (.0386)	.3535 (.0235)
ALS 21	.3781 (.0215)	.4355 (.2397)	.2507 (.0414)	.4243 (.0259)
ALS 22 or over	.2827 (.0122)	.2400 (.0758)	.2464 (.0296)	.2857 (.0138)
Studying	.3030 (.0248)	.2168 (.0580)	.2176 (.0333)	.2567 (.0594)
Married	.3053 (.0101)	.2097 (.0224)	.3847 (.0178)	.3050 (.0135)

Live together	.0369 (.0206)	−.0200 (.0641)	.1368 (.0292)	.0007 (.0305)
Divorced	−.5792 (.0231)	−1.1528 (.0955)	−.5973 (.0707)	−.5722 (.0256)
Separated	−.7265 (.0338)	−1.0049 (.3178)	−.6432 (.0814)	−.7164 (.0378)
Widowed	−.3257 (.0163)	−.6949 (.3623)	−.5517 (.1089)	−.3102 (.0182)
Belgium	.9210 (.0145)	.8073 (.0521)	.9826 (.0269)	.8969 (.0172)
Netherlands	1.4938 (.0148)	1.2348 (.0549)	1.5094 (.0276)	1.4988 (.0176)
Germany	.6052 (.0143)	.0047 (.0505)	.3803 (.0270)	.6884 (.0169)
Italy	−.1609 (.0142)	−.3512 (.0483)	−.1571 (.0264)	−.1682 (.0169)
Luxembourg	1.2885 (.0209)	.7975 (.0730)	1.1277 (.0396)	1.3458 (.0246)
Denmark	2.0542 (.0150)	1.7368 (.0557)	2.0482 (.0285)	2.0651 (.0177)
Ireland	1.0596 (.0149)	.5961 (.0471)	.9047 (.0267)	1.1251 (.0181)
Great Britain	.9714 (.0146)	.5922 (.0523)	.8561 (.0278)	1.0185 (.0173)
Northern Ireland	1.0735 (.0218)	.5024 (.0710)	.8651 (.0392)	1.1681 (.0263)
Greece	−.3825 (.0165)	−.4659 (.0573)	−.3484 (.0309)	−.3987 (.0195)
Spain	.4067 (.0189)	.3393 (.0607)	.4622 (.0341)	.3759 (.0228)
Portugal	−.3173 (.0184)	−.4169 (.0609)	−.2300 (.0340)	−.3813 (.0220)
Cut1	−3.1037 (.0356)	−12.934 (1.9671)	−5.3165 (.2023)	−2.7274 (.2023)
Cut2	−1.4792 (.0350)	−11.2165 (1.9669)	−3.6327 (.2017)	−1.1201 (.2017)
Cut3	1.3002 (.0350)	−8.3124 (1.9664)	−.7586 (.2014)	1.6294 (.2014)
N	371,440	32,887	108,574	262,866
Pseudo R^2	.0730	.0623	.0739	.0741
X^2	59,826.06	4,272.66	17,274.11	43,393.8
Log likelihood	−379,787.5	−32,178.6	−108,215.1	−271,016.6

Source: Eurobarometer series.

Note: Excluded categories are age left school (ALS) under 15, single, France, and self-employed farmers and fishermen (skippers). Self-employed 2 = professional self-employed (lawyers, accountants, etc.), and Self-employed 3 = business self-employed (owners of shops, craftsmen, proprietors, etc.). Numbers in parentheses are standard errors.

2.05 for Denmark to −.38 for Greece. It should be borne in mind that these are pure cross-sectional effects. Such divergent numbers are likely to reflect cultural and linguistic differences. This may stem partly from the difficulty of translation (words like "happiness," "contentment," and "satisfaction" have subtle distinctions in English and in other languages). It is not necessarily all variation in language, however. As Inglehart (1990) points out, Switzerland makes an ideal laboratory to test this. German-speaking Swiss, French-speaking Swiss, and Italian-speaking Swiss all express higher satisfaction levels than do native Germans, French, and Italians. There is something intrinsically nicer about Switzerland. Nevertheless, it seems unwise to take too literally the country dummy coefficients.

Do all these European countries have youth populations who are becoming more contented? It is not possible to answer this question by looking at the pooled equation of table 7.4. Hence table 7.5 disaggregates by nation. It reports the time trends on life satisfaction equations estimated for each country separately. Separate results by age and educational group are included. In all countries except Belgium and Ireland, the well-being gradient is greater for those under 30 than for those over 30.

One other point is worth recording. Taking the under-thirties in the 13 countries, in each nation except Great Britain and Northern Ireland there is a positive and statistically significant upward time trend over the most recent decade, 1983–92 (results not reported). Why the British Isles misses out on this recent growth of well-being among the young is a puzzle.

7.4 The Source of Young People's Growing Well-Being

Young people in the West say they are becoming relatively happier and more satisfied with life. This section tries to understand why.

One possibility is that the *cessation of the cold war* has raised young people's well-being by diminishing the likelihood of war with the former USSR. This is a difficult hypothesis to address convincingly. However, one approach (suggested to us by Rafael Di Tella) is to test whether those nations closest to the ex–Soviet Union have the largest upward trends in well-being. The underlying argument is that greater distance—for example, for Britain and to a greater extent the United States—from the old Eastern Bloc gave some safety in the event of war. Nations contiguous to the USSR should have been most vulnerable and ought thus to show the greatest recent increases in youth well-being. Table 7.5 can be used to explore this. However, it reveals little correlation between the time trend in happiness and distance from the old USSR. Germany, for example, both borders the Eastern Bloc and had one of the smallest increases in youth well-being. Portugal, despite being relatively far from the Eastern Bloc, had a strong rise in young people's satisfaction.

Table 7.6 suggests that the rising happiness of youth is not because of

Table 7.5   Life Satisfaction Ordered Logits by Country and Level of Education: Europe, 1970s–1990s

	Under Age 30			Age 30 and Over		
	Overall	Less Educated	More Educated	Overall	Less Educated	More Educated
All	.0183 (15.07)	.0094 (4.98)	.0246 (15.26)	.0061 (8.13)	.0094 (10.54)	−.0055 (3.84)
France	.0255 (7.25)	−.0031 (0.51)	.0417 (9.57)	−.0009 (0.41)	.0035 (1.28)	−.0131 (3.39)
Belgium	−.0403 (10.88)	−.0578 (7.76)	−.0354 (8.09)	−.0311 (13.79)	−.0304 (10.54)	−.0365 (9.64)
Netherlands	.0355 (8.10)	.0283 (3.75)	.0366 (6.70)	.0142 (5.78)	.0157 (5.14)	.0096 (2.29)
Germany	.0256 (618)	.0273 (4.63)	.0235 (3.96)	.0329 (14.35)	.0355 (13.33)	.0234 (5.09)
Italy	.0705 (20.50)	.0499 (8.86)	.0838 (19.06)	.0379 (17.70)	.0417 (16.86)	.0230 (5.12)
Luxembourg	.0398 (5.89)	.0358 (3.21)	.0411 (4.73)	.0206 (5.18)	.0199 (3.95)	.0191 (2.88)
Denmark	.0312 (7.60)	.0207 (2.99)	.0357 (6.87)	.0205 (7.96)	.0260 (8.26)	.0022 (0.45)
Ireland	−.0171 (4.93)	−.0249 (4.99)	−.0121 (2.48)	−.0259 (11.30)	−.0261 (9.79)	−.0354 (7.47)
Great Britain	.0106 (2.85)	.0105 (2.28)	.0074 (1.14)	.0045 (2.10)	.0061 (2.58)	−.0067 (1.23)
Northern Ireland	.0346 (4.94)	.0414 (4.59)	.0273 (2.40)	.0244 (5.40)	.0238 (4.82)	.0220 (1.84)
Greece	.0200 (2.86)	.0187 (1.42)	.0206 (2.45)	−.0243 (5.55)	−.0138 (2.61)	−.0527 (2.15)
Spain	.0261 (1.93)	−.0256 (1.20)	.0691 (3.89)	−.0015 (0.17)	.0050 (0.49)	−.0290 (1.46)
Portugal	.1234 (7.90)	.0729 (3.41)	.1810 (7.77)	.0761 (7.94)	.0756 (7.29)	.0765 (2.91)

Source: Eurobarometer series.

Note: Equations include five marital status dummies, nine labor force status dummies, age and its square, a gender dummy, and ten schooling dummies (three if age left school is under 18 and five if over 17). The overall equations also include twelve country dummies. "Less educated" = age left school under 18. "More educated" = age left school 18 or over. Numbers in parentheses are *t*-statistics.

Table 7.6   Happiness Ordered Logits by Sex and Whether White: United States, 1970s–1990s

Variable	Male (1)	Female (2)	Male under Age 30 (3)	Female under Age 30 (4)	Nonwhite under Age 30 (5)	Male Nonwhite under Age 30 (6)
Time trend	.0107 (.0029)	−.0036 (.0027)	.0274 (.0061)	.0076 (.0057)	.0461 (.0102)	.0721 (.0162)
Male					.0968 (.1276)	
Black	−.4210 (.0572)	−.6133 (.0474)	−.5840 (.1135)	−.8989 (.0948)		
Other nonwhite	.1347 (.1249)	−.1890 (.1125)	−.1168 (.2319)	−.2620 (.2064)		
Part time	−.2031 (.0739)	.0021 (.0522)	−.3166 (.1224)	−.0869 (.0991)	−.3513 (.1947)	−.6508 (.3180)
Job but absent	−.1994 (.1123)	−.2381 (.1182)	−.3157 (.2566)	−.0022 (.2534)	−1.3557 (.4572)	−1.3822 (.7341)
Unemployed	−.8882 (.0860)	−.5635 (.1339)	−.8462 (.1384)	−.4556 (.2103)	−.6895 (.2348)	−1.0675 (.3114)
Retired	−.0637 (.0731)	.0113 (.0717)				
In school	.0648 (.1064)	.1705 (.1001)	−.0484 (.1280)	.2127 (.1289)	−.3006 (.2078)	−.7514 (.3248)
Keeping house	−.5053 (.1875)	−.0667 (.0409)	−.1946 (.3706)	−.0635 (.0855)	.1075 (.1689)	.2764 (.5702)
Other	−.6952 (.1433)	−.4896 (.1525)	−.5311 (.4079)	.4094 (.3672)	−.1662 (.4474)	−.8668 (.6922)
Age	−.0176 (.0067)	−.0121 (.0051)	−.2822 (.1982)	−.2561 (.180)	−.3221 (.3106)	−.6731 (.4896)
Age²	.0003 (.00007)	.0002 (.00005)	.0049 (.0040)	.0053 (.0037)	.0062 (.0064)	.0119 (.0102)
Years schooling	.6461 (.0541)	.6258 (.0529)	.6064 (.0901)	.5768 (.0828)	.5481 (.1431)	.7839 (.2460)
Married	−.5355 (.1099)	−.3598 (.0713)	−.4033 (.8468)	−.0656 (.5126)	.5480 (.1430)	−1.2712 (1.276)
Widowed	−.3344 (.0832)	−.3069 (.0677)	−.4028 (.2318)	−.3924 (.1515)	−1.4963 (.7378)	−.2517 (.6850)
Divorced	−.4270 (.1213)	−.5181 (.0926)	−.7156 (.2865)	−.8341 (.1796)	−.1874 (.3025)	−.8099 (.5334)
Separated	.0301 (.0056)	.0726 (.0060)	.1278 (.0180)	.1106 (.0168)	−.7864 (.2687)	.1282 (.0549)
Cut1	−1.6807 (.1779)	−1.1370 (.1589)	−4.2549 (2.3420)	−3.5082 (2.1443)	−3.9647 (3.685)	−8.6271 (5.779)
Cut2	1.2486 (1.775)	1.7056 (.1590)	−1.0446 (2.3405)	−.5387 (2.1434)	−1.0874 (3.684)	−5.4934 (5.770)
N	12,431	15,860	3,117	3,702	1,207	493
Pseudo R^2	.0417	.0438	.0469	.0502	.0448	.0782
χ^2	978.73	1,326.7	266.3	350.7	104.31	73.1
Log likelihood	−11,255.7	−14,483.6	−2,703.2	−3,318.7	−1,112.2	−430.6

Source: General Social Surveys.

Note: Equation also includes eight census area dummies. "Nonwhite" includes black and other nonwhite. Numbers in parentheses are standard errors.

declining discrimination against women or blacks. The well-being trend is strong for men; it is not merely young women who have become happier. For the United States, the GSS reveals that from the 1970s to the 1990s there has been a rapid increase in black men's reported well-being, but part of the rise has been among older black men.[7] Young white men, moreover, have enjoyed improved well-being—especially relative to older white men. Among whites aged 30 or over, there was actually a small decline among those giving the answer "very happy" (from 37 percent in the 1970s to 35 percent in the 1990s). More formally, the time-trend coefficient in column (6) of table 7.6 is not large enough to explain the whole improvement in young people's well-being.

Another potential argument is that the increasing contentment of the younger generation is somehow linked to *work or education.* Table 7.7 suggests that this is unlikely to be the explanation. Both employed and not employed groups of young men show—in columns (3) and (4)—a positive time trend. The trend is in fact greater for those out of work. Columns (1) and (2) find that more educated men have a time trend of .04 compared to less than .02 for the less educated. This seems worth knowing. However, the ranking is reversed for women. While further exploration in this area might yield insights, our judgment is that the reason for growing youth happiness will probably not be found here.

It is well known that over the past two decades, marriage has become less common in both the United States and Europe (as table 7.8 shows). Does the *changing nature of marital relationships* have a role to play in the growth of young people's happiness?

Consider table 7.9, which breaks down the trends in happiness scores of Americans by marital status. The highest happiness level is "very happy"; the medium level is "pretty happy"; the lowest level is "not too happy." Data are presented for two periods. The first runs from 1972 to 1984, the second from 1985 onward.

Table 7.9 uncovers a simple fact. It is predominantly the unmarried who account for the rise in reported happiness among young people in the United States. In the first period, 21.3 percent of young unmarried people gave the survey answer "very happy." In the following decade, 26.1 percent said they were very happy. This contrasts with the data for married young people. In the first period, for example, 36.9 percent of married people said they were very happy. In the second period, an almost unchanged 36.6 percent did so.

For this to be persuasive, a broadly similar effect would have to be found at the bottom of the happiness distribution, namely, for those giving the response "not too happy." Apparently it is. According to table 7.9, in

---

7. In an equation for blacks only, the time trend has a coefficient of .0206 ($t = 3.9$), whereas for older black men (age 30 or over), the coefficient is .0154 ($t = 2.5$).

Table 7.7   Happiness Ordered Logits by Education and Employment for Males under Age 30: United States, 1970s–1990s

Variable	Less Educated (1)	More Educated (2)	Employed (3)	Not Employed (4)
Time trend	.0174 (.0085)	.0427 (.0092)	.0219 (.0070)	.0464 (.0129)
Black	−.5743 (.1407)	−.6137 (.1980)	−.5485 (.1361)	−.7239 (.2114)
Other nonwhite	.1227 (.3019)	−.5318 (.3683)	.1945 (.2727)	−1.0106 (.4400)
Part time	−.4084 (.1723)	−.3296 (.1822)	.0007 (.2785)	
Job but absent	−.5507 (.3356)	−.0653 (.3985)	.3203 (.2582)	
Unemployed	−.8702 (.1597)	−.8693 (.2872)		
In school	−.3820 (.2066)	.1758 (.1761)		.7192 (.2029)
Keeping house	−.1961 (.4045)	−.3982 (.8685)		.5628 (.3855)
Other	−.3137 (.4742)	−1.4257 (.7613)		.2204 (.4299)
Age	−.7160 (.2545)	.2321 (.3988)	−.3411 (.2358)	−.2440 (.4163)
Age²	.0144 (.0052)	−.0062 (.0080)	.0060 (.0048)	.0048 (.0088)
Married	.4835 (.1232)	.7598 (.1346)	.6506 (.0989)	.3478 (.2294)
Widowed	.1323 (1.034)	−1.6998 (.4355)	−.6184 (.9492)	1.2845 (.9788)
Divorced	−.6056 (.2957)	−.0302 (.3754)	−.2067 (.2567)	−1.3381 (.5580)
Separated	−.9051 (.3602)	−.3759 (.4854)	−.5876 (.3082)	−1.5296 (.8921)
Years schooling	.0595 (.0425)	.1788 (.0388)	.1263 (.0200)	.1380 (.0424)
Cut1	−9.8783 (3.0271)	2.0978 (4.8428)	−4.7224 (2.835)	−2.8441 (4.715)
Cut2	−6.8431 (3.0207)	5.6521 (4.8454)	−1.4792 (2.833)	.3148 (4.713)
N	1,744	1,373	2,430	687
Pseudo R^2	.0398	.0547	.0322	.0848
χ^2	129.8	129.0	139.41	110.7
Log likelihood	−1,567.0	−1,114.7	−2,096.5	−597.6
	Females under Age 30: Time Trends from Separate Equations			
Time trend	.0099 (.0075)	.0027 (.0089)	.0123 (.0076)	.0037 (.0087)

Source: General Social Surveys.

Note: Equations also include eight census area dummies. "Less educated" is less than 13 years of schooling. "More educated" is 13 or more years of schooling. Numbers in parentheses are standard errors.

1972–84, 17.5 percent of unmarried young Americans said they were not happy; for the period 1985 onward, this number fell to 11.1 percent. The trend for married people was also down, but less steeply. In the early period, 9.6 percent of married young people reported themselves as not happy; this became 6.2 percent by the later period of 1985 onward. There was a slight overall rise, therefore, in the reported happiness of young married Americans from the 1970s to the 1990s. However, this rise was dwarfed by the considerable change in unmarried young people's happiness. The conclusion appears to be that the trend of rising well-being among young Americans is explained largely by what happened among a single subsample—those not married.

Rather less appears to have happened to the well-being of those over age 30. Table 7.9 shows that the percentages giving the answer "very

Table 7.8   **Decline in Marriage: United States and Europe (percent married)**

Country	Under Age 30			Age 30 and Over		
	1970s	1980s	1990s	1970s	1980s	1990s
United States	53.8	41.6	36.5	72.5	61.4	57.3
Europe	46.7	33.1	25.3	85.0	73.1	70.1

Source: General Social Surveys and Eurobarometer series.

Note: Only three years are available for the 1990s. Europe-wide weights are imposed to obtain the European estimates.

Table 7.9   **Distribution of Happiness by Marital Status: United States**

Happiness	1972–84		1985–92	
	Married	Not Married	Married	Not Married
	Under Age 30			
Not too happy	.096	.175	.062	.111
Pretty happy	.535	.612	.572	.628
Very happy	.369	.213	.366	.261
	Age 30 and Over			
Not too happy	.090	.209	.068	.172
Pretty happy	.499	.562	.532	.616
Very happy	.411	.229	.401	.212

Source: General Social Surveys.

Note: Table reports the proportion giving each response. Only three years are available for the 1990s.

happy" altered little between the periods. There was an improvement, nevertheless, at the lower end of the happiness distribution. For both the married and unmarried, the numbers responding "not too happy" fell approximately 3 percentage points.

Table 7.10 provides the same message using an ordered logit for U.S. data. An extended set of variables is included.[8] As well as the findings discussed earlier in the paper, this specification shows that reported happiness for both age groups is lower among those whose parents were divorced (by the time the respondent was age 16) and those who state that

8. In addition to the variables used in earlier tables we also include controls for the number of siblings, religion, the number of children, household size, and whether the respondent's parents were divorced when the respondent was age 16. We included a variable that identified whether one or both of the parents had died when the respondent was age 16, but it was always insignificant different from zero and hence was excluded. Further, we used two variables suggested to us by Jim Davis and used in Davis (1984) to represent a (qualitative) measure of income and a change in financial circumstances. In the former case the respondents were asked, "Compared with American families in general, would you say your family income is far below average, below average, average or above average?" In the latter case the question was, "During the last 5 years has your financial situation been getting better, worse or has it stayed the same?" Unsurprisingly income buys happiness.

Table 7.10   **Happiness Ordered Logits by Marital Status: United States, 1970s–1990s**

	Age 30 and Over		Under Age 30		
Variable	Married (1)	Not Married (2)	Married (3)	Not Married (4)	All (5)
Time trend	−.0041 (.0023)	−.0069 (.0032)	−.0025 (.0055)	.0131 (.0049)	−.0031 (.0017)
Part time	.0777 (.0591)	.1597 (.0821)	.2068 (.1272)	−.1720 (.0939)	.0712 (.0393)
Job but absent	−.0604 (.1094)	−.2073 (.1389)	−.1146 (.2600)	−.4763 (.2341)	−.1591 (.0766)
Unemployed	−.4844 (.1291)	−.5141 (.1202)	−.5085 (.2110)	−.4000 (.1388)	−.4660 (.0684)
Retired	.1563 (.0672)	−.0842 (.0783)			.0682 (.0482)
In school	−.0643 (.2057)	.2244 (.2105)	.2477 (.2186)	.2047 (.1035)	.3329 (.0704)
Keeping house	.1488 (.0509)	−.1896 (.0737)	.2198 (.1050)	−.2268 (.1369)	.0142 (.0358)
Other	.1679 (.1529)	−.8031 (.1401)	1.0325 (.6569)	−.0030 (.3241)	−.2879 (.0967)
Male	−.0588 (.0393)	−.2586 (.0486)	−.2919 (.0870)	−.3251 (.0674)	−.1817 (.0257)
Black	−.5157 (.0609)	−.1935 (.0611)	−.6641 (.1349)	−.5664 (.0955)	−.4265 (.0369)
Other nonwhite	.1108 (.1076)	−.0038 (.1415)	.1763 (.2236)	−.2207 (.1737)	.0354 (.0719)
Parents divorced[a]	−.1375 (.0605)	−.1847 (.0682)	−.2111 (.1010)	−.1174 (.0814)	−.1705 (.0363)
Years schooling	.0177 (.0060)	.0434 (.0074)	.0927 (.0191)	.0609 (.0184)	.0316 (.0043)
Age	.0068 (.0094)	−.0158 (.0098)	.1507 (.2348)	−.3725 (.1693)	−.0107 (.0044)
Age^2 * 10^2	.0031 (.0091)	.0272 (.0088)	−.0027 (.0047)	.7594 (.0035)	.0209 (.0046)
Income far below average	−.4625 (.0992)	−.7122 (.0858)	−.6087 (.2044)	−.4866 (.1392)	−.6076 (.0553)
Income below average	−.2996 (.0455)	−.3013 (.0502)	−.4082 (.0914)	−.2855 (.0807)	−.3136 (.0289)
Income above average	.1227 (.0419)	.1635 (.0685)	.0376 (.1112)	.3267 (.0916)	.1404 (.0315)

Income far above average	.3126 (.1124)	.0843 (.1737)	−.5468 (.4049)	.0383 (.2589)	.1669 (.0857)
Married		−.2702 (.0758)		.3474 (.4398)	.6168 (.0363)
Widowed		−.1288 (.0615)		−.1894 (.1315)	−.4127 (.0551)
Divorced		−.2983 (.0864)		−.4023 (.1583)	−.2311 (.0475)
Separated					−.3939 (.0689)
Finances getting better	.2818 (.0375)	.3541 (.0525)	.3904 (.0850)	.3671 (.0752)	.3288 (.0265)
Finances getting worse	−.5927 (.0446)	−.5416 (.0541)	−.5079 (.1121)	−.5817 (.0925)	−.5681 (.0308)
No. of siblings	.0057 (.0053)	−.0023 (.0066)	−.0246 (.0131)	−.0243 (.0122)	−.0025 (.0037)
No. of children	−.0229 (.0099)	.0266 (.0123)	−.0736 (.0390)	−.1147 (.0513)	−.0033 (.0074)
Protestant	.3482 (.0726)	.1919 (.0817)	.2493 (.1322)	.3568 (.0947)	.2984 (.0436)
Catholic	.2578 (.0766)	.0952 (.0877)	.1227 (.1436)	.3394 (.1018)	.2103 (.0465)
Jewish	.2124 (.1255)	−.5290 (.1703)	.1974 (.3478)	−.1474 (.2482)	−.0162 (.0882)
Other	.1973 (.1343)	.0151 (.1589)	.5053 (.2789)	.0653 (.1949)	.1636 (.0851)
Cut1	−2.0672 (.2744)	−1.3908 (.3186)	.7568 (2.8842)	−5.3049 (1.9695)	−1.5668 (.1329)
Cut2	.9488 (.2735)	1.6169 (.3188)	3.9925 (2.8848)	−1.9302 (1.9674)	1.4829 (.1326)
N	15,575	9,435	3,254	4,302	32,566
Pseudo R^2	.0357	.0486	.0646	.0784	.0679
χ^2	1,004.2	954.2	379.0	614.8	4,173.7
Log likelihood	−13,563.7	−8,497.3	−2,744.6	−3,611.4	−28,643.4

Source: General Social Surveys.

Note: "Not married" includes widowed, separated, divorced, and single. Excluded categories are full-time job, white, income average, finances same, and no religion. Equations also include 44 state dummies. Numbers in parentheses are standard errors.

[a] Parents were divorced by the time the child was 16 years old.

their "finances are getting worse." For the young, the number of siblings and the number of children enter negatively, but they are insignificant for the older age group. In column (1), the time trend for married older people enters with a coefficient of approximately −.004. It is not possible, at normal confidence levels, to reject the null of zero. Thus life satisfaction has been flat or slightly declining through time for the older married subsample in the United States. For older unmarried people, the time trend is also negative and statistically significant. In column (4), there is evidence of a strong upward movement in well-being levels. This is for the young unmarried subsample. The coefficient is .0131 with a standard error of .0049. By contrast, in column (3), the time trend for married young people is −.0025 with a standard error of .0055.

To begin to explore the possible causes of the rising well-being of the young in Europe, table 7.11 contains life satisfaction ordered logits for four subgroups. There is a positive time trend for three of these groups: employees, students and those on military service, and the unemployed. For the remaining category, housewives and the retired (at this age, presumably predominantly because of poor health), there is a slight downward trend in life satisfaction. The sample in column (2) is approximately 13,000, so this is unlikely to be a chance result generated by inadequate sample size.

Another way to divide the data is by education. Table 7.12 does so. "Low education" is defined as those who left school at age 18 or less. "High education" is the group who left school when older. In columns (1) and (2) it emerges that in Europe it is the high-education young who are experiencing the most rapid increase in well-being. In fact, individuals with high education who are over age 30 show up with a negative time trend. For them, average life satisfaction fell over the two decades of the data. Thus education may be somehow connected to the phenomenon of rising youth well-being. But the major force appears to lie elsewhere.

Table 7.13 successfully replicates for Europe the main finding from the U.S. data. The time trend in well-being predominantly results from the unmarried having become more content. Whether using measures for European life satisfaction or European happiness (available for 1975–79 and 1982–86 only), the time trend in well-being in table 7.13 is more than five times larger for young people who are not married.

These findings appear to provide evidence against another possible explanation for the trend in young people's well-being. It might be argued—as Nick Crafts has suggested to us—that this era has seen particular growth in *new consumer goods aimed at the young.* If this were the reason for young people's greater reported happiness, however, it would presumably show up as strongly for married as for unmarried people. It seems that the rise in youth well-being in the West is not somehow the product of changed income or consumption patterns.

Table 7.11

Life Satisfaction Ordered Logits by Labor Market Status for People under Age 30: Europe, 1970s–1990s

Variable	Employed (1)	Housewife/ Retired (2)	Student/ Military Service (3)	Unemployed (4)
Time trend	.0143 (.0017)	−.0041 (.0035)	.0336 (.0023)	.0142 (.0053)
Male	−.1159 (.0180)	−.2046 (.1118)	−.0264 (.0224)	−.2889 (.0408)
Self-employed 2	.1841 (.0684)			
Self-employed 3	.0766 (.0614)			
Manual	−.2324 (.0523)			
White collar	−.0425 (.0535)			
Executive	.2098 (.0622)			
Retired		−.1107 (.1076)		
Age	−.1494 (.0306)	−.1935 (.0590)	−.1490 (.0395)	−.2963 (.0686)
Age^2	.0022 (.0007)	.0036 (.0012)	.0018 (.0009)	.0054 (.0015)
ALS 15	−.0542 (.0391)	−.0153 (.0617)	.2802 (.1578)	−.0896 (.0839)
ALS 17	.0645 (.0376)	.2630 (.0642)	.2671 (.1460)	.2215 (.0832)
ALS 18	.0834 (.0365)	.3545 (.0629)	.1686 (.1467)	.2292 (.0782)
ALS 19	.1115 (.0427)	.2294 (.0874)	.2278 (.1616)	.2572 (.0918)
ALS 20	.1750 (.0476)	.4070 (.1164)	.2738 (.1778)	.2203 (.1094)
ALS 21	.1627 (.0503)	.3601 (.1222)	.2725 (.2114)	.3485 (.1245)
ALS 22 or over	.1719 (.0384)	.1924 (.0824)	.3869 (.1299)	.3128 (.0840)
Studying	.0815 (.0592)	.2368 (.1462)	.3365 (.1195)	.3619 (.1485)
Married	.3442 (.0212)	.5398 (.0619)	.2757 (.0731)	.5213 (.0598)
Live together	.1139 (.0365)	.5011 (.1167)	.0925 (.0695)	.2858 (.0909)
Divorced	−.4847 (.0890)	−.7842 (.1636)	−.6677 (.3239)	−.5107 (.2029)
Separated	−.5926 (.1065)	−.7074 (.1832)	−.9971 (.4284)	−.3729 (.1938)
Widowed	−.7744 (.2009)	−.3661 (.1498)	.1127 (.4705)	.1161 (.4151)
Belgium	1.1825 (.0378)	1.1649 (.0886)	.6692 (.0498)	.7271 (.0875)
Netherlands	1.7903 (.0408)	1.5930 (.0706)	1.1204 (.0500)	1.2451 (.1086)
Germany	.5723 (.0377)	.6568 (.0819)	−.0094 (.0506)	.3874 (.1032)
Italy	.0271 (.0401)	−.1560 (.0802)	−.5382 (.0469)	−.1122 (.0827)
Luxembourg	1.3009 (.0535)	1.6709 (.1223)	.7514 (.0726)	.4048 (.2654)
Denmark	2.3061 (.0395)	1.9800 (.1204)	1.7128 (.0513)	1.7537 (.1011)
Ireland	1.2232 (.0384)	1.0056 (.0758)	.6659 (.0503)	.1046 (.0864)
Great Britain	1.1258 (.0383)	.9603 (.0715)	.5136 (.0605)	.3907 (.0956)
Northern Ireland	1.1391 (.0555)	.8166 (.0993)	.5693 (.0842)	.6890 (.1161)
Greece	−.3696 (.0471)	.0458 (.0809)	−.7097 (.0559)	−.0365 (.1032)
Spain	.5928 (.0531)	.7164 (.1014)	.0936 (.0588)	.4719 (.1019)
Portugal	−.0846 (.0473)	.0147 (.1063)	−.6035 (.0647)	−.1956 (.1202)
Cut1	−4.7874 (.3558)	−4.7452 (.6814)	−4.9675 (.4149)	−5.2562 (.7634)
Cut2	−3.0522 (.3551)	−3.1162 (.6802)	−3.1564 (.4137)	−3.7098 (.7624)
Cut3	−.1027 (.3548)	−.3802 (.6796)	−.1144 (.4132)	−1.3841 (.7615)
N	53,961	13,110	32,474	9,029
Pseudo R^2	.0732	.0559	.0666	.0438
χ^2	8,319.8	1,590.3	4,363.4	997.8
Log likelihood	−52,708.3	−13,422.2	−30,588.7	−10,883.8

Source: Eurobarometer series.

Note: Numbers in parentheses are standard errors.

Table 7.12 **Life Satisfaction Ordered Logits by Education: Europe, 1970s–1990s**

Variable	Under Age 30		Age 30 and Over	
	Low Education (1)	High Education (2)	Low Education (3)	High Education (4)
Time trend	.0067 (.0017)	.0285 (.0018)	.0063 (.0008)	−.0075 (.0017)
Male	−.1736 (.0193)	−.0577 (.0179)	−.1071 (.0109)	−.2109 (.0195)
Self-employed 2	.1119 (.0913)	.3016 (.1292)	.3052 (.0405)	.5130 (.07423)
Self-employed 3	−.0188 (.0680)	.2414 (.1325)	.1306 (.0272)	.3380 (.07613)
Manual	−.2428 (.0567)	−.1210 (.1196)	−.0422 (.0233)	.0863 (.07259)
White collar	−.0845 (.0587)	.0303 (.1180)	.1828 (.0250)	.2746 (.06986)
Executive	.1695 (.0816)	.2802 (.1230)	.3139 (.0340)	.5418 (.07082)
Retired	−.2637 (.1013)	−.2226 (.2361)	.0588 (.0240)	.4110 (.0735)
Housewife	−.2177 (.0607)	−.0780 (.1253)	.0645 (.0238)	.2330 (.07281)
Student/military	−.2323 (.0708)	−.0261 (.1203)	.0284 (.1560)	.0116 (.1115)
Unemployed	−1.2377 (.0609)	−.9972 (.1226)	−.9678 (.0320)	−.7954 (.08347)
Age	−.2021 (.0276)	−.1783 (.0242)	−.0341 (.0023)	−.0243 (.0049)
Age²	.0036 (.0006)	.0026 (.0005)	.0003 (.00002)	.0003 (.00004)
ALS 15	−.0055 (.0303)		.0532 (.0137)	
ALS 17	.0960 (.0282)		.1429 (.0141)	
ALS 18	.1805 (.0299)		.2282 (.0164)	
ALS 19	.2055 (.0290)		.2893 (.0153)	
ALS 20		.0514 (.0417)		.0611 (.0305)
ALS 21		.0828 (.0444)		.1459 (.0325)
ALS 22 or over		.0600 (.0337)		−.0012 (.0240)
Studying		.0239 (.0412)		.0111 (.0663)
Married	.3336 (.0225)	.4486 (.0298)	.2850 (.0160)	.3542 (.0256)
Live together	.1265 (.0415)	.1686 (.0412)	−.0354 (.0385)	.0891 (.0507)
Divorced	−.7116 (.0800)	−.2151 (.1481)	−.6194 (.0305)	−.4769 (.0478)
Separated	−.6752 (.0924)	−.5409 (.1697)	−.7313 (.0441)	−.7110 (.0743)
Widowed	−.5861 (.1178)	−.3320 (.2769)	−.3012 (.0205)	−.4027 (.0455)
Belgium	1.1762 (.0399)	.8171 (.0366)	.9570 (.0199)	.7512 (.0348)
Netherlands	1.6899 (.0421)	1.3578 (.0369)	1.5384 (.0208)	1.4230 (.0336)
Germany	.5788 (.0380)	.1848 (.0388)	.7016 (.0191)	.6856 (.0372)
Italy	.0611 (.0402)	−.3510 (.0356)	−.1358 (.0191)	−.2578 (.0370)
Luxembourg	1.3269 (.0584)	.9464 (.0541)	1.3696 (.0287)	1.3024 (.0484)
Denmark	2.1338 (.0421)	1.9580 (.0391)	2.0842 (.0209)	2.0593 (.0346)
Ireland	.9969 (.0363)	.8521 (.0404)	1.1338 (.0201)	1.1383 (.0432)
Great Britain	.9988 (.0363)	.7165 (.0460)	1.0399 (.0193)	.9663 (.0408)
Northern Ireland	.9821 (.0491)	.8055 (.0681)	1.1873 (.0285)	1.0948 (.0720)
Greece	−.1597 (.0455)	−.5306 (.0426)	−.4063 (.0222)	−.3582 (.0419)
Spain	.6637 (.0517)	.2883 (.0458)	.4027 (.0258)	.2746 (.0494)
Portugal	.0450 (.0472)	−.4964 (.0500)	−.3477 (.0244)	−.5512 (.0524)
Cut1	−5.1917 (.3179)	−5.4507 (.2909)	−2.7437 (.0689)	−3.0365 (.1412)
Cut2	−3.5783 (.3173)	−3.6474 (.2899)	−1.1454 (.0684)	−1.3699 (.1397)
Cut3	−.8103 (.3169)	−.6394 (.2893)	1.5643 (.0685)	1.5470 (.1398)
N	55,381	53,193	205,017	57,849
Pseudo R^2	.0683	.0792	.0696	.0831
χ^2	8,399.4	8,727.08	32,163.9	10,114.2
Log likelihood	−575,253.5	−50,744.5	−215,015.5	−55,796.8

Source: Eurobarometer series.

Note: "Low education" = age left school 18 or under. "High education" = age left school over 18.

Table 7.13 **Life Satisfaction and Happiness Ordered Logits by Marital Status for People under Age 30: Europe, 1970s–1990s**

Variable	Life Satisfaction Married (1)	Life Satisfaction Not Married (2)	Happiness Married (3)	Happiness Not Married (4)
Time trend	.0044 (.0021)	.0227 (.0015)	.0041 (.0050)	.0250 (.0037)
Male	−.2689 (.0274)	−.0734 (.0150)	−.3314 (.0457)	−.1675 (.0272)
Self-employed 2	.3272 (.1139)	.0640 (.0839)	.3444 (.2088)	.0231 (.1585)
Self-employed 3	.0858 (.1021)	.0635 (.0760)	.0354 (.1734)	.3608 (.1327)
Manual	−.1350 (.0908)	−.2574 (.0627)	−.0670 (.1559)	−.0880 (.1088)
White collar	.0207 (.0919)	−.0994 (.0638)	.0773 (.1569)	.0420 (.1106)
Executive	.3504 (.1043)	.0856 (.0752)	.3798 (.1899)	.3634 (.1583)
Retired	.0799 (.1448)	−.5126 (.1265)	−.3651 (.4604)	.1862 (.3713)
Housewife	−.0959 (.0922)	−.4006 (.0761)	−.0362 (.1578)	−.0558 (.1357)
Student/military	−.2279 (.1379)	−.2124 (.0669)	−.0918 (.2217)	−.0448 (.1164)
Unemployed	−.9203 (.1021)	−1.3114 (.0653)	−.5778 (.1743)	−.9848 (.1138)
Age	−.1126 (.0490)	−.1613 (.0215)	.0146 (.0970)	−.1715 (.0394)
Age²	.0019 (.0010)	.0023 (.0005)	−.0005 (.0020)	.0026 (.0009)
ALS 15	−.0022 (.0445)	−.0627 (.0409)	.0520 (.0692)	−.0268 (.0682)
ALS 16	.0798 (.0410)	.0297 (.0366)	.0362 (.0650)	.0024 (.0626)
ALS 17	.1895 (.0446)	.1078 (.0388)	.0921 (.0697)	.0963 (.0662)
ALS 18	.2574 (.0431)	.1069 (.0374)	.1745 (.0691)	.0726 (.0649)
ALS 19	.2094 (.0540)	.1477 (.0438)	.3384 (.0872)	.1494 (.0773)
ALS 20	.3214 (.0626)	.1734 (.0498)	.2700 (.1059)	.0612 (.0910)
ALS 21	.3367 (.0654)	.1793 (.0541)	.2491 (.1076)	.0744 (.0968)
ALS 22 or over	.2320 (.0473)	.2383 (.0386)	.1534 (.0862)	.0741 (.0793)
Studying	.3178 (.1028)	.1772 (.0391)	.3642 (.1523)	.0127 (.0673)
Single		−.1649 (.0298)		−.2896 (.0560)
Divorced		−.6779 (.0748)		−1.0695 (.1357)
Separated		−.7278 (.0853)		−1.0841 (.1441)
Widowed		−.5941 (.1173)		−1.1308 (.2419)
Belgium	1.2039 (.0449)	.8719 (.0338)	1.1319 (.0702)	1.0977 (.0702)
Netherlands	1.7780 (.0457)	1.3592 (.0349)	1.6355 (.0702)	1.3780 (.0702)
Germany	.6579 (.0488)	.2674 (.0327)	.3738 (.0815)	−.0235 (.0815)
Italy	−.0423 (.0528)	−.2273 (.0312)	−.4158 (.0849)	−.6137 (.0849)
Luxembourg	1.5249 (.0753)	.9594 (.0468)	.5230 (.1190)	.3865 (.1190)
Denmark	2.3610 (.0545)	1.9108 (.0338)	1.3616 (.0813)	.9423 (.0813)
Ireland	1.1260 (.0501)	.8032 (.0321)	.9871 (.0779)	.7725 (.0779)
Great Britain	1.1083 (.0460)	.7251 (.0352)	.7097 (.0723)	.4287 (.0723)
Northern Ireland	1.0698 (.0641)	.7813 (.0499)	.7911 (.0995)	.5184 (.0995)
Greece	−.1037 (.0577)	−.4559 (.0369)	−.7783 (.1025)	−1.0457 (.1025)
Spain	.6432 (.0676)	.3658 (.0398)	.5106 (.1412)	.2604 (.1412)
Portugal	−.1499 (.0637)	−.2892 (.0404)	−.2281 (.1385)	−.2200 (.1385)
Cut1	−4.3586 (.6016)	−5.2884 (.2429)	−1.5090 (1.1971)	−3.9706 (.4428)
Cut2	−2.6920 (.6011)	−3.5955 (.2423)	1.5983 (1.1971)	−.8614 (.4418)
Cut3	.2168 (.6009)	−.7270 (.2419)	n.a.	n.a.
N	32,876	75,698	12,977	24,326
Pseudo R²	.0706	.0757	.0642	.0764
χ²	4,872.7	12,453.8	1,553.7	3,547.2
Log likelihood	−32,072.46	−82,219.0	−11,332.3	−21,426.9

Source: Eurobarometer series.

Note: Excluded categories are age left school (ALS) under 15, single, France, and self-employed farmers and fishermen (skippers). Self-employed 2 = professional self-employed (lawyers, accountants, etc.). Self-employed 3 = business self-employed (owners of shops, craftsmen, proprietors, etc.).

Further evidence for these conclusions is included as tables 7.14, 7.15, and 7.16. Using the General Social Surveys, these tables estimate ordered logit equations for other kinds of satisfaction answers. In these surveys, Americans are asked how satisfied they are with their financial situation, job, friends, family, hobbies, health, and city. The exact forms of the questions are reported at the end of tables 7.14 and 7.15. Table 7.14 shows no evidence of an upward time trend—for the young or the old—in satisfaction with finances or job. But table 7.15 is more interesting. Column (2), which is for young people's satisfaction with their family life, uncovers a statistically significant positive time trend. Of the seven aspects of life covered in tables 7.14 and 7.15, young people's satisfaction with family is the only one that is rising through time. In table 7.16 we report further ordered logits for those under age 30 for satisfaction with friends and family according to whether the individual was married or not. Here we find a positive and significant coefficient on the time trend in both cases for the unmarried, whereas the two coefficients are insignificant and considerably smaller in magnitude for the married. These tables might be viewed as corroborative evidence for the paper's suggestion that rising youth happiness is connected to changes in marriage and relationships.

7.5 Conclusions

This paper is an attempt to understand what has been happening to the well-being of young people in the United States and Europe. It studies what random samples of people say about their own levels of happiness and satisfaction with life. Economists are not experienced at interpreting patterns in such data. Nevertheless, something may be learned from this kind of information.

The main finding of the paper is a potentially surprising one. Young Americans and Europeans seem to be getting happier through time. In 1972, for example, 16 percent of young Americans reported themselves as not too happy and 30 percent said that they were very happy. By 1990, 9 percent of young Americans were not too happy and 33 percent were very happy. Older people in the United States, by contrast, report numbers that are little changed. For Europe, the paper uncovers similar evidence. Life satisfaction has been growing noticeably faster among people under age 30. This result emerges in pooled microeconomic data for 13 European nations, and in 11 of them individually.

The evidence suggests, therefore, that in the West the well-being of the young is rising. Explaining why is more difficult. This paper has not gotten to the bottom of the phenomenon. On balance, we believe it is not explained by the decline in the chance of war with the Eastern Bloc, falling discrimination, changing education and work, or the rise of youth-oriented consumer goods. The paper demonstrates that most of the

Table 7.14 Satisfaction with Finances and Job Ordered Logits by Age: United States, 1970s–1990s

Variable	Finances[a]		Job[b]		
	Under Age 30	Age 30 and Over	Under Age 30	Age 30 and Over	Age 30 and Over Working
Time trend	−.0034 (.0045)	−.0123 (.0025)	−.0001 (.0047)	−.0158 (.0028)	−.0147 (.0033)
Part time	.0664 (.0797)	.1240 (.0540)	−.2071 (.0752)	−.0111 (.0537)	−.0173 (.0547)
Job but absent	−.2351 (.1826)	.0748 (.0975)	−.3998 (.1700)	.0736 (.0976)	.0736 (.0982)
Unemployed	−.5385 (.1248)	−.8596 (.1136)	−.2846 (.1243)	−.3762 (.1024)	
Retired	1.2225 (1.715)	.2507 (.0532)			
In school	.1197 (.0952)	.2678 (.1657)			
Keeping house	.0172 (.0832)	.2638 (.0448)	−.1650 (.0823)	−.4348 (.0474)	
Other	.2032 (.3034)	−.3517 (.1229)			
Male	−.1581 (.0555)	−.0380 (.0342)	−.0012 (.0568)	−.1944 (.0380)	−.1780 (.0397)
Black	.2103 (.0776)	−.4026 (.0465)	−.3129 (.0784)	−.2872 (.0498)	−.3572 (.0589)
Other nonwhite	.3508 (.1543)	.0935 (.1044)	−.1687 (.1625)	−.1960 (.1044)	−.1323 (.1235)
Parents divorced	−.2437 (.0701)	−.1587 (.0544)	.0009 (.0700)	−.1486 (.0563)	−.1226 (.0663)
Unemployment rate	.0022 (.0092)	.0109 (.0101)	.0065 (.0095)	.0238 (.0105)	.0234 (.0125)
Years schooling	.0291 (.0139)	.0116 (.0051)	.0424 (.0139)	.0056 (.0058)	.0104 (.0068)
Age	−.2347 (.1477)	.0655 (.0073)	.2757 (.1531)	.0395 (.0088)	.0280 (.0125)
Age^2	.0043 (.0029)	−.0002 (.0000)	−.0048 (.0030)	−.0001 (.0001)	.0000 (.0001)
Income below average	.6538 (.1451)	.6390 (.0821)	.1274 (.1278)	.1879 (.0818)	.0393 (.1117)
Income average	−1.7227 (.1420)	1.7197 (.0809)	.3943 (.1256)	.4638 (.0803)	.3380 (.1086)
Income above average	−2.6105 (.1556)	2.4232 (.0885)	.5962 (.1416)	.6699 (.0877)	.5788 (.1144)
Income far above average	−2.4917 (.2710)	2.4387 (.1390)	.3730 (.2756)	.9145 (.1463)	.7133 (.1741)
Married	.7810 (.4627)	−.1969 (.0512)	.2080 (.4822)	−.2222 (.0647)	−.0372 (.0935)
Widowed	−.2354 (.1264)	−.5587 (.0518)	−.2572 (.1213)	−.1227 (.0540)	.0020 (.0609)

(continued)

Table 7.14 (continued)

Variable	Finances[a]		Job[b]		
	Under Age 30	Age 30 and Over	Under Age 30	Age 30 and Over	Age 30 and Over Working
Divorced	.0792 (.1561)	−.4089 (.0841)	.0627 (.1523)	−.0203 (.0864)	.3103 (.1031)
Separated	−.0664 (.0651)	−.2256 (.0604)	−.3086 (.0652)	−.2340 (.0647)	−.1943 (.0724)
Finances getting better	.6128 (.0586)	.7275 (.0345)	.3315 (.0603)	.2951 (.0376)	.3507 (.0435)
Finances getting worse	−1.1136 (.0772)	−1.3527 (.0396)	−.3083 (.0760)	−.2996 (.0419)	−.2864 (.0513)
No. of siblings	.0005 (.0094)	−.0000 (.0046)	−.0135 (.0094)	−.0049 (.0051)	.0090 (.0062)
No. of children	−.2275 (.0362)	−.0156 (.0092)	.0005 (.0358)	.0147 (.0108)	.0096 (.0140)
Household size	.1203 (.0203)	−.0632 (.0128)	.0199 (.0212)	.0038 (.0137)	.0180 (.0167)
Cut1	−2.0066 (1.8517)	2.4410 (.2747)	1.7731 (1.925)	−1.4633 (.3091)	−1.7420 (.3996)
Cut2	.5363 (1.8514)	5.0511 (.2766)	3.1868 (1.925)	−.1652 (.3076)	−.4103 (.3976)
Cut3	n.a.	n.a.	5.1753 (1.926)	1.8198 (.3078)	1.6362 (.3978)
N	6,343	19,980	5,496	15,653	11,292
Pseudo R^2	.1517	.1867	.0306	.0336	.0326
χ^2	2,038.6	7,977.0	397.01	1,102.8	750.17
Log likelihood	−5,700.7	−17,379.9	−6,287.2	−15,862.1	−11,122.6

Source: General Social Surveys.

Note: Equations also include eight census area dummies. Numbers in parentheses are standard errors.

[a]Answers are to the question "We are interested in how people get along financially these days. So far as you and your family are concerned, would you say that you are pretty well satisfied with your present financial situation, more or less satisfied, or not satisfied at all?"

[b]Answers are to the question (asked of those currently working, temporarily not at work, or keeping house) "On the whole how satisfied are you with the work you do—would you say you are very satisfied, moderately satisfied, a little dissatisfied, or very dissatisfied?"

Table 7.15 Various Types of Life Satisfaction Ordered Logits for People under Age 30: United States, 1970s–1990s

Variable	Friends (1)	Family (2)	Hobby/Leisure (3)	Health (4)	City (5)
Time trend	.0056 (.0046)	.0119 (.0047)	.0019 (.0045)	−.0073 (.0046)	.0047 (.0044)
Part time	.0152 (.0796)	−.0213 (.0809)	.0202 (.0781)	−.0725 (.0788)	−.0566 (.0769)
Job but absent	−.1474 (.1814)	−.1265 (.1900)	−.0478 (.1743)	−.6435 (.1783)	−.2985 (.1792)
Unemployed	−.0133 (.1122)	.0737 (.1135)	−.0639 (.1099)	−.0400 (.1111)	−.1522 (.1087)
Retired	−2.4489 (1.4471)	−.7124 (1.4514)	−1.3048 (1.456)	−2.3411 (1.486)	.1616 (1.485)
In school	−.0178 (.0950)	.1772 (.0962)	.1829 (.0937)	−.1307 (.0938)	−.0171 (.0928)
Keeping house	−.1688 (.0808)	−.0393 (.0842)	−.1983 (.0794)	.0354 (.0810)	.0077 (.0786)
Other	.3176 (.3093)	.1587 (.3030)	.0487 (.2984)	−.0499 (.3267)	.0636 (.3082)
Male	−.3627 (.0552)	−.4407 (.0565)	.2190 (.0542)	.1348 (.0547)	−.1520 (.0535)
Black	−.7279 (.0750)	.0456 (.0764)	−.3495 (.0739)	.3569 (.0748)	−.3023 (.0727)
Other nonwhite	−.0026 (.1583)	.1735 (.1654)	.0184 (.1568)	.3650 (.1634)	.3154 (.1576)
Parents divorced	−.1304 (.0692)	−.0320 (.0709)	−.1074 (.0681)	−.0922 (.0692)	−.3106 (.0668)
Unemployment rate	−.0036 (.0088)	.0126 (.0090)	−.0007 (.0086)	.0163 (.0088)	.0012 (.0085)
Years schooling	.0909 (.0138)	.0577 (.0143)	.1281 (.0137)	.0449 (.0137)	.0446 (.0134)
Age	−.0944 (.1438)	.2310 (.1472)	−.2941 (.1409)	−.1803 (.1436)	−.0810 (.1397)
Age^2	.0012 (.0029)	−.0048 (.0029)	.0058 (.0028)	.0036 (.0029)	.0021 (.0028)
Income below average	.1136 (.1218)	−.0274 (.1217)	−.0288 (.1198)	.0794 (.1191)	.0869 (.1184)
Income average	.3914 (.1202)	.1300 (.1197)	.1081 (.1180)	.2916 (.1172)	.3413 (.1167)
Income above average	.5568 (.1345)	.1654 (.1348)	.2196 (.1320)	.3107 (.1312)	.4790 (.1307)
Income far above average	.4966 (.2595)	−.0893 (.2577)	−.2638 (.2468)	.3336 (.2521)	.2088 (.2488)
Married	.9741 (.4425)	−.2566 (.5043)	.8827 (.4637)	.6692 (.4690)	.9535 (.4183)
Widowed	−.1826 (.1206)	−1.0435 (.1231)	−.3062 (.1190)	−.1877 (.1190)	−.3684 (.1162)
Divorced	−.0033 (.1512)	−1.1974 (.1549)	.1403 (.1498)	−.0217 (.1508)	−.2355 (.1468)

(continued)

Table 7.15 (continued)

Variable	Friends (1)	Family (2)	Hobby/Leisure (3)	Health (4)	City (5)
Separated	−.0301 (.0643)	−1.3042 (.0676)	−.1328 (.0633)	−.2267 (.0641)	−.1211 (.0620)
Finances getting better	.1076 (.0584)	.2096 (.0601)	.3234 (.0577)	.1727 (.0581)	.1352 (.0567)
Finances getting worse	−.0696 (.0724)	−.1673 (.0732)	−.0354 (.0706)	−.2304 (.0719)	−.2355 (.0703)
No. of siblings	−.0333 (.0092)	−.0239 (.0094)	−.0324 (.0091)	−.0070 (.0091)	−.0171 (.0091)
No. of children	−.0588 (.0340)	−.0372 (.0348)	−.0921 (.0340)	−.0735 (.0341)	−.0532 (.0334)
Household size	.0272 (.0196)	.1023 (.0196)	.0048 (.0196)	.0374 (.0196)	.0366 (.0194)
Cut1	−5.8933 (1.814)	−1.3712 (1.842)	−6.0587 (1.767)	−6.3573 (1.807)	−3.0911 (1.752)
Cut2	−4.0179 (1.805)	−.2760 (1.840)	−4.9277 (1.765)	−4.9398 (1.801)	−1.7842 (1.751)
Cut3	−3.2631 (1.804)	.4044 (1.839)	−4.1283 (1.764)	−4.0845 (1.800)	−.9725 (1.751)
Cut4	−2.1161 (1.803)	1.3404 (1.839)	−3.2377 (1.764)	−2.8744 (1.799)	.2382 (1.751)
Cut5	−1.1487 (1.803)	2.1658 (1.839)	−2.3685 (1.763)	−2.0043 (1.799)	1.1155 (1.751)
Cut6	.5224 (1.803)	3.7215 (1.840)	−.8845 (1.763)	−.4614 (1.799)	2.5413 (1.752)
N	5,526	5,521	5,518	5,523	5,525
Pseudo R^2	.0273	.0491	.0279	.0115	.0165
χ^2	446.6	780.5	517.0	188.3	327.6
Log likelihood	−7,942.7	−7,563.7	−8,995.3	−8,086.9	−9,747.7
		Age 30 and Over: Time Trends from Separate Equations			
Time trend	−.0011 (.0044)	.0082 (.0026)	−.0004 (.0025)	−.0078 (.0025)	−.0057 (.0025)
N	17,066	17,021	16,994	17,063	17,071

Source: General Social Surveys.

Note: Answers are to the question "For each area of life I am going to name, tell me the number that shows how much satisfaction you get from that area (1 = a very great deal, 2 = a great deal, 3 = quite a bit, 4 = a fair amount, 5 = some, 6 = a little, 7 = none): (a) the city or place you live in (city); (b) your nonworking activities—hobbies and so on (hobby/leisure); (c) your family life (family); (d) your friendships (friends); (e) your health and physical condition (health)." All equations include eight census area dummies. Numbers in parentheses are standard errors.

Table 7.16   Satisfaction with Friends and Family Ordered Logits for People under Age 30: United States, 1970s–1990s

	Friends		Family	
Variable	Married	Unmarried	Married	Unmarried
Time trend	-.0019 (.0066)	.0186 (.0059)	.0013 (.0071)	.0186 (.0059)
Part time	-.0046 (.1311)	-.0653 (.0986)	.1622 (.1436)	-.0653 (.0986)
Job but absent	.2786 (.2601)	-.3213 (.2561)	.1926 (.2877)	-.3213 (.2561)
Unemployed	-.0145 (.2034)	.0733 (.1319)	.0269 (.2157)	.0733 (.1319)
In school	-.2794 (.2195)	.1797 (.1076)	-.0439 (.2280)	.1797 (.1076)
Keeping house	.0136 (.1045)	.0223 (.1403)	.0150 (.1126)	.0223 (.1403)
Other	.3394 (.3395)	-.0788 (.3155)	.8461 (.7429)	-.0788 (.3155)
Male	-.2767 (.0894)	-.5546 (.0702)	-.1796 (.0962)	-.5546 (.0702)
Black	-.4928 (.1277)	.2332 (.0909)	-.4894 (.1333)	.2332 (.0910)
Other nonwhite	.0473 (.2445)	.1157 (.2018)	.4145 (.2833)	.1157 (.2018)
Parents divorced	-.0864 (.1053)	-.0798 (.0886)	.0146 (.1115)	-.0798 (.0886)
Years schooling	.0722 (.0192)	.0371 (.0196)	.0844 (.0208)	.0371 (.0196)
Age	.0994 (.2301)	.3308 (.1738)	.0183 (.2436)	.3307 (.1738)
Age^2	-.0019 (.0046)	-.0075 (.0036)	-.0004 (.0049)	-.0075 (.0036)
Income far above average	-.4614 (.2068)	-.2127 (.1431)	-.0762 (.2146)	-.2127 (.1431)
Income below average	-.3033 (.0909)	-.1371 (.0847)	-.2377 (.0961)	-.1371 (.0847)
Income above average	.2117 (.1130)	.0586 (.0951)	.0489 (.1231)	.0586 (.0951)
Income far above average	-.3839 (.3994)	-.1284 (.2682)	.5981 (.4131)	-.1284 (.2682)
Divorced		-.6362 (.5114)		-.6362 (.5114)
Separated		-.9566 (.5193)		-.9566 (.5193)
Single		-.8663 (.5049)		-.8663 (.5049)

(continued)

Table 7.16   (continued)

| | Friends | | | Family | | |
Variable	Married	Unmarried	Married	Unmarried
Finances getting better	.2114 (.1076)	.2923 (.0964)	.4664 (.1133)	.2923 (.0964)
Finances getting worse	.0728 (.1109)	.1807 (.0932)	.1105 (.1157)	.1807 (.0932)
No. of siblings	−.0378 (.0132)	−.0116 (.0128)	−.0255 (.0137)	.0144 (.0555)
No. of children	−.0615 (.0564)	.0144 (.0555)	−.0706 (.0597)	.0896 (.0214)
Household size	−.0129 (.0514)	.0896 (.0214)	.0993 (.0557)	.0371 (.0196)
Cut1	−3.9131 (2.8512)	−.3655 (2.0995)	−5.0057 (3.0310)	−.3655 (2.0995)
Cut2	−1.8579 (2.8345)	.6831 (2.0973)	−3.3372 (2.9973)	.6831 (2.0973)
Cut3	−1.0884 (2.8334)	1.3498 (2.0968)	−2.3564 (2.9923)	1.3498 (2.0968)
Cut4	.1352 (2.8326)	2.2667 (2.0967)	−1.2891 (2.9902)	2.2667 (2.0967)
Cut5	1.1047 (2.8326)	3.0715 (2.0972)	−.3616 (2.9894)	3.0715 (2.0972)
Cut6	2.7177 (2.8330)	4.5296 (2.0981)	1.3975 (2.9894)	4.5296 (2.0981)
N	2,582	3,051	2,582	3,051
Pseudo R^2	.0196	.0159	.0204	.0159
χ^2	149.35	156.39	117.54	156.39
Log likelihood	−3,727.14	−4,847.12	−2,824.91	−4,847.121

Source: General Social Surveys.

Note: Numbers in parentheses are standard errors.

increase in young people's well-being is to be found in the group who are unmarried. It may be that young men and women have benefited from society's recently increased tolerance of those living outside marriage, and from their consequent ability to live in less formal relationships. While this is not an explanation, it suggests that the ultimate answer is somehow connected to the role of family life and personal freedom. Perhaps this hunch will help future researchers to find an answer.

The paper produces some other findings. As in earlier work on U.S. data alone (Blanchflower et al. 1993), happiness and life satisfaction are greatest among women, whites, married people, the highly educated, and those with high income. It is especially low among the unemployed. Well-being is U-shaped in age. In principle, the methods in the paper provide tools for a kind of happiness calculus that might be used to measure the underlying utility value of all kinds of characteristics and life events. Before that, however, economists have more to learn about the strengths and weaknesses of well-being data.

Appendix A
Data

U.S. General Social Surveys, 1972–93

The General Social Surveys have been conducted by the National Opinion Research Center at the University of Chicago since 1972. Interviews are undertaken during February, March, and April. There were no surveys in 1979 and 1981. There are approximately 25,000 completed interviews. The median length of the interview is about one and a half hours. Each survey is an independently drawn sample of English-speaking persons 18 years of age or over, living in noninstitutional arrangements within the United States. Block quota sampling was used in the 1972–74 surveys and in half of the 1975 and 1976 surveys. Full probability sampling was employed in half of the 1975 and 1976 surveys and in the 1977, 1978, 1980, and 1982–88 surveys. In this paper we make use of data from 1974 because of the unavailability of earnings data in 1972 and 1973.

The initial survey, in 1972, was supported by grants from the Russell Sage Foundation and the National Science Foundation (NSF). The NSF provided support for the 1973–78, 1980, and 1982–87 surveys. The NSF will continue to support the project. Supplemental funding for 1984–91 came from Andrew M. Greeley.

The items appearing on the surveys are one of three types: permanent questions that occur on each survey, rotating questions that appear on two out of every three surveys (1973, 1974, and 1976, or 1973, 1975, and

1976), and a few occasional questions such as split ballot experiments that occur in a single survey. In recent years the GSS has expanded in two significant ways: first, by adding annual topical modules that explore new areas or expand existing coverage of a subject and, second, by expanding its cross-national collaboration. Bilateral collaboration with the Zentrun für Unfragen, Methoden and Analysen in the Federal Republic of Germany dates from 1982. In 1985 the first multinational collaboration was carried out with the United States, Britain, Germany, Italy, and Australia. The 1985 topic was the role of government and included questions on (1) civil liberties and law enforcement, (2) education and parenting, (3) economic regulation, and (4) social welfare and inequality. The 1986 topic was social support covering information on contact with family and friends and hypothetical questions about where one would turn for help when faced with various problems. The 1987 topic was social inequality dealing with social mobility, intergroup conflicts, beliefs about reasons for inequality, and perceived and preferred income differentials between occupations.

Eurobarometer Surveys, 1973–92

The European Commission organized the Eurobarometer surveys, which have been held approximately annually since 1970. The usual sampling method was nationwide stratified quota samples of individuals older than 14 years of age. Summing across years, approximately 35,000 individuals were interviewed from each of Belgium, Great Britain, Denmark, France, Germany, Ireland, Italy, and the Netherlands. Slightly smaller samples are available from Northern Ireland, Greece, Portugal, and Spain. The surveys collect both attitudinal information and standard data on personal characteristics. Most of the econometric analysis in the paper uses data from 1973–92, providing a total sample of approximately 370,000 people. Data files from 1974 were not used because they were missing values for some relevant variables.

Appendix B

Background Notes

There is a literature on the quantitative social science of well-being. Much of the work appears in the journal *Social Indicators Research* and in a variety of psychology journals. Recent research on well-being includes Andrews (1991), Fox and Kahneman (1992), Thomas and Hughes (1986), Inglehart (1990), and Veenhoven (1991, 1993). Although little read by economists, the pioneering work on the statistical study of well-being includes Cantril (1965), Andrews and Withey (1976), Andrews and Inglehart

(1978), Campbell, Converse, and Rodgers (1976), Campbell (1981), Diener (1984), Douthitt, MacDonald, and Mullis (1992), Larsen, Diener and Emmons (1984), Smith (1979), Shin (1980), and Weaver (1980). Argyle (1989) is an introduction to the literature. Myers (1993) is informal and especially easy to read and has extensive references to the technical literature. Economists interested in dipping into these writings might also look at Andrews (1991), Mullis (1992), and Warr (1987, 1990a, 1990b).

Birdi, Warr, and Oswald (1995), Clark et al. (1996), and Warr (1992) show that job satisfaction is U-shaped in age and give other results.

Hirsch (1976) and Easterlin (1974) are well-known skeptics about the value to society of increased real national income. Oswald (1997) discusses recent evidence. Relevant data are also examined in MacCulloch (1996). Early British results on the distress caused by unemployment are due to Peter Warr (1978, 1987, 1990a, 1990b, 1992), Jackson et al. (1983), and Warr, Jackson, and Banks (1988). The findings are now conventional in the psychology literature but probably still not well known among economists (see, however, Clark and Oswald 1994). Important early work in the economics literature was done by Bjorklund (1985) and Edin (1988).

If well-being depends on relative income, most of economists' tax theory is wrong or incomplete. Some of the few attempts to change this are Boskin and Sheshinski (1978), Layard (1980), and Oswald (1983). Clark and Oswald (1996) finds evidence for relative wages in satisfaction equations.

International well-being comparisons using the multinational International Social Survey Programme are given in Birdi et al. (1995), Blanchflower (1997), and Blanchflower and Freeman (1997). Blanchflower (1997) specifically looks at the well-being of the young. Recent work by Di Tella, MacCulloch, and Oswald (1996) suggests that macroeconomic variables may help to explain movements in happiness in a country. Blanchflower et al. (1993) is an earlier look at adult well-being using the U.S. GSS. It also reports information about the time trend in job satisfaction in Britain and the United States. Blanchflower and Oswald (1998) estimates well-being equations for various countries showing that other factors held constant, the self-employed appear to be happier and more satisfied with their jobs than employed people. The paper also uses a British birth cohort sample to estimate a well-being equation based on a 10-point life satisfaction scale.

Appendix C

Table 7C.1 Life Satisfaction by Country (percent)

Country	Year																		
	1973	1975	1976	1977	1978	1979	1980	1981	1982	1983	1984	1985	1986	1987	1988	1989	1990	1991	1992
France																			
Not at all satisfied	5	7	7	8	8	9	8	7	5	7	6	7	6	6	7	5	7	6	9
Not very satisfied	18	17	21	22	21	22	22	22	17	19	21	20	21	19	26	15	15	16	18
Fairly satisfied	62	60	60	60	59	58	61	59	62	61	61	61	61	62	54	64	64	64	60
Very satisfied	16	16	12	12	12	11	10	12	15	13	11	12	12	13	14	16	14	14	14
N = 38,516	2,198	2,391	2,555	2,246	2,122	997	984	979	2,130	1,993	2,000	1,994	1,970	1,986	1,981	4,016	1,998	1,986	1,990
Belgium																			
Not at all satisfied	2	3	3	3	2	2	3	3	4	4	7	3	5	4	3	3	3	2	3
Not very satisfied	6	7	7	7	9	7	8	10	12	14	15	14	17	13	17	10	9	9	8
Fairly satisfied	49	52	52	48	47	48	54	50	57	61	55	61	60	56	57	59	60	55	60
Very satisfied	44	38	38	42	42	43	35	36	27	21	23	22	18	27	23	28	29	34	29
N = 36,791	1,261	2,510	2,026	1,975	2,004	964	970	929	2,151	1,991	2,029	2,004	1,974	1,978	2,020	3,967	1,925	2,056	2,057
Netherlands																			
Not at all satisfied	1	2	2	2	1	1	1	2	1	2	1	2	1	1	1	1	0.5	1	1
Not very satisfied	5	7	8	6	5	4	4	5	5	6	5	6	6	6	6	4	5	4	5
Fairly satisfied	53	56	51	52	48	48	48	47	48	53	48	54	54	53	53	48	49	46	45
Very satisfied	41	36	40	41	45	47	48	46	46	40	46	38	39	39	40	47	46	49	50
N = 36,941	1,451	1,974	2,012	1,977	2,065	1,013	977	1,084	2,260	2,030	1,993	2,032	2,011	1,948	2,005	3,987	2,092	2,023	1,998
Germany																			
Not at all satisfied	2	2	2	2	2	2	2	3	2	3	2	2	2	2	1	1	2	2	1
Not very satisfied	16	17	17	14	13	11	12	16	14	15	13	16	13	13	14	9	8	9	11
Fairly satisfied	66	67	61	62	64	63	69	64	66	66	66	64	65	67	61	64	64	64	64
Very satisfied	17	14	21	22	21	24	17	17	18	16	19	18	20	18	24	25	27	26	24
N = 37,838	1,931	1,995	1,985	1,984	1,972	985	989	966	2,387	2,029	2,008	2,005	2,051	1,932	2,045	4,387	2,061	2,058	2,068

Italy

Not at all satisfied	7	11	13	10	12	11	9	9	9	8	9	9	9	8	9	5	5	5	6	4	7
Not very satisfied	28	30	29	29	25	30	27	24	24	24	25	25	25	23	24	17	24	17	18	16	18
Fairly satisfied	57	51	49	52	53	50	54	54	57	54	56	53	55	55	55	63	55	63	60	61	62
Very satisfied	8	8	8	9	10	9	10	14	10	13	11	12	11	13	15	16	15	16	15	19	14
N = 39,149	1,888	2,099	1,959	2,172	2,197	1,173	1,112	1,181	2,058	2,314	2,148	2,162	2,186	2,078	2,070	4,111	2,078	2,076	2,087		

Luxembourg

Not at all satisfied	2	5	3	1	2	1	1	1	2	3	2	2	1	2	1	1	1	1	1		
Not very satisfied	9	12	7	9	11	5	7	5	6	7	6	6	5	3	11	5	6	5	5		
Fairly satisfied	49	49	59	52	50	61	58	53	54	53	56	52	53	55	50	57	57	47	47	46	54
Very satisfied	40	34	31	38	37	33	35	40	38	37	36	40	40	39	37	37	37	47	48	41	
N = 11,578	329	595	557	644	608	295	297	300	591	694	590	596	595	577	593	1,195	599	931	992		

Denmark

Not at all satisfied	1	1	1	1	1	1	1	1	1	1	1	1									
Not very satisfied	4	4	5	4	4	4	4	4	4	4	3	3	3	4	4	9	3	2	1		
Fairly satisfied	45	49	43	42	39	44	41	36	40	39	37	37	37	41	42	38	36	36	34		
Very satisfied	51	47	50	54	56	51	55	59	55	57	58	59	59	54	48	57	61	61	63		
N = 36,209	1,197	1,961	1,926	1,994	1,977	1,063	985	996	2,015	2,187	1,953	1,997	2,007	1,982	2,006	3,995	1,984	1,994	1,990		

Ireland

Not at all satisfied	2	3	3	4	4	5	3	4	3	3	7	5	6	6	8	7	3	4	4		
Not very satisfied	6	8	9	7	7	11	11	13	10	12	10	12	14	18	10	9	9	11			
Fairly satisfied	39	51	52	48	48	47	52	49	49	50	51	54	53	48	50	53	46	48			
Very satisfied	53	38	36	40	41	37	34	34	38	31	33	29	24	27	34	35	41	37			
N = 36,255	1,197	1,993	1,980	1,998	2,000	994	1,004	997	1,980	2,174	1,996	2,004	1,994	1,988	1,993	3,941	2,022	2,001	1,999		

Great Britain

Not at all satisfied	3	4	5	4	3	3	4	5	4	4	3	4	4	3	3	3	4	4			
Not very satisfied	11	11	2	11	10	11	8	10	9	9	10	10	10	11	17	10	9	11			
Fairly satisfied	59	52	52	51	56	59	52	52	51	56	55	55	56	55	52	53	57	56	54		
Very satisfied	27	36	32	36	30	27	37	36	32	36	31	32	31	30	28	35	29	31	31		
N = 38,148	1,006	1,152	1,050	2,149	1,985	1,006	1,152	1,050	2,149	1,985	2,095	2,168	2,037	1,960	2,018	3,831	2,085	2,112	2,061		

(continued)

Table 7C.1   (continued)

Country	1973	1975	1976	1977	1978	1979	1980	1981	1982	1983	1984	1985	1986	1987	1988	1989	1990	1991	1992
Norhern Ireland																			
Not at all satisfied		4	4	4	3	4	4	5	3	4	3	4	3	5	4	4	2	3	3
Not very satisfied		9	11	13	10	10	15	11	8	10	9	7	8	8	16	7	11	10	9
Fairly satisfied		55	59	56	56	53	49	58	57	56	56	54	56	55	47	53	54	53	49
Very satisfied		32	25	27	31	32	31	26	31	30	32	36	33	32	33	36	33	35	41
N = 10,719		592	611	596	608	307	297	306	591	625	633	646	640	636	636	1,164	631	600	600
Greece																			
Not at all satisfied								22	13	15	13	13	13	16	12	12	15	11	11
Not very satisfied								20	25	22	23	24	19	23	26	20	21	35	34
Fairly satisfied								38	44	46	47	46	46	43	46	47	47	47	47
Very satisfied								19	18	18	17	16	21	18	16	21	17	8	9
N = 10,719								998	2,182	1,994	1,998	1,985	1,992	1,994	1,981	3,993	2,004	1,990	1,995
Spain																			
Not at all satisfied												7	6	5	6	3	4	3	4
Not very satisfied												22	20	21	25	18	18	17	20
Fairly satisfied												47	47	46	46	57	53	55	53
Very satisfied												24	27	28	24	22	24	24	23
N = 16,913												988	1,980	1,998	2,002	3,964	1,990	1,998	1,993
Portugal																			
Not at all satisfied												16	10	7	9	7	8	6	6
Not very satisfied												28	25	22	30	23	18	20	19
Fairly satisfied												53	60	66	51	65	67	67	69
Very satisfied												3	5	6	9	5	7	7	6
N = 16,864												989	1,986	1,972	1,983	3,971	1,975	1,991	1,997

(Year)

Source: Eurobarometer series.

References

Andrews, F. M. 1991. Stability and change in levels and structure of subjective well-being: USA 1972 and 1988. *Social Indicators Research* 25:1–30.

Andrews, F. M., and R. F. Inglehart. 1978. The structure of subjective well-being in nine Western societies. *Social Indicators Research* 6:73–90.

Andrews, F. M., and S. B. Withey. 1976. *Social indicators of well-being.* New York: Plenum.

Argyle, M. 1987. *The psychology of happiness.* London: Routledge.

Birdi, K. M., P. B. Warr, and A. J. Oswald. 1995. Age differences in employee well-being: A multi-national study. *Applied Psychology: An International Review* 44: 345–73.

Bjorklund, A. 1985. Unemployment and mental health: Some evidence from panel data. *Journal of Human Resources* 20:469–83.

Blanchflower, D. G. 1999. Youth labor markets in twenty-three countries: A comparison using micro data. In *International perspectives on the school-to-work transition,* ed. D. Stern and D. Wagner. Cresskill, N.J.: Hampton.

Blanchflower, D. G., and R. B. Freeman. 1997. The attitudinal legacy of communist labor relations. *Industrial and Labor Relations Review* 50:438–59.

Blanchflower, D. G., and A. J. Oswald. 1998. What makes an entrepreneur? *Journal of Labor Economics* 16:26–60.

Blanchflower, D. G., A. J. Oswald, and P. B. Warr. 1993. Well-being over time in Britain and the USA. London: London School of Economics. Mimeograph.

Boskin, M., and E. Sheshinski. 1978. Optimal redistributive taxation when individual welfare depends upon relative income. *Quarterly Journal of Economics* 92:589–601.

Campbell, A. 1981. *The sense of well-being in America.* New York: McGraw-Hill.

Campbell, A., P. E. Converse, and W. L. Rodgers. 1976. *The quality of American life.* New York: Russell Sage Foundation.

Cantril, H. 1965. *The pattern of human concerns.* New Brunswick, N.J.: Rutgers University Press.

Clark, A. E., and A. J. Oswald. 1994. Unhappiness and unemployment. *Economic Journal* 104:648–59.

Clark, A. E., A. J. Oswald, and P. B. Warr. 1996. Is job satisfaction U-shaped in age? *Journal of Occupational and Organizational Psychology* 69:57–81.

Diener, E. 1984. Subjective well-being. *Psychological Bulletin* 95:542–75.

Di Tella, R., R. MacCulloch, and A. J. Oswald. 1996. The macroeconomics of happiness. Oxford: University of Oxford, November. Mimeograph.

Douthitt, R. A., M. MacDonald, and R. Mullis. 1992. The relationship between measures of subjective and economic well-being: A new look. *Social Indicators Research* 26:407–22.

Easterlin, R. 1974. Does economic growth improve the human lot? Some empirical evidence. In *Nations and households in economic growth: Essays in honour of Moses Abramowitz,* ed. P. A. David and M. W. Reder. New York: Academic Press.

Edin, P.-A. 1988. *Individual consequences of plant closures.* Doctoral diss., Uppsala University, Uppsala.

Fox, C. R., and D. Kahneman. 1992. Correlations, causes and heuristics in surveys of life satisfaction. *Social Indicators Research* 27:221–34.

Hirsch, F. 1976. *The social limits of growth.* Cambridge, Mass.: Harvard University Press.

Inglehart, R. 1990. *Culture shift in advanced industrial society.* Princeton, N.J.: Princeton University Press.

Jackson, P. R., E. M. Stafford, M. H. Banks, and P. B. Warr. 1983. Unemployment and psychological distress in young people: The moderating role of employment commitment. *Journal of Applied Psychology* 68:525–35.

Larsen, R. J., E. Diener, and R. A. Emmons. 1984. An evaluation of subjective well-being measures. *Social Indicators Research* 17:1–18.

Layard, R. 1980. Human satisfactions and public policy. *Economic Journal* 90: 737–50.

MacCulloch, R. 1996. The structure of the welfare state. Doctoral thesis, University of Oxford, Oxford.

Mullis, R. J. 1992. Measures of economic well-being as predictors of psychological well-being. *Social Indicators Research* 26:119–35.

Myers, D. G. 1993. *The pursuit of happiness.* London: Aquarian.

Oswald, A. J. 1983. Altruism, jealousy and the theory of optimal non-linear taxation. *Journal of Public Economics* 20:77–87.

———. 1997. Happiness and economic performance. *Economic Journal* 107: 1815–31.

Pavot, W., et al. 1991. Further validation of the satisfaction with life scale: Evidence for the cross-method convergence of wellbeing measures. *Journal of Personality Assessment* 57:149–61.

Shin, D. C. 1980. Does rapid economic growth improve the human lot? Some empirical evidence. *Social Indicators Research* 8:199–221.

Smith, T. W. 1979. Happiness: Time trends, seasonal variation, inter-survey differences and other mysteries. *Social Psychology Quarterly* 42:18–30.

Thomas, M. E., and M. Hughes. 1986. The continuing significance of race: A study of race, class, and quality of life in America, 1972–1985. *American Sociological Review* 5:830–41.

Veenhoven, R. 1991. Is happiness relative? *Social Indicators Research* 24:1–34.

———. 1993. *Happiness in nations: Subjective appreciation of life in 56 nations, 1946–1992.* Rotterdam: Erasmus University Risbo.

Warr, P. B. 1978. A study of psychological well-being. *British Journal of Psychology* 69:111–21.

———. 1987. *Work, unemployment, and mental health.* Oxford: Oxford University Press.

———. 1990a. Decision latitude, job demands, and employee well-being. *Work and Stress* 4:285–94.

———. 1990b. The measurement of well-being and other aspects of mental health. *Journal of Occupational Psychology* 63:193–210.

———. 1992. Age and occupational well-being. *Psychology and Aging* 7:37–45.

Warr, P. B., P. Jackson, and M. Banks. 1988. Unemployment and mental health: Some British studies. *Journal of Social Issues* 44:47–68.

Watson, D., and L. Clark. 1991. Self versus peer ratings of specific emotional traits: Evidence of convergent and discriminant validity. *Journal of Personality and Social Psychology* 60:927–40.

Weaver, C. N. 1980. Job satisfaction in the United States in the 1970s. *Journal of Applied Psychology* 65:364–67.

III

The Effect of Programs

The Sensitivity of Experimental Impact Estimates
Evidence from the National JTPA Study

James J. Heckman and Jeffrey A. Smith

8.1 Introduction

The experimental estimates of the impact of youth training funded under the Job Training Partnership Act (JTPA) from the recent National JTPA Study (NJS) resulted in large budget cuts in the JTPA program. The experiment, which included only 16 of the more than 600 JTPA training centers, found negative and statistically significant impacts on the earnings of male youths in the 18 months after random assignment and negligible impacts on the earnings of female youths. In response to these estimates, Congress cut funding for the youth component of JTPA from $540 million in 1994 to only $110 million in 1995, a cut of over 80 percent.

In light of the dramatic changes in JTPA resulting from the NJS impact estimates, it is of interest to consider their sensitivity to issues of construction and interpretation. In this paper, we address the following questions: (1) How sensitive are the estimates to the set of training centers included in the evaluation? (2) Does it matter how the impact estimates from the individual training centers in the evaluation are combined? (3) How sensi-

James J. Heckman is the Henry Schultz Distinguished Service Professor of Economics and director of the Center for Social Program Evaluation at the University of Chicago, a senior fellow of the American Bar Foundation, and a research associate of the National Bureau of Economic Research. Jeffrey A. Smith is associate professor of economics at the University of Western Ontario and a faculty research fellow of the National Bureau of Economic Research.

This research was supported by National Science Foundation grants SBR 91-11-445 and SBR 93-21-048 and by grants from the Russell Sage Foundation and the Social Science and Humanities Research Council of Canada. The authors thank David Blanchflower, Richard Freeman, Lawrence Katz, Gerd Ronning, and NBER workshop participants for helpful comments and Robert LaLonde for useful suggestions and a very close reading of a draft of this paper.

tive are the estimates to the treatment of outliers in the earnings data? (4) How sensitive are the estimates to the construction of the earnings measure used in the evaluation? (5) How sensitive are the estimates to the manner in which dropouts from the experimental treatment group are handled? (6) How sensitive are the conclusions of the evaluation to the manner in which substitution by control group members into alternative sources of training similar to that provided by JTPA is dealt with?

We find the following: (1) The dispersion in impacts across centers is large enough that choosing a different set of centers could have produced a fundamentally different pattern of impact estimates. (2) Combining the centers in the NJS in a manner that takes account of the fact that some centers dropped out of the experiment early leads to negative and statistically significant impact estimates for female youth. (3) The magnitude and statistical significance of the male youth estimates depend on how outliers in the earnings data are handled. (4) The different methods used to construct the earnings variables in the two official NJS impact reports lead estimated impacts on important subgroups to change by up to $1,000 and to switch signs. (5) Taking account of the 40 percent of experimental treatment group members who drop out substantially increases the magnitude of the impact estimates. (6) Substitution by control group members in the NJS is empirically important, and taking account of it in the construction and interpretation of the estimates requires recourse to nonexperimental evaluation methods. Estimates of the impact of JTPA classroom training that account for both treatment group dropout and control group substitution present a substantially more positive picture of the effects of JTPA youth training than the unadjusted experimental impact estimates.

Our work has an important methodological motivation. No social program has ever been the subject of multiple experimental evaluations. It is well known in the literature that factors such as those we consider in this paper can have a major influence on the estimates obtained from nonexperimental evaluations, even holding constant the data sources and econometric methods employed. The prime example of such sensitivity is the multiple evaluations of JTPA's predecessor, the Comprehensive Employment and Training Act (CETA). Dickinson, Johnson, and West (1987) show that the widely divergent estimates in these evaluations resulted in large part from seemingly minor choices in the construction of the estimates.

While analysts using data from a social experiment do not have to choose a nonexperimental evaluation method, they must still make many choices regarding how to construct, report, and interpret their estimates. Some of these choices, such as the selection of locations at which to evaluate the program, are more problematic in experiments than in nonexperimental analyses. Others, such as what to do about control group members who obtain close substitutes for the experimental treatment, are unique to experiments. The claim that experiments are superior to nonexperimental methods because they produce "one number" is false. Correcting this mistaken view by showing the sensitivity of experimental estimates to the numerous choices that must be made to produce them is one of the primary goals of this paper.

The strategy we adopt makes use of the data at hand. An important reason why multiple experimental evaluations have never been conducted for the same program is that experimental evaluations are quite expensive. For example, the NJS cost around $30 million. Thus, rather than answering the sensitivity question directly by conducting and reporting on the results from multiple experimental evaluations, we examine the sensitivity of estimates constructed from a single experimental data set to alternative choices regarding construction and interpretation.[1]

The remainder of this paper proceeds as follows. Sections 8.2 and 8.3 describe the institutional structure of the JTPA program and characterize the data from the NJS, respectively. Section 8.4 examines the effects of variation in the set of JTPA training centers included in the analysis. Section 8.5 examines how the method used to combine the data from the individual training centers affects the impact estimates. Section 8.6 considers the effects of alternative methods for handling outliers in the earnings data, and section 8.7 shows how the construction of the earnings measure affects the impact estimates. In section 8.8 we consider ways to adjust and reinterpret the impact estimates to take account of treatment group members who drop out and control group members who obtain close substitutes to the experimental treatment. In section 8.9 we summarize our findings and discuss their implications for the interpretation of the NJS estimates, for our understanding of the effectiveness of training programs for disadvantaged youth, and for future evaluations of employment and training programs.

8.2 The JTPA Program

The JTPA program was, until recently, one of the largest federal training programs in the United States. With an annual budget of around $1 billion, JTPA provided employment and training services to several hundred thousand economically disadvantaged persons each year. The JTPA program was highly decentralized, with more than 600 JTPA training centers across the United States. While JTPA was a major provider of training in most areas, it was usually not the only provider of subsidized training to the disadvantaged. The federal government provided the funding and set

---

1. There is some evidence of this type from earlier experiments. An important example is the long-standing debate on the effect of a negative income tax on marital stability. Both Cain and Wissoker (1990) and Hannan and Tuma (1990) use data from the U.S. negative income tax experiments, but they come to dramatically different conclusions.

the broad outlines of the JTPA program but left local training centers a substantial amount of flexibility in determining whom to serve and how to serve them.

Devine and Heckman (1996) show that the JTPA-eligible population included nearly everyone below the poverty line and many persons above it. Because its budget allowed JTPA to serve only about 3 percent of those eligible for it each year, program operators had wide latitude in choosing whom to serve. Moreover, even if program operators had picked at random from among the eligible (and they did not), they would have ended up with widely different participant populations due to the heterogeneity across training centers in the characteristics of the eligible population.[2]

Local operators also had control over what services to offer to JTPA participants. The most common services provided by JTPA were classroom training in occupational skills, subsidized on-the-job training at private firms, and job search assistance. Less common were basic education (typically GED preparation) and work experience. The relative proportions of trainees receiving each type of training, as well as the form, content, and duration of training within each type, varied widely across centers (Kemple, Doolittle, and Wallace 1993).

8.3   The National JTPA Study

Our data come from the National JTPA Study, a recent experimental evaluation of the JTPA program commissioned by the U.S. Department of Labor.[3] Due to the high fixed costs of setting up random assignment at a given training center, the NJS includes only 16 centers. The original design called for a random sample of training centers, but these plans had to be abandoned when most of the centers initially contacted refused to participate. In the end, it was necessary to approach over 200 training centers in order to find 16 willing to take part in the experiment (Doolittle and Traeger 1990). In addition, training centers in large urban areas and training centers serving fewer than 500 persons per year were excluded for cost and sample size reasons, respectively. Random assignment took place between 1987 and 1989, with the exact dates varying across training centers. A total of 20,601 persons were randomly assigned, of whom 2,558 were male youths and 3,132 were female youths.

8.4   Selection of Training Centers

In this section we examine the sensitivity of the overall experimental impact estimates to the set of centers included in the evaluation. The selec-

---

2. Smith (1997a) documents this heterogeneity for four centers in the NJS at which data on the eligible population were collected.
3. Doolittle and Traeger (1990) and Bloom et al. (1993) describe the NJS in detail.

tion of training centers is more problematic in experimental than non-experimental evaluations. The high fixed costs of setting up random assignment limit the number of centers. In addition, centers often refuse to participate because of the political and budgetary costs associated with random assignment[4] or because of the increased recruitment necessary to fill the experimental control group.

We present experimental impact estimates for each center in the NJS. In order for the set of centers included in the evaluation to affect the overall impact estimates, it must be the case that the impact differs across centers. While the point estimates do vary widely, formal statistical tests do not reject the null hypothesis of equal impacts across centers. In light of this, we perform a simulation analysis that shows the effect of the variability we do observe in center-level impacts on the overall impact estimate. The simulation provides strong evidence of the sensitivity of the overall impact estimates for youths to the set of included centers. In addition, the statistical significance of the overall estimate for male youths is very sensitive to center selection.

We also consider whether the variation across centers in the estimated impact of JTPA can be traced to specific factors operating at the center level, such as the center's administrative structure or the local labor market. We find little evidence for the importance of center-level factors.

8.4.1   Impacts by Training Center in the National JTPA Study

Table 8.1 presents experimental estimates of the mean impact of JTPA training on earnings in the first 18 months after random assignment for male and female youths in the NJS.[5] Two important patterns emerge from these estimates. First, the point estimates differ substantially across training centers within each demographic group. For example, for male youths, the center-specific impact estimates range from a low of −$6,554.68 at center 2 to a high of $4,432.61 at center 8. Second, only one estimate in table 8.1 is statistically distinguishable from zero at the 5 percent level, though some of the extreme positive and negative estimates are statistically distinguishable from one another.

Statistical tests of the equality of impacts across training centers do not reject that hypothesis at conventional levels. Two F-tests were carried out for each group, one with covariates included in the regression used to estimate the impacts and one without. We use the same regression specification as in the official report of Bloom et al. (1993). For male youths, the

---

4. The U.S. Department of Labor spent nearly $1 million on payments to centers to cover the budgetary costs of participating in the NJS. Doolittle and Traeger (1990) note that ethical and public relations difficulties with random assignment and the denial of services to control group members were the concerns cited most often by centers declining to participate in the NJS.

5. The centers are not identified by name due to an agreement between the centers in the NJS and the U.S. Department of Labor.

Table 8.1   **Experimental Estimates of Impact on Self-Reported Earnings in First 18 Months after Random Assignment**

Training Center[a]	Male Youths	Female Youths
Center 1	−2,364.73	−440.97
	(1,304.04)	(701.85)
Center 2	−6,554.68	−929.94
	(3,048.81)	(1,772.11)
Center 3	531.76	−106.22
	(1,335.79)	(681.21)
Center 4	−153.10	−806.40
	(2,385.74)	(1,514.22)
Center 5	−644.58	−626.51
	(1,084.94)	(796.94)
Center 6	−1,645.31	−1,418.03
	(1,607.93)	(893.77)
Center 7	1,501.57	−460.12
	(1,280.66)	(784.37)
Center 8	4,432.61	1,491.85
	(3,037.43)	(1,542.14)
Center 9	−1,278.52	333.92
	(3,266.78)	(2,491.02)
Center 10	−2,611.03	789.43
	(2,599.02)	(2,069.87)
Center 11	−1,570.64	−2,489.35
	(2,064.25)	(1,665.46)
Center 12	−1,958.44	−377.75
	(2,252.27)	(1,065.39)
Center 13	318.39	775.10
	(2,044.43)	(1,323.22)
Center 14	−1,150.37	1,090.70
	(1,208.29)	(860.41)
Center 15	−2,265.58	985.84
	(1,525.25)	(945.40)

Source: National JTPA Study 18 Month Impact Sample.

Note: The self-reported earnings variable used here includes the Bloom et al. (1993) hand imputations for outliers. These impact estimates are regression-adjusted using the same specification as in Bloom et al. (1993); results differ slightly from those in Bloom et al. because we were unable to exactly replicate their construction of some of the covariates. Numbers in parentheses are estimated standard errors.

[a]Only 15 training centers are listed because youth were not randomly assigned at one of the 16 centers in the NJS.

p-values are 0.3945 and 0.3940 with and without covariates, respectively. For female youths, they are 0.7284 and 0.3162, respectively.

In thinking about the lack of statistically significant estimates at the individual centers, and the failure to reject the null of equal impacts, it is important to note that the available sample sizes are rather small, particularly given the large variance in earnings (even conditional on covariates) in the JTPA participant population. The average center sample size is 117 for male youths and 153 for female youths.

One good reason to think that small sample sizes, and not actual equality of impacts across centers, underlie the lack of statistically significant findings is that such findings appear in other evaluations of employment and training programs for the disadvantaged with larger sample sizes. For example, the experimental evaluation of California's Greater Avenues to Independence (GAIN) program reported in Riccio, Friedlander, and Freedman (1994) reveals earnings impacts (over the 36 months after random assignment) for AFDC single family heads ranging from $260 in Los Angeles County to $3,113 in Riverside County. With an average sample size of over 3,000 per county, the larger estimates in the GAIN study are statistically distinguishable from zero and from the smaller estimates. Similar differences across centers are found in the experimental evaluation of the National Supported Work (NSW) program described in Hollister, Kemper, and Maynard (1984), where again the sample sizes per center are larger than for youths in the NJS.

8.4.2   Effect of Center Selection on Variability of Overall Impact Estimates

This subsection examines the effect of variation in center-level impacts from the NJS on the overall impact estimates. We conduct a simulation in which we calculate overall impact estimates based on random samples of 15 centers drawn, with replacement, from the NJS data. The data from the centers in each random sample are combined to produce overall impact estimates for male and female youths. In formal terms, we treat the estimated impacts from the NJS training centers as providing a nonparametric estimate of the distribution of center-level impacts for the population of JTPA training centers. Because we use the nonrandom sample of JTPA training centers participating in the NJS, our results likely understate the variability in overall impacts that would be obtained from repeated random sampling from the *population* of JTPA training centers.

Table 8.2 reports characteristics of the distribution of overall impacts obtained when 100,000 samples of 15 centers are randomly drawn from the observed distribution. The top panel reports percentiles of the distribution of overall impacts from the 100,000 samples, as well as the mean and standard deviation of the overall impact estimates. The figures reveal remarkable variability in the overall impacts obtained from random samples of 15 centers. For female youths, the interquartile range is around $380. For male youths, it is over $600. Looking in the tails, the variation in estimates is particularly large for female youths, for whom the 5th percentile estimate is −$647.80 while the 95th percentile estimate is $312.45. This variability is large relative to the overall experimental impact estimates reported in Bloom et al. (1993).

Table 8.2   **Sensitivity of Experimental Impact Estimates to Set of Training Centers Included**

	Male Youths	Female Youths
Parameters of the Distribution of Overall Impact Estimates from 100,000 Random Samples of 15 Training Centers		
1st Percentile	−1,969.51	−885.33
5th Percentile	−1,663.78	−647.80
25th Pecentile	−1,227.08	−341.91
Median	−920.00	−146.10
75th Percentile	−613.19	42.32
95th Percentile	−158.22	312.45
99th Percentile	167.91	503.27
Mean	−917.81	−154.36
Standard deviation	457.96	292.52
Characteristics of the Distribution of Overall Impact Estimates from 100,000 Random Samples of 15 Training Centers		
Fraction negative and significant at 1%	.2846	.0142
Fraction negative and significant at 5%	.5265	.0626
Fraction negative and significant at 10%	.6490	.1149
Fraction negative	.9767	.6990
Fraction positive and significant at 1%	.0000	.0006
Fraction positive and significant at 5%	.0001	.0050
Fraction positive and significant at 10%	.0003	.0127
Fraction positive	.0233	.3010

Source: National JTPA Study 18 Month Impact Sample.

Note: Each set of 15 training centers is drawn at random from the NJS data, with replacement. The self-reported earnings variable used here includes the Bloom et al. (1993) hand imputations for outliers. This analysis uses simple mean-difference experimental impact estimates.

The bottom panel of table 8.2 summarizes the sign and statistical significance of the overall impact estimates obtained from the 100,000 random samples of centers. The overall estimates are essentially always negative for male youths. For female youths, they are negative 70 percent of the time and positive 30 percent of the time. Varying the set of included training centers has strong effects on the statistical significance of the overall estimates. In almost half the samples, the negative overall impact estimate for male youths is not statistically significant at the 5 percent level. Given the common practice of treating statistically insignificant estimates as zero, these findings are very important.

8.4.3   Do Center-Level Factors Account for Heterogeneous Impacts?

Linking the differing impacts across centers to specific factors associated with each center, such as their approach to treatment or their local economic conditions, serves two purposes. First, it may allow the problem of "external validity" that results from allowing centers to self-select into the evaluation to be overcome. Provided the support of the distribution of center characteristics affecting program impacts among centers in the evaluation spans the support in the population, the relevant characteristics can be conditioned on in the evaluation and then used in combination with the distribution of factors across centers for the program as a whole in generating estimated impacts for the population of centers. Second, such links have obvious policy relevance, particularly for factors controlled by center staff, such as the approach to treatment.

We investigate this question indirectly using the JTPA data. If center-level factors drive the differences in impact estimates, then the impact estimates across demographic groups should be correlated. That is, if centers that have strong local economies, or are run by private rather than public agencies, have higher (or lower) impacts, this should hold across demographic groups because these center characteristics are fixed for a given center. Thus positive correlations between the center-specific impacts for pairs of demographic groups provide evidence of the importance of center-level characteristics.

Table 8.3 displays estimated Pearson product-moment correlations and Spearman rank correlations between the center-level impact estimates for pairs of demographic groups in the NJS. In this case, we include all four NJS demographic groups because doing so increases the available evidence from one correlation to six. The table also displays *p*-values from tests of the null hypothesis that the true correlation is zero, along with the number of estimates used in calculating the correlation.

None of the estimated correlations in table 8.3 is statistically distinguishable from zero at the 5 percent level. All but one of the point estimates is below .3 in absolute value, and all but two are below .2. A few of the point estimates are negative. Overall, the table provides little evidence that center-level factors are important determinants of the impact of JTPA.

Another possible source of heterogeneous impacts at the center level is that certain centers perform well or poorly at providing certain treatment types. In the NJS, it is possible to produce experimental impact estimates that condition, not on the services actually received, which are determined after random assignment, but on the services for which potential participants are recommended by JTPA staff prior to random assignment. The three treatment streams based on recommended services are the classroom training in occupational skills (CT-OS) stream, the on-the-job training (OJT) stream, and the "other services" stream. We calculated the Pearson product-moment and Spearman rank correlations between center-level impact estimates within each treatment stream for each demographic

Table 8.3   Correlations of Experimental Impact Estimates across Training Centers

Demographic Group	Adult Males	Adult Females	Male Youths
Pearson Product-Moment Correlation			
Adult females	.1906		
	(.4704)		
	[16]		
Male youths	.0835	.0582	
	(.7675)	(.8368)	
	[15]	[15]	
Female youths	−.3528	.2473	.5001
	(.2160)	(.3939)	(.0686)
	[14]	[14]	[14]
Spearman Rank Correlation			
Adult females	.0235		
	(.9311)		
	[16]		
Male youths	.1821	.1321	
	(.5159)	(.6387)	
	[15]	[15]	
Female youths	−.4066	.0198	.2835
	(.1491)	(.9465)	(.3260)
	[14]	[14]	[14]

Source: National JTPA Study 18 Month Impact Sample.

Note: The self-reported earnings variable used here includes the Bloom et al. (1993) hand imputations for outliers along with the imputed values generated by Bloom et al. for adult female nonrespondents using information from state unemployment insurance earnings records. Training centers with fewer than 30 experimental sample members are excluded. The correlations are calculated using simple mean-difference experimental impact estimates. Numbers in parentheses are *p*-values from tests of the null hypothesis that the true correlation is zero. Numbers in brackets are numbers of impact estimates used to construct correlations. The estimated standard errors do not account for the fact that the impacts being correlated are themselves estimates. Doing so would make the estimated standard errors larger and therefore reinforce the conclusions drawn in the text.

group. The results of this analysis match those reported in table 8.3. If anything, the evidence for the treatment streams is even weaker, as the estimated correlations are more often negative than in table 8.3.

8.5 Pooling

In the preceding section, we considered the sensitivity of the experimental impact estimates to the set of training centers included in the evaluation under the assumption that the best way to combine the data across centers was to pool it into a single large sample of individuals. In this

Table 8.4   **Sensitivity of Experimental Impact Estimates to Method of Pooling Training Centers**

Weighting Variable	Male Youths	Female Youths
Center sample size	−893.05	−191.52
	(466.93)	(293.11)
	[.0548]	[.5156]
Inverse variance of estimated impact	−506.30	−78.61
	(429.26)	(276.95)
	[.2380]	[.7794]
Number of program year 1989 terminees	−660.89	−609.05
	(553.77)	(341.41)
	[.2340]	[.0750]

Source: National JTPA Study 18 Month Impact Sample.

Note: The self-reported earnings variable used here includes the Bloom et al. (1993) hand imputations for outliers. Simple mean-difference experimental impact estimates are used for each training center in computing the overall impacts. The overall estimates obtained when the training center estimates are weighted by the training center sample sizes differ slightly from the overall mean difference estimates obtained using the full sample of individuals because the ratio of control to treatment group members differs slightly across training centers. At some centers, random assignment ratios higher than 2:1 were used for short periods. Numbers in parentheses are estimated standard errors. Numbers in brackets are *p*-values from tests of the null hypothesis that the true impact is zero.

section, we examine the sensitivity of the experimental estimates to two alternative pooling methods.[6]

The desirability of using an alternative pooling method depends on how the impact of JTPA and the variance of the outcome variable, earnings, vary across training centers. If both the impact and the outcome variance are the same across centers, then there is no gain from doing anything other than combining the data from each training center into a single large sample of individuals. Doing so is equivalent to weighting the center-level impact estimates by the center sample sizes. Impact estimates produced in this way appear in the first row of table 8.4.

If the variance of earnings itself varies across centers, while the impact is constant or varies independently of the variance in earnings, then the efficiency of the estimates can be increased without adding any bias by calculating the overall impact as a weighted average of the impact estimates for the individual centers, with the weights inversely proportional to the variance of the impact estimate at each center. Impact estimates

6. When, as in the NJS, the sample of centers is not randomly selected from the population of centers, the justification for combining the centers in any way to produce an overall impact estimate is unclear. Whatever estimate is obtained from doing so is not externally valid, which means that it is not a valid estimate of the impact of training at centers other than those included in the evaluation.

obtained in this way appear in the second row of table 8.4. For male youths, weighting cuts the magnitude of the impact estimate almost in half, indicating that point estimates for this group are lower (more negative) at centers where the variance of the impact estimate is relatively large. This effect is less pronounced for female youths.

Another type of weighting is useful if the representation of each center in the experimental sample differs from its representation in the overall JTPA participant population. To see why, suppose that large training centers are underrepresented in the experimental sample and that the impact of the program is bigger in large training centers due to economies of scale. In this case, simply combining the samples from the individual training centers results in an overall impact estimate that is biased downward relative to the true impact of JTPA on a randomly selected participant. Note that underrepresentation of particular centers in the experimental sample is not an issue if the impact of JTPA is the same at every training center, or if whether or not a training center is underrepresented is independent of its impact.

In the NJS data, the participating centers are not represented in proportion to the number of participants they serve because several centers dropped out of the experiment early. The third row of table 8.4 presents impact estimates constructed by weighting the center-specific impacts with weights proportional to the number of JTPA terminees at each center in program year 1989, where program year 1989 is selected because it overlaps with the period of random assignment at most of the centers.[7] This weighting has a large effect on the impact estimate for female youths, which becomes nearly as large in absolute value as that for male youths and statistically significant at the 10 percent level.

8.6 Treatment of Earnings Outliers

Unusually large earnings observations, or outliers, can have important effects on experimental impact estimates based on conditional means. Outliers may represent invalid values, or they may represent valid values with a very low probability of being observed. In either case, it may be desirable to adopt a systematic procedure to minimize their influence on the impact estimates.

Table 8.5 shows the sensitivity of the experimental impact estimates for youths in the NJS data to alternative methods of handling earnings outliers. The first row of the table presents impact estimates constructed using the raw earnings data. The second row presents the estimates from Bloom et al. (1993), in which the top 2 percent of the earnings values for each group were examined by hand for coding errors or inconsistencies and

7. Program year 1989 runs from July 1989 to June 1990.

Table 8.5   **Sensitivity of Experimental Impact Estimates to Method of Handling Earnings Outliers**

	Male Youths	Female Youths
Unadjusted earnings data	−1,141.55	−72.78
	(492.05)	(291.12)
	[.02]	[.81]
Bloom et al. (1993) hand corrections	−867.33	−163.00
	(429.37)	(262.90)
	[.04]	[.53]
Top 1% trimmed within groups	−946.14	−119.47
	(411.37)	(248.90)
	[.02]	[.63]
Top 2% trimmed within groups	−805.66	−140.60
	(387.34)	(238.31)
	[.04]	[.56]
Top 3% trimmed within groups	−737.64	−141.75
	(374.44)	(232.38)
	[.05]	[.54]
Top 4% trimmed within groups	−656.59	−125.35
	(364.77)	(223.84)
	[.07]	[.58]
Top 5% trimmed within groups	−679.72	−119.21
	(355.87)	(216.75)
	[.06]	[.58]

Source: National JTPA Study 18 Month Impact Sample.

Note: These impact estimates are regression-adjusted using the same specification as in Bloom et al. (1993); results for the case using the hand corrections differ slightly from those in Bloom et al. because we were unable to exactly replicate their construction of some of the covariates. Estimates with trimming are obtained by dropping the indicated percentage of the earnings values from the top of the earnings distribution for each of the control and treatment groups for each demographic group in each month prior to calculating the impact estimates. Numbers in parentheses are estimated standard errors. Numbers in brackets are *p*-values from two-tailed tests of the null hypothesis that the true value of the coefficient is zero.

then corrected if necessary.[8] These hand corrections have a large effect for male youth, where they reduce the absolute value of the estimate by almost $300, or around 25 percent.

The remaining rows examine the alternative strategy of trimming off the top 1 to 5 percent of the raw earnings values in each month in each of the treatment and control groups prior to calculating the experimental impact

8. The estimates in the first row of table 8.4 differ slightly from those in the second row of table 8.5 because the estimates in table 8.4 are not regression adjusted and because the random assignment ratio was changed from two treatment group members to each control group member at some centers for short periods. The latter causes the weighted (by the center sample sizes) average of the center-specific impact estimates to differ from the impact estimates obtained from the pooled sample of individuals.

estimates. The trimming procedure has the advantage that it is easier to replicate than the hand correction procedure. Estimates are obtained with trimming of the top 1, 2, 3, 4, and 5 percent of the earnings values. In the case where the outliers represent invalid values, the raw data can be thought of as a mixture of two distributions, one valid and one invalid, and the trimming acts to remove the invalid values. In the case where the outliers represent valid values, reporting estimates based on trimmed means can be justified on robustness grounds. For male youths, trimming has a marked effect on the magnitude of the impact estimates. The point estimate falls as the amount of trimming increases and ceases to be statistically significant at the 5 percent level when more than 3 percent of the observations are trimmed. There is little effect of trimming on the estimates for female youths.

8.7 Earnings Measures

We have assumed throughout this paper that earnings represent the outcome measure of interest in an evaluation. However, there are many alternative ways to measure earnings, and the specific measure chosen may affect the impact estimates obtained.[9] For example, earnings data from surveys may do a better job of capturing earnings in the underground economy but a poorer job of capturing regular earnings than administrative data from unemployment insurance (UI) records.

This section presents two pieces of evidence on the sensitivity of the NJS experimental impact estimates to the earnings measure used. The first piece of evidence is a comparison of 12-month impacts constructed using self-reported and UI administrative earnings data for a subsample of the NJS data with valid values for both measures. The second piece of evidence compares the 18-month impact estimates from the two official NJS impact reports submitted to the U.S. Department of Labor. Our evidence reveals surprising sensitivity of the experimental impact estimates for youth to seemingly modest changes in the construction of the earnings variable. This sensitivity is sufficient to affect the policy conclusions drawn from the NJS in some respects.

Table 8.6 compares 12-month impact estimates constructed using self-reported and UI administrative earnings data on a common sample. Confining the impact estimate to the first 12 months after random assignment

---

9. A related issue that we do not address in detail here is whether other outcome measures should be included in an evaluation. The choice of whether to examine other outcome measures will affect the results of a cost-benefit analysis as benefits not measured are often not included. In some past evaluations, such as the nonexperimental evaluation of the Job Corps program described in Mallar et al. (1982), program impacts on factors other than earnings, such as crime, have been responsible for much of the overall benefit attributed to the program. Recent evaluations, such as the NJS, have tended to downplay these other outcomes.

Table 8.6   **Comparison of Experimental Impact Estimates Calculated Using Self-reported and Administrative Earnings Data**

Earnings Measure	Male Youths	Female Youths
Impact using self-reported data	−555*	6[a]
Impact using UI administrative data	−240[a]	21[a]
Difference in impacts	−315	−15
N	1,447	1,939

Source: Estimates drawn from Bloom et al. (1993, exhibit E.10).

Note: The estimates are calculated over the first 12 months after random assignment rather than the first 18 months after random assignment in order to maximize the number of observations with valid values for both earnings measures. The sample includes persons with valid values for both self-reported earnings and administrative earnings from state unemployment insurance (UI) records for the first year after random assignment. All persons at the Jersey City, New Jersey, and Marion, Ohio, training centers are excluded as UI earnings data are not available for those states.

[a]Not statistically significantly different from zero.

*Significant at the 10 percent level.

maximizes the size of the sample with valid values for both measures. For male youths, the estimate constructed using the self-reported earnings data is nearly twice as large as that constructed using the UI data and is statistically significant at the 10 percent level. For female youths, the difference is essentially zero. The findings for adults (not reported here) match those for male youths and reinforce the conclusion that which of the two earnings measure is used makes a difference in the resulting impact estimates.[10]

Table 8.7 compares the experimental impact estimates for the first 18 months after random assignment presented in the official 18- and 30-month impact reports submitted to the U.S. Department of Labor (Bloom et al. 1993; Orr et al. 1995) These estimates are broken down by the experimental treatment streams described earlier, which divide the sample based on the services recommended by JTPA staff prior to random assignment. The two sets of estimates differ in their construction in a number of important ways. In particular, in the 30-month impact report (1) persons with fewer than 18 months of self-reported earnings data had the remaining months filled in with UI earnings data when the UI data were available,

---

10. Bloom et al. (1993) examine and reject explanations based on recall bias in self-reported earnings, missing UI earnings at centers near state borders, and measurement problems at specific centers for the differences between the self-reports and the UI administrative data. Smith (1997b) argues, based on comparisons with other earnings measures in the NJS and with other samples of similar populations, that the difference in impacts results from an apparent upward bias in the survey-based earnings measure. Inflating the means of both the treatment and control groups by a common factor increases the absolute value of the experimental impact estimate.

Table 8.7   **Comparison of Experimental Impact Estimates in Official NJS 18- and 30-Month Impact Reports**

Treatment Stream	18-Month Report	30-Month Report	Ratio of Estimates[a]
	Male Youths[b]		
CT-OS	−380	795 (899)	−.48
OJT	−2,392*	−1,814 (1,082)	1.32
Other services	−1,976*	249 (721)	−7.94
	Female Youths		
CT-OS	−792	174 (376)	−4.55
OJT	762	321 (892)	2.37
Other services	−271	−130 (759)	2.08

Source: Bloom et al. (1993, exhibits 6.7 and 6.12) for 18-month impact report. Orr et al. (1995, exhibit 5.17) for 30-month impact report.

Note: Table reports impact per enrollee calculated using Bloom (1984) estimator. No standard errors are reported for the estimates in the 18-month impact report. Numbers in parentheses are estimated standard errors for estimates from the 30-month impact report.

[a]Estimates from the two impact reports differ due to changes in sample composition, rescaling of self-reported overtime earnings in the 30-month impact report, and use of rescaled data from matched unemployment insurance earnings records in the 30-month impact report. See the text for more details.

[b]Male youth results refer to the full sample for the 18-month impact report and to the subsample of persons without a self-reported arrest between their sixteenth birthdays and the date of random assignment for the 30-month impact report.

*Significant at the 10 percent level.

(2) the UI earnings data were rescaled up by the ratio between the mean self-reported and UI earnings for each demographic group, (3) some persons who were excluded from the 18-month evaluation because they were randomly assigned late in 1989 were included, (4) only male youths without self-reported arrests between their sixteenth birthdays and the time of random assignment were included because it was found that the negative impact of the program for this group reported in the 18-month evaluation was concentrated among those with self-reported arrests, and (5) the overtime component of the self-reported earnings measure was scaled down in light of evidence of an upward bias in the reporting of this component of earnings. The most important of these factors are the use and rescaling of the UI data because they affect the largest fraction of the sample.

The table shows surprisingly large differences in impact estimates across official reports. The largest percentage effects are for female youths, where the ratio of the two estimates is at least 2.0 for all three treatment streams. The point estimate for the CT-OS treatment stream reverses sign and changes by nearly $1,000 between the two reports. For male youths, the statistical significance of the estimates in the 18-month report disappears in the 30-month report, and the CT-OS and other services stream estimates change sign. The estimates in table 8.6 make clear that much of the change in the male youth estimates results from changes in the earnings measure, not from the arbitrary restriction of the sample to persons without self-reported arrests prior to random assignment.[11]

8.8   Treatment Group Dropout and Control Group Substitution

In this section we discuss two issues that can have important effects on the impact estimates reported in an experimental evaluation and, more important, on the interpretation of those estimates. The first is treatment group members who drop out of the program prior to receiving treatment. The second is control group members who obtain substitutes for the experimental treatment from other sources.

8.8.1   Treatment Group Dropout

In order to reduce costs and minimize the disruption of normal JTPA operating procedures, random assignment took place at the JTPA office after recommendation for services, rather than at the service provider location prior to the start of services. This led to a substantial dropout problem in the NJS data, with around 40 percent of the treatment group never enrolling in JTPA (see Heckman, Smith, and Taber 1998).

In the presence of dropouts, the treatment group earnings distribution mixes the distributions of earnings for persons who have and have not received the treatment, instead of providing a clean estimate of the distribution of earnings conditional on treatment. The literature offers three strategies for dealing with dropouts. The first consists of reinterpreting the impact estimates as estimating the impact of "assignment to the treatment group"—sometimes called "intent to treat"—rather than of actual receipt of treatment. While the impact of assignment to treatment is often of interest in medical contexts, it is less interesting in the case of training programs.

The second strategy, developed in Bloom (1984), assumes that dropouts in the treatment group experience the same outcome they would have ex-

---

11. Similar variability across the official reports is observed for the adult groups (Heckman, LaLonde, and Smith 1999). E.g., a reader of Bloom et al. (1993) would conclude that on-the-job training has the largest impact on adult women, while a reader of Orr et al. (1995) would conclude that "other services" is the best treatment for that group.

perienced had they been in the control group. Under this assumption, an estimate of the impact of treatment on the treated can be obtained by dividing the experimental impact estimate by one minus the fraction of the treatment group that drops out. This strategy is often plausible but fails when dropouts receive partial treatment, as they appear to in the NJS case.[12] Heckman, Smith, and Taber (1998) propose alternative identifying assumptions based on prior knowledge of the impact of partial treatment or prior knowledge of the ratio of the mean earnings in the untreated (control) state of persons who would and would not have been dropouts had they been randomly assigned to the experimental treatment group.

Heckman, Smith, and Taber (1998) find large differences between the unadjusted NJS experimental impact estimates and those provided by the Bloom (1984) method and their alternative identifying assumptions. For example, Bloom et al. (1993) report that the impact of assignment to treatment on the earnings of male youths aged 16–21 in the 18 months after random assignment is −$854, while the estimate of the effect of treatment on the treated for this group obtained using the Bloom (1984) method is −$1,356. At the same time, differences between the Bloom (1984) estimates and the alternatives in Heckman, Smith, and Taber (1998) are modest, given reasonable assumptions about the effectiveness of partial treatment or about the ratio of earnings of control group members who would and would not have been dropouts.

8.8.2   Control Group Substitution

Control group substitution arises in the evaluation of many training programs because there are often multiple programs serving the same clientele and because these programs often contract out to service providers who offer the same services to the general public. Cave and Quint (1991) find substitution in their evaluation of the Career Beginnings program, Puma et al. (1990) find it in their evaluation of the Food Stamp Employment and Training Program, and Riccio et al. (1994) find it in their evaluation of the GAIN program.[13]

Heckman, Hohmann, Smith, and Khoo (1999) document the importance of control group substitution in the NJS. Table 8.8, taken from their paper, shows the percentage of the treatment and control group members recommended to receive classroom training prior to random assignment (the CT-OS treatment stream) that actually received classroom training

---

12. Doolittle and Traeger (1990) estimate that about half of the persons in the treatment group who did not formally enroll in JTPA, and who are therefore counted as dropouts in the official reports, received some form of JTPA services following random assignment. In most cases, these services were fairly minimal such as counseling or job search assistance.

13. Heckman, LaLonde, and Smith (1999) provide evidence on control group substitution for a large number of social experiments.

Table 8.8   **Percentages of Experimental Treatment and Control Groups Receiving Classroom Training Services**

	Male Youths	Female Youths
Treatment group	55.7	58.6
Control group	34.5	40.1
Difference	22.2	18.5
p-Value for difference[a]	0.00	0.00

Source: National JTPA Study 18 Month Rectangular Sample. Statistics taken from Heckman, Hohmann, Smith, and Khoo (1999, table II).

Note: Sample consists of all persons in the CT-OS treatment stream in the NJS with valid values of earnings and training in the 18 months after random assignment. The CT-OS treatment stream consists of persons recommended to receive classroom training by JTPA staff prior to random assignment. The training measure used here includes only classroom training. Some persons in each group received other training services but not classroom training.

[a]*p*-Values are from tests of the null hypothesis that the difference between the percentages receiving training in the two groups is zero.

in the 18 months after random assignment, along with the *p*-value from a test of the null hypothesis of equality of the two percentages. For both youth groups, the data reveal substantial substitution into alternative classroom training services by controls, as well as a high rate of dropping out among the treatment group.[14] Substitution and dropping out also characterize the other two treatment streams in the NJS, though the rates of substitution are less because some other JTPA services, such as subsidized on-the-job training at private firms, are not widely available from alternative sources.

There are three standard methods for handling control group substitution. The first reinterprets the experimental impact estimate as estimating the marginal impact of the additional training provided by the program being evaluated relative to that received by the control group, rather than estimating the impact of training relative to no training. When the latter parameter is the object of interest, as it often is, this approach is unsatisfactory.

The other two methods use the experimental data to estimate the impact of training relative to no training. The second method relies on the assumption of either a common impact of training incidence (or of each hour of training) across persons or a varying impact of training incidence (or of each hour of training) whose idiosyncratic portion is either unknown to the person deciding to participate in training or not used in

14. Some treatment group members in the CT-OS treatment stream enrolled in JTPA but received services other than classroom training. See Heckman, Hohmann, Smith, and Khoo (1999) for details.

making that decision. We call this (very strong) assumption A-1. Under
assumption A-1,

$$\hat{\Delta} = \frac{\overline{Y_t} - \overline{Y_c}}{\overline{p_t} - \overline{p_c}}$$

estimates the mean impact of training relative to no training, where $\overline{Y_t}$ is
mean earnings in the treatment group, $\overline{Y_c}$ is mean earnings in the control
group, and $\overline{p_t}$ and $\overline{p_c}$ are either the fractions of the treatment and control
group members receiving training or the mean hours of training received
by treatment and control group members, respectively.

The third method uses the treatment group data to conduct a standard
nonexperimental evaluation using the techniques in Heckman and Robb
(1985), Heckman, LaLonde, and Smith (1999), and elsewhere. By comparing persons who receive training with persons who do not, these nonexperimental techniques also address both substitution and dropout.

Table 8.9 displays unadjusted experimental impact estimates, adjusted
estimates based on assumption A-1, and estimates from two standard nonexperimental estimation procedures. The dependent variable is earnings
in the first 12 months after training (for persons with a post-random-
assignment classroom training spell) or the first 12 months after random
assignment (for persons without such a spell). Using this dependent variable makes the estimates net of the opportunity costs (in terms of forgone
earnings) of training and is consistent with the usual practice in nonexperimental evaluations. The sample for the experimental and adjusted experimental estimates consists of persons in the classroom training treatment
stream with valid values of the dependent variable. The sample for the
nonexperimental estimates consists only of treatment group members in
the CT-OS treatment stream. Thus the nonexperimental comparison
group consists of the treatment group dropouts.

The first panel of table 8.9 presents benchmark experimental impact
estimates for this sample and dependent variable. The next panel presents
estimates obtained under assumption A-1 expressed in terms of either
training incidence or hours of training. The adjusted estimates are substantially larger in absolute value than the benchmark experimental estimates. Furthermore, the two versions of assumption A-1 yield very different estimates for male youths—$1,883 when A-1 applies to the incidence
of training and $693 when A-1 applies to each hour of training.

The final panel presents nonexperimental estimates of the impact of
training relative to no training. The first is the coefficient on a training
receipt indicator from an OLS regression of earnings on the indicator and
a vector of individual characteristics, while the second is the coefficient on
the training indicator in the same regression with the difference between
earnings before random assignment and earnings after training as the

Table 8.9   **Sensitivity of Impact Estimates to Method of Accounting for Control Group Substitution and Treatment Group Dropout**

	Male Youths	Female Youths
Unadjusted Experimental Estimate		
Experimental estimate	334.16	−52.61
	(510.57)	(290.74)
Adjusted Experimental Estimates Based on Assumption A-1[a]		
A-1 for training incidence	1,883.10	−253.90
	(2,877.28)	(1,403.12)
A-1 for each hour of training	693.31	−80.84
	(1,059.35)	(544.18)
Nonexperimental Impact Estimates Using the Experimental Treatment Group		
OLS[b]	1,653.61	1,645.79
	(542.13)	(309.24)
Difference in differences[c]	2,114.79	1,542.44
	(593.81)	(365.37)

Source: National JTPA Study 12 Month Post-Training Sample.

Note: The dependent variable in all cases except the difference-in-differences estimator consists of self-reported earnings in the 12 months after the first spell of classroom training following random assignment, for those with a classroom training spell, or the first 12 months after random assignment, for those without a classroom training spell. The sample for the unadjusted and adjusted experimental estimates consists of all NJS sample members in the CT-OS treatment stream with valid self-reported earnings and training data for the 12-month period indicated in the preceding sentence. The sample for the nonexperimental estimates consists of treatment group members meeting the same criteria. The measure of training includes only self-reported classroom training. Numbers in parentheses are estimated standard errors.

[a]The adjusted experimental estimates are constructed using the experimental treatment and control groups as described in the text. Assumption A-1 is that either training incidence (or each hour of training) has the same impact on everyone or the impact of training incidence (or each hour of training) varies but individuals do not know the idiosyncratic portion of their impact or do not use that information in deciding whether to take training. Reported estimates for the per hour case are at the mean hours of classroom training in the treatment group.

[b]The OLS estimates consist of the coefficient on an indicator variable for classroom training receipt in a regression of earnings on the training indicator and a vector of background variables. The comparison group for these estimates is the treatment group dropouts.

[c]The difference-in-differences estimates consist of the coefficient on an indicator variable for classroom training receipt in a regression of the difference between earnings before random assignment and earnings after random assignment or training on the training indicator and a vector of background variables. The comparison group for these estimates is the treatment group dropouts.

dependent variable. The two sets of nonexperimental estimates are quite close, and both sets are larger than the unadjusted experimental estimates.[15]

The lessons from this section are as follows. First, treatment group dropout and control group substitution are empirically important in the NJS. Second, taking account of them makes a difference in both the magnitude and the interpretation of the impact estimates. Moreover, doing so involves making the same type of nonexperimental assumptions that experiments attempt to avoid. We show that the impact estimates depend on which among the set of plausible assumptions is invoked in solving the substitution and dropout problems.

8.9   Summary and Conclusions

In this paper, we examine the sensitivity of the NJS experimental impact estimates for youth along several dimensions. Our analysis emphasizes that experimental impact estimates differ from nonexperimental estimates only in that they rely on random assignment. All of the normal issues that arise in any empirical evaluation, such as how to measure the outcome variable, what to do about outliers, and how to combine data from different training centers, arise in experiments just as they do in nonexperimental analyses. Other issues, such as treatment group dropout, control group substitution, and selection of the training centers to include in the evaluation, are unique to experiments or are more problematic in an experimental context.

We show that the magnitude and interpretation of the experimental estimates depend crucially on a number of these factors. We find the selection of which training centers to include in the evaluation and the construction and interpretation of estimates of the effect of training relative to no training in the presence of treatment group dropout and control group substitution to be the most important factors in the NJS youth data. In addition, we demonstrate the importance of the construction of the earnings variable used in the evaluation. The fact that the two official NJS impact reports submitted to the U.S. Department of Labor provide 18-month impact estimates for youth that change by over $1,000 in one case and that switch signs in several others illustrates this importance.

While our analysis does not indicate that experiments should be

---

15. Heckman, Hohmann, Smith, and Khoo (1999) consider a number of other nonexperimental estimators. The nonexperimental estimates almost always exceed the unadjusted experimental estimates. At the same time, they emphasize that whether JTPA classroom training passes a cost-benefit test after taking account of substitution and dropout depends on assumptions about the longevity of training's impact on earnings and about the discount rate. For most demographic groups, plausible assumptions imply that JTPA classroom training produces a private benefit to its recipients but has negative net social benefits.

dropped in favor of a return to nonexperimental methods, it suggests the importance of examining the sensitivity of experimental impact results and the potential value of conducting multiple independent experimental evaluations of the same program. It also makes clear that experiments do not constrain the ability of an investigator to find what he or she wants to find as strongly as many advocates of experimentation hoped they would.

Our findings support moderation in the interpretation of the NJS youth results. The magnitudes of the impact estimates for male youths are sensitive along nearly every dimension we examine. The statistical significance of the negative male youth impact estimates is extremely fragile; it appears more likely that JTPA has a zero impact on male youths than a negative one. At the same time, the estimates for both youth groups are sensitive to the adjustments for control group substitution and treatment group dropout. Like Heckman, Hohmann, Smith, and Khoo (1999), we find that the effect of JTPA classroom training on earnings measured relative to no training, rather than relative to the available alternatives, is positive, though probably not positive enough to pass a social cost-benefit test.

Finally, the results presented in this paper emphasize the consistency of the JTPA impact estimates with earlier findings for other programs. For youths, the record of government training programs for the disadvantaged is almost uniformly negative.[16] Impacts on the earnings of dropouts in the NSW demonstration were negligible (Hollister et al. 1984). The CETA estimates for youth reported in Bassi (1984) are negative for males and negligible for females. Cave and Doolittle (1991) present experimental impact estimates from Jobstart, a youth program similar to the Job Corps but lacking its residential component. Its effect on earnings is negative for male youths and negligible for female youths. The one bright spot is the somewhat dated nonexperimental evaluation of the Job Corps by Mallar et al. (1982), which found a positive effect on participant earnings and criminal behavior sufficient to pass a cost-benefit test.[17] Unlike the other programs, the Job Corps involves a residential component, in which youth are removed from their neighborhoods to a separate camp with other Job Corps participants. It is also, unlike JTPA, quite expensive.

Though sensitive along several dimensions and, for JTPA classroom training, perhaps somewhat more positive than found for previous programs once adjusted for substitution and dropping out, the NJS impact estimates for youth fit comfortably into the pattern of several decades of research that finds very limited earnings effects for the types of services offered by JTPA.

---

16. Heckman, Roselius, and Smith (1994), Heckman, LaLonde, and Smith (1999), Heckman, Lochner, Smith, and Taber (1997), and LaLonde (1995), among others, provide extended surveys of the literature on training.

17. Their cost-benefit analysis does not include the deadweight costs associated with raising the funds for the program through taxation.

References

Bassi, Laurie. 1984. Estimating the effect of training programs with non-random selection. *Review of Economics and Statistics* 66 (1): 36–43.

Bloom, Howard. 1984. Accounting for no-shows in experimental evaluation designs. *Evaluation Review* 82 (2): 225–46.

Bloom, Howard, Larry Orr, George Cave, Stephen Bell, and Fred Doolittle. 1993. *The National JTPA Study: Title IIA impacts on earnings and employment at 18 months.* Bethesda, Md.: Abt Associates.

Cain, Glen, and Douglas Wissoker. 1990. A reanalysis of marital stability in the Seattle-Denver Income Maintenance Experiment. *American Journal of Sociology* 95:1235–69.

Cave, George, and Fred Doolittle. 1991. *Assessing Jobstart: Interim impacts of a program for school dropouts.* New York: Manpower Demonstration Research Corporation.

Cave, George, and Janet Quint. 1991. *Career beginnings impact evaluation: Findings from a program for high school students.* New York: Manpower Demonstration Research Corporation.

Devine, Theresa, and James Heckman. 1996. The structure and consequences of the eligibility rules for a social program: A study of the Job Training Partnership Act (JTPA). In *Research in labor economics,* ed. Solomon Polachek, 15:111–70. Greenwich, Conn.: JAI.

Dickinson, Katherine, Terry Johnson, and Richard West. 1987. An analysis of the sensitivity of quasi-experimental net impact estimates of CETA programs. *Evaluation Review* 11 (4): 452–72.

Doolittle, Fred, and Linda Traeger. 1990. *Implementing the National JTPA Study.* New York: Manpower Demonstration Research Corporation.

Hannan, Michael, and Nancy Tuma. 1990. A reassessment of the effect of income on marital dissolution in the Seattle-Denver experiment. *American Journal of Sociology* 95:1270–98.

Heckman, James, Neil Hohmann, Jeffrey Smith, and Michael Khoo. 1999. Substitution and dropout bias in social experiments: A study of an influential social experiment. *Quarterly Journal of Economics.* Forthcoming.

Heckman, James, Robert LaLonde, and Jeffrey Smith. 1999. The economics and econometrics of active labor market policies. In *Handbook of labor economics,* vol. 3, ed. Orley Ashenfelter and David Card. Amsterdam: North-Holland.

Heckman, James, Lance Lochner, Jeffrey Smith, and Christopher Taber. 1997. The effects of government policy on human capital investment and wage inequality. *Chicago Policy Review* 1 (2): 1–40.

Heckman, James, and Richard Robb. 1985. Alternative methods for evaluating the impact of interventions. In *Longitudinal analysis of labor market data,* ed. James Heckman and Burton Singer, 156–245. New York: Cambridge University Press.

Heckman, James, Rebecca Roselius, and Jeffrey Smith. 1994. U.S. education and training policy: A re-evaluation of the underlying assumptions behind the "new consensus." In *Labor markets, employment policy and job creation,* ed. A. Levenson and L. C. Solomon, 83–122. Boulder, Colo.: Westview.

Heckman, James, and Jeffrey Smith. 1996. Experimental and nonexperimental evaluation. In *International handbook of labour market policy and evaluation,* ed. Günter Schmid, Jacqueline O'Reilly, and Klaus Schömann, 37–88. London: Edward Elgar.

Heckman, James, Jeffrey Smith, and Christopher Taber. 1998. Accounting for dropouts in evaluations of social experiments. *Review of Economics and Statistics* 80 (1): 1–14.

Hollister, Robinson, Peter Kemper, and Rebecca Maynard, eds. 1984. *The National Supported Work demonstration.* Madison: University of Wisconsin Press.

Kemple, James, Fred Doolittle, and John Wallace. 1993. *The National JTPA Study: Final implementation report.* New York: Manpower Demonstration Research Corporation.

LaLonde, Robert. 1995. The promise of public sector-sponsored training programs. *Journal of Economic Perspectives* 9 (2): 149–68.

Mallar, Charles, David Long, Stewart Kerachsky, and Craig Thornton. 1982. *Evaluation of the impact of the Job Corps program: Third follow-up report.* Princeton, N.J.: Mathematica Policy Research.

Orr, Larry, Howard Bloom, Stephen Bell, Winston Lin, George Cave, and Fred Doolittle. 1995. *The National JTPA Study: Impacts, benefits and costs of Title II-A.* Bethesda, Md.: Abt Associates.

Puma, Michael, Nancy Burstein, Katie Merrell, and Gary Silverstein. 1990. *Evaluation of the Food Stamp Employment and Training Program: Final report.* Bethesda, Md.: Abt Associates.

Riccio, James, Daniel Friedlander, and Stephen Freedman. 1994. *GAIN: Benefits, costs and three-year impacts of a welfare-to-work program.* New York: Manpower Demonstration Research Corporation.

Smith, Jeffrey. 1997a. The JTPA selection process: A descriptive analysis. Manuscript.

———. 1997b. Measuring earnings levels among the poor: A comparison of two samples of JTPA eligibles. Manuscript.

The Swedish Youth Labor Market in Boom and Depression

Per-Anders Edin, Anders Forslund, and Bertil Holmlund

9.1 Introduction

The Swedish labor market experienced a dramatic change in the early 1990s. The overall unemployment rate was 1.5 percent in 1989 and 1.6 percent in 1990. By 1993, the unemployment rate had increased to 8.2 percent. Since then unemployment has remained high (8.1 percent in 1996). The slump induced a sharp expansion of various labor market programs; the number of people in programs increased from 1 percent of the labor force in 1990 to 5 percent in 1994. Most program participants are classified as being out of the labor force, so a mirror image of these developments was a substantial fall in labor force participation ratios (from 87 to 80 percent for males and 82 to 76 percent for females). The employment-population ratio fell by over 10 percentage points during the same period, from 83.1 percent in 1990 to 72.6 percent in 1993 and 71.6 percent in 1996.

The sources of the steep fall in employment have been discussed elsewhere, and we do not attempt to summarize or contribute to this debate here. Suffice it to say that macroeconomic shocks played an important role, partly driven by external forces (such as higher real interest rates) and partly by internal policy failures. In addition to the macroeconomic shocks that hit the economy in the late 1980s and the early 1990s, a number of plausible supply-side factors, such as an increasingly generous un-

Per-Anders Edin is professor of industrial relations in the Department of Economics, Uppsala University, and research economist of the National Bureau of Economic Research. Anders Forslund is associate professor of economics at Uppsala University and deputy director of the Office of Labour Market Policy Evaluation. Bertil Holmlund is professor of economics at Uppsala University.

The authors are grateful to Susanne Ackum Agell, Peter Fredriksson, Lawrence Kahn, and participants at the NBER conference for useful comments.

employment insurance system, may have caused some trend rise in the equilibrium unemployment rate over the past three decades.

It is well known that the burden of unemployment is not shared equally among people; the young and the less skilled are particularly prone to unemployment. The present paper is concerned with the labor market experience of Swedish youths during the 1980s and the 1990s. The first objective is to portray early economic attainment among young Swedes. We make use of two data sets with information on labor market outcomes and education among school leavers. Are parental resources and early educational choices crucial for school leavers' success in the labor market and in the educational system? Are there distinct differences between the patterns prevailing in the years of boom in the late 1980s and the years of slump in the 1990s? Has the slump been particularly costly for disadvantaged youths?[1]

The second objective of the paper is to examine the impact of labor market programs on youth employment. The sharp deterioration of the labor market situation in the 1990s has been met by an unprecedented increase in various active labor market programs, such as educational programs and measures to put people into work (or worklike activities). Several programs have been explicitly targeted at unemployed youths. What is the impact of these programs on regular youth employment? We use panel data on employment by Swedish municipalities to examine to what extent the programs crowd out regular employment.

9.2 Youth Employment and Unemployment in Sweden

Youth relative wages increased substantially in Sweden between the late 1960s and the mid-1980s, along with a sharp decline in overall wage differentials. The ratio between hourly wages of 18–19-year-olds and wages of 35–44-year-olds stood at 0.55 in 1968 and had increased to 0.80 in 1986. After 1986 there has been a modest drop in relative wages among teenagers. Relative wages among 20–25-year-olds have been much more stable around 80 percent, with a minor increase between 1968 and 1974. The causes of pay compression in Sweden have been explored elsewhere. In our view, they have to be found in fundamental demand and supply forces as well as egalitarian wage policies pursued by the strong trade unions. (See Edin and Holmlund 1995 for further details and discussion.)

To the extent that the rise in youth relative wages has been institutionally driven one would expect adverse employment responses. To what extent, then, are there signs of deteriorating labor market outcomes for Swedish youths? Somewhat surprisingly, perhaps, the period of marked pay compression in Sweden from the late 1960s to the mid-1980s does

---

1. For discussions of the youth labor market before the downturn in the 1990s, see, e.g., Schröder (1995), Blomskog (1997), and Blomskog and Schröder (1997).

not seem have been accompanied by substantially increasing inequality in employment outcomes.

There is evidence of some trend deterioration in youth labor market performance, however. From the mid-1960s to the early 1980s there was a trend increase in youth unemployment rates and also a trend increase in youth relative to adult unemployment. Youth participation in labor market programs increased substantially in the mid-1980s. For example, over 10 percent of the 16–19-year-old population were engaged in public employment programs in 1984. Program activity declined rapidly, however, during the strong labor market improvement of the late 1980s.

A comparison between the structure of employment and unemployment in 1970 and in 1990 is sufficient to capture the main trends over the 1970s and the 1980s; these two years are characterized by a very tight labor market with very low unemployment (1.4 percent in 1970 and 1.6 percent in 1990). The unemployment rate among 18–24-year-olds increased from 2.5 to 3.5 percent between 1970 and 1990 (table 9.1). There was a substantial increase in the youth employment-population rate, primarily driven by rising labor force participation among young women. School enrollment among teenagers increased as senior high school was extended. Rising school enrollment has made teenage labor force participants an increasingly selected group with relatively low educational attainment, which contributes to relatively high unemployment.

Youth unemployment skyrocketed as a slump hit the Swedish economy in the early 1990s. Overall unemployment increased from 1.6 percent to 8.2 percent between 1990 and 1993 and has remained stubbornly high. Unemployment among 18–24-year-olds increased from 3.5 to 19.1 percent during the same three-year period. The overall employment-population ratio declined by 10 percentage points, whereas the youth employment rate declined by no less than 25 percentage points. There has also been a substantial increase in school enrollment, including activities organized as active labor market policies. We will return to a discussion of these policies in section 9.4. Suffice here to note that they were traditionally not targeted

Table 9.1   **Labor Market Activities and School Enrollment among 18–24-Year-Olds**

Year	Unemployment[a]	Employment[b]	School Enrollment[b]		Labor Market Programs[b]
			Ages 16–19	Ages 20–24	
1970	2.5	66.9	38.4	12.8	n.a.
1990	3.5	75.1	46.4	11.1	2.1
1993	19.1	49.5	63.2	18.9	10.4
1995	18.9	49.1	65.0	21.7	7.4

Sources: Labor Force Surveys, Statistics Sweden, and Thoursie (1996).

[a]Percentage of labor force.

[b]Percentage of population.

particularly at unemployed youths, but this changed as early as the mid-1980s. By 1993, 10 percent of 18–24-year-olds were enrolled in various labor market programs.

Another group that was hit very hard by the slump in the Swedish economy in the 1990s was immigrants. Unemployment rates among recent immigrants (foreign citizens) are much higher than among Swedish citizens. Whereas average unemployment among 20–24-year-olds increased from 3 to 17 percent between 1990 and 1994, unemployment among foreign citizens in this age group rose from 6 to 30 percent. Unemployment among recent immigrants aged 35–44 was as high as 20 percent in 1994.

The depression that hit the Swedish economy in the early 1990s has affected all age groups and all educational groups. Unemployment among 16–24-year-olds increased by a factor of five whereas unemployment among 35–44-year-olds increased by a factor of six. The ratio between youth (16–24) and adult (35–44) unemployment was 3.7 in 1990 and 2.9 in 1993. The ratio between low-education (compulsory schooling) unemployment and university unemployment stood at 2.5 in 1990 and at 2.4 in 1993. Indeed, there is considerable evidence from a number of countries that unemployment relativities for age and educational groups are fairly stable over the business cycle. (See Nickell and Bell 1994 for evidence and interpretations.)

9.3   Labor Market Outcomes in the 1980s and the 1990s

9.3.1   Labor Market Status among Disadvantaged Youths

To provide a somewhat more detailed background for our discussion of disadvantaged youth in the 1980s and 1990s, we start by describing the main trends in employment and nonemployment for various age-education groups since 1971. We choose to concentrate on males to abstract from the massive increase in female labor force participation during the period in question.

Since 1971 a number of major changes may have affected the youth labor market. The combination of (1) an increasingly selected group that do not stay on at school, (2) adverse labor demand shifts, and (3) pay compression could have created a large increase in joblessness among disadvantaged youths. Some evidence on this issue is presented in figure 9.1, where we graph employment-population rates for males of different ages (16–19, 20–24, and 35–44) with different levels of schooling (no high school, one or two years of high school, and three or four years of high school).[2]

These graphs have two striking features. The first is the dramatic

2. The corresponding graphs for unemployment-population rates and nonparticipation rates appear in the appendix.

A. 16-19 years

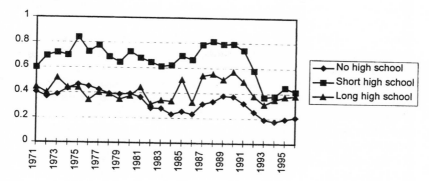

B. 20-24 years

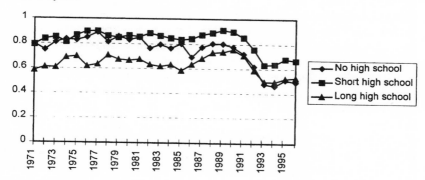

C. 35-44 years

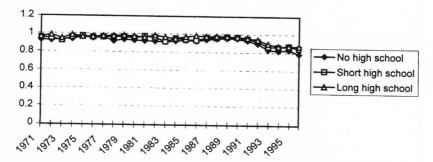

Fig. 9.1   Employment-population rates for males by age and level of schooling
Source: Labor Force Surveys.

development of the 1990s; the second is the absence of strong long-run trends in employment. The only trend in the data is for teenagers (with no high school). Employment rates fall rather steadily for this group with the exception of the boom in the late 1980s. The reason for this trend seems to be the increased school enrollment of teenagers with no previous high school education (see table 9.1 above). Apart from this it seems difficult to discern any sizable long-run trends in these data. Edin, Harkman, and Holmlund (1995) contains a more detailed analysis of these data in terms of employment and nonemployment for different parts of the skill distribution, and they come to similar conclusions. Apart from the teenagers, there is very little evidence of increasing inequality in employment outcomes.

The patterns of employment and nonemployment rates in the Swedish labor market are not easily interpreted in terms of the popular hypothesis about global pervasive trends in labor demand that are particularly harmful for less skilled workers. The empirical work reported in Edin et al. (1995) documents some trend increase in nonemployment among the less skilled, and some increase in mismatch. These trends are exclusively driven by deteriorating labor market performance among 16–19-year-olds. Employment rates among prime-aged men in the bottom decile of the wage distribution were roughly constant during the period 1971–91. This stability is in marked contrast to the sharp fall in employment rates among the least skilled men in the U.S. labor market (see Juhn, Murphy, and Topel 1991).

One might speculate that the growth of the Swedish public sector has counteracted negative relative demand shifts for low-skilled workers, thereby being particularly helpful for the less skilled in the labor market. The share of public employment in the labor force increased from 20 percent in the early 1960s to almost 40 percent in the mid-1980s. Public sector employment increased by 4 to 5 percent per year during the 1970s, with almost all of the expansion taking place in the local government sector. Is there any evidence that low-skilled workers who have been priced out of the private sector have been employed by the rapidly expanding public sector? The fact is that the public sector does not employ many low-educated men (see Edin and Holmlund 1994 for further discussion). The number of men in the public sector with only basic (compulsory) education has been around 40,000 to 50,000 during the past 20 years, to be compared with over one million low-educated men in the private sector during the 1970s (and over 600,000 in the early 1990s). It does not seem very plausible that the expanding public sector has been an important alternative employer for low-skilled men who have lost their jobs in the private sector.[3]

---

3. The role of the public sector is much larger for women. Between 1971 and 1984, female employment grew by 39 percent. Expansion of the public sector accounted for 96 percent of these jobs (Edin and Topel 1997).

9.3.2 Labor Market Outcomes and Socioeconomic Background in the 1980s and the 1990s

We will in this section portray labor market outcomes among Swedish youths at age 22 by means of data sets from 1986 and 1995. During those two years, Statistics Sweden made surveys among those who left the compulsory nine-year school seven years earlier, in 1979 and 1988. The respondents were asked in detail about their present labor market situation, and to some degree about their labor market history in the past few years. The data for 1995 include information on parental socioeconomic background as well as immigrant status; the data for 1986 do not have this information.[4]

We begin by looking at labor market status in 1995, which allows us to examine the role of parental background and immigrant status. We estimate linear probability models for ease of interpretation and focus on five states in February 1995: (regular) employment, unemployment, labor market programs, education, and nonparticipation. The results are reported in table 9.2. The first column for each case only includes parental characteristics in addition to gender and immigrant status; the second includes in addition the high school choice of the respondent.[5] The results suggest that parental background does matter for labor market outcomes. These results become somewhat weaker but are still strongly significant when education is accounted for. This suggests that parental effects work partly through educational choice. The effects of parental background are very strong for employment and education, much weaker for unemployment and nonparticipation, and of no importance for program participation.

What do these estimates say about the situation for disadvantaged youths? The results here are not quite clear-cut. First, if we define disadvantaged youths by parents' skill, we find that youths with blue-collar parents (SEI-1 and -2) are not worse off on all dimensions. They have lower school enrollment rates and possibly somewhat higher unemployment, at least when we do not control for education, but they have higher employment rates. A similar pattern is true also for youths with farmer parents (SEI-8). Their lower school enrollment is offset by higher employment rates.

Second, as could be expected, the situation of youths from immigrant backgrounds seems quite problematic.[6] Lower employment rates and higher unemployment rates are only partly offset by higher school enrollment. Furthermore, the higher school enrollment rate disappears when we

---

4. For further information on the data, see Statistics Sweden (1987, 1996).

5. We choose to use high school curriculum instead of highest level of schooling as our education variable, since a majority of those choosing to continue to college have not graduated by the date of the survey. Most of those who attend college have a three-year theoretical high school degree.

6. Immigrant background is defined as having both parents born abroad.

Table 9.2   Labor Market Status by Family Background and Education, February 1995

	Employment		Unemployment		Programs		Education		Nonparticipation (excl. education)	
Variable	(1)	(2)	(3)	(4)	(5)	(6)	(7)	(8)	(9)	(10)
Constant	.447	.309	.108	.044	.044	.041	.368	.603	.034	.004
	(34.2)	(20.3)	(12.67)	(4.42)	(9.22)	(7.18)	(32.20)	(47.42)	(4.64)	(.44)
Female	−.048	−.036	−.046	−.043	−.017	−.017	.037	.020	.074	.076
	(4.72)	(3.59)	(6.91)	(6.60)	(4.73)	(4.54)	(4.13)	(2.41)	(13.23)	(13.52)
Foreign citizen	−.108	−.062	.026	.040	.005	.006	.072	.004	.005	.011
	(10.12)	(5.76)	(3.73)	(5.67)	(1.20)	(1.57)	(7.73)	(.50)	(0.92)	(1.83)
Family background										
SEI-1	.167	.111	.039	.014	−.003	−.005	−.244	−.148	.041	.028
	(10.78)	(7.13)	(3.86)	(1.38)	(.60)	(.85)	(18.02)	(11.39)	(4.78)	(3.16)
SEI-2	.172	.112	.044	.025	−.003	−.006	−.229	−.139	.017	.008
	(10.45)	(6.82)	(4.06)	(2.30)	(.56)	(.91)	(15.94)	(10.13)	(1.84)	(.81)
SEI-3	.151	.118	.009	.000	−.004	−.005	−.156	−.108	−.001	−.005
	(7.95)	(6.29)	(.73)	(.01)	(.60)	(.79)	(9.36)	(6.89)	(.07)	(.47)
SEI-4	.069	.054	.011	.013	−.007	−.009	−.066	−.054	−.006	−.004
	(4.09)	(3.25)	(.98)	(1.19)	(1.21)	(1.39)	(4.52)	(3.93)	(.62)	(.43)
SEI-5 (omitted)	0	0	0	0	0	0	0	0	0	0
SEI-6	−.074	−.008	−.013	.014	.037	−.035	.115	.004	.009	.025
	(−.75)	(.08)	(.20)	(.22)	(1.02)	(.96)	(1.33)	(.05)	(.17)	(.45)

	(1)	(2)	(3)	(4)	(5)	(6)	(7)	(8)	(9)	(10)
SEI-7	.186	.149	.011	.001	−.007	−.009	−.180	−.126	−.010	−.015
	(8.12)	(6.59)	(.72)	(.09)	(.89)	(1.08)	(8.96)	(6.70)	(.79)	(1.17)
SEI-8	.214	.157	−.007	−.020	−.012	−.015	−.204	−.124	.009	.002
	(5.85)	(4.38)	(.28)	(−.86)	(.93)	(1.11)	(6.40)	(4.14)	(.45)	(.10)
High school education										
No		.122		.124		−.002		−.317		.072
		(7.50)		(11.58)		(.32)		(23.29)		(7.88)
One-year		.204		.113		.002		−.367		.048
		(8.21)		(6.95)		(.23)		(17.73)		(3.42)
Two-year vocational		.238		.088		.008		−.376		.042
		(18.17)		(10.20)		(1.55)		(34.38)		(5.72)
Three-year vocational		.975		.052		.013		−.362		.022
		(12.48)		(3.59)		(1.62)		(19.70)		(1.77)
Two-year theoretical		.124		.073		.000		−.211		.014
		(5.99)		(5.40)		(.03)		(12.26)		(1.21)
Three-year theoretical (omitted)		0		0		0		0		0
R^2	0.031	0.068	0.010	0.028	0.003	0.003	0.051	0.166	0.024	0.031
N	9,515	9,515	9,515	9,515	9,515	9,515	9,515	9,515	9,515	9,515

Note: Linear probability models. The family background socioeconomic indicators (SEI) are as follows: (1) unskilled blue-collar worker; (2) skilled blue-collar worker; (3) white-collar worker, lower level; (4) white-collar worker, intermediate level; (5) white-collar worker, upper level; (6) self-employed professional; (7) owner of business; and (8) farmer. Numbers in parentheses are *t*-values.

control for high school choice. Even if youths from immigrant backgrounds do worse than "native" youths, their situation seems reasonably good compared with recent immigrants (see Wadensjö 1996). One should bear in mind that the group of "immigrants" we have in our sample have completed Swedish compulsory school and spent several years in the country.

Finally, we note that youths who decided not to go on to high school experience a tough situation in the labor market. Their high unemployment rates and low school enrollment rates are not much compensated by higher employment rates. This group also has a substantially higher rate of nonparticipation. Also, it seems that youths who choose vocational high schools or short theoretical high schools are worse off than those who choose long theoretical high schools, even if these differences are smaller than those between no high school and long theoretical high schools.

We have also undertaken a direct comparison of labor market outcomes in 1986 and 1995. In addition to gender, we include dummies for early education (whether the individual continued to high school and the type of high school education). The education variable is the only measure of skill that is available in both samples. The estimates of linear probability models for employment, unemployment, education, and nonparticipation in one week in February 1986 and one week in February 1995 are shown in table 9.3.[7]

Once again the results suggest that early schooling decisions are strongly associated with labor market outcomes for youths. Youths with no or short high school education have higher unemployment rates, lower schooling rates, and higher rates of nonparticipation. However, they also have higher employment rates. The labor market situation for youths has of course deteriorated substantially between 1986 and 1995. It is still true that low-skilled youths have higher unemployment and nonparticipation rates as well as lower rates of school enrollment. It is unclear, though, to what extent the 1990s crisis has hit low-skilled youths more than other youths. Low-skilled youths have reduced their school enrollment and increased their rates of nonparticipation, but the development of employment and unemployment rates may be interpreted somewhat differently. Youths with no high school have about 18 percentage point higher employment rates than youths with long theoretical high school in both 1986 and 1995. The entire fall in youth employment between these years is attributed to a shift in the intercept. Thus high-skilled youths experienced a larger relative drop in their employment rate, since they had a lower employment rate initially.

---

7. Employment programs organized by the labor market agency are included in regular employment. These were not reported separately in 1986, when they accounted for about 1 percent of the sample (SCB 1996).

Table 9.3   Labor Market Status by Education, February 1986 and February 1995

Variable	Employment 1986	Employment 1995	Unemployment 1986	Unemployment 1995	Education 1986	Education 1995	Nonparticipation (excl. education) 1986	Nonparticipation (excl. education) 1995
Constant	.564	.343	.025	.057	.402	.566	.009	.005
	(49.59)	(22.68)	(4.26)	(5.85)	(42.36)	(45.84)	(1.63)	(0.58)
Female	−.033	−.051	.001	−.039	.005	.023	.027	.06
	(3.75)	(4.13)	(.30)	(4.87)	(0.69)	(2.25)	(6.58)	(11.24)
High school education								
No	.186	.176	.061	.123	−.296	−.398	.049	.093
	(13.35)	(8.31)	(8.36)	(9.11)	(25.53)	(23.05)	(7.73)	(7.93)
One year	.236	.277	.052	.096	−.320	−.434	.032	.054
	(12.20)	(9.09)	(5.19)	(4.93)	(19.87)	(17.48)	(3.56)	(3.21)
Two-year vocational	.253	.302	.026	.083	−.293	−.440	.015	.045
	(20.42)	(17.94)	(4.03)	(7.72)	(28.45)	(32.13)	(2.55)	(4.82)
Three-year vocational		.350		.058		−.440		.018
		(13.97)		(3.60)		(21.53)		(1.29)
Two-year theoretical	.178	.169	.025	.074	−.203	−.268	.011	.020
	(11.17)	(6.80)	(4.26)	(4.66)	(15.32)	(13.22)	(1.52)	(1.46)
Three-year theoretical (omitted)	0	0	0	0	0	0	0	0
R^2	0.045	0.062	0.009	0.019	0.091	0.159	0.011	0.031
N	9,770	6,188	9,770	6,188	9,770	6,188	9,770	6,188

Note: Linear probability models. Numbers in parentheses are *t*-values.

Low-skilled youths have experienced a larger absolute increase in their unemployment rate than high-skilled youths. The unemployment differential between no high school and long theoretical high school increased from 6 to 12 percentage points between 1986 and 1995. However, this increase is less striking in relative terms. The unemployment rate for youths with long theoretical high school also more than doubled during this period (from 2.5 to 5.7 percent). Thus the pattern of stable unemployment relativities observed across educational groups in aggregate data also appears within this group of youths.

The estimates reported above refer to a snapshot of the labor market situation of two cohorts at age 22 at different points in time with very different overall labor market conditions. To get some idea of the dynamics of labor market entry, we summarize in table 9.4 the labor force status of each cohort by six-month periods for two and a half years prior to the interview. The respondents were asked to report their main activity by six-month period. Here we report these data for the full samples. The same exercise for low-skilled (no high school) youths tells a similar story.

Apart from large differences in levels across years, there is a striking difference in the development over time across cohorts. In the 1980s there is a strong and steady increase in employment rates over time—from 59 percent in fall 1983 to 71 percent in fall 1985. There is no such trend in the 1990s. The employment rate actually falls early on to recover during

Table 9.4   **Labor Market Status by Six-Month Period, 1980s versus 1990s (percent)**

A. 1986 Sample

	Fall 1983	Spring 1984	Fall 1984	Spring 1985	Fall 1985
Employment	59.3	62.2	66.8	69.7	71.3
Programs	4.5	3.4	2.0	1.7	1.2
Unemployment	4.6	3.2	3.6	2.8	3.6
Education	15.6	16.3	17.4	17.4	18.2
Nonparticipation (excluding education)	14.9	14.1	8.5	7.7	5.4

B. 1995 Sample

	Fall 1992	Spring 1993	Fall 1993	Spring 1994	Fall 1994
Employment	40.6	38.4	39.5	41.4	44.9
Programs	12.8	14.8	12.8	14.0	9.7
Unemployment	7.8	8.8	10.8	8.2	9.3
Education	22.3	22.1	22.9	23.3	24.8
Nonparticipation (excluding education)	13.3	13.0	11.0	10.4	7.7

the last year and a half. The long-run consequences of these problems of entering the labor market for the 1990 cohort will probably depend crucially on what alternative routes of entering the labor market they have access to. The table illustrates that the lower employment rates (26 percentage points) are "compensated" for mainly by higher participation in public employment programs (8 points), higher unemployment rates (6 points), and higher school enrollment rates (7 points).

The notion that unemployment can have serious long-run consequences for youths is probably not controversial. The question is then whether participation in public employment programs or regular education can counteract these negative effects. We will return to a discussion of labor market programs in section 9.4. Concerning the effects of increased school enrollment rates we have no direct evidence. Judging from the type of education these youths enroll in—all of the increase is in regular college and university education—it is plausible that increasing education has a counteracting effect.

9.3.3   Evidence on Wage Behavior

To what extent has the slump been associated with widening wage differentials among age and educational categories? We have used data from two surveys, augmented with information on wages based on the respondents' own reports, to estimate standard wage equations with age and education dummies. The surveys are the Household Market and Non-market Activities (HUS)[8] and the Labor Force Survey (AKU); the latter is undertaken by Statistics Sweden and has included questions on wages in later years. The wage data in the AKU seem to be plagued with substantial measurement errors. The standard deviation of log hourly wages in the 1991 sample is about twice the size of that reported by Edin and Holmlund (1995) from the HUS data for the same year. A comparison of the 90th and 10th wage percentiles, however, shows an almost identical differential. In the empirical analysis below we report only estimates from samples where we have excluded the top and bottom percentiles. There is also some evidence that self-reported schooling levels in the AKUs tend to overstate actual schooling. On the whole, however, we believe that the AKU data should say something about changes over time in the wage structure, even if one should be careful in interpreting the magnitude of various wage differentials using these data.

Estimated relative wages of youths are presented in table 9.5. Since the earlier HUS teenage estimates are based on 18–19-year-olds, we report AKU estimates for both 16–19- and 18–19-year-olds. The teenage relative wages tend to vary across years, but there is no clear change between 1991 and 1994. The relative wages of young adults (ages 20–24) are stable

---

8. For a description, see Klevmarken and Olovsson (1993).

Table 9.5   Youth Relative Wages

| | Age 16–19 vs. Age 35–44 | | | Age 20–24 vs. Age 35–44 | |
| | HUS | AKU | AKU | | |
Year	Ages 18–19	Ages 16–19	Ages 18–19	HUS	AKU
1984	.66	–	–	.80	–
1986	.80	–	–	.80	–
1988	.76	–	–	.83	–
1991	.74	.67	.72	.81	.82
1992	–	.68	.69	–	.82
1993	–	.76	.79	–	.82
1994	–	.75	.74	–	.81

Note: All entries are based on regressions with education and gender controls. The HUS estimates are reproduced from Edin and Holmlund (1995).

around 80 percent. The overall impression is that the results do not indicate any relative wage adjustments for potentially disadvantaged youths during the major slump in the early 1990s.

9.4   Labor Market Programs and Youth Employment: Crowding In or Crowding Out?

In the previous section, we saw that much of the rise in nonemployment among youth is accounted for by an increase in participation in active labor market programs (ALMPs). This raises a question about the effects of ALMPs on regular employment. This is the main theme of the present section. We begin by giving very brief background information on Swedish ALMPs in general and programs targeted at youths in particular, as well as some figures describing the volume of the programs. We then present some new evidence on the effects of ALMPs targeted at youths on regular youth employment.

Over the years since the 1950s, when the foundations of modern Swedish ALMPs were laid down, a large number of different measures have been used. The programs are financed by the central government and implemented by the central Labor Market Board and its regional bodies. Apart from the public employment service, Swedish ALMPs can be broadly classified as employment creation, training, and mobility-enhancing measures.[9] The two principal programs that have been employed over the whole period since the 1950s are temporary public sector jobs, called relief work, and labor market training. During the first half of the 1980s these programs were supplemented by a number of new pro-

9. Since the volumes of mobility-enhancing measures have been very modest since the 1960s and since displacement is hardly an issue related to these programs, we will not discuss them here.

Table 9.6   **Youth Participation in Labor Market Programs, 1978–93**

Year	Relief Work	Labor Market Training	Temporary Replacement Scheme	Job Introduction Projects	Youth Measures	Total
1978	28,584	18,000				46,584
1979	29,431	19,631				49,062
1980	12,581	15,689				28,270
1981	12,527	11,071				23,598
1982	30,418	12,298				42,716
1983	38,260	12,914				51,174
1984	19,310	13,123			17,743	50,176
1985	7,891	11,977			30,542	50,410
1986	6,423	12,030			24,473	42,926
1987	5,019	12,465			17,869	35,353
1988	3,668	14,988			10,096	28,752
1989	2,189	11,842			4,487	18,518
1990	1,598	10,236			2,959	14,793
1991	2,265	17,439	762		9,617	30,083
1992	2,369	25,862	3,805		29,738	61,774
1993	238	11,580	3,296	4,751	58,330	78,195

Source: Skedinger (1995).

grams, one of which was explicitly targeted at youths. In the wake of rapidly growing unemployment in the early 1990s, participation in many programs (the most notable exception being relief work)[10] has grown considerably, and a number of new measures have been introduced.

Before 1984, the dominant measure for youths in terms of participation was relief work (see table 9.6). Since their introduction in 1984 in the form of "youth teams," which provided teenagers with half-time employment and encouraged job seeking, special youth measures have taken a number of forms. After a few years, youth teams were succeeded by "job introduction" schemes, providing work experience for teenagers. As is evident from table 9.6, these programs had a rather modest volume. In 1992, a form called "youth practice" was introduced at the same time as the volume was increased rapidly.

Youth practice is targeted at youths under age 25. The objective is to provide the participants with practice and professional experience. The introduction of this measure was accompanied by instructions aimed at minimizing displacement (participants should not replace ordinary recruitees; the measure is to be seen as a "measure of last resort"). The employer receives free labor, whereas the participant receives a grant. The normal duration is six months. A final thing to note about the program is that it,

---

10. This is a notable exception, because relief work traditionally has been the prime measure used to deal with cyclical swings in the labor market.

in contrast to previous measures, primarily is directed to the private sector.

The number of studies dealing with displacement effects of Swedish ALMPs is small, and the number of those dealing explicitly with youth measures even smaller. The main thrust of these studies is that the displacement effect of job creation programs is significant, estimates ranging between 40 percent and more than 100 percent.[11] The results of the two studies explicitly treating youth measures are no exceptions.

Skedinger (1995) uses quarterly data for the period 1970:3–91:4 to estimate a VAR including youth (ages 18–24) participation in labor market programs and youth employment. The derived impulse-response function implies more than 100 percent crowding out during the first quarter and significant crowding out for two quarters. Skedinger's results have been questioned by, among others, Holmlund (1995), who shows that a reasonable reformulation of the VAR gives an estimated displacement of around 40 percent, rather than above 100 percent. Still, this is significant crowding out. Forslund (1996) analyzes a panel of the Swedish municipalities for the period 1990–94. His estimates indicate that youth programs crowd out 95 percent of total employment in the short run and about 75 percent in the long run.

To throw more light on the effects of youth measures on regular youth employment, we use the data set constructed by Forslund (1996) to estimate a model of the demand for youth labor. The dependent variable is the employment-population share of youths aged 18–24. In addition to time dummies, the right-hand-side variables include the lagged dependent variable to take care of sluggish adjustment, the adult employment rate to control for "aggregate" employment shocks, an index for municipality-specific labor demand for youth, and the (average annual) labor income of youth as a proxy for the youth wage rate. We also include the participation rate in youth measures, which is the fraction of the population aged 18–24 that is enrolled in a youth program. Finally, we include the youth share of the population in the age interval 18–65 to control for relative supply effects to the extent that these are imprecisely captured by the youth income variable. All variables are available for all Swedish municipalities for the years 1990–94.

Most variables are straightforward, but the demand variable warrants some explanation. Time dummies are used in the estimations to control for aggregate demand shifts, but to purge the estimates of spurious correlation between municipality employment and youth programs, we want to control for municipality-specific shifts in the demand for youths. The variable is constructed in the following way: the industry distribution of youth employment by municipality in 1990 is used to generate municipality-specific

---

11. The studies include Gramlich and Ysander (1981), Forslund and Krueger (1997), Calmfors and Skedinger (1995), Ohlsson (1995), and Forslund (1996).

Table 9.7   **Sample Means of Variables in Estimated Model, 1990–94**

Variable	1990	1991	1992	1993	1994
Youth income	89,200	93,400	97,700	99,100	97,000
Youth employment rate	.749	.670	.537	.434	.462
Adult employment rate[a]	.649	.626	.598	.558	.562
Demand index	5.49	5.34	5.09	4.78	4.96
Youth population share[b]	.155	.151	.148	.145	.142
Youth programs	.004	.013	.032	.082	.083

[a]Number of employed over age 24 relative to population over age 24.
[b]Population aged 18–24 relative to population aged 18–65.

weights. The demand index is constructed by applying these weights to the aggregate employment development in each of about 60 industries and dividing by the number of youths in each of the years.

The model is estimated in fixed-effect form. The presence of the lagged dependent variable as well as measurement errors and simultaneity problems caution against OLS estimation. Thus, in addition to estimating the model by OLS on within-group transformed data, we have used the IV estimator of Arellano and Bond (1991) implemented in the OX program DPD (Arellano, Bond, and Doornik 1997).

The major simultaneity problem in this study, as well as in other studies of displacement, is related to the reasonable hypothesis that programs are adjusted in response to the labor market situation. A negative correlation between youth employment and youth program participation, thus, may as well reflect this policy reaction as crowding out. Instrumenting is one way to deal with this problem. Another way that we have used is related to the dating of the variables. Employment is measured in November each year, whereas program participation is measured as a twelve-month average preceding November.

Another reason to introduce instruments is the presence of the adult employment rate in the equation. To the extent that both youth and adult employment are driven by common shocks, this will introduce bias into OLS estimates. The choice of instruments for the adult employment rate is based on the estimates in Forslund (1996).[12] The main instrument for the youth program variable in addition to its own lag is the lagged unemployment rate, because it is known that the allocation of resources to labor market programs is based on the past unemployment history of a region.

The sample means of the data are presented in table 9.7, and the preferred estimated models are presented in table 9.8. Looking at the data in table 9.7, some tendencies are worth noting. First, the fall in youth employment is dramatic: the youth employment rate falls from just below

---

12. See the note to table 9.8 for a list of all instruments used in the GMM estimations.

Table 9.8   Estimated Models of Youth Employment

Variable	1: OLS Within-Group Estimates of Basic Dynamic Model	2: GMM Estimates of Basic Dynamic Model	3: Alternative GMM Estimates of Dynamic Model	4: GMM Estimates of Static Model
Lagged dependent variable	.482	.001	−.032	
	(14.75)	(.01)	(−.30)	
Demand index	.218	.197		
	(2.18)	(.59)		
Adult employment rate	1.658	2.44	2.59	2.24
	(13.66)	(7.86)	(6.25)	(6.50)
Youth income	−.103	−.186		
	(−1.573)	(−.90)		
Youth programs	−.006	−.057	−.056	−.079
	(−1.71)	(−5.05)	(−5.44)	(−4.76)
Youth population share	−.156	−.453	−.537	−.562
	(−1.82)	(−1.96)	(−3.07)	(−2.88)
σ̂ (levels)	.046	.045	.045	.049

Note: The number of municipalities is 284. The estimation period is 1991–94 for models 1 and 4, 1992–94 for models 2 and 3. Time dummies are used in all models to control for aggregate variables. Numbers in parentheses are t-statistics. All variables are in natural logarithms. The instruments used are the lags of the dependent variable, the demand index, the youth employment share, the unemployment rate (by municipality), the population share of the elderly (over age 65), the population share of children (under age 18), average incomes, youth incomes, employment-creating labor market programs (excluding youth programs), retraining programs, and demand index for total employment. The ordinary least squares (OLS) standard errors are two-step, heteroscedasticity-consistent estimates. All general method of moments (GMM) models pass the usual tests: absence of second-order serial correlation and a Sargan test for instrument validity. The reported t-values in the GMM estimations are based on the second-step standard errors, which are known from Monte Carlo studies to be biased downward for a number of data-generating processes, see Bergström (1997).

75 percent in 1990 to around 45 percent in 1993 and 1994. This fall is much more pronounced than the corresponding fall in the adult employment rate. Second, the fraction of youths in youth programs rises drastically from below half a percent in 1990 to above 8 percent in 1993 and 1994.

The estimated model[13] pass specification tests at conventional levels,[14] and the signs of the point estimates are the expected ones (with the exception of the negative coefficient on the lagged dependent variable in model 3). Thus we find an insignificant negative effect of youth income (which proxies the youth wage rate), an insignificant positive effect of municipality-specific demand, a negative effect of youth population share, and, most important for our present purposes, a significant negative effect of youth programs on relative youth employment. It is also instructive to note that the estimates of the elasticity of the youth employment rate with respect to the adult employment rate fall between a bit below 2 (the OLS estimate) and just above 2.5, thus confirming that youth employment is indeed more volatile than the employment of adults.

Leaving the OLS estimates aside, the reported short-run elasticities of youth employment with respect to youth programs fall between $-.056$ and $-.079$ and seem rather robust to at least small changes in model specification (compare models 2, 3, and 4). Noting that the point estimate effect of the lagged variable is very close to zero, implying rapid adjustment, the long-run effects virtually coincide with their short-run counterparts.[15] A change in program participation from, say, 3 to 9 percent[16] would then be expected to drive down youth employment by between 6.2 and 8.7 percent (taking the two extreme estimates of the elasticity), or between 3.5 and 4.9 percentage points. Thus the estimates provide evidence for the hypothesis that youth measures may actually have made a significant contribution to the fall in youth employment between the mid-1980s and the mid-1990s.

Looking at the development in the sample, the fall in the youth employment rate between 1990 and 1994 is 28.7 percentage points. The estimates, taken at face value, ascribe between 12.5 and 17.7 of these percentage points, or around half of the fall, to the expansion of youth programs.

13. With the exception of the OLS within-group model, where, in addition to all possible simultaneity and other reasons to believe in biased estimates, the residuals are strongly serially correlated.

14. The Sargan test concerns instrument validity and basically tests for correlations between instruments and estimated residuals. The estimator relies on absence of first-order serial correlation in the residuals of the model in level form, which translates into absence of second-order serial correlation in the estimated residuals, as the model is estimated in first-difference form.

15. The estimate of long-run crowding out derived from model 2, evaluated at sample means, is 76 percent.

16. These figures would be in the neighborhood of the actual figures in table 9.8, although they actually understate the change between the mid-1980s and the mid-1990s.

9.5   Concluding Remarks

We have taken a look at the labor market experience of Swedish youths during the depression of the 1990s and made some comparisons with youth employment and unemployment during earlier decades. For the 1970s and the 1980s there is not much evidence of deteriorating labor market performance among Swedish youths, despite sharply increasing youth relative wages (particularly for teenagers). There is no obvious explanation for the lack of "action" in employment despite the marked pay compression. We have considered the role of the public sector as an employer of last resort for disadvantaged youths. The support for this hypothesis is not overwhelming, however.

The slump in the 1990s has been associated with dramatic increases in youth unemployment and youth participation in active labor market programs. The impact on unemployment rates by age and education has been roughly proportional, however; unemployment rates among the young and the less skilled have increased most in absolute terms, but the relative increases have been similar across age and educational groups. The evolution of employment and unemployment does not offer much support for the popular hypothesis that the recent rise in unemployment is driven by large and pervasive shifts in the demand for labor by skill attributable to technological innovation. Wage differentials have been roughly stable during the slump, which also cautions against interpretations in terms of adverse labor demand shifts against the young and the less skilled.

The employment crisis has been met by an unprecedented increase in active labor market programs, in large part targeted at unemployed youths. The risk is that these programs may crowd out regular youth employment, a hypothesis that is supported in our empirical investigation of regular youth employment in Swedish municipalities. Of course, participation in active labor market programs has potential long-run benefits relative to open unemployment, although these have been difficult to confirm in the existing evaluation studies (Forslund and Krueger 1997). There is, however, an obvious risk that the exceptional volumes of programs in the 1990s have put them into the region with decreasing marginal returns. A strategy for viable employment growth must have other ingredients than more of the same active labor market programs.

Appendix

A. 16-19 years

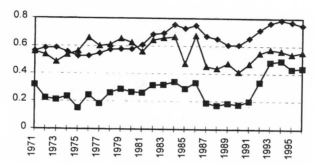

B. 20-24 years

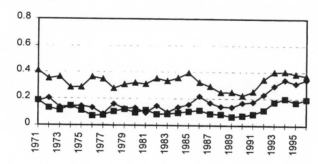

C. 35-44 years

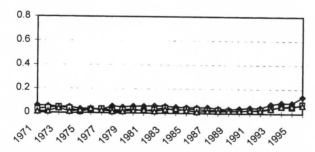

Fig. 9A.1   Nonparticipation rates for males by age and level of schooling
Source: Labor Force Surveys.
Note: Levels of schooling are no high school (*diamonds*), short high school (*squares*), and long high school (*triangles*).

A. 16-19 years

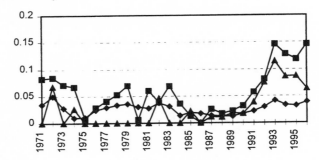

B. 20-24 years

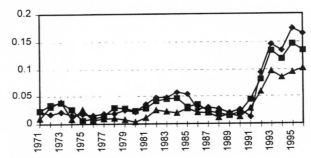

C. 35-44 years

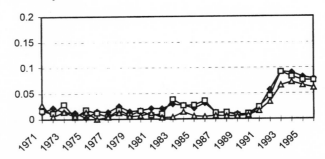

Fig. 9A.2   Unemployment-population rates for males by age and level of schooling
Source: Labor Force Surveys.
Note: Levels of schooling are no high school (*diamonds*), short high school (*squares*), and long high school (*triangles*).

References

Arellano, M., and S. Bond. 1991. Some tests of specification for panel data: Monte Carlo evidence and an application to employment equations. *Review of Economic Studies* 58:277–97.

Arellano, M., S. Bond, and J. Doornik. 1997. Dynamic panel data estimation using DPD for Ox. Oxford: Oxford University. Mimeograph.

Bergström, P. 1997. On bootstrap standard errors in dynamic panel data models. Working Paper no. 1997:23. Uppsala: Uppsala University, Department of Economics.

Blomskog, S. 1997. Long-run persistence effects arising from unstable youth labour market careers: The case of Sweden. In *Essays on the functioning of the Swedish labour market*, by S. Blomskog. Ph.D. diss., Swedish Institute for Social Research, Stockholm University, Stockholm.

Blomskog, S., and L. Schröder. 1997. Labour market entry, vocational training, and mobility in the Swedish young work force, 1950–1991. In *Essays on the functioning of the Swedish labour market*, by S. Blomskog. Ph.D. diss., Swedish Institute for Social Research, Stockholm University, Stockholm.

Calmfors, L., and P. Skedinger. 1995. Does active labour market policy increase employment? Theoretical considerations and some empirical evidence from Sweden. *Oxford Review of Economic Policy* 11:91–108.

Edin, P.-A., A. Harkman, and B. Holmlund. 1995. Unemployment and wage inequality in Sweden. Uppsala: Uppsala University, Department of Economics. Mimeograph.

Edin, P.-A., and B. Holmlund. 1994. *Arbetslösheten och arbetsmarknadens funktionssätt* (Unemployment and labor market performance). Report on the Medium Term Survey 1994. Stockholm: Ministry of Finance.

———. 1995. The Swedish wage structure: The rise and fall of solidarity wage policy? In *Differences and changes in wage structures*, ed. R. Freeman and L. Katz. Chicago: University of Chicago Press.

Edin, P.-A., and R. Topel. 1997. Wage policy and restructuring: The Swedish labor market since 1960. In *The welfare state in transition*, ed. R. Freeman, R. Topel, and B. Swedenborg. Chicago: University of Chicago Press.

Forslund, A. 1996. *Direkta undanträngningseffekter av arbetsmarknadspolitiska åtgärder* (Direct displacement effects of labor market policy measures). Report to the Parliamentary Auditors.

Forslund, A., and A. Krueger. 1997. An evaluation of the active Swedish labor market policy: New and received wisdom. In *The welfare state in transition*, ed. R. Freeman, R. Topel, and B. Swedenborg. Chicago: University of Chicago Press.

Gramlich, E., and B.-C. Ysander. 1981. Relief work and grant displacement in Sweden. In *Studies in labor market behavior*, ed. G. Eliasson, B. Holmlund, and F. Stafford. Stockholm: Industriens Utredningsinstitut.

Holmlund, B. 1995. Comments on Per Skedinger: Employment policies and displacement in the youth labour market. *Swedish Economic Policy Review* 2: 173–79.

Juhn, C., K. Murphy, and R. Topel. 1991. Why has the natural rate of unemployment increased over time? *Brookings Papers on Economic Activity*, no. 2:75–142.

Klevmarken, A., and P. Olovsson. 1993. *Household market and nonmarket activities.* Gothenburg, Sweden: Industriens Utredningsinstitut.

Nickell, S., and B. Bell. 1994. The collapse in demand for the unskilled and unemployment across the OECD. *Oxford Review of Economic Policy* 11:40–62.

Ohlsson, H. 1995. Labor market policy, unemployment and wages: A VAR-model for Sweden, 1969–1990. Uppsala: Uppsala University, Department of Economics. Mimeograph.

Schröder, L. 1995. *Ungdomars etablering på arbetsmarknaden—från femtiotal till nittiotal* (The labor market entry of youths—from the 1950s to the 1990s). Stockholm: Ministry of Labor, Delegation for Labor Market Policy Research.

Skedinger, P. 1995. Employment policies and displacement in the youth labour market. *Swedish Economic Policy Review* 2:135–71.

Statistics Sweden. 1987. Ungdomars verksamhet efter grundskolan (Youth's activities after compulsory school). No. U44 SM8701. Stockholm: Statistics Sweden.

———. 1996. Ungdomars verksamhet sju år efter grundskolan (Youth's activities seven years after compulsory school). No. U82 SM9601. Stockholm: Statistics Sweden.

Thoursie, A. 1996. Post-Essen seminar in Sweden: Background material for "Engaging with the Essen Themes." Working Paper no. 6/1996. Stockholm: Stockholm University, Swedish Institute for Social Research.

Wadensjö, E. 1996. Den mörka bilden: Invandrarna på 1990-talets svenska arbetsmarknad (The dark picture: Immigrants in the Swedish labor market in the 1990s). In *Invandrare på arbetsmarknaden*. Rådet för arbetslivsforskning.

Young and Out in Germany
On Youths' Chances of Labor Market Entrance in Germany

Wolfgang Franz, Joachim Inkmann,
Winfried Pohlmeier, and Volker Zimmermann

10.1 Introduction

The youth labor market in Germany often fascinates labor economists and policymakers: youth unemployment rates in Germany are considerably below the OECD average and are beaten only by Japan, Luxembourg, and Switzerland. Moreover, the German apprenticeship training system is frequently cited as a promising model for vocational education.

Whatever the merits of the institutional regulations and the functioning of the German youth labor market are, this paper focuses on those youths who fail in this system at one point or another. Hence, our study deliber-

Wolfgang Franz is president of the Centre for European Economic Research (ZEW), Mannheim, and professor of economics at the University of Mannheim. Joachim Inkmann is a research associate of the University of Konstanz. Winfried Pohlmeier is professor of econometrics at the University of Konstanz and a research associate of the Center of Finance and Econometrics and of the Centre for European Economic Research. Volker Zimmermann is a research associate of the Centre for European Economic Research, Mannheim.

Some of the data used in this paper are from the Central Documentation Center for Empirical Social Research (Zentralarchiv für Empirische Sozialforschung, Universität zu Köln). The interview entitled "Acquisition and Utilization of Vocational Qualification" ("Erwerb und Verwertung beruflicher Qualifikation") was conducted by the Federal Office of Vocational Training (Bundesinstitut für Berufsbildung) and the Institute for Employment Research (Institut für Arbeits- und Berufsbildung). These data were processed and documented by the Central Documentation Center for Empirical Social Research. The Federal Office of Vocational Training, the Institute for Employment Research, and the Central Documentation Center for Empirical Social Research are not responsible for any analysis or interpretation of the data in this paper.

Early versions of the paper were presented at a preconference in Konstanz and at the Konstanz-Florence workshop. Financial support by the Rockefeller Foundation and the Deutsche Forschungsgemeinschaft is gratefully acknowledged. The authors thank David Blanchflower, Richard Freeman, François Laisney, Andrew Oswald, and John Abowd for helpful comments. All remaining errors are the authors'.

ately refrains from joining the literature analyzing the advantages of the dual system in Germany (without denying that there are a lot of them). Rather, our concern is the group of young people who either do not find an apprenticeship training opportunity or do not successfully complete such training for whatever reason, or fail to get a job after apprenticeship training. More specifically, the paper is devoted to a treatment of the following type of questions: How does youth unemployment evolve in comparison to adult joblessness? Are there any differences in the risk or the duration of unemployment? To what extent does the apprenticeship training system relegate unemployment to higher age groups? Who does not get an apprenticeship and what happens to him or her? Which individual characteristics of a youth make him or her most likely to fail at one stage or another in early work history? To what extent can a disadvantageous family background be blamed for failures? Are early failures permanent scars or temporary blemishes?

Since our approach is empirically oriented—including a microeconometric analysis of some of the aforementioned aspects—a serious caveat is in order. Focusing on youths and, moreover, concentrating on problematic groups of young people means a substantial reduction in sample size even if the entire data set is large. Therefore, some of our findings represent case studies, the robustness of which is in question.

The paper is organized as follows. Section 10.2 not only offers an overview of the youth labor market, including its dynamics and institutional framework, but also provides a quantitative assessment of those youths who fail during several transition stages from school to work. Section 10.3 analyzes the duration of the first spell of nonemployment after completion of formal vocational training. The estimates are based on a proportional hazard function approach for grouped durations. Section 10.4 addresses the extent to which failures early in the work history have long-lasting effects on future income. Section 10.5 summarizes our findings.

10.2 Problematic Groups in the Youth Labor Market in Germany: An Overview

10.2.1 Youth Unemployment: Getting the Questions Right

As an obvious starting point figures 10.1 and 10.2 display time series of youth and adult unemployment rates for West Germany distinguishing between males and females and several age groups. The definition of the unemployment rate follows official statistics in Germany: registered unemployed persons divided by members of the labor force (including self-employed persons). Note, however, that youths looking exclusively for apprenticeship training are not counted in official unemployment statistics because they are "not at the disposal of the labor office" (see below).

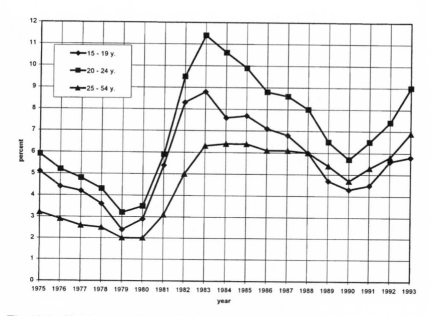

Fig. 10.1   Youth and adult unemployment rates: males

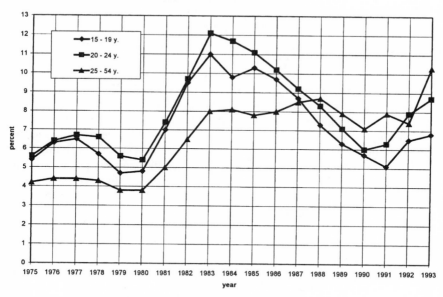

Fig. 10.2   Youth and adult unemployment rates: females

Both figures reveal that youth unemployment in Germany is, to some extent, relegated to the age group 20–24. Male unemployment rates for youths aged 20–24 exceeded those for youths aged 15–19 by 2.2 percentage points on average during the time period 1983–93, with a maximum of more than 3 percentage points in the recession year 1993. These differences with respect to age groups are less marked for females. Hence, the question arises as to why youth unemployment rates differ so much between age and sex groups (see Franz 1982 for an earlier study). In section 10.2 we therefore investigate the extent of possible failures during the transition from school to work using aggregate data, while section 10.3 is devoted to a microeconometric analysis concerning failures to enter a first job.

A second striking feature emerges if we compare youth and adult unemployment rates. Between 1980 and 1988 all youth unemployment rates displayed in figures 10.1 and 10.2 exceeded adult unemployment rates, sometimes by a considerable amount. With males aged 20–24 as an exception, all but one youth unemployment rate fell short of adult unemployment rates afterward.

We have noted already that official unemployment figures do not include youths looking exclusively for apprentice training. Information on those is available for September of each year and refers to youths registered at the labor office and looking for apprenticeship training. They are far from negligible in number. For example, in West Germany during the recession year 1993 about 67,500 youths under the age of 20 were officially registered as being unemployed (in East Germany, 22,600). In September of the same year 14,800 youths were not yet recruited for an apprenticeship training position in West Germany (in East Germany, 2,900). When a boom year such as 1991 is considered the figures for West Germany are 54,200 unemployed youths and 11,200 applicants; that is, official youth unemployment figures for West Germany have to be multiplied by a factor of around 1.2 for a broader definition of youth joblessness. It should be stressed, however, that these calculations represent a crude approximation at best. Many applicants receive an apprenticeship training position soon after September because a considerable number of these positions are blocked for some time by multiple applications (it is not required that the labor office be involved, either by applicants or by firms offering apprentice training). Moreover, an unsuccessful search for an apprenticeship training position does not necessarily mean unemployment but may end in further school education, for example. Under these caveats figure 10.3 nevertheless gives an impression of the size of problematic groups among the young in the labor market. The figure converts official unemployment rates for youths less than 20 years old into youth joblessness rates by including yet unsuccessful applicants for apprenticeship training.

As is well known, unemployment rates are of limited importance because they are silent on the dynamics of unemployment, such as the risk

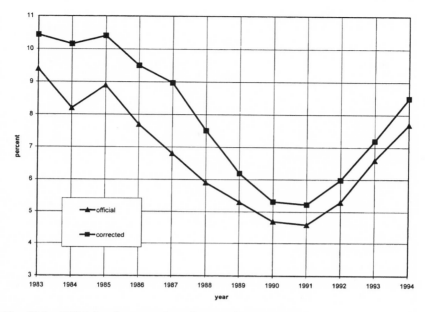

Fig. 10.3   Official and corrected youth unemployment rates

and duration of unemployment or the occurrence of multiple spells. To begin with, table 10.1 shows annual figures averaged over five-year periods on risk and on duration by age and sex. The risk of becoming unemployed for a group is measured by the ratio of the annual sum of inflows into the unemployment pool to the labor force of that group. Thus "risk" also includes multiple entries into unemployment by the same individual (per year). "Duration" means completed unemployment duration of those individuals who left the unemployment register during one year, where annual data for each individual are taken in the period between 1 October of the previous year and 30 September of the current year. In light of these definitions, dictated by the data set, it is obvious that the figures in table 10.1 suffer from various deficiencies. They do not allow a distinction between single and multiple spells of unemployment per individual, and moreover, the long-term unemployed may be underrepresented in the calculation of unemployment duration. Under these caveats they support an observation made in many, if not in most countries, namely, that youths suffer from a higher risk of becoming unemployed compared to older members of the labor force, such as those aged 55–59, but that they face a considerably shorter duration for each unemployment spell (though not necessarily of unemployment insofar as they experience multiple spells of unemployment). Both risk and duration are higher for males aged 20–24 than for the younger age group. For females, however, only duration in-

Table 10.1   **Dynamics of Unemployment in West Germany: Risk and Duration**

	1984–88		1989–93	
Age Group	Males	Females	Males	Females
Risk (%)				
Below 20	22.7	28.0	21.6	23.1
20–24	28.7	25.1	25.0	19.4
55–59	14.8	14.9	13.0	13.9
15–65	15.6	18.3	14.4	14.5
Duration (weeks)				
Below 20	16.5	19.1	12.1	14.4
20–24	18.6	22.0	15.1	17.1
55–59	44.0	54.5	52.7	67.1
15–65	27.0	31.1	26.6	30.6

Source: Bundesanstalt für Arbeit, *Amtliche Nachrichten der Bundesanstalt für Arbeit* (Bonn, various issues); calculations by authors.

Note: See text for details.

creases with age, and the reverse is true for risk. Hence, we are left asking why the aforementioned distribution of risk and duration among age groups exists. A tentative explanation as to why males aged 20–24 face considerably higher risk than females may be that males can escape from unemployment by entering military service already at ages under 20. This only means, however, a postponement of the risk from the lowest age group to the next higher one.[1] The comparatively short duration of youth unemployment leaves it open whether such a short episode has long-lasting effects on a worker's later career. Hence, in section 10.4 we elaborate on this question by estimating earnings functions depending on, among other variables, unemployment experience at the beginning of working life.

In the presence of multiple spells of unemployment a distinction is in order between the duration per spell of unemployment and the duration of unemployment per person. Put differently, the first dimension times the number of unemployment spells per individual gives the latter dimension. Information on this issue with an emphasis on youth unemployment is not very rich for Germany. Karr and John (1989) is still the most in-depth study. The authors base their investigation on all unemployed persons who received unemployment compensation between July 1979 and June 1984, around 7.9 million persons. In addition, they match data from employment statistics to the data stemming from unemployment benefits statistics in order to capture those unemployed who are not entitled to any unemployment benefits. While the results of this study tend to be somewhat historical they are based on a huge data set and provide information some-

---

1. Note that figures on the labor force include soldiers.

Table 10.2   Cumulated Unemployment in West Germany, 1979–84

Age Group	Number of Persons (million)	Number of Spells per Individual	Duration per Spell (weeks)	Cumulated Duration (weeks)
Below 20	1.965	1.14	17.9	20.4
20–24	2.260	1.86	18.4	34.2
25–29	1.440	1.96	22.2	43.6
30–54	3.723	1.86	25.7	47.8
55–59	.665	1.20	46.7	55.8
All	10.053	1.71	23.7	40.5

Source: Karr and John (1989).

what more reliable than that obtained from case studies of a few hundred unemployed individuals.

Table 10.2 highlights some results of Karr and John's study. Note that all numbers refer to the period 1979–84, so that an unemployed youth under age 20 had 1.14 spells of unemployment during the whole five-year period. Each spell lasted 17.9 weeks, so that the cumulated unemployment duration amounted to 20.4 weeks. Disregarding the lowest and highest age groups, there is little variation in the number of spells per individual. By and large, the relation between age and number of spells follows the shape of an inverted U. This does not hold for duration per spell, which increases with age.

In order to obtain more recent empirical evidence on this aspect we carry out a similar analysis based on several waves of the German Socio-Economic Panel covering the time period 1984–93 (West Germany). While our calculations also refer to a five-year period they differ from those in Karr and John (1989) in that all persons are included who became unemployed at any point of time and could be observed for five years (Karr and John consider only those who became unemployed at the beginning of the five-year period 1979–84). As a consequence our figures are not strictly comparable to those obtained by Karr and John. The main reason for our approach is, of course, to obtain more observations. Our sample size remains small nevertheless. The number of spells per individual amounts to 1.22 for youths under age 25, with a cumulated duration of 23.4 weeks as displayed in table 10.3. As in table 10.2 there is no clear tendency for the number of spells to unambiguously decrease with age, whereas the cumulated duration of unemployment is positively correlated with age.

10.2.2   Demand and Supply of Apprenticeship Training

Over the past two years concern about the supply of apprenticeship training positions has again taken center stage in public discussions. Figure 10.4 reveals that no substantial new developments have appeared in

Table 10.3   Multiple Spells and Duration of Unemployment in West Germany, 1984–93

Age Group	Number of Persons	Number of Spells per Individual	Cumulated Duration (weeks)
Below 25	525	1.22	23.4
25–30	314	1.25	27.0
31–40	312	1.14	30.0
41–50	221	1.16	33.3
51–60	217	1.11	55.8

Source: German Socio-Economic Panel; calculations by authors.

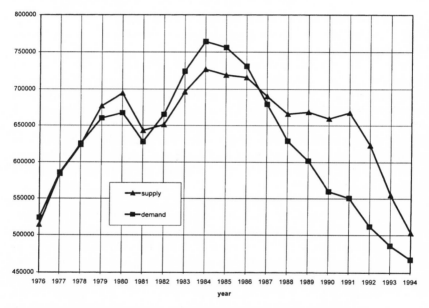

Fig. 10.4   Demand and supply of apprenticeship training positions in West Germany

the market for apprenticeship training positions underlying this debate. Periods of excess demand for apprenticeship training such as 1976–78 and 1982–86 were followed by periods of excess supply. Note that the numbers in figure 10.4 refer only to those positions and applicants registered at the labor office.[2] There is only very limited information on those employers and applicants who act without contacting the labor office.

2. "Supply" means the sum of new contracts for apprenticeship training and vacancies for apprenticeship training. "Demand" is defined as the sum of new apprenticeship training applicants and applicants for apprenticeship training who have not (yet) received a contract.

As can be seen, the years after 1986 are characterized by considerable excess supply, with a peak in 1991. This helps to explain why unemployment rates of youths fall short of adult unemployment rates in this time period. The increase in demand for apprenticeship training positions in the first half of the 1980s is due to the entrance of the baby boom birth cohort of the second half of the 1960s into the labor market. The decline in demand after 1984 is not only a consequence of smaller birth cohorts but also due to lower labor force participation rates. For example, participation rates of males under age 20 fell from 45.8 percent in 1985 to 37.1 percent in 1993 (for females from 39.6 percent to 32.8 percent) due to increased demand for higher education. This issue will be taken up again in the next section. Reasons for the shrinking supply of apprenticeship training positions are, among other things, increasing costs, institutional regulations, and lower expected demand for qualified workers.[3]

10.2.3 From School to Work: Success or Failure?

What follows is a quantitatively oriented analysis of the transition process from school to work, including a brief description of major institutional regulations concerning vocational education. Special attention is given to those youths who at one point or another fail in the system. In addition, subsection 10.2.4 is entirely concerned with measures for those youths who fail or drop out of an apprenticeship.

While this section is based on an interpretation of various statistics and institutional regulations, an econometric analysis of some aspects of this transition process is relegated to section 10.3. In view of the numerous variations in the system, for example, according to which state of the Federal Republic of Germany is under consideration, it goes without saying that only some stylized facts can be displayed here.

By and large, three stages of the educational process can be distinguished for the topics dealt with here: (1) the transition from the school system into apprenticeship training, (2) dropouts and failures during apprenticeship training, and (3) the transition to employment after apprenticeship training.

First Stage: Transition from School to Vocational Training

To begin with, three different school types and certificates of general education are distinguished in figure 10.5, where all numbers refer to West Germany in the year 1990.[4] All calculations in this figure are based on a national accounts system for education (Bildungsgesamtrechnung). This system uses various aggregate flows and stocks and merges them with tran-

---

3. See Franz and Soskice (1995) and Winkelmann (1996) for a brief overview and analytical treatment.
4. This is the most recent year for which numbers are available.

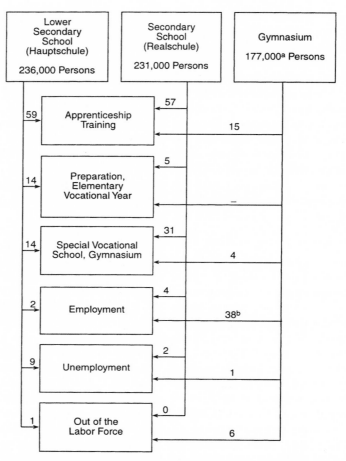

Fig. 10.5   Transitions from general education in West Germany, 1990
Source: Institut für Arbeitsmarkt- und Berufsforschung (1993, 17).
Note: See text for details. Numbers labeling arrows are percentages.
[a]Thirty-five percent of these youths enter universities or advanced colleges for higher education.
[b]Twenty-nine percent military service and 9 percent employment.

sition probabilities obtained from other sources (e.g., individual data sets) in order to get a consistent flow diagram for different types of school education, vocational training, and the labor market. It is, however, set up for some years only (for details, see Tessaring, Reinberg, and Fischer 1993). Note that other flows will be discussed later, such as flows from apprentice training or vocational schools (see fig. 10.6 below).

A nine- or ten-year lower secondary school (*Hauptschule*) education is compulsory for all youths aged 7–15 unless they switch after four years, typically at age 10, to a nine-year gymnasium or a six-year secondary school (*Realschule*).[5] The lower secondary school provides basic general education and provides a certificate (*Hauptschulabschluß*) to those who successfully pass all classes. The student at the gymnasium, after examinations, ends up with a certificate called an *Abitur*, which entitles this youth to continue his or her education at a university or an advanced college for higher education (*Fachhochschule*). The secondary school also provides successful youths with a certificate (*Mittlere Reife*), which, for example, entitles its holders—provided that they have completed apprenticeship training—to attend the aforementioned three-year advanced college for higher education, which specializes in fields such as engineering or business administration. These colleges differ from universities not only in their shorter period of education (three years) but also in that they attempt to provide an education that is more oriented to applications and practice.

As figure 10.5 indicates, 236,000 youths left lower secondary school in 1990. Note that "leaving" does not necessarily mean that all youths passed all classes in this school.[6] Those who fail in one class or another have to repeat the class but may leave lower secondary school after finishing the nine-year compulsory full-time school period. Many of those youths, however, stay at this school in order to complete all nine classes successfully and to receive the lower secondary school certificate. In case of serious deficiencies some youths change from lower secondary school to a specialized school for disabled persons. Of the 236,000 lower secondary school leavers, 59 percent embark on apprenticeship training more or less immediately afterward, 14 percent enroll in a preparation or elementary vocational year, 14 percent continue vocational education at a special vocational school, but 9 percent enter unemployment. Indeed, the transition from lower secondary school to apprenticeship training is a critical point. Moreover, the suspicion may be raised that an unknown share of youths continue their education involuntarily.

Hence, the obvious question arises as to what happens with those youths without an apprenticeship training position. Whether employed or unemployed a youth has to attend a part-time vocational training school, which is compulsory until age 18, unless the youth departs for another school. "Part time" usually refers to one full day per week. Youths may, however, continue their educations, and the German vocational training system offers a variety of possibilities, such as a preparation year for vocational training (*Berufsvorbereitungsjahr*) or an elementary vocational year (*Berufsgrundbildungsjahr*). The first alternative is a full-time school specially designed to assist youths who found it difficult to obtain an appren-

---

5. See the glossary of some features of the German educational system in appendix C.
6. In 1988 roughly 20 percent of all youths leaving lower secondary school did not have a lower secondary school certificate (Bundesministerium für Bildung, Wissenschaft, Forschung und Technologie 1994, 76).

Table 10.4   **Youths in Vocational Education (thousands)**

Year	Vocational School	Special Vocational School	Elementary Vocational Year		Preparation Year for Vocational Training
			Full Time	Part Time	
1980[a]	1,848	326	66	14	42
1985[a]	1,893	330	80	16	36
1990[a]	1,469	246	37	47	26
1993[b]	1,323	246	30	63	32

Source: Bundesministerium für Bildung, Wissenschaft, Forschung und Technologie (1994, 48).
[a]West Germany.
[b]West Germany and East Berlin.

ticeship by offering broad prevocational training. On the other hand, the elementary vocational year, which is now mostly part-time schooling (see table 10.4), [7] provides instruction in subjects common to a range of similar occupations and replaces six to twelve months of normal apprenticeship training. To some unknown extent both variants of the preparation year serve as "waiting loops" for school leavers without apprenticeship contracts. As a third example, those youths who leave lower secondary school with a certificate may attend a, usually one-year, full-time special vocational school (*Berufsfachschule*). Although some of these special (higher) vocational schools provide a complete education, such as that needed to work as a medical-technical assistant, the great majority of these schools are of a kind where attendance counts toward the training period in a recognized skilled occupation and among these there is a preponderance of the clerical-administrative variety (known as commercial schools) and a second type providing training for home economics or social care occupations. An exceptionally high proportion of students (roughly two-thirds) are female and want to continue their training in the dual system (Münch 1991, 122–23).

We are now in a position to take a closer look at those lower secondary school leavers in figure 10.5 who undergo training within the "preparation year for vocational training" and the "elementary vocational year" or attend special (higher) vocational schools. What do these youths do after this time period? Our own calculations based on the Socio-Economic Panel reveal that more than half of these youths enter an apprenticeship afterward, although this result should be viewed with caution because the number of persons involved is small.

---

7. The shift toward the part-time form of the elementary vocational year since the second half of the 1980s may, to some extent, stem from the emphasis that has been placed on this type of school by several employers' associations; see Münch (1991, 113).

As is displayed in figure 10.5, 9 percent of those youths who leave lower secondary school (with or without a certificate of successful completion) enter the unemployment pool.

Going back to figure 10.5, the second major school type is the *Real-schule,* or secondary school. The typical youth enters this school after completing the first four years of elementary school, that is, at age 10. Schooling at the secondary school lasts six years and culminates, after examinations, with a secondary school certificate. Ambitious apprentice training positions more or less formally require such a certificate. As can be seen from figure 10.5 slightly more than one-half of all secondary school leavers enter apprenticeship training. By and large, the remaining school leavers continue their educations. Compared with leavers from lower secondary school only a small fraction of secondary school leavers enter unemployment. Table 10.5 shows the status of school leavers from lower secondary and secondary school one year and five years after they have left school. One year after completion of general education, about 80 percent are still in school or in vocational training. Only about 7.5 percent of them are employed. Five years after completion of general education 16.5 percent are still in vocational training and 3.8 percent attend university or an advanced college for higher education.

Table 10.5   **School and Employment Status of Lower Secondary School and Secondary School Leavers in West Germany (percent)**

	After One Year				
School Cohorts 1984–93	School	Vocational Training	Employed	Unemployed	Not in Labor Market
Males	25.0	57.3	7.9	2.2	7.6
Females	19.9	60.0	7.1	2.4	12.1
German	22.2	66.2	4.5	2.0	5.1
Foreign	23.3	45.8	11.5	3.4	16.0
Total	22.5	57.6	7.5	2.6	9.8
	After Five Years				
School Cohorts 1984–89	School[a]	Vocational Training	Employed	Unemployed	Not in Labor Market
Males	5.7	16.3	63.8	9.9	4.3
Females	1.6	16.8	60.0	8.0	13.6
German	5.2	27.2	59.4	6.5	7.1
Foreign	1.8	9.0	65.8	12.6	10.8
Total	3.8	16.5	62.0	9.0	8.6

Source: German Socio-Economic Panel; calculations by authors.

[a]University or advanced college for higher education.

Finally, the third school type is the nine-year gymnasium. As with secondary school youths enter gymnasium after four years of elementary school and leave it at age 19–20 or so. As has been mentioned the gymnasium awards, after examinations, a certificate called an *Abitur,* which entitles the holder to enter a university. Some 15 percent of all gymnasium leavers, however, decide to undergo apprenticeship training first, as figure 10.5 indicates. For example, a youth might obtain an apprenticeship training position at a bank and after that study business economics (perhaps with an emphasis on banking). The largest group of gymnasium leavers (35 percent) continues school education mostly at universities (28 percent). Some 9 percent become employed, and 29 percent enter military service, voluntarily or involuntarily, or community service (in lieu of military service). Roughly 1 percent become unemployed, and 6 percent leave the labor force. The latter group consists mostly of females.

Most youths experience a smooth transition from school to vocational training. One reason for this is their high flexibility toward their future occupations. In 1994/95, 65 percent of youths named more than one occupation that they wanted to get training for, and 28 percent named more than three occupations. Roughly 51 percent started apprenticeship training in an occupation that was not their first choice. Tables 10.6 and 10.7 show the 10 most desired occupations of young males and females one or two years before completion of schooling and the 10 most frequent newly concluded apprenticeship training contracts. Besides the differences between males and females, the high flexibility of youths in the transition process can be seen.

Taken together, in 1990 about 12 percent of all youths did not experience a smooth transition from the three school types under consideration into apprenticeship training or further education, and another 7 percent dropped out of the labor force. With respect to the first group, the labor office offers several measures to assist school leavers, such as providing vocational counseling, matching seekers of apprenticeship training with such positions (as far as they are registered at the labor office), and providing financial aid not only to enable youths to receive apprenticeship training (such as reimbursing costs of applications or moving) but also to maintain their livelihood during apprenticeship training if they do not live with their parents, are at least 18 years old, or are married. A description and quantitative assessment of measures for the "hard to employ" is relegated to subsection 10.2.4.

Failures in the transition from school to apprentice training have long-lasting effects on later occupational careers. Table 10.8 takes a closer look at those transitions by distinguishing two groups of persons in the age 20–24 category depending on whether they had complete vocational training in 1988. For each group it was then investigated what they had done immediately after school (being then 14–15 years old). For example, 10

Table 10.6   Desired Occupations and Newly Concluded Apprenticeship Training Contracts of Male Youths, 1994/95

Rank	Desired Occupation	Percentage	New Apprenticeship Training Contract	Percentage
1	Motor vehical mechanic	18.6	Motor vehicle mechanic	6.8
2	Joiner/woodworker	12.4	Bricklayer/skilled construction worker	6.8
3	Bricklayer	11.0	Joiner/woodworker	5.4
4	Bank clerk	9.8	Electrician	4.9
5	Electrician	9.1	Painter/varnisher	4.6
6	Mechanical electrician	8.3	Industrial worker	4.0
7	Office clerk	7.2	Plumber/fitter	3.6
8	Radio/television technician	5.6	Import/export and wholesaler trader	3.4
9	Carpenter	5.4	Retail trader	3.1
10	Draftsman	4.8	Industrial clerk	2.6

Note: See text for details.

Table 10.7 Desired Occupations and Newly Concluded Apprenticeship Training Contracts of Female Youths, 1994/95

Rank	Desired Occupation	Percentage	New Apprenticeship Training Contract	Percentage
1	Office clerk	14.5	Office clerk	10.7
2	Doctor's assistant	14.4	Doctor's assistant	7.6
3	Bank clerk	10.8	Retail trader	6.7
4	Hotel manageress	9.4	Dental assistant	6.3
5	Hairdresser	8.3	Hairdresser	6.1
6	Animal keeper	7.7	Industrial clerk	5.0
7	Veterinary assistant	7.6	Bank clerk	4.2
8	Florist	6.3	Sales assistant	4.0
			Food industry	
9	Photographer	6.0	Lawyer's/notary's clerk	4.0
10	Shop assistant	5.9	Hotel manageress	3.5

Note: See text for details.

Table 10.8   **Transitions from School by Vocational Education in West**
                        Germany, 1988

	Persons with or without Complete Vocational Education in 1988 (%)	
Previous Exits after School Into	With	Without
Job without qualification requirements	10	54
Apprenticeship training	64	16
Unemployment	1	4
Further education	22	21

Source: Bundesminister für Bildung und Wissenschaft (1991, 33, 35).
Note: See text for details.

percent of those persons who completed vocational training in 1988 did not embark on apprenticeship training immediately after school but first had a job without qualification requirements. The data are based on a special survey of youths aged 20–24 collected in West Germany around 1988. Each group consists of about 1,800 youths. Some 54 percent of those without a complete vocational education had failed already in the transition from school, in that they embarked on a job that did not require further vocational education. This figure stands in marked contrast to the corresponding figure of 10 percent for those with a complete vocational education. Thus the suspicion may be raised that those early failures represent "permanent scars rather than temporary blemishes" (Ellwood 1982). This is also evidenced by the subsequent transition of youths without a complete vocational education. Among those who had a job some 27 percent changed to another job (again without further requirements with respect to vocational education), 13 percent entered the unemployment pool, 6 percent temporarily entered apprenticeship training, and 11 percent took up further vocational training, unsuccessfully, however.

Table 10.9 reveals that youths' failures to receive apprenticeship training stem from both sides, supply and demand. Figures are based on the same survey mentioned before and include youths aged 20–24 who do not have a complete vocational education. A distinction is made between youths looking for apprenticeship training and those who were not. Both groups of youths were asked for their reasons for not embarking on apprenticeship training. For example, 57 percent of youths who had been looking for apprenticeship training did not start such training because offers were lacking in the desired occupation,[8] but this figure is clearly

8. Those who did not look for apprenticeship training answered this question, too. This may be due to anticipations (correct or not).

Table 10.9   Reasons for Not Starting Apprenticeship Training, 1988 (percent)

	Searching for Apprenticeship Training	
Reason[a]	Yes	No
Poor performance (certificates, tests)	65	35
No interest in further learning	7	30
No offer of apprentice training in desired profession	57	10
No offer at all	41	15
No idea about what type of profession	9	25
More labor income wanted	12	21
Marriage, pregnancy	8	19
No confidence in himself or herself	4	15

Source: Bundesminister für Bildung und Wissenschaft (1991, 49).
Note: See text for details.
[a]Multiple answers are possible.

overshadowed by poor performance as the major reason for not starting apprenticeship training. In total (and not displayed in table 10.9) 56 percent of youths without a complete vocational education did not search for apprenticeship training, and reasons for that can mainly be found in individual circumstances such as poor performance, unwillingness to undertake further learning, lack of ideas about what to do, and family formation.

Second Stage: During Vocational Training

As pointed out in the previous subsection, inflows into apprenticeship training stem from various school types. This is also highlighted by table 10.10, which differentiates trainees according to their level of school education. The age structure of the apprenticeship trainees mirrors school leaving dates and shows that the traditional picture of the 15-year-old youth leaving lower secondary school and embarking on apprentice training is not (or at least no longer) a representative description of reality. In 1990, around one-quarter of all apprenticeship trainees were under age 18; the corresponding figures for 1980 and 1960 were 52 and 82 percent, respectively.[9] The average age of an apprenticeship trainee increased from 16.6 years in 1970 to 19.0 years in 1993 (Bundesminister für Bildung und Wissenschaft 1991, 40). Our own calculation on the basis of the Socio-Economic Panel shows that in West Germany during the period 1984–93 the average age of youths successfully completing their apprenticeship training increased from around 22 to 24 years. There are several reasons

---

9. Bundesminister für Bildung und Wissenschaft (1995, 56); figure for 1990 includes East Germany.

Table 10.10   **Apprenticeship Trainees by School Education (percent)**

Education	1983	1989	1993
Without lower secondary school certificate	3.0	2.5	3.5
With lower secondary school certificate	39.9	35.5	34.2
Preparation year for vocational training, basic vocational year	4.4	6.2	4.9
Special vocational school	11.1	10.2	7.9
Graduation from secondary school	31.7	31.8	35.8
Graduation from gymnasium	8.4	13.8	13.7

Source: Bundesminister für Bildung und Wissenschaft (1985, 38; 1991, 36; 1995, 56).

for this change: First, in the past decade an increasing number of gymnasium leavers have undergone apprenticeship training before entering, say, university (see fig. 10.5 for the respective flow in 1990). Not only have qualification standards for several professions risen, so that completing (lower) secondary school is no longer enough, but in addition firms increasingly value work experience among academics leaving universities. Second, those males with higher school experience increasingly try to finish their military service before embarking on apprenticeship training in order to ensure a smooth transition from training to work.

In the course of apprenticeship training, malfunctioning may arise from three sources: the trainee changes the type of vocational training or the firm providing such training; the trainee drops out to take up full-time school education, to become (un)employed, or to leave the labor force; or finally the trainee fails to pass examinations. To begin with, aggregate data on premature terminations of training contracts as a percentage of annual newly signed contracts (averaged over three previous years) display an average figure of 16.2 percent for the 1980s, ranging between 14.4 percent (1982) and 21.2 percent (1989), where the first year was during a recession while 1989 was characterized by much better economic conditions (Bundesminister für Bildung und Wissenschaft 1991, 42). In the boom year 1991 we observe a figure of more than 24 percent. Thus the suspicion may be raised that premature terminations are procyclical. Moreover, in 1989 some 83 percent of all premature terminations were initiated by trainees. Reasons in declining order of importance are difficulties with the trainers or entrepreneurs, dissatisfaction with the chosen profession, another more promising training firm, deficiencies in training courses, and duties that have nothing to do with vocational training. Premature terminations are above average in small and medium-size firms.

Finally, the overwhelming majority of trainees succeed in final examinations. The average percentage of passed exams was about 90 percent in the 1980s with a slightly decreasing trend (Tessaring 1993, 136). Those who fail are allowed to repeat, of course. Information on trainees who ultimately fail is sparse, however.

Third Stage: After Vocational Training

In order to give a first impression figure 10.6 summarizes transitions from the apprenticeship training system into the labor market or the school system for 1990. This year has been chosen to facilitate comparison with figure 10.5. Note, however, that the data do not indicate whether a trainee successfully completed his or her training. Calculations are again based on the national accounts for education. Seventy-eight percent of all trainees got a job, but more than 11 percent became unemployed or left the labor market. Unsurprisingly, transitions into the labor market exhibit a cyclical pattern. For example, the transition into employment declined in the recession years 1982–83 to about 70 percent but increased to 76 percent in the boom year 1990.

More information can be gained from individual data sets. Figure 10.7 presents our own calculations using the third wave (taken in 1991–92) from a data set collected by the Federal Institute of Vocational Education (Bundesinstitut für Berufsbildung—BiBB). People born between 1960 and 1970—that is, between ages 32 and 22 when the survey was taken— were interviewed about personal characteristics, school and work history, and the like. Their school and work experience covers the time period from around 1975 onward. In total, the data set contains 4,651 youths leaving (lower) secondary school. About 64 percent completed training successfully, and most were employed in the same firm afterward. On the

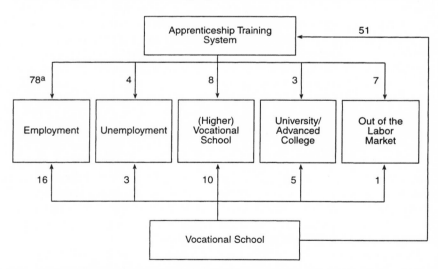

Fig. 10.6   Transitions from apprenticeship training and vocational schools in West Germany, 1990
Source: Institut für Arbeitsmarkt- und Berufsforschung (1993, 19).
[a]Includes military service and community service.

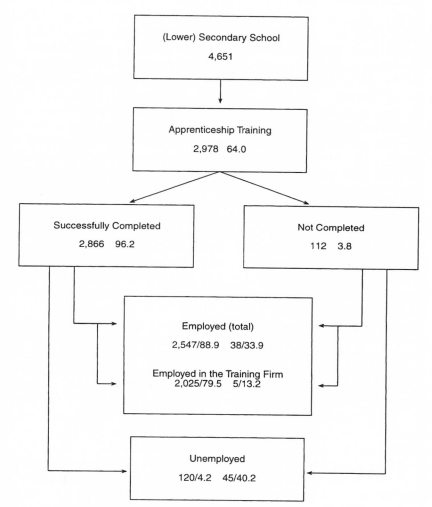

Fig. 10.7   Transitions from school to work in West Germany, 1975–91
Source: Bundesinstitut für Berufsbildung; calculations by authors.
Note: See text for details. First number is number of persons; second number is percentage of directly preceding status.

other side, some 40 percent of those who failed in the training system became unemployed.

10.2.4   Special Measures for the "Hard to Employ"

This subsection is devoted to an overview and assessment of measures designed for special groups on the youth labor market. The major question to be dealt with is how to make the less and the least able youths reasonably productive. Three types of measures are offered: prevocational measures for those youths who have not yet found an apprenticeship training position, special measures for handicapped youths, and special measures for youths without reasonable school experience or with social problems.

To begin with, prevocational measures aim to assist young persons during the transition process from school to apprenticeship training. These youths are not necessarily disabled but need some orientation and basis to prepare for vocational education. These measures include, first, basic training in order to find an adequate vocational training position for the youth in question; second, special classes for youths with physical or mental deficiencies who are not yet ready for vocational training but who may, in principle, be considered for vocational training; and, third, courses that provide information and motivation to those youths who are on the brink of dropping out of vocational life or have done so already. Taking all three measures together, some 68,000 youths entered such prevocational training in West Germany in 1994, with an emphasis on the second type. This figure amounts to roughly 15 percent of those who started apprenticeship training in that year.[10]

Measures of the second type are exclusively concerned with mentally or physically disabled youths. These measures provide either vocational training or vocational reintegration into work by further training or recruiting. The overwhelming share of all this training takes place in special training schools and workshops for disabled youths and is concerned mostly with recruiting. The number of disabled youths who left one of these programs in West Germany in 1993 was about 38,000. Of these, some 70 percent completed this training successfully in that they passed examinations in order to receive a certificate in an officially recognized profession. Some of the rehabilitation centers that provide such training report that in 1993 about 72 percent of all disabled youths got employment afterward, some 18 percent became unemployed, and the remaining persons could not be integrated into the labor market.

Measures of the third type are mainly devoted to assisting youths during apprenticeship training who have difficulties coping with the training due to school deficiencies or social problems. For the most part these measures take the form of accompanying courses while the youth stays in apprenticeship training. By the end of 1994 around 75,000 disadvantaged youths were subject to these measures in West Germany.

On the whole and referring to West Germany in 1993, around 150,000 hard-to-employ youths were covered by measures described in this section.

---

10. The figures in this subsection are from Bundesminister für Bildung und Wissenschaft (1995, 77–84).

To get an impression of this magnitude, at the same time about 1.3 million youth were apprentices. Note, however, that the two figures have about 50,000 persons in common.

10.3   Finding the First Job

Referring to the third stage mentioned above, economists generally agree that the German vocational training system is rather efficient in preventing youths from becoming unemployed. However, there is little empirical evidence on the effectiveness of the system in placing youths into stable and adequate employment. Therefore, this section focuses on the duration of nonemployment after participation in a formal vocational training program. This formal training can be a traditional apprenticeship training program within the dual vocational training system (consisting of education in a public vocational school and vocational training within a firm) or some other vocational training offered solely in a profession-specific vocational school. Schools of this type include schools for professions in the health care system (*Schulen des Gesundheitswesens*), special vocational schools,[11] and schools for the civil service (see the glossary in appendix C for details).

In the following empirical study we take a closer look at the process of growing into work in general by analyzing the duration of nonemployment after graduation from a vocational training program, as well as the duration of youth unemployment for those who report being unemployed. We define a nonemployed youth as someone who is either unemployed or out of the labor force. The latter group of people, for instance, consists of youths participating in brief additional vocational training programs (without receiving official degrees from them) or youths who, for some reason, are not willing to search for permanent jobs, for example, because they plan to continue schooling in the near future. On the other hand, the subsample of the unemployed can be regarded as the sample of those individuals who are likely to be more restricted in their choice sets. However, our measure of unemployment is rather weak because we have to define an unemployed youth as somebody who is registered as being unemployed at the labor office. Since registration at the labor office is, for example, a prerequisite for the parents to receive child support benefits (*Kindergeld*) this measure captures to some extent individuals who are not actively searching for jobs, as well. For simplicity we disregard compulsory military service (or alternative service) as a specific option to escape the nonemployment pool and compute the length of nonemployment spells net of military service.

---

11. These schools train young people to become, e.g., bilingual secretaries, interpreters, or children's or old people's nurses.

The first step into the labor market is likely to be the most crucial one. Hence we focus on the first spell of nonemployment (unemployment) after the completion of formal vocational training using a subsample of the German Socio-Economic Panel for the years 1984–92. The sample consists of 1,071 individuals aged 17–30 who have successfully completed their final vocational training programs. A more detailed description of the data construction and some basic descriptive statistics of the sample are given in appendix A. Our estimates are based on the proportional hazard function approach proposed by Han and Hausman (1990) for grouped durations. The estimation of this model does not require a parametric specification of the baseline hazard. Moreover, unlike Cox's (1972) partial likelihood method the Han-Hausman approach can easily tackle the problem of ties as well as the inclusion of parametric heterogeneity. For the case of individual heterogeneity resulting from an exponentially distributed individual effect it can be shown that the log likelihood is that of a conventional ordered logit model (without censoring). The additional nuisance parameter due to the exponential compounder is not separately identifiable and is estimated as a part of the nonparametric baseline hazard.

Figure 10.8 depicts the shape of the baseline hazard of a representative youth based on estimates displayed in table 10.11. The probability of finding a job after the completion of a vocational training program decreases sharply in the first few months and remains fairly constant afterward; that

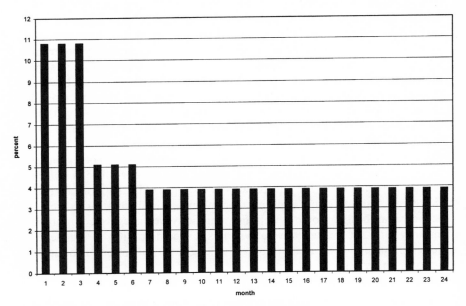

Fig. 10.8   Baseline hazard rates for a representative youth

Table 10.11   **Parameter Estimates of the Grouped Hazard Rate Model**

Variable[a]	Coefficient	t-Value[b]
Socioeconomic background		
Age/100	−13.57	−2.7
Sex	.00	.0
Nationality	−.02	−.1
Family status	−.07	−.2
Handicapped	.54	2.2
General educational background (no certificate)[c]		
Lower secondary, secondary school	−.69	−2.3
Entitlement for advanced college, gymnasium	−1.08	−2.7
Type of vocational training (special vocational school)		
Apprenticeship	−1.40	−4.3
Higher vocational school	−.84	−2.2
Vocational school: civil service	−1.97	−2.7
Other vocational training including health care	−.33	−.9
Socioeconomic background of head of household		
Household head not missing	1.67	1.6
Age	−2.49	−1.4
Sex	.56	1.2
Family status	−.15	−.4
Vocational background of head of household (nonemployed)		
Blue collar without formal training	−.87	−2.8
Blue collar with formal training	−.64	−2.0
Foreman, senior craftsman	−1.15	−2.6
White collar with low training	−.90	−2.7
White collar with high training	−1.01	−2.1
Civil servant	−.14	−.3
Self-employed	−.72	−1.8
Replacement ratio	−1.18	−1.4
Mean log likelihood	−.5391	
N	1,071	

Note: Dependent variable is duration of nonemployment.

[a]Reference categories in parentheses.

[b]Robust *t*-values on the sandwich form of the variance-covariance estimates.

[c]Contains very few persons who obtained instruction at other schools not included in the following categories.

is, youths who do not find jobs shortly after their graduation from vocational training have to face comparatively long episodes of nonemployment on average. The low hazard rate for the long-term nonemployed points to a potential malfunctioning of the youth labor market, which does not offer great chances of a successful transition from school to work.

The estimated effects of the covariates on the hazard function are given in table 10.11, where a positive coefficient implies a positive impact of the corresponding variable on the duration of nonemployment. Our results show that being particularly young turns out to be a severe handicap in finding a first job. Looking at employment probabilities of apprentices, Helberger, Rendtel, and Schwarze (1994) cannot find significant evidence of commonly supposed discrimination against foreign and female youths. Our estimates point in the same direction. Although there is no significant difference between foreign and German youths in terms of the probability of finding a job, foreign youths can be regarded as less "choosy" with respect to the quality of jobs. While more than 80 percent of German youths find jobs for which they have been trained in the vocational training program, the corresponding figure for foreign youths is 66 percent. Hence the difference in the labor market entry behavior of German and foreign youths is characterized by different choices between the short-run gain of a quick escape into employment and the long-run gain of choosing a job corresponding to one's vocational training with a lower probability of unemployment and higher earnings in later stages of one's career. Such a search strategy might be reasonable for foreign youths who plan to return to their home countries, where they cannot expect significant positive returns from the vocational training program.

Although a number of statutory measures to promote employment for the handicapped exist, physical disability significantly reduces the chances of finding a job. Of little surprise is the effect of the level of general education on the duration of unemployment. Those with the highest schooling (gymnasium, entitlement for advanced colleges for higher education) face significantly shorter episodes of nonemployment than youths holding no general educational degree from a German school. This finding clearly contradicts the notion that employers are sometimes reluctant to employ "overqualified" workers who hold degrees that qualify them for academic professions.

Youths being trained within the dual system reveal significantly shorter spells of nonemployment after vocational training than those who are trained in any other vocational school. This, however, is only limited evidence for the hypothesis that the dual system is an efficient vehicle for promoting youth employment because the dummies for the type of vocational training proxy the occupational demand conditions as well.[12] Moreover, in contrast to other types of vocational training programs an apprenticeship guarantees a first employment relationship during the training period. In the past decade around 80 percent of apprentices stayed with their training firms after completion of apprenticeship (see figure 10.7 and Harhoff and Kane 1997). In comparison to youths who receive their training solely in conventional vocational schools, graduates from higher

---

12. Unfortunately, given our data source, we are not able to distinguish between individuals of the same occupational degree by their training background (apprenticeship within the dual system vs. training in occupational training centers).

vocational schools (*Fachschulen für Meister* or *Technikerschulen*) and vocational schools for the civil service can expect a quick start into employment. For the latter group this is mainly due to the fact that the public sector adjusts the recruitment of apprentices to its own demand for skilled employees.

Most interesting are the effects of the family background variables. Occupational status is a decisive determinant of the length of the nonemployment spell. We are able to distinguish between various levels of occupational states of the household head. Using "nonemployed household head" as the reference category, we find that children of blue-collar workers are more likely to escape from the nonemployment pool than children of nonemployed parents. In particular, children of highly qualified blue-collar workers (foremen and senior craftsmen) have the greatest chances of finding jobs. A similar pattern can be observed for youths with parents belonging to the group of white-collar workers. Here again we find a positive correlation between the qualification of the parent and the likelihood of finding a job. To some extent our estimates support the notion that apprenticeships serve as a partial gift exchange, where the qualified staff receives an extra premium by having their children favored in the recruitment process. In particular, such policies are well known at large companies. This view is also supported by estimates for the remaining two parental background variables. Children of self-employed parents or civil servants do not have significantly better chances of finding jobs than children belonging to the reference group. Other parental background variables, such as gender of household head, age, marital status, and the dummy for whether there is information on the household head in the sample at all, do not significantly contribute to the explanation of the duration of nonemployment.

Graduates of apprenticeship programs are eligible for unemployment benefits while graduates of vocational training programs outside the dual system are not. This suggests that the type of vocational training has an decisive impact on the youth's reservation wage. Using the replacement ratio as a crude measure for the opportunity costs of not working we cannot find any positive impact of the level of unemployment benefits on the duration of nonemployment.[13]

In order to assess the relevance of long-term unemployment for specific subgroups we compute the average predicted probability of long-term nonemployment.[14] In figure 10.9 we distinguish by the type of vocational training. With an average long-term nonemployment probability of more than 30 percent, youths who were trained in a special vocational school

---

13. See Wurzel (1993, chap. 7) and Hunt (1995) for a more elaborate analysis of the effect unemployment compensation schemes on the hazard rate using samples of youth and adult unemployment.

14. Long-term nonemployment is defined as nonemployment having a duration of more than a year.

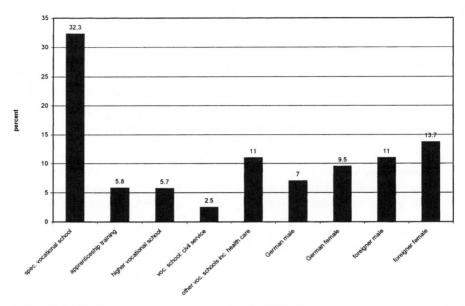

Fig. 10.9   Twelve-month average survival probabilities in nonemployment

outside the dual system are the ones most likely to face long-term nonemployment. This may reflect the rather limited opportunities for these graduates. In contrast, graduates of other training schemes face a much lower average probability of long-term nonemployment.

Also in figure 10.9 we repeat the exercise comparing the average predicted probability of long-term nonemployment distinguished by gender and nationality. Although neither the coefficient of the gender dummy nor the coefficient of the nationality dummy are significant, a comparison of the average predicted probabilities of long-term nonemployment for the four subgroups reveals substantial differences in employment chances. While the average probability of long-term nonemployment for German males is 7.03 percent, the corresponding figure for foreign females is almost twice as high (13.7 percent).

In a final step, we try to detect hard-to-employ youths by looking at socioeconomic characteristics of youths who reveal significantly higher probabilities of long-term nonemployment. This is done by estimating the probability of long-term nonemployment for each individual in the sample and testing this probability against the null hypothesis that it is not greater than the long-term nonemployment ratio in the sample (8.85 percent). Individuals with significantly higher long-term nonemployment probabilities are defined as belonging to the hard-to-employ group. Given rather brief average spells of nonemployment this criterion is fairly extreme and leaves us with 74 observations in the hard-to-employ subsample. However, our main conclusions remain valid for less extreme selection procedures (e.g., choosing hard-to-employ youths on the basis of a six-month criterion).

Descriptive statistics for the subsample of outsiders are given in table 10.12. In comparison to the overall sample the outsiders are slightly

Table 10.12   Descriptive Statistics for Hard-to-Employ Subsample

Characteristic	Mean for Hard to Employ	Mean for Overall Sample
Socioeconomic background		
Age	19.22	21.66
Sex	.65	.45
Nationality	.35	.19
Family status (married)	.03	.12
Handicapped	.20	.13
General educational background		
No certificate[a]	.15	.08
Lower secondary, secondary school	.84	.79
Entitlement for advanced college, gymnasium	.01	.13
Type of vocational training		
Special vocational school	.94	.12
Apprenticeship	.03	.72
Higher vocational school	.00	.07
Vocational school: civil service	.00	.03
Other vocational training including health care	.03	.06
Socioeconomic background of head of household		
Household head not missing	.97	.82
Age	47.92	41.91
Sex	.12	.09
Family status (not married)	.09	.11
General educational background of head of household		
No certificate[a]	.33	.12
Lower secondary, secondary school	.60	.57
Entitlement for advanced college, gymnasium	.04	.13
Vocational background of head of household		
Nonemployed	.20	.15
Blue collar without formal training	.34	.18
Blue collar with formal training	.20	.13
Foreman, senior craftsman	.03	.06
White collar with low training	.04	.11
White collar with high training	.01	.05
Civil servant	.11	.06
Self-employed	.05	.08
Replacement ratio	.04	.30
N	74	1,071

[a]Contains very few persons who obtained instruction at other schools not included in the following categories.

younger (19 vs. 22 years) and have almost the same general educational background. The most distinguishing feature is background with respect to vocational training. While in the overall sample 70 percent of the youths are trained within the dual system, only 3 percent of the hard-to-employ youths have received such training. We interpret this result as striking evidence of the efficiency of the dual system in promoting access to the labor market.

Again, the importance of family background is striking. The hard-to-employ group contains on average substantially more youths whose parents have a bad general educational background (36 vs. 20 percent). A similar pattern is observable with respect to occupational background of the parent. Contrary to the inferences based on the parameter estimates our selection procedure points out that females (65 vs. 44 percent) and foreign youths (35 vs. 19 percent) are overrepresented in the group of outsiders. Of course, the results based on our selection procedure should not be interpreted in a causal manner. The fact that we find females overrepresented in the hard-to-employ subgroup reflects to some extent the reality of their occupational choices (e.g., vocational training outside the dual system).

It seems worth mentioning that our selection procedure also reveals the "hotel mom syndrome."[15] Youths with a high probability of long-term nonemployment have on average older parents (49 vs. 42 years) and are less likely to live with a household head that is not married (9 vs. 11 percent).

Appendix table 10B.2 contains parameter estimates of the grouped duration model where we use duration of unemployment as the dependent variable. The sign pattern of the parameter estimates is very similar to that for duration of nonemployment, leading to the conclusion that the two dependent variables capture similar phenomena. However, two distinctive features are present. First, while the duration of nonemployment decreases significantly with age there is no significant evidence that older unemployed youths are easier to employ. The higher probability of nonemployment for the young turns out to be the result of lower opportunity costs of time. Second, being trained in a profession related to the civil service almost guarantees a job afterward when the youth is willing to delay her or his entrance into the labor market.

10.4 Permanent Scars or Temporary Blemishes?

In contrast to the U.S. literature (e.g., Ellwood 1982; Lynch 1985, 1989) there has been little research on the long-run effects of youth unemployment in Germany. The vast majority of studies for Germany such as Flaig,

---

15. The "hotel mom syndrome" denotes the recent trend among youths and young adults toward attending a local occupational school in order to enjoy the convenience of staying home.

Licht, and Steiner (1993) or Mühleisen and Zimmermann (1993) concentrate on the effects of previous unemployment on the probability of unemployment by controlling for occurrence dependence or some type of duration dependence. None of these studies center on youth unemployment in particular. To our knowledge no study has been devoted to the long-run effects of youth unemployment on earnings. The following analysis attempts to gain some insight into the quantitative importance of long-term effects of failure during apprenticeship and the effects of initial unemployment on an individual's earnings in subsequent years.

The following analysis is based on a cross section conducted in 1991–92 by the BiBB in cooperation with the Institute for Employment Research (Institut für Arbeits- und Berufsbildung). The data set contains information on roughly 34,000 East and West German employees. For the purposes of our study the BiBB data are of particular interest because they include extensive retrospective information on an individual's labor force history. Questions about vocational training, in particular those related to apprenticeship training, are covered in great detail. We restrict the analysis to regularly employed West German employees who were not over age 25 when they passed their vocational training in the period 1965–90. Hence the oldest individuals in our sample are in their fifties and can look back on a work history of more than 20 years. Contrary to the studies by Ellwood (1982) for the United States and Ackum (1991) for Sweden we are able to trace the long-run effects on earnings of early failure in the labor market. The final sample used for the analysis consists of 6,970 males and 2,221 females. The reader is referred to appendix B for a more detailed description of the sample construction and some basic descriptive statistics.

Table 10.13 compares the distribution of monthly gross earnings for persons who faced problems at the beginning of their careers with that for people who successfully completed apprenticeship and entered the labor market without any friction. About 5.2 percent of all persons either dropped out of a training program or became unemployed after apprenticeship. Every fifth youth who dropped out of a training program became unemployed afterward.

The descriptive evidence is striking. While about 50 percent of those who experienced at least one of the two types of friction in the early stages of their careers are located in the lower tail of the earnings distribution (less than DM4,000), only 26 percent of the successful labor market entrants fall into this category. Moreover, those who accept jobs that are inadequate with respect to their previous vocational training have to face substantially lower earnings. A comparison of the figures in columns (4) and (5) reveals no serious differences in earnings between those who stay with the training firm and those who get an appropriate job outside the training firm.

In order to obtain empirical evidence on whether entry problems into

Table 10.13 **Earnings Distribution of Former Apprenticeship Trainees**

		Apprenticeship Training Completed and Immediately Followed By			
Income[a] (thousand DM)	Apprenticeship Training Not Completed (1)	Unemployment (2)	Inadequate Occupation outside Training Firm (3)	Adequate Occupation outside Training Firm (4)	Adequate Occupation inside Training Firm (5)
Less than 4	60 (52.6)	59 (49.2)	70 (35.4)	115 (26.5)	704 (26.5)
4–5	38 (33.3)	42 (35.0)	86 (43.4)	183 (42.2)	1,148 (43.1)
More than 5	16 (14.1)	19 (15.8)	42 (21.2)	136 (31.3)	810 (30.4)
Total	114	120	198	434	2,662

Source: Bundesinstitut für Berufsbildung; calculations by authors.

Note: Numbers in parentheses are percentages of column totals.

[a]Monthly gross earnings for a sample of 3,871 West German males employed in 1991 at least 30 hours a week who passed (or failed) an apprenticeship in the period 1965–90.

the labor market have long-run effects on an individual's earnings we estimate a conventional earnings function augmented by explicit information on entry problems into the labor market and the background of the training firm. Since there is only information on earnings in categorical form we estimate the parameters of a log earnings function by ML-ordered probit. Since the income brackets (thresholds) are known we are able to identify the parameters of the earnings function (including the variance of the error term) completely.

Table 10.14 presents estimates for two different specifications of the earnings function for males and females, where we try to distinguish between the hypothesis of a permanent shift in earnings due to entry problems and the hypothesis that the scar effects may decay with time. For the sake of brevity we do not comment on the effects of the conventional regressors, which in general are comparable in size and significance to the effects found in other studies using different samples.

For workers graduating from any vocational training program gross earnings increase with the general level of education. To some extent this reflects not only the effect of higher human capital accumulation but also the fact that apprentices with *Abitur* certificates (graduation from gymnasium) are mainly recruited by high-paying sectors.[16]

In order to capture the effects of quality of training we use sectoral and firm size dummies for the training firm. Both sets of regressors have only a quantitatively weak impact on current earnings. Due to the high proportion of males who stayed in the training sector the sectoral dummies for the training firm and the current firm are highly correlated. We can only observe marginal differences in earnings with regard to the training sector. Similar arguments hold for the firm size dummies for the training and the current firm. However, in this case the firm size effects of the training firm are more pronounced than the effects of the current firm. Receiving training in a large firm significantly increases earnings prospects in later years. The well-known positive correlation between firm size and income vanishes if one controls for the size of the training firm. The opposite is true for female earnings, where the firm size effect of the training firm disappears. Since for females we observe a proportion of employees not working in the jobs for which they have been trained due to career interruptions we can conclude that the quality of the training firm captured by the firm size dummies vanishes.

Somewhat problematic is the inclusion of three variables capturing the effect of job mobility on earnings, since they may be affected by endogeneity. Both male and female workers can expect a positive return to chang-

16. E.g., Winkelman (1996, 1997) points out that 15.8 percent of all apprentices with *Abitur* certificates were trained in the banking sector, where the majority of apprentices (58.2 percent) graduated from gymnasium.

Table 10.14   Earnings Functions: ML-Ordered Probit Estimates with Known Thresholds

| | Males | | | | Females | | | |
| | (1) | | (2) | | (3) | | (4) | |
Variable[a]	Coefficient	t-Value[b]	Coefficient	t-Value[b]	Coefficient	t-Value[b]	Coefficient	t-Value[b]
Intercept	7.75	179.8	7.75	179.6	7.66	86.7	7.66	86.7
Socioeconomic background								
Age/10	.15	8.7	.15	8.7	.14	3.3	.14	3.3
Potential experience/10	.14	6.8	.14	6.8	.06	1.4	.06	1.4
Squared potential experience/100	-.05	-15.9	-.05	-15.9	-.04	-5.2	-.04	-5.2
Married	.07	5.4	.07	5.3	.05	2.9	.05	2.9
Schooling (secondary school)								
Lower secondary school	-.11	-12.6	-.11	-12.6	-.10	-5.7	-.10	-5.7
Entitlement for advanced college for higher education	.15	8.0	.15	8.0	.09	2.9	.09	2.8
Gymnasium	.19	10.4	.19	10.4	.11	3.6	.11	3.6
Type of failure (none)								
Vocational training failed	-.12	-5.1	-.10	-1.7	-.13	-3.0	-.09	-1.1
× Potential experience			-.01	-.4			-.02	-.5
Unemployment after vocational graduation	-.01	-.5	-.02	-.5	-.03	-.9	-.01	-.2
× Potential experience			.01	.3			-.02	-.5
Changes in employment (none)								
Profession changed	.08	4.2	.08	4.2	.11	1.9	.10	1.8
Employer changed	.03	3.3	.03	3.3	.01	.7	.01	.7
Profession and employer changed	-.08	-3.8	-.07	-3.8	-.14	-2.4	-.14	-2.3

	χ²	p-value	χ²	p-value	χ²	p-value	χ²	p-value
Size of training firm (less than 10 employees)								
10–49 Employees	.03	3.2	.03	3.2	.04	2.2	.04	2.3
50–99 Employees	.04	3.3	.04	3.3	−.01	−.2	−.01	−.2
100–499 Employees	.06	5.5	.06	5.5	−.01	−.3	−.01	−.3
500 Employees or more	.09	7.4	.09	7.4	.00	.0	.00	.0
Size of current firm (less than 10 employees)								
10–49 Employees	−.02	−2.0	−.02	−2.0	.07	3.3	.07	3.2
50–99 Employees	−.01	−.8	−.01	−.8	.08	2.8	.08	2.8
100–499 Employees	−.02	−1.5	−.02	−1.5	.11	4.6	.11	4.6
500 Employees or more	.01	.8	.01	.8	.18	7.1	.18	7.1
Sector of training firm (service)								
Manufacturing	−.02	−2.0	−.02	−2.0	.04	1.5	.04	1.5
Craft	−.01	−1.2	−.01	−1.2	−.02	−.6	−.01	−.6
Trade	.02	1.1	.02	1.1	−.01	−.2	.00	−.2
Sector of current firm (service)								
Manufacturing	.08	8.8	.08	8.8	−.01	−.5	−.01	−.6
Craft	.03	3.0	.03	3.0	−.09	−2.5	−.09	−2.5
Trade	.06	4.4	.06	4.4	−.07	−3.1	−.07	−3.1
δ	.26	62.0	.26	62.0	.31	32.6	.31	32.6
N	6,970		6,970		2,221		2,221	
Log likelihood	−14,775.01		−14,774.87		−4,656.82		−4,656.46	
	χ²	p-value	χ²	p-value	χ²	p-value	χ²	p-value
Joint significance of slope coefficients	2,015.76	.0	2,047.97	.0	484.37	.0	486.39	.0

[a] Reference categories in parentheses.

[b] Robust t-values based on the sandwich form of the variance-covariance estimates.

ing original professions during their careers. For males earnings are increased by 8 percent if they change profession but not employer and 3 percent for the reverse. A change of employer corresponds to an increase in current earnings of 3 percent for males while this effect is insignificant for females. The joint effect of both, a change in profession and employer, is captured by the sum of the two respective estimated coefficients and the one obtained from the interaction of the two variables. It turns out that the joint returns are different for males and females. While males profit from a 3 percent income increase, females have to suffer a 2 percent reduction. However, at least for males our results are in contrast with the common belief that a highly institutionalized German labor market punishes those who leave the professional track because of existing institutional barriers to entry into another occupation.

Most important for the purposes of our study is the set of regressors capturing the long-run effects of entry problems into the labor market. Assuming that the shift in earnings due to entry problems into the labor market is permanent, the estimates of the first specification (cols. [1] and [3]) imply a reduction of 12 percent (13 percent for females) in earnings if the youth drops out of an apprenticeship training program. Starting a professional career with a spell of unemployment does not generate a significant reduction in earnings. For the second specification we introduce interaction terms between the failure variables and the length of work history. This allows us to check whether the effects of entry problems become less relevant over the life cycle or can be regarded as permanent scars. Using the likelihood ratio test we cannot reject the hypothesis of a permanent earnings reduction in favor of a temporary blemish.

Since we are using cross-sectional information the usual caveats apply. In the first place we have to mention unobserved heterogeneity that cannot be controlled for. Thus both reduced earnings in later years and failure during apprenticeship years can be driven by unobservable components such as motivation and intellectual capabilities. Therefore, the size of the scar effects found may be smaller if unobserved heterogeneity is properly controlled for. Because of a different methodology and quality of data our results are not directly comparable to the earlier findings by Ellwood and Ackum. Unlike Ellwood's study we are able to focus on long-term effects that last over several decades. Moreover, we only use the incidence of youth unemployment as a predictor for earnings rather than forgone experience in terms of time out of the labor force. All in all our results suggest that the scar effects are much more severe in Germany than in the United States. Our results seem to differ also from those obtained by Ackum for Sweden. She finds that an additional year of unemployment reduces hourly earnings only by 2 percent. Having in mind that youth unemployment spells in Germany are fairly short and that the incidence of an early failure (particularly dropping out of a training program) plays such a crucial role, our results suggest that a central role of firm-specific training within the dual system is that of screening device.

10.5 Conclusions

The main intent of this study has been an analysis of problematic groups in the youth labor market in Germany, that is, the nature and causes of failures during the school-to-work process. Briefly, the more important findings are the following:

1. To some extent youth unemployment is relegated to the age group 20–24 because teenagers are absorbed by the apprenticeship training system. This can be seen, for example, by inspection of table 10.5: Leaving lower secondary school and secondary school, roughly two-thirds of all German youths are in vocational training one year later and only 3 percent are unemployed. But four years later, nearly 9 percent of all those youths are unemployed, whereas the majority (around 60 percent) are employed. For all figures marked differences can be observed with respect to gender and nationality. For example, foreign youths are underrepresented in the share of youths in vocational training but overrepresented in the group of employed as well as unemployed youths. Since the supply of apprenticeship training positions is subject to considerable fluctuations this role of absorber is anything but perfect, as evidenced by the procyclical behavior of youth unemployment rates and a reversal of ordering between youth and adult unemployment rates at the end of the 1980s.

2. The dynamics of youth unemployment exhibit the familiar pattern. By and large, youths face a higher risk of becoming unemployed than do adult members of the labor force, but their duration of unemployment is relatively short. This observation still holds if multiple spells of unemployment by the same person are taken into account.

3. Failures are most prominent in the following three stages of the transition process from school to work. First, in 1990 about 4 percent of youths did not experience a smooth transition from schools of various types to apprenticeship training or further education, and another 2 percent dropped out of the labor force at this stage for whatever reason. Moreover, those early failures in the transition from school to apprenticeship training have long-lasting effects on later occupational careers. Second, in the course of apprenticeship training several sources of malfunction can arise, such as dropping out or failing to pass examinations. More precisely, as an average figure for the 1980s the number of premature terminations of training contracts as a fraction of annually signed contracts amounted to some 16 percent. The overwhelming share of all premature terminations were initiated by the trainees. With respect to examinations, roughly 10 percent failed to pass them. Around 40 percent of those who

did not complete apprenticeship training entered unemployment. Third, the transition from apprenticeship training, even if successfully completed, is not always smooth. During past decades on average nearly 90 percent embarked on employment (80 percent in the same firm where they had undergone their training), but 4 percent became unemployed. The suspicion may be raised that the latter figure has increased during past years.

4. A more in-depth investigation of the last mentioned transition process has been carried out on the basis of an econometric hazard rate approach. More precisely, we elaborate on the duration of the first spell of nonemployment (and unemployment) after the completion of formal vocational training. Our estimates are based on a proportional hazard function approach for grouped durations. The shape of the baseline hazard of a representative youth reveals that youths who do not have luck finding jobs shortly after their graduation from vocational training face comparatively long episodes of nonemployment. Interestingly, we do not find evidence of discrimination against foreign youths, perhaps due to a higher willingness of foreigners to accept less qualified jobs or greater assimilation with German youths if their parents have been in Germany for a long time. Similarly, there is no clear-cut correspondence between gender and the probability of becoming employed. However, overall background matters—that is, the choice of type of general education and type of vocational training scheme. These factors drive our findings that females and foreign nationals face high average probabilities of long-term nonemployment. Previous studies of the labor market entry behavior of youths in Germany have neglected the relevance of family background. We find an outstanding impact of family background on the labor market entry behavior of youths.

5. Finally, we focus again on the question as to whether early failures represent temporary blemishes or permanent scars by estimating earnings functions on the basis of an ordered probit approach with known thresholds. While the incidence of youth unemployment does not generate a permanent scar we find that failure in an apprenticeship training program is an important predictor of an individual's income opportunities in later stages of working life.

As with most empirical work a lot of questions cannot be (adequately) dealt with due to data limitations. These are of great concern, especially in this study, since we are dealing with a fairly small group of youths failing in the labor market. For example, attempts to estimate more elaborate models, such as a competing risk model for different risks of escaping from nonemployment, turned out to be difficult due to, say, an overparameterization that calls for more parsimonious specifications compared with the single risk model.

Appendix A

Table 10A.1   **Descriptive Statistics for German Socio-Economic Panel Data Set**

Characteristic	Mean	Standard Deviation	Minimum	Maximum
Nonemployment duration (months)	3.25	9.25	.00	83.0
Unemployment duration (months)	.81	3.23	.00	47.0
Socioeconomic background				
Age	21.66	2.60	17	29
Sex	.45			
Nationality	.19			
Family status (married)	.12			
Handicapped	.13			
General educational background				
No certificate[a]	.08			
Lower secondary, secondary school	.79			
Entitlement for advanced college, gymnasium	.13			
Type of vocational training				
Special vocational school	.12			
Apprenticeship	.72			
Higher vocational school	.07			
Vocational school: civil service	.03			
Other vocational training including health care	.06			
Socioeconomic background of head of household				
Household head not missing	.82			
Age	50.83			
Sex	.09			
Family status (not married)	.11			
General educational background of head of household				
No certificate[a]	.12			
Lower secondary, secondary school	.57			
Entitlement for advanced college, gymnasium	.13			
Vocational background of head of household				
Nonemployed	.15			
Blue collar without formal training	.18			
Blue collar with formal training	.13			
Foreman, senior craftsman	.06			
White collar with low training	.11			
White collar with high training	.05			
Civil servant	.06			
Self-employed	.08			
Replacement ratio	.03	.22		
N	1,071			

[a]Contains very few persons who obtained instruction at other schools not included in the following categories.

Table 10A.2   Parameter Estimates of Grouped Hazard Rate Model

Variable[a]	Coefficient	t-Value[b]
Socioeconomic background		
Age/100	10.24	1.6
Sex	.14	.4
Nationality	.45	1.2
Family status	−.46	−.9
Handicapped	.49	1.3
General educational background (no certificate)[c]		
Lower secondary, secondary school	−.18	−.4
Entitlement for advanced college, gymnasium	−1.32	−2.0
Type of vocational training (special vocational school)		
Apprenticeship	−.34	−.7
Higher vocational school	−1.03	−1.8
Vocational school: civil service	−11.92	−22.6
Other vocational training including health care	−.55	−.9
Socioeconomic background of head of household		
Household head not missing	.63	.4
Age	−1.22	−.4
Sex	−.34	−.6
Family status	.72	1.6
Vocational background of head of household		
Blue collar without formal training	−.96	−2.1
Blue collar with formal training	−.94	−1.9
Foreman, senior craftsman	−2.10	−1.9
White collar with low training	−.20	−.5
White collar with high training	−.48	−.7
Civil servant	−.27	−.5
Self-employed	−1.11	−1.7
Replacement ratio	−.88	−.6
Mean log likelihood	−0.3011	
N	1,071	

Note: Dependent variable is duration of unemployment.

[a]Reference categories in parentheses.

[b]Robust t-values based on the sandwich form of the variance-covariance estimates.

[c]Contains very few persons who obtained instruction at other schools not included in the following categories.

Appendix B
The BiBB/IAB Data

The earnings function estimates in section 10.4 are based on the cross-sectional interview entitled "Acquisition and Utilization of Vocational Qualification" ("Erwerb und Verwertung beruflicher Qualifikation"), which was conducted in 1991–92 by the Federal Office of Vocational Training (Bundesinstitut für Berufsbildung—BiBB) in cooperation with the Institute for Employment Research (Institut für Arbeits- und Berufs-bilding—IAB). This data set is the third wave of a repeated cross-sectional study with earlier waves collected in 1979 and 1985–86. The third wave consists of 34,277 persons employed at the date of the interview, including 10,187 former citizens of the GDR and 614 foreigners living in West Germany.

The data set contains extensive information on the complete labor force history of each individual. Questions about vocational training, in particular those related to apprenticeship training, are covered in great detail. Monthly gross earnings, which serves as a dependent variable in the proposed earnings functions, is classified in one of fifteen categories, which is only a minor drawback compared to a more detailed recording. Twelve categories remain after a pairwise aggregation of the six lowest earning classes containing only a few observations. Table 10B.1 displays the resulting earnings distributions for males and females.

We restricted our analysis to individuals who grew up in the former West Germany because we focused on earnings impacts of failures during the transition process from apprenticeship training to employment. The East German vocational system did not offer a direct counterpart to West German apprenticeship training. In addition, we excluded self-employed persons and part-time workers with less than 30 hours of regular weekly work. Finally, we dropped individuals who completed their apprenticeship training either before 1965 or at more than 25 years of age. The resulting data set covers 6,970 males and 2,221 females with nonmissing information. Table 10B.2 displays descriptive statistics of the sample underlying the analysis given in section 10.4.

Table 10B.1   Earnings Distribution in the BiBB/IAB Sample

		Male Percentages		Female Percentages	
Cell	Earnings Interval (DM)	Cell	Cumulated	Cell	Cumulated
1	Less than 1000	.30	.30	1.44	1.44
2	1,001–2,000	.42	.72	5.18	6.62
3	2,001–3,000	2.34	3.06	12.83	19.45
4	3,001–3,500	6.79	9.84	21.34	40.79
5	3,501–4,000	13.37	23.21	20.80	61.59
6	4,001–4,500	18.09	41.31	18.37	79.96
7	4,501–5,000	19.21	60.52	10.09	90.05
8	5,001–5,500	12.17	72.68	4.46	94.51
9	5,501–6,000	9.12	81.81	2.61	97.12
10	6,001–7,000	5.71	87.52	.77	97.88
11	7,001–8,000	4.03	91.55	.77	98.65
12	More than 8,000	8.45	100.00	1.35	100.00

Source: Bundesinstitut für Berufsbildung; calculations by the authors.

Table 10B.2   **Descriptive Statistics for BiBB/IAB Data Used**

Characteristic	Males		Females	
	Mean	Standard Deviation	Mean	Standard Deviation
Earnings	7.27	2.37	5.12	1.99
Socioeconomic background				
Age/10	4.14	1.12	3.55	1.09
Potential experience/10	2.21	1.17	1.61	1.14
Squared potential experience/100	6.26	5.40	3.88	4.57
Married	.92	.27	.78	.41
Schooling (secondary school)				
Lower secondary school	.65	.48	.44	.50
Secondary school	.25	.43	.46	.50
Entitlement for advanced college				
for higher education	.05	.22	.04	.19
Gymnasium	.05	.22	.06	.24
Vocational training				
Apprenticeship training				
completed	.96	.20	.90	.31
Vocational training completed	.07	.26	.13	.34
Apprenticeship failed	.03	.16	.04	.19
Unemployment after vocational				
training graduation	.03	.18	.04	.21
Changes in employment				
Profession changed	.35	.48	.26	.44
Employer changed	.68	.47	.64	.48
Profession and employer				
changed	.31	.46	.23	.42
Size of training firm				
Less than 10 employees	.27	.45	.35	.48
10–49 Employees	.29	.45	.23	.42
50–99 Employees	.10	.30	.10	.30
100–499 Employees	.16	.36	.15	.36
500 Employees or more	.17	.37	.11	.31
Size of current firm				
Less than 10 employees	.15	.36	.30	.46
10–49 Employees	.24	.43	.22	.42
50–99 Employees	.11	.31	.11	.31
100–499 Employees	.22	.41	.20	.40
500 Employees or more	.28	.45	.17	.37
Sector of training firm				
Service	.45	.50	.11	.32
Manufacturing	.29	.45	.20	.40
Craft	.08	.27	.25	.44
Trade	.16	.37	.36	.48
Sector of current firm				
Service	.36	.48	.20	.40
Manufacturing	.24	.43	.12	.32
Craft	.10	.29	.24	.43
Trade	.30	.46	.44	.50
N	6,970		2,221	

Appendix C

Glossary of Some Features of the German Educational System

General Education

Elementary school (*Grundschule*)	Compulsory for all children aged 6–7; four years of schooling
Lower secondary school (*Hauptschule*)	After elementary school pupils have to enroll unless they change to higher educational schools; five years of schooling; certificate of successful completion of compulsory general education (*Hauptschulabschluß*)
Secondary school (*Realschule*)	Optional after elementary school; six years of schooling; certificate of successful completion (*Realschulabschluß*) entitles enrollment in several schools of further education and, if apprenticeship training is successfully completed, in advanced colleges of higher education (*Fachhochschulen*)
Gymnasium	Optional after elementary school (or secondary school); nine years of schooling; certificate of successful completion (*Abitur*) entitles enrollment at universities

Vocational Education

Elementary vocational year (*Berufsgrundbildungsjahr*)	Optional part-time or full-time school after elementary school, especially for youths who do not have apprenticeship training positions; prepares for vocational education
Preparation year for vocational training (*Berufsvorbereitungsjahr*)	Optional full-time school after elementary school for youths without apprenticeship training positions; prepares for vocational education (in a broader sense compared with the elementary vocational year)
Vocational school (*Berufsschule*)	Compulsory for leavers of lower secondary school until age 18; mainly three years of schooling; part of the dual system in that an apprenticeship trainee

	has to attend this school usually one day per week during apprenticeship training
Special vocational school (*Berufsfachschule*)	Provides full-time instruction lasting at least one year; does not demand vocational training or occupational experience as a prerequisite for admission; a first type enables the student to acquire a qualifying certificate in a recognized profession where attendance counts toward the training period in the profession
Higher vocational school	Provides part-time or full-time instruction for those who have successfully completed apprenticeship training and aim at a craftsman certificate, for example
Advanced vocational school (*Fachoberschule* or *Fachgymnasium*)	Provides full-time instruction lasting three years; these schools require certificate of secondary school for admission; *Fachoberschule* entitles student to study at a *Fachhochschule; Fachgymnasium* entitles a student to study at a university
Advanced college for higher education (*Fachhochschule*)	Colleges with near-university status; three years of education; mostly specialized in various fields of studies, for example, engineering, commerce, social work, fine arts

References

Ackum, S. 1991. Youth unemployment: Labor market programs and subsequent earnings. *Scandinavian Journal of Economics* 93 (4): 531–43.

Bundesministerium für Bildung und Wissenschaft. 1991. *Daten und Fakten über Jugendliche ohne abgeschlossene Berufsausbildung.* Bonn: Bundesministerium für Bildung und Wissenschaft.

———. Various issues. *Berufsbildungsbericht.* Bonn: Bundesministerium für Bildung und Wissenschaft.

Bundesministerium für Bildung, Wissenschaft, Forschung und Technologie. 1994. *Grund- und Strukturdaten, Ausgabe 1994/95.* Bonn: Bundesministerium für Bildung, Wissenschaft, Forschung und Technologie.

Cox, D. R. 1972. Regression models and life-tables. *Journal of the Royal Statistical Society B* 26:186–220.

Ellwood, D. T. 1982. Teenage unemployment: Permanent scars or temporary blemishes? In *The youth labor market problem: Its nature, causes, and conse-*

quences, ed. R. B. Freeman and D. A. Wise. Chicago: University of Chicago Press.

Flaig, G., G. Licht, and V. Steiner. 1993. Testing for state dependence effects in a dynamic model of male unemployment behavior. ZEW Discussion Paper no. 93–07. Mannheim: Centre for European Economic Research.

Franz, W. 1982. *Youth unemployment in the Federal Republic of Germany: Theory, empirical results and policy implications: An economic analysis.* Tübingen: Mohr.

Franz, W., and D. Soskice. 1995. The German apprenticeship system. In *Institutional frameworks and labor market performance: Comparative views on the U.S. and German economies,* ed. F. Buttler, W. Franz, R. Schettkat and D. Soskice, 208–34. London: Routledge.

Han, A., and J. A. Hausman. 1990. Flexible parametric estimation of duration and competing risk models. *Journal of Applied Econometrics* 5:1–28.

Harhoff, D., and T. J. Kane. 1997. Is the German apprenticeship system a panacea for the U.S. labor market? *Journal of Population Economics* 10:171–96.

Helberger, C., U. Rendtel, and J. Schwarze. 1994. Labor market entry of young people analyzed by a double threshold model. In *Labor market dynamics in present day Germany,* ed. J. Wagner, F. Buttler, and G. Wagner, 142–64. Frankfurt: Campus.

Hunt, J. 1995. The effect of unemployment compensation on unemployment duration in Germany. *Journal of Labor Economics* 13:88–120.

Institut für Arbeitsmarkt- und Berufsforschung. 1993. *Übergänge zwischen Bildung, Ausbildung und Beschäftigung und die Entwicklung der Qualifikationsstruktur in den alten und neuen Bundesländern.* Nürnberg: Institut für Arbeitsmarkt- und Berufsforschung. Mimeograph.

Karr, W., and K. John. 1989. Mehrfacharbeitslosigkeit und kumulative Arbeitslosigkeit. *Mitteilungen aus der Arbeitsmarkt- und Berufsforschung* 1:1–16.

Lynch, L. 1985. State dependency in youth unemployment: A lost generation? *Journal of Econometrics* 28:71–84.

———. 1989. The youth labor market in the eighties: Determinants of reemployment probabilities for young men and women. *Review of Economics and Statistics* 71:37–45.

Mühleisen, M., and K. F. Zimmermann. 1993. A panel analysis of job changes and unemployment. *European Economic Review* 38:793–801.

Münch, J. 1991. *Vocational training in the Federal Republic of Germany,* 3d ed. Berlin: European Center for the Development of Vocational Training.

Tessaring, M. 1993. Das duale System der Berufsausbildung in Deutschland: Attraktivität und Beschäftigungsperspektiven. *Mitteilungen aus der Arbeitsmarkt- und Berufsforschung* 26:131–61.

Tessaring, M., A. Reinberg, and G. Fischer. 1993. Beschäftigung und Qualifikation in den alten Bundesländern: Konzeption und Ergebnisse der Bildungsgesamtrechnung des IAB. In *Bestand und Bewegung im Bildungs- und Beschäftigungssystem der Bundesrepublik Deutschland,* ed. G. Fischer et al., 7–178. Nürnberg: Institut für Arbeitsmarkt- und Berufsforschung.

Winkelmann, R. 1996. Employment prospects and skill acquisition of apprenticeship-trained workers in Germany. *Industrial and Labor Relations Review* 49: 658–72.

———. 1997. How young workers get their training: A survey of Germany versus the United States. *Journal of Population Economics* 10:159–70.

Wurzel, E. 1993. *An econometric analysis of individual unemployment duration in West Germany.* Heidelberg: Physica.

11

Minimum Wages and Youth Employment in France and the United States

John M. Abowd, Francis Kramarz, Thomas Lemieux, and David N. Margolis

11.1 Introduction

In this paper we examine the link between changes in the minimum wage and employment outcomes for the youth (under age 31) labor market, in France and the United States. We make use of longitudinal data on employment status and earnings to see how individuals are affected by real increases (in the case of France) or real decreases (in the case of the United States) in the minimum wage conditional on the individual's loca-

John M. Abowd is professor of labor economics at Cornell University, distinguished senior research fellow at the U.S. Bureau of the Census, research associate at the Centre de Recherche en Economie et Statistique (CREST, Paris), and a research associate of the National Bureau of Economic Research. Francis Kramarz is head of the research department at INSEE-CREST, the French statistical institute; an associate professor at Ecole Polytechnique; and a research fellow of the Centre for Economic Policy Research, London. Thomas Lemieux is associate professor of economics at the University of British Columbia, a research director of the Centre Interuniversitaire de Recherche en Analyse des Organisations (CIRANO, Montréal), and a research associate of the National Bureau of Economic Research. David N. Margolis is a researcher with the Centre National de la Recherche Scientifique, working at the Université de Paris 1 Panthéon–Sorbonne in the Laboratoire de Microéconomie Appliquée and the Centre de Recherche en Economie et Statistique. Part of this paper was written while Margolis was assistant professor at the Université de Montréal and a research associate at the Centre de Recherche et Developement en Economie and the Centre Interuniversitaire de Recherche et d'Analyse des Organisations.

The authors gratefully acknowledge financial support from CIRANO, the National Science Foundation (SBR-93-21053 to Abowd and Margolis), and the Fonds pour la Formation de Chercheurs et l'Aide à la Recherche (97-NC-1676 to Margolis). Much of this work was completed while Margolis was visiting the CREST Laboratoire de Microéconométrie. The authors thank David Blanchflower, Richard Freeman, Shulamit Kahn, Lawrence Katz, Alan Krueger, John Martin, and participants at the NBER Summer Institute, CIRANO Summer Workshop, CREST Département de la Recherche Internal Workshop, CREST Microéconométrie Workshop, and the Université de Paris 1 Panthéon–Sorbonne for comments on previous versions of this paper. The American data used in this study were taken from public-tion in the earnings distribution. We take particular care to distinguish subpopulations that might be affected differently by the minimum wage, focusing in particular on low-wage workers and (in the case of France, where the data are available) on the use of employment promotion contracts that allow the payment of subminimum wages.

Although little attention has been paid to the situation in Europe,[1] some European countries provide interesting alternatives to the much studied U.S. case. France, in particular, seems a perfect contrast to the United States. Whereas in the United States the nominal federal minimum wage remained constant for most states during most of the 1980s (thus implying a declining real federal minimum wage), nominal minimum wages in France rose steadily over the 1980s, as did real minimum wages. In this paper we exploit the different growth patterns in real minimum wages in a symmetric manner to more clearly understand their effect on employment.

Most existing studies of the French minimum wage system use aggregate time-series data and find no effect of the minimum wage system on youth employment (see, e.g., Bazen and Martin 1991). This is surprising because, since the inception of the minimum wage, a significant percentage of the French labor force has been employed at wages close to that level. One reason for the orientation in the empirical analyses done in France is, certainly, the tendency of American applied researchers to rely on aggregate time-series analyses[2] prior to the widespread dissemination of public-use microeconomic data such as the Current Population Survey (CPS). Another reason is that research access to French microdata was extremely limited until the 1990s. In the present study we use microdata from France and the United States collected in household surveys that are quite comparable. In particular, we use longitudinal information on the workers. Consequently, we are able to analyze both French and American minimum wage systems using individual-level panel data.

Because of the dramatic differences between the evolution of both nominal and real French minimum wages and that of the national U.S. minimum,[3] we have designed statistical comparisons that address the same be-

---

use Current Population Survey (CPS) files provided by the Bureau of Labor Statistics and the Bureau of the Census. David Card graciously provided the computer code for implementing the Census Bureau CPS matching algorithms used in this paper. The French data were taken from the Enquête Emploi research files constructed by the Institut National de la Statistique et des Etudes Economiques (INSEE, the French national statistical agency). The French data are also public-use samples. For further information contact INSEE, Département de la Diffusion, 18 bd Adolphe Pinard, 75675 Paris Cedex 14, France. The opinions expressed in this paper are those of the authors, not the U.S. Census Bureau. The paper was completed before Abowd assumed his appointment.

1. See Dolado et al. (1996) for a summary of minimum wage studies for France, the Netherlands, Spain, and the United Kingdom.

2. See Brown, Gilroy, and Kohen (1982) for a review.

3. We do not consider state-specific minimum wages or youth subminimum wages in the United States, which became increasingly important at the end of the 1980s. See Neumark

havior using the different variations in the national minimum wage systems to identify the relevant effects. We use two different statistical approaches based on the same idea: analysis of employment transition probabilities conditional on the position of an individual in the wage distribution. In each approach, we decompose the wage distribution into four components (under, around, marginally over, and over the minimum wage). We then, in our first approach, use a multinomial logit model to analyze the factors that affect the probability of making a transition between a particular position in the wage distribution and employment or nonemployment (in the case of France) or between employment or nonemployment and the position in the wage distribution (in the case of the United States). We find that young workers paid around the minimum wage in France were more likely to transition to a nonemployment state (unemployment or inactivity) than those paid over the minimum wage and that, for French men, such differences were greater in years where major increases in the minimum wage occurred. In the United States, we find that among workers currently employed around the minimum wage, a larger share were in a nonemployment state the previous period than among workers above the minimum wage. In both cases, the effects are strongest for the youngest workers. We find some minor "spillover" effects in both cases and provide evidence to suggest that these effects capture some of the heterogeneity between low-wage and high-wage labor markets.

In the second approach, we exploit the size of the movements in the real minimum wage more directly.[4] For France, we use the automatic and legislated increases in the nominal minimum wage that occur (at least) each July to identify groups of workers whose current wage rate will fall below the new minimum wage rate after the increase. We also identify workers whose present employment is part of a special youth program that permits wage payments below the statutory minimum. We use the limited duration of employment spells in such programs to identify a second group of minimum wage employment effects. Our statistical analysis identifies the change in future employment probabilities given an individual's minimum wage status in the present period. We show that individuals whose reference year wage was between the two real minimum wages, as defined above, have substantially lower subsequent employment probabilities than those who were not. The conditional elasticity of subsequent nonemployment as a function of the real minimum wage for young male workers in France in this situation, evaluated at sample means, is -2.5. This effect is present even when unobserved labor market heterogeneity

---

and Wascher (1992) for an explicit treatment of this variation in the U.S. data. Similarly, we do not explicitly control for minimum wages specified by collective agreement in France that exceed the national minimum. See Margolis (1993) for a detailed treatment of the effects of the collective bargaining agreement salary grids on employment.

4. Our analysis bears some resemblance to that of Linneman (1982).

and supply behavior are partially controlled for by the inclusion of a separate category for workers marginally over the minimum. However, the impact of the minimum wage decreases with experience. We also show that youths who participated in employment programs had lower subsequent employment probabilities. For the United States we use the constancy of the nominal minimum wage between 1981 and 1987 to identify groups of employed workers whose real wage in the present period would have been below the real minimum wage in the previous period. We show that young men whose wages were between the two real minimum wages, as described above, had lower employment probabilities in the previous period than individuals who were not (the conditional elasticity, evaluated at sample means, is 2.2). These effects get worse with age in the United States and are mitigated by eligibility for special employment promotion contracts in France.

The structure of this paper is as follows. Section 11.2 provides some institutional background on the systems of minimum wages in both France and the United States and provides some preliminary indications of the potential impact in each case based on empirical wage distributions. Section 11.3 describes the data that we use to analyze the impact of minimum wages, and section 11.4 lays out the statistical models used to evaluate the employment effects of minimum wage changes. Section 11.5 details the results of our multinomial logit analysis, and section 11.6 discusses the conditional logit analyses. Section 11.7 concludes.

11.2 Institutional Background

11.2.1 France

The first minimum wage law in France was enacted in 1950, creating a guaranteed hourly wage rate that was partially indexed to the rate of increase in consumer prices. Beginning in 1970, the original minimum wage law was replaced by the current system (called the *salaire minimum interprofessionnel de croissance*—SMIC) linking the changes in the minimum wage to both consumer price inflation and growth in the hourly blue-collar wage rate. In addition to formula-based increases in the SMIC, the government legislated increases many times over the next two decades. The statutory minimum wage in France regulates the hourly regular cash compensation received by an employee, including the employee's part of any payroll taxes.[5]

---

5. In theory, no provisions in any of the minimum wage laws allow regional variation in the SMIC. In some sectors in the French economy, however, the effective minimum wage was determined by (often extended) collective bargaining agreements. These agreements typically covered entire regions and industries, especially when extended to nonbargaining employers. Although relatively important in the 1970s, these provisions became increasingly irrelevant

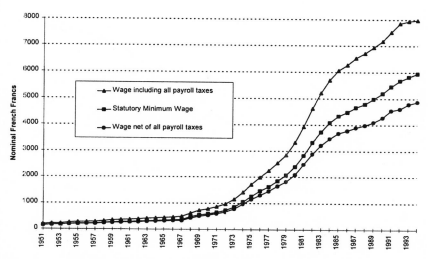

Fig. 11.1   Monthly minimum wage: France

Figure 11.1 shows the time series for the French minimum wage and the associated employee-paid and employer-paid payroll taxes. Because of the extensive use of payroll taxes to finance mandatory employee benefits, by the 1980s the French minimum wage imposed a substantially greater cost on the employer than its statutory value. Employees share in the legal allocation of the payroll taxes, as the figure shows; however, low-wage workers benefit substantially more than the average worker from the social security systems financed through these taxes in proportion to their revenue (unemployment insurance, health care, retirement income, and employment programs, in particular). Appendix table 11A.1 provides a complete statistical history of the real and nominal SMIC, including employer and employee payroll tax components.

Figure 11.2 shows the real hourly French minimum wage from 1951 to 1994. Although the original minimum wage program (called the *salaire minimum interprofessionnel garanti*—SMIG) was only partially indexed—in particular the inflation rate had to exceed 5 percent per year (2 percent from 1957 to 1970) to trigger the indexation—the real minimum wage did not decline measurably over the entire postwar period and increased substantially during most decades.

The French minimum wage lies near most of the mass of the wage rate distribution for the employed workforce. To show the location of the SMIC in this distribution, we plotted the empirical distribution of hourly

---

during the 1980s (our period of analysis) as the collective agreement nominal salary grids remained fixed in the face of an increasing nominal SMIC. See Margolis (1993) for a discussion of extended collective agreements and their relation to the SMIC.

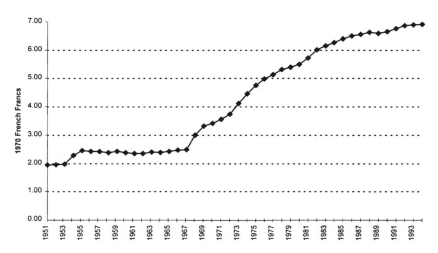

Fig. 11.2   Real hourly minimum wage: France

wage rates for 1990, the earliest year for which the Labor Force Survey reports continuous wage data. Figure 11.3 shows these data. We have indicated the SMIC directly on the figure. Notice that the first mode of the wage distribution is within F 5 of the minimum wage and the second mode is within F 10 of the minimum. In the overall distribution, 13.6 percent of the wage earners lie at or below the minimum wage and an additional 14.4 percent lie within an additional F 5 per hour of the SMIC.

Dolado et al. (1996) discuss the incidence of the SMIC with respect to household income. They find that although people employed at the SMIC do tend to be in the poorest households, the distribution of *"smicards"* (people paid the SMIC) is not monotonically decreasing in household income. For example, they find that the share of individuals paid the SMIC in each decile of household income increases from 10.1 percent in the lowest decile to 13.1 percent in the third lowest decile, then decreases to 6.6 percent for the fifth decile, increases to 7.4 percent for the sixth decile and declines monotonically to 0.6 percent in the highest decile of household income.

11.2.2   United States

The first national minimum wage in the United States was a part of the original Fair Labor Standards Act (FLSA) of 1938. The American national minimum wage has never been indexed and increases only when legislative changes are enacted. The national minimum applies only to workers covered by the FLSA, whose coverage has been extended over the years to include most jobs. The statutory minimum wage regulates the

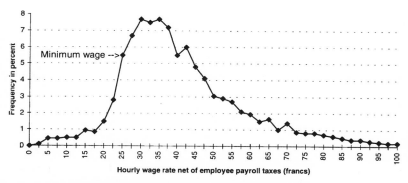

Fig. 11.3   Empirical distribution of hourly wages: France, 1990

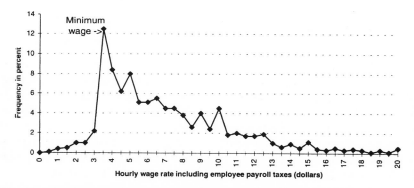

Fig. 11.4   Empirical distribution of hourly wages: United States, 1981

hourly regular cash compensation received by an employee including the employee's part of any payroll taxes.

Figures 11.4 and 11.5 show the distribution of the American hourly wage rate and the location of the minimum wage in that distribution for 1981 and 1987, the beginning and ending years of our analyses.[6] For 1981, 17.7 percent of the employed workforce had wage rates at or below the minimum wage and an additional 14.6 percent had wage rates within an additional $1.00 per hour of the minimum. For 1987, only 9.5 percent of employed persons had hourly wage rates at or below the minimum while an additional 9.9 percent lay within an additional $1.00 per hour of the minimum.

6. It should be noted that the federal minimum wage was increased to $3.35 per hour in 1980.

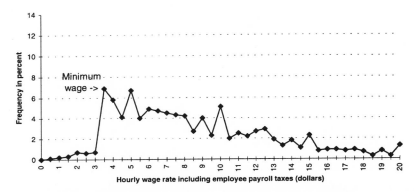

Fig. 11.5   Empirical distribution of hourly wages: United States, 1987

11.3   Data Description

11.3.1   France

The French data were extracted from the Enquête Emploi (Labor Force Survey) for the years 1982–89. The 60,000 households included in the Labor Force Survey sample are interviewed in March of three consecutive years with one-third of the households replaced each year. Every member of the household is surveyed and followed provided that he or she does not move during the three years. We used the INSEE research files for each of the indicated years. These files include identifiers that allowed us to follow individuals from year to year. Using these identifiers we created year-to-year matched files for the years 1982–83 to 1988–89.

The survey measures usual monthly earnings, net of employee payroll taxes but including employee income taxes, and usual weekly hours. Usual monthly earnings is measured in 20 intervals of widths varying from F 500 to F 5,000. It is important to note that the narrowest intervals were used for the lowest salaries. We take the categorical nature of our wage data explicitly into account in our analyses, in that we compare the declared wage category against the wage category in which an individual working the same number of hours per month at the SMIC would be found.

Certain young workers were employed in publicly funded programs that either combined classroom education with work ("*apprentis,*" "*stage de qualification,*" or "*stage d'insertion, contrat emploi–formation*") or provide subsidized low-wage employment ("*travaux d'utilité collective*" or "*stage d'initiation à la vie professionnelle,*" both from 1985 to 1989). All of these programs provide a legal exemption from the SMIC and from certain payroll taxes. Most of these programs are limited to workers 25 years old and under.

The employment status in year t is equal to one for all individuals who are employed in March of the survey year and equal to zero otherwise. The French Labor Force Survey definition of employment is the same as the one used by the International Labour Office: a person is employed if he or she worked for pay for at least one hour during the reference week. The definition is thus consistent with the American Bureau of Labor Statistics (BLS) definition used below.

Our control variables consisted of education, labor force experience, seniority, region of France, date of labor force entry, and year. Education was constructed as eight categories: none, completed elementary school, completed junior high school, completed basic vocational/technical school, completed advanced vocational/technical school, completed high school (*baccalauréat*), completed technical college or undergraduate university, and completed graduate school or postcollege professional school. Labor force experience was computed as the difference between current age and age at school exit. Seniority was measured as the response to a direct question on the survey (years with the present employer). Region is an indicator variable for the Ile de France (Paris metropolitan area) as the region of residence.

The SMIC data were taken from Bayet (1994), which reports official INSEE statistics. We selected the hourly SMIC for March of the indicated year, net of employee payroll taxes.

11.3.2   United States

We used the official BLS public-use outgoing rotation group files from the CPS for the months January to May and September to December and the years 1981–87. We applied the Census Bureau matching algorithm to create year-to-year linked files for the years 1981–82 to 1986–87.

The outgoing rotation groups (households being interviewed for the fourth or eighth time in the CPS rotation schedule) are asked to report usual weekly wage and usual weekly hours. Individuals who normally are paid by the hour are asked to report that wage rate directly. We created an hourly wage rate using the directly reported hourly wage rate when available and the ratio of usual weekly earnings to usual weekly hours otherwise. Respondents are asked to report these wage measures gross of employee payroll taxes, so they are not directly comparable to the measures constructed from the French data, which are reported net of employee payroll taxes. We created real hourly wage rates by dividing by the 1982–84-based Consumer Price Index for All Urban Workers for the appropriate month.

We created a second set of hourly wage measures for the United States that included income from tips in the hourly wage. To do this we computed a second hourly wage rate as usual weekly earnings divided by usual weekly hours for workers who reported that they were paid by the hour.

When this second hourly wage rate exceeded the one directly reported, we used the computed measure. This measure of hourly wage rate is used below in the analysis labeled "including income from tips."

An individual is employed in year t if he or she worked at least one hour for pay during the second week of the survey month. We used the CPS employment status recode variable to determine employment. The BLS definition is thus consistent with the one used in the French Labor Force Survey.

Our control variables consist of education, potential labor force experience, race, marital status, and region. Education was constructed as the number of years required to reach the highest grade completed. For the multinomial logit analysis, this was decomposed into six categories: less than junior high school (no diploma), junior high school, high school, less than four years of college, four years of college, and more than four years of college. Potential labor force experience is age minus years of education minus five. Race is one for nonwhite individuals. Marital status is one for married persons. Region is a set of three indicator variables for the northeastern, north-central, and southern parts of the United States.

The U.S. national nominal minimum wage was $3.35 throughout our analysis period.[7]

11.3.3 Empirical Transition Probabilities

A preliminary analysis of the empirical transition probabilities of young workers into or out of employment based on their positions in the wage distribution relative to the minimum wage suggests that one might expect to see significant impacts of the minimum wage on employment probabilities in both France and the United States. In the case of France, we are concerned with that probability that an individual is employed at the date $t + 1$ given the person's employment status and wage rate relative to the SMIC (if employed) at date t. In the case of the United States, the question is whether or not an individual was employed at date t given his or her employment status and wage rate relative to the minimum wage (if employed) at date $t + 1$.

Let miw_t be the nominal hourly minimum net wage in year t, $rmiw_t$ be the real hourly minimum net wage in year t, and h_t represent the number of monthly hours worked in the sample month in year t. For France let $wcat_t$ be the category in which the individual's nominal net monthly earnings falls in year t, and for the United States let w_t be the individual's hourly net wage rate in year t and rw_t be the real net wage for year t.

---

7. Throughout the period, and particularly toward the end, some states independently increased their nominal wages above the national level. We do not explicitly account for state-by-state variation in the nominal minimum wage. See Neumark and Wascher (1992) for an analysis, using a different methodology, of the effects of interstate variation of minimum wages in the United States.

For France define $micat_t$ as the earnings category into which expected nominal monthly earnings at the SMIC ($h_t \times miw_t$) would fall, and order the categories from 1 (less than F 500 per month) to 15 (over F 45,000 per month). Then we define the following six departure (occupied at date t) states:

out of the labor force at t,
unemployed at t,
employed at t and paid under the SMIC: $I(wcat_t < micat_t) = 1$,
employed at t and paid the SMIC: $I(wcat_t = micat_t) = 1$,
employed at t and paid marginally over the SMIC: $I(wcat_t = micat_t + 1) = 1$, and
employed at t and paid over the SMIC: $I(wcat_t > micat_t + 1) = 1$,

where $I(\cdot)$ is the indicator function taking the value one when the condition is true and zero otherwise. We also define two arrival (occupied at date $t + 1$) states:

employed at $t + 1$ and
not employed at $t + 1$.

For the United States recall that the nominal minimum wage was constant over the entire sample period at $3.35 per hour. Thus we construct six arrival states:

out of the labor force at $t + 1$,
unemployed at $t + 1$,
employed at $t + 1$ and paid under the minimum wage: $I(w_{t+1} < \$3.25) = 1$,
employed at $t + 1$ and paid the minimum wage: $I(\$3.25 \le w_{t+1} < \$3.50) = 1$,
employed at $t + 1$ and paid marginally over the minimum wage: $I(\$3.50 \le w_{t+1} < \$4.00) = 1$, and
employed at $t + 1$ and paid over the minimum wage: $I(w_{t+1} \ge \$4.00) = 1$.

We have the same two departure states:

employed at t and
not employed at t.

Using these definitions, figures 11.6 and 11.7 describe the breakdown of the population and the change in the real hourly minimum wage for French young men and women, respectively, and figures 11.8 and 11.9 show the corresponding breakdowns and changes for U.S. young men and women, respectively. Table 11.1 describes the distribution of transitions over the sample periods for the French data, and table 11.2 describes the distribution of transitions for the American data.

In the case of the United States, it is clear from looking at the raw transition probabilities that minimum wage workers are different from

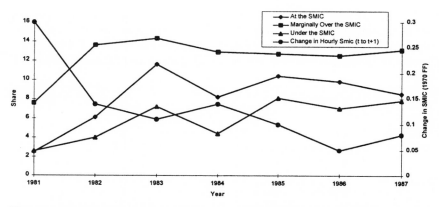

Fig. 11.6   **Population breakdown by earnings and evolution of real SMIC: French young men**

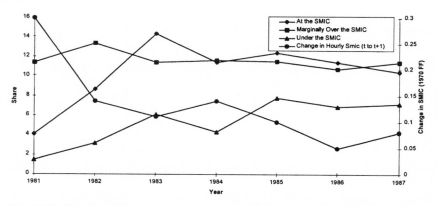

Fig. 11.7   **Population breakdown by earnings and evolution of real SMIC: French young women**

their higher paid counterparts. A much larger share of the population employed at the minimum wage at date $t + 1$ comes from the nonworking pool (42.92 percent) than does the share of the population employed far over the minimum wage (only 12.28 percent). The case in France is less clear, since the difference between the share of workers paid at the SMIC who are not employed the following period (6.63 percent) and the share paid over the SMIC who are not employed the following period (12.16 percent) is much less dramatic, and even goes in the opposite direction from the U.S. result. These effects may, however, be due to the presence of various sorts of employment promotion contracts, which might shield workers paid at or under the SMIC from layoffs. Such effects would not

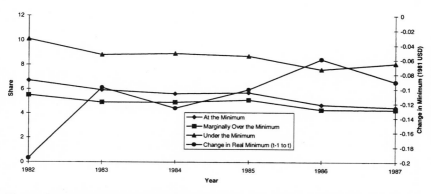

Fig. 11.8   Population breakdown by earnings and evolution of real minimum wage: U.S. young men

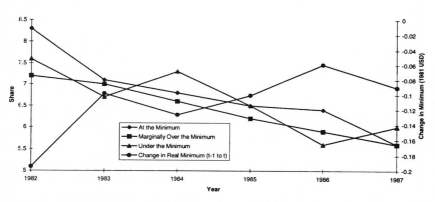

Fig. 11.9   Population breakdown by earnings and evolution of real minimum wage: U.S. young women

be visible in these cross-tabulations, and our conditional logit results go to great lengths to try to discriminate between the effects of the contracts and the effects of the minimum wage.

It should be noted that the transition behavior of workers paid marginally over the minimum is, in both countries, intermediate between the transitions made by those paid at the minimum and those paid over the minimum. This "spillover" effect could be capturing a degree of heterogeneity between low-wage and high-wage workers, and we will exploit this control group in what follows.

Clearly, this descriptive analysis is not sufficient to discredit the hypothesis that low-wage workers are, in some way, qualitatively different from high-wage workers; in fact, the spillover effect noted above suggests that

Table 11.1 **Transition Probabilities for France**

From	To Nonemployment			To Employment					Total
	Out of LF	Unemployed	Total	Under SMIC	At SMIC	Marginal SMIC	Over SMIC	Total	
Out of labor force	10,081	2,150	12,231	556	574	452	852	2,434	14,665
Overall %	11.67	2.49	14.15	0.64	0.66	0.52	0.99	2.82	16.97
Row %	68.74	14.66	83.40	3.79	3.91	3.08	5.81	16.60	100
Column %	67.54	18.10	45.64	11.85	7.40	4.64	2.28	4.08	111.8
Unemployed	2,328	5,733	8,061	856	723	595	1,041	3,215	11,276
Overall %	2.69	6.63	9.33	0.99	0.84	0.69	1.20	3.72	13.05
Row %	20.65	50.84	71.49	7.59	6.41	5.28	9.23	28.51	100
Column %	15.60	48.27	30.08	18.25	9.32	6.11	2.78	5.39	100.33
Under SMIC	6	14	20	1410	474	210	220	2,314	2,334
Overall %	0.01	0.02	0.02	1.63	0.55	0.24	0.25	2.68	2.70
Row %	0.26	0.60	0.86	60.41	20.31	9.00	9.43	99.14	100
Column %	0.04	0.12	0.07	30.06	6.11	2.16	0.59	3.88	39.1
At SMIC	133	150	283	880	2,144	661	300	3,985	4,268
Overall %	0.15	0.17	0.33	1.02	2.48	0.76	0.35	4.61	4.94
Row %	3.12	3.51	6.63	20.62	50.23	15.49	7.03	93.37	100
Column %	0.89	1.26	1.06	18.76	27.63	6.79	0.80	6.69	56.1
Marginal SMIC	175	451	626	540	2,465	3,194	1,166	7,365	7,991
Overall %	0.20	0.52	0.72	0.62	2.85	3.70	1.35	8.52	9.25
Row %	2.19	5.64	7.83	6.76	30.85	39.97	14.59	92.17	100
Column %	1.17	3.80	2.34	11.51	31.77	32.79	14.59	12.36	84.1
Over SMIC	2,202	3,378	5,580	449	1,380	4,630	33,837	40,296	45,876
Overall %	2.55	3.91	6.46	0.52	1.60	5.36	39.16	46.63	53.09
Row %	4.80	7.36	12.16	0.98	3.01	10.09	73.76	87.84	100
Column %	14.75	28.44	20.82	9.57	17.78	47.53	90.43	67.60	208.5
Total	14,925	11,876	26,801	4,691	7,760	9,742	37,416	59,609	86,410
Overall %	17.27	13.74	31.02	5.43	8.98	11.27	43.30	68.98	100
Row %	99.8	82.62	182.4	100.1	114.72	82.91	119.85	417.62	600
Column %	100	100	100	100	100	100	100	100	600

Source: French Labor Force Survey, 1982–89, matched year to year.

Note: Table reports on people aged 30 or under.

Table 11.2   **Transition Probabilities for the United States**

From	To						
	Out of LF	Unemployed	Under Minimum	At Minimum	Marginal Minimum	Over Minimum	Total
Nonemployment							
Out of labor force	25,245	3,124	1,586	2,278	1,617	4,547	38,397
Overall %	19.27	2.38	1.21	1.74	1.23	3.47	29.31
Row %	65.75	8.14	4.13	5.93	4.21	11.84	100
Column %	72.53	31.21	16.40	30.79	22.69	7.33	181.0
Unemployed	2,466	2,819	574	897	773	3,065	10,594
Overall %	1.88	2.15	0.44	0.68	0.59	2.34	8.09
Row %	23.28	26.61	5.42	8.47	7.30	28.93	100
Column %	7.09	28.16	5.94	12.12	7.30	4.94	69.10
Total	27,711	5,943	2,160	3,175	2,390	7,612	48,991
Overall %	21.15	4.54	1.65	2.42	1.82	5.81	37.40
Row %	56.56	12.13	4.41	6.48	4.88	15.54	100
Column %	79.62	59.37	22.34	42.92	33.53	12.28	250.06
Employment							
Under minimum	1,511	471	5,038	674	490	2,018	10,202
Overall %	1.15	0.36	3.85	0.51	0.37	1.54	7.79
Row %	14.81	4.62	49.38	6.61	4.80	19.78	100
Column %	4.34	4.71	52.11	9.11	6.88	3.25	80.40
At minimum	1,445	668	424	2,002	1,502	2,231	8,272
Overall %	1.10	0.51	0.32	1.53	1.15	1.70	6.31
Row %	17.47	8.08	5.13	24.20	18.16	26.97	100
Column %	4.15	6.67	4.39	27.06	21.07	3.60	66.95

(*continued*)

Table 11.2 (continued)

From		Out of LF	Unemployed	Under Minimum	At Minimum	Marginal Minimum	Over Minimum	Total
					To			
Marginal minimum		1,091	485	323	673	1,534	3,467	7,573
	Overall %	0.83	0.37	0.25	0.51	1.17	2.65	5.78
	Row %	14.41	6.40	4.27	8.89	20.26	45.78	100
	Column %	3.13	4.85	3.34	9.10	21.52	5.59	47.53
Over minimum		3,046	2,443	1,723	874	1,211	46,674	55,971
	Overall %	2.33	1.86	1.32	0.67	0.92	35.63	42.72
	Row %	5.44	4.36	3.08	1.56	2.16	83.39	100
	Column %	8.75	24.41	17.82	11.81	16.99	75.28	155.06
Total		7,093	4,067	7,508	4,223	4,737	54,390	82,018
	Overall %	5.41	3.10	5.73	3.22	3.62	41.52	62.60
	Row %	8.65	4.96	9.15	5.15	5.78	66.31	100
	Column %	20.38	40.63	77.66	57.08	66.47	87.72	349.94
Total		34,804	10,010	9,668	7,398	7,127	62,002	131,009
	Overall %	26.57	7.64	7.38	5.65	5.44	47.33	100
	Row %	141.2	58.21	71.4	55.66	56.89	216.70	600
	Column %	100	100	100	100	100	100	600

Source: U.S. Current Population Survey, 1981–87, January–May and September–December, matched year to year.

Note: Table reports on people aged 30 or under.

such heterogeneity may exist. To separate out this effect, we need to control for worker characteristics and analyze more carefully the transitions between employment and nonemployment.[8]

11.4   Statistical Models for the Minimum Wage Effects on Employment

In order to control for the impact that variables, including the minimum wage and its movements, might have on labor market transitions, we applied two different statistical techniques. In the first approach, we use a multinomial logit analysis to try to control for factors that might render low-wage workers different from other workers and could thereby affect their transition probabilities. We analyze the raw transitions and describe the factors that increase or reduce the probability of transitions involving nonemployment and how these factors differentially affect minimum wage and above minimum wage workers. In the second approach, we exploit the size of the increases to categorize workers as "between" old and new values of the real minimum wage (i.e., with an hourly real wage rate lying between the old and the new real minimum wage), and we use a logit analysis of subsequent (or prior) employment probabilities to see if workers who might be directly affected by minimum wage increases have significantly different subsequent (or prior) employment probabilities.

11.4.1   Multinomial Logit Analysis

Using the same definitions of states as in subsection 11.3.3, we regroup the unemployed and inactive states into a single state, nonemployment. Using the notation N = nonemployment, E = employment, U = under the minimum, A = at the minimum, M = marginally over the minimum, and O = over the minimum, we can define the set of possible transitions for each country. Thus for France there are 10 possible transitions: O to E or O to N, M to E or M to N, A to E or A to N, U to E or U to N, and N to E or N to N. For the United States there are 10 symmetric transitions: E to O or N to O, E to M or N to M, E to A or N to A, E to U or N to U, and E to N or N to N. We use a multinomial logit approach to control for observable factors while allowing for a common shock. For interpretation, however, we are particularly concerned with the conditional transition probabilities.

In the French case, we are interested in the probability of transition out of employment conditional on the position in the earnings distribution.

---

8. There remains a possibility that unobserved worker heterogeneity might bias our results in sections 11.5 and 11.6. Because of selection considerations and sample sizes, we were not able to use standard (Hsiao 1986) or nonstandard (Abowd, Kramarz, and Margolis 1999) techniques to control for these effects. Thus we are forced to suppose that the inclusion of the "marginally above" the minimum wage group is sufficient to capture any heterogeneity in transition rates that is correlated with wages.

For the United States, we are interested in the initial state of a worker conditional on his or her ex post position in the earnings distribution. In each of these cases, we have in mind the hypothesis of a competitive labor market, and thus a model in which a worker with a given marginal productivity (equal to the wage) closer to the minimum wage might be more at risk to transit out of employment in France or to have come from nonemployment in the United States than an observationally equivalent worker paid above the minimum wage. We suppose that those workers employed at wages marginally above the minimum share unobservable characteristics that affect transition probabilities in the absence of a minimum wage, and that all differences in their transition behavior can be attributed to the more direct impact of the minimum wage on those paid at it relative to those paid marginally over it. We can use our parameter estimates from the multinomial logit to see how the differences in these conditional transition probabilities evolve over time, thus seeing if the difference is correlated with movements in the real minimum wage. This approach is particularly useful not only for seeing how minimum wage movements affect the probability of job loss conditional on employment (or on having come from nonemployment conditional on being employed) but also for determining whether minimum wage movements play a role in excluding workers completely from the labor market. We can also see which workers are the most likely to transition out of employment in France or come from nonemployment in the United States based on observable characteristics, such as age, conditional on the individual's position in the earnings distribution. Furthermore, since our estimates are based on the entire population, interpretation of these results can be more easily generalized than the results based on the employed subsample of our data, as in the conditional logit analysis described below.

11.4.2   Conditional Logit Analysis

Once again, let $rmiw_t$ be the real hourly minimum net wage in year t and let rw_t be the real hourly net wage for year t. Let age_t represent an individual's age at the date t and $stage_t$ indicate that the person was employed under some employment promotion contract that allows for subminimum wages in year t. Finally, let e_t indicate the individual's employment status in year t $(e_t = 1$ if employed$)$.

We define a person as "between" in France if the mean of the cell in which the person is located at the date t is at or above the minimum wage at date t but below the minimum wage (in date t francs) at date $t + 1$. Algebraically, after defining rw_t to be the mean of the cell in which the individual is located, this is equivalent to

$$I(rmiw_t \leq rw_t \leq rmiw_{t+1}) = 1.$$

We also break up the subminimum population (those for whom rw_t $rmiw_t$) into two groups in France: those on employment promotion contracts ($stage_t$) and those not on employment promotion contracts. Thus for France we estimate variants of the following equation for individuals:

$$\Pr[e_{t+1} = 1 | e_t = 1]$$

$$= F(x_t\beta + \alpha_1 I(rw_t < rmiw_t) \times stage_1 \times (rmiw_{t+1} - rmiw_t)$$

$$+ \alpha_2 I(rw_t < rmiw_t) \times (1 - stage_1) \times (rmiw_{t+1} - rmiw_t)$$

(1)

$$+ \alpha_3 I(rmiw_t \leq rw_t \leq rmiw_{t+1}) \times (rmiw_{t+1} - rmiw_t) \times age_t$$

$$+ \alpha_4 I(rmiw_{t+1} < rw_t \leq (rmiw_{t+1} \times 1.1)) \times (rmiw_{t+1} - rmiw_t)$$

$$\times age_t),$$

where $F(\cdot)$ is the standard logistic function. The logit described in equation (1) allows us to test the hypothesis, implied by the theory of competitive labor markets, that if marginal productivity stays constant, increases in the real minimum wage render previously employed individuals, whose wages fall between the old and new minima, currently unemployable. In particular, this specification also us to see if the effects of the minimum wage vary with age, and we experiment with different degrees of age aggregation to evaluate particular labor market phenomena such as the end of eligibility for employment promotion contracts or mandatory military service.

We define a person as "between" in the United States if the person's wage at date $t + 1$ is at or above the minimum wage at date $t + 1$ but below the minimum wage (in date $t + 1$ dollars) at date t. Algebraically, this is equivalent to

$$I(rmiw_{t+1} \leq rw_{t+1} \leq rmiw_t) = 1.$$

We also define the variable $rmarg_t$ as the deflated value of $4.00 at date t. Thus for the United States we estimate variants of the following equation:

$$\Pr[e_t = 1 | e_{t+1} = 1]$$

$$= F(x_t\beta + \alpha_1 I(rw_{t+1} < rmiw_{t+1}) \times (rmiw_t - rmiw_{t+1}) \times age_t$$

(2)

$$+ \alpha_2 I(rmiw_{t+1} \leq rw_{t+1} \leq rmiw_t) \times (rmiw_t - rmiw_{t+1})$$

$$\times age_t + \alpha_3 I(rmiw_t < rw_{t+1} \leq rmarg_t) \times (rmiw_t - rmiw_{t+1})$$

$$\times age_t).$$

The interpretation of equation (2) is symmetric to that of equation (1). Does a relatively large decrease in the real minimum wage allow previously unemployable individuals to be employed? Furthermore, in the United States, we explicitly examine the impact that tips might have on our measure of the position of a person in the wage distribution.

Notice that the equations for the United States have empirical content because the nominal minimum wage rate does not change during our sample period whereas the real minimum wage rate declines because of general price inflation. In contrast, the equations for France have empirical content because the indexation formula is tied to general price inflation and to the growth in average hourly earnings among blue-collar workers, and as noted in subsection 11.2.1, real minimum wages increased steadily throughout the sample period.[9]

11.5   Multinomial Logit Results

11.5.1   France

Appendix table 11A.2 shows some of the results of estimating the multinomial logit for France. We have reported only the coefficients on certain key variables; the reference state is the transition U to E. The multinomial logit models for both France and the United States were estimated on the entire population, and not just on the youth subpopulation (as is the case for the conditional logit models), in order to highlight differences between younger and older workers. A large number of the coefficients are significantly different from zero, and the differences in the intercepts are consistent with the raw transition probabilities (O-E is more probable than O-N, N-N is more probable than N-E, etc.). Having completed one's *baccalauréat* (roughly the equivalent of high school in the United States) is an advantage for those employed over the minimum wage (0.62 vs. 0.29 for men, 1.34 vs. 1.06 for women); however, men with *baccalauréats* who are employed at the minimum wage seem relatively worse off (−0.31 vs. −0.49). This might be coherent with a signaling explanation in which only the low-productivity *baccalauréat* holders are willing to accept jobs at the minimum wage.

In general, the coefficients corresponding to transitions from marginally over the SMIC are intermediate between transitions from at the SMIC and transitions from over the SMIC. This is consistent with the idea of using workers paid marginally over the SMIC as a comparison group for the purposes of analyzing the effects of the minimum wage on the popula-

9. Our conditional logit estimates are performed on the set of individuals who are employed at some point in the sample. Thus the coefficients should not necessarily be interpreted as representative of the entire potential labor force, but rather as appropriate for the sample of workers who satisfy the selection criterion.

tion of workers being paid at the minimum. For French women in particular, the time-series transition behavior of women paid marginally over the minimum strongly resembles that of women paid at the minimum. We exploit these results in the conditional logit models that follow in section 11.6.

Since the interpretation of the raw regression coefficients is not immediately informative, figure 11.10 explores the variation in conditional transition probabilities out of employment with age for a French man in 1984 who entered the labor market between 1962 and 1972, living in the Paris region with a *baccalauréat,* and figure 11.11 shows the same conditional transition probabilities for a French woman with the same characteristics. All conditional transition probabilities are conditional on the date *t* posi-

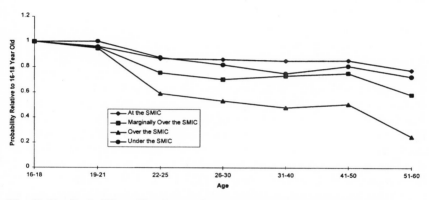

Fig. 11.10   Probability of leaving employment (relative to 16–18-year-olds): French men, 1984

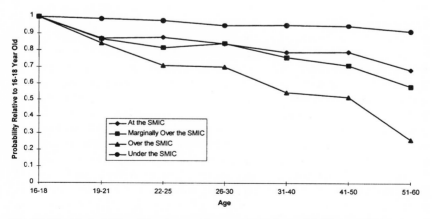

Fig. 11.11   Probability of leaving employment (relative to 16–18-year-olds): French women, 1984

tion in the earnings distribution. The general downward trends in both figures are due simply to the fact that young people are more likely to transition out of employment independent of position in the wage distribution. Still, it is worth noting that while 51–60-year-olds paid over the minimum are about a third as likely to transition out of employment than 16–18-year-olds, workers paid at the minimum seem to benefit much less from the reduction in the probability of transitioning out of employment as they age. Furthermore, it seems that aging does not reduce at all the probability of transitioning out of the labor force for women being paid under the minimum. This suggests that the subminimum population of older women is characterized by much weaker labor force attachment than comparable women paid elsewhere in the wage distribution.

11.5.2   United States

Appendix table 11A.3 shows some of the results of estimating the multinomial logit for the United States. Once again, we have reported only the coefficients on certain key variables; the reference state is the transition E to U. A certain number of the coefficients are significantly different from zero, and the differences in the intercepts are consistent with the raw transition probabilities (E-O is more probable than N-O, E-O is more probable than E-A, etc.). Having completed high school is associated with a relative higher share coming from employment for those employed over the minimum wage (0.75 vs. 0.49 for men, 0.65 vs. 0.37 for women); however, men with high school diplomas who are employed at the minimum wage come disproportionately from nonemployment (0.13 vs. 0.08) whereas the effect is opposite for women (−0.02 vs. 0.05), although the differences in the estimated coefficients are small. The subminimum transitions do not seem dramatically different from the at minimum transitions (the coefficients in the E-A column are rarely significantly different from zero), although a significantly smaller share of young women paid under the minimum were employed in the previous period, relative to those paid at the minimum. This suggests that low-wage employers hire relatively more from the pool of nonemployed, and it thus could be interpreted as running counter to the idea that subminimum sectors in the United States (particularly jobs that receive income from tips) provide more stable employment than jobs that pay the minimum wage.

As in the French case, the time-series behavior of the transitions of workers paid marginally over the minimum closely mimics that of workers paid at the minimum, further reinforcing the idea that the group of workers paid marginally over the minimum might be a reasonable control group for minimum wage workers. Also, as in the French case, the interpretation of the raw coefficients can be difficult. Figure 11.12 explores the variation in conditional (on arrival state) transition probabilities into employment with age for an American man in 1984 who entered the labor

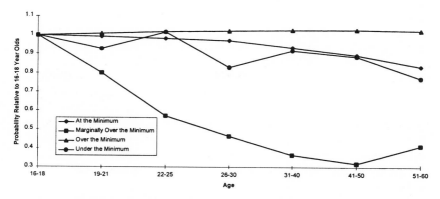

Fig. 11.12   Probability of moving into employment (relative to 16–18-year-olds): U.S. men, 1984

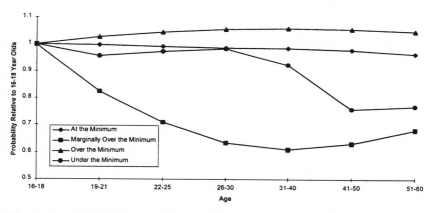

Fig. 11.13   Probability of moving into employment (relative to 16–18-year-olds): U.S. women, 1984

market between 1962 and 1972 with a high school diploma, and figure 11.13 shows the variation of the conditional transition probabilities for an American woman with the same characteristics.

Clearly, in the United States, the effect of age on the transition probabilities differs dramatically from the French case. The two figures are similar in form, although the relative reduction in the conditional probability of transitioning from nonemployed to marginally over the minimum is stronger for men and turns back up sooner for women. The most remarkable difference between the French and U.S. cases is that while in France the probability of making a O-N transition decreases with age, there is either no effect or a slight increase in the relative probability of N-O transitions (the U.S. equivalent) for older workers relative to younger workers in our results for the United States. This could be due to the high stability in general of jobs that pay substantially over the minimum wage; the intercepts for E-O transitions are significantly larger than all other estimated intercepts in the model. On the other hand, in the United States it seems that the probability of transitioning from nonemployment to marginally over the minimum wage is the transition the most affected by aging, while in France the order of magnitude of the change is about half for 31–40-year-olds relative to 16–18-year-olds (a 63 percent drop vs. a 27 percent drop for men, a 39 percent drop vs. a 24 percent drop for women). If workers paid marginally over the minimum are indeed a reasonable control group for minimum wage workers, the relatively feeble decline in the probability of having come from nonemployment experienced by workers paid at the minimum suggests that in the United States at least, the minimum wage is playing a role in determining the sorts of transitions that low-wage workers make in the labor market.

11.6   Conditional Logit Results

11.6.1   France

Table 11.3 shows the results of estimating equation (1) for France on young people, using broad age categories.[10] We have reported the coefficients for the key real minimum wage variables, as well as variables for several types of employment contracts in France.[11]

The coefficients show that French men aged 25–30 with real wage rates in period t that are above the real minimum in t but below the real minimum wage in period $t + 1$ have much lower subsequent employment probabilities than similar men paid substantially over the period $t + 1$ real minimum wage. The elasticity is very large: an increase of 1 percent in the minimum wage entails an decrease in the probability of keeping one's job of 4.6 percent, relative to men aged 25–30 who are paid marginally over the minimum. One interpretation of these results is that although low-wage workers do differ from high-wage workers (as the fairly consistent negative coefficients suggest), the minimum wage hits workers whose real wages are between the two minima much harder than other low-wage workers.

Similar results hold for women and people 20–24 years old, but these coefficients are less significant. In general, the employment loss effects worsen with age among the young employed population, but the level of

10. Appendix table 11A.4 provides descriptive statistics for the French data used in these regressions.

11. We explicitly consider fixed-term contracts (CDD), youth employment schemes (young *stagiaire*), and apprenticeships, with the reference being long-term contracts (CDI). See Abowd, Corbel, and Kramarz (1999) for more detail on the differences between CDD and CDI.

Table 11.3   Estimated Effect of Real French Minimum Wage Increases on Subsequent Employment Probabilities: Broad Age Categories

Name of Effect	Coefficient	Standard Error	p-Value	Elasticity
Young Men, Hourly Wage				
Fixed-term contract	−.5129	.0819	.0001	−.0478
Young stagiaire	−.8777	.1263	.0001	−.0818
Apprentice	−.1490	.1364	.2747	−.0139
Real wage$_t$ < Real SMIC$_t$ and Not young stagiaire	2.9500	2.2341	.1867	.7765
Real wage$_t$ < Real SMIC$_t$ and Young stagiaire	9.0935	5.5130	.0990	5.4727
(Real SMIC$_t$ ≤ Real wage$_t$ ≤ Real SMIC$_{t+1}$)*(16 ≤ Age$_t$ ≤ 19)	5.4614	8.5478	.5229	2.0094
(Real SMIC$_t$ ≤ Real wage$_t$ ≤ Real SMIC$_{t+1}$)*(20 ≤ Age$_t$ ≤ 24)	−7.7651	8.2247	.3451	−1.2017
(Real SMIC$_t$ ≤ Real wage$_t$ ≤ Real SMIC$_{t+1}$)*(25 ≤ Age$_t$ ≤ 30)	−33.2708	9.9755	.0009	−4.8928
(Real SMIC$_{t+1}$ ≤ Real wage$_t$ ≤ (1.1*Real SMIC$_{t+1}$))*(16 ≤ Age$_t$ ≤ 19)	2.9869	5.2162	.5669	1.1201
(Real SMIC$_{t+1}$ ≤ Real wage$_t$ ≤ (1.1*Real SMIC$_{t+1}$))*(20 ≤ Age$_t$ ≤ 24)	−3.4111	4.2892	.4264	−.4256
(Real SMIC$_{t+1}$ ≤ Real wage$_t$ ≤ (1.1*Real SMIC$_{t+1}$))*(25 ≤ Age$_t$ ≤ 30)	−3.7791	5.8713	.5198	−.2914
Young Women, Hourly Wage				
Fixed-term contract	−.9351	.0826	.0001	−.0879
Young stagiaire	−1.4152	.1150	.0001	−.1331
Apprentice	−1.0683	.1954	.0001	−.1005
Real wage$_t$ < Real SMIC$_t$ and Not young stagiaire	−.8857	2.3804	.7098	−.1604
Real wage$_t$ < Real SMIC$_t$ and Young stagiaire	8.3441	5.0400	.0978	4.4279
(Real SMIC$_t$ ≤ Real wage$_t$ ≤ Real SMIC$_{t+1}$)*(16 ≤ Age$_t$ ≤ 19)	−1.6553	9.8606	.8667	−.2759
(Real SMIC$_t$ ≤ Real wage$_t$ ≤ Real SMIC$_{t+1}$)*(20 ≤ Age$_t$ ≤ 24)	−8.7397	6.8185	.1999	−1.2485
(Real SMIC$_t$ ≤ Real wage$_t$ ≤ Real SMIC$_{t+1}$)*(25 ≤ Age$_t$ ≤ 30)	−11.6779	7.8799	.1383	−1.5537
(Real SMIC$_{t+1}$ ≤ Real wage$_t$ ≤ (1.1*Real SMIC$_{t+1}$))*(16 ≤ Age$_t$ ≤ 19)	−5.1875	7.6857	.4997	−.7447
(Real SMIC$_{t+1}$ ≤ Real wage$_t$ ≤ (1.1*Real SMIC$_{t+1}$))*(20 ≤ Age$_t$ ≤ 24)	.3164	4.4018	.9427	.0354
(Real SMIC$_{t+1}$ ≤ Real wage$_t$ ≤ (1.1*Real SMIC$_{t+1}$))*(25 ≤ Age$_t$ ≤ 30)	−1.6632	4.7962	.7288	−.1734

Source: French Labor Force Survey, 1982–89, matched year to year.

Note: Equations estimated by maximum likelihood logit. All equations include indicators for year, education (eight groups), region (Ile de France), and age (three groups), as well as the continuous variables labor force experience (through quartic), seniority, seniority squared, and hourly wage in year t (through cubic). All displayed coefficients except fixed-term contract, young stagiaire, and apprentice are equal to the indicated group multiplied by the real percentage increase in the SMIC between years t and $t + 1$ (1981 = 100). The coefficients and elasticities show the partial effects on the probability of employment in year $t + 1$, given t. A separate equation was estimated for each demographic panel. Sample sizes are young men, 30,804; young women, 26,434.

detail is not sufficient to speculate on why certain age groups are more affected than others. It is clear from the estimates of the coefficients on the different contract types that all of the types of contract studied here lead to more precarious labor force attachment than an indefinite term contract on average, but the employment promotion contracts (young *stagiaire*) seem to provide relative security for the subminimum popula-tion.[12] Looking at these populations in more detail, in particular at what happens to 25-year-olds (who will no longer be eligible for employment promotion contracts the following year), will give us more information on whether the dramatic differences seen between 25–30-year-old and 20–24-year-old men with wages between the two minima are due to the expira-tion of the protection provided by the employment promotion contracts. Table 11.4 gives these detailed results.

Looking first at the men, the most remarkable feature is in fact the huge negative coefficient affecting 25-year-old men whose wages are between the two minima. This elasticity of -15.9 (expressed as a difference from the marginally above category) and the subsequent negative coefficients for "between" men are consistent with the idea that the minimum wage has a strong negative impact on subsequent employment probabilities. However, the presence of employment promotion contracts, and the re-duction in employer social insurance contributions that they imply, helps workers who are under age 25 to retain their jobs in the face of a steadily increasing real SMIC. When workers are no longer eligible for such con-tracts, their probability of losing their jobs increases dramatically. Relative to the control group of workers marginally above the SMIC, the coeffi-cients for 25- and 26-year-olds are significantly larger. In fact, there is no significant bump in the coefficients at 25 years old for the marginally above workers, suggesting that this phenomenon is only pertinent to minimum wage workers. This further reinforces the interpretation that "between" workers who are eligible for employment promotion contracts are shielded from the negative effects of movements in the SMIC, but "older" young workers are not.

On average, the coefficients for workers between the two SMICs are more negative than for workers marginally over the date t SMIC. The av-erage difference (excluding the 25-year-olds) is 7.8, suggesting that the "be-tween" population might be different from the "marginal" population. Unfortunately, none of these differences (except for 25-year-olds) is sig-nificant, and in fact, none of the other coefficients for men are significantly different from zero. Although there are also a few significant coefficients in the results for women, interpretation of these results is much more dif-ficult. Although 23-year-old women with wages between the two minima

12. See Bonnal, Fougère, and Sérandon (1997) for an analysis centered on the impact of the youth employment schemes.

Table 11.4   Estimated Effect of Real French Minimum Wage Increases on Subsequent Employment Probabilities: Detailed Age Categories

Name of Effect	Coefficient	Standard Error	p-Value	Elasticity
Young Men, Hourly Wage				
(Real SMIC$_t$ ≤ Real wage$_t$ ≤ Real SMIC$_{t+1}$)*(16 ≤ Age$_t$ ≤ 19)	4.9184	8.5415	.5647	1.8096
(Real SMIC$_t$ ≤ Real wage$_t$ ≤ Real SMIC$_{t+1}$)*(Age$_t$ = 20)	9.4237	17.3312	.5866	1.8847
(Real SMIC$_t$ ≤ Real wage$_t$ ≤ Real SMIC$_{t+1}$)*(Age$_t$ = 21)	−14.4978	13.9315	.2980	−2.9995
(Real SMIC$_t$ ≤ Real wage$_t$ ≤ Real SMIC$_{t+1}$)*(Age$_t$ = 22)	−16.5940	18.9398	.3810	−2.0742
(Real SMIC$_t$ ≤ Real wage$_t$ ≤ Real SMIC$_{t+1}$)*(Age$_t$ = 23)	−21.2335	19.3804	.2732	−3.6252
(Real SMIC$_t$ ≤ Real wage$_t$ ≤ Real SMIC$_{t+1}$)*(Age$_t$ = 24)	24.3191	32.6535	.4564	1.1581
(Real SMIC$_t$ ≤ Real wage$_t$ ≤ Real SMIC$_{t+1}$)*(Age$_t$ = 25)	−63.8672	19.4477	.0010	−15.0276
(Real SMIC$_t$ ≤ Real wage$_t$ ≤ Real SMIC$_{t+1}$)*(Age$_t$ = 26)	−48.3802	22.1020	.0286	−7.7408
(Real SMIC$_t$ ≤ Real wage$_t$ ≤ Real SMIC$_{t+1}$)*(Age$_t$ = 27)	−10.1344	41.6355	.8077	−.8108
(Real SMIC$_t$ ≤ Real wage$_t$ ≤ Real SMIC$_{t+1}$)*(28 ≤ Age$_t$ ≤ 30)	−18.1628	15.4336	.2393	−2.0957
(Real SMIC$_t$ ≤ Real wage$_t$ ≤ (1.1*Real SMIC$_{t+1}$))*(16 ≤ Age$_t$ ≤ 19)	2.9091	5.2114	.5767	1.0909
(Real SMIC$_t$ ≤ Real wage$_t$ ≤ (1.1*Real SMIC$_{t+1}$))*(Age$_t$ = 20)	−1.2895	7.5889	.8651	−.3281
(Real SMIC$_t$ ≤ Real wage$_t$ ≤ (1.1*Real SMIC$_{t+1}$))*(Age$_t$ = 21)	−5.3057	7.6142	.4859	−.8079
(Real SMIC$_t$ ≤ Real wage$_t$ ≤ (1.1*Real SMIC$_{t+1}$))*(Age$_t$ = 22)	−14.2510	9.4418	.1312	−1.3538
(Real SMIC$_t$ ≤ Real wage$_t$ ≤ (1.1*Real SMIC$_{t+1}$))*(Age$_t$ = 23)	9.8803	11.9823	.4096	.8084
(Real SMIC$_t$ ≤ Real wage$_t$ ≤ (1.1*Real SMIC$_{t+1}$))*(Age$_t$ = 24)	5.1411	12.0952	.6708	.3054
(Real SMIC$_t$ ≤ Real wage$_t$ ≤ (1.1*Real SMIC$_{t+1}$))*(Age$_t$ = 25)	7.3424	13.7843	.5943	.8811
(Real SMIC$_t$ ≤ Real wage$_t$ ≤ (1.1*Real SMIC$_{t+1}$))*(Age$_t$ = 26)	−2.0793	13.6645	.8791	−.1368
(Real SMIC$_t$ ≤ Real wage$_t$ ≤ (1.1*Real SMIC$_{t+1}$))*(Age$_t$ = 27)	−6.7963	13.8000	.6224	−.2281
(Real SMIC$_t$ ≤ Real wage$_t$ ≤ (1.1*Real SMIC$_{t+1}$))*(28 ≤ Age$_t$ ≤ 30)	−8.2901	8.4234	.3250	−.6564

(continued)

Table 11.4 (continued)

Name of Effect	Coefficient	Standard Error	p-Value	Elasticity
Young Women, Hourly Wage				
(Real SMIC$_t$ ≤ Real wage$_t$ ≤ Real SMIC$_{t+1}$)*(16 ≤ Age$_t$ ≤ 19)	-1.7276	9.8645	.8610	-.2879
(Real SMIC$_t$ ≤ Real wage$_t$ ≤ Real SMIC$_{t+1}$)*(Age$_t$ = 20)	38.9118	23.1330	.0926	3.0882
(Real SMIC$_t$ ≤ Real wage$_t$ ≤ Real SMIC$_{t+1}$)*(Age$_t$ = 21)	-2.5471	12.7138	.8412	-.3069
(Real SMIC$_t$ ≤ Real wage$_t$ ≤ Real SMIC$_{t+1}$)*(Age$_t$ = 22)	-14.8695	14.2127	.2955	-2.2876
(Real SMIC$_t$ ≤ Real wage$_t$ ≤ Real SMIC$_{t+1}$)*(Age$_t$ = 23)	-35.7959	14.0221	.0107	-7.8100
(Real SMIC$_t$ ≤ Real wage$_t$ ≤ Real SMIC$_{t+1}$)*(Age$_t$ = 24)	-26.8167	17.8484	.1330	-4.3098
(Real SMIC$_t$ ≤ Real wage$_t$ ≤ Real SMIC$_{t+1}$)*(Age$_t$ = 25)	4.9443	23.7480	.8351	.5494
(Real SMIC$_t$ ≤ Real wage$_t$ ≤ Real SMIC$_{t+1}$)*(Age$_t$ = 26)	-17.3310	15.5787	.2659	-2.3788
(Real SMIC$_t$ ≤ Real wage$_t$ ≤ Real SMIC$_{t+1}$)*(Age$_t$ = 27)	.3354	18.9002	.9858	.0419
(Real SMIC$_t$ ≤ Real wage$_t$ ≤ Real SMIC$_{t+1}$)*(28 ≤ Age$_t$ ≤ 30)	-18.7008	11.4752	.1032	-2.6715
(Real SMIC$_{t+1}$ ≤ Real wage$_t$ ≤ (1.1*Real SMIC$_{t+1}$))*(16 ≤ Age$_t$ ≤ 19)	-5.2027	7.6973	.4991	-.7469
(Real SMIC$_{t+1}$ ≤ Real wage$_t$ ≤ (1.1*Real SMIC$_{t+1}$))*(Age$_t$ = 20)	26.3323	11.6838	.0242	2.7296
(Real SMIC$_{t+1}$ ≤ Real wage$_t$ ≤ (1.1*Real SMIC$_{t+1}$))*(Age$_t$ = 21)	7.0573	8.8323	.4243	.7876
(Real SMIC$_{t+1}$ ≤ Real wage$_t$ ≤ (1.1*Real SMIC$_{t+1}$))*(Age$_t$ = 22)	-14.9729	8.3171	.0718	-1.7468
(Real SMIC$_{t+1}$ ≤ Real wage$_t$ ≤ (1.1*Real SMIC$_{t+1}$))*(Age$_t$ = 23)	-4.4278	9.8576	.6533	-.5009
(Real SMIC$_{t+1}$ ≤ Real wage$_t$ ≤ (1.1*Real SMIC$_{t+1}$))*(Age$_t$ = 24)	-6.0435	9.7212	.5341	-.6784
(Real SMIC$_{t+1}$ ≤ Real wage$_t$ ≤ (1.1*Real SMIC$_{t+1}$))*(Age$_t$ = 25)	-.0432	10.5009	.9967	-.0054
(Real SMIC$_{t+1}$ ≤ Real wage$_t$ ≤ (1.1*Real SMIC$_{t+1}$))*(Age$_t$ = 26)	1.5230	9.9692	.8786	.1488
(Real SMIC$_{t+1}$ ≤ Real wage$_t$ ≤ (1.1*Real SMIC$_{t+1}$))*(Age$_t$ = 27)	7.7465	12.2241	.5263	.7173
(Real SMIC$_{t+1}$ ≤ Real wage$_t$ ≤ (1.1*Real SMIC$_{t+1}$))*(28 ≤ Age$_t$ ≤ 30)	-7.2571	7.0661	.3044	-.7392

Source: French Labor Force Survey, 1982–89, matched year to year.

Note: Equations estimated by maximum likelihood logit. All equations include indicators for year, education (eight groups), region (Ile de France), and age (ten groups), fixed-term contract, young *stagiaire*, apprentice, paid under the SMIC and young *stagiaire*, and paid under the SMIC and not young *stagiaire*, as well as the continuous variables labor force experience (through quartic), seniority, seniority squared, and hourly wage in year t (through cubic). All displayed coefficients are equal to the indicated group multiplied by the real percentage increase in the SMIC between years t and $t+1$ (1981 = 100). The coefficients and elasticities show the partial effects on the probability of employment in year $t+1$, given employment in year t. Sample sizes are young men, 30,804; young women, 26,434.

are significantly more likely to be nonemployed the following year than women who are paid over the SMIC, the difference from 23-year-old women paid marginally over the SMIC is not significant. And the large, positive coefficients on 20-year-old women, again present in both the "between" and "marginal" populations, is hard to explain. These results may reflect the added opportunities available for women as men go off to perform their military service (and thus withdraw from the labor market), but such an interpretation can neither be accepted not rejected exclusively on the basis of the evidence presented here.

In addition to estimating the conditional logits with "marginally over" the SMIC defined as 1.10 times the SMIC, we also estimated these models with two alternative definitions (1.15 and 1.20 times the SMIC). Table 11.5 analyzes the robustness of the coefficients for the between and marginal categories to these changes in the definition of "marginally over." It seems clear that our results are quite robust to changes in the definition of "marginal."

11.6.2   United States

Table 11.6 shows the results of estimating equation (2) using both the hourly wage measure that excludes income from tips and the measure that

Table 11.5   **Robustness of Conditional Logit Results to Variations in Definition of "Marginally over" the Minimum**

	Narrow		Medium		Wide	
	Between	Marginally Over	Between	Marginally Over	Between	Marginally Over
French youth						
Men	4.0888	.7317	5.3906	4.0222	6.5107	5.0473
	(6.6196)	(3.8171)	(6.6543)	(2.6087)	(6.7083)	(2.4817)
Women	−6.0281	−.04525	−6.0108	−.4013	−5.8400	−.1178
	(8.2804)	(4.2333)	(8.3134)	(3.1828)	(8.3809)	(3.0601)
U.S. youth						
Men	1.9965	−1.6196	2.0827	−1.9342	1.5043	−2.6988
	(1.6373)	(1.8837)	(1.7436)	(1.7077)	(1.7871)	(1.6751)
Women	3.9599	−.8667	4.6514	−.5443	3.8852	−1.6244
	(1.5578)	(1.8022)	(1.6694)	(1.6615)	(1.7297)	(1.6484)

Sources: French Labor Force Survey, 1982–89, matched year to year, and U.S. Current Population Survey, 1981–87, January–May and September–December, matched year to year.

Note: Coefficients come from logistic regressions conditional on employment at date t for France and date $t+1$ for the United States. For France, the categories are defined as "narrow" = SMIC to 1.10*SMIC, "Medium" = SMIC to 1.15*SMIC, and "wide" = SMIC to 1.20*SMIC. For the United States, the categories are defined as "narrow" = $3.35 to $3.75, "medium" = $3.35 to $4.00, and "wide" = $3.35 to $4.25. For this table, "youth" is defined as ages 25 and under. See notes to tables 11.3, 11.4, 11.6, 11.7, and 11.8 for details on other variables in the regressions. Numbers in parentheses are standard errors.

Table 11.6   **Estimated Effect of Real U.S. Minimum Wage Decreases on Prior Employment Probabilities: Total Labor Market Experience**

Name of Effect	Coefficient	Standard Error	p-Value	Elasticity
Young Men, Hourly Wage—No Tips				
Real wage$_{t+1}$ < Real min$_{t+1}$	−.4567	2.5368	.8571	−.1498
Real min$_{t+1}$ ≤ Real wage$_{t+1}$ ≤ Real min$_t$	−3.0723	1.6532	.0631	−1.3287
Real min$_t$ ≤ Real wage$_{t+1}$ ≤ Real ($4.00)$_t$	.3153	1.6178	.8455	.0977
(Real wage$_{t+1}$ ≤ Real min$_{t+1}$)*Experience	.2406	.4178	.5648	.4046
(Real min$_{t+1}$ ≤ Real wage$_{t+1}$ ≤ Real min$_t$)*Experience	−1.4714	.2841	.0001	−2.5115
(Real min$_t$ ≤ Real wage$_{t+1}$ ≤ Real ($4.00)$_t$)*Experience	−.8961	.2497	.0003	−1.3746
Young Women, Hourly Wage—No Tips				
Real wage$_{t+1}$ < Real min$_{t+1}$	−.0535	2.1856	.9805	−.0340
Real min$_{t+1}$ ≤ Real wage$_{t+1}$ ≤ Real min$_t$	−8.3538	1.5107	.0001	−4.8544
Real min$_t$ ≤ Real wage$_{t+1}$ ≤ Real ($4.00)$_t$	−2.6704	1.5055	.0761	−1.8436
(Real wage$_{t+1}$ ≤ Real min$_{t+1}$)*Experience	−.6488	.2570	.0116	−1.3900
(Real min$_{t+1}$ ≤ Real wage$_{t+1}$ ≤ Real min$_t$)*Experience	−.9277	.2007	.0001	−1.8917
(Real min$_t$ ≤ Real wage$_{t+1}$ ≤ Real ($4.00)$_t$)*Experience	−.8574	.1894	.0001	−1.5564

Young Men, Hourly Wage—With Tips

Real wage$_{t+1}$ < Real min$_{t+1}$	-2.6088	2.4905	.2949	-1.7404
Real min$_{t+1}$ ≤ Real wage$_{t+1}$ ≤ Real min$_t$	-4.3814	1.6346	.0074	-2.4823
Real min$_t$ ≤ Real wage$_{t+1}$ ≤ Real ($4.00)$_t$	-.7521	1.6034	.6390	-.5111
(Real wage$_{t+1}$ ≤ Real min$_{t+1}$)*Experience	.1059	.4154	.7988	.1805
(Real min$_{t+1}$ ≤ Real wage$_{t+1}$ ≤ Real min$_t$)*Experience	-1.5673	.2849	.0001	-2.6350
(Real min$_t$ ≤ Real wage$_{t+1}$ ≤ Real ($4.00)$_t$)*Experience	-.9464	.2491	.0001	-1.4794

Young Women, Hourly Wage—With Tips

Real wage$_{t+1}$ < Real min$_{t+1}$	-3.0938	2.0570	.1326	-1.8775
Real min$_{t+1}$ ≤ Real wage$_{t+1}$ ≤ Real min$_t$	-9.1702	1.4879	.0001	-5.2774
Real min$_t$ ≤ Real wage$_{t+1}$ ≤ Real ($4.00)$_t$	-3.3196	1.4939	.0263	-2.2658
(Real wage$_{t+1}$ ≤ Real min$_{t+1}$)*Experience	-.7841	.2570	.0023	-1.7565
(Real min$_{t+1}$ ≤ Real wage$_{t+1}$ ≤ Real min$_t$)*Experience	-.9762	.2009	.0001	-1.9923
(Real min$_t$ ≤ Real wage$_{t+1}$ ≤ Real ($4.00)$_t$)*Experience	-.8851	.1894	.0001	-1.6186

Source: Current Population Survey, 1981–87, January–May and September–December, matched year to year.

Note: Equations estimated by maximum likelihood logit. All equations include indicators for year, region (three groups), nonwhite, and married; and years of schooling, labor force experience (through quartic), and log hourly real wage (1982 prices, through cubic). All displayed coefficients are equal to the indicated group times the real decrease (absolute value of the change in logarithms) in the minimum wage between years t and $t+1$. The coefficients and elasticities show the partial effects on the probability of employment in year t, given employment in year $t+1$. A separate equation was estimated for each panel. Sample sizes are young men, 41,001; young women, 38,992.

includes income from tips, and interacting with total labor market experience instead of age.[13] In every case, individuals who are employed in year $t + 1$ were more likely to have been unemployed or not in the labor force in t if their real wage in $t + 1$ was between the real minimum wage in years t and $t + 1$. The magnitudes of these effects are large, with elasticities for men with zero experience of -1.42 to -1.97 and for women with no experience of -3.01. Once again, we refer to comparisons with the "marginal" group—that is, workers who are paid marginally above the old (date t) minimum wage—to get at the direct effect of movements in the real minimum wage on transitions into employment. By weighting the different experience groups, a decrease in the real minimum wage of 1 percent between $t - 1$ and t is related to an increased probability of having been nonemployed at $t - 1$ of 2.2 percent (in difference from the marginal workers) for those men who are paid between the t and $t + 1$ minimum wages. These results are consistent with the neoclassical idea that decreases in the real minimum wage make nonemployed workers easier to employ and these workers enter disproportionately between the two minimum wages. This decreases the share of those employed at date $t + 1$ who were employed at date t for the "between" group more than for other groups.

It is interesting to note the differences, or rather lack of differences, between the results that measure wages with and without tips. None of the qualitative results seem sensitive to the manner in which we define wages; however, some intuition can be gleaned from how the coefficients seem to shift when passing from measures without tips to measures with tips. All of the coefficients shown in table 11.6 become more negative when tips are included in the wage measure. This is also consistent with the standard neoclassical model, which would imply that the measure with tips more accurately describes a worker's marginal productivity and would conclude that the less significant coefficients in the estimation without tips are affected by measurement error. Nevertheless, due to the lack of any qualitative difference between the results with and without tips, and because our measure without tips uses reported rather than constructed data,[14] the rest of our results for the United States will be based on the wage measure that excludes tips.

Table 11.7 reestimates equation (2) using the broad age categories, as in table 11.3. As was suggested by the negative coefficients on the experience interaction terms in table 11.6, the effects of the minimum wage worsen as young workers get older. The differences between workers paid between the two minima and workers paid marginally over the t minimum are still

13. Appendix table 11A.5 provides descriptive statistics for the U.S. data used in these regressions.

14. Welch (1997) provides evidence on various sorts of measurement error in the CPS and hints that hours are likely to be a greater source of measurement error than wages.

Table 11.7 Estimated Effect of Real U.S. Minimum Wage Increases on Prior Employment Probabilities (excluding tips): Broad Age Categories

Name of Effect	Coefficient	Standard Error	p-Value	Elasticity
Young Men, Hourly Wage				
Real wage$_{t+1}$ < Real min$_{t+1}$	.6119	1.9147	.7493	.2007
(Real min$_{t+1}$ ≤ Real wage$_{t+1}$ ≤ Real min$_t$)*(16 ≤ Age, ≤ 19)	−6.1455	1.3807	.0001	−2.9233
(Real min$_{t+1}$ ≤ Real wage$_{t+1}$ ≤ Real min$_t$)*(20 ≤ Age, ≤ 24)	−11.8902	1.9536	.0001	−4.2095
(Real min$_{t+1}$ ≤ Real wage$_{t+1}$ ≤ Real min$_t$)*(25 ≤ Age, ≤ 30)	−19.4188	3.1495	.0001	−5.9588
(Real min$_t$ ≤ Real wage$_{t+1}$ ≤ Real (4.00)$_t$)*(16 ≤ Age, ≤ 19)	−.9696	1.3901	.4855	−.3767
(Real min$_t$ ≤ Real wage$_{t+1}$ ≤ Real (4.00)$_t$)*(20 ≤ Age, ≤ 24)	−5.9107	1.7693	.0008	−1.4697
(Real min$_t$ ≤ Real wage$_{t+1}$ ≤ Real (4.00)$_t$)*(25 ≤ Age, ≤ 30)	−9.8243	2.4330	.0001	−1.8055
Young Women, Hourly Wage				
Real wage$_{t+1}$ < Real min$_{t+1}$	−3.2195	1.6924	.0571	−1.1762
(Real min$_{t+1}$ ≤ Real wage$_{t+1}$ ≤ Real min$_t$)*(16 ≤ Age, ≤ 19)	−9.1433	1.3730	.0001	−4.3346
(Real min$_{t+1}$ ≤ Real wage$_{t+1}$ ≤ Real min$_t$)*(20 ≤ Age, ≤ 24)	−14.0812	1.6675	.0001	−4.8644
(Real min$_{t+1}$ ≤ Real wage$_{t+1}$ ≤ Real min$_t$)*(25 ≤ Age, ≤ 30)	−19.8125	1.8812	.0001	−7.1220
(Real min$_t$ ≤ Real wage$_{t+1}$ ≤ Real (4.00)$_t$)*(16 ≤ Age, ≤ 19)	−3.0577	1.4261	.0320	−1.1732
(Real min$_t$ ≤ Real wage$_{t+1}$ ≤ Real (4.00)$_t$)*(20 ≤ Age, ≤ 24)	−8.4481	1.4757	.0001	−2.2399
(Real min$_t$ ≤ Real wage$_{t+1}$ ≤ Real (4.00)$_t$)*(25 ≤ Age, ≤ 30)	−12.5349	1.5423	.0001	−3.2334

Source: Current Population Survey, 1981–87, January–May and September–December, matched year to year.

Note: Equations estimated by maximum likelihood logit. All equations include indicators for year, region (three groups), nonwhite, married, and age (three groups); and years of schooling, labor force experience (through quartic), and log hourly real wage (1982 prices, through cubic). All displayed coefficients are equal to the indicated group times the real decrease (absolute value of the change in logarithms) in the minimum wage between years t and $t+1$. The coefficients and elasticities show the partial effects on the probability of employment in year t, given employment in year $t+1$. A separate equation was estimated for each demographic panel. Sample sizes are young men, 41,001; young women, 38,992.

significant for all age groups, and the elasticities are still large. For the oldest age group, a decrease of 1 percent in the real minimum wage at t is associated with a 5.96 percent higher chance that a given "between" worker came from nonemployment, whereas such a change is associated with only an 1.81 percent higher chance for "marginal" workers. Unlike the French case, although 25–30-year-olds with date $t + 1$ wages between the two minima have a higher chance of having come from nonemployment than do 20–24-year-olds, the difference is not nearly as dramatic. This is not surprising, as there existed no nationwide employment promotion schemes in the United States in the 1980s that would have induced effects similar to the French case.

One might think that our approach of considering *previous* employment in the United States could be subject to the possibility, especially among young people, that many of the transitions from nonemployment to employment are first jobs after the end of schooling.[15] Since we control for schooling as a set of regressors reflecting different levels of educational attainment, looking at the pattern of age coefficients for "between" workers and "marginal" workers should allow us to ignore such considerations to the extent that entry into the labor force does not occur disproportionately in a particular wage category. Table 11.8, which provides our conditional logit analysis at the same level of aggregation as table 11.4, therefore allows us to concentrate more precisely on how minimum wage movements affect the stability of early career employment at different points in the wage distribution.

As was the case in our earlier results, the probability that a worker came from nonemployment is higher among the set of workers with date $t + 1$ real wages between the two minima than among the set of workers with date $t + 1$ real wages marginally above the date t real minimum. The same holds true for a comparison of "between" workers with workers earning substantially more than the date t real minimum, and these differences are often significant. Despite a lot of variation across the different ages, there appears to be a secular trend toward a higher and higher share of workers coming from nonemployment as age increases, and this trend is steeper among "between" workers than among "marginal" workers, particularly for young men. This is not the case in France, and it may suggest that information is revealed faster in the United States and that as workers age, the sorts of low-wage jobs they can find become increasingly precarious.

Since there do not exist systematic, targeted programs that should affect transitions among young people throughout the United States in the same manner (with the exception of education), interpretation of these coefficients is not as straightforward as in the French case. However, if (as men-

---

15. See Topel and Ward (1992), among others, for an analysis of early career mobility in the United States.

Table 11.8   Estimated Effect of Real U.S. Minimum Wage Increases on Prior Employment Probabilities (excluding tips): Detailed Age Categories

Name of Effect	Coefficient	Standard Error	p-Value	Elasticity
Young Men, Hourly Wage				
Real wage$_{t+1}$ < Real min$_{t+1}$	.2962	1.9152	.8771	.0971
(Real min$_{t+1}$ ≤ Real wage$_{t+1}$ ≤ Real min$_t$)*(16 ≤ Age$_t$ ≤ 19)	−6.5106	1.3857	.0001	−3.0970
(Real min$_{t+1}$ ≤ Real wage$_{t+1}$ ≤ Real min$_t$)*(Age$_t$ ≤ 20)	−11.6092	3.1697	.0002	−4.4924
(Real min$_{t+1}$ ≤ Real wage$_{t+1}$ ≤ Real min$_t$)*(Age$_t$ ≤ 21)	−9.0680	3.4352	.0083	−3.2645
(Real min$_{t+1}$ ≤ Real wage$_{t+1}$ ≤ Real min$_t$)*(Age$_t$ ≤ 22)	−7.3453	4.7357	.1209	−2.0986
(Real min$_{t+1}$ ≤ Real wage$_{t+1}$ ≤ Real min$_t$)*(Age$_t$ ≤ 23)	−22.0209	5.2597	.0001	−8.4499
(Real min$_{t+1}$ ≤ Real wage$_{t+1}$ ≤ Real min$_t$)*(Age$_t$ ≤ 24)	−15.1148	5.2426	.0039	−4.6784
(Real min$_{t+1}$ ≤ Real wage$_{t+1}$ ≤ Real min$_t$)*(Age$_t$ ≤ 25)	−16.6557	6.2664	.0079	−4.7588
(Real min$_{t+1}$ ≤ Real wage$_{t+1}$ ≤ Real min$_t$)*(Age$_t$ ≤ 26)	−17.9004	6.9347	.0098	−5.3701
(Real min$_{t+1}$ ≤ Real wage$_{t+1}$ ≤ Real min$_t$)*(Age$_t$ ≤ 27)	−15.9424	8.5432	.0620	−5.1813
(Real min$_{t+1}$ ≤ Real wage$_{t+1}$ ≤ Real ($4.00)$_t$)*(28 ≤ Age$_t$ ≤ 30)	−22.0514	4.5378	.0001	−6.9252
(Real min$_{t+1}$ ≤ Real wage$_{t+1}$ ≤ Real ($4.00)$_t$)*(16 ≤ Age$_t$ ≤ 19)	−1.2309	1.3918	.3765	−.4783
(Real min$_{t+1}$ ≤ Real wage$_{t+1}$ ≤ Real ($4.00)$_t$)*(Age$_t$ ≤ 20)	−4.7686	3.0687	.1202	−1.2724
(Real min$_{t+1}$ ≤ Real wage$_{t+1}$ ≤ Real ($4.00)$_t$)*(Age$_t$ ≤ 21)	−4.4151	3.3797	.1914	−1.2184
(Real min$_{t+1}$ ≤ Real wage$_{t+1}$ ≤ Real ($4.00)$_t$)*(Age$_t$ ≤ 22)	−5.2612	3.9467	.1825	−1.2314
(Real min$_{t+1}$ ≤ Real wage$_{t+1}$ ≤ Real ($4.00)$_t$)*(Age$_t$ ≤ 23)	−9.3349	4.0392	.0208	−2.0277
(Real min$_{t+1}$ ≤ Real wage$_{t+1}$ ≤ Real ($4.00)$_t$)*(Age$_t$ ≤ 24)	−8.6274	4.7811	.0712	−1.9071
(Real min$_{t+1}$ ≤ Real wage$_{t+1}$ ≤ Real ($4.00)$_t$)*(Age$_t$ ≤ 25)	−6.4574	4.8991	.1875	−1.1170
(Real min$_{t+1}$ ≤ Real wage$_{t+1}$ ≤ Real ($4.00)$_t$)*(Age$_t$ ≤ 26)	−8.4370	5.7535	.1425	−1.5576
(Real min$_{t+1}$ ≤ Real wage$_{t+1}$ ≤ Real ($4.00)$_t$)*(Age$_t$ ≤ 27)	−12.1263	5.3991	.0247	−2.4804
(Real min$_{t+1}$ ≤ Real wage$_{t+1}$ ≤ Real ($4.00)$_t$)*(28 ≤ Age$_t$ ≤ 30)	−10.7899	3.5679	.0025	−1.9561

(continued)

Table 11.8   (continued)

Name of Effect	Coefficient	Standard Error	p-Value	Elasticity
Young Women, Hourly Wage				
Real wage$_{t+1}$ < Real min$_{t+1}$	-3.7559	1.6913	.0264	-1.3722
(Real min$_{t+1}$ ≤ Real wage$_{t+1}$ ≤ Real min$_t$)*(16 ≤ Age$_t$ ≤ 19)	-9.8220	1.3730	.0001	-4.6564
(Real min$_{t+1}$ ≤ Real wage$_{t+1}$ ≤ Real min$_t$)*(Age$_t$ ≤ 20)	-12.2205	2.8456	.0001	-4.6320
(Real min$_{t+1}$ ≤ Real wage$_{t+1}$ ≤ Real min$_t$)*(Age$_t$ ≤ 21)	-12.8276	3.1141	.0001	-4.6853
(Real min$_{t+1}$ ≤ Real wage$_{t+1}$ ≤ Real min$_t$)*(Age$_t$ ≤ 22)	-13.4058	3.6339	.0002	-4.4009
(Real min$_{t+1}$ ≤ Real wage$_{t+1}$ ≤ Real min$_t$)*(Age$_t$ ≤ 23)	-14.1311	4.2524	.0009	-4.1771
(Real min$_{t+1}$ ≤ Real wage$_{t+1}$ ≤ Real min$_t$)*(Age$_t$ ≤ 24)	-14.0301	4.2585	.0010	-4.1895
(Real min$_{t+1}$ ≤ Real wage$_{t+1}$ ≤ Real min$_t$)*(Age$_t$ ≤ 25)	-23.5188	4.2544	.0001	-9.5817
(Real min$_{t+1}$ ≤ Real wage$_{t+1}$ ≤ Real min$_t$)*(Age$_t$ ≤ 26)	-18.8257	4.0242	.0001	-6.4372
(Real min$_{t+1}$ ≤ Real wage$_{t+1}$ ≤ Real min$_t$)*(Age$_t$ ≤ 27)	-20.1282	4.6770	.0001	-6.8814
(Real min$_{t+1}$ ≤ Real wage$_{t+1}$ ≤ Real min$_t$)*(28 ≤ Age$_t$ ≤ 30)	-19.6787	2.4999	.0001	-6.9948
(Real min$_{t+1}$ ≤ Real wage$_{t+1}$ ≤ Real ($4.00)$_t$)*(16 ≤ Age$_t$ ≤ 19)	-3.4490	1.4233	.0154	-1.3234
(Real min$_{t+1}$ ≤ Real wage$_{t+1}$ ≤ Real ($4.00)$_t$)*(Age$_t$ ≤ 20)	-2.3108	2.8808	.4225	-.5968
(Real min$_{t+1}$ ≤ Real wage$_{t+1}$ ≤ Real ($4.00)$_t$)*(Age$_t$ ≤ 21)	-4.9630	2.9318	.0905	-1.3019
(Real min$_{t+1}$ ≤ Real wage$_{t+1}$ ≤ Real ($4.00)$_t$)*(Age$_t$ ≤ 22)	-9.1566	3.0945	.0031	-2.5897
(Real min$_{t+1}$ ≤ Real wage$_{t+1}$ ≤ Real ($4.00)$_t$)*(Age$_t$ ≤ 23)	-13.4398	3.2502	.0001	-3.4858
(Real min$_{t+1}$ ≤ Real wage$_{t+1}$ ≤ Real ($4.00)$_t$)*(Age$_t$ ≤ 24)	-14.1707	3.4026	.0001	-3.7468
(Real min$_{t+1}$ ≤ Real wage$_{t+1}$ ≤ Real ($4.00)$_t$)*(Age$_t$ ≤ 25)	-16.7514	3.1826	.0001	-4.7081
(Real min$_{t+1}$ ≤ Real wage$_{t+1}$ ≤ Real ($4.00)$_t$)*(Age$_t$ ≤ 26)	-7.2195	3.7185	.0522	-1.5576
(Real min$_{t+1}$ ≤ Real wage$_{t+1}$ ≤ Real ($4.00)$_t$)*(Age$_t$ ≤ 27)	-6.5597	3.5805	.0669	-1.4072
(Real min$_{t+1}$ ≤ Real wage$_{t+1}$ ≤ Real ($4.00)$_t$)*(28 ≤ Age$_t$ ≤ 30)	-15.0802	2.0915	.0001	-4.2146

Source: Current Population Survey, 1981–87, January–May and September–December, matched year to year.

Note: Equations estimated by maximum likelihood logit. All equations include indicators for year, region (three groups), nonwhite, married, and age (ten groups); and years of schooling, labor force experience (through quartic), and log hourly real wage (1982 prices, through cubic). All displayed coefficients are equal to the indicated group times the real decrease (absolute value of the change in logarithms) in the minimum wage between years t and $t+1$. The coefficients and elasticities show the partial effects on the probability of employment in year t, given employment in year $t+1$. A separate equation was estimated for each demographic panel. Sample sizes are young men, 41,001; young women, 38,992.

tioned above) the coefficients corresponding to a given age are particularly strong, and if this age corresponds to the age at which many students typically finish a certain diploma, one might conclude that the coefficients are capturing disproportionate entry into the labor force at particular places in the wage distribution. Unfortunately, the most remarkable coefficients (23 years old for men and 25 years old for women) are not concurrent with ages at which a significant portion of the future workforce is in their last year of schooling. There does not seem to be any clear interpretation for the particular age pattern of the coefficients in the United States.

Finally, to promote comparability between our analysis, which is done conditional on the employment state in either year t (France) or year $t + 1$ (United States), and other analyses, which consider the effects of the minimum wage unconditional on the previous or future employment state, we compute the implied unconditional elasticities implied by our estimates. To calculate an unconditional elasticity we apply Bayes law to obtain the relation between the forms of the analysis equations we used for France and the United States. Hence, we have

(3)
$$\Pr[e_{t+1} = 1 | e_t = 1, rmiw_t, rmiw_{t+1}]$$
$$= \Pr[e_t = 1 | e_{t+1} = 1, rmiw_t, rmiw_{t+1}] \frac{\Pr[e_{t+1} = 1 | rmiw_t, rmiw_{t+1}]}{\Pr[e_t = 1 | rmiw_t]}.$$

To calculate the elasticity we use the following derivative formula:

(4)
$$\frac{\partial \ln \Pr[e_{t+1} = 1]}{\partial \ln rmiw_{t+1}} = \frac{\partial \ln \Pr[e_{t+1} = 1 | e_t = 1, rmiw_t, rmiw_{t+1}]}{\partial \ln rmiw_{t+1}}$$
$$- \frac{\partial \ln \Pr[e_t = 1 | e_{t+1} = 1, rmiw_t, rmiw_{t+1}]}{\partial \ln rmiw_{t+1}}.$$

Notice that the derivative in equation (4) simplifies because the denominator in the ratio of unconditional probabilities in equation (3) does not depend on the future minimum wage. The right-hand side of equation (4) has two terms. For France, we can estimate only the first of these two terms because the real minimum wage is always increasing. The conditions necessary for estimating the second term occur in the United States, where the real minimum wage is always decreasing. To estimate the unconditional elasticity in equation (4) we must make an assumption regarding the term that cannot be estimated in the particular country. We assume that this term is zero, which means that increases in the real minimum wage do not change the rate at which nonemployed workers become employed and, conversely, decreases in the real minimum wage do not change

Table 11.9	Elasticity Estimates for Young Men and Women: Rate of Change of Employment Probability for 1 Percent Increase in Real Minimum Wage

	France	United States
Conditional (aggregated over age groups)		
Young men	−2.489	−2.234
Young women	−1.044	−1.873
Unconditional (aggregated over age groups)		
Young men	−.203	−.123
Young women	−.108	−.127

Source: France, table 11.3, figs. 11.6 and 11.7, and Labor Force Survey. United States, table 11.7, figs. 11.8 and 11.9, and Current Population Survey.

Note: The conditional elasticity is the weighted average of the elasticities for each age group in tables 11.3 and 11.7 reported as the difference between the elasticity for the "at minimum" group as compared to the "marginally above" group. The unconditional elasticity is an estimate of the rate of change of the employment probability in period $t+1$ given a 1 percent increase in the real minimum wage between periods t and $t+1$.

the rate at which employed workers at t remain employed at $t + 1$. Our results are summarized in table 11.9. To take advantage of the structure of our estimates in tables 11.3 and 11.7, we computed the required conditional elasticities in equation (4) according to the following formula for France, which assumes that the appropriate control group is individuals who are marginally over the minimum wage:

$$\frac{\partial \ln \Pr\left[e_{t+1} = 1 \middle| e_t = 1\right]}{\partial \ln rmiw_{t+1}}$$

$$= \Pr[\text{at minimum}] \sum_{\ell} \left[\frac{\partial \ln \Pr\left[e_{t+1} = 1 \middle| e_t = 1, \ell, \text{at minimum}\right]}{\ell \ln rmiw_{t+1}} \right.$$

$$\left. - \frac{\partial \ln \Pr\left[e_{t+1} = 1 \middle| e_t = 1, \ell, \text{marginal}\right]}{\ell \ln rmiw_{t+1}} \right] \Pr[\ell],$$

where the summation is taken over the three age groups. We use the comparable formula for the United States.

11.7   Conclusion

This paper has shown that for young people in both France and the United States, movements in the real minimum wage are associated with significant employment effects, typically in the direction predicted by competitive labor market theory. In France, as the real SMIC increased over the period 1982–89, a certain share of young French workers had real wages that fell between the increasing consecutive real minimum wages.

For workers in this situation, subsequent employment probabilities fell significantly. However, participation in employment promotion programs seemed to shield these workers from some of the effects of the increasing real SMIC, and when this eligibility ended, the probability of subsequent nonemployment shot up dramatically. In the United States, a comparable effect of a real minimum wage moving in the opposite direction occurred, as many workers had market wage rates that were passed by the declining real minimum wage over the period 1981–87. American workers whose current real wage rate would have been below the real minimum wage in earlier periods were much less likely to have been employed in those earlier periods.

By comparing effects of minimum wage movements on workers employed at the minimum with the effects on those employed marginally above it, we identify the direct effects of the minimum wage, as distinct from heterogeneity across the wage distribution in labor force attachment and response to macroeconomic shocks. We suppose that these workers have identical labor supply behavior, but they also have much higher subsequent reemployment probabilities in France as well as much higher prior employment probabilities in the United States. Within the youth population, these strong effects increase with age in the United States, and the pattern in France is dominated by eligibility for employment promotion contracts. Across the population as whole, however, our multinomial logit results suggest that in both countries, it is youths who are most affected by movements in the real minimum wage.

Even if the conditional elasticities in question are large, the at-risk groups (workers between two minimum wages) are relatively small—8 percent of young men and 10 percent of young women in France, 6 percent of young men and 7 percent of young women in the United States. Thus overall unconditional elasticities tend to be much lower than the elasticities conditional on being between the two minima. If the relevant policy question concerns the impact of the minimum wage on those individuals most likely to be affected by it (i.e., those currently paid at the minimum wage), our results suggest that there are much larger negative employment effects on this group, especially as compared to the group in the wage distribution marginally above the minimum, than other research has found.

Appendix

Table 11A.1   Statistical History of the *Salaire Minimum Interprofessionnel de Croissance* (SMIC)

Year	Statutory Hours per Month	Gross Hourly SMIC (francs)	Gross Real Hourly SMIC (1970) (francs)	Gross Monthly SMIC (francs)	Net Monthly SMIC (francs)	Monthly Total Compensation Cost (francs)	Employee Payroll Tax Rate (% at SMIC)	Employer Payroll Tax Rate (% at SMIC)	Consumer Price Index (1970 = 100)
1951	173.3	0.89	1.95	154.41	145.15	195.78	6.00	26.79	45.60
1952	173.3	1.00	1.96	173.33	162.93	220.74	6.00	27.35	50.98
1953	173.3	1.00	1.98	173.33	182.33	222.47	6.00	28.35	50.39
1954	173.3	1.15	2.29	199.98	187.98	256.67	6.00	28.35	50.21
1955	173.3	1.25	2.46	216.45	203.46	277.81	6.00	28.35	50.80
1956	173.3	1.26	2.43	218.40	205.30	280.32	6.00	28.35	51.80
1957	173.3	1.29	2.42	223.78	210.35	287.22	6.00	28.35	53.21
1958	173.3	1.46	2.39	253.87	238.64	319.50	6.00	28.85	61.19
1959	173.3	1.58	2.43	270.62	253.84	349.51	6.20	29.15	64.98
1960	173.3	1.61	2.39	279.19	261.88	360.57	6.20	29.15	67.40
1961	173.3	1.64	2.36	284.69	267.04	370.52	6.20	30.15	69.59
1962	173.3	1.72	2.36	298.77	278.45	393.33	7.05	31.65	72.91
1963	173.3	1.84	2.41	319.62	297.09	418.88	7.05	31.05	76.38
1964	173.3	1.89	2.39	328.27	305.13	430.20	7.05	31.05	78.98
1965	173.3	1.97	2.43	342.28	318.15	448.56	7.05	31.05	80.98
1966	173.3	2.06	2.48	358.27	331.15	468.00	7.05	31.36	83.22
1967	173.3	2.13	2.49	368.32	339.66	498.45	8.15	35.33	85.41
1968	173.3	2.68	3.00	484.81	426.84	617.17	8.17	32.78	89.28
1969	173.3	3.16	3.32	548.16	503.32	728.07	8.18	32.82	95.12

1970	173.3	3.42	3.42	591.92	543.50	786.13	8.18	32.81	100.00
1971	173.3	3.76	3.56	651.72	598.15	867.31	8.22	33.08	105.52
1972	173.3	4.19	3.74	725.96	668.00	971.62	8.26	33.84	111.99
1973	173.3	4.95	4.12	858.27	786.52	1,151.28	8.36	34.14	120.20
1974	173.3	6.10	4.46	1,053.74	967.78	1,421.63	8.42	34.53	136.71
1975	173.3	7.26	4.75	1,260.25	1,150.86	1,711.87	8.68	35.82	152.80
1976	173.3	8.34	4.98	1,466.01	1,306.18	1,981.47	9.67	37.03	167.49
1977	173.3	9.40	5.13	1,629.59	1,464.19	2,239.06	10.15	37.40	183.22
1978	173.3	10.61	5.31	1,839.61	1,650.68	2,536.45	10.27	37.88	199.82
1979	173.3	11.94	5.40	2,068.69	1,817.14	2,843.62	12.14	38.91	221.30
1980	173.3	13.80	5.49	2,391.67	2,085.54	3,324.42	12.80	39.00	251.30
1981	173.3	16.30	5.72	2,824.41	2,478.98	3,925.93	12.23	39.00	285.00
1982	169.0	19.17	6.02	3,323.46	2,892.07	4,623.60	12.98	39.12	318.70
1983	169.0	21.50	6.16	3,725.87	3,216.92	5,221.43	13.66	40.14	349.29
1984	169.0	23.53	6.27	4,077.88	3,465.79	5,693.33	15.01	39.62	375.19
1985	169.0	25.44	6.41	4,335.00	3,676.51	6,056.88	15.19	39.72	397.04
1986	169.0	26.53	6.51	4,482.87	3,777.27	6,270.64	15.74	39.88	407.62
1987	169.0	27.60	6.56	4,663.84	3,894.77	6,528.91	16.49	39.99	420.43
1988	169.0	28.65	6.64	4,791.71	3,977.60	6,715.10	16.99	40.14	431.74
1989	169.0	29.54	6.60	4,991.42	4,093.46	6,943.58	17.99	39.11	447.33
1990	169.0	30.80	6.66	5,205.20	4,269.83	7,182.13	17.97	37.89	462.38
1991	169.0	32.30	6.77	5,458.70	4,547.95	7,527.66	17.39	37.90	477.20
1992	169.0	33.58	6.87	5,674.46	4,606.38	7,860.94	17.98	38.53	488.60
1993	169.0	34.45	6.91	5,821.21	4,794.70	7,945.37	18.38	36.49	498.86
1994	169.0	35.20	6.92	5,947.96	4,881.38	7,981.57	18.64	34.19	508.84

Source: Friez and Julhès (1998).

Note: Data for 1950–69 are for the earlier minimum wage system (*salaire minimum interprofessionnel garantie*).

Table 11A.2   Multinomial Logit Results for France

	Transition																	
	Men									Women								
Effect	U-N	A-N	A-E	M-N	M-E	O-N	O-E	N-N	N-E	U-N	A-N	A-E	M-N	M-E	O-N	O-E	N-N	N-E
Intercept	1.39	-2.98	-3.81	-5.95	-5.77	-3.96	-3.36	-.42	-4.52	2.44	-1.55	-.93	-1.71	-1.02	1.03	2.77	2.08	-3.10
	(.91)	(.87)	(.53)	(.75)	(.45)	(.47)	(.40)	(.41)	(1.02)	(.73)	(.59)	(.37)	(.66)	(.35)	(.48)	(.32)	(.31)	(.96)
1982	-.11	-.13	-.18	.13	.01	.38	.40	.26	.32	.02	.04	-.02	.19	.13	.35	.35	.23	.30
	(.12)	(.12)	(.08)	(.09)	(.07)	(.07)	(.06)	(.06)	(.13)	(.10)	(.08)	(.05)	(.08)	(.05)	(.06)	(.04)	(.04)	(.12)
1983	-.28	-.11	-.23	.41	.18	.79	.79	.53	.64	-.05	.13	.00	.53	.40	.78	.69	.45	.64
	(.12)	(.12)	(.08)	(.09)	(.06)	(.06)	(.06)	(.06)	(.13)	(.10)	(.08)	(.05)	(.08)	(.05)	(.06)	(.04)	(.04)	(.13)
1984	-.07	-.14	-.21	.23	.13	.62	.57	.30	.45	.03	.08	.00	.40	.28	.65	.51	.34	.52
	(.12)	(.12)	(.08)	(.09)	(.07)	(.07)	(.06)	(.06)	(.13)	(.10)	(.07)	(.05)	(.08)	(.05)	(.06)	(.04)	(.04)	(.13)
1985	-.16	.06	-.07	.64	.37	1.00	.94	.59	.57	-.07	.30	.11	.62	.44	.87	.72	.51	.46
	(.12)	(.12)	(.08)	(.09)	(.06)	(.06)	(.06)	(.06)	(.13)	(.10)	(.08)	(.05)	(.08)	(.05)	(.06)	(.04)	(.04)	(.12)
1986	-.30	.00	-.08	.50	.33	.82	.81	.44	.64	-.23	.13	.08	.42	.36	.61	.57	.40	.30
	(.12)	(.12)	(.08)	(.09)	(.06)	(.07)	(.06)	(.06)	(.13)	(.10)	(.07)	(.05)	(.08)	(.05)	(.06)	(.04)	(.04)	(.12)
1987	-.39	.00	.05	.45	.34	.80	.79	.43	.33	-.26	.23	.12	.36	.37	.63	.57	.41	.38
	(.12)	(.12)	(.08)	(.09)	(.06)	(.07)	(.06)	(.06)	(.13)	(.10)	(.08)	(.05)	(.08)	(.05)	(.06)	(.04)	(.04)	(.12)
1988	-.34	.24	.14	.66	.47	.99	.92	.56	.49	-.24	.37	.26	.64	.54	.77	.74	.56	.46
	(.12)	(.13)	(.08)	(.11)	(.07)	(.07)	(.06)	(.06)	(.14)	(.10)	(.09)	(.05)	(.09)	(.05)	(.06)	(.05)	(.04)	(.12)
Baccalauréat	-.26	-.31	-.49	-.35	-.50	.29	.62	-.02	.42	.08	.01	.04	.30	.38	1.06	1.34	.38	1.04
	(.16)	(.13)	(.08)	(.13)	(.07)	(.07)	(.06)	(.06)	(.13)	(.11)	(.09)	(.06)	(.10)	(.05)	(.06)	(.05)	(.05)	(.14)
Age = 22-25	.60	-.68	-.81	-.90	-1.01	-1.50	-1.78	-1.29	-1.02	.77	.04	-.22	.00	-.19	-.53	-.69	-.39	.12
	(.11)	(.13)	(.07)	(.12)	(.06)	(.08)	(.06)	(.06)	(.16)	(.10)	(.09)	(.06)	(.11)	(.05)	(.08)	(.05)	(.05)	(.17)

Source: French Labor Force Survey, 1982–89, matched year to year.

Note: Equations estimated by multinomial logit. Transitions identified by U = under the minimum, A = at the minimum, M = marginally over the minimum, N = nonemployment, and E = employment. In addition to the coefficients shown, the regression included indicator variables for region (Ile de France), eight education categories, and three entry cohorts. The reference categories for the indicator variables were year = 1981, education = no degree, age = 41–50 years old, and year of entry into labor market = before 1961. Separate equations were estimated for men and women. Sample sizes were men, 145,646; women, 166,716. Numbers in parentheses are standard errors.

Table 11A.3   Multinomial Logit Results for the United States

| | | | Men | | | | | | | | | | Women | | | | | |
Effect	N-U	N-A	E-A	N-M	E-M	N-O	E-O	N-N	E-N	N-U	N-A	E-A	N-M	E-M	N-O	E-O	N-N	E-N
Intercept	-1.61	.11	.30	.80	1.20	4.28	6.60	-.80	-.39	-.89	2.74	.81	3.45	1.94	5.56	6.91	.34	1.40
	(1.06)	(.86)	(.58)	(.91)	(.54)	(.51)	(.44)	(.44)	(.46)	(.67)	(.57)	(.40)	(.61)	(.38)	(.42)	(.32)	(.32)	(.34)
1982	.04	.17	.02	.13	.10	.26	.07	.16	.06	.06	.09	.04	.09	-.02	.14	.09	.06	.02
	(.07)	(.05)	(.04)	(.06)	(.04)	(.04)	(.04)	(.04)	(.04)	(.05)	(.04)	(.03)	(.04)	(.03)	(.03)	(.03)	(.03)	(.03)
1983	-.07	.22	.00	.18	.05	.34	.09	.15	-.05	.00	.13	.00	.07	-.06	.17	.11	.05	-.01
	(.08)	(.05)	(.04)	(.06)	(.04)	(.04)	(.04)	(.04)	(.04)	(.05)	(.04)	(.03)	(.04)	(.03)	(.03)	(.03)	(.03)	(.03)
1984	.01	.22	.05	.20	.08	.30	.16	.20	.03	.01	.16	-.06	.12	-.01	.24	.19	.10	.05
	(.09)	(.06)	(.06)	(.07)	(.05)	(.05)	(.05)	(.05)	(.05)	(.06)	(.04)	(.04)	(.05)	(.04)	(.04)	(.03)	(.03)	(.03)
1985	.01	.16	.02	.22	.17	.34	.27	.27	.06	-.08	.11	-.12	.21	-.04	.26	.22	.06	.02
	(.12)	(.08)	(.07)	(.09)	(.07)	(.07)	(.06)	(.06)	(.06)	(.08)	(.06)	(.05)	(.06)	(.05)	(.05)	(.04)	(.04)	(.04)
1986	-.06	.09	-.08	.20	.06	.35	.20	.21	.05	-.05	.09	-.07	.16	-.06	.36	.29	.10	.08
	(.08)	(.05)	(.05)	(.06)	(.05)	(.05)	(.04)	(.04)	(.04)	(.05)	(.04)	(.03)	(.04)	(.03)	(.03)	(.03)	(.03)	(.03)
High school	-.12	.13	.08	.16	.12	.49	.75	.12	.38	-.14	.05	-.02	.19	.20	.37	.65	-.05	.22
	(.09)	(.07)	(.05)	(.07)	(.05)	(.05)	(.04)	(.04)	(.04)	(.06)	(.05)	(.04)	(.06)	(.04)	(.04)	(.03)	(.03)	(.03)
Age = 22–25	.09	.13	.10	.25	.14	.20	-.11	-.86	-.71	.13	.63	.21	.76	.25	.52	.21	-.64	-.21
	(.27)	(.21)	(.14)	(.22)	(.13)	(.12)	(.11)	(.11)	(.11)	(.16)	(.13)	(.10)	(.14)	(.09)	(.10)	(.08)	(.08)	(.08)

Source: Current Population Survey, 1981–87, January–May and September–December, matched year to year.

Note: Equations estimated by multinomial logit. Transitions identified by U = under the minimum, A = at the minimum, M = marginally over the minimum, O = over the minimum, N = nonemployment, and E = employment. In addition to the coefficients shown, the regression included indicator variables for six education categories, eight age categories, and three entry cohorts. The reference transition was E-U. The reference categories for the indicator variables were year = 1981, education = no diploma, age = 61 years old or older, and year of entry into labor market = before 1961. Separate equations were estimated for men and women. Sample sizes were men, 162,073; women, 199,682. Numbers in parentheses are standard errors.

Table 11A.4   Descriptive Statistics Conditional on Employment: France

| | Entire Population | | | | Youth | | | |
| | Men | | Women | | Men | | Women | |
Indicator	Mean	S.D.	Mean	S.D.	Mean	S.D.	Mean	S.D.
Age	37.5769	10.7732	36.9156	10.9116	25.0472	3.6006	24.9998	3.4430
Seniority	10.9995	9.0239	9.5347	8.1790	4.2628	5.7013	4.4259	6.1117
Experience	20.5879	14.7257	19.6161	13.1948	7.5144	12.0523	6.8722	10.8535
Fixed-term contract	.0144	.1191	.0178	.1322	.0342	.1697	.0357	.1756
Apprentice	.0064	.0795	.0021	.0462	.0216	.0671	.0065	.0389
Youth *stagiaire*	.0037	.0611	.0057	.0750	.0124	.0818	.0173	.0986
Paris region	.2031	.4023	.2350	.4240	.1907	.3924	.2217	.4151
Year = 1988	.0692	.2538	.0724	.2592	.0641	.2449	.0629	.2428
Year = 1987	.1386	.3455	.1444	.3515	.1343	.3410	.1349	.3415
Year = 1986	.1374	.3443	.1420	.3490	.1342	.3409	.1352	.3419
Year = 1985	.1413	.3484	.1430	.3501	.1385	.3453	.1401	.3471
Year = 1984	.1437	.3508	.1399	.3469	.1427	.3498	.1402	.3471
Year = 1983	.1455	.3526	.1411	.3481	.1481	.3552	.1490	.3561
Year = 1982	.1479	.3550	.1443	.3514	.1554	.3623	.1567	.3635
No education	.2407	.4275	.1821	.3859	.2361	1.4579	.1635	1.5493
Elementary school	.1845	.3879	.2114	.4083	.0978	.2941	.0963	.2908
Junior high school	.0610	.2394	.0920	.2890	.0794	.2701	.1055	.3072
Basic vocational/technical	.2997	.4581	.2344	.4236	.3989	.4896	.3129	.4632
Advanced vocational/technical school	.0509	.2199	.0689	.2533	.0477	.2103	.0887	.2831
Baccalauréat (high school)	.0434	.2038	.0709	.2566	.0460	.2050	.0921	.2878
Technical college or university	.0495	.2169	.0841	.2776	.0554	.2157	.1008	.2891
Grad school or postcollege professional school	.0639	.2445	.0541	.2263	.0387	.1727	.0401	.1815
Employed next period?	.9285	.2577	.9209	.2699	.9068	.2666	.9060	.2871
Observations under SMIC and *Stagiaire*	329		422		329		424	
Observations under SMIC and Not *stagiaire*	5,548		9,826		3,256		3,617	
Observations between two real SMICs	849		1,292		494		645	
Observations marginally over SMIC	4,146		5,441		2,155		2,206	
Total observations	104,081		80,993		30,804		26,434	

Source: French Labor Force Survey, 1982–89, matched year to year.

Note: S.D. = standard deviation. "Youth" is defined as ages 30 and under.

Table 11A.5   Descriptive Statistics Conditional on Employment: United States

	Entire Population				Youth			
	Men		Women		Men		Women	
Indicator	Mean	S.D.	Mean	S.D.	Mean	S.D.	Mean	S.D.
Years of education	12.8629	2.8842	12.8531	2.4770	12.7341	2.2514	12.9628	2.0845
Experience	20.5188	12.9620	20.1023	12.9669	7.3809	4.0105	6.9846	3.9707
Nonwhite	.1156	.3198	.1399	.3469	.1177	.3223	.1312	.3376
Married	.7055	.4558	.5973	.4905	.4366	.4960	.4342	.4957
Year = 1981	.2005	.4004	.1937	.3952	.2048	.4035	.2019	.4014
Year = 1982	.2004	.4003	.2000	.4000	.2007	.4005	.2061	.4045
Year = 1983	.2049	.4036	.2023	.4017	.2076	.4056	.2043	.4032
Year = 1984	.1133	.3169	.1151	.3191	.1137	.3174	.1138	.3176
Year = 1985	.0706	.2561	.0721	.2587	.0694	.2542	.0695	.2542
Northeastern region	.2326	.4225	.2316	.4219	.2249	.4175	.2304	.4211
North-central region	.2618	.4396	.2613	.4393	.2679	.4429	.2684	.4431
Southern region	.3215	.4670	.3249	.4683	.3251	.4684	.3176	.4655
Employed previous period?	.9170	.2760	.8705	.3358	.8397	.3668	.7977	.4017
Observations under minimum wage	2,571		5,367		1,475		2,481	
Observations between two real minimum wages	4,085		7,645		3,177		4,434	
Observations marginally over minimum wage	6,799		13,218		4,664		6,097	
Total observations	121,356		110,287		41,001		38,993	

Source: Current Population Survey, 1981–87, January–May and September–December, matched year to year.

Note: S.D. = standard deviation. "Youth" is defined as ages 30 and under.

References

Abowd, John M., Patrick Corbel, and Francis Kramarz. 1999. The entry and exit of workers and the growth of employment: An analysis of French establishments. *Review of Economics and Statistics* 81 (May): 170–87.

Abowd, John M., Francis Kramarz, and David N. Margolis. 1999. High wage workers and high wage firms. *Econometrica* 67 (March): 251–333.

Bayet, Alain. 1994. Les salaires de 1991 à 1993 dans le secteur privé et semi-public. INSEE Résultats, no. 64. Paris: Institut National de la Statistique et des Etudes Economiques.

Bazen, S., and J. P. Martin. 1991. L'impact du salaire minimum sur les salaires et l'emploi en 1994. *Note du Bureau Emploi-Salaires* no. 95BD4.

Bonnal, Liliane, Denis Fougère, and Anne Sérandon. 1997. Evaluating the impact of French employment policies on individual labour market histories. *Economic Studies* 64:683–713.

Brown, Charles, C. Gilroy, and A. Kohen. 1982. The effect of the minimum wage on employment and unemployment. *Journal of Economic Literature* 20 (June): 487–528.

Dolado, Juan, Francis Kramarz, Steven Machin, Alan Manning, David Margolis, and Coen Teulings. 1996. The economic impact of minimum wages in Europe. *Economic Policy* 23 (October): 319–72.

Friez, Adrien, and Mathieu Julhès. 1998. Séries longues sur les salaires, edition 1998. INSEE Résultats, no. 605. Paris: Institut National de la Statistique et des Etudes Economiques.

Hsiao, Cheng. 1986. *The analysis of panel data.* Cambridge: Cambridge University Press.

Linneman, Peter. 1982. The economic impacts of minimum wage laws: A new look at an old question. *Journal of Political Economy* 90 (June): 443–69.

Margolis, David. 1993. *Compensation practices and government policies in Western European labor markets.* Ph.D. diss., Cornell University, Ithaca, N.Y.

Neumark, David, and William Wascher. 1992. Employment effects of minimum and subminimum wages: Panel data on state minimum wage laws. *Industrial and Labor Relations Review* 46 (October): 55–81.

Topel, Robert H., and Michael P. Ward. 1992. Job mobility and the careers of young men. *Quarterly Journal of Economics* 107 (May): 439–79.

Welch, Finis. 1997. Wages and participation. *Journal of Labor Economics* 15 (January): S77–S103.

Contributors

John M. Abowd
School of Industrial and Labor
  Relations
259 Ives Hall
Cornell University
Ithaca, NY 14853

David G. Blanchflower
Department of Economics
6106 Rockefeller Hall
Dartmouth College
Hanover, NH 03755

Francine D. Blau
School of Industrial and Labor
  Relations
265 Ives Hall
Cornell University
Ithaca, NY 14853

David Card
Department of Economics
University of California, Berkeley
549 Evans Hall #3880
Berkeley, CA 94720

Per-Anders Edin
Department of Economics
Uppsala University
Box 513
751 20 Uppsala, Sweden

Anders Forslund
Department of Economics
Uppsala University
Box 513
751 20 Uppsala, Sweden

Wolfgang Franz
Centre for European Economic
  Research
PO Box 103443
68034 Mannheim, Germany

Richard B. Freeman
National Bureau of Economic
  Research
1050 Massachusetts Avenue
Cambridge, MA 02138

Paul Gregg
Centre for Economic Performance
London School of Economics
Houghton Street
London WC2A 2AE England

James J. Heckman
Department of Economics
University of Chicago
1126 East 59th Street
Chicago, IL 60637

Bertil Holmlund
Department of Economics
Uppsala University
Box 513
751 20 Uppsala, Sweden

Joachim Inkmann
Faculty of Economics and Statistics
University of Konstanz
Box D124
78457 Konstanz, Germany

Lawrence M. Kahn
School of Industrial and Labor
   Relations
265 Ives Hall
Cornell University
Ithaca, NY 14853

Sanders Korenman
School of Public Affairs
Baruch College
17 Lexington Avenue
Box F-1228
New York, NY 10010

Francis Kramarz
CREST-INSEE
15 boulevard Gabriel Péri
92245 Malakoff Cedex, France

Thomas Lemieux
Department of Economics
University of British Columbia
1873 East Mall
Vancouver, British Columbia V6T 1Z1
   Canada

Stephen Machin
Department of Economics
University College London
Gower Street
London WC1E 6BT England

David N. Margolis
Laboratoire de Microéconomie
   Appliquée (LAMIA)
Université de Paris 1
   Pantheon–Sorbonne
Maison des Sciences Economiques
Boulevard de l'Hôpital
Paris Cedex 13 France

David Neumark
Department of Economics
Michigan State University
101 Marshall Hall
East Lansing, MI 48824

Andrew J. Oswald
Department of Economics
University of Warwick
Coventry CV4 7AL England

Winfried Pohlmeier
Faculty of Economics and Statistics
University of Konstanz
Box D124
78457 Konstanz, Germany

Jeffrey A. Smith
Department of Economics
University of Western Ontario
Social Sciences Centre
London, Ontario N6A 5C2 Canada

Volker Zimmermann
Centre for European Economic
   Research
PO Box 103443
68034 Mannheim, Germany

Author Index

Abowd, John, 443n8, 450n11
Abraham, Katherine, 108, 111n4, 120n16, 130
Ackum, S., 411, 416
Adler, Patricia, 233
Allen, Steven G., 92n29
Altonji, Joseph G., 176n5
Andrews, F. M., 322, 323
Arellano, M., 373
Argyle, M., 289, 323

Baker, Regina M., 79n20
Bane, Mary Jo, 145
Banks, M., 323
Bassi, Laurie, 353
Bayet, Alain, 435
Bazen, S., 428
Beach, Charles M., 178n7
Bell, Brian, 110, 154, 360
Berger, Mark, 1, 63t, 99, 102
Birdi, K. M., 323
Björklund, Anders, 109, 111, 323
Blackburn, McKinley L., 172n2
Blanchflower, David G., 21, 35n4, 42n5, 43, 47n7, 49, 54, 93nn30, 31, 111n6, 249n2, 262n13, 290, 321, 323
Blank, Rebecca, 92, 95, 182, 183, 193
Blau, Francine D., 107n1, 109, 111, 112, 114, 121n17, 130n21, 138n25, 145n29
Blomskog, S., 358n1
Bloom, David E., 60, 61, 172n2

Bloom, Howard, 334n3, 335–36, 337, 342, 345, 346t, 347–48
Blyth, C., 93
Bok, Derek, 6
Bond, S., 373
Bonnal, Liliane, 452n12
Börsch-Supan, Axel, 60, 102n39
Boskin, M., 323
Bound, John, 79n20, 107n1
Bowden, Roger J., 83n23
Braga, Anthony A., 240
Brown, Charles, 194, 428n2
Buechtemann, Christoph, 110, 111, 115, 119n15
Bundesministerium für Bildung und Wissenschaft, 398, 399, 402n10
Bureau of National Affairs, 111
Burkhauser, Richard V., 114n10
Burtless, Gary, 93, 107

Cain, Glen, 333n1
Calmfors, L., 93, 372n11
Campbell, A., 323
Cantril, H., 322
Cappelli, Peter, 95
Card, David, 43, 93n31, 95, 111nn5, 6, 194n17, 195n19
Cavanaugh, David P., 242n19
Cave, George, 348, 353
Center for Human Resource Research, 219
Christenson, R. L., 240

Clark, A. E., 294, 323
Clark, Kim B., 11, 19, 68, 99
Clark, L., 290
Cohen, Mark A., 241
Converse, P. E., 323
Corbel, Patrick, 450n11
Cox, D. R., 404
Crouch, Colin, 93
Currie, Janet, 248n1

Davis, James, 307
Davis, Steven J., 83
Dearden, Lorraine, 283n16
Deere, Donald, 111n5
Demleitner, Nora V., 112, 113
Devine, Theresa, 334
Dickinson, Katherine, 332
Diener, E., 290, 323
DiIulio, John, 241, 242
DiNardo, John, 187
Di Tella, R., 323
Dolado, Juan, 428n1, 432
Dominguez, Kathryn, 60–61, 63t, 99
Doolittle, Fred, 334, 335n4, 348n12, 353
Doornik, J., 373
Douthitt, R. A., 323
Driffill, J., 93

Easterlin, R., 290, 291t, 292, 323
Edin, Per-Anders, 109, 111n6, 112, 323,
    358, 362, 369, 370t
Eggenbeen, David J., 171n1
Ehrenberg, Ronald, 149
Eissa, Nada, 114n9
Elais, Peter, 262n13
Ellwood, David, 145, 397, 410, 411, 416
Emmons, R. A., 323

Fair, Ray, 60–61, 63t, 99
Ferber, Marianne A., 138n25
Fischer, G., 390
Flaig, G., 410–11
Flaim, Paul O., 63t, 98
Flinn, Christopher J., 64t, 100
Forslund, Anders, 95n32, 372, 373, 376
Fougère, Denis, 452n12
Fox, C. R., 322
Fox, James Alan, 219
Franz, W., 384, 389n3
Freedman, Stephen, 337
Freeman, Richard B., 1, 2, 8, 11, 21, 35n4,
    42n5, 43, 47n7, 49, 54, 60, 92, 93nn30,

31, 95, 102, 109, 111, 188, 194n17, 218,
    219, 234, 249n2, 323
Friedlander, Daniel, 337

Gilroy, Curtis, 194, 428n2
Gould, Eric D., 8
Gramlich, E., 372n11
Gregg, Paul, 248n1
Grogger, Jeffrey, 8, 219
Gustaffson, B., 102

Haltiwanger, John C., 83
Ham, John C., 176n5
Han, A., 404
Hannan, Michael, 333n1
Hanratty, Maria J., 182, 183, 193
Harhoff, D., 406
Harkman, A., 362
Harkness, Susan, 248n1
Hartog, Joop, 64t, 101
Hausman, J. A., 404
Heckman, James, 334, 347, 348, 349, 350,
    352n15, 353
Helberger, C., 406
Hindelang, M. J., 221
Hirsch, F., 323
Hirschi, T., 221
Hisao, Cheng, 443n8
Hohmann, Neil, 348, 349, 352n15, 353
Hollister, Robinson, 337, 353
Holmlund, Bertil, 358, 362, 369, 370t, 372
Holzer, Harry J., 2
Houseman, Susan, 108, 111n4, 120n16, 130
Hughes, M., 322
Hyland, Stephanie L., 113

Inglehart, R., 297, 322
International Labour Office (ILO), 108,
    113n8
International Social Survey Programme, 51t

Jackman, Richard, 96
Jackson, P. R., 323
Jaeger, David A., 79n20
John, K., 386, 387
Johnson, George, 107n1
Johnson, Terry, 332
Jonsson, A., 102
Juhn, Chinhui, 107n1, 109n2, 143, 144, 362

Kahn, Lawrence M., 107n1, 109, 111, 112,
    114, 121n17, 130n21

Kahneman, D., 322
Kane, Thomas J., 8, 406
Karr, W., 386, 387
Katz, Lawrence, 107, 111n6, 114n10
Kemper, Peter, 337
Kemple, James, 334
Kennedy, David M., 240
Khoo, Michael, 348, 349, 352n15, 353
Kiernan, Kathleen, 262n13
Killingsworth, Mark R., 99n38, 143
Kimmel, Jean, 143
Klaus, Patsy, 241
Kleiman, Mark A. R., 242n19
Klerman, Jacob Alex, 116, 153n30
Klevmarken, N. Anders, 64t, 102, 369n8
Kohen, Andrew, 194, 428n2
Korenman, Sanders, 60, 187
Kramarz, Francis, 93n31, 111n6, 443n8, 450n11
Krebs, John R., 234
Krueger, Alan B., 95n32, 111n5, 116, 117n14, 194n17, 195n19, 372n11, 376
Kuh, Diana, 286n17

LaLonde, Robert, 347n11, 348n13, 350, 353n16
Larsen, R. J., 323
Layard, Richard, 96, 323
Leibowitz, Arleen, 116, 153n30
Leigh, Duane, 62n5, 93n31, 95
Lemieux, Thomas, 43, 93n31, 111n6, 187
Levine, Phillip B., 63t
Levitt, Steven, 241, 242n20
Levy, Frank, 171
Licht, G., 410–11
Lichter, Daniel T., 171n1
Liebman, Jeffrey B., 114n9
Lillydahl, Jane H., 74n12
Linneman, Peter, 429n4
Lipsey, Mark W., 243
Lochner, Lance, 353n16
Loveman, Gary W., 111n6
Lynch, Lisa, 2, 92, 410

MacCulloch, R., 323
MacDonald, M., 323
Machin, Stephen, 111n6, 248n1, 283n16, 284
Macunovich, Diane J., 12
Maguire, Kathleen, 218f, 226n10, 230n11
Mallar, Charles, 344n9, 353
Manning, Alan, 111n6

Margolis, David, 428–29n3, 430–31n5, 443n8
Martin, J. P., 428
Martin, Linda G., 102
Marvell, Thomas, 242n20
Maynard, Rebecca, 337
Micklewright, John, 253n9
Miller, Ted R., 241
Mincer, Jacob, 109n2, 114
Mitchell, B. R., 65
Mitchell, Olivia S., 63t
Moffitt, Robert, 114, 145
Moody, Carlisle, 242n20
Moore, J. P., 239–40
Moulton, Brent, 198
Mühleisen, M., 411
Mullis, R., 323
Münch, J., 392
Murnane, Richard J., 171
Murphy, Kevin, 102, 107, 111n5, 114n10, 362
Mustard, David B., 8
Myers, D. G., 289, 290, 323

Nardone, Thomas, 63t, 99
Needels, Karen, 188
Neumark, David, 111n5, 187, 428n3, 436n7
Nickell, Stephen, 64t, 96, 102, 110, 112, 154, 360

Ogawa, Naohiro, 102
Ohlsson, H., 372n11
Olovsson, P., 369n8
O'Neill, June, 114
Oosterbeck, Hessel, 64t, 101
Organization for Economic Cooperation and Development (OECD), 2, 10, 12, 20n1, 21, 33t, 34t, 37t, 39t, 40t, 48t, 61n2, 108, 113, 137n24
Orr, Larry, 345
Oswald, Andrew J., 43, 93n31, 290, 294, 323

Padilla, F., 233, 240
Pastore, Ann L., 218f, 226n10, 230n11
Pavot, W., 290
Piehl, Anne M., 240, 241, 242
Pierce, Brooks, 107n1
Pischke, Jörn-Steffen, 116, 117n14
Plant, Mark, 102
Polachek, Solomon, 114
Puma, Michael, 348

Quint, Janet, 348

Reed, Howard, 283n16
Reinberg, A., 390
Rendtel, U., 406
Riccio, James, 337, 348
Robb, Richard, 350
Robinson, Peter, 252n6
Rodgers, W. L., 323
Rodgers, William, 11
Roselius, Rebecca, 353n16
Rossman, Shelli B., 241

Schmidt, Christoph M., 64t, 101–2
Schröder, L., 358n1
Schuh, Scott, 83
Schultz, T. Paul, 143
Schupp, Juergen, 110, 111
Schwarze, J., 406
Sérandon, Anne, 452n12
Sheshinski, E., 323
Shin, D.C., 323
Sickmund, Melissa, 216n6
Singell, Larry D., 74n12
Skedinger, P., 371t, 372
Slotsve, George A., 178n7
Smith, Jeffrey, 334n2, 345n10, 347, 348,
      349, 350, 352n15, 353
Smith, Robert, 149
Smith, T. W., 323
Soloff, Dana, 110, 111
Sorrentino, Constance, 76n14
Soskice, David, 110n3, 389n3
Stapleton, David C., 63t, 99, 102
Statistics Sweden, 363n4
Steedman, Hilary, 110n3
Steiner, V., 410–11
Stephens, David W., 234
Suits, Daniel B., 87
Sullivan, Mercer, 233
Summers, Lawrence, 11, 19, 68, 99

Taber, Christopher, 347, 348, 353n16
Tasiran, A., 102
Taylor, C., 233, 240
Tessaring, M., 390, 399
Teulings, Coen, 64t, 101
Thomas, M. E., 322

Thornberry, Terence, 240
Thoursie, A., 359t
Topel, Robert, 109, 111n6, 112, 362, 460n15
Traeger, Linda, 334, 335n4, 348n12
Tuma, Nancy, 333n1
Turkington, Darrell A., 83n23

United Nations, 46t
U.S. Bureau of Labor Statistics (BLS), 108
U.S. Bureau of the Census, 5t, 7t, 239n16
U.S. Department of Health and Human Ser-
      vices (USDHHS), 237
U.S. Department of Justice, 216, 217, 218,
      219, 236t, 238t, 240t
U.S. Office of Technology Assessment
      (OTA), 92
U.S. Social Security Administration, 114

Veenhoven, R., 290, 322

Wadensjö, E., 366
Wadsworth, Michael, 286n17
Waldfogel, Jane, 130
Wallace, John, 334
Ward, Michael P., 460n15
Warr, P. B., 290, 294, 323
Wascher, William, 111n5, 428n3, 436n7
Watson, D., 290
Weaver, C. N., 323
Weinberg, Bruce A., 8
Weis, J., 221
Welch, Finis, 1, 102, 111n5, 458n14
West, Richard, 332
Williams, Terry, 233
Winkelmann, R., 389n3, 413n16
Wise, David, 194n17
Wissoker, Douglas, 333n1
Withey, S. B., 322
World Health Organization, 44–45t
Wright, Robert E., 64t, 101, 102
Wurzel, E., 407n13

Yankelovitch Partners, 14
Young, Douglas J., 63t, 99, 102
Ysander, B.-C., 372n11

Zedlewski, Edwin, 242
Zimmermann, Klaus F., 64t, 100–101, 411

Subject Index

Apprenticeship training, Austria, 11
Apprenticeship training system, West Germany: demand and supply (1976–94), 387–89; dual system, 110–11; school leavers entering, 392–98; success of program, 9; youth experience in, 398–99, 417–18; for youths, 10, 11, 381–82
Armed Forces Qualifying Test (AFQT): scores of incarcerated youths, 222–23

Baby boom cohort: effect on employment in Canada and United States (1950–95), 171, 173, 174–75; effect on labor market supply, 1; labor market entry in West Germany, 389; in OECD time series, 65–66

Child allowances, Germany, 113–14
Child development, Britain: age 16 economic and social outcomes, 252–62; age 23 economic and social outcomes, 262–76; age 33 economic and social outcomes, 276–84; estimation of age 16 outcomes, 257–61
Cohort crowding: specifying effects of, 83–85; test of hypothesis, 61
Cohort size: analysis of effect on OECD youth labor market, 62–91; history of changes in OECD countries, 71–74; literature on effects on labor markets of, 60–64, 98–102. *See also* Baby boom cohort

Collective bargaining, West Germany, 111
Crime: committed by young men, 226–32; decision to engage in, 232–35; effect of reducing youth involvement in, 241–43; increased involvement of U.S. and U.K. youths in, 7–8; as response to labor market deterioration, 7–8; role of youth gangs in, 239–41

Data sources: for analysis of cohort size effects, 62, 65; for analysis of correlation of youth cohorts and unemployment, 62, 65; Canadian census (1971, 1981, 1991), 207–8; data file of youths employed or in school, 35; Eurobarometer Surveys, 297–302, 322; OECD International Social Survey Programme (ISSP), 49; for well-being (1946–57), 291t; youth cohort size for fifteen countries (1970–94), 65–69
Data sources, Britain: National Child Development Study (NCDS), 248, 252–53
Data sources, Canada: census (1971, 1981, 1991), 207–8; Survey of Consumer Finances (SCF), 178n6, 179–80, 191, 208–9
Data sources, France: Institut National de la Statistique et des Etudes Economiques (INSEE), 427–28n, 434–35; Labor Force Survey (Enquête Emploi), 427–28n, 434

Data sources, Germany: BiBB/IAB data, 400, 410, 411, 420–22; German Socio-Economic Panel (GSOEP) data, 108, 114–16, 392, 398, 404, 419–20

Data sources, Sweden: Household Market and Nonmarket Activities (HUS), 369–70; Labor Force Survey (AKU), 369–70

Data sources, United States: Current Population Survey (CPS), 108, 114–16, 117, 119, 178n6, 179, 191, 206–7, 427–28n, 435–36; General Social Surveys (GSS), 291–97, 321–22; National JTPA Study (NJS), 331–34; National Longitudinal Survey of Youth (NLSY), 42, 219, 221–32; Panel Study of Income Dynamics (PSID), 114; Public Use Microdata One Percent Sample (PUMS), 119

Demographics: in analysis of cohort size and cohort crowding, 75–91; decline in youth proportion of workforce, 4; institutional response to changes in, 91–96

Disadvantages, economic and social: effect for age 16 in Britain, 252–62; effect for age 23 in Britain, 262–76; effect for age 33 in Britain, 276–84

Earnings: of youths in Canada and United States, 186–87; of youths in West Germany and United States, 129–36. *See also* Wages

Economic conditions: related to youth labor market and cohort size, 60–64; schooling and employment with varying, 38–39; shocks in Sweden (1990s), 357–59

Educational levels: correlation of unemployment with, 31–32; effect in Sweden of low, 366; of incarcerated youths, 219–25; related to earnings in West Germany and United States, 129–36; related to youth employment outcomes in West Germany and United States, 121–29. *See also* School enrollment

Educational system, Britain: changes (1970s–1990s), 252

Educational system, United States: provision of basic skills, 108–9; youth preparedness for employment, 116–21

Educational system, West Germany: glossary of some features of, 423–24; products of, 110; provision of basic skills, 108–9; secondary school leavers,

392–93; transition to apprentice and vocational training from, 110–11, 389–98, 417–18; youth preparedness for employment, 116–21

Employment: determinants for ages 18–29 and 25–36 in Germany and United States, 156–57t, 158–59t; at different levels of education in Germany and United States, 160–61t; effect of educational attainment in Sweden on, 359, 362–69; effect of youth cohort size on, 75–91; gap between adult and youth (1980s–1990s), 2; by gender and enrollment status, 38–40; low-skilled in Germany and United States, 5, 108; of low-skilled youths in Sweden, 366–68; modeling behavior in Canada and United States related to, 194–205, 209–10t; prime-age men in Sweden (1987–91), 362; regional and cyclical variation in Canada and United States, 176, 177f; sensitive to economic conditions, 38–39; students in workforce (1984, 1994), 25, 30t, 31; trends in British youth labor market, 249–52; of women in Germany and United States, 164; of youths in Canada and United States, 187–93; of youths in West Germany and United States, 121–29

Employment, full-time: determinants for ages 18–29 and 25–36 in Germany and United States, 156–57t, 158–59t; of women in Germany and United States, 164t; of youths in Canada and United States, 187–93

Employment, public sector: probabilities related to education levels, 163t; Sweden (1960s–1980s), 359, 362

Employment policy, United States: maternity and parental leave, 109, 112–14, 151–53

Employment policy, West Germany: active labor market policies, 110–12; maternity and parental leave, 109–10, 112–13, 151–53

Employment rates: three and five years after leaving education, 31, 33t

Employment transition probabilities, France, 429, 436–43; conditional logit analysis, 444–46, 450–55, 470t; multinomial logit analysis, 443–44, 446–48, 468t

Employment transition probabilities,

United States, 429, 436–43; conditional logit analysis, 444–46, 455–64, 471t; multinomial logit analysis, 443–44, 448–50, 469t

Enrollment. *See* School enrollment

Eurobarometer Surveys, 297–302, 322

Family and Medical Leave Act (1993), United States, 113

Gender differences: in British youth work-school decisions, 249–52; in earnings of youths in Canada and United States, 186–87; education levels related to employment in Germany and United States, 160–61t; employment in Germany and United States, 156–59t; of immigrants related to education and employment, 162t; public sector employment probabilities in Germany and United States, 163t; youth earnings in West Germany and United States, 129–36; youth employment in West Germany and United States, 121–29; in youth living arrangements in Canada and United States, 182–86, 209–11; of youth work-school activities in Canada and United States, 188–93. *See also* Men; Women

Happiness: levels in United States (1972–96), 291–97; for men under 30 by education and employment, 305–6; ordered logits by age in United States, 294–97; related to marital status, 305–10; of youths, 13; of youths in United States, 302, 304–5. *See also* Life satisfaction; Well-being

Household Market and Nonmarket Activities (HUS), Sweden, 369–70

Immigrants, youth: education levels, employment, and wages (1984, 1991), 135, 137–38, 162t; Sweden (1980s–1990s), 363–66

Incarceration: as remedy for youth crime, 241–43

Income: distribution in families, Canada and United States, 176, 178–82; of youths living away from home in Canada and United States, 180–82, 209–11

Institutions, labor market: response to demographic change, 91–96

Joblessness: lack of youth response to, 12–13; of younger workers, 1

Job market. *See* Labor market, youth

Job Training Partnership Act (JTPA): evaluation (1995), 10; program, 333–34; programs for disadvantaged young men, 10. *See also* National JTPA Study (NJS)

Juvenile delinquency, Britain, 260, 262–63

Labor force participation: modes of entry, 41–42; status for 16/17-year-olds in Britain (1975), 287t; of women in West Germany and United States, 109, 112–14

Labor Force Survey (AKU), Sweden, 369–70

Labor market, Britain: trends, 249

Labor market, Sweden: change (1990s), 357–60; factors influencing youth market outcomes (1971–95), 360–69; youth labor market (1960s–1980s), 359, 363–65; youths in programs, 360, 370–71

Labor market, United States: conditions and institutions (1980s), 110–14; less-educated youths in, 138–40; mobility in, 42; youth outcomes in, 116–38

Labor market, West Germany: conditions and institutions (1980s), 110–14; effect of public sector employment on, 154–55; overview of youths in, 382–403; for special groups of youths in, 401–10; youth outcomes in, 116–38; for youths, 381

Labor market, youth: Canada and United States (1950–95), 173–76; combining work and crime, 233–35; comparison of young men and women in German and U.S., 4–5; continuing problem of, 11–12; demographics in OECD countries, 43–47, 58; deterioration in OECD countries, 57–58; effect of cohort size on, 62–91; effect of influx of women, 4–5, 11; effect on youth work-school decisions of regional, 202–5; factors influencing, 3–6; literature on effect of cohort size on, 60–64; 1970s period, 1–2; OECD countries, 19; policies helping youths in, 9–11; regional differences in Canadian and U.S., 195–97, 202–5; response of youths to deteriorated, 6–9; response of youths to

Labor market, youth (*cont.*)
opportunities in, 172; sectoral employment in OECD countries, 47–49; social
outcomes of worsening, 42–43; status
in OECD countries (1984, 1997), 21,
23, 26–28t
Labor market programs, Sweden: displacement effect of active programs
(ALMPs), 370–76; second-chance,
9–10
Labour Force Survey (LFS), Britain, 248
Life satisfaction: by country, 324–26t; Europe, 297–303; over and under age 30,
310–14. *See also* Happiness; Well-
being

Maternity Protection Act, Germany, 112
Men: characteristics of prisoners aged 18–
34, 236–37; income and work prior to
incarceration for prisoners aged 18–34,
238–39
Minimum wage, France: current system,
SMIC (salaire minimum interprofessionel de croissance), 10, 430–32, 466–
67t; employee and employer payroll
tax for, 431; impact on youth employment, 436–43; impact on youth employment, conditional logit analysis,
444–46, 450–55, 470t; impact on youth
employment, multinomial logit analysis, 443–44, 446–48, 468t; location in
distribution of hourly wage (1990),
432–33; original, SMIG (salaire minimum interprofessionel garanti), 431;
real hourly (1951–93), 431–32
Minimum wage, United States: impact on
youth employment, 436–43; impact on
youth employment, conditional logit
analysis, 444–46, 455–64, 471t; impact
on youth employment, multinomial
analysis, 443–44, 448–50, 469t; location in distribution of hourly wages
(1981, 1987), 432–34; relative low levels, 109; statutory national, 432–33
Mothers, single: in Canada and United
States, 183, 186; in West Germany and
United States, 145–51

National Child Development Study
(NCDS), 248, 252–53
National Crime Victimization Survey, 241
National JTPA Study (NJS): impacts of
JTPA training centers on, 335–40;
JTPA training center selection, 334–40

National Longitudinal Survey of Youth
(NLSY), 42, 219, 221–32
National Youth Gang Survey (1995),
239–40
NJS. *See* National JTPA Study (NJS)
NLSY. *See* National Longitudinal Survey
of Youth (NLSY)

Public sector: as employer of last resort in
Sweden, 111–12; youths employed in
West German and American, 139–45
Public sector, West Germany: as employer
of last resort, 154–55; employment of
low-skilled youths, 5, 110–12

Rochester Youth Study, 240

School enrollment: after age 16 in Europe,
Canada, and United States, 20, 22–
23f; in OECD countries (1980s–1990),
6–7; relation to labor market conditions, 6–7, 69–71; sensitive to economic conditions, 38–39; of Swedish
youths (1970–95), 359, 362–69; of
youths in Canada and United States,
187–93
School-to-work transition: in OECD countries, 20–42, 54; West Germany, 389–
403; youth joblessness, 1. *See also* Economic conditions; Educational levels;
Labor market (*specific countries*);
School enrollment; Work-school decisions
Suicide rates, youth, 13, 42–45

Training programs. *See* Apprenticeship
training system, West Germany; Job
Training Partnership Act (JTPA); Labor market programs, Sweden
Transition to work. *See* School-to-work
transition

Unemployment: effects on youths of aggregate, 36–38; Sweden (1990s), 357–59;
of young women workers, 4; of youths
in Canada and United States (1970–
95), 174t, 176; of youths in European
Union, 4; of youths in Western Europe, 2
Unemployment, Germany: effects of youth,
410–17; youth and adult rates in West
Germany (1975–93), 382–84, 389; for
youths, 107–8, 381–82, 417
Unemployment, youth: correlated with co-

hort size in fifteen countries (1970–94), 65–69; effect of youth cohort size on, 75–91; five-year period after leaving education, 31, 34t, 35; in household where no one is employed (1985, 1996), 35, 36t; levels in United States (1970–94), 57; in Sweden (1960s–1990s), 359–62. *See also* Joblessness
U.S. Department of Justice: prison inmate survey (1991), 240–41

Vocational training, West Germany: hazard function in transition from, 404–6, 418; school leavers in, 398–99; transition from school to, 389–98; youth experiences after, 400–401, 417–18; youth nonemployment after, 403–10; youth participation in, 108; youths enrolled in, 392–93. *See also* Apprenticeship training system, West Germany

Wage discounts, youth, 49–54
Wages: adult-youth wage differential, 2, 49–54; of low-skilled youths in West Germany, 109, 111; regional differences in Canada and United States, 212f; Sweden (1960s–1980s), 358; of younger workers, 1; of young women (1990s), 4; of youths in European Union, 4; youth wage discount in OECD countries, 49–54. *See also* Minimum wage, France; Minimum wage, United States

Welfare system: differences in West German and American, 145–51; payroll tax to finance benefits in France, 431; youths in Canada and United States receiving benefits, 193–94
Well-being: data (1946–57), 291t; literature on, 322–23; youth sources of, 302–14. *See also* Happiness; Life satisfaction
Women: employment in Swedish public sector, 362; as single mothers in Canada and United States, 183, 186; in Swedish labor market (1970–90), 359–60. *See also* Mothers, single
Work, legal and illegal opportunities, 232–35
Workers, young: factors influencing economic position of, 11–12; with influx of women in labor market, 11
Work-school decisions: in Britain (1975–95), 249–52; effect of wages and cyclical factors in Canada and United States, 197–205; labor force status in Britain (1975), 286t

Youths: characteristics with crime/no crime involvement, 219–23; hard-to-employ, 116; living with parents in Canada and United States, 178–80, 182–86, 209–11; position in family income distribution in Canada and United States, 176, 178–82; receiving welfare in Canada and United States, 193–94; response to labor market deterioration, 6–9, 12–15